To Sue, Clare, Frances and Robert
for their love and support.

MATHEMATICS IN ECONOMICS

David Bailey

McGRAW-HILL PUBLISHING COMPANY

London · New York · St Louis · San Francisco · Auckland
Bogota · Caracas · Lisbon · Madrid · Mexico · Milan
Montreal · New Delhi · Panama · Paris · San Juan
Sao Paulo · Singapore · Sydney · Tokyo · Toronto

Published by
McGraw-Hill Publishing Company
Shoppenhangers Road, Maidenhead, Berkshire, SL6 2QL, England
Telephone 01628 23432
Facsimile 01628 770224

The LOC data for this book has been applied for and may be obtained from the Library of Congress, Washington, D.C.

A catalogue record for this book is available from the British Library.

Further information on this and other McGraw-Hill titles is to be found at
http://www.mcgraw-hill.co.uk

ISBN 0 07 707860 8

McGraw-Hill
A Division of The McGraw·Hill Companies

Copyright © 1998 McGraw-Hill International (UK) Limited.
All rights reserved. No part of this publication may be reproduced, stored in a retrieval system, or transmitted, in any form or by any means, electronic, mechanical, photocopying, recording, or otherwise, without the prior permission of McGraw-Hill International (UK) Limited.

Typeset by Mackreth Media Services, Hemel Hempstead
Printed and bound in Great Britain at the University Press, Cambridge

CONTENTS

CHAPTER 1	INTRODUCTION	1
CHAPTER 2	VECTORS	9
	2.1 Introduction	9
	2.2 Operations on vectors	9
	2.3 Linear combinations	16
	2.4 Summary	20
	2.5 Exercises	20
CHAPTER 3	AN INTRODUCTION TO MATRICES	22
	3.1 Introduction	22
	3.2 Operations on matrices	22
	3.3 Some special matrices	25
	3.4 Summary	29
	3.5 Exercises	30
CHAPTER 4	DETERMINANTS	31
	4.1 Introduction	31
	4.2 The evaluation of the determinants	31
	4.3 Determinants and the inverse of a matrix	38
	4.4 The solution to a set of linear simultaneous equations	39
	4.5 A simple macroeconomic model	42
	4.6 Summary	43
	4.7 Exercises	43
CHAPTER 5	SIMULTANEOUS LINEAR EQUATIONS	46
	5.1 Introduction	46
	5.2 The rank of a matrix	47
	5.3 The solution to a set of linear equations	48
	5.4 Elementary operations on a matrix	50
	5.5 Elementary operations and the inverse of a matrix	52
	5.6 Echelon matrices	54
	5.7 Summary	58
	5.8 Exercises	59

CHAPTER 6	AN INTRODUCTION TO LINEAR PROGRAMMING	61
	6.1 Introduction	61
	6.2 Linear programming: a graphical treatment	62
	6.3 Basic feasible solutions to the problem	65
	6.4 The simplex method	67
	6.5 The choice of an initial basic feasible solution	70
	6.6 A tabular approach to solving linear programs	73
	6.7 More on the initial basic feasible solution	74
	6.8 Techniques for solving minimisation problems	75
	6.9 Conclusion	78
	6.10 Exercises	79
CHAPTER 7	DUALITY AND LINEAR PROGRAMMING	82
	7.1 Introduction	82
	7.2 The dual of a linear program	83
	7.3 The solution to the dual	95
	7.4 The dual simplex method	99
	7.5 Sensitivity analysis	102
	7.6 Conclusion	105
	7.7 Exercises	106
CHAPTER 8	THE TRANSPORTATION PROBLEM	109
	8.1 Introduction	109
	8.2 How to solve the transportation problem	110
	8.3 The dual of the transportation problem	117
	8.4 A practical hint for solving transportation problems	121
	8.5 The solution to unbalanced problems	122
	8.6 The assignment problem	123
	8.7 Conclusion	127
	8.8 Exercises	128
CHAPTER 9	EIGENVALUES AND EIGENVECTORS	131
	9.1 Introduction	131
	9.2 Eigenvalues and eigenvectors	132
	9.3 Diagonalisation of a matrix	134
	9.4 Eigenvalues and eigenvectors of symmetric matrices	139
	9.5 A non-symmetric matrix with a repeated eigenvalue	143
	9.6 Quadratic forms	144
	9.7 Summary	148
	9.8 Exercises	148
CHAPTER 10	NON-NEGATIVE SQUARE MATRICES	151
	10.1 Introduction	151
	10.2 The Cayley–Hamilton Theorem	151
	10.3 Decomposable and indecomposable matrices	153
	10.4 Input–output economics	157
	10.5 Stochastic matrices	163
	10.6 Summary and conclusions	163
	10.7 Exercises	164

CHAPTER 11   AN INTRODUCTION TO DIFFERENTIAL CALCULUS   166
11.1 Introduction   166
11.2 The concept of a derivative   167
11.3 Differentiation using first principles   171
11.4 Some simple rules of differentiation   172
11.5 Concavity and convexity   178
11.6 Some more rules of differentiation   181
11.7 Summary   187
11.8 Exercises   187

CHAPTER 12   FURTHER DIFFERENTIAL CALCULUS AND APPLICATIONS TO ECONOMICS   191
12.1 Introduction   191
12.2 Partial differentiation   192
12.3 Homogeneous functions and Euler's theorem   194
12.4 Differentials and total derivatives   197
12.5 An introduction to comparative static analysis   200
12.6 Summary   212
12.7 Exercises   212

CHAPTER 13   OPTIMISATION WITH A SINGLE CHOICE VARIABLE   214
13.1 Introduction   214
13.2 Optimisation   215
13.3 The general conditions for a relative extremum   218
13.4 Some economic applications of maxima and minima   224
13.5 Some comparative static analysis   228
13.6 Summary   229
13.7 Exercises   230

CHAPTER 14   OPTIMISATION WITH MORE THAN ONE CHOICE VARIABLE   234
14.1 Introduction   234
14.2 The first- and second-order conditions   235
14.3 Some economic applications   239
14.4 Some comparative static analysis   245
14.5 Summary   247
14.6 Exercises   248

CHAPTER 15   AN INTRODUCTION TO INTEGRAL CALCULUS   251
15.1 Introduction   251
15.2 Some rules of integration   251
15.3 Definite and improper integrals   259
15.4 Some economic applications of integral calculus   261
15.5 Summary   268
15.6 Exercises   269

CHAPTER 16   CONSTRAINED OPTIMISATION   273
16.1 Introduction   273
16.2 Solution methods for constrained optimisation problems   274

16.3	The second-order conditions	277
16.4	Quasi-concavity and quasi-convexity	281
16.5	Some economic applications of constrained optimisation	285
16.6	More on the interpretation of the Lagrangean multiplier	291
16.7	Summary	300
16.8	Exercises	301

CHAPTER 17 AN INTRODUCTION TO NON-LINEAR PROGRAMMING — 304

17.1	Introduction	304
17.2	The solution to a non-linear program	305
17.3	Non-linear programming and public enterprise economics	319
17.4	Quadratic programming	323
17.5	Summary	328
17.6	Exercises	329

CHAPTER 18 FIRST-ORDER DIFFERENTIAL EQUATIONS — 333

18.1	Introduction	333
18.2	The solution to simple first-order linear differential equations	334
18.3	First-order non-linear differential equations	341
18.4	Summary	349
18.5	Exercises	349

CHAPTER 19 SECOND-ORDER LINEAR DIFFERENTIAL EQUATIONS — 353

19.1	Introduction	353
19.2	How to solve second-order linear differential equations	353
19.3	More on the particular integral	365
19.4	Higher-order linear differential equations	368
19.5	Summary	370
19.6	Exercises	370

CHAPTER 20 FIRST-ORDER DIFFERENCE EQUATIONS — 373

20.1	Introduction	373
20.2	How to solve first-order linear differential equations	374
20.3	Some economic applications	378
20.4	Summary	382
20.5	Exercises	383

CHAPTER 21 SECOND-ORDER LINEAR DIFFERENCE EQUATIONS — 385

21.1	Introduction	385
21.2	The characteristic equation	385
21.3	An economic application of second-order difference equations: a model of the trade cycle	393
21.4	More on the particular integral	396
21.5	A brief note on higher-order difference equations	398
21.6	Summary	398
21.7	Exercises	399

CHAPTER 22 SIMULTANEOUS DIFFERENTIAL AND DIFFERENCE EQUATIONS — 402

22.1	Introduction	402

22.2	Simultaneous differential equations	402
22.3	The phase diagram	410
22.4	Simultaneous linear difference equations	414
22.5	Summary	417
22.6	Exercises	417

SOLUTIONS TO EXERCISES 420

INDEX 479

CHAPTER ONE
INTRODUCTION

The aim of this volume is to provide students with a thorough introduction to those mathematical techniques which are commonly used in economics. The student reading economics at first degree level is typically required to study a set of courses in macroeconomic and microeconomic theory, as well as mathematics for economists, basic statistics and introductory econometrics, often with the option of pursuing these quantitative subjects at a more technically advanced level.

Students can obviously make some progress in developing their abilities in both macroeconomics and microeconomics through verbal and diagrammatic analysis. However, as the subject has developed over the years, an ability to understand key mathematical concepts and techniques and to be able to apply them in modelling economic behaviour has become an essential skill for economists. To acquire a knowledge and understanding of these techniques requires a substantial investment on the part of the student, but the potential pay-off is large indeed. The use of mathematics as a tool of analysis in the study of economics enables many results to be derived in a much neater and more efficient way than if the analyst was required to eschew the use of mathematics and rely solely on his or her verbal and diagrammatic skills.

A famous economist, and one well known for his contributions to mathematical economics, once remarked in jest that God would have made it easier for us to construct three-dimensional diagrams had there been more than two factors of production. Two-dimensional diagrams for example of indifference curves, budget constraints and production possibility curves do indeed enable us to make some important statements about the conditions for efficient resource allocation, for example. Diagrammatic analysis using aggregate demand and aggregate supply curves or IS and LM curves allows us to draw some important conclusions about the impact of certain changes on such important macroeconomic variables as the level of real output, the general price level, the interest rate, etc. However, consumers spend their income on thousands of different products, and firms employ many different types of factor of production and typically also produce many different products. Not only does the use of mathematics in economics enable us to derive in a neat and aesthetically pleasing manner results that can be obtained in other ways, it also makes possible the derivation of general results which could not be obtained by reliance on purely verbal or diagrammatic methods of argument.

Students come to economics courses from a variety of backgrounds. Some have studied mathematics to advanced or equivalent level, whereas others have not taken the subject beyond GCSE level and approach with some trepidation the requirement to study mathematics for economists. This book assumes no knowledge of mathematics beyond that possessed by the GCSE student. It is assumed that the student is familiar with simple algebraic manipulation, co-ordinate geometry and curve-plotting, but it assumes no prior knowledge of either calculus or linear algebra.

The organisation of the book is as follows. Chapters 2 to 5 provide an introduction to some key concepts in linear algebra. Linear algebra is a particularly powerful and effective tool for analysing multi-dimensional problems. For example, an understanding of the techniques of linear algebra is a prerequisite for being able to deal effectively with econometric estimation and hypothesis testing in general models, as well as for understanding linear economic models such as input–output economics and optimisation problems such as linear programming.

In Chapter 2, the topic of vectors, which are one-dimensional arrays of numbers, is introduced, and standard operations such as addition, subtraction and multiplication by a scalar are discussed, along with a simple geometric depiction of these operations. The notions of a vector space and of a set of vectors constituting a basis for n-dimensional Euclidean space are also introduced.

In Chapter 3 we turn to matrices which are multi-dimensional arrays of numbers, and discuss the conditions which must be satisfied for matrix addition, subtraction and multiplication to be defined for a pair of matrices, and given that these conditions are met, how the operations are performed. We also consider special kinds of matrices, including identity matrices (the matrix equivalent of the scalar one), transposes and symmetric matrices.

Associated with any square matrix is a scalar, a single number which is known as the determinant of the matrix. In Chapter 4 we demonstrate how to calculate the determinant of a 2×2 and 3×3 matrix, and show how a technique known as the Laplace expansion process enables determinants of higher-order matrices to be calculated. We discuss the various properties that determinants possess, knowledge of which can in some cases simplify the calculations required to obtain their numerical values. When we divide a scalar by itself, the quotient is obviously equal to one. The equivalent operation in linear algebra is to find a matrix such that when we pre- or post-multiply a given square matrix by this matrix we end up with an identity matrix, a diagonal matrix with one along the diagonal and zeroes everywhere else. Such a matrix known as the inverse of the given square matrix will exist provided that the latter's determinant is not equal to zero. We outline a method of solving for the inverse of a matrix which involves the use of determinants and co-factors which are themselves a type of sub-determinant. We show how the solution to a set of simultaneous equations, where it exists, can be solved using the inverse of a matrix. Alternatively, an approach based on forming the quotient of two determinants, known as Cramer's rule may be employed to the same effect. We then provide a simple economic example of a linear Keynesian income determination model to illustrate this procedure.

In Chapter 5 we introduce into the analysis the concept of the rank of a matrix, which measures the number of linearly independent rows and columns in a matrix. Understanding of the concept of rank then enables us to develop a more comprehensive discussion of simultaneous linear equations. We are particularly interested in how to proceed in the case where there are as many unknowns as there are equations, which was the situation considered in the previous chapter, and in addition the determinant of the matrix vanishes so the matrix does not have full rank. We then generalise the discussion to consider rectangular matrices where there are more unknowns than equations. We demonstrate how the concept of elementary row operations can be applied to derive solutions to a set of linear simultaneous equations. These elementary row operations also constitute an alternative method of deriving the inverse of a matrix where it exists.

Chapter 6 to 8 make use of the techniques discussed in the preceding four chapters to explain how to solve a particular set of optimisation problems. The common features of these problems are as follows: (1) the function whose value we seek to optimise, either maximise or minimise, is a linear function of the choice variables whose values are to be selected in order to achieve the particular objective; (2) these choice variables are not permitted to take on negative values; and (3) the values that they may take are further constrained by the existence of a set of linear inequalities. Such problems are known as linear programming problems.

In Chapter 6, we first show how to solve some simple linear programming problems diagrammatically. An example of a maximising problem would be that of a firm faced with given prices for the goods that it can produce. The manufacture of these goods is subject to a linear technology, that is one characterised by a fixed production coefficients technology in which in order to produce a unit of output of each good given quantities of certain productive inputs are required. The firm has a restricted supply of these inputs. Naturally, the non-negativity requirements most hold: it would not make economic sense for output of any of these goods to be negative. As an example of a typical minimisation problem, we may consider the diet problem. Such a problem involves an individual choosing to purchase given quantities of certain foodstuffs at fixed prices so as to ensure a sufficient intake of certain key nutrients; these dietary requirements give rise to the set of linear inequalities. The cost of the diet should be made as small as possible subject to these nutritional requirements being satisfied, and again naturally that the quantities selected of each foodstuff are non-negative. A given foodstuff may obviously not be consumed and therefore take on a zero value as a result of a combination of relatively high price and/or relatively low nutritional content, but we do not consume negative quantities of a good.

A general solution to linear programming problems is provided by the simplex method. Essentially the solution to a linear programming problem must contain as many variables as there are linear inequalities in the problem with all of these variables being assigned non-negative values. Such a solution is known as a basic feasible solution and coincides with a vertex or extreme point of the set of points which satisfy the linear inequalities and non-negativity requirements of the problem. The simplex method involves identifying such points, and then moving to an adjacent point for as long as the value of the function continues to rise or fall, depending on whether we are dealing with a maximisation or a minimisation problem. The simplex method contains criteria that guarantee that the movement is in the right direction as far as optimality is concerned, and secondly that the new point selected is indeed feasible.

In Chapter 7, we discuss the important concept of the dual of a linear program. Associated with any given linear program, known as the primal, is another linear program which is known as its dual. If the original problem is a maximisation problem then its dual will be a minimisation problem, and vice versa. The dual objective function will be a linear function of a set of dual variables, where there are as many dual variables as there are linear inequalities in the primal problem. These dual variables must also satisfy a set of linear inequalities, there being as many such inequalities as there are choice variables in the primal problem. There are some important results connecting the values taken by the primal and dual variables on the one hand and whether the constraints of the dual and primal problems are satisfied as equalities on the other hand. These results have great economic significance and these are discussed in detail in this chapter.

Chapter 8 is concerned with a special type of linear program, known as the transportation problem. The essential feature of such problems is that goods available at certain sources, for example factories or warehouses, are to be shipped to certain destinations, e.g. supermarkets, in order to minimise total shipping costs. The chosen shipping plan must not ship more from a source than is available there, nor ship more to a destination than is required there. Once again, it is clear from the context of the problem that negative amounts cannot be shipped over any route. The structure of these problems makes them particularly straightforward to solve, and two alternative approaches for finding the optimal solution are outlined in this chapter. One of these methods draws directly on the dual of the transportation problem to motivate the procedure for finding feasible allocations, and then to move in the direction of eliminating a route and replacing it with a new one so as to reduce shipment costs. The chapter ends with a discussion of so-called assignment problems in which, for example, individuals are allocated to tasks so as to maximise profits or minimise costs. No individual may be allocated to more than one task, and no task may be performed by more than one individual. These problems are very basic transportation problems, and have a particularly straightforward method of solution.

Chapters 9 and 10 are devoted to further topics in linear algebra. In Chapter 9 the concepts of eigenvalues and eigenvectors are introduced. We then go on to show how in certain circumstances a matrix can be diagonalised such that the eigenvalues of the original matrix appear in the principal diagonal. Though we do not neglect to consider the eigenvalues and eigenvectors of non-symmetric matrices, we are particularly concerned in this chapter with the case of symmetric matrices. Such matrices always have real eigenvalues, and can always be diagonalised even when the matrix does not have distinct roots. These characteristics of symmetric matrices are of great significance when we seek to assess whether a particular function of many variables known as a quadratic form always take a positive or negative value regardless of the values taken by these variables. Quadratic forms are discussed towards the end of Chapter 9, and we shall subsequently see in Chapter 14 how the results we have derived here can be utilised in order to assess whether a particular point gives rise to a maximum or minimum value of a function of many variables.

In Chapter 10 we continue to investigate the properties of some square matrices. Our topic of interest here is that of non-negative square matrices. Non-negative matrices are matrices, all of whose elements are non-negative. We show that in certain cases, by interchanging rows and columns of a square matrix, we may be able to partition a matrix into a set of submatrices such that one of the submatrices is a null matrix, a matrix all of whose elements are equal to zero. If such a result emerges the matrix is said to be decomposable, otherwise the matrix is indecomposable. We then state some properties possessed by indecomposable matrices. The significance of these properties becomes apparent in our discussion of input–output economics which then follows.

Input–output economics is a technique of analysis which can be applied for investigating the pattern of production in an economy characterised by a linear production technology. In such a system goods are produced by combining primary factors of production such as land, labour and capital equipment with produced intermediate inputs. There are fixed production coefficients, such that in order to produce a unit of one good, say a tonne of steel, then fixed quantities of both the intermediate inputs, so many tonnes of coal, so many kW hours of electricity etc., as well as fixed quantities of the primary inputs are required. Such a linear structure to the technology also implies the existence of constant returns to scale such that a doubling of the use of inputs leads to a doubling of outputs. It is clear that the production technology is quite complicated since in order to produce the coal, electricity and other produced inputs to produce the steel, we shall need inputs of steel, coal, electricity and other produced inputs in order to produce these intermediate inputs, and so on. We demonstrate how the techniques of linear algebra can be applied in order to investigate what will have to be produced in total in order to make available a certain bundle of goods to, for example, consumers.

Chapter 10 ends with a brief discussion of stochastic matrices, which are non-negative square matrices, all of whose columns sum to one. We shall meet such matrices again in the final chapter where we discuss simultaneous difference equations.

In the next section, Chapters 12 to 17, we deal with the calculus and applications of the calculus to economics. Chapter 12 is devoted to an introduction to differential calculus, where the functions which are our focus of analysis are functions of a single variable. The first derivative of a function is shown to measure the slope of that function at a particular point, and we look at the conditions that must be satisfied for the slope to be defined and hence for the function to be differentiable. We then go on to discuss how to find the first derivative of a function from first principles. Obviously it is inefficient to apply first principles every time we wish to find the derivative of a function, so we then in the rest of the chapter provide some important rules for finding the derivatives of different kinds of functions. The derivative and marginal concepts in economics are essentially measuring the same thing. If a firm producing a single product, say computers, increases its production by one unit, then we may calculate the impact that this discrete change in the firm's output has on the firm's costs of production: this is a measure of marginal cost. Alternatively, if we differentiate the firm's cost function with respect to output, then we will obtain the change in the firm's total costs which results from an infinitesimally small change in the firm's output. We may define this derivative as equalling marginal cost, even though we have taken an infinitesimally small rather than a discrete change in output. We also concern ourselves with higher-order derivatives, and discuss the concepts of concavity and convexity. For example, if marginal cost is increasing as output is increasing, then the second derivative of the total cost function will be positive. This derivative is obviously nothing more than the first derivative of the marginal cost function with respect to output.

Chapter 12 further extends our discussion of differential calculus by now turning to functions of more than one variable. We introduce the concepts of partial and total differentiation, and provide economic applications of these concepts. Consider a firm manufacturing computers. Its production function informs us of the manner in which its output of computers depends upon inputs of capital services and labour services. By varying the employment of labour by an infinitesimally small amount and assessing the impact that this has on the firm's output yields the partial derivative of output with respect to labour input. This is what the economist calls the marginal product of labour. Note again we have dealt with an infinitesimally small change in the labour services input rather than a discrete change.

An interesting question that we often ask about a firm's production function is whether it exhibits constant returns to scale with a doubling of all inputs leading to a doubling of output. The relevant mathematical concept in this context is that of linear homogeneity or alternatively homogeneity of degree one. We show how to evaluate the degree of homogeneity of a function, and then discuss Euler's theorem. Euler's theorem demonstrates in the context of economics that only if the production technology exhibits constant returns to scale, i.e. is homogeneous of degree one, will payments to factors of production equal to the respective factors' value of their marginal productivities just exhaust the total value of output produced.

A common method of economic analysis is to evaluate how the equilibrium of a particular model will be affected by varying one of the parameters of the model. This comparison of the new equilibrium with the one prevailing before the change is known as comparative static analysis. The analysis is static in that it tells us nothing about the transition path taken in moving from one equilibrium to the other. It is comparative in that it shows how the characteristics of the new position differ from what prevailed prior to the postulated change. In the penultimate section of the chapter, we consider some closed and open economy macroeconomic models. Our objective is to examine the impact that changes in the money supply or in the level of government expenditure have on the equilibrium values of real output, the rate of interest rate and the exchange rate in some macroeconomic models of the economy.

Chapters 13 and 14 are devoted to a consideration of the important topic of optimisation. In Chapter 13 we restrict our analysis to the case of functions of a single variable. We investigate the first- and second-order conditions for a particular value of the dependent variable to give rise to a maximum or minimum value of the function. We then move on to provide a wide-ranging discussion of maxima and minima in economics. In particular, we look at profit-maximising behaviour by firms operating in different market structures and examine the conditions which if satisfied will guarantee that profits are maximised. Again, we engage in some comparative static analysis by assessing the effect that changes in taxes or subsidies have on market price and output at the level of both the representative firm and the industry.

We widen our discussion of optimisation in Chapter 14 by examining functions of more than one variable. Here we need to draw upon the techniques of partial and total differentiation which were the subject of Chapter 12. For distinguishing whether a particular point gives rise to a maximum or minimum value of the function under consideration, we make use of the results on quadratic forms from Chapter 9. Economic applications of these optimisation methods which are dealt with at length include: price discrimination by a monopolist; profit-maximisation in a multi-plant monopoly; and the optimal employment of factors of production. The penultimate section once more shows how to analyse the effect that parametric changes have on the equilibrium outcome in models in which agents are optimisers.

In Chapter 15 we provide an introduction to integral calculus. In differential calculus we start with a function and then differentiate it in order to obtain its derivative. In integral calculus, on the other hand, we are presented with a derivative and are then asked to work backwards in order to find the original function whose derivative is equal to the one we have been given. Our first task, therefore, is to work through the standard rules of integral calculus, which obviously bear a close relationship to the rules of differentiation discussed in Chapter 11. We distinguish between definite and indefinite integrals, showing that the former involves evaluating the area under a curve. We then move on to provide numerous economic applications of the use of integral calculus. Problems which have a temporal or spatial dimension to them are ones in which such techniques can be effectively applied, and we look at a number of examples concerned with such matters as optimal harvesting of resources, investment projects in which time is treated as a continuous variable, the analysis of a firm faced with potential consumers who are located at different distances from the firm's factory etc.

In the next two chapters we return to optimisation problems, dealing in Chapter 16 with constrained optimisation problems and in Chapter 17 with non-linear programming. The essential difference between these two kinds of optimisation problem is that in the former we require the constraints of the problem to hold as equalities, whereas slack is permitted in the constraints of the latter. Furthermore, the variables whose values we are free to choose in a constrained optimisation problem are restricted only by the equality constraints attached to the problem, whereas in non-linear programming there exist further restrictions that confine the choice variables to be non-negative. In Chapter 16 we describe alternative methods of solving simple constrained optimisation problems with a single constraint. The most useful and general approach is the one involving optimising a new function known as the Lagrangean function, which is made up of the objective function plus a term containing the constraint multiplied by a scalar known as the Lagrangean multiplier. We shall see in this chapter how to interpret the Lagrangean multiplier: it simply measures the impact that a very small relaxation of the constraint has on the value of the function we are seeking to optimise. As in all optimisation problems, we need to consider both first- and second-order conditions. This chapter therefore points out the significance of the concepts of quasi-concavity and quasi-convexity for the satisfaction of the second-order conditions.

Constrained optimisation plays a major role in economic analysis. Consider the following examples. A consumer wishes to choose that bundle of goods which maximises her utility, but is constrained by the fact that her income is limited; a firm wishes to choose that combination of the factors of production which minimises its costs subject to the firm producing a specified level of output; a government wishes to choose the rate of indirect tax to levy on different goods in order to minimise the deadweight loss which results from such indirect taxes subject to a given amount of tax revenue being realised. We work through some problems of this type in this chapter.

In Chapter 17 we further develop the analysis of optimisation subject to constraints by restricting the values that can be taken by the variables under consideration to be non-negative and allowing for there to be slack in the constraints. We find that for maximisation problems in which the function we are seeking to maximise is concave and the constraint functions are convex, then the solution to the problem is given by a set of conditions known as the Kuhn–Tucker maximum conditions. Regarding minimisation problems, we also have, provided that the objective function is convex and the constraints concave, that the solution is given by the Kuhn–Tucker minimum conditions. As we shall see in this chapter, these conditions are analogous and have a similar economic interpretation to the complementary/slackness conditions of linear programming discussed in Chapter 7. The Lagrangean multipliers of the non-linear program have the same interpretation as the dual variables in the linear program. If there is slack in the relevant constraint in each problem, the corresponding Lagrangean multiplier (dual variable) will be zero. If a given Lagrangean multiplier (dual variable) is positive, then the corresponding constraint will hold as an equality. We further see that for solving certain kinds of non-linear programming problems, we may apply some of the techniques that are applicable in the context of linear programming. We then discuss some economic examples of non-linear programming problems.

The final section of the book, Chapters 18 to 22, is devoted to dynamic analysis. Here we are concerned with how variables evolve through time. Time may be treated in one of two ways: we may assume that it is a continuous variable so that we have infinitesimally small changes in time, or alternatively we may consider time to be a discrete variable, i.e. it just takes integer values: 0, 1, 2..., and the smallest change in time is then one time period. We begin our analysis by making the former assumption that time varies continuously. In the continuous time case we draw upon the techniques of integral calculus outlined in Chapter 15 in order to solve differential equations, with first-order differential equations being the topic of analysis in Chapter 18 and second-order differential equations being treated in Chapter 19. A first-order differential equation is an equation in which the derivative of some variable with respect to time appears as a function of the variable itself. We shall be mainly concerned with differential equations in which the time derivative is a linear function of the variable itself, though note the discussion of first-order non-linear differential equations in Chapter 18. The solution to such equations can be decomposed into two components: (1) a part known as the complementary function, and (2) a part known as the particular integral. One important issue that we are concerned with in these chapters is whether the variable whose time-path we have solved for converges on some particular value or not. Amongst the economic applications we consider in this chapter is the famous Solow model of economic growth.

In Chapter 19 we deal with second-order linear differential equations. In such equations both the first and second derivatives of the variable with respect to time as well as the variable itself enter the equation in a linear manner. We show that in order to solve a second-order linear differential equation we must find the roots of a quadratic equation. These roots give us one part of the solution: the complementary function; the other component is found by setting the two derivatives equal to zero and then solving in order to obtain what is known as the particular integral, which gives us the long-run equilibrium of the variable. In some circumstances the long-run equilibrium may involve a constant value for the variable, or alternatively we may have the variable following some trend or cycle. Again, we are interested in whether convergence on this long-run equilibrium value or time-path occurs.

We turn in Chapters 20 and 21 to the case where time changes discretely. The equation we must now solve to obtain the time-path of the variable which is the focus of our interest is known as a difference equation. We confine ourselves to the case of linear difference equations. In Chapter 20 we consider how to solve first-order linear difference equations where the value of some variable depends linearly upon the value of the same variable in the immediately preceding period. As in the case of our differential equations, the solution to difference equations consists of two parts: the complementary function and the particular integral. Amongst economic applications of first-order difference equations is the famous cobweb theorem applied to certain agricultural products. It is the presence of the lagged price in the supply function of the agricultural product along with an assumption of market clearing which generates a first-order difference equation in the price of the product.

In Chapter 21 we deal with the case of second-order linear difference equations where the value of some variable depends linearly upon the value of the same variable in the two immediately preceding periods. As with the second-order linear differential equation, finding the complementary function involves the solution of a quadratic equation. A famous economic application of second-order linear difference equations is the Samuelson model of the trade cycle where the combined operation of the multiplier and the accelerator can give rise to cyclical fluctuations in real output.

In Chapter 22, the final chapter of the book, we present a brief discussion of some simultaneous differential and difference equations. We restrict our discussion to situations where there are two variables whose time-paths are to be determined, and where the two simultaneous equations are both first-order and linear. We show that for both the differential and difference equation cases, the solution involves solving a second-order equation in each unknown.

The book is organised in a sequential manner, and there are good arguments for working through the chapters in the order in which they are written, though individuals may wish to deviate to some extent from this. The book starts with material on linear algebra. A case can be made for deferring the study of linear optimising techniques which are discussed in Chapters 6 to 8 until after the discussion of optimising in Chapters 16 and 17 where the techniques of differential calculus are used to analyse classical constrained optimisation and non-linear programming problems. I chose to put the chapters on linear programming and associated topics earlier in the book so that students could make use in an economic context of some of the techniques they have covered in the first five chapters on linear algebra earlier than would otherwise have been the case. Others may prefer to defer gratification and wait until differential calculus and optimisation techniques dependent upon the calculus have also been mastered.

A significant amount of the material in the calculus chapters can be understood without a knowledge of linear algebra. However, the material on comparative statics and the discussion of the second-order conditions for a maximum in the multi-variate case do require understanding of some basic linear algebra.

In each chapter there are exercises provided. Students are advised to attempt these exercises as they work through the various chapters. Solutions to the exercises are provided at the end of the book.

CHAPTER TWO
VECTORS

2.1 INTRODUCTION

In this chapter we commence our discussion of linear algebra by introducing the concept of a vector. We discuss the arithmetic operations that can be performed on vectors, and provide a geometric analysis of these operations. In Section 2.2 we introduce the idea of a column vector and row vector, and discuss the operations of multiplying a vector by a scalar; adding and subtracting two vectors; and forming the product of two vectors. The operation of multiplying a vector by a scalar can be performed on any vector, but for us to be able to add one vector to another, subtract one vector from another, or form the product of two vectors, then the two vectors must each have the same number of elements in them. In this section, we also introduce the concept of a vector space, discuss how to measure the length of a vector, and deal with the special cases of orthogonal and orthonormal vectors.

In Section 2.3, we discuss the concepts of linear dependence and linear independence. We show that if one vector in a set of vectors can be written as a linear combination of the other vectors in the set, then the set exhibits linear dependence. If a set of vectors is linearly independent, then it is not possible to write one of these vectors as a linear combination of the other vectors in the set. We end this section by introducing the concepts of a set of vectors which (1) spans n-dimensional Euclidean space and (2) forms a basis for n-dimensional Euclidean space. In the first case, a set of vectors spans n-dimensional Euclidean space if any other n-dimensional vector can be expressed as a linear combination of this set of vectors. If in addition to spanning n-dimensional Euclidean space, the set of vectors is also linearly independent, then it is said to form a basis for n-dimensional Euclidean space.

2.2 OPERATIONS ON VECTORS

Whereas a scalar is a single number such as *5, 100, 125* etc., a vector is an ordered one-dimensional array of scalars, a list of numbers the order in which the numbers appear being of crucial significance. (*3, 2, 500, 1, 1000*) is an example of a vector containing five elements; such a vector for instance might represent the quantities of certain goods purchased by a consumer: *3* kilos of apples, *2* kilos of butter, *500* kilos of coal, *1* kilo of dates, and *1000* kW hours of electricity. Clearly the vector (*3, 2, 500, 1, 1000*) is not the same as the vector (*1, 3, 1000, 2, 500*), though the five same numbers appear in the two vectors, the order is different.

We shall adopt the usual notational convention of using bold typeface to represent vectors and normal typeface for scalars. Vectors may be written as an array of numbers appearing in a row or as an array of numbers appearing in a column. We shall let *x* represent a column vector. Hence, we have the following *n*-component column vector:

$$x = \begin{bmatrix} x_1 \\ x_2 \\ \vdots \\ x_n \end{bmatrix}$$

Instead of a column vector, we may order our set of numbers in a row. In order to distinguish between a column and a row vector we shall use the symbol x^T for the latter: this is known as the transpose of *x*. We have simply converted the vector such that the ith element in the column vector now appears as the ith element in the row vector. An *n*-component row vector takes the following form:

$$x^T = (x_1, x_2, \ldots, x_n)$$

Multiplication by a scalar

What kind of arithmetical operations may we perform on vectors? Firstly we may multiply a vector by a scalar. A new vector *y* can be obtained by multiplying each element of the original vector *x* by some scalar λ.

$$y = \lambda x$$
$$y_i = \lambda x_i \quad i = 1, 2, \ldots, n$$

Consider Fig. 2.1 in which we have represented a two-dimensional vector *x*. The effect of multiplying the vector by a scalar is to alter the position of the point drawn on the ray through the

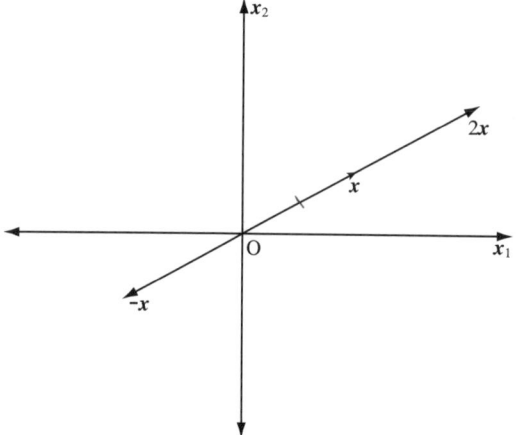

Figure 2.1 A two-dimensional vector. The original vector is labelled *x* on the ray through the origin. Multiplying this vector by a scalar equal to 2 leads to the new point 2*x* which is twice as far along the ray through origin as *x* is. Multiplying *x* by the scalar -1 shifts the vector to $-x$ in the non-negative quadrant.

origin. If λ were equal to 2, then the new point would lie twice as far from the origin as the original point did; if λ were equal to 0.5, then the distance from the origin to the new point would be only half the original distance. Multiplication by a negative scalar reverses the direction of the vector; for λ equal to −1, the new point would be the mirror image in the negative quadrant of the old one.

Addition and subtraction of vectors

Assume we have two *n*-component vectors, *x* and *y*. We may define a third *n*-component vector *z* which is obtained by addition of *x* and *y* where

$$z_i = x_i + y_i \quad \forall i$$

Note that such an operation requires the two vectors which are to be added to have the same number of components or elements. The subtraction of two vectors can be similarly performed provided the two vectors have the same number of elements. Note that the subtraction of the first vector from the second is equivalent to multiplying the first vector by −1 and then adding this new vector to the second vector.

Example 2.1

Given the following two vectors

$$x = \begin{bmatrix} 2 \\ 10 \end{bmatrix}, \quad y = \begin{bmatrix} 6 \\ 4 \end{bmatrix}$$

we have

$$x + y = \begin{bmatrix} 8 \\ 14 \end{bmatrix}, \quad x - y = \begin{bmatrix} -4 \\ 6 \end{bmatrix}, \quad y - x = \begin{bmatrix} 4 \\ -6 \end{bmatrix}$$

In Fig. 2.2 we show how geometrically the new vector *z* which is given by the summation of the vectors *x* and *y* can be obtained. The co-ordinates of the new vector *z* are obtained by

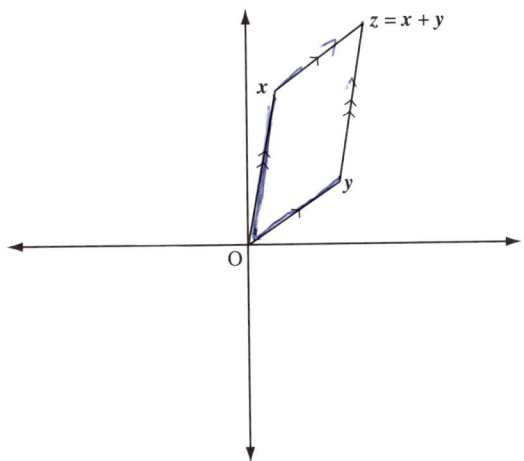

Figure 2.2 The summation of two vectors. To depict diagrammatically the vector *z* which is given by *x* + *y*, first draw a line through *x* which is parallel to O*y* and a line through *y* which is parallel to O*x*. Where these two lines intersect determines the position of *z*.

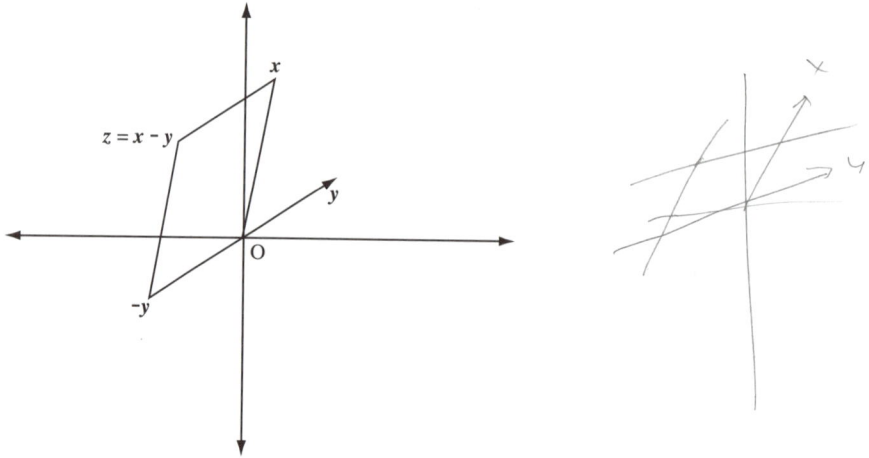

Figure 2.3 The subtraction of two vectors. To depict diagrammatically the vector z which is given by $x - y$, first multiply x by -1 and then draw a line through $-y$ which is parallel to Ox. Where a line drawn through x which is parallel to the ray through the origin to $-y$ meets the earlier line determines the position of z.

completing the parallelogram three of whose corners are the origin, the point x, and the point y. We construct a line through x which is parallel to the ray drawn from the origin to y and similarly we construct a line through y which is parallel to the ray drawn from the origin to x. Where these two lines intersect determines the position of the new vector z.

The procedure for diagrammatically finding z for the case where $z = x - y$ is depicted in Fig. 2.3. Firstly we multiply y by -1, and then construct a line through $-y$ which is parallel to the ray drawn from the origin to x. Where this line meets the one drawn through x which is parallel to the ray drawn from the origin through y determines the position of the new vector. A similar procedure is used to find diagrammatically the position of the vector $y - x$.

The operations on vectors which we have discussed to date have the usual properties which will be familiar to the reader as also holding for operations on scalars, pure and simple. These are:

1. the associative property

$$(a + b) + c = a + (b + c)$$

2. the commutative property

$$a + b = b + a$$

3. the distributive property

$$(\lambda + \mu)a = \lambda a + \mu a$$

$$\lambda(a + b) = \lambda a + \lambda b$$

Vector spaces

A vector space is made of a set of vectors for which the following conditions are satisfied.

1. It must be possible to carry out the operation of addition on any two vectors which are members of the set. In other words, all vectors in the set must have the same dimension.

2. It must be possible to carry out the operation of multiplying any vector in the set by any scalar quantity.
3. Those vectors which arise as a result of the operations of addition and scalar multiplication discussed in the above two conditions are also members of the vector space.
4. The normal associative, commutative and distributive rules apply to the operations of vector addition and multiplication by a scalar.

The vector space which is made up of all real n-component vectors is referred to as an n-dimensional Euclidean space, for which the usual symbol is R^n.

The inner product of two vectors

We have seen that we may multiply a vector by a scalar. In addition we may form the scalar product of two vectors as long as the two vectors contain the same number of elements. The procedure is as follows: we multiply together the first element in each vector, then repeat for the second element in each vector, and so on until we multiply together the last element in each vector. We then form the sum of these n product terms. In notation, we have:

$$x \cdot y = x_1 y_1 + x_2 y_2 + \cdots + x_n y_n$$

$$= \sum_{i=1}^{i=n} x_i y_i$$

The result is a scalar, hence the name scalar product for this operation. Alternative terminology for this operation is the dot product or the Euclidean inner product of two vectors.

Example 2.2

Given the following two vectors

$$x = \begin{bmatrix} 5 \\ 2 \\ -6 \\ 8 \end{bmatrix} \quad \text{and} \quad y = \begin{bmatrix} -3 \\ 5 \\ -10 \\ 4 \end{bmatrix}$$

we may easily find their inner product.

$$x \cdot y = 5(-3) + 2(5) + (-6)(-10) + 8(4) = 87$$

Given a vector x we may calculate the dot product of this vector with itself, i.e. $x \cdot x$. If we then take the square root of this inner product we end up with a measure of the length of the vector, known as the Euclidean norm, the symbol for which is $\|x \cdot x\|$.

$$\|x \cdot x\| = \sqrt{\sum_{i=1}^{i=n} x_i^2}$$

Note for a two-dimensional vector the Euclidean norm is just the length of the hypotenuse of a right-angled triangle. Consider the vector (4, 3). Then its length is easily seen to be 5, and is depicted in Fig. 2.4.

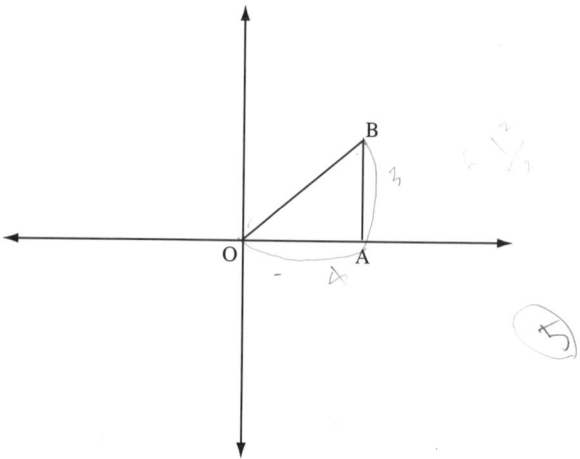

Figure 2.4 The length of a vector. The first element in the vector (4, 3) is measured along the horizontal axis, and the second element along the vertical axis. Hence the distance OA is *4* and the distance AB is *3*. The length of the vector is the length of OB, the hypotenuse of the right-angled triangle OAB, which is equal to 5.

Orthogonal vectors

We may find that when we form the inner product of two vectors that the result is zero. Such vectors are said to be orthogonal to each other. A simple case of a pair of vectors that are orthogonal to each other is the following.

Example 2.3

$$x = \begin{bmatrix} 1 \\ 0 \end{bmatrix}, \quad y = \begin{bmatrix} 0 \\ 1 \end{bmatrix}$$

We plot these two vectors in Fig. 2.5, it is immediately apparent that the angle between two vectors is a right angle. This is always the case when two vectors are orthogonal to each other. Consider another example.

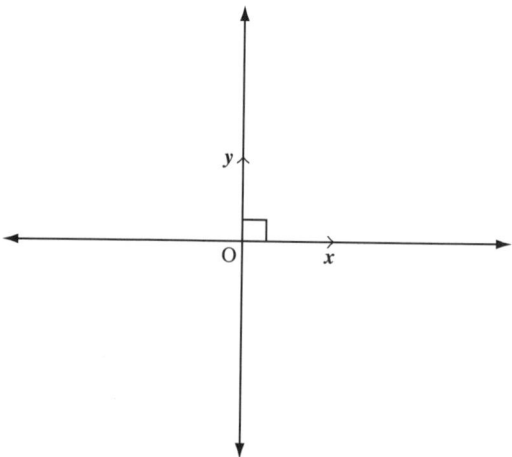

Figure 2.5 A pair of orthogonal vectors. The vector *x* lies along the horizontal axis with the distance from the origin being unity. The vector *y* was along the vertical axis with the distance from the origin being unity. It is straightforward to see that the angle between these two vectors is 90 degrees.

Example 2.4

$$x = \begin{bmatrix} 5 \\ -4 \end{bmatrix}, \quad y = \begin{bmatrix} 12 \\ 15 \end{bmatrix}$$

$$x \cdot y = 5(12) + (-4)(15) = 0$$

Plotting these two vectors accurately in Fig. 2.6, we see that they do indeed stand at a right angle to each other.

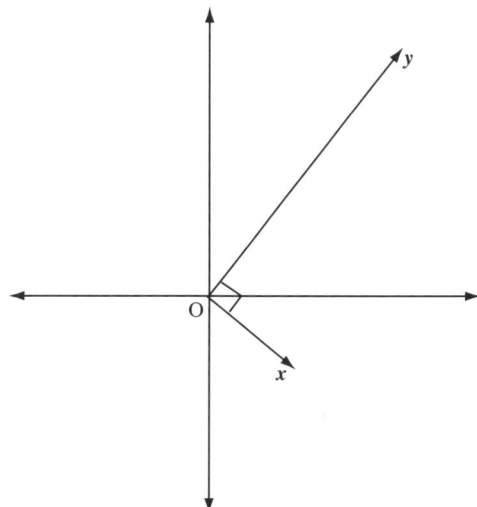

Figure 2.6 Another pair of orthogonal vectors. The first element in the x vector is measured along the horizontal axis and the second element along the vertical axis, and similarly for the y vector. Measuring the angle formed by the two rays, Ox and Oy yields a right angle.

Orthonormal vectors

Whereas a pair of vectors are orthogonal to each other when their inner product is zero, they will in addition be a pair of orthonormal vectors if they are each of unit length. Hence the vectors x and y are orthonormal if

$$x \cdot x = y \cdot y = 1$$

$$x \cdot y = 0$$

Any pair of orthogonal vectors may be converted to a pair of orthonormal vectors by multiplying each vector by an appropriate scalar. This appropriate scalar is the reciprocal of the length of the vector. Return to our earlier orthogonal pair of vectors, and calculate the length of x and y respectively.

$$\|x \cdot x\| = \sqrt{5^2 + (-4)^2} = \sqrt{41}$$

$$\|y \cdot y\| = \sqrt{12^2 + 15^2} = \sqrt{369}$$

If we now multiply the respective original vectors by the reciprocal of their Euclidean norms, λ_1 and λ_2 respectively, we shall have converted them into vectors whose length is unity. Naturally, these new vectors will still be orthogonal to each other. We now have:

$$\lambda_1 x = \begin{bmatrix} \dfrac{5}{\sqrt{41}} \\ \dfrac{-4}{\sqrt{41}} \end{bmatrix}, \quad \lambda_2 y = \begin{bmatrix} \dfrac{12}{\sqrt{369}} \\ \dfrac{15}{\sqrt{369}} \end{bmatrix}$$

$$\lambda_1^2 x \cdot x = \lambda_2^2 y \cdot y = 1$$

$$\lambda_1 \lambda_2 x \cdot y = 0$$

2.3 LINEAR COMBINATIONS

Assume we have a set of m vectors, each vector having n elements in it. We write this set as:

$$a_1, a_2, \ldots, a_m$$

This set of vectors is said to be linearly independent if it is impossible to express one of the vectors in the set as a linear combination of the other vectors in the set. In other words it must be the case for linear independence that

$$\lambda_1 a_1 + \lambda_2 a_2 + \cdots + \lambda_m a_m = 0$$

only holds when

$$\lambda_1 = \lambda_2 = \cdots = \lambda_m = 0$$

Correspondingly this set of vectors will exhibit linear dependence if at least one of the λ_is is not equal to zero.

A vector b is then defined as a linear combination of these m vectors if

$$b = \lambda_1 a_1 + \lambda_2 a_2 + \cdots + \lambda_m a_m$$

$$= \sum_{i=1}^{i=m} \lambda_i a_i$$

where the λ_is are scalars, at least one of which is non-zero. In Fig. 2.7, we present a case where b is indeed a linear combination of two vectors a_1 and a_2. The two original vectors have each been multiplied by a different scalar, λ_1 and λ_2. A parallelogram has then been formed whose corners are the origin and the two new points on the original rays through the origin. The fourth corner gives us the vector b. Given two linearly independent vectors which each contain two components, any other two-component vector can be written as a linear combination of these two original vectors. The diagrammatic approach we have just outlined shows how we can express any point in this two-dimensional space as a linear combination (weighted average) of the two linearly independent vectors with which we started.

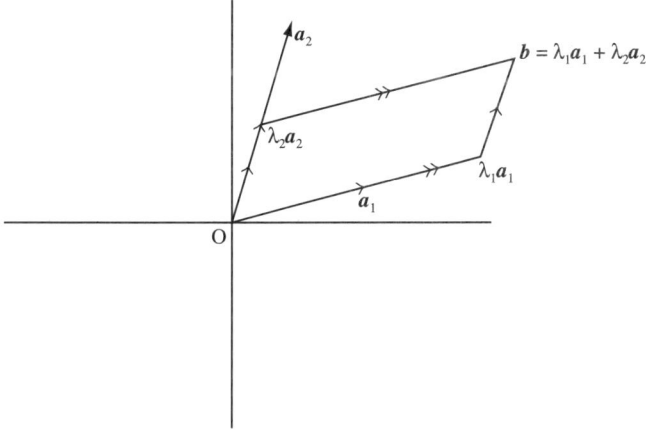

Figure 2.7 A linear combination of two vectors. The vector b is a linear combination of the vectors a_1 and a_2. To find b diagrammatically we first multiply a_1 and a_2 by λ_1 and λ_2 respectively. We then form a parallelogram, three of whose corners are given by the origin, $\lambda_1 a_1$ and $\lambda_2 a_2$; the fourth corner gives us the vector b.

Example 2.5

Given the following two vectors

$$a_1 = \begin{bmatrix} 2 \\ 1 \end{bmatrix}, \quad a_2 = \begin{bmatrix} 1 \\ 4 \end{bmatrix}$$

Are these two vectors linearly independent? If, so, express the following two vectors each as a linear combination of a_1 and a_2.

$$b_1 = \begin{bmatrix} 5 \\ -1 \end{bmatrix}, \quad b_2 = \begin{bmatrix} 1 \\ 11 \\ 8 \end{bmatrix}$$

It is immediately apparent that the two vectors lie on different rays through the origin, so that one of the vectors cannot be expressed as a linear function of the other one. Any other two-component vector can, therefore, be expressed as a linear combination of these two vectors. In the first case, we have:

$$2\lambda_1 + \lambda_2 = 5$$

$$\lambda_1 + 4\lambda_2 = -1$$

Solving these two linear simultaneous equations, we find

$$\lambda_1 = 3, \quad \lambda_2 = -1$$

Hence $b_1 = 3a_1 - a_2$

In the second case, we have

$$2\lambda_1 + \lambda_2 = 1$$

$$\lambda_1 + 4\lambda_2 = \frac{11}{8}$$

Solving these two linear simultaneous equations, we find

$$\lambda_1 = \frac{3}{8}, \quad \lambda_2 = \frac{1}{4}$$

Hence $b_2 = \frac{3}{8}a_1 + \frac{1}{4}a_2$

Example 2.6

Now consider the case where the two initial vectors take the following form.

$$a_1 = \begin{bmatrix} 4 \\ 10 \end{bmatrix}, \quad a_2 = \begin{bmatrix} 6 \\ 15 \end{bmatrix}$$

Note that in this case we do indeed have linear dependence, and one of the vectors can be expressed as a linear combination of the other. Setting λ_1 equal to *1.5* and λ_2 equal to *−1*, it is clear that

$$\lambda_1 a_1 + \lambda_2 a_2 = 0$$

and the second vector is simply *1.5* times the first vector. These two vectors lie on the same ray through the origin; only those other vectors which also lie on this same ray through the origin can be written as a linear combination of these two vectors. All other points which lie in this two-dimensional space cannot be expressed as a linear combination of these two particular vectors.

When a set of vectors is linearly dependent, then it must be the case that at least one vector is a linear combination of the others. Correspondingly, if one vector in a set can be written as a linear combination of the other vectors in the set, then the set is linearly dependent.

Now consider a situation in which we have $n + 1$ vectors, each vector containing n elements in it. It is impossible for these $n + 1$ vectors to be linearly independent. Assume for purposes of simplification that $n = 2$, and that any two of the three vectors in our set are indeed linearly independent. Then as we have already seen, any other two-component vector including the third one in our set can be written as a linear combination of the particular two vectors we have chosen. So they are not all linearly independent of each other: one can always be written as a linear combination of the other two.

Example 2.7

Assume we have the following two linearly independent vectors:

$$\begin{bmatrix} 4 \\ 1 \end{bmatrix}, \quad \begin{bmatrix} 2 \\ 3 \end{bmatrix}$$

Then any two-component vector can be expressed as a linear combination of these two vectors. We have:

$$\begin{cases} x_1 = 4\lambda_1 + 2\lambda_2 \\ x_2 = \lambda_1 + 3\lambda_2 \end{cases}$$

Solving these two linear simultaneous equations, we can express the required weights, the λs, as functions of the components of the particular x vector we wish to obtain from our two given vectors.

$$\lambda_1 = 0.3x_1 - 0.2x_2$$

$$\lambda_2 = -0.1x_1 + 0.4x_2$$

Say we wish to obtain the vector

$$\begin{bmatrix} 10 \\ -5 \end{bmatrix}$$

then we must have $\lambda_1 = 4$ and $\lambda_2 = -3$.

Furthermore, if it were now the case that our three vectors all lay on the same ray through the origin, then it would be self-evident that our set was not linearly independent in this case either.

Vectors spanning an *n*-dimensional Euclidean space

Assume there exists a set of vectors, $a_1, a_2, \ldots, a_n$, such that every vector with n elements can be expressed as a linear combination of these vectors. This set of vectors is then said to span *n*-dimensional Euclidean space. As we have seen above our two vectors

$$\begin{bmatrix} 4 \\ 1 \end{bmatrix}, \begin{bmatrix} 2 \\ 3 \end{bmatrix}$$

span R^2; we can always find values of λ_1 and λ_2 which will generate the required x vector from our two vectors.

Vectors forming a basis for *n*-dimensional Euclidean space

We now need to distinguish between a set of vectors that spans R^n and a set of vectors that forms a basis for R^n. The latter property of forming a basis is satisfied if in addition to spanning R^n the set of vectors is also linearly independent. In other words, for a set of vectors to constitute a basis for R^n it must contain just n vectors which are linearly independent, whereas a set which spans R^n may contain more than n vectors, which could not then all be linearly independent. Hence, our two two-component vectors above constitute a basis for two-dimensional Euclidean space, whereas these two vectors along with any other two-component real vectors span R^2. If b, the number of vectors, is less than n, the dimension of each vector, then the vectors will only span a sub-space of R^n.

When a set of vectors constitute a basis for R^n, then there exists one and only one way in which some other *n*-dimensional vector can be expressed as a linear combination of these basis vectors. This can be easily shown to be the case.

Assume to the contrary that there are two ways in which x can be expressed as a function of the set of basis vectors, $b_1, b_2, \ldots, b_n$. Then we would have

$$x = \sum_{i=1}^{i=n} \lambda_i b_i = \sum_{i=1}^{i=n} \mu_i b_i$$

$$\lambda_j \neq \mu_j \text{ for some } j$$

from which it would follow that

$$\sum_{i=1}^{i=n} (\lambda_i - \mu_i) \boldsymbol{b}_i = \boldsymbol{0}$$

$\lambda_i - \mu_i \neq 0$ *for some i*

But this would then require the *b* vectors to be linearly dependent, and therefore, they could not constitute a basis for R^n in the first place.

2.4 SUMMARY

In this chapter we have been looking at operations on vectors which are one-dimensional arrays of numbers. The elements of the vector may appear in either a column or a row. We have demonstrated how to carry out simple arithmetic operations, such as addition, subtraction, and multiplication of a vector by a scalar or by another vector, the outcome of this latter operation being known as the inner product of the two vectors. For the above operations to be defined, apart obviously for multiplication by a scalar, the two vectors must contain the same number of elements. We have also introduced the notion of the length of a vector: this involves taking the square root of the inner product of a vector with itself. Two vectors are said to be orthogonal to each other if the inner product which results from multiplying the two vectors together is zero, and they will constitute a pair of orthonormal vectors if their respective lengths are both unity, and the inner product of the two vectors is zero.

An important question we have raised in this chapter is whether a set of vectors is linearly independent. This will be the case if it is impossible to express one of the vectors in the set as a linear combination of the remaining vectors. If there are *n* vectors, each containing *n* elements, and these vectors are linearly independent, then this set is said to form a basis for *n*-dimensional Euclidean space. Any other *n*-component vector can then be expressed as a linear combination of this particular set of vectors.

If the number of vectors in a set of vectors each containing *n* elements is larger than *n*, then at most *n* of these vectors are linearly independent. If we do indeed have *n* linearly independent vectors, then the set is said to span *n* dimensional Euclidean space. However, if less than *n* of the vectors are *L.I.*, then only a subspace of *n* dimensional Euclidean space will be spanned by these vectors.

2.5 EXERCISES

2.1 (a) Calculate the lengths of the following vectors:

$$(i) \begin{bmatrix} 9 \\ -7 \end{bmatrix}, \quad (ii) \begin{bmatrix} 12 \\ 16 \end{bmatrix}, \quad (iii) \begin{bmatrix} -3 \\ -21 \end{bmatrix}, \quad (iv) \begin{bmatrix} -10 \\ 5 \end{bmatrix}$$

$$(v) \begin{bmatrix} 2 \\ -7 \\ 3 \end{bmatrix}, \quad (vi) \begin{bmatrix} -11 \\ 7 \\ 4 \end{bmatrix}, \quad (vii) \begin{bmatrix} 8 \\ 6 \\ 10 \end{bmatrix}, \quad (viii) \begin{bmatrix} 2 \\ -2 \\ 5 \end{bmatrix}$$

(b) Calculate the inner product of the following pairs of vectors:

(i) $x = \begin{bmatrix} 7 \\ -2 \end{bmatrix}$, $y = \begin{bmatrix} 3 \\ 10 \end{bmatrix}$, (ii) $x = \begin{bmatrix} 8 \\ 4 \end{bmatrix}$, $y = \begin{bmatrix} -3 \\ 6 \end{bmatrix}$

(iii) $x = \begin{bmatrix} 12 \\ 7 \\ 4 \end{bmatrix}$, $y = \begin{bmatrix} -4 \\ 6 \\ 3 \end{bmatrix}$, (iv) $x = \begin{bmatrix} 5 \\ -7 \\ 10 \end{bmatrix}$, $y = \begin{bmatrix} 3 \\ -5 \\ -5 \end{bmatrix}$

(v) $x = \begin{bmatrix} -4 \\ 2 \\ 9 \\ 3 \end{bmatrix}$, $y = \begin{bmatrix} 6 \\ 6 \\ 4 \\ -8 \end{bmatrix}$, (vi) $x = \begin{bmatrix} -1 \\ 13 \\ -8 \\ 5 \end{bmatrix}$, $y = \begin{bmatrix} 6 \\ 2 \\ -3 \\ -10 \end{bmatrix}$

(c) Which pairs of vectors in (b) are orthogonal to each other? Convert these pairs of orthogonal vectors into orthonormal vectors.

2.2 (a) Are the following sets of vectors linearly dependent or independent?

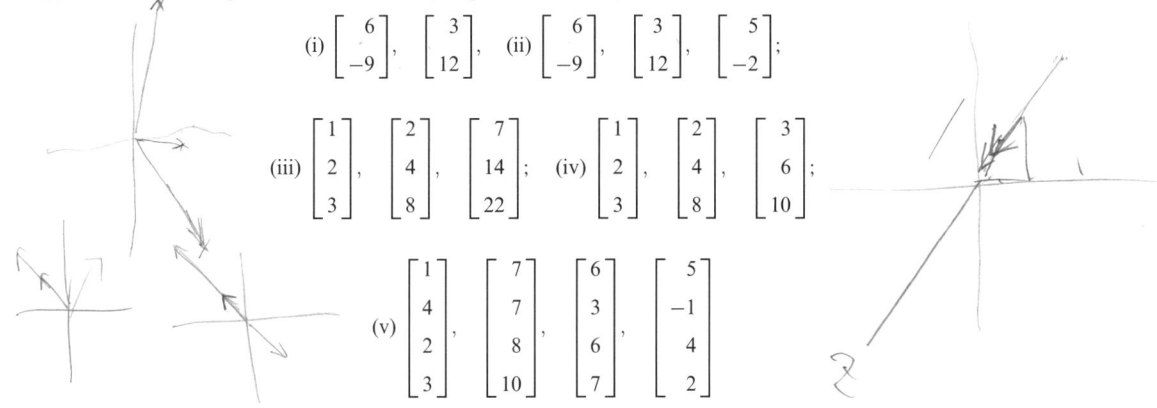

(i) $\begin{bmatrix} 6 \\ -9 \end{bmatrix}$, $\begin{bmatrix} 3 \\ 12 \end{bmatrix}$; (ii) $\begin{bmatrix} 6 \\ -9 \end{bmatrix}$, $\begin{bmatrix} 3 \\ 12 \end{bmatrix}$, $\begin{bmatrix} 5 \\ -2 \end{bmatrix}$;

(iii) $\begin{bmatrix} 1 \\ 2 \\ 3 \end{bmatrix}$, $\begin{bmatrix} 2 \\ 4 \\ 8 \end{bmatrix}$, $\begin{bmatrix} 7 \\ 14 \\ 22 \end{bmatrix}$; (iv) $\begin{bmatrix} 1 \\ 2 \\ 3 \end{bmatrix}$, $\begin{bmatrix} 2 \\ 4 \\ 8 \end{bmatrix}$, $\begin{bmatrix} 3 \\ 6 \\ 10 \end{bmatrix}$;

(v) $\begin{bmatrix} 1 \\ 4 \\ 2 \\ 3 \end{bmatrix}$, $\begin{bmatrix} 7 \\ 7 \\ 8 \\ 10 \end{bmatrix}$, $\begin{bmatrix} 6 \\ 3 \\ 6 \\ 7 \end{bmatrix}$, $\begin{bmatrix} 5 \\ -1 \\ 4 \\ 2 \end{bmatrix}$

(b) If the n-component vectors a, b, c are linearly independent, show that $a + b$, $b + c$, $a + c$ are also linearly independent. Is this true of $a - b$, $b + c$, $a + c$?

(c) Given the following vectors in vectors in R^3.

$$a = \begin{bmatrix} 1 \\ -15 \\ 2 \end{bmatrix}, \quad b = \begin{bmatrix} 3 \\ 5 \\ 1 \end{bmatrix}$$

(i) Calculate the lengths of a and b.
(ii) Find k so that $c = a + kb$ is orthogonal to b.
(iii) Is $[a, b, c]$ a basis for R^3, where c is defined in (ii) above? Give a reason for your answer.
(iv) Find another vector d so that $[b, c, d]$ is an orthogonal basis for R^3, where c is defined in (ii) above.
(v) Convert the basis in (iv) to an orthonormal basis.

CHAPTER THREE
AN INTRODUCTION TO MATRICES

3.1 INTRODUCTION

In the last chapter we introduced the reader to the concept of a vector. In this chapter we turn to the concept of a matrix and discuss the various operations that can be carried out on matrices, which are rectangular arrays of numbers. In Section 3.2 we outline some arithmetical operations that can be performed on matrices. We first discuss the conditions that must be satisfied for the operations of addition and subtraction to be performed on two matrices, and then look at the operations themselves. We then turn to the question of multiplication, looking first at the case of multiplying a matrix by a scalar, before moving on to the more complicated case of matrix multiplication. In Section 3.3 we introduce some special types of matrix. Here we deal with the concept of an identity matrix, which is the matrix equivalent of the scalar unity. An identity matrix is a matrix whose elements are all unity along the principal diagonal, and zero everywhere else. A diagonal matrix is a matrix where one, or more, of the elements along the principal diagonal is non-zero, and all off-diagonal elements are zero. An identity matrix is, therefore, a special kind of diagonal matrix. The matrix equivalent of the scalar zero is a null matrix, all of whose elements are zero. We end Section 3.3 by discussing transposed matrices, symmetric and skew-symmetric matrices. A matrix whose transpose is equal to itself is a symmetric matrix. We finally show that any matrix may be written as the sum of two matrices, one of which is symmetric and one which is skew-symmetric.

3.2 OPERATIONS ON MATRICES

A matrix is a rectangular array of numbers. An example of a square 3 × 3 matrix is:

$$A = \begin{bmatrix} 2 & 3 & 1 \\ 0 & 4 & 6 \\ 7 & 9 & 2 \end{bmatrix}$$

More generally we have for a matrix with m rows and n columns:

$$A = \begin{bmatrix} a_{11} & a_{12} & \cdots & a_{1n} \\ a_{11} & a_{22} & \cdots & a_{2n} \\ \vdots & \vdots & \cdots & \vdots \\ a_{m1} & a_{m2} & \cdots & a_{mn} \end{bmatrix}$$

where a_{ij} is the element which appears in the ith row and jth column of the matrix A.

Operations on matrices

1. addition and subtraction

First of all, we consider the operations of addition and subtraction. For these operations to be defined for two matrices then the matrices must have the same dimensions, i.e. the same number of rows and columns. Assume we have the following two matrices:

$$A = \begin{bmatrix} a_{11} & a_{12} & a_{13} \\ a_{21} & a_{22} & a_{23} \\ a_{31} & a_{32} & a_{33} \end{bmatrix} ; \quad B = \begin{bmatrix} b_{11} & b_{12} & b_{13} \\ b_{21} & b_{22} & b_{23} \\ b_{31} & b_{32} & b_{33} \end{bmatrix}$$

Then the matrix C which is formed from the addition of A and B is defined, and is given by:

$$C = A + B = \begin{bmatrix} a_{11}+b_{11} & a_{12}+b_{12} & a_{13}+b_{13} \\ a_{21}+b_{21} & a_{22}+b_{22} & a_{23}+b_{23} \\ a_{31}+b_{31} & a_{32}+b_{32} & a_{33}+b_{33} \end{bmatrix}$$

$$c_{ij} = a_{ij} + b_{ij} \quad \forall i,j$$

We deal with the subtraction of one matrix from another in a similar manner. This operation is obviously also defined if the two matrices have the same number of rows and columns. Let

$$D = B - A$$
$$d_{ij} = b_{ij} - a_{ij} \quad \forall i,j$$

The addition (and subtraction) of two matrices follows the commutative rule:

$$A + B = B + A$$
$$A - B = -(B - A)$$

Matrix addition also follows the associative rule:

$$(A + B) + C = A + (B + C)$$

2. Multiplication

We first deal with the multiplication of a matrix by a scalar before going to consider the circumstances under which it is possible to form the product of two matrices. Multiplication of a matrix by a scalar λ is very straightforward. We simply multiply each element of the matrix by the scalar. Hence

$$\lambda A = \lambda \begin{bmatrix} a_{11} & a_{12} & \cdots & a_{1n} \\ a_{21} & a_{22} & \cdots & a_{2n} \\ \vdots & \vdots & \cdots & \vdots \\ a_{m1} & a_{m2} & \cdots & a_{mn} \end{bmatrix}$$

$$= \begin{bmatrix} \lambda a_{11} & \lambda a_{12} & \cdots & \lambda a_{1n} \\ \lambda a_{21} & \lambda a_{22} & \cdots & \lambda a_{2n} \\ \vdots & \vdots & \cdots & \vdots \\ \lambda a_{m1} & \lambda a_{m2} & \cdots & \lambda a_{mn} \end{bmatrix}$$

Multiplication of matrices, however, is more complicated than multiplying a matrix by a scalar. Given two matrices A and B, the product AB or the product BA may or may not be defined, and if they both are in fact defined, it will not normally be the case that AB is equal to BA, or even that these two products, assuming they do exist, actually have the same dimensions.

For us to be able to pre-multiply matrix B by matrix A, the number of columns of A must equal the number of rows of B, and the new matrix $C = AB$ will have the same number of rows as A and the same numbers of columns as B. Let A be of dimension $m \times n$ and B be of dimension $n \times p$, then the product $C = AB$ is defined and is of dimension $m \times p$. Is it possible to post-multiply B by A in order to find $D = BA$? The two matrices will only be conformable for multiplication in this way if $p = m$. If this condition is met the number of columns of B will equal the number of rows of A, D will be defined and will have dimension $n \times n$. Assume both C and D exist, they will only be of the same dimension if $m = n$.

Assume we can form the product $C = AB$. How do we generate the elements of this new matrix, the c_{ij}s? The element c_{ij} is equal to the inner product of two vectors: the ith row of A and the jth column of B:

$$c_{ij} = a_{i1}b_{1j} + a_{i2}b_{2j} + \cdots + a_{in}b_{nj}$$

$$= \sum_{k=1}^{k=n} a_{ik}b_{kj}$$

Example 3.1

Given the following two matrices

$$A = \begin{bmatrix} 4 & 5 \\ 2 & 0 \\ 1 & 2 \end{bmatrix}, \quad B = \begin{bmatrix} 2 & 3 & 1 \\ 0 & 4 & 6 \end{bmatrix}$$

Since A is 3×2 and B is 2×3, then the products AB and BA are both defined.

$$AB = C = \begin{bmatrix} 4(2)+5(0) & 4(3)+5(4) & 4(1)+5(6) \\ 2(2)+0(0) & 2(3)+0(4) & 2(1)+0(6) \\ 1(2)+2(0) & 1(3)+2(4) & 1(1)+2(6) \end{bmatrix}$$

$$= \begin{bmatrix} 8 & 32 & 34 \\ 4 & 6 & 2 \\ 2 & 11 & 13 \end{bmatrix}$$

$$D = BA = \begin{bmatrix} 2(4)+3(2)+1(1) & 2(5)+3(0)+1(2) \\ 0(4)+4(2)+6(1) & 0(5)+4(0)+6(2) \end{bmatrix}$$

$$= \begin{bmatrix} 15 & 12 \\ 14 & 12 \end{bmatrix}$$

What is clear from the above is that the commutative law of multiplication does not hold:

$$AB \ne BA$$

even when both AB and BA are defined.

However it is the case given that AB and BC are both defined that $A(BC) = (AB)C$; so the associative law continues to hold.

3.3 SOME SPECIAL MATRICES

An identity matrix

If we multiply a scalar by 1, we do not change its value. Now can we find a matrix such that if we were to pre- or post-multiply any arbitrary square matrix by this matrix the product of the two matrices would equal the arbitrary matrix? In other words we seek to find the form of the square matrix of dimension n, I, where

$$IA = AI = A$$

where A is an arbitrary square matrix of dimension n. It is easy to check that if I is such that each element along the principal diagonal is unity, and all off-diagonal elements are zero, then the above result will be satisfied. The inner product of the ith row of I and the jth column of A would be given by:

$$0(a_{1j}) + 0(a_{2j}) + \cdots + 1(a_{ij}) + \cdots + 0(a_{nj}) = a_{ij}$$

And if we were to consider the case where A is post-multiplied by I, we would have the inner product of the ith row of A and the jth column of I

$$a_{i1}(0) + a_{i2}(0) + \cdots + a_{ij}(1) + \cdots + a_{in}(0) = a_{ij}$$

The matrix I is known as an identity matrix, and is the linear algebra equivalent of the scalar unity.

$$I = \begin{bmatrix} 1 & 0 & \cdots & 0 \\ 0 & 1 & \cdots & 0 \\ \vdots & \vdots & \cdots & \vdots \\ 0 & 0 & \cdots & 1 \end{bmatrix}$$

If A is $m \times n$, then pre-multiplying by an $m \times m$ identity matrix or post-multiplying by an $n \times n$ identity matrix will obviously yield A.

A diagonal matrix

A diagonal matrix is a square matrix in which the off-diagonal elements are all zero, and at least one of the elements in the principal diagonal is not zero.

$$D = \begin{bmatrix} a_{11} & 0 & \cdots & 0 \\ 0 & a_{22} & \cdots & 0 \\ \vdots & \vdots & \cdots & \vdots \\ 0 & 0 & \cdots & a_{nn} \end{bmatrix}$$

An identity matrix is, therefore, a particular type of diagonal matrix, where all the elements in the principal diagonal are unity.

A null matrix

A null matrix is a matrix all of whose elements are zero.

$$\begin{bmatrix} 0 & 0 & \cdots & 0 \\ 0 & 0 & \cdots & 0 \\ \vdots & \vdots & \cdots & \vdots \\ 0 & 0 & \cdots & 0 \end{bmatrix}$$

Whereas a diagonal matrix is always a square matrix, such a restriction does not apply to a null matrix.

The transpose of a matrix

For a matrix A, we may derive an associated matrix by converting the rows (columns) of A into the columns (rows) of the new matrix. The first row of A becomes the first column of the new matrix, the second row of A becomes the second column of the new matrix, and so on. This matrix is known as the transpose of A, and is symbolised by A^T or by A'. If A is $m \times n$, then A^T will be $n \times m$.

$$\text{If } A = \begin{bmatrix} 5 & 8 \\ 1 & 4 \\ 6 & 3 \end{bmatrix}, \quad \text{then } A^T = \begin{bmatrix} 5 & 1 & 6 \\ 8 & 4 & 3 \end{bmatrix}$$

Symmetric matrices

If A is equal to A^T, then A is a symmetric matrix.

$$\text{If } A = \begin{bmatrix} 12 & -4 & 6 \\ -4 & 5 & 1 \\ 6 & 1 & -2 \end{bmatrix}, \text{ then } A^T = \begin{bmatrix} 12 & -4 & 6 \\ -4 & 5 & 1 \\ 6 & 1 & -2 \end{bmatrix}$$

If we pre-multiply or post-multiply a matrix by its transpose, then we obtain a symmetric matrix. Consider pre-multiplying A by its transpose, then the element in row i column j of the new matrix is given by the product of row i of A^T and column j of A; and the element in row j column i of the new matrix is given by the product of row j of A^T and column i of A. However, by definition of the transpose, row $i(j)$ of A^T equals column $i(j)$ of A. Hence the new matrix is symmetric. The similar argument will show that post-multiplying A by A^T will also yield a symmetric matrix.

If A itself is a symmetric matrix, then we obviously have

$$AA^T = A^TA = A^2$$

and by our argument above, A^2 is symmetric.

Transposed matrices possess the following properties:

1. The transpose of the transpose of a matrix is equal to the original matrix:

$$(A^T)^T = A$$

2. The transpose of the sum (difference) of two matrices is equal to the sum (difference) of the transposes of the two matrices:

$$(A \pm B)^T = A^T \pm B^T$$

3. The transpose of the product of two matrices is equal to the product of the transpose of the first matrix pre-multiplied by the transpose of the second matrix:

$$(AB)^T = B^T A^T$$

The first two properties are straightforward, and the reader should check that they do in fact hold. The third result can be derived as follows. Let $C = AB$ and c_{ij} be a typical element of this matrix; c_{ij} is the scalar product of two vectors: the ith row of A and the jth column of B. Now transpose C; then

$$C^T = (AB)^T$$

and the element in the jth row and ith column of this matrix is c_{ij}. Now consider the matrix $B^T A^T$; the element in the jth row and ith column of this matrix is given by the inner product of the jth row of the transpose of B and the ith column of the transpose of the transpose of A. However, the jth row of the transpose of B is the jth column of B, and the ith column of the transpose of A is the ith row of A. But this element is equal to c_{ij}, which proves the rule.

Skew-symmetric matrices

A is a skew-symmetric matrix if

$$A = -A^T$$

Such a matrix will, therefore, have zeroes in the principal diagonal. Regarding the off-diagonal elements, it must be the case for a skew-symmetric matrix that

$$a_{ij} = -a_{ij} \quad \forall i \neq j$$

The following is an example of a skew-symmetric matrix:

$$A = \begin{bmatrix} 0 & -3 & 9 \\ 3 & 0 & 7 \\ -9 & -7 & 0 \end{bmatrix}, \quad \text{then } A^{\text{T}} = \begin{bmatrix} 0 & 3 & -9 \\ -3 & 0 & -7 \\ 9 & 7 & 0 \end{bmatrix}$$

$$\text{and } -A^{\text{T}} = \begin{bmatrix} 0 & -3 & 9 \\ 3 & 0 & 7 \\ -9 & -7 & 0 \end{bmatrix}$$

In fact any square matrix can be expressed as the sum of a symmetric and skew-symmetric matrix. Let

$$A = B + C$$

$$\text{where } B = \frac{A + A^{\text{T}}}{2} \text{ and } C = \frac{A - A^{\text{T}}}{2}$$

Given our definitions, we have:

$$b_{ii} = \frac{a_{ii} + a_{ii}}{2} = a_{ii}$$

$$b_{ij} = \frac{a_{ij} + a_{ji}}{2} \text{ and } b_{ji} = \frac{a_{ji} + a_{ij}}{2}$$

hence $b_{ij} = b_{ji}$ and B is symmetric

It also follows that:

$$c_{ii} = \frac{a_{ii} - a_{ii}}{2} = 0$$

$$c_{ij} = \frac{a_{ij} - a_{ji}}{2} \text{ and } c_{ji} = \frac{a_{ji} - a_{ij}}{2}$$

Hence since $c_{ii} = 0$, and $c_{ij} = -c_{ji}$, C is skew-symmetric.

Example 3.2

Let

$$A = \begin{bmatrix} 4 & 7 & 2 \\ 3 & -6 & 6 \\ -8 & 8 & 5 \end{bmatrix}, \quad \text{then } A^\text{T} = \begin{bmatrix} 4 & 3 & -8 \\ 7 & -6 & 8 \\ 2 & 6 & 5 \end{bmatrix}$$

$$\text{hence } B = \begin{bmatrix} 4 & 5 & -3 \\ 5 & -6 & 7 \\ -3 & 7 & 5 \end{bmatrix}, \quad \text{and } C = \begin{bmatrix} 0 & 2 & 5 \\ -2 & 0 & -1 \\ -5 & 1 & 0 \end{bmatrix}$$

$$\text{and } A = B + C$$

3.4 SUMMARY

In this chapter, we have started to discuss matrices, which are rectangular arrays of numbers, and to outline some simple arithmetic operations which can be performed on them. For the operations of addition and subtraction to be performed on two matrices, they must both have the same dimensions: the number of rows and the number of columns respectively must be the same for the two matrices. In matrix multiplication, we need to distinguish between pre-multiplying a matrix by another matrix, and post-multiplying a matrix by another matrix. For it to be possible to pre-multiply a matrix B of dimension $p \times q$ by another matrix A of dimension $m \times n$ to form the product AB, then A must have as many columns as B has rows, i.e. we must have $n = p$. The element in row i column j of this new matrix is given by the inner product of two vectors, row i of A and column j of B. On the other hand, for it to be possible to postmultiply B by A to form BA, then B must have as many columns as A has rows, i.e. $q = m$. The element in row i column j of the new matrix is then given by the product of row i of B and column j of A. There will be some situations then where both the operations, pre- and post-multiplication can be performed, i.e. when $n = p$ and $q = m$. However, even when this is the case, the new matrices will not have the same dimensions unless $m = n = p = q$; and even if this is the case, the two new matrices will not normally be equal to each other.

Following our discussion of how to perform simple arithmetic operations on matrices, we then turned to consider some special types of matrices. An identity matrix, which is the matrix algebra equivalent of the scalar unity, is a square matrix whose diagonal elements are all equal to one, and all its other elements are zero. A null matrix, which is the matrix algebra equivalent of the scalar zero, has all its elements equal to zero. Assume we have two matrices, A and B whose elements are a_{ij} and b_{ij} respectively. Then if it is the case for all values of i and j that $a_{ij} = b_{ji}$, then B is said to be the transpose of A. In transposing a matrix, the first row of the new matrix is equal to the first column of the original matrix, and so on. If in transposing a matrix we find that the new matrix is identical to the original matrix, then the matrix is symmetric: we have $a_{ij} = a_{ji}$. A skew-symmetric matrix is a matrix where for all i and j, we have $a_{ij} = -a_{ji}$. We have seen that any square matrix can be expressed as the sum of a symmetric matrix and a skew-symmetric matrix.

In the next chapter, we continue our discussion of matrices by introducing the concept of a determinant of a matrix and showing how to find, where it exists, the inverse of a matrix. When we divide a non-zero scalar by itself, we obtain the value unity. When we pre- or post-multiply a square matrix by its inverse, we obtain an identity matrix.

3.5 EXERCISES

3.1 (a) Given

$$A = \begin{bmatrix} 3 & 4 & 1 \\ -2 & 0 & 4 \\ 5 & -1 & 7 \end{bmatrix}, \quad B = \begin{bmatrix} 1 & -3 & 2 \\ 0 & 5 & -1 \\ 9 & 6 & 3 \end{bmatrix},$$

$$\lambda = 4 \text{ and } \mu = 5$$

Calculate the following:

(a) $A + B$; (b) $B - A$; (c) $\lambda A - \mu B$;
(d) AB; (e) BA; (f) μBA.

(b) Given

$$A = \begin{bmatrix} -9 & 5 \\ 1 & 0 \\ 2 & -8 \end{bmatrix}, \quad B = \begin{bmatrix} 12 & 5 & -2 \\ 4 & -3 & 0 \end{bmatrix}$$

$$x = \begin{bmatrix} 3 \\ 10 \\ 17 \end{bmatrix}, \quad y = \begin{bmatrix} -1 \\ 6 \end{bmatrix}$$

Calculate the following:

(a) Bx, (b) Ay, (c) $x^T A$
(d) $y^T B$, (e) AB, (f) BA.

3.2 (a) Calculate where possible (a) AB, (b) $A^T B$, (c) BA^T, (d) $B^T A$, (e) $C^T - B$ and (f) $A^T - AC^T B^T$ when

$$A = \begin{bmatrix} 4 & 6 \\ 3 & 5 \end{bmatrix}, \quad B = \begin{bmatrix} 2 & 0 & 7 \\ 3 & 8 & 1 \end{bmatrix}, \quad C = \begin{bmatrix} 4 & 1 \\ 3 & 0 \\ 1 & 5 \end{bmatrix}$$

(b) Given the following matrices, compute A^2, A^3 and A^4.

(a) $A = \begin{bmatrix} 0.25 & \sqrt{0.1875} \\ \sqrt{0.1875} & 0.75 \end{bmatrix}$;

(b) $A = \begin{bmatrix} 1 & 5 & -3 \\ 0 & 1 & 0 \\ 6 & -3 & 2 \end{bmatrix}$

(c) Express the following square matrices as the sum of a symmetric and skew-symmetric matrix:

(i) $\begin{bmatrix} 5 & 10 \\ -4 & 3 \end{bmatrix}$, (ii) $\begin{bmatrix} -2 & 8 \\ 6 & 9 \end{bmatrix}$

(iii) $\begin{bmatrix} 1 & 7 & 4 \\ 2 & 5 & -8 \\ 3 & -4 & 6 \end{bmatrix}$, (iv) $\begin{bmatrix} 2 & 4 & -6 & 3 \\ 8 & -1 & 7 & -2 \\ 1 & 11 & 0 & 5 \\ 2 & 6 & 9 & 4 \end{bmatrix}$

CHAPTER FOUR
DETERMINANTS

4.1 INTRODUCTION

In this chapter, we show that associated with a square matrix is a scalar known as the determinant of that matrix. In section 4.2 we demonstrate how to find the determinants of 2×2 and 3×3 matrices. By further introducing the concepts and co-factors, we show how higher-order determinants can be evaluated using a method known as the Laplace expansion process. Section 4.2 ends by discussing some useful and important results relating to determinants. If the determinant of a matrix A is not zero, then it is possible to find another matrix which when pre- or post-multiplied by A yields an identity matrix. Such a matrix is known as the inverse of A. In Section 4.3 we discuss how the determinants and co-factors of a matrix can be made use of in order to find the inverse of a matrix. Section 4.4 is concerned with finding the solution to a set of equations which are linearly independent and contain just as many unknowns as there are equations. We demonstrate that the solution to such a set of equations can be obtained by evaluating ratios of determinants. This approach is known as Cramer's rule. Alternatively, we shall see that the solution can be obtained by matrix inversion. In the final section, we apply the mathematical techniques we have discussed in this chapter to the determination of the equilibrium levels of output and the rate of interest in a simple macro-economic model, a linearised version of the Hicks–Hansen *IS/LM* model.

4.2 THE EVALUATION OF DETERMINANTS

Associated with any square matrix is a scalar known as a determinant. The determinant of a 2×2 matrix is given by:

$$\det . A = \begin{vmatrix} a_{11} & a_{12} \\ a_{21} & a_{22} \end{vmatrix} = a_{11}a_{22} - a_{12}a_{21}$$

For the case of a 3×3 matrix, the determinant takes the following form:

$$\det . A = \begin{vmatrix} a_{11} & a_{12} & a_{13} \\ a_{21} & a_{22} & a_{23} \\ a_{31} & a_{32} & a_{33} \end{vmatrix}$$

$$= a_{11}a_{22}a_{33} - a_{11}a_{23}a_{32} + a_{12}a_{23}a_{31} - a_{12}a_{21}a_{33} + a_{13}a_{21}a_{32} - a_{13}a_{22}a_{31}$$

Example 4.1

Given

$$A = \begin{bmatrix} 4 & 2 & -1 \\ -2 & 3 & 0 \\ 7 & 8 & 1 \end{bmatrix}$$

then $\det . A = (4 \times 3 \times 1) - (4 \times 0 \times 8) + (2 \times 0 \times 7) - (2 \times -2 \times 1) + (-1 \times -2 \times 8) - (-1 \times 3 \times 7) = 12 - 0 + 0 + 4 + 16 + 21 = 53$.

Note there are six terms to evaluate for the 3×3 case, compared with the two terms for the 2×2 case. Now consider a matrix of dimension n. Each term in the determinant of this matrix involves the product of a subset of elements (n in number), with each term containing one and only one element from each row and column of the matrix. These terms include all possible combinations of n elements subject to the above restrictions; and there are $n!$ such combinations where

$$n! = n(n-1)(n-2)(n-3)\ldots(2)(1)$$

For a 4×4 matrix there will, therefore, be *24* terms in total, and for a 5×5 matrix there will be *120* terms in total. This makes the evaluation of higher-order determinants a complex matter, and the complexity is increased by the fact that half of these terms will enter with a positive sign, and half with a negative sign. Whilst it is relatively straightforward to remember the sign that is attached to a particular term for the 3×3 case, for higher-order determinants this is no longer the case. As we have already pointed out, the determinant of a matrix of dimension *4* contains *24* terms in total ($4! = 24$, and each a_{ij} appears in six ($3!$) of the terms. The terms containing a_{11} are as follows:

$a_{11}a_{22}a_{33}a_{44}$	$a_{11}a_{22}a_{34}a_{43}$
$a_{11}a_{23}a_{34}a_{42}$	$a_{11}a_{23}a_{32}a_{44}$
$a_{11}a_{24}a_{32}a_{43}$	$a_{11}a_{24}a_{33}a_{42}$

The terms in the left-hand column enter with a positive sign, whilst the terms in the right-hand column enter with a negative sign. Why this should be so is not obvious, and in order to set the scene for a consideration of how to evaluate higher-order determinants, we must first introduce two new concepts: minors and co-factors.

Minors and co-factors

Associated with each element of a matrix is a subdeterminant, called a minor: the minor of the element a_{ij} is formed by calculating the determinant from the elements which remain when row i and column j of the matrix have been deleted. An example will clarify the discussion. For the standard 3×3 matrix, the minor of the element a_{23} is given by:

$$|M_{23}| = \begin{vmatrix} a_{11} & a_{12} \\ a_{31} & a_{32} \end{vmatrix}$$

$$= a_{11}a_{32} - a_{12}a_{31}$$

Associated with each minor is a scalar known as a co-factor. The following relationship exists between a minor and its co-factor:

$$|C_{ij}| = (-1)^{i+j}|M_{ij}|$$

Hence if $i + j$ is an even number, then the values of the minor and the co-factor are the same, whereas for the case where $i + j$ is an odd number, the value of the co-factor is the negative of the value of the minor.

For the matrix given above in example 4.1, the reader should check that the matrix of co-factors is as follows:

$$\begin{bmatrix} 3 & 2 & -37 \\ -10 & 11 & -18 \\ 3 & 2 & 16 \end{bmatrix}$$

The concept of a co-factor is a particularly useful one, and higher-order determinants are usually much more appropriately estimated by using what is known as the Laplace expansion process, which relies on the use of co-factors. The determinant of a matrix of dimension n may be obtained as follows:

$$\det . A = \sum_{j=1}^{j=n} a_{ij}|C_{ij}|$$

We multiply each element in a row by its co-factor and then sum over these products. Alternatively, instead of performing the Laplace expansion along a row, column expansion may also be utilised. In this case, we would have:

$$\det . A = \sum_{i=1}^{i=n} a_{ij}|C_{ij}|$$

Practical considerations should determine which row or column is selected for the Laplace expansion. Ease of calculation would be enhanced by the choice of a row or column which had a number of zero elements in it (assuming one existed). As we shall see later in this chapter, if there are no rows or columns with zeroes, we may still be able to simplify the calculations by deducting a scalar multiple of a row or column from another row or column in order to generate some zeroes.

For the calculation of the determinant of a 3×3 matrix, the Laplace expansion of the third column would yield:

$$\det . A = a_{13}\begin{vmatrix} a_{21} & a_{22} \\ a_{31} & a_{32} \end{vmatrix} - a_{23}\begin{vmatrix} a_{11} & a_{12} \\ a_{31} & a_{32} \end{vmatrix} + a_{33}\begin{vmatrix} a_{11} & a_{12} \\ a_{21} & a_{22} \end{vmatrix}$$

For our numerical example we would have:

$$\det . A = -1(-37) - 0(-18) + 1(16) = 53$$

Obviously we need not have bothered to calculate the co-factor of the element a_{23}.

Properties of determinants

The determinant of A is equal to the determinant of A^T. Since the Laplace expansion process can be applied to any row or column to calculate the determinant of a matrix, then we get the same answer whether we use the ith row or the jth column on which to perform the expansion. But the ith row of A is the ith column of A^T, and the jth column of A is the jth row of A^T. Hence the determinants of the two matrices are equal to each other.

Example 4.2

$$\begin{vmatrix} 6 & -1 \\ 2 & 3 \end{vmatrix} = 6(3) - (-1)2 = 20$$

$$\begin{vmatrix} 6 & 2 \\ -1 & 3 \end{vmatrix} = 6(3) - 2(-1) = 20$$

The determinant of λA is equal to λ^n times the determinant of A where λ is a scalar and n is the dimension of A. This follows from the fact that each term in the determinant of the new matrix is λ^n times greater than before. If just one row or column of a matrix is multiplied by λ, then the new determinant will be λ times greater than the old one.

Example 4.3

$$A = \begin{bmatrix} 5 & 2 & 0 \\ 6 & 8 & 1 \\ 4 & -1 & 0 \end{bmatrix} \text{ and } B = \begin{bmatrix} 10 & 4 & 0 \\ 12 & 16 & 2 \\ 8 & -2 & 0 \end{bmatrix}$$

Then taking the Laplace expansion of the third column, we have:

$$|A| = -1\begin{vmatrix} 5 & 2 \\ 4 & -1 \end{vmatrix} = 13$$

$$|B| = -2\begin{vmatrix} 10 & 4 \\ 8 & -2 \end{vmatrix} = 104$$

Note that each element of B is equal to twice the corresponding element of A, and the value of the determinant of B is eight (2^3) times that of A.

If two rows or columns of a matrix are interchanged, the absolute value of the determinant is unchanged; there is simply a change of sign. Interchange two adjacent rows (i and $i+1$) or columns (j and $j + 1$): then the minors of the new row $i + 1$ (column $j + 1$) are the same as the minors of the old row i (column j), but the co-factors have a sign change, since a typical element has moved from position i,j (i,j) to $i + 1, j$ ($i, j + 1$). Such an interchange obviously just changes the sign of the determinant. Now interchange row i and row $i + k$ (column j and column $j + k$). If we break this interchange down into a series of successive changes were we interchange adjacent rows (columns), we will have to undertake $2k - 1$ changes. Each change just changes the sign of the determinant as we have seen, and since there is an odd number of changes to make, the new determinant will just be the negative of the old one.

Example 4.4

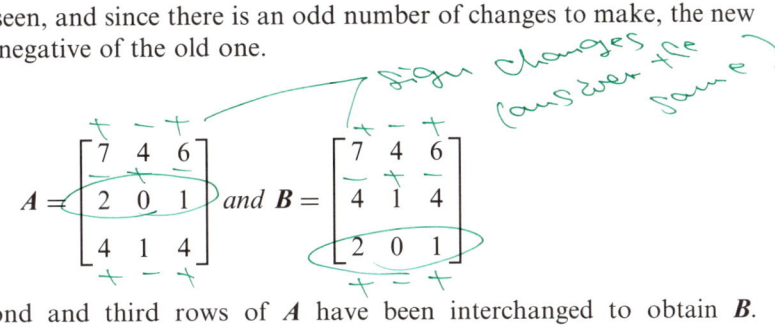

$$A = \begin{bmatrix} 7 & 4 & 6 \\ 2 & 0 & 1 \\ 4 & 1 & 4 \end{bmatrix} \text{ and } B = \begin{bmatrix} 7 & 4 & 6 \\ 4 & 1 & 4 \\ 2 & 0 & 1 \end{bmatrix}$$

Note that the second and third rows of A have been interchanged to obtain B. Evaluating the determinants of these two matrices, we find

$$|A| = -2 \begin{vmatrix} 4 & 6 \\ 1 & 4 \end{vmatrix} - \begin{vmatrix} 7 & 4 \\ 4 & 1 \end{vmatrix}$$

$$= -2(10) - (-9) = -11$$

$$|B| = 2 \begin{vmatrix} 4 & 6 \\ 1 & 4 \end{vmatrix} + \begin{vmatrix} 7 & 4 \\ 4 & 1 \end{vmatrix}$$

$$= 2(10) + (-9) = 11$$

Now consider a matrix which has two identical rows or columns: then interchanging these two rows (columns) must, as we have seen above, just change the sign of the determinant. The new matrix, however, which results from this operation is indistinguishable from the old one, and must therefore have the same determinant. To satisfy both these conditions, the determinant must be zero. This will also be the case if one row (column) is a multiple of some other row (column), since as we have seen above multiplying a row or column by a scalar just increases the value of the determinant by a multiple equal to the scalar. Choosing the scalar equal to the reciprocal of the original multiple will yield a matrix with two identical rows (columns), and such a matrix has a zero-valued determinant.

Example 4.5

$$\begin{vmatrix} 2 & 1 & 3 \\ 5 & 2 & 6 \\ 1 & -1 & -3 \end{vmatrix} = 2 \begin{vmatrix} 2 & 6 \\ -1 & -3 \end{vmatrix} - \begin{vmatrix} 5 & 6 \\ 1 & -3 \end{vmatrix} + 3 \begin{vmatrix} 5 & 2 \\ 1 & -1 \end{vmatrix}$$

$$= 2(0) - (-21) + 3(-7) = 0$$

Note the third column of the matrix is three times the second column.

The value of a determinant is not altered by adding the multiple of one row or column to another row or column. If in carrying out the Laplace expansion process, we employ co-factors applicable to the elements in row i along with the elements of row j, we shall find that expansion by such alien co-factors yields a value of zero. Why should this be so? Using the co-factors of row i and the elements of row j to carry out the expansion is equivalent to evaluating the determinant of a matrix in which row i is simply the negative of row j. If we multiply row i by -1, rows i and j will now be identical (but when two rows are identical, as we have already seen, the determinant vanishes). The determinant of this matrix will now be the negative of the determinant of the old one, but we know that the determinant of the new matrix is zero, hence so must the determinant of the original one.

Example 4.6

Consider the following 3×3 matrix:

$$A = \begin{bmatrix} a & b & c \\ d & e & f \\ g & h & i \end{bmatrix}$$

The co-factors of row 3 are as follows:

$$bf - ce, \quad cd - af, \quad ae - bd$$

The reader should check that if we multiply these co-factors by the elements of the first row of the matrix, all the terms will cancel out leaving us with a value of zero. If the co-factors of row three had also been the co-factors of row one, then the matrix would have looked like this:

$$A = \begin{bmatrix} a & b & c \\ d & e & f \\ -a & -b & -c \end{bmatrix}$$

Row three is the negative of row one and it is straightforward to check that the co-factors of row one are indeed equal to the co-factors of row three. Multiplying row three by minus one just changes the sign of the determinant and also yields a matrix with two identical rows. The determinant of this new matrix is zero. Hence the original matrix also had a determinant of zero.

Given a matrix A, let us now derive a new matrix A^* which differs from A only in that its ith row is equal to the old ith row plus k times the mth row. Hence a typical element of this row, a^*_{ij}, is equal to $a_{ij} + ka_{mj}$. Evaluating the determinant of A^* by using the Laplace expansion of row i we have:

$$|A| = \sum_{j=1}^{j=n} a^*_{ij} |C^*_{ij}|$$

However, the co-factors of the new ith row are identical to those of the old ith row since no other rows of the original matrix have been altered. Given this equality and substituting for a^*_{ij} in the above equation, we have:

$$|A^*| = \sum_{j=1}^{j=n} a_{ij}|C_{ij}| + k\sum_{j=1}^{j=n} a_{mj}|C_{ij}|$$

$$= \sum_{j=1}^{j=n} a_{ij}|C_{ij}|$$

$$= |A|$$

Since adding the multiple of a row (column) to another row (column) does not change the value of the determinant, then it is clear that if a row (column) of a matrix is a linear combination of other rows (columns) of the matrix, then the determinant must vanish. Assume row can be written as a linear combination of the other $n - 1$ rows. Now deducting this linear combination from the first row will not change the value of the determinant, but will leave a set of zeroes there. Hence the determinant must have a value of zero.

This property of determinants is particularly useful for the evaluation of higher order determinants.

Example 4.7

Consider the following matrix:

$$A = \begin{bmatrix} 5 & 2 & -2 & 1 \\ 12 & 6 & -6 & 3 \\ 7 & -3 & 2 & -1 \\ 6 & 4 & 9 & 2 \end{bmatrix}$$

Multiply the first row by -3 and add to the second row to obtain:

$$\begin{bmatrix} 5 & 2 & -2 & 1 \\ -3 & 0 & 0 & 0 \\ 7 & -3 & 2 & -1 \\ 6 & 4 & 9 & 2 \end{bmatrix}$$

We now evaluate the determinant using the Laplace expansion process on the second row.

$$\det. A = 3\begin{vmatrix} 2 & -2 & 1 \\ -3 & 2 & -1 \\ 4 & 9 & 2 \end{vmatrix}$$

However, we may further simplify our calculations by adding the second row to the first row:

$$\det. A = 3\begin{vmatrix} -1 & 0 & 0 \\ -3 & 2 & -1 \\ 4 & 9 & 2 \end{vmatrix}$$

$$= 3(-1)\begin{vmatrix} 2 & -1 \\ 9 & 2 \end{vmatrix}$$

$$= -39$$

4.3 DETERMINANTS AND THE INVERSE OF A MATRIX

Let A be a square matrix; then if $AB = BA = I$, then B is said to be the inverse of A, which is written as A^{-1}. Given some square matrix A, how can we find its inverse, assuming that it exists? Note that we must have the inner product of the ith row of $A(B)$ and the jth column of $B(A)$ equal to unity for $i = j$, and 0 otherwise. To proceed we introduce the concept of an adjoint matrix. The adjoint of A, written $adj.A$, is a matrix formed by first calculating the co-factors of all the elements of A, stacking these co-factors in a matrix, and finally transposing this matrix of co-factors. We, therefore, have:

$$adj.A = \begin{bmatrix} |C_{11}| & |C_{21}| & \ldots & |C_{n1}| \\ |C_{12}| & |C_{22}| & \ldots & |C_{n2}| \\ \vdots & \vdots & \ldots & \vdots \\ |C_{1n}| & |C_{2n}| & \ldots & |C_{nn}| \end{bmatrix}$$

Now consider the matrix formed by pre-multiplying $adj.A$ by A. The inner product of the ith row of A and the ith column of $adj.A$ is by the Laplace expansion process equal to the determinant of A, whereas the inner product of the ith row of A and the jth column of $adj.A$ is equal to zero when i is not equal to j, since this involves a Laplace expansion using alien co-factors. It must, therefore, be the case that $A\,adj.A$ is a diagonal matrix in which the determinant of A appears everywhere in the principal diagonal, and we have zeroes everywhere else. If we then multiply this matrix by a scalar equal to the reciprocal of the determinant of A, we shall end up with an identity matrix. It, therefore, follows that:

$$A^{-1} = \frac{1}{\det.A} adj.A$$

Since it is impermissible to divide by zero, the inverse of A only exists if its determinant does not vanish. A matrix whose determinant is zero is called a singular matrix.

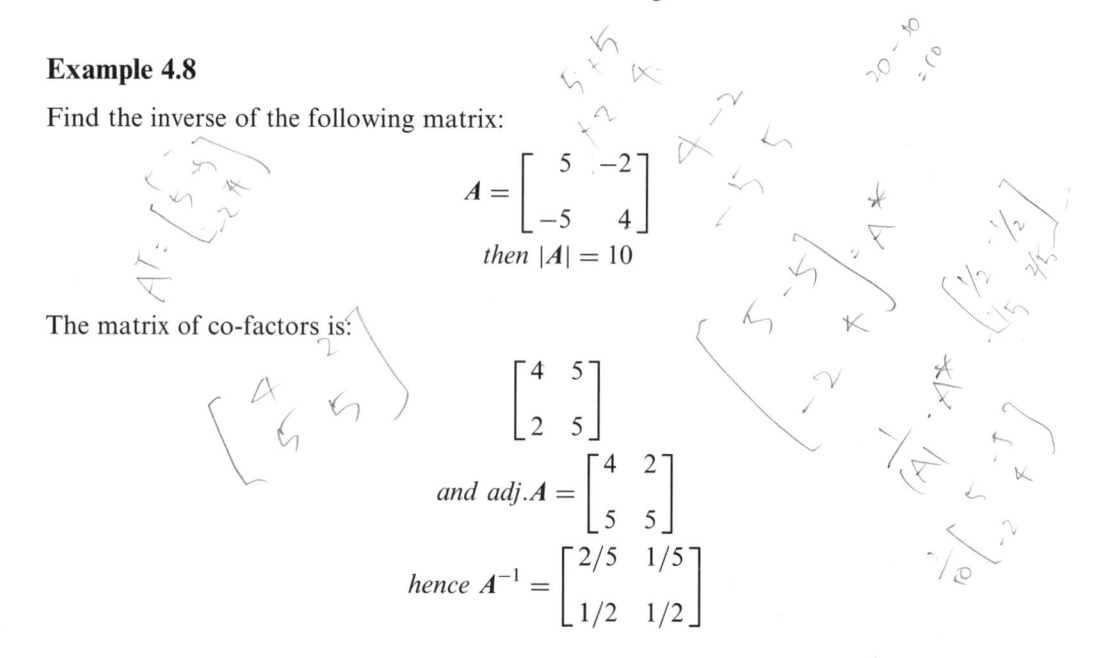

Example 4.8

Find the inverse of the following matrix:

$$A = \begin{bmatrix} 5 & -2 \\ -5 & 4 \end{bmatrix}$$

then $|A| = 10$

The matrix of co-factors is:

$$\begin{bmatrix} 4 & 5 \\ 2 & 5 \end{bmatrix}$$

and $adj.A = \begin{bmatrix} 4 & 2 \\ 5 & 5 \end{bmatrix}$

hence $A^{-1} = \begin{bmatrix} 2/5 & 1/5 \\ 1/2 & 1/2 \end{bmatrix}$

Example 4.9

Is it possible to find the inverse of the following matrix?

$$A = \begin{bmatrix} 6 & 3 \\ 8 & 4 \end{bmatrix}$$

It is a straightforward matter to see that the determinant of this matrix is zero. The matrix is not therefore invertible: A is a singular matrix in this case.

4.4 THE SOLUTION TO A SET OF LINEAR SIMULTANEOUS EQUATIONS

In this section, we consider the solution to the following set of equations:

$$Ax = b$$

where A is a non-singular matrix. If we pre-multiply the equation by the inverse of A, we shall obtain the solution we are seeking:

$$A^{-1}Ax = Ix = x = A^{-1}b$$

Alternatively, we may make use of the result derived in the previous section where we demonstrated that

$$A^{-1} = \frac{adj.A}{det.A}$$

Hence the solution may be expressed in the following way:

$$x = \frac{adj.A}{det.A}b$$

and the value taken by the variable, x_j, is given by

$$x_j = \frac{1}{det.A}[|C_{1j}|b_1 + |C_{2j}|b_2 + \cdots + |C_{nj}|b_n]$$

Note that the expression inside the square brackets, which is the inner product of the *j*th row of the adjoint of A and the column vector of constants, b, is itself equal to the determinant of a particular matrix. This matrix is one which has been created by replacing the *j*th column of A with the b vector. In calculating the co-factors which make up the *j*th row of the adjoint of A, we utilised all the columns of A except the *j*th one. These co-factors now appear in a row as a result of transposing the matrix of co-factors. Post-multiplying this row by the column b yields by the Laplace expansion process the determinant of the matrix described above: an amended A matrix in which the original *j*th column has been replaced by b. Each of the unknown xs can, therefore, be found by evaluating the ratio of two determinants. This procedure is known as Cramer's rule.

Example 4.10

Consider the following set of equations:

$$\begin{bmatrix} 1 & 3 & 2 \\ -1 & 2 & 1 \\ 3 & 0 & 4 \end{bmatrix} \begin{bmatrix} x_1 \\ x_2 \\ x_3 \end{bmatrix} = \begin{bmatrix} 14 \\ 7 \\ 11 \end{bmatrix}$$

We now proceed to apply Cramer's rule in order to find the values of the xs which satisfy the three equations. We have:

$$x_1 = \frac{\begin{vmatrix} 14 & 3 & 2 \\ 7 & 2 & 1 \\ 11 & 0 & 4 \end{vmatrix}}{\begin{vmatrix} 1 & 3 & 2 \\ -1 & 2 & 1 \\ 3 & 0 & 4 \end{vmatrix}}$$

$$x_2 = \frac{\begin{vmatrix} 1 & 14 & 2 \\ -1 & 7 & 1 \\ 3 & 11 & 4 \end{vmatrix}}{\begin{vmatrix} 1 & 3 & 2 \\ -1 & 2 & 1 \\ 3 & 0 & 4 \end{vmatrix}}$$

$$x_3 = \frac{\begin{vmatrix} 1 & 3 & 14 \\ -1 & 2 & 7 \\ 3 & 0 & 11 \end{vmatrix}}{\begin{vmatrix} 1 & 3 & 2 \\ -1 & 2 & 1 \\ 3 & 0 & 4 \end{vmatrix}}$$

First, we evaluate the determinant of A, i.e. the determinant which appears in the denominator of the above three expressions. Since a zero appears in the third row, it makes sense to calculate the determinant by employing the Laplace expansion process on the third row.

$$\det A = 3 \begin{vmatrix} 3 & 2 \\ 2 & 1 \end{vmatrix} + 4 \begin{vmatrix} 1 & 3 \\ -1 & 2 \end{vmatrix} = 3(-1) + 4(5) = 17$$

To find the determinant in the numerator of the expression for x_1, again it makes sense to use the Laplace expansion of the third row. Hence we have

$$\begin{vmatrix} 14 & 3 & 2 \\ 7 & 2 & 1 \\ 11 & 0 & 4 \end{vmatrix} = 11 \begin{vmatrix} 3 & 2 \\ 2 & 1 \end{vmatrix} + 4 \begin{vmatrix} 14 & 3 \\ 7 & 2 \end{vmatrix} = 11(-1) + 4(7) = 17$$

and x_1 is equal to *1*.

To find the determinant in the numerator of the expression for x_2, we first add the second row to the first row to obtain a new first row. As we have seen, such an operation does not change the value of the determinant, but this operation will yield a zero in the first row, thus simplifying the calculation of the determinant. Note also in this case that we multiply the first subdeterminant by -21 rather than by 21 since the element lies in an odd position in row 1 column 2, and the subdeterminant is, therefore, the minor but not the co-factor of the element.

$$\begin{vmatrix} 1 & 14 & 2 \\ -1 & 7 & 1 \\ 3 & 11 & 4 \end{vmatrix} = \begin{vmatrix} 0 & 21 & 3 \\ -1 & 7 & 1 \\ 3 & 11 & 4 \end{vmatrix}$$

$$= -21 \begin{vmatrix} -1 & 1 \\ 3 & 4 \end{vmatrix} + 3 \begin{vmatrix} -1 & 7 \\ 3 & 11 \end{vmatrix} = -21(-7) + 3(-32) = 51$$

Hence x_2 is equal to 3.

Finally we evaluate:

$$\begin{vmatrix} 1 & 3 & 14 \\ -1 & 2 & 7 \\ 3 & 0 & 11 \end{vmatrix} = 3 \begin{vmatrix} 3 & 14 \\ 2 & 7 \end{vmatrix} + 11 \begin{vmatrix} 1 & 3 \\ -1 & 2 \end{vmatrix} = 3(-7) + 11(5) = 34$$

Hence x_3 is equal to 2.

Alternatively we could instead of applying Cramer's rule which required us to evaluate four 3×3 determinants, we could have proceeded by finding the inverse of A.

$$adj.A = \begin{bmatrix} 8 & -12 & -1 \\ 7 & -2 & -3 \\ -6 & 9 & 5 \end{bmatrix}$$

We have already shown that the determinant of A is equal to 17 in this instance, and hence we have:

$$x = \frac{adj.A}{\det.A} b = \frac{1}{17} \begin{bmatrix} 8 & -12 & -1 \\ 7 & -2 & -3 \\ -6 & 9 & 5 \end{bmatrix} \begin{bmatrix} 14 \\ 7 \\ 11 \end{bmatrix}$$

$$= \frac{1}{17} \begin{bmatrix} 8(14) + (-12)(7) + (-1)(11) \\ 7(14) + (-2)(7) + (-3)(11) \\ (-6)(14) + 9(7) + 5(11) \end{bmatrix}$$

$$= \begin{bmatrix} 1 \\ 3 \\ 2 \end{bmatrix}$$

4.5 A SIMPLE MACROECONOMIC MODEL

Consider the following linear macroeconomic model:

$$C = a + CD \tag{1}$$
$$D = Y - T = (1 - t)Y \tag{2}$$
$$I = d - eR \tag{3}$$
$$G = \tilde{G} \tag{4}$$
$$X = \tilde{X} \tag{5}$$
$$MP = mY \tag{6}$$
$$Y = C + I + G + X - MP \tag{7}$$
$$M^d = f + gY - hR \tag{8}$$
$$M^s = \tilde{M} \tag{9}$$
$$M^d = M^s \tag{10}$$

where C is planned consumption expenditure, D disposable income, Y national income, T total taxation, I planned investment, G planned government expenditure, X exports, MP imports, R the rate of interest, M^d the demand for money, M^s the supply of money. The lower case letters are all positive parameters, with the marginal propensity to consume, c, the marginal propensity to import, m, and the tax rate, t, all constrained to be less than unity.

Substituting equations (1) through (6) into (7) yields the equation defining the locus of points in income–interest rate space for which the goods market is in equilibrium: planned expenditure is equal to income. This is the equation of the *IS* curve, which is downward sloping in (Y, R) space. Substituting equations (8) and (9) into (10) yields the equation defining the locus of points in income–interest rate space for which the money market is in equilibrium: this is the equation of the *LM* curve, which is upward sloping in (Y, R) space.

$$[1 - c(1 - t) + m]Y + eR = a + d + \tilde{G} + \tilde{X} \quad (IS)$$

$$-gY + hR = f - \tilde{M} \quad (LM)$$

Applying Cramer's rule, we obtain:

$$Y = \frac{\begin{vmatrix} a + d + \tilde{G} + \tilde{X} & e \\ f - \tilde{M} & h \end{vmatrix}}{\begin{vmatrix} 1 - c(1 - t) + m & e \\ -g & h \end{vmatrix}}$$

$$= \frac{(a + d + \tilde{G} + \tilde{X})h + e(\tilde{M} - f)}{(1 - c(1 - t) + m)h + eg}$$

$$R = \frac{\begin{vmatrix} 1-c(1-t)+m & a+d+\tilde{G}+\tilde{X} \\ -g & f-\tilde{M} \end{vmatrix}}{\begin{vmatrix} 1-c(1-t)+m & e \\ -g & h \end{vmatrix}}$$

$$= \frac{(f-\tilde{M})(1-c(1-t)+m)+(a+d+\tilde{G}+\tilde{X})g}{(1-c(1-t)+m)h+eg}$$

Note that income increases when either government expenditure or the money supply is increased, whereas the rate of interest rises with an increase in government expenditure, but falls with an increase in the money supply.

4.6 SUMMARY

In this chapter we have discussed the concept of determinants, outlined their properties, and shown how to calculate them. The most straightforward procedure for finding the numerical value of the determinant of a matrix is to apply the Laplace expansion process which relies on the calculation of co-factors. Co-factors and the related concept of a minor, which is just a subdeterminant formed by eliminating the row and column in which the particular element of the matrix appears, at most differ from each other by a sign change.

We went on to show that a matrix whose determinant is not equal to zero can be inverted. Such a matrix is known as a non-singular matrix. Matrix inversion can be used to find the solution to a set of linear simultaneous equations. An alternative approach is to make use of Cramer's rule to calculate the ratio of two determinants in order to solve for the values of the variables. The chapter ended with a discussion of a simple macroeconomic model, to which the techniques discussed in this chapter could be applied.

As we have seen, Cramer's rule can be used to solve a set of equations in the case where there are as many unknowns as there are equations, and the matrix of coefficients is invertible. In the next chapter we shall investigate how to tackle the more complicated cases where the number of unknowns is not equal to the number of equations, or where A is a singular matrix.

4.7 EXERCISES

4.1 (a) Evaluate the determinants of the following matrices:

(i) $\begin{vmatrix} 2 & -5 \\ 4 & -8 \end{vmatrix}$, (ii) $\begin{vmatrix} 3 & 5 & 2 \\ 4 & 6 & -1 \\ 2 & 1 & 8 \end{vmatrix}$

(iii) $\begin{vmatrix} -1 & -1 & 3 \\ 4 & 6 & -1 \\ 2 & 1 & 8 \end{vmatrix}$, (iv) $\begin{vmatrix} 2 & 2 & -6 \\ -8 & -12 & 2 \\ -4 & -2 & -16 \end{vmatrix}$

(v) $\begin{vmatrix} 5 & 6 & 1 \\ 3 & 4 & 2 \\ 2 & -1 & 8 \end{vmatrix}$, (vi) $\begin{vmatrix} 0 & 3 & -9 \\ 3 & 4 & 2 \\ 2 & -1 & 8 \end{vmatrix}$

$$\text{(vii)}\begin{vmatrix} 0 & 1 & 1 & 7 \\ 1 & 3 & 3 & -6 \\ 1 & 3 & 4 & -6 \\ 7 & -6 & -6 & 9 \end{vmatrix}, \quad \text{(viii)}\begin{vmatrix} 5 & 4 & 0 & 5 \\ 1 & 0 & 1 & 2 \\ 3 & 4 & -2 & 1 \\ 1 & -3 & 7 & 5 \end{vmatrix}$$

4.2 (a) Find the inverses of the matrices given in Exercise 4.1. Note the inverse of (viii) is not defined since its determinant is equal to zero.

4.3 (a) Use Cramer's rule to solve the following sets of equations:

(i) $2x_1 + x_2 = 44$
$x_1 + 3x_2 = 72$

(ii) $3x_1 + 2x_2 = 41$
$2x_1 + 5x_2 = 53$

(iii) $3x_1 + 5x_3 = 69$
$2x_2 + 4x_3 = 46$
$x_1 + x_2 + 4x_3 = 30$

(iv) $5x_1 + 2x_2 + 3x_3 = 76$
$x_2 + 2x_3 = 34$
$4x_1 + 5x_2 = 20$

(b) Solve the following sets of equations by matrix inversion:

(i) $\begin{bmatrix} 2 & -3 \\ 1 & 5 \end{bmatrix}\begin{bmatrix} x_1 \\ x_2 \end{bmatrix} = \begin{bmatrix} 4 \\ 54 \end{bmatrix}$

(ii) $\begin{bmatrix} 2 & 6 \\ -1 & 2 \end{bmatrix}\begin{bmatrix} x_1 \\ x_2 \end{bmatrix} = \begin{bmatrix} 18 \\ 21 \end{bmatrix}$

(iii) $\begin{bmatrix} 5 & 2 & 7 \\ 0 & 1 & 0 \\ 3 & 0 & -2 \end{bmatrix}\begin{bmatrix} x_1 \\ x_2 \\ x_3 \end{bmatrix} = \begin{bmatrix} 0 \\ 25 \\ 32 \end{bmatrix}$

(iv) $\begin{bmatrix} 2 & -1 & 1 \\ 4 & 0 & 3 \\ -1 & 4 & 0 \end{bmatrix}\begin{bmatrix} x_1 \\ x_2 \\ x_3 \end{bmatrix} = \begin{bmatrix} 10 \\ 45 \\ 30 \end{bmatrix}$

4.4 (a) For the above macroeconomic model, derive the equilibrium values of output and the rate of interest for the following numerical values of the parameters of the model:

$a = 50, \quad c = 4/5, \quad t = 1/4, \quad m = 1/5, \quad d = 300, \quad e = 20,$

$\tilde{G} = 300, \quad \tilde{X} = 200, \quad f = 1000, \quad g = 1, \quad h = 50, \quad \tilde{M} = 2000$

(i) How large is equilibrium output and what is the equilibrium value of the rate of interest?
(ii) What are the numerical values of the fiscal and money multipliers?
(iii) If the full employment level of output is *1400*, calculate the increase in government expenditure required to achieve full employment. What is the resultant change in the rate of interest?

(iv) Calculate the increase in the money supply that is required to achieve full employment. What is the resultant change in the rate of interest?

(v) Determine the set of all possible combinations of rates of government expenditure and levels of the money supply which will yield full employment. How will the composition of full employment output be affected by the government's choice of policy?

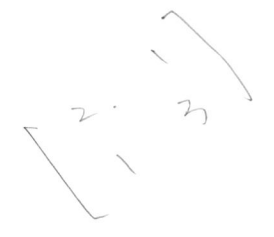

CHAPTER FIVE

SIMULTANEOUS LINEAR EQUATIONS

5.1 INTRODUCTION

In Chapter 4 we examined the simple case where the solution to a set of linear equations was unique. Here, we open up the discussion to consider more generally the subject of simultaneous linear equations. A key concept that we need to throw light on this subject is that of the rank of the matrix. This concept is discussed in Section 5.2. We may distinguish between the row rank and the column rank of a matrix: the row rank of a matrix is the number of linearly independent rows of a matrix, whereas the column rank is the number of linearly independent columns of a matrix. However, row and column rank of a matrix are always the same, so we may refer unambiguously just to the rank of a matrix. In Section 5.3 we consider the solution to a set of linear equations where the number of equations is equal to the number of unknowns. We are concerned with the conditions which must be satisfied for there to exist a solution to a set of linear equations. If a solution exists, under what circumstances will the solution be unique or non-unique?

In Section 5.4 we introduce the concept of elementary row and column operations and the associated concept of elementary matrices. Here what we are concerned with are the techniques of multiplying a row or column of a matrix by a scalar, and of multiplying a row or column of a matrix by a scalar and then adding this new row (column) to another row (column) of the matrix. In Chapter 4, we showed how to invert a non-singular matrix by multiplying the transposed matrix of co-factors of the original matrix, which is known as the adjoint, by the reciprocal of its determinant. In Section 5.5 we demonstrate how elementary row operations can be used in order to invert a non-singular matrix, and to find thereby the solution to a set of equations. In the case where the matrix is non-singular, the solution will be unique. The advantage of this approach to solving simultaneous linear equations over the determinantal one is that we can also automatically find, when they exist, the set of non-unique solutions when the matrix is singular. In Section 5.6 we introduce the concept of echelon matrices, and show again how elementary row operations can be employed to derive such matrices. Echelon matrices are a particularly useful means of solving a set of equations when the number of unknowns is greater than the number of equations. The procedure of using elementary row operations on a matrix to obtain the solution to a set of linear equations is known as Gaussian elimination. When we have more variables than unknowns, we shall have to predetermine the values of some of the variables in order so solve for the values of the remaining ones. We shall obtain what is known as a basic solution to the set of equations when the value assigned to each predetermined variable is zero. We shall see when we come to analyse linear programming problems, starting in Chapter 6, that a key role is played by basic solutions to a set of linear simultaneous equations.

5.2 THE RANK OF A MATRIX

We define a matrix to have row rank k if the number of linearly independent rows is k. Similarly column rank refers to the number of linearly independent columns. However, it so happens that the row rank of any matrix is equal to its column rank, and so we may simply refer without ambiguity to the rank of the matrix A, which we write as rank(A).

Assume for the moment that A is a square matrix of dimension n. If the rank of this matrix is n, then all its rows (columns) are linearly independent, and as we know from our earlier discussion of determinants, its determinant will be non-zero and its inverse will exist. Alternatively, we may say that A is a non-singular matrix, and that both the rows and columns of A provide a basis for R^n.

Now more generally, let A be an $m \times n$ matrix. Given that a matrix's row and column rank are the same, the rank of this matrix cannot be greater than the smaller of m and n. A will have full rank if rank(A) is min(m, n). A will be of rank k if we can find at least one non-zero valued determinant of order k associated with a submatrix consisting of k rows and columns of A, whilst there are no non-zero valued determinants associated with higher dimension submatrices of A. To find the rank of A where $m > n$, we first look at the largest square submatrices that we can form from A; these will be of dimension n. We check whether any of these submatrices are non-singular, i.e. whether any have a non-zero determinant. If all these submatrices are singular, we then examine the next largest square submatrices of A for non-singularity; these will be of dimension $n - 1$. The procedure continues until we have found the first non-singular matrix; rank(A) is equal to the dimension of the first non-singular matrix.

Example 5.1

Let us evaluate the rank of the following 3×4 matrix:

$$A = \begin{bmatrix} 4 & 3 & 2 & 1 \\ 0 & -1 & -2 & -3 \\ 8 & 3 & -2 & -7 \end{bmatrix}$$

Its rank cannot exceed three; so, we first try to find a non-vanishing 3×3 determinant. There are four 3×3 determinants to evaluate:

$$\begin{vmatrix} 4 & 3 & 2 \\ 0 & -1 & -2 \\ 8 & 3 & -2 \end{vmatrix} = -1 \begin{vmatrix} 4 & 2 \\ 8 & -2 \end{vmatrix} + 2 \begin{vmatrix} 4 & 3 \\ 8 & 3 \end{vmatrix} = 0$$

$$\begin{vmatrix} 4 & 3 & 1 \\ 0 & -1 & -3 \\ 8 & 3 & -7 \end{vmatrix} = -1 \begin{vmatrix} 4 & 1 \\ 8 & -7 \end{vmatrix} + 3 \begin{vmatrix} 4 & 3 \\ 8 & 3 \end{vmatrix} = 0$$

$$\begin{vmatrix} 4 & 2 & 1 \\ 0 & -2 & -3 \\ 8 & -2 & -7 \end{vmatrix} = -2\begin{vmatrix} 4 & 1 \\ 8 & -7 \end{vmatrix} + 3\begin{vmatrix} 4 & 2 \\ 8 & -2 \end{vmatrix} = 0$$

$$\begin{vmatrix} 3 & 2 & 1 \\ -1 & -2 & -3 \\ 3 & -2 & -7 \end{vmatrix} = 3\begin{vmatrix} -2 & -3 \\ -2 & -7 \end{vmatrix} - 2\begin{vmatrix} -1 & -3 \\ 3 & -7 \end{vmatrix} + 1\begin{vmatrix} -1 & -2 \\ 3 & -2 \end{vmatrix} = 0$$

Since all these four determinants vanish, the matrix cannot be of rank(3). However in applying the Laplace expansion process to evaluate the 3×3 determinants we found many non-vanishing minors of order 2; hence the matrix is of rank(2). The reader should check that we may write the third row as the sum of twice the first row and three times the second row. As regards linear dependence of the columns of A, we may write the third column as twice the second column less the first column, whereas the fourth column may be written as three times the second column less twice the first column.

Given two matrices, A and B, which are conformable for multiplication, then rank(AB) = min(rank(A), rank(B)). It also follows that if BA exists its rank is the same as that of AB.

Assume we have two matrices: A which is 3×2, and B which is 2×3. The matrix $C = AB$ is, therefore, defined and is 3×3. Let both A and B be of full rank. Hence we may write:

$$A = \begin{bmatrix} \alpha_1 \\ \alpha_2 \\ k_1\alpha_1 + k_2\alpha_2 \end{bmatrix}, \quad B = [b_1 \; b_2 \; m_1 b_1 + m_2 b_2]$$

where α_i is the ith row of A and b_j is the jth column of B. The reader should form the product $C = AB$ and then check that:

$$c_3 = m_1 c_1 + m_2 c_2$$

$$\gamma_3 = k_1 \gamma_1 + k_2 \gamma_2$$

where γ_i is the ith row and c_j is the jth column of C.

5.3 THE SOLUTION TO A SET OF LINEAR EQUATIONS

Consider the solution to the set of equations: $Ax = b$ where A is a square matrix. If A is non-singular, its inverse exists and the solution is given by: $x = A^{-1}b$. How may we proceed, however, in the case where A is a singular matrix? In this situation the columns of A are linearly dependent, and accordingly only span a sub-space of R^n. If b does lie in the subspace spanned by the columns of A, then it will be possible to express b as a linear combination of the columns of A. The solution, however, will not be unique.

Example 5.2

Assume we have

$$A = \begin{bmatrix} 5 & -15 \\ 2 & -6 \end{bmatrix}, \quad b = \begin{bmatrix} 10 \\ 4 \end{bmatrix}$$

It is clear that the columns of A are linearly dependent, and that b lies in the subspace spanned by these columns (i.e. the b vector lies on the same ray through the origin as the column vectors of A). Therefore, b may be expressed as a linear combination of the columns of A, but there is an uncountable number of ways of doing this; letting x_1 and x_2 be the weights attached to the two columns of A, the only restriction is that $x_1 = 2 + 3x_2$. However, if b lies on some other ray through the origin, then it lies outside the subspace spanned by the columns of A. There is no way in which b can be expressed as a linear combination of the columns of A. Let

$$b = \begin{bmatrix} 1 \\ 3 \end{bmatrix}$$

Then again applying weights, x_1 and x_2, to the columns of A we have

$$5x_1 - 15x_2 = 1$$

$$2x_1 - 6x_2 = 3$$

The system of equations is inconsistent; there is no way that x_1 can equal both $0.2 + 3x_2$ and $1.5 + 3x_2$.

We may summarise the position. If rank($[A, b]$) is greater than rank(A), the system of equations is inconsistent. On the other hand, if rank($[A, b]$) is the same as rank(A), given that A is singular, we have a consistent system, but one in which the number of solutions is infinite.

Example 5.3

Let us consider the following system of equations:

$$\begin{bmatrix} 5 & 6 & 1 \\ 2 & 4 & -6 \\ 1 & 2 & -3 \end{bmatrix} \begin{bmatrix} x_1 \\ x_2 \\ x_3 \end{bmatrix} = \begin{bmatrix} 25 \\ 18 \\ 9 \end{bmatrix}$$

Note A is singular since the second row is twice the third row. Rank(A) is two; we can easily find non-singular submatrices of order two. What about the rank of $[A, b]$? Note this is also two, since we still have a situation in which the second row of the extended matrix is still twice the third row. In this example, therefore, we have a consistent system of equations with an infinite number of solutions.

Dropping the third row, we may write the system as follows:

$$\begin{bmatrix} 5 & 6 & 1 \\ 2 & 4 & -6 \end{bmatrix} \begin{bmatrix} x_1 \\ x_2 \\ x_3 \end{bmatrix} = \begin{bmatrix} 25 \\ 18 \end{bmatrix}$$

Note that we now have a rectangular matrix on the left-hand side, but we can convert this into a square matrix by taking some terms over to the right-hand side. In this matter we have a choice: we may take over the terms containing either x_1, x_2 or x_3. Let us take over the terms containing x_1 to obtain:

$$\begin{bmatrix} 6 & 1 \\ 4 & -6 \end{bmatrix} \begin{bmatrix} x_2 \\ x_3 \end{bmatrix} = \begin{bmatrix} 25 - 5x_1 \\ 18 - 2x_1 \end{bmatrix}$$

Solving these two equations we find:

$$x_2 = 4.2 - 0.8x_1$$
$$x_3 = -0.2 - 0.2x_1$$

5.4 ELEMENTARY OPERATIONS ON A MATRIX

Given a matrix A there are some simple operations that we may perform on this matrix. These operations, known as elementary operations, take one of three different forms:

1. the interchanging of two rows (columns) of the original matrix;
2. the multiplication of a row (column) of the original matrix by a scalar;
3. the addition of a scalar multiple of one row (column) of the original matrix to another row (column) of the original matrix.

If we perform such elementary operations on an identity matrix, we obtain what are known as elementary matrices. For instance the operation of interchanging the first and third rows of a 3×3 identity matrix is given by the following elementary matrix:

$$E_1 = \begin{bmatrix} 0 & 0 & 1 \\ 0 & 1 & 0 \\ 1 & 0 & 0 \end{bmatrix}$$

The same matrix obviously also represents the operation of changing the first and third columns of an identity matrix.

Multiplying the second row (column) of a 3×3 identity matrix by a scalar, λ, is represented by the following elementary matrix:

$$E_2 = \begin{bmatrix} 1 & 0 & 0 \\ 0 & \lambda & 0 \\ 0 & 0 & 1 \end{bmatrix}$$

Finally, multiplying the second row of a 3×3 identity matrix by a scalar, λ, and then adding it to the first row is given by:

$$E_3 = \begin{bmatrix} 1 & \lambda & 0 \\ 0 & 1 & 0 \\ 0 & 0 & 1 \end{bmatrix}$$

To apply elementary row operations to some matrix A, we pre-multiply A by the relevant elementary matrices, whereas to apply elementary column operations, we must post-multiply A by the relevant elementary matrices.

Example 5.4

To interchange the first and third rows of A where

$$A = \begin{bmatrix} 1 & 1 & 4 \\ 2 & 4 & 1 \\ 1 & 3 & 2 \end{bmatrix}$$

then

$$E_1 A = \begin{bmatrix} 0 & 0 & 1 \\ 0 & 1 & 0 \\ 1 & 0 & 0 \end{bmatrix} \begin{bmatrix} 1 & 1 & 4 \\ 2 & 4 & 1 \\ 1 & 3 & 2 \end{bmatrix}$$

$$= \begin{bmatrix} 1 & 3 & 2 \\ 2 & 4 & 1 \\ 1 & 1 & 4 \end{bmatrix}$$

Example 5.5

To interchange the first and third columns of A, we must post-multiply A by E_1:

$$AE_1 = \begin{bmatrix} 1 & 1 & 4 \\ 2 & 4 & 1 \\ 1 & 3 & 2 \end{bmatrix} \begin{bmatrix} 0 & 0 & 1 \\ 0 & 1 & 0 \\ 1 & 0 & 0 \end{bmatrix}$$

$$= \begin{bmatrix} 4 & 1 & 1 \\ 1 & 4 & 2 \\ 2 & 3 & 1 \end{bmatrix}$$

Example 5.6

Multiplying the second row of A by 2 and adding to the first row of A is given by EA where

$$EA = \begin{bmatrix} 1 & 2 & 0 \\ 0 & 1 & 0 \\ 0 & 0 & 1 \end{bmatrix} \begin{bmatrix} 1 & 1 & 4 \\ 2 & 4 & 1 \\ 1 & 3 & 2 \end{bmatrix}$$

$$= \begin{bmatrix} 5 & 9 & 6 \\ 2 & 4 & 1 \\ 1 & 3 & 2 \end{bmatrix}$$

Example 5.7

Multiplying the second column of A by 2 and adding to the first column of A is given by

$$AE = \begin{bmatrix} 1 & 1 & 4 \\ 2 & 4 & 1 \\ 1 & 3 & 2 \end{bmatrix} \begin{bmatrix} 1 & 0 & 0 \\ 2 & 1 & 0 \\ 0 & 0 & 1 \end{bmatrix}$$

$$= \begin{bmatrix} 3 & 1 & 4 \\ 10 & 4 & 1 \\ 7 & 3 & 2 \end{bmatrix}$$

If a matrix B can be obtained by applying elementary matrices to some other matrix A, then the two matrices are said to be equivalent to each other. Letting P and Q be both products of elementary matrices, then A and B are equivalent matrices if it is the case that

$$PAQ = B$$

For the case of two square matrices, A and B, A and B are congruent matrices if

$$B = R^T A R$$

where R is a non-singular matrix.

For the case of two square matrices, A and B, A and B are similar matrices if $B = S^{-1}AS$.

5.5 ELEMENTARY OPERATIONS AND THE INVERSE OF A MATRIX

We now provide an example to show that the inverse of A can be obtained by carrying out a series of elementary row operations on an identity matrix.

Example 5.8

Given the following matrix A, extend it by adding on additional columns where these additional columns constitute an identity matrix. Hence, we have:

$$[A, I] = \begin{bmatrix} 4 & 1 & 1 & 0 \\ 3 & 1 & 0 & 1 \end{bmatrix}$$

We now carry out elementary row operations on the above extended matrix in order to end up with a matrix of the form $[I, B]$. The inverse of A will be equal to B. We first multiply the first row by $1/4$ to obtain:

$$\begin{bmatrix} 1 & 1/4 & 1/4 & 0 \\ 3 & 1 & 0 & 1 \end{bmatrix}$$

SIMULTANEOUS LINEAR EQUATIONS   53

We now multiply the new first row by -3 and add to the second row; this yields:

$$\begin{bmatrix} 1 & 1/4 & 1/4 & 0 \\ 0 & 1/4 & -3/4 & 1 \end{bmatrix}$$

Next we multiply the new second row by 4 to obtain:

$$\begin{bmatrix} 1 & 1/4 & 1/4 & 0 \\ 0 & 1 & -3 & 4 \end{bmatrix}$$

Finally we multiply this new second row by $-1/4$ and add to the first row:

$$\begin{bmatrix} 1 & 0 & 1 & -1 \\ 0 & 1 & -3 & 4 \end{bmatrix}$$

The inverse of A is given in columns 3 and 4 of the final extended matrix. It is the product of the following set of elementary matrices:

$$A^{-1} = \begin{bmatrix} 1 & -1/4 \\ 0 & 1 \end{bmatrix} \begin{bmatrix} 1 & 0 \\ 0 & 4 \end{bmatrix} \begin{bmatrix} 1 & 0 \\ -3 & 1 \end{bmatrix} \begin{bmatrix} 1/4 & 0 \\ 0 & 1 \end{bmatrix}$$

$$= \begin{bmatrix} 1 & -1/4 \\ 0 & 1 \end{bmatrix} \begin{bmatrix} 1 & 0 \\ 0 & 4 \end{bmatrix} \begin{bmatrix} 1/4 & 0 \\ -3/4 & 1 \end{bmatrix}$$

$$= \begin{bmatrix} 1 & -1/4 \\ 0 & 1 \end{bmatrix} \begin{bmatrix} 1/4 & 0 \\ -3 & 4 \end{bmatrix}$$

$$= \begin{bmatrix} 1 & -1 \\ -3 & 4 \end{bmatrix}$$

The inverse of a non-singular matrix can be obtained by carrying out elementary row operations on the original matrix. These row operations involve multiplying a row of an identity matrix by a scalar, and adding some multiple of a row of an identity matrix to another row. Pre-multiplying the original matrix by these square elementary matrices, we eventually end up with an identity matrix.

It clearly also follows that any square non-singular matrix can be obtained as the product of a set of elementary matrices. Given that

$$E_1 E_2 \ldots E_n A = I$$

then we must have

$$A = E_n^{-1} E_{n-1}^{-1} \ldots E_2^{-1} E_1^{-1} I$$

Consider example 5.8 above where we derived the inverse of

$$A = \begin{bmatrix} 4 & 1 \\ 3 & 1 \end{bmatrix}$$

The inverse was given by the product of the following elementary matrices:

$$E_1 = \begin{bmatrix} 1 & -1/4 \\ 0 & 1 \end{bmatrix}, \quad E_2 = \begin{bmatrix} 1 & 0 \\ 0 & 4 \end{bmatrix}$$

$$E_3 = \begin{bmatrix} 1 & 0 \\ -3 & 1 \end{bmatrix}, \quad E_4 = \begin{bmatrix} 1/4 & 0 \\ 0 & 1 \end{bmatrix}$$

It is a straightforward matter to show that the inverses of the above elementary matrices are given by:

$$E_1^{-1} = \begin{bmatrix} 1 & 1/4 \\ 0 & 1 \end{bmatrix}, \quad E_2^{-1} = \begin{bmatrix} 1 & 0 \\ 0 & 1/4 \end{bmatrix}$$

$$E_3^{-1} = \begin{bmatrix} 1 & 0 \\ 3 & 1 \end{bmatrix}, \quad E_4^{-1} = \begin{bmatrix} 4 & 0 \\ 0 & 1 \end{bmatrix}$$

The reader should then check that

$$\begin{bmatrix} 4 & 0 \\ 0 & 1 \end{bmatrix} \begin{bmatrix} 1 & 0 \\ 3 & 1 \end{bmatrix} \begin{bmatrix} 1 & 0 \\ 0 & 1/4 \end{bmatrix} \begin{bmatrix} 1 & 1/4 \\ 0 & 1 \end{bmatrix} = \begin{bmatrix} 4 & 1 \\ 3 & 1 \end{bmatrix}$$

A corollary of the result that a non-singular matrix can be written as the product of elementary matrices is that the determinant of this matrix is equal to the product of the determinants of the elementary matrices. As we saw in our discussion of determinants, the operation of multiplying a row of an identity matrix by a scalar simply leads to an outcome where the determinant of the new matrix is equal to the scalar multiple. Remember the determinant of an identity matrix is unity. The operation of multiplying the row of an identity matrix by a scalar and adding it to another row does not change the value of the determinant: it stays equal to unity. Hence, we have

$$|A| = |E_1||E_2|\ldots|E_n|$$

The result is of general applicability. If a matrix is the product of two non-singular square matrices, then its determinant is equal to the product of the determinants of the two matrices. What is the position if one of the square matrices is singular? We know from our earlier discussion of rank that a matrix which is the product of two square matrices, one of which is singular, cannot have full rank. Its determinant must be zero. Hence, regardless of whether our two matrices are non-singular or not, we shall always have:

$$|C| = |A||B|$$

given that

$$C = AB$$

5.6 ECHELON MATRICES

Now consider a matrix A of dimension m by n. We may carry out elementary row operations on this matrix so as to convert it into one of two forms.

$$\begin{bmatrix} a_{11} & a_{12} & \cdots & a_{1k} & \cdots & a_{1n} \\ 0 & a_{22} & \cdots & a_{2k} & \cdots & a_{2n} \\ \vdots & \vdots & \cdots & \vdots & \cdots & \vdots \\ 0 & 0 & \cdots & a_{kk} & \cdots & a_{kn} \\ 0 & 0 & \cdots & 0 & \cdots & 0 \\ \vdots & \vdots & \cdots & \vdots & \cdots & \vdots \\ 0 & 0 & \cdots & 0 & \cdots & 0 \end{bmatrix}$$

$$\begin{bmatrix} a_{11} & a_{12} & \cdots & a_{1m} & \cdots & a_{1n} \\ 0 & a_{22} & \cdots & a_{2m} & \cdots & a_{2n} \\ \vdots & \vdots & \cdots & \vdots & \cdots & \vdots \\ 0 & 0 & \cdots & a_{mm} & \cdots & a_{mn} \end{bmatrix}$$

Matrices of this form are known as echelon matrices.

If we carry out elementary operations on a set of equations, $Ax = b$, we do not alter the solution to that set of equations. Consider the following set:

$$a_{11}x_1 + a_{12}x_2 + a_{13}x_3 = b_1$$
$$a_{12}x_1 + a_{22}x_2 + a_{23}x_3 = b_2$$

If we multiply the first equation by a scalar λ, we obtain:

$$\lambda a_{11}x_1 + \lambda a_{12}x_2 + \lambda a_{13}x_3 = \lambda b_1$$
$$a_{12}x_1 + a_{22}x_2 + a_{23}x_3 = b_2$$

Its solution is obviously identical to that of our original set. Similarly, if we multiply the first equation in the original set by λ and add it to the second equation, we obtain:

$$a_{11}x_1 + a_{12}x_2 + a_{13}x_3 = b_1$$
$$(a_{21} + \lambda a_{11})x_1 + (a_{22} + \lambda a_{12})x_2 + (a_{23} + \lambda a_{13})x_3 = b_2 + \lambda b_1$$

The solution is again unchanged by this operation.

Let us assume that we have performed elementary operations on the set of equations $Ax = b$, and have obtained $Cx = d$, where C is an echelon matrix. This approach to solving a set of simultaneous equations is known as Gaussian elimination. If we further assume that C has rank k, then the equivalent set of equations will take the following form:

$$c_{11}x_1 + c_{12}x_2 + \cdots + c_{1k}x_k + \cdots + c_{1n}x_n = d_1$$
$$c_{22}x_2 + \cdots + c_{2k}x_k + \cdots + c_{2n}x_n = d_2$$
$$\vdots + \vdots + \vdots + \cdots + \vdots = \vdots$$
$$c_{kk}x_k + \cdots + c_{kn}x_n = d_k$$

If $k < m$, the remaining $m - k$ equations are redundant, and they will have disappeared as a consequence of our applying elementary row operations. If we assign values to $x_{k+1}, x_{k+2}, \ldots, x_n$, and substitute these values in the above set of equations, then we can solve for the remaining variables, $x_1, x_2, \ldots, x_k$, first obtaining the value of x_k, then x_{k-1}, and so on up to x_1.

A further simplification can be obtained by deriving the following equivalent set of equations:

$$x_1 + e_{1k+1}x_{k+1} + \cdots + e_{1n}x_n = f_1$$
$$x_2 + e_{2k+1}x_{k+1} + \cdots + e_{2n}x_n = f_2$$
$$\vdots + \vdots + \vdots + \cdots + \vdots = \vdots$$
$$x_k + e_{kk+1}x_{k+1} + \cdots + e_{kn}x_n = f_n$$

Note that the coefficient on the ith non-arbitrary variable is unity in the ith equation and zero in every other equation. In the general m by n equation system, some of the variables have to be given arbitrary values; these variables are known as independent variables, whereas the remaining variables are dependent or basic variables. If we assign a value of zero to each of the independent variables, then the solution which then emerges to the system of equations is known as a basic solution. If it so happens that one or more of the basic variables takes on a value of zero, then the basic solution is said to be degenerate.

Example 5.9

Consider the following set of equations:

$$\begin{bmatrix} 1 & 1 & 4 & 1 & 0 & 0 \\ 2 & 4 & 1 & 0 & 1 & 0 \\ 1 & 3 & 2 & 0 & 0 & 1 \end{bmatrix} \begin{bmatrix} x_1 \\ x_2 \\ x_3 \\ x_4 \\ x_5 \\ x_6 \end{bmatrix} = \begin{bmatrix} 12 \\ 16 \\ 14 \end{bmatrix}$$

We immediately have a basic solution by setting x_1, x_2 and x_3 all equal to zero. Then $x_4 = 12$, $x_5 = 16$ and $x_6 = 14$. Assume we now wish to obtain a basic solution containing the first three variables. We carry out elementary row operations to obtain an echelon matrix in which the first three columns constitute an identity matrix.

Firstly we add -2 times the first row to the second row, and -1 times the first row to the third row to obtain:

$$\begin{bmatrix} 1 & 1 & 4 & 1 & 0 & 0 \\ 0 & 2 & -7 & -2 & 1 & 0 \\ 0 & 2 & -2 & -1 & 0 & 1 \end{bmatrix} \begin{bmatrix} x_1 \\ x_2 \\ x_3 \\ x_4 \\ x_5 \\ x_6 \end{bmatrix} = \begin{bmatrix} 12 \\ -8 \\ 2 \end{bmatrix}$$

We now multiply the second row by *0.5*, add *−0.5* times the second row to the first row, and add *−1* times the second row to the third row to obtain:

$$\begin{bmatrix} 1 & 0 & 15/2 & 2 & -1/2 & 0 \\ 0 & 1 & -7/2 & -1 & 1/2 & 0 \\ 0 & 0 & 5 & 1 & -1 & 1 \end{bmatrix} \begin{bmatrix} x_1 \\ x_2 \\ x_3 \\ x_4 \\ x_5 \\ x_6 \end{bmatrix} = \begin{bmatrix} 16 \\ -4 \\ 10 \end{bmatrix}$$

Finally we multiply the third row by *1/5*, add *−3/2* times the third row to the first row, and add *7/10* times the third row to the second row.

$$\begin{bmatrix} 1 & 0 & 0 & 1/2 & 1 & -3/2 \\ 0 & 1 & 0 & -3/10 & -1/5 & 7/10 \\ 0 & 0 & 1 & 1/5 & -1/5 & 1/5 \end{bmatrix} \begin{bmatrix} x_1 \\ x_2 \\ x_3 \\ x_4 \\ x_5 \\ x_6 \end{bmatrix} = \begin{bmatrix} 1 \\ 3 \\ 2 \end{bmatrix}$$

Hence we have as our basic solution: $x_1 = 1$, $x_2 = 3$, $x_3 = 2$. The last three columns of this matrix constitute the inverse of the matrix made up of the first three columns of the original matrix; hence we have:

$$B = \begin{bmatrix} 1 & 1 & 4 \\ 2 & 4 & 1 \\ 1 & 3 & 2 \end{bmatrix}$$

$$B^{-1} = \begin{bmatrix} 1/2 & 1 & -3/2 \\ -3/10 & -1/5 & 7/10 \\ 1/5 & -1/5 & 1/5 \end{bmatrix}$$

Example 5.10

We now carry out a set of elementary operations on the following set of equations which we have referred to earlier in the chapter.

$$\begin{bmatrix} 5 & 6 & 1 \\ 2 & 4 & -6 \\ 1 & 2 & -3 \end{bmatrix} \begin{bmatrix} x_1 \\ x_2 \\ x_3 \end{bmatrix} = \begin{bmatrix} 25 \\ 18 \\ 9 \end{bmatrix}$$

Firstly, multiply the first row by *1/5*, multiply the first row by *−2/5* and add to the second, and multiply the first row by *−1/5* and add to the third row.

$$\begin{bmatrix} 1 & 6/5 & 1/5 \\ 0 & 8/5 & -32/5 \\ 0 & 4/5 & -16/5 \end{bmatrix} \begin{bmatrix} x_1 \\ x_2 \\ x_3 \end{bmatrix} = \begin{bmatrix} 5 \\ 8 \\ 4 \end{bmatrix}$$

Now multiply the second row by *5/8*, then multiply the second row by *−3/4* and add to the first row, and lastly multiply the second row by *−1/2* and add to the third row.

$$\begin{bmatrix} 1 & 0 & 5 \\ 0 & 1 & -4 \\ 0 & 0 & 0 \end{bmatrix} \begin{bmatrix} x_1 \\ x_2 \\ x_3 \end{bmatrix} = \begin{bmatrix} -1 \\ 5 \\ 0 \end{bmatrix}$$

The third equation is redundant, leaving us with two equations in three unknowns. We can solve for two of these variables in terms of the third variable; for example

$$x_1 = -1 - 5x_3$$
$$x_2 = 5 + 4x_3$$

5.7 SUMMARY

In this chapter we have been concerned with finding the solution to a set of linear simultaneous equations. We have seen that a key concept in explaining the nature of the solution to a set of such equations is that of the rank of a matrix: the number of linearly independent rows of the matrix of coefficients on the unknowns, *A*. In dealing with the case of an equal number of equations and unknowns, then there will exist a unique solution provided that *A* has a full rank. However, if this matrix is not of full rank, then its rows are not linearly independent. In these circumstances, there will exist an infinite number of solutions to the set of equations provided that the augmented matrix, i.e. the matrix of coefficients on the unknowns plus the column of constants, [*A*, *b*], has the same rank as *A*.

We then discussed the concept of elementary operations on a matrix, and demonstrated that elementary row operations could be employed to obtain the inverse of a non-singular matrix. Applying elementary row operations to a matrix, it can be transformed into an echelon matrix in which zeroes appear beneath the principal diagonal. The method of Gaussian elimination which makes use of elementary row operations and the conversion of matrices into echelon form can be used to derive the solution to a set of equations. An advantage of this procedure is that it can be applied when the number of unknowns is greater than the number of equations. When this is the case, then some of the variables will have to be treated as being exogenously determined with given values being assigned to them. It will then be possible to solve for the remaining variables.

In the next three chapters of the book, we shall be applying the techniques of linear algebra which we have discussed in Chapters 2 to 5 to examine how to solve what are known as linear programming problems. These are problems in which we seek to find non-negative values of a set of variables which maximise or minimise a linear function subject to a set of linear inequalities.

5.8 EXERCISES

5.1 (a) What is the rank of each of the following matrices?

$$\text{(i) } A = \begin{bmatrix} 5 & -1 \\ 4 & 2 \end{bmatrix}, \quad \text{(ii) } B = \begin{bmatrix} 1 & -3 & 2 \\ -2 & 0 & 1 \\ 5 & -1 & 5 \end{bmatrix},$$

$$\text{(iii) } C = \begin{bmatrix} 6 & -2 & 0 \\ -12 & 4 & 1 \end{bmatrix}, \quad \text{(iv) } D = \begin{bmatrix} 2 & -4 & 6 \\ -1 & 2 & -3 \\ 7 & -14 & 21 \end{bmatrix},$$

$$\text{(v) } E = \begin{bmatrix} -2 & 1 & 5 \\ 0 & 1 & -1 \\ 1 & 5 & 1 \\ 5 & 3 & -2 \end{bmatrix}, \quad \text{(vi) } F = \begin{bmatrix} 2 & -1 & 4 & 5 \\ 3 & 0 & -4 & 6 \\ 0 & -1 & 9 & -1 \\ 1 & 0 & 1 & 0 \end{bmatrix}$$

(b) For the matrices given above, what is the rank of each of the following:

(i) CB,   (ii) BE^T,   (iii) DC^T
(iv) BD^T,   (v) CE^T,   (vi) FE

5.2 (a) For the set of equations in Example 5.3 on page 49, express (a) x_1 and x_2 as functions of x_3, and (b) x_1 and x_3 as functions of x_2.

(b) (i) Obtain the solution to the following set of equations:

$$\begin{bmatrix} 1 & -3 & -1 \\ 2 & 5 & 4 \\ 1 & 8 & 5 \end{bmatrix} \begin{bmatrix} x_1 \\ x_2 \\ x_3 \end{bmatrix} = \begin{bmatrix} 19 \\ 16 \\ -3 \end{bmatrix}$$

(ii) What would have happened had the element in the right-hand side vector been 3 rather than -3?

5.3 (a) Use elementary row operations to find the inverses of the following matrices.

$$\text{(i) } \begin{bmatrix} 2 & 1 \\ 3 & 4 \end{bmatrix}, \quad \text{(ii) } \begin{bmatrix} 2 & 3 & 8 \\ 1 & 0 & 1 \\ 4 & 2 & 0 \end{bmatrix}$$

$$\text{(iii) } \begin{bmatrix} 5 & 1 & 2 \\ 8 & 6 & 3 \\ 5 & 4 & 2 \end{bmatrix}, \quad \text{(iv) } \begin{bmatrix} 5 & 0 & 1 & 2 \\ 0 & 5 & 0 & 0 \\ 3 & 0 & 5 & 1 \\ 10 & 0 & 8 & 4 \end{bmatrix}$$

(b) (i) What are the elementary matrices implied by the row operations you carried out in deriving the inversion in (a)(i) and (a)(ii) above.

(ii) Show that in the two cases the product of the determinants of these elementary matrices is equal to the reciprocal of the determinant of the original matrix.

(iii) Obtain the set of elementary matrices which will convert an identity matrix into the matrix given in 1(a).

(iv) Show that the product of the determinants of these elementary matrices is equal to the determinant of the original matrix.

5.4 (a) Reduce the following matrices to echelon form:

$$\text{(i)} \begin{bmatrix} 4 & -1 & 2 \\ 1 & 2 & -2 \\ 5 & -3 & 1 \end{bmatrix}, \quad \text{(ii)} \begin{bmatrix} 4 & -1 & 2 \\ 1 & 2 & -2 \\ 7 & -4 & 6 \end{bmatrix}$$

$$\text{(iii)} \begin{bmatrix} 2 & 3 & 0 & 1 \\ 4 & -1 & 2 & 0 \\ -1 & 0 & 0 & 5 \\ 2 & -1 & 1 & 2 \end{bmatrix}, \quad \text{(iv)} \begin{bmatrix} 2 & 3 & 0 & 1 \\ 6 & 2 & 2 & 1 \\ 4 & -1 & 2 & 0 \\ 2 & -4 & 2 & -1 \end{bmatrix}$$

(b) Solve the following sets of equations, using the Gaussian elimination method discussed in this section:

$$\text{(i)} \begin{bmatrix} 1 & -2 & 0 \\ 3 & 1 & 1 \\ -2 & -3 & 5 \end{bmatrix} \begin{bmatrix} x_1 \\ x_2 \\ x_3 \end{bmatrix} = \begin{bmatrix} 14 \\ 16 \\ 10 \end{bmatrix}$$

$$\text{(ii)} \begin{bmatrix} 2 & 1 & -1 \\ -1 & 2 & 1 \\ 0 & 5 & 1 \end{bmatrix} \begin{bmatrix} x_1 \\ x_2 \\ x_3 \end{bmatrix} = \begin{bmatrix} 28 \\ 6 \\ 40 \end{bmatrix}$$

$$\text{(iii)} \begin{bmatrix} 4 & 0 & 0 & 1 \\ 0 & -2 & 5 & 0 \\ -1 & 5 & 0 & 0 \\ 0 & 0 & 6 & -1 \end{bmatrix} \begin{bmatrix} x_1 \\ x_2 \\ x_3 \\ x_4 \end{bmatrix} = \begin{bmatrix} 30 \\ 26 \\ 5 \\ 26 \end{bmatrix} \quad \text{(iv)} \begin{bmatrix} 1 & 2 & 1 & 0 \\ 3 & 4 & 0 & 1 \\ 5 & 6 & -1 & 2 \\ 0 & 2 & 3 & -1 \end{bmatrix} \begin{bmatrix} x_1 \\ x_2 \\ x_3 \\ x_4 \end{bmatrix} = \begin{bmatrix} 8 \\ 20 \\ 32 \\ 4 \end{bmatrix}$$

CHAPTER SIX
AN INTRODUCTION TO LINEAR PROGRAMMING

6.1 INTRODUCTION

In this chapter we consider how to solve a particular type of optimisation problem. We shall be looking at both maximisation and minimisation problems, but in our initial discussion we shall confine our attention to maximisation problems. The basic features of a linear programming problem are as follows:

1. the objective function, i.e. the function whose value we are seeking to maximise, is a linear function of the choice variables;
2. the choice variables are restricted to take on non-negative values;
3. the values which the choice variables may take are further constrained by a set of linear inequalities.

Our representative linear programming problem with n choice variables and m constraints may, therefore, be written out mathematically as:

$$Max\ c_1 x_1 + c_2 x_2 + \cdots + c_n x_n$$

$$s.t.\ \begin{bmatrix} a_{11} & a_{12} & \cdots & a_{1n} \\ a_{21} & a_{22} & \cdots & a_{2n} \\ \vdots & \vdots & \cdots & \vdots \\ a_{m1} & a_{m2} & \cdots & a_{mn} \end{bmatrix} \begin{bmatrix} x_1 \\ x_2 \\ \vdots \\ x_n \end{bmatrix} \leq \begin{bmatrix} b_1 \\ b_2 \\ \vdots \\ b_m \end{bmatrix}$$

$$x_j \geq 0\ \forall j$$

More compactly, we have:

$$Max\ \mathbf{c}^T \mathbf{x}$$
$$s.t.\ \mathbf{A}\mathbf{x} \leq \mathbf{b}$$
$$\mathbf{x} \geq \mathbf{0}$$

where c and x are both n component column vectors, A is an $m \times n$ matrix, and b is a column vector with m components.

We shall be utilising techniques in linear algebra which we have discussed in the preceding chapters to show how to obtain solutions to such problems. In Section 6.2 in order to set the scene, we show how some simple problems can be solved graphically. We shall find that the solution to an LP problem occurs at a vertex of the feasible region. In Section 6.3 we show that at each vertex of the feasible region, we have a basic feasible solution to a set of linear equations. By converting the inequalities of the problem into equalities by introducing slack variables, we now have m equations in $m + n$ unknowns. We then obtain a basic solution to this set of m equations by setting n of the unknowns equal to zero, and then solving for the remaining m unknowns. The solution will be feasible if all the unknowns take on non-negative values.

In Section 6.4, we discuss the simplex method which is a general method of solving LP problems. We shall discuss two important criteria: the optimality criterion and the feasibility criterion. Satisfaction of the optimality criterion ensures that the value of the objective function increases when a new variable is introduced into the basis, whereas satisfaction of the feasibility criterion guarantees that the new basis remains feasible when we eliminate one of the existing basic variables to make way for the new one.

The choice of an initial basic feasible solution is dealt with in Section 6.5, and a user-friendly way of presenting the move from one basic feasible solution to the next is given in Section 6.6. The scene is set for discussion of how to solve minimisation problems in Section 6.7 where the problem of finding an initial basic feasible solution in the absence of the availability of the origin is touched upon. This is then followed in Section 6.8 with an analysis of two methods of solving minimisation problems: the big-M technique and the two-phase method.

6.2 LINEAR PROGRAMMING: A GRAPHICAL TREATMENT

In order to throw light on the nature of the solution to such problems, we first consider a simple linear programming problem which can be solved diagrammatically.

$$Max\ 4x_1 + 6x_2$$
$$s.t.\ 2x_1 + x_2 \leq 26$$
$$x_1 + 5x_2 \leq 40$$
$$x_1, x_2 \geq 0$$

In Fig. 6.1, we plot the feasible region for this problem. The constraints including the non-negativity requirements are satisfied by any point lying inside or on the boundaries of the shaded area, $OABC$. Turning to the objective function, we may define a set of iso-value downward-sloping straight lines; along a given such line, the value of the objective function is unchanging, and the further such a line lies to the right of the origin, the larger is the value of the objective function. It is clear from the diagram that the solution to our problem will lie at the vertex B, where x_1 is *10*, and x_2 is *6*; the value of the objective function is *76*. The value of the absolute slope of an iso-value line in this example is intermediate between those of the two inequality constraints, thereby yielding the optimal position at B.

If we were to increase the coefficient on x_1 in the objective function, the vertex B would remain optimal until the coefficient had been increased beyond *12*. At a value of *12*, anywhere along the line segment BC would yield the same value of the function since the absolute slopes of the objective function and the first constraint would coincide. Once the coefficient on x_1 in the objective had risen beyond *12*, the optimal position would change to the vertex C. Similarly, if we

x_2 ▲

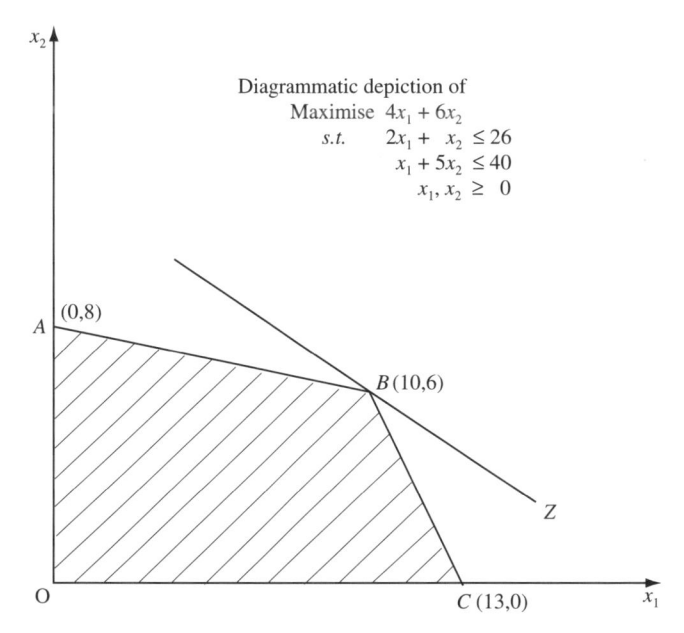

Diagrammatic depiction of
Maximise $4x_1 + 6x_2$
s.t. $2x_1 + x_2 \leq 26$
$x_1 + 5x_2 \leq 40$
$x_1, x_2 \geq 0$

A (0,8)

B (10,6)

Z

O   C (13,0) x_1

Figure 6.1 The optimal position is the vertex B. As the coefficient on x_1 in the objective function increases, the slope of the iso-revenue line, Z, becomes absolutely steeper. The converse applies as the coefficient on x_2 in the objective function increases.

were to increase the coefficient on x_2 in the objective function, the vertex B would remain optimal until the coefficient had been increased beyond *20*. At a value of *20*, anywhere along the line segment AB would yield the same value of the function since the absolute slopes of the objective function and the second constraint would coincide. Once the coefficient on x_2 in the objective function had risen beyond *20*, the optimal position would change to the vertex A. Note that at B, both constraints hold as equalities, whereas there is slack in the first constraint at A, and slack in the second constraint at C. For completeness, we may add that the origin would have been the solution to the problem had both coefficients in the objective function been negative.

What this simple example then suggests is that regardless of the precise nature of the objective function, at least one of the vertices of the feasible region will constitute a solution to the problem. In the vast majority of cases, the solution to the problem will be unique, involving just one vertex, but as we have seen, we cannot rule out the possibility of multiple solutions, involving a linear combination of two vertices.

We may also consider the possibility that there exists no feasible solution to an LP problem. If we were to plot the two constraints for the following problem, we would indeed find that our problem has no solution. The two constraints are mutually contradictory.

$$\text{Max } 2x_1 + 5x_2$$
$$\text{s.t. } 2x_1 + x_2 \leq 10$$
$$-x_1 - 2x_2 \leq -24$$
$$x_1, x_2 \geq 0$$

It is clearly impossible when x_2 is zero, for x_1 to be no greater than *5* and no smaller than *24*; similarly when x_1 is zero, we cannot have x_2, no greater than *10* and no smaller than *12*. The set of feasible points is empty, as shown in Fig. 6.2.

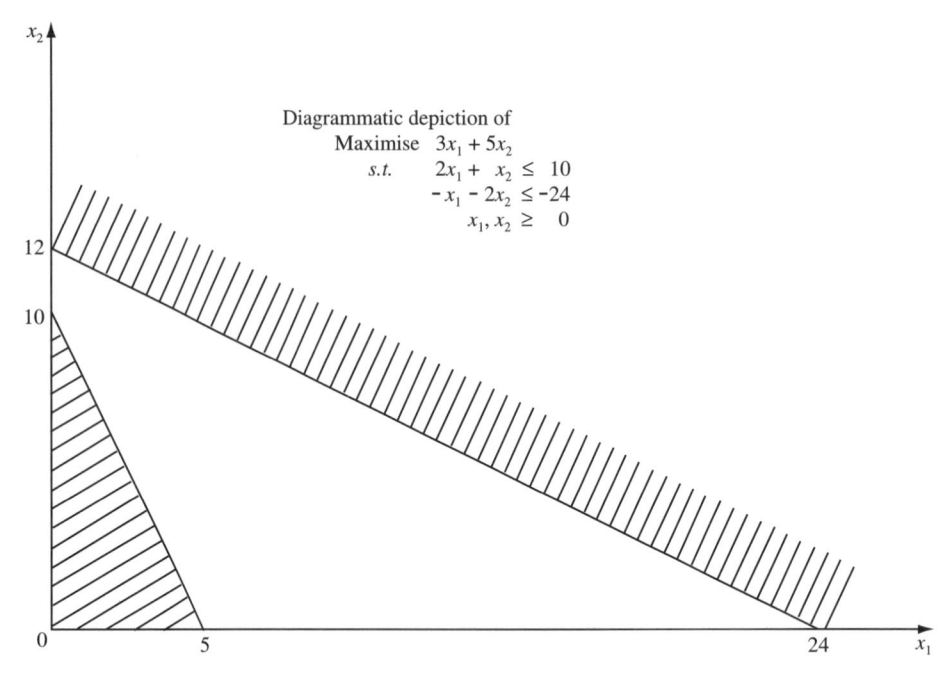

```
                    Diagrammatic depiction of
                    Maximise    3x₁ + 5x₂
                         s.t.   2x₁ +  x₂ ≤  10
                               -x₁ - 2x₂ ≤ -24
                                  x₁, x₂ ≥  0
```

Figure 6.2 There are no points which satisfy the constraints in this problem.

Now we turn to a different case: one where there is no bounded solution to the problem, it being possible to increase the value of the objective function without limit. Assume we have:

$$Max\ 3x_1 + 10x_2$$

$$s.t.\ 2x_1 \leq 12$$

$$-x_1 - 2x_2 \leq -12$$

$$x_1,\ x_2 \geq 0$$

Whereas x_1 may not exceed 6, there is no upper limit on the value which may be taken by x_2, and hence the value of the objective function can be increased without limit. We can keep on reaching higher valued iso-value lines which lie further to the right of the origin, and yet still remain in the feasible region. This problem is depicted in Fig. 6.3.

When a solution to an LP problem exists, it will always be the case that the set of feasible points will be convex. A set of points is convex if any weighted average of a pair of points that lies in the set also lies in the set. For a two-dimensional problem, all the points lying on the straight line joining up two points which lie in the feasible region will also lie in the feasible region; for a three-dimensional problem, all the points lying on the plane passing through two points which lie in the feasible region will also lie in the feasible region; for an n-dimensional problem, it will be the case that all the points lying on the hyperplane which passes through two points which lie in the feasible region will also lie in the feasible region.

Now consider the objective function, and in particular the characteristics of the set of points which all give the same value of the objective function. For a two-dimensional problem, such points lie on a straight line, for a three-dimensional problem, such points lie on a plane, and for an n-dimensional problem, such points lie on a hyperplane. As we have seen in our simple two-dimensional problem, the optimal solution to the problem involves an outcome in which such an iso-value line just touches the feasible region. If the solution is unique, the point of contact just

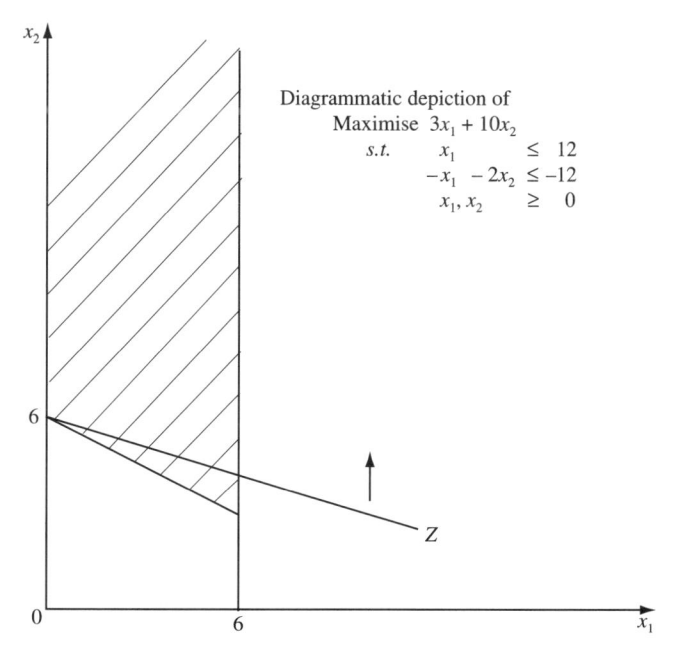

[Figure 6.3 depiction: graph with axes x_1 and x_2, showing feasible region.]

Diagrammatic depiction of
Maximise $3x_1 + 10x_2$
s.t. $\quad x_1 \leq 12$
$\quad -x_1 - 2x_2 \leq -12$
$\quad x_1, x_2 \geq 0$

Figure 6.3 The constraints of the problem are such that though x_1 cannot exceed 6, there is no upper limit on the value that can be taken by x_2, so the value of the objective function can be increased without limit.

involves a vertex, an extreme point of the feasible region; in the case of a non-unique solution, however, the line and part of the boundary of the feasible region coincide with each other. The iso-value line divides up R^2 into two subspaces with all points in the feasible region lying in the same subspace. For the general n-dimensional problem, the solution is given by the hyperplane which similarly divides up R^n with the convex set of feasible points lying in the same subspace. Such a hyperplane is known as a supporting hyperplane.

6.3 BASIC FEASIBLE SOLUTIONS TO THE PROBLEM

In the general LP problem we have n choice variables and m constraints. A typical interpretation that we could give to such a problem is that of a firm deciding the quantities to produce of certain goods in order to maximise the value of its output when it is subject to constraints on the availability of inputs necessary for production. Hence, we have n goods and m inputs.

We first convert the inequality constraints into equality constraints by introducing into the left-hand side of each constraint a slack variable with a coefficient of unity. Such a variable must also satisfy the non-negativity requirements of the problem: a positive value for the slack variable in the ith constraint would mean that not all the ith input was being utilised, with a zero value signifying that there was full utilisation of this particular input. We now have m equations in $(m + n)$ unknowns. As far as these equations are concerned, we are interested in a subset of basic solutions to these equations. Remember our discussion of basic solutions in Chapter 5. A basic solution is obtained by arbitrarily setting n of the $(m + n)$ unknowns equal to zero, and then solving for the remaining m unknowns. Some of these basic solutions will not be of interest to us since they will require one or more of the basic variables to take on negative values, thereby violating the non-negativity requirements of the linear programming problem. Our attention will be restricted to what are known as basic feasible solutions, i.e. solutions in which all the basic variables take on non-negative values. We shall also wish to distinguish between those cases where all the basic variables are positive from those in which at least one of the basic variables is equal to zero. Solutions in which one or more basic variables take on a value of zero are referred to as degenerate solutions.

It is extremely important to note that a basic feasible solution to a set of equality constraints of the LP problem is nothing more than an extreme point of the feasible region of that problem. Return to the earlier simple example in Fig. 6.1, and consider the extreme points of the feasible region. At O the basic variables are the two slack variables, at A the basic variables are x_2 and the first slack variable, at B the basic variables are x_1 and x_2, and at C the basic variables are x_1 and the second slack variable. Furthermore we know that the solution to the problem does in fact occur at an extreme point. So in solving our problem we need only concern ourselves with basic feasible solutions to the set of equality constraints (extreme points of the feasible region).

In our simple example with two choice variables in the objective function and two constraints, there are, in total, six basic solutions to the two equality constraints, four of which, as we have seen, are feasible; there were two infeasible solutions, those containing x_1 and the first slack variable, and x_2 and the second slack variable. Typically, however, even for quite small problems, there is a large number of such solutions, not all of which will be feasible; and as the number of choice variables or constraints increases, the number of basic solutions increases very rapidly. If $m = 4$ and $n = 3$, then the number of basic solutions is *35*; if $m = 4$ and $n = 4$, then the number of basic solutions is *70*; if $m = 4$ and $n = 5$, then the number of basic solutions is *504*. More generally, the number of basic solutions is given by $[(m+n)!/m!n!]$. Note that these numbers relate to the maximum number of possible basic solutions. In practice, the actual number of solutions may fall short of this. This will be the case if the equations containing a particular set of basic variables are inconsistent with each other.

Consider the following problem:

$$\text{Maximise } 10x_1 + 8x_2 + 18x_3$$
$$\text{s.t. } 2x_1 + x_2 + 4x_3 \leq 44$$
$$3x_1 + 3x_2 + x_3 \leq 56$$
$$x_1 + x_2 + 3x_3 \leq 32$$
$$x_1, x_2, x_3 \geq 0$$

Converting the constraints of this problem into equalities, we obtain three equations in six unknowns.

$$2x_1 + x_2 + 4x_3 + x_4 = 44$$
$$3x_1 + 3x_2 + x_3 + x_5 = 56$$
$$x_1 + x_2 + 3x_3 + x_6 = 32$$

Hence, there will be at most *20* basic solutions. In fact, in this particular example, there are only *19* basic solutions, since for the basic solution containing x_1, x_2 and x_4 we have:

$$2x_1 + x_2 + x_4 = 44$$
$$3x_1 + 3x_2 = 56$$
$$x_1 + x_2 = 32$$

The second and third equations in this set are clearly inconsistent with each other. Note, however, what would have happened had the constant in the third equation equalled *56/3* rather than *32*.

We would have had a situation in which the second equation in the set was equal to three times the third equation with the result that there would have existed an infinite number of solutions to the set of equations.

One way, but an extremely inefficient one, of solving our problem would be to find all the basic solutions to our three equations, check for feasibility, and for the feasible solutions, evaluate the value of the objective function, choosing the one with the highest value. The value of the objective function is given in the final column for each basic feasible solution. The basic solutions are given in the following table.

Table 6.1 The set of basic solutions

1.	$x_4 = 44$, $x_5 = 56$, $x_6 = 32$	feasible	0
2.	$x_1 = 32$, $x_4 = -20$, $x_5 = -40$	infeasible	n.a.
3.	$x_1 = 56/3$, $x_4 = 20/3$, $x_6 = 40/3$	feasible	560/3
4.	$x_1 = 22$, $x_5 = -10$, $x_6 = 10$	infeasible	n.a.
5.	$x_2 = 32$, $x_4 = 12$, $x_5 = -40$	infeasible	n.a.
6.	$x_2 = 56/3$, $x_4 = 76/3$, $x_6 = 40/3$	feasible	448/3
7.	$x_2 = 44$, $x_5 = -76$, $x_6 = -12$	infeasible	n.a.
8.	$x_3 = 88/3$, $x_4 = 4/3$, $x_5 = 136/3$	feasible	576/3
9.	$x_3 = 56$, $x_4 = -180$, $x_6 = -136$	infeasible	n.a.
10.	$x_3 = 11$, $x_5 = 45$, $x_6 = -1$	infeasible	n.a.
11.	$x_1 = 76/3$, $x_2 = -20/3$, $x_6 = 40/3$	infeasible	n.a.
12.	$x_1 = 12$, $x_2 = 20$, $x_5 = -40$	infeasible	n.a.
13.	$x_1 = 17$, $x_3 = 5$, $x_4 = -10$	infeasible	n.a.
14.	$x_1 = 2$, $x_3 = 10$, $x_5 = 40$	feasible	196
15.	$x_1 = 18$, $x_3 = 2$, $x_6 = 8$	feasible	216
16.	$x_2 = 17$, $x_3 = 5$, $x_4 = 7$	feasible	226
17.	$x_2 = -4$, $x_3 = 12$, $x_5 = 56$	infeasible	n.a.
18.	$x_2 = 180/11$, $x_3 = 76/11$, $x_6 = -56/11$	infeasible	n.a.
19.	$x_1 = 7$, $x_2 = 10$, $x_3 = 5$	feasible	240

The optimal solution, therefore, occurs at the vertex at which x_1, x_2 and x_3 are the basic variables.

6.4 THE SIMPLEX METHOD

The above procedure of finding all the basic feasible solutions to the problem has enabled us to find the solution to our problem, but it is long-winded and tedious. What we need is an efficient computational technique which will enable us, starting out from an initial basic feasible solution (an extreme point of the feasible region), to move to an adjacent basic feasible solution (extreme point) which is associated with an increase in the value of our objective function, and to continue to move to adjacent feasible solutions until the value of the objective function no longer increases. By an adjacent basic feasible solution, we mean one in which all bar one of the previous basic variables are still present in the basis. Such an approach, known as the simplex method, is available and it is highly efficient in that it requires us (at least in medium- or large-sized problems) to find only a small proportion of the total number of basic feasible solutions.

The simplex method, involving as it does a move from one basic feasible solution to an adjacent basic feasible solution, provides us with the answer to two important questions:

1. Which non-basic variable should be introduced into the basis in order for the value of the objective function to increase?
2. Having decided which non-basic variable should be introduced into the basis, which of the current basic variables should be eliminated in order to make way for the new basic variable?

Naturally, if there is no non-basic variable which, if introduced into the basis, would increase the value of the objective function, then the current basis is optimal. There may be circumstances in which the introduction of a non-basic variable would leave unchanged the value of the objective function, in which case the solution to the problem would be non-unique. The crucial factor in determining which of the current basic variables should be removed from the basis is the need to ensure that the new basis is indeed feasible: i.e. all the variables in it must take on non-negative values.

We now proceed to derive the optimality and feasibility criteria of the simplex method. To do this we shall assume we have a problem with three constraints and three non-slack variables; hence we have $m = 3$, $n = 3$. Our problem is to find non-negative values of x which maximise $c^T x$ s.t. $Ax = b$ where

$$c^T = (c_1 \ c_2 \ c_3 \ 0 \ 0 \ 0)$$

$$A = \begin{bmatrix} a_{11} & a_{12} & a_{13} & 1 & 0 & 0 \\ a_{21} & a_{22} & a_{23} & 0 & 1 & 0 \\ a_{31} & a_{32} & a_{33} & 0 & 0 & 1 \end{bmatrix}, \quad \text{and } b = \begin{bmatrix} b_1 \\ b_2 \\ b_3 \end{bmatrix}$$

We start out with a particular basic feasible solution. We defer discussion of how to find an initial basic solution until the next section. Let B be a 3×3 matrix made up of columns of A with the columns appearing in the same order in which the basic variables appear in the basis. If

$$x_B = \begin{bmatrix} x_4 \\ x_3 \\ x_1 \end{bmatrix}, \quad \text{then } B = \begin{bmatrix} 1 & a_{13} & a_{11} \\ 0 & a_{23} & a_{21} \\ 0 & a_{33} & a_{31} \end{bmatrix}$$

The basic variables must satisfy the following equation:

$$Bx_B = b$$

Pre-multiplying by B^{-1}, we obtain

$$x_B = B^{-1} b$$

which for feasibility must be non-negative. The value of the objective function is given by:

$$Z = c_B^T x_B$$

where c_B^T is a subvector of c^T and contains the coefficients of the particular basic variables in the objective function, again in the order in which the variables appear in the basis. For our previous example of a basis, we would have:

$$c_B^T = (0 \ c_3 \ c_1)$$

Now consider introducing a non-basic variable into the basis, say x_j. The following equation must still continue to hold:

$$Bx_B + a_j x_j = b$$

where a_j is the jth column of A. Pre-multiplying by B^{-1} and rearranging, we obtain:

$$x_B = B^{-1} b - B^{-1} a_j x_j$$

The new value of the objective function is given by
$$\tilde{Z} = c_B^T B^{-1} b - [c_B^T B^{-1} a_j - c_j] x_j$$
$$= Z - [z_j - c_j] x_j$$
$$\text{where } z_j = c_B^T B^{-1} a_j$$

By introducing x_j into the basis the value of the objective function will, therefore, be increased if $z_j - c_j$ is negative. We should calculate this measure for each non-basic variable, and the variable which has the most negative value of $z_j - c_j$ should be introduced into the basis. If there are no non-basic variables for which $z_j - c_j$ is negative, then the current basis is optimal. If there is a non-basic variables for which $z_j - c_j$ is zero, then the current basis is optimal, but the solution to the problem is non-unique, since if this particular non-basic variable were to be introduced into the basis the value of the objective function would not change.

It should be clear that if our problem is a minimisation rather than a maximisation problem, then we should introduce a non-basic variable into the basis if $z_j - c_j$ is positive, for then the value of the objective function would fall as a result of introducing such a non-basic variable into the basis.

Assume we have found that it would be optimal to introduce some non-basic variable into the basis. We must now consider which of the current basic variables should be eliminated in order to make way for it. The crucial factor is that feasibility must be retained. We have earlier derived an expression defining the new values which the original basic variables must take when the non-basic variable, x_j, is introduced into the basis. This was given by
$$x_B = B^{-1} b - B^{-1} a_j x_j$$

and for feasibility no element of this vector may be negative. This obviously imposes an upper limit on the value which can be taken by the variable we wish to introduce into the basis. A unit increase in x_j will increase the value of the objective function by an amount equal to $-(z_j - c_j)$, and so we obviously wish to make x_j as large as possible subject to the proviso that none of the prior basic variables become negative. What does this imply about the variable that leaves the basis? Let us write out in full the equation defining the value of some pre-existing basic variable, x_i, as a function of x_j:
$$x_i = \beta_{i1} b_1 + \beta_{i2} b_2 + \beta_{i3} b_3 - [\beta_{i1} a_{1j} + \beta_{i2} a_{2j} + \beta_{i3} a_{3j}] x_j \geq 0$$

where β_{ij} is the element in row i column j of B^{-1}. The sum of the first three terms gives us the initial value of the basic variable, which given feasibility is non-negative. The bracketed term on x_j in the above equation is given by the product of the ith row of the inverse of B^{-1} and the column of A referring to the non-basic variable x_j. If this bracketed term takes on a non-positive value, then x_i will be a non-decreasing function of x_j. We may, therefore, let x_j take on an infinitely large value without driving x_i below zero. If the bracketed term on x_j is non-positive for all the current basic variables, then there clearly exists no bounded solution to the problem. We need, therefore, in considering which of the current basic variables should be eliminated from the basis, only concern ourselves with those basic variables which give rise to a positive bracketed term, for only in such cases is an upper limit imposed upon the value of x_j. We must have
$$x_j \leq \frac{\beta_{i1} b_1 + \beta_{i2} b_2 + \beta_{i3} b_3}{\beta_{i1} a_{1j} + \beta_{i2} a_{2j} + \beta_{i3} a_{3j}} \quad \forall i$$

The basic variable which is then eliminated in order to make way for the new basic variable is the one which gives rise to the smallest non-negative value of x_j in the above expression. Note that the numerator on the right-hand side is necessarily non-negative, since it is simply equal to the initial value of the particular basic variable, and for the reasons stated above we are only concerned with cases where the denominator of the right-hand side of the above expression is also positive.

In determining the leaving basic variable, we are essentially comparing the ratios of the respective elements in the following two column vectors:

$$\boldsymbol{B}^{-1}\boldsymbol{b} \text{ and } \boldsymbol{B}^{-1}\boldsymbol{a}_j$$

The leaving variable is the one with the smallest non-negative ratio.

Whereas the optimality criterion changes its sign when we move from a maximisation to a minimisation problem, the feasibility criterion is unchanged: the basic variable which is eliminated is found by calculating the ratio of the value taken by each current basic variable to the corresponding element in the column vector $\boldsymbol{B}^{-1}\boldsymbol{a}_j$. The one with the smallest non-negative ratio is the one to be removed.

6.5 THE CHOICE OF AN INITIAL BASIC FEASIBLE SOLUTION

We now need to address the matter of finding an initial basic feasible solution. The simplest case to deal with is where all the initial constraints before the introduction of slack variables are of the form: $\boldsymbol{Ax} \leq \boldsymbol{b}$. An initial basic feasible solution is immediately available once the slack variables are introduced to convert the weak inequalities into equalities. It is one which just consists of slack variables. Diagrammatically, we start out at the origin. We would then make use of the optimality and feasibility criteria of the simplex method to derive the optimal solution.

Consider the following example:

$$\text{Maximise } 10x_1 + 8x_2 + 18x_3$$
$$\text{s.t. } 2x_1 + x_2 + 4x_3 \leq 44$$
$$3x_1 + 3x_2 + x_3 \leq 56$$
$$x_1 + x_2 + 3x_3 \leq 32$$
$$x_1, x_2, x_3 \geq 0$$

Converting the constraints into equalities by introducing slack variables, our initial basic feasible solution just consists of the three slack variables.

$$\boldsymbol{B}_1 = \boldsymbol{B}_1^{-1} = \begin{bmatrix} 1 & 0 & 0 \\ 0 & 1 & 0 \\ 0 & 0 & 1 \end{bmatrix}$$

$$\boldsymbol{x}_{B_1} = \boldsymbol{B}_1^{-1}\boldsymbol{b} = \begin{bmatrix} 44 \\ 56 \\ 32 \end{bmatrix}$$

$$\boldsymbol{c}_{B_1}^T \boldsymbol{B}_1^{-1} = (0\ 0\ 0)\boldsymbol{I} = (0\ 0\ 0)$$

At the origin $z_j - c_j$ is, therefore, just equal to $-c_j$ for each non-basic variable, x_j, and we would therefore wish to enter into the basis the variable with the largest positive value of c_j. The variable to be eliminated is found by calculating the ratio of each element in the b vector to the corresponding element in the column a_j. We, therefore, wish to introduce into the basis x_3 and eliminate the third slack variable x_6. Hence we have:

$$B_2 = \begin{bmatrix} 1 & 0 & 4 \\ 0 & 1 & 1 \\ 0 & 0 & 3 \end{bmatrix}$$

The inverse of this matrix can be easily obtained:

$$B_2^{-1} = \begin{bmatrix} 1 & 0 & -4/3 \\ 0 & 1 & -1/3 \\ 0 & 0 & 1/3 \end{bmatrix}$$

from which it follows that:

$$x_{B_2} = \begin{bmatrix} 4/3 \\ 136/3 \\ 32/3 \end{bmatrix}$$

$$c_{B_2}^T B_2^{-1} = (0 \ 0 \ 6)$$

$$z_1 - c_1 = -4, \quad z_2 - c_2 = -2, \quad z_6 - c_6 = 6$$

Introducing either x_1 or x_2 into the basis will further increase the value of the objective function, but the more negative value of $z_j - c_j$ refers to x_1, so we introduce that non-basic variable. To determine which variable should leave, we first calculate

$$B_2^{-1} a_1 = \begin{bmatrix} 1 & 0 & -4/3 \\ 0 & 1 & -1/3 \\ 0 & 0 & 1/3 \end{bmatrix} \begin{bmatrix} 2 \\ 3 \\ 1 \end{bmatrix}$$

$$= \begin{bmatrix} 2/3 \\ 8/3 \\ 1/3 \end{bmatrix}$$

Calculating the ratio of each element in the vector of basic variables to this vector, given that all elements in this vector are positive reveals that the smallest ratio refers to the basic variable x_4. So this variable must be removed from the basis. The new basis matrix is given by

$$B_3 = \begin{bmatrix} 2 & 0 & 4 \\ 3 & 1 & 1 \\ 1 & 0 & 3 \end{bmatrix}$$

72 MATHEMATICS IN ECONOMICS

and the inverse of this matrix is equal to

$$B_3^{-1} = \begin{bmatrix} 3/2 & 0 & -2 \\ -4 & 1 & 5 \\ -1/2 & 0 & 1 \end{bmatrix}$$

hence $x_{B_3} = \begin{bmatrix} 2 \\ 40 \\ 10 \end{bmatrix}$, $c_{B_3}^T B_3^{-1} = (6 \; 0 \; -2)$

and $z_2 - c_2 = -4$, $z_5 - c_5 = 0$, $z_6 - c_6 = -2$

We, therefore, now introduce x_2 into the basis since this non-basic variable has the more negative value of $z_j - c_j$. Since

$$B_3^{-1} a_2 = \begin{bmatrix} 3/2 & 0 & -2 \\ -4 & 1 & 5 \\ -1/2 & 0 & 1 \end{bmatrix} \begin{bmatrix} 1 \\ 3 \\ 1 \end{bmatrix} = \begin{bmatrix} -1/2 \\ 4 \\ 1/2 \end{bmatrix}$$

$$x_{B_3} = \begin{bmatrix} 2 \\ 40 \\ 10 \end{bmatrix}$$

and the relevant ratios are then

$$\begin{bmatrix} -4 \\ 10 \\ 20 \end{bmatrix}$$

Since the first element in this column is negative, the basic variable x_1 imposes no restriction upon the value which can be taken by the non-basic variable x_2 when it is introduced into the basis. The smaller positive ratio refers to the basic variable x_5, and this variable is therefore the one to be removed.

We therefore have

$$B_4 = \begin{bmatrix} 2 & 1 & 4 \\ 3 & 3 & 1 \\ 1 & 1 & 3 \end{bmatrix}$$

from which it follows that

$$B_4^{-1} = \begin{bmatrix} 1 & 1/8 & -11/8 \\ -1 & 1/4 & 5/4 \\ 0 & -1/8 & 3/8 \end{bmatrix}$$

$$x_{B_4} = \begin{bmatrix} 7 \\ 10 \\ 5 \end{bmatrix}, \quad \text{and} \quad c_{B_4}^T B_4^{-1} = (2 \ 1 \ 3)$$

The optimal solution has now been reached, with $x_1 = 7$, $x_2 = 10$, and $x_3 = 5$; the value of the objective function is 240. $z_j - c_j$ is positive for each non-basic variable, and for the ith slack variable this is simply given by the ith element in the $c_B^T B^{-1}$ vector.

6.6 A TABULAR APPROACH TO SOLVING LINEAR PROGRAMS

An alternative and more user-friendly approach to obtain the solution to a linear programming maximisation problem by means of the simplex method is to use the following tabular form. We have converted all the constraints into equalities by including slack variables, and these equations appear in the last three rows of the first tableau. In the $z_j - c_j$ row, we have the equation for the objective function including the slack variables, having taken all the terms over onto the left-hand side.

	x_1	x_2	x_3	x_4	x_5	x_6	solution
$z_j - c_j$	-10	-8	-18	0	0	0	0
x_4	2	1	4	1	0	0	44
x_5	3	3	1	0	1	0	56
x_6	1	1	3	0	0	1	32

In the final column of the tableau appear the values taken by the current basic variables; these are the elements of the vector: $B^{-1}b$. In the first row of each tableau are the values of $z_j - c_j$ for both the basic and non-basic variables. Note that for the basic variables, these values are always zero. Turning now to the left-hand side of the equations for the constraints, what we have here is the matrix $B^{-1}A$. In each column of this matrix, we therefore have $B^{-1}a_j$. Given that the columns of A referring to the slack variables constitute an identity matrix, the current inverse matrix appears under the slack variables in the equations for the constraints.

Applying the rules of the simplex method, we introduce x_3 into the basis and eliminate x_6 from the basis. To do this, we carry out elementary row operations to convert the x_3 column into one in which zeros appear everywhere except in the last row where we require a coefficient of unity. Remember x_3 is replacing x_6 in the new basis. The necessary row operations are as follows:

1. multiply the x_6 row by $1/3$;
2. multiply the x_6 row by 6 and add to the $z_j - c_j$ row;
3. multiply the x_6 row by $-4/3$ and add to the x_4 row;
4. multiply the x_6 row by $-1/3$ and add to the x_5 row.

Having carried out these operations, we obtain the new tableau:

	x_1	x_2	x_3	x_4	x_5	x_6	solution
$z_j - c_j$	-4	-2	0	0	0	6	192
x_4	2/3	$-1/3$	0	1	0	$-4/3$	4/3
x_5	8/3	8/3	0	0	1	$-1/3$	136/3
x_6	1/3	1/3	1	0	0	1/3	32/3

We now introduce x_1 in place of x_4. In this case, the necessary row operations are as follows:

1. multiply the x_4 row by *3/2*;
2. multiply the x_4 row by *6* and add to the $z_j - c_j$ row;
3. multiply the x_4 row by *-4* and add to the x_5 row;
4. multiply the x_4 row by *-1/2* and add to the x_3 row.

Having carried out these operations, we obtain the new tableau:

	x_1	x_2	x_3	x_4	x_5	x_6	solution
$z_j - c_j$	0	-4	0	6	0	-2	200
x_1	1	-1/2	0	3/2	0	-2	2
x_5	0	4	0	-4	1	5	40
x_3	0	1/2	1	-1/2	0	1	10

At the next iteration, we introduce x_2 in place of x_5. The row operations are as follows:

1. multiply the x_5 row by *1/4*;
2. add the x_5 row to the $z_j - c_j$ row;
3. multiply the x_5 row by *1/8* and add to the x_1 row;
4. multiply the x_4 row by *-1/8* and add to the x_3 row.

Having carried out these operations, we obtain the new tableau:

	x_1	x_2	x_3	x_4	x_5	x_6	solution
$z_j - c_j$	0	0	0	2	1	3	240
x_1	1	0	0	1	1/8	-11/8	7
x_2	0	1	0	-1	1/4	5/4	10
x_3	0	0	1	0	-1/8	3/8	5

There is now no non-basic variable for which $z_j - c_j$ is negative. We have therefore reached the optimal solution to the problem with $x_1 = 7$, $x_2 = 10$, $x_3 = 5$, and the value of the objective function is *240*.

6.7 MORE ON THE INITIAL BASIC FEASIBLE SOLUTION

Where we have equality constraints or weak inequalities where the inequality sign has been reversed, then the initial basic feasible solution is somewhat less straightforward to find. First of all, consider the case where all the constraints are equalities. Here, it would obviously be illegitimate to introduce slack variables into the analysis. One or more of them might appear in the optimal solution, but if this were indeed the case, then the constraints of the problem would not be satisfied. The way to proceed in these circumstances is to introduce artificial variables rather than slack variables into the constraints. Like a slack variable in the standard LP problem, for each equality constraint an artificial variable would enter with a coefficient of unity in that particular constraint and would appear with a coefficient of zero in all the other constraints. We would need to ensure that such an artificial variable does not enter the optimal solution to avoid violating the equality constraint. For a maximisation problem, we could then proceed by introducing the artificial variables into the objective function, assigning to them arbitrarily large negative values in order to guard against the possibility that they might appear in the optimal solution.

When the constraints are of the form $Ax \geq b$, then it will be necessary not only to introduce artificial variables, but also slack variables. Whereas the submatrix of coefficients on the artificial variables constitutes an identity matrix, the submatrix of coefficients on the slack variables constitutes the negative of an identity matrix. Once again, an initial basic feasible solution can be found: this too will be solely made up of artificial variables, and the same procedure as above can be used to ensure that they are all eliminated before the optimal solution is reached.

When the problem consists of a mixed set of constraints, then the initial basic feasible solution will consist of a mixture of artificial variables and slack variables. Slack variables will be the initial basic variables in constraints of the form: $Ax \leq b$. Artificial variables will be the initial basic variables in equality constraints and in constraints of the form: $Ax \geq b$.

6.8 TECHNIQUES FOR SOLVING MINIMISATION PROBLEMS

In a typical minimisation problem, the origin is not available as the initial basic feasible solution. We must proceed by introducing both artificial and slack variables into the constraints. There are two procedures available for finding the solution: the big M technique and the two-phase method. We shall discuss each of these approaches in turn.

The big M technique

We now demonstrate how to solve the following simple minimisation problem using the big M technique:

$$\text{Minimise } x_1 + x_2$$
$$\text{s.t. } x_1 + 2x_2 \geq 34$$
$$4x_1 + x_2 \geq 52$$
$$x_1, x_2 \geq 0$$

Adding an artificial variable, R_i, and a slack variable, S_i, to each constraint, and assigning a large positive coefficient, M, to each artificial variable in the objective function, we may set up the following tableau. Carrying out a succession of row operations on this and subsequent tableaux, we shall arrive at the optimal solution.

	x_1	x_2	R_1	R_2	S_1	S_2	solution
$z_j - c_j$	-1	-1	$-M$	$-M$	0	0	0
R_1	1	2	1	0	-1	0	34
R_2	4	1	0	1	0	-1	52

The row operations to be performed are as follows. We must first adjust the tableau by expressing the $z_j - c_j$ row in terms of the non-basic variables. To do this we multiply the R_1 and R_2 rows both by M and add to the $z_j - c_j$ row.

	x_1	x_2	R_1	R_2	S_1	S_2	solution
$z_j - c_j$	$5M-1$	$3M-1$	0	0	$-M$	$-M$	$86M$
R_1	1	2	1	0	-1	0	34
R_2	4	1	0	1	0	-1	52

We are now in a position to apply the simplex method for a minimisation problem. We wish to enter the non-basic variable with the largest positive value in the $z_j - c_j$ row since this is a minimisation problem. This is x_1 and for the new basis to remain feasible, we eliminate R_2. The row operations we carry out to derive the third tableau are:

1. multiply the R_2 row by $1/4$;
2. multiply the R_2 row by $-1/4$ and add to the R_1 row;
3. multiply the R_2 row by $(1 - 5M)/4$ and add to the $z_j - c_j$ row.

	x_1	x_2	R_1	R_2	S_1	S_2	solution
$z_j - c_j$	0	$(7M - 3)/4$	0	$(1 - 5M)/4$	$-M$	$(M - 1)/4$	$13 + 21M$
R_1	0	$7/4$	1	$-1/4$	-1	$1/4$	21
x_1	1	$1/4$	0	$1/4$	0	$-1/4$	13

Applying the optimality criterion, we now introduce x_2, and to retain feasibility R_1 must leave the basis. The row operations we perform in order to obtain the next tableau are:

1. multiply the R_1 row by $4/7$;
2. multiply the R_1 row by $-1/7$ and add to the R_2 row;
3. multiply the R_1 row by $(3 - 7M)/7$ and add to the $z_j - c_j$ row.

	x_1	x_2	R_1	R_2	S_1	S_2	solution
$z_j - c_j$	0	0	$(3 - 7M)/7$	$(1 - 7M)/7$	$-3/7$	$-1/7$	22
x_2	0	1	$4/7$	$-1/7$	$-4/7$	$1/7$	12
x_1	1	0	$-1/7$	$2/7$	$1/7$	$-2/7$	10

We have now reached the optimal solution. There are no non-basic variables for which $z_j - c_j$ is positive. We have $x_1 = 10$, $x_2 = 12$, and the value of the objective function is equal to 22.

The two-phase method

An alternative procedure is available for solving linear programming problems which require the inclusion of artificial variables. This method is known as the two-phase method, and it enables us to dispense with the use of the large M coefficient on the artificial variables in the objective function. When solving problems by hand, the use of the big M approach can make the carrying out of the row operations quite tedious. When using computer software, obviously a specific numerical value must be assigned to M, and this may cause problems to the unwary which can be avoided by using the two-phase method.

In the first phase, the objective function is specified solely in terms of the artificial variables. The constraints are as in the big M method. We do not wish the artificial variables to appear in the final solution. To avoid this, we simply write the initial objective function as either

$$\text{Minimise } \sum R_i \text{ or Maximise } - \sum R_i$$

If the problem has a feasible solution, then adopting this initial objective function will lead to the artificial variables being removed from the basis. We proceed by applying the simplex method to our new problem after first carrying out row operations to write the $z_j - c_j$ row in terms of the non-basic variables. The first phase ends when we have eliminated all the artificial variables from the basis. If it is impossible to do this, then there is no feasible solution to our problem. Having eliminated the artificial variables from the basis, we then introduce the original objective function back into the problem. As in the first phase, it will first be necessary to express the $z_j - c_j$ row in terms of the non-basic variables before it will be possible to proceed with the simplex method.

We provide an example of the method by applying the two-phase method to the problem we have just solved using the big M technique. If the objective function of the first phase is to minimise the sum of the artificial variables, we have the following tableau.

	x_1	x_2	R_1	R_2	S_1	S_2	solution
$z_j - c_j$	0	0	−1	−1	0	0	0
R_1	1	2	1	0	−1	0	34
R_2	4	1	0	1	0	−1	52

The row operations we perform are as follows. We must adjust the first tableau by expressing the $z_j - c_j$ row in terms of the non-basic variables. To do this we multiply the R_1 and R_2 rows both by *1* and add to the $z_j - c_j$ row.

	x_1	x_2	R_1	R_2	S_1	S_2	solution
$z_j - c_j$	5	3	0	0	−1	−1	86
R_1	1	2	1	0	−1	0	34
R_2	4	1	0	1	0	−1	52

We are now in a position to apply the simplex method for a minimisation problem. We wish to enter the non-basic variable with the largest positive value. This is x_1 and for the new basis to remain feasible, we eliminate R_2. The row operations we carry out to derive the third tableau are:

1. multiply the R_2 row by *1/4*;
2. multiply the R_2 row by *−1/4* and add to the R_1 row;
3. multiply the R_2 row by *−5/4* and add to the $z_j - c_j$ row.

	x_1	x_2	R_1	R_2	S_1	S_2	solution
$z_j - c_j$	0	7/4	0	−5/4	−1	1/4	21
R_1	0	7/4	1	−1/4	−1	1/4	21
x_1	1	1/4	0	1/4	0	−1/4	13

Applying the optimality criterion, we now introduce x_2, and to retain feasibility R_1 must leave the basis. The row operations we perform in order to obtain the next tableau are:

1. multiply the R_1 row by *4/7*;
2. multiply the R_1 row by *−1/7* and add to the R_2 row;
3. multiply the R_1 row by *−1* and add to the $z_j - c_j$ row.

	x_1	x_2	R_1	R_2	S_1	S_2	solution
$z_j - c_j$	0	0	−1	−1	0	0	0
x_2	0	1	4/7	−1/7	−4/7	1/7	12
x_1	1	0	−1/7	2/7	1/7	−2/7	10

We have now eliminated the two artificial variables from the basis. This is the end of the first phase. In the second phase we return to the original objective function. We, therefore modify the last tableau as follows, having omitted the columns pertaining to the artificial variables:

	x_1	x_2	S_1	S_2	solution
$z_j - c_j$	-1	-1	0	0	0
x_2	0	1	$-4/7$	$1/7$	12
x_1	1	0	$1/7$	$-2/7$	10

Once we express the $z_j - c_j$ row in terms of the non-basic variables, we find that the current basis in this case is indeed optimal.

	x_1	x_2	S_1	S_2	solution
$z_j - c_j$	0	0	$-3/7$	$-1/7$	22
x_2	0	1	$-4/7$	$1/7$	12
x_1	1	0	$1/7$	$-2/7$	10

Had it not been so, then we would have continued to apply the simplex method until we reached the optimal basis.

6.9 CONCLUSION

We shall now briefly summarise the key findings of this chapter which has introduced linear programming. The solution to a linear program where it exists always occurs at an extreme point or vertex of the feasible region, though the solution is not necessarily unique. Such a vertex constitutes a basic feasible solution to a set of equations obtained by converting the inequality constraints of the problem into equalities by introducing slack variables into them. The simplex method provides a general method of solution. For a maximisation problem, the optimality criterion tell us that the introduction of a non-basic variable x_j will lead to an increase in the value of the objective function as long at $z_j - c_j$ is negative. We shall provide an economic interpretation of this criterion in the next chapter where we discuss the important topic of the dual of a linear program. For a minimisation problem, then introducing a non-basic variable x_j into the basis will reduce the value of the objective function provided that $z_j - c_j$ is positive. For the new basis to remain feasible in both the maximisation and minimisation cases, then the basic variable which is to be eliminated from the basis is the one which has the smallest positive ratio of the element in the solution column ($\boldsymbol{B}^{-1}\boldsymbol{b}$) to the corresponding element in the column of the entering variable ($\boldsymbol{B}^{-1}\boldsymbol{a}_j$). If all the elements in the column of the entering variable are negative, then the problem has no bounded solution.

In the next chapter, we shall extend out discussion of linear programming by introducing the concept of the dual of a linear program.

6.10 EXERCISES

6.1 (a) Solve the following linear programming problems graphically, enumerating in each case the extreme points of the feasible region:

(i) Maximise $2x_1 + 3x_2$

s.t. $2x_1 + 4x_2 \leq 36$

$3x_1 + 2x_2 \leq 34$

$x_1, x_2 \geq 0$

(ii) Minimise $4x_1 + x_2$

s.t. $x_1 + 2x_2 \geq 24$

$3x_1 + x_2 \geq 22$

$x_1, x_2 \geq 0.$

(iii) Maximise $3x_1 + x_2$

s.t. $2x_1 + x_2 \geq 28$

$5x_1 + 2x_2 \leq 64$

(iv) Maximise $3x_1 + x_2$

s.t. $2x_1 + x_2 \geq 28$

$5x_1 + 2x_2 \leq 64$

$x_2 \leq 10$

(b) A firm can produce three products, each of which requires the use of two scarce inputs. To produce a unit of the first good, the firm must employ two units of the first input and four units of the second input. To produce unit output of the second good requires one unit of the first input and two units of the second input, and unit output of the third good requires three units of the first input and one unit of the second input. The prices of the three goods are *10, 4* and *5* respectively. The firm has available *48* units of the first input and *56* units of the second input. Its objective is to maximise its sales revenue subject to the two input requirement constraints.

(i) Draw diagrams with two of the three goods measured along the axes. Find the extreme points and hence determine the sales-maximising output bundle.

(ii) Why does producing two goods at a time solve the problem?

6.2 (a) Use the simplex method to solve the following problems:

(i) Maximise $10x_1 + 15x_2 + 18x_3$

s.t. $2x_1 + x_2 + x_3 \leq 64$

$x_1 + 2x_2 + x_3 \leq 43$

$4x_2 + 5x_3 \leq 80$

$x_1, x_2, x_3 \geq 0$

(ii) Maximise $11x_1 + 7x_2 + 10x_3$

s.t. $2x_1 + x_2 + 3x_3 \leq 30$

$4x_1 + 2x_2 + x_3 \leq 40$

$x_1 + x_2 + x_3 \leq 17$

$x_1, x_2, x_3 \geq 0$

(iii) *Maximise* $18x_1 + 20x_2 + 16x_3$

s.t. $2x_1 + 3x_2 + x_3 \leq 48$

$x_1 + x_2 + 2x_3 \leq 27$

$4x_1 + x_2 \leq 36$

$x_1, x_2, x_3 \geq 0$

(iv) *Maximise* $14x_1 + 18x_2 + 20x_3$

s.t. $3x_1 + x_2 + 2x_3 \leq 42$

$4x_1 + 2x_2 + x_3 \leq 40$

$x_1 + 3x_2 + 3x_3 \leq 30$

$x_1, x_2, x_3 \geq 0$

(v) *Maximise* $5x_1 + 16x_2 + 11x_3$

s.t. $2x_1 + x_2 + 3x_3 \leq 41$

$x_1 + 2x_2 + x_3 \leq 22$

$4x_2 + 5x_3 \leq 68$

$x_1, x_2, x_3 \geq 0$

(b) Suppose that the basis B is proposed as the optimal basis, where the problem is to maximise $c^T x$ subject to $Ax = b$ ($x \geq 0$), and we have

$$B = \begin{bmatrix} 2 & 1 & 0 \\ 1 & 2 & 1 \\ 4 & 3 & 0 \end{bmatrix}$$

$$c^T = (28 \ 17 \ 21 \ 0 \ 0 \ 0)$$

$$A = \begin{bmatrix} 2 & 1 & 1 & 1 & 0 & 0 \\ 1 & 4 & 2 & 0 & 1 & 0 \\ 4 & 1 & 3 & 0 & 0 & 1 \end{bmatrix}, \quad \text{and} \quad b = \begin{bmatrix} 44 \\ 60 \\ 100 \end{bmatrix}$$

Given that

$$B^{-1} = \begin{bmatrix} \frac{3}{2} & 0 & \frac{-1}{2} \\ -2 & 0 & 1 \\ \frac{5}{2} & 1 & \frac{-3}{2} \end{bmatrix}$$

determine whether the basis is indeed optimal. If it is not, proceed to find the optimal solution to the problem.

6.3 (a) Solve the following problem by means of:

(i) the big M technique;

(ii) the two-phase method.

Minimise $2x_1 + x_2$

s.t. $x_1 + 3x_2 \geq 36$

$4x_1 + x_2 \geq 34$

$x_1, x_2 \geq 0$

(b) Use the two-phase method to solve the following problem:

$$\text{Maximise } x_1 + x_2$$
$$\text{s.t. } x_1 + 4x_2 = 36$$
$$x_1 + 2x_2 \leq 22$$
$$2x_1 + x_2 \leq 30$$
$$x_1, x_2 \geq 0$$

(c) Use the two-phase method to show that there exists no feasible solution to the following problem:

$$\text{Maximise } 2x_1 + 3x_2$$
$$\text{s.t. } 2x_1 + x_2 \leq 8$$
$$3x_1 + x_2 \geq 18$$
$$x_1, x_2 \geq 0$$

CHAPTER SEVEN
DUALITY AND LINEAR PROGRAMMING

7.1 INTRODUCTION

In this chapter, we consider the important topic of duality. In Section 7.2 we show that associated with any linear program is another optimisation problem known as its dual. We refer to the original problem as the primal. If the primal problem is a maximisation problem, then its dual is a minimisation problem, and vice versa, if the primal is a minimisation problem. Dual variables have an important economic interpretation: they are, as we shall see, measures of marginal valuation. A dual variable measures the impact on the value of the objective function of the primal problem of marginally relaxing the corresponding constraint of the primal. If the primal problem is one of maximising the value of a firm's bundle of outputs subject to constraints on the availability of productive inputs, then the dual variables are the marginal revenue productivities or shadow prices of these productive inputs. We derive a number of important results connecting the primal and its dual, and provide an economic interpretation of the significance of the optimality criterion of the simplex method. A good which the firm is not currently producing should be produced if its price exceeds the value of the inputs required to produce a unit of the good. If the primal basis is not currently optimal, then we shall see that the dual is currently infeasible. We also discuss and provide an economic interpretation of the dual of a minimisation problem. Finally in this section we look at the complication caused to the analysis by the presence of equality constraints in a linear program.

In Section 7.3 we discuss the solution to the dual of a maximisation problem, and provide in this case too an economic interpretation of the optimality criterion of the dual. We shall see that a non-basic dual variable should be introduced into the basis if there is excess demand for the relevant productive input. As with the primal, if the dual is not currently optimal, then the primal will be currently infeasible.

In Chapter 6 we discussed two techniques which can be applied to solve linear programming problems where the origin is not available as an initial basic feasible solution as is the case in minimisation problems. In Section 7.4 we discuss a further technique: the dual simplex method which can be applied to solve problems which are currently optimal but infeasible. We shall see that many minimisation problems can be converted into a form in which these conditions are indeed met. This method is not a general one, but when it can be applied it avoids the necessity of introducing artificial variables into the problem.

In Section 7.5 we provide a brief discussion of sensitivity analysis. Drawing upon our knowledge of the nature of the optimal solutions to both the primal problem and its dual, we investigate the impact that certain key parametric changes might have for the solutions to both the primal and dual. In particular we investigate the impact that a change in a product price, a change in the availability of a productive input; or a change in a technological coefficient might have on the solution. We shall see that where the effect of the parametric change is to lead the current basis to be infeasible we can make use of the dual simplex method in order to eliminate the infeasibility.

7.2 THE DUAL OF A LINEAR PROGRAM

If we return to the representative linear programming problem of the previous chapter:

$$\text{Max } c_1 x_1 + c_2 x_2 + \cdots + c_n x_n$$

$$\text{s.t.} \begin{bmatrix} a_{11} & a_{12} & \cdots & a_{1n} \\ a_{21} & a_{22} & \cdots & a_{2n} \\ \vdots & \vdots & \cdots & \vdots \\ a_{m1} & a_{m2} & \cdots & a_{mn} \end{bmatrix} \begin{bmatrix} x_1 \\ x_2 \\ \vdots \\ x_n \end{bmatrix} \leq \begin{bmatrix} b_1 \\ b_2 \\ \vdots \\ b_m \end{bmatrix}$$

$$x_j \geq 0 \ \forall \ j$$

More compactly, we have:

$$\text{Max } c^T x$$
$$\text{s.t. } Ax \leq b$$
$$x \geq 0$$

where c and x are both n component column vectors, A is an $m \times n$ matrix, and b is a column vector with m components. We shall refer to this problem as the primal.

For every LP problem, whether it be a maximisation or minimisation problem, there exists a related problem which is known as the dual of the original problem. The dual of our representative problem takes the following form:

$$\text{Min } b_1 y_1 + b_2 y_2 + \cdots + b_m y_m$$

$$\text{s.t.} \begin{bmatrix} a_{11} & a_{21} & \cdots & a_{m1} \\ a_{12} & a_{22} & \cdots & a_{m2} \\ \vdots & \vdots & \cdots & \vdots \\ a_{1n} & a_{2n} & \cdots & a_{mn} \end{bmatrix} \begin{bmatrix} y_1 \\ y_2 \\ \vdots \\ y_m \end{bmatrix} \geq \begin{bmatrix} c_1 \\ c_2 \\ \vdots \\ c_n \end{bmatrix}$$

$$y_i \geq 0 \ \forall \ i$$

More compactly, we have:

$$\text{Min } y^T b$$
$$\text{s.t. } y^T A \geq c^T$$
$$y \geq 0$$

where y and b are both m component vectors, A is an $m \times n$ matrix, and c is a column vector with n components. y is the vector of dual variables, the interpretation of which we will discuss below.

Links between the primal and dual problems

1. When the primal problem is a maximisation problem, its dual is a minimisation problem. Conversely if the primal is a minimisation problem, its dual will be a maximisation problem.
2. The coefficients on the dual variables in the dual objective function are the right-hand side values of the primal constraints.
3. The coefficients on the primal variables in the primal objective function appear in the dual on the right-hand side of the dual constraints.
4. In comparing the weak inequality constraints of the primal and the dual problems, note two important points:
   i. the left-hand side of the jth dual constraint is equal to the inner product of the vector of dual variables, y, and the jth column of A, whereas the left-hand side of the ith primal constraint is given by the inner product of the vector of primal variables, x, and the ith row of A. In other words, in moving from the primal to the dual constraints we have transposed A.
   ii. The inequality sign in the dual constraints is the opposite of that in the primal constraints.
5. Both the primal and dual variables must be non-negative.

Two important theorems

Having outlined the main comparative features of the primal and dual problems, we now turn to two important results. In the first place, at the optimal solutions to the primal and the dual, the value of the primal objective function is equal to the value of the dual objective function. Let $\hat{x}$ and $\hat{y}$ be feasible solutions to the primal and dual respectively. Given that the constraints of the two problems must be satisfied, then we must have:

$$A\hat{x} \leq b \text{ and } \hat{y}^T A \geq c^T$$

Pre-multiply the primal constraint by $\hat{y}^T$ and post-multiplying the dual constraint by $\hat{x}$, we obtain:

$$\hat{y}^T A\hat{x} \leq \hat{y}^T b \text{ and } \hat{y}^T A\hat{x} \geq c^T \hat{x}$$

Furthermore, assume that at the feasible vectors x^* and y^* the value of the primal objective function is equal to the value of the dual objective function. Hence, we have

$$y^{*T} b = y^{*T} A x^* = c^T x^*$$

We shall now show that no other basic feasible solution to the primal can give rise to a larger value of the primal objective function than x^* does. We know from above that

$$y^{*T} b \geq y^{*T} A\hat{x} \geq c^T \hat{x}$$

and since by assumption $c^T x^* = y^{*T} b$, it must be the case that $c^T x^* \geq c^T \hat{x}$. A similar line of argument would show that there can be no other feasible solution to the dual which would give rise to a smaller value of the dual objective function than that associated with y^*.

Given that feasible solutions exist to primal and dual problems such that the value of the primal and dual objective functions are equal, then these two vectors, x^* and y^*, do in fact constitute the optimal solutions to the two problems.

We now demonstrate that if x^* is the optimal solution to the primal, then the optimal solution to the dual will be given by y^* where $y^{*T}b$ is actually equal to $c^T x^*$. Given that by assumption the primal basis is the optimal one, for all primal variables we have $z_j - c_j \geq 0$ where z_j is given by $c_B^T B^{-1} a_j$. If we now let y^{*T} equal $c_B^T B^{-1}$, then the fact that the primal is optimal will ensure that the constraints of the dual are met, since we have $y^{*T} a_j \geq c_j$. Note that the values taken by the dual variables depend upon the variables entering the primal basis. However, not only must the dual constraints be satisfied, but the dual variables must also be non-negative. Will this, in fact, be the case?

Let us consider this by returning to the primal variables, and in particular the slack variables. For each slack primal variable, c_j is equal to zero and a_j is a column with unity in the row referring to the particular primal constraint in which the slack primal variable appears and with zeros everywhere else. If x_j is the first slack variable, then a_j has unity in the first row and zeros everywhere else and y_1 is equal to $c_B^T B^{-1} a_j$, which is the first element of the vector $c_B^T B^{-1}$. Since the primal basis is optimal and c_j is zero, then y_1 must be non-negative. A similar argument applies to all the other dual variables. So the vector of dual variables is feasible, but is it optimal?

The value of the dual objective function is given by $y^{*T}b$, which is equal to $c_B^T B^{-1} b$. However x^* is equal to $B^{-1} b$, and $c_B^T B^{-1} b$ is the value of the primal objective function. Hence the value of the primal objective function is equal to the value of the dual objective function. But as we have seen above, this means that y^* is then also optimal.

We have seen above that if feasible solutions exist to both the primal problem and its dual, then optimal solutions exist to the two problems, with the value of the primal objective function equal to the value of the dual objective function. However, if no vector exists which satisfies the constraints of one of the two problems, then its dual will have no feasible solution. In stating that the dual has no feasible solution, we allow for two possibilities: (1) that there is no feasible vector which satisfies the constraints of the dual or (2) that the dual has an unbounded solution.

Consider the following problem:

$$\text{Maximise } 4x_1 + 2x_2$$
$$\text{s.t. } x_1 + 2x_2 \leq 10$$
$$3x_1 + x_2 \geq 36$$
$$x_1, x_2 \geq 0$$

It is straightforward to see that the set of feasible points which satisfy the constraints of this problem is empty. When x_2 is zero, it is impossible for x_1 to be both no larger than *10*, and no smaller than *12*. The situation is depicted in Fig. 7.1(a). Regarding the dual of the above problem, we have, after multiplying the second primal constraint by -1:

$$\text{Minimise } 10y_1 - 36y_2$$
$$\text{s.t. } y_1 - 3y_2 \geq 4$$
$$2y_1 - y_2 \geq 2$$
$$y_1, y_2 \geq 0$$

Plotting the constraints of the dual in Fig. 7.1(b), we observe that the solution to the dual problem is unbounded.

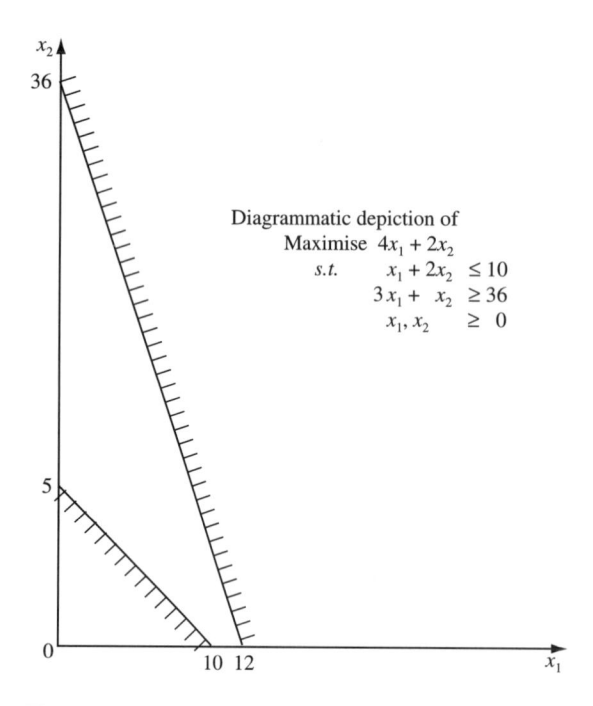

Figure 7.1(a). There are no points which satisfy the constraints of the problem. When x_1 is zero, x_2 cannot simultaneously be no greater than 36 and no smaller than 5. Similarly, when x_2 is zero, x_1 cannot simultaneously be no greater than 12 and no smaller than 5.

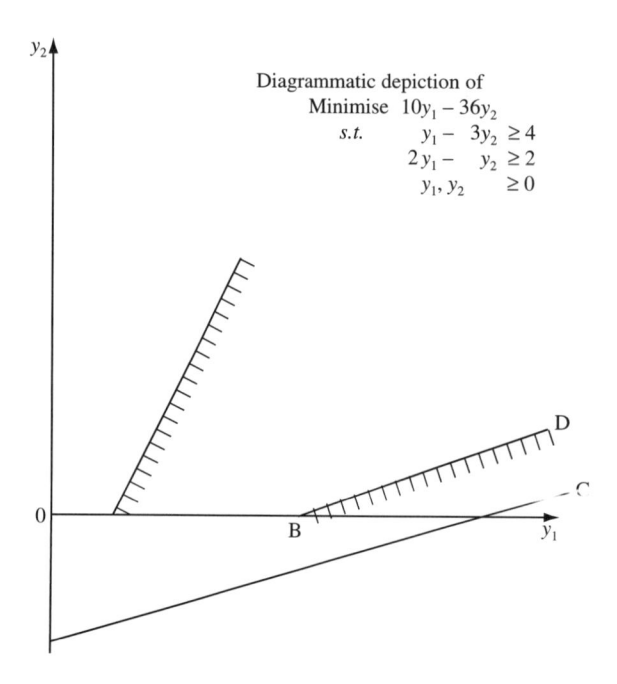

Diagrammatic depiction of
Maximise $4x_1 + 2x_2$
s.t. $x_1 + 2x_2 \leq 10$
$3x_1 + x_2 \geq 36$
$x_1, x_2 \geq 0$

Diagrammatic depiction of
Minimise $10y_1 - 36y_2$
s.t. $y_1 - 3y_2 \geq 4$
$2y_1 - y_2 \geq 2$
$y_1, y_2 \geq 0$

Figure 7.1(b). The feasible region is that part of the non-negative quadrant whose boundaries are the y_1 axis and the line BD extended. An upward shift of the C function will be associated with a smaller value of the objective function. There is no limit on the extent to which this function can be shifted upwards.

Now consider another example where there is no feasible vector for the primal problem.

$$Maximise\ 4x_1 + 2x_2$$
$$s.t.\ -x_1 - 2x_2 \leq -10$$
$$x_1 \leq -6$$
$$x_1,\ x_2 \geq 0$$

Turning to the dual, we have:

$$Minimise\ -10y_1 - 6y_2$$
$$s.t.\ -y_1 + y_2 \geq 4$$
$$-2y_1 \geq 2$$
$$y_1,\ y_2 \geq 0$$

The dual possesses no feasible vector either. When the primal (dual) has no feasible vector, then the dual (primal) is either unbounded, or does not possess a feasible vector.

The second important result concerns the relationship between primal variables and dual constraints, and between dual variables and primal constraints. We have shown above that

$$y^{*T}b = y^{*T}Ax^* = c^T x^*$$

We may, therefore, write

$$y^{*T}[b - Ax^*] = 0$$

and

$$[y^{*T}A - c^T]x^* = 0$$

Consider first the relationship between dual variables and primal constraints. Inside the square bracket, we have a column vector of primal slack variables, where S_i is the ith slack variable; so we may alternatively express the result as

$$(y_1\ y_2\ \cdots\ y_m) \begin{bmatrix} S_1 \\ S_2 \\ \vdots \\ S_m \end{bmatrix} = 0$$

$$y_1 S_1 + y_2 S_2 + \cdots + y_m S_m = 0$$

Since both the dual variables and the slack variables must be non-negative, then we must have a zero value for each term in the summation. In other words, if there is slack in the ith constraint of the primal, then the ith dual variable must be zero. If the ith dual variable is positive, then the corresponding primal constraint must hold as an equality. Furthermore we cannot rule out the possibility that in certain circumstances both the dual variable and the corresponding slack variable are both zero.

Let us turn now to the relationship between the primal variables and the dual constraints. Inside the square bracket, we have a row vector of slack variables for the dual constraints. Letting T_j represent the slack variable in the jth dual constraint, we may express the conditions as follows:

$$(T_1 \ T_2 \ \ldots \ T_n) \begin{bmatrix} x_1 \\ x_2 \\ \vdots \\ x_n \end{bmatrix} = 0$$

$$T_1 x_1 + T_2 x_2 + \cdots + T_n x_n = 0$$

Since both the primal variables and the slack dual variables must be non-negative, then we must have a zero value for each term in the summation. In other words, if there is slack in the jth constraint of the dual, then the jth primal variable must be zero. If the jth primal variable is positive, then the corresponding dual constraint must hold as an equality. Furthermore we cannot rule out the possibility that in certain circumstances both the primal variable and the corresponding slack variable are both zero. These results are known as the complementary-slackness conditions, or alternatively as the equilibrium theorem of linear programming.

Having outlined the mathematical aspects of these relationships, we will consider their application in economics. First we shall interpret the dual variables in the problem of a firm maximising the value of its total output when it is subject to constraints on the availabilities of inputs which are necessary in the production process.

We have earlier seen that introducing a non-basic variable into the basis will only lead to an increase in the value of the objective function if $z_j - c_j$ is negative, and that the current value of the ith dual variable is given by the ith element in the row vector $\boldsymbol{c}_B^T \boldsymbol{B}^{-1}$. Let x_j be the slack variable associated with the kth primal constraint and assume that it is non-basic. Then $z_j - c_j$ is equal to y_k, and if x_j were to be introduced into the basis, the value of the objective function would fall by an amount equal to y_k for each unit increase in x_j. Introducing x_j into the basis means in these circumstances that some of the kth input is left unutilised. We may therefore interpret y_k as measuring the marginal value to the firm of the kth input. We may alternatively refer to the dual variable as the shadow price of the relevant input. Remember that the values of the dual variables depend upon which particular primal variables are in the current basis, and changes in the composition of the primal basis will lead to changes in the values of the dual variables.

If a production input is not being fully utilised, then its shadow price will be zero. This follows from the equilibrium theorem of linear programming. There would be no way that the firm could benefit from a unilateral relaxation of this particular primal constraint. It would not be able to produce a more valuable bundle of outputs. All that would happen is that there would be an increase in the quantity of the input that was not used; the slack variable in this particular primal constraint would simply be larger. If, however, the dual variable was positive, then a relaxation of the primal constraint would make it possible to produce a more valuable bundle of outputs. What is the maximum the firm would be prepared to pay to have one more unit of this scarce input? Obviously no more than the increase in the value of the output made possible by having one more unit of the input, but this is precisely what is measured by the dual variable.

Now let us look at the economic significance of $z_j - c_j$ for non-basic non-slack variables. Let x_j be a product which the firm is not currently producing; in this case the column vector $\boldsymbol{a}_j$ informs us of the quantities of the various inputs which are necessary to produce unit output of this particular product, and z_j, being the product of the vector of dual variables and the column $\boldsymbol{a}_j$, measures the imputed values of the inputs necessary to produce unit output of good j. Since in this problem c_j is to be interpreted as the price of good j, then the significance of the optimality criterion is that the good should be produced (x_j should be introduced into the basis) if its price exceeds the imputed value of the resources necessary to produce a unit of it (for if this is so, then $z_j - c_j$ is negative).

In equilibrium a good would not be produced if the value of the inputs required to produce a unit of the good was greater than the price of the good. Since the objective is to maximise the value of the firm's total output, these inputs are put to much better use by being used to produce other goods. This again stems from the equilibrium theorem.

Example 7.1

You are informed that at the solution to the following problem the first and third dual variables are positive, and that x_3 is a non-basic variable:

$$\text{Maximise } 22x_1 + 24x_2 + 18x_3$$
$$\text{s.t.} \quad 4x_1 + 5x_2 + 3x_3 \leq 120$$
$$2x_1 + 3x_2 + x_3 \leq 80$$
$$3x_1 + 2x_2 + 4x_3 \leq 76$$
$$x_1, x_2, x_3 \geq 0$$

(a) Find the solution to the primal problem without using the simplex method or graphical techniques.

(b) What values are taken by the dual variables? How large would the coefficient on x_3 in the objective function have to be for it to be worthwhile to introduce x_3 into the basis?

From the information we are given that the first and third dual variables are positive, we know that the first and third primal constraints must hold as equalities. Furthermore given that x_3 is a non-basic variable, we must have:

$$4x_1 + 5x_2 = 120$$
$$3x_1 + 2x_2 = 76$$

from which it follows that $x_1 = 20$, and $x_2 = 8$, and the value of the objective function is equal to 632. Note that there is indeed slack in the second constraint of the primal at this point, and hence y_2 must be zero.

The dual of our example is given by:

$$\text{Minimise } 120y_1 + 80y_2 + 76y_3$$
$$\text{s.t.} \quad 4y_1 + 2y_2 + 3y_3 \geq 22$$
$$5y_1 + 3y_2 + 2y_3 \geq 24$$
$$3y_1 + y_2 + 4y_3 \geq 18$$
$$y_1, y_2, y_3 \geq 0.$$

Given that x_1 and x_2 are both in the optimal primal basis, as is the slack variable in the second constraint, then the first and second dual constraints must hold as equalities with y_2 equal to zero. Hence we have:

$$4y_1 + 3y_2 = 22$$
$$5y_1 + 2y_3 = 24$$

from which it follows that $y_1 = 4$ and $y_2 = 2$. Note there is slack in the third dual constraint:

$$z_3 - c_3 = 3(4) + 1(0) + 4(2) - 18 = 2$$

and it will not be worth introducing x_3 into the basis. However, if c_3 were to increase from *18* to *20*, then $z_3 - c_3$ would now equal *0*, and introducing x_3 into the basis would not change the value of the objective function. We would have a non-unique solution. If c_3 were to be increased beyond *20*, then the current basis would no longer be optimal, and introducing x_3 into the basis would increase the value of the objective function.

The dual of a minimisation problem

Let us now turn to consider the dual of a minimisation problem. The diet problem is a well known example of a minimisation problem. The objective in the diet problem is to choose quantities of various foodstuffs so as to satisfy certain nutritional requirements at minimum cost. The chosen diet must provide the consumer with at least minimal quantities of protein, fat, carbohydrate, certain vitamins etc. The dual of this problem, therefore, is a maximisation problem, and we know from our first theorem of linear programming that the value of the primal will equal the value of the dual. The dual objective function is the sum of the products of each required nutrient and its dual variable. Hence the dual variable must be a kind of price; in fact, the dual variables in this case must effectively measure the imputed values or shadow prices of the nutrients.

What can we say about the interpretation of the dual constraints of the diet problem? On the left-hand side of the constraint we have the value of the nutrients contained in a unit of a particular foodstuff, and on the right-hand side we have the price of a unit of the foodstuff. The value of these nutrients must not exceed the price of the foodstuff. If the value of the nutrients falls short of the price of the foodstuff, then we know from the equilibrium theorem of linear programming that the foodstuff will not be consumed. Since the consumer's objective is to minimise the cost of the diet, then it is clearly in their interests to abstain from consuming such products as these are an inefficient way of providing the required nutrients. However, when a good is consumed, again it follows from the equilibrium theorem that the corresponding dual constraint will hold as an equality. If the optimal diet is one which yields the consumer more than is minimally necessary of a particular nutrient, then that nutrient will have no implicit value to the consumer. Again from the equilibrium theorem, the dual variable will be zero since there is a corresponding slack in the relevant primal constraint.

The possibility of negative dual variables

To date our dual variables have either taken on positive or zero values. We now consider the possibility that a dual variable takes on a negative value in the optimal solution. Let us return to our standard maximisation problem of a firm maximising the value of its output subject to constraints on the availability of inputs used in the production process. So that the dual variable can potentially be negative we must modify the form the constraint takes, and therefore instead of permitting the possibility of slack in the constraint, require the constraint to hold as an equality.

Assume we have the following problem in which the third constraint must hold as an equality:

$$\text{Maximise } c_1x_1 + c_2x_2 + c_3x_3$$
$$\text{s.t. } a_{11}x_1 + a_{12}x_2 + a_{13}x_3 \leq b_1$$
$$a_{21}x_1 + a_{22}x_2 + a_{23}x_3 \leq b_2$$
$$a_{31}x_1 + a_{32}x_2 + a_{33}x_3 = b_3$$
$$x_1, x_2, x_3 \geq 0$$

Note that we may express the equality constraint in the form of two weak inequalities:

$$a_{31}x_1 + a_{32}x_2 + a_{33}x_3 \leq b_3$$
$$a_{31}x_1 + a_{32}x_2 + a_{33}x_3 \geq b_3$$

Multiplying the second of these two constraints by -1 yields the following problem:

$$\text{Maximise } c_1x_1 + c_2x_2 + c_3x_3$$
$$\text{s.t. } a_{11}x_1 + a_{12}x_2 + a_{13}x_3 \leq b_1$$
$$a_{21}x_1 + a_{22}x_2 + a_{23}x_3 \leq b_2$$
$$a_{31}x_1 + a_{32}x_2 + a_{33}x_3 \leq b_3$$
$$-a_{31}x_1 - a_{32}x_2 - a_{33}x_3 \leq -b_3$$
$$x_1, x_2, x_3 \geq 0$$

The dual of this problem is:

$$\text{Minimise } b_1y_1 + b_2y_2 + b_3y_3^+ - b_3y_3^-$$
$$\text{s.t. } a_{11}y_1 + a_{21}y_2 + a_{31}y_3^+ - a_{31}y_3^- \geq c_1$$
$$a_{12}y_1 + a_{22}y_2 + a_{32}y_3^+ - a_{32}y_3^- \geq c_2$$
$$a_{13}y_1 + a_{23}y_2 + a_{33}y_3^+ - a_{33}y_3^- \geq c_3$$
$$y_1, y_2, y_3^+, y_3^- \geq 0$$

Note that we appear to have four dual variables, all of which are constrained to be non-negative. Yet we only have three separate inputs; the fact that the third input must be fully utilised means that there are two dual variables associated with that equality constraint. We may define

$$y_3 = y_3^+ - y_3^-$$

This dual variable will, in fact, be unrestricted in sign. What would be the significance of this dual variable actually being negative? Since the third dual variable measures the value to the firm of having an additional unit of the third input, a negative value for y_3 means that the value of the objective function would fall if there were to be an increase in b_3 and the constraint were still required to hold as an equality. The value of the objective function is lower than it would have been with slack permitted in the third constraint.

Example 7.2

Consider the following example

$$\text{Maximise } 8x_1 + 4x_2$$
$$\text{s.t. } 3x_1 + x_2 \leq 56$$
$$x_1 + x_2 \leq 32$$
$$x_1 + 2x_2 = 54$$

For the moment assume that slack is permitted in the third constraint. The feasible region is given by the area $OABCD$ in Fig. 7.2. Since the absolute slope of the objective function lies in the interval formed by the absolute slopes of the line segments BC and CD, the optimal solution would occur at the vertex C where the first and second constraints hold as equalities, and there is slack in the third constraint. However, with the requirement that the third constraint hold as an equality, the solution must be somewhere along the line segment AB. The optimal position is at B with $x_1 = 10$ and $x_2 = 22$, whereas at C we would have had $x_1 = 12$ and $x_2 = 20$. At B there is slack in the first constraint, hence must have y_1 equal to zero. Now solve for the remaining two dual variables:

$$y_2 + y_3 = 8$$
$$y_2 + 2y_3 = 4$$
$$\text{Hence } y_2 = 12 \quad \text{and} \quad y_3 = -4$$

Compare this outcome with the solution where slack is indeed permitted in the third constraint. The third dual variable would be zero. Solving the following two equations for

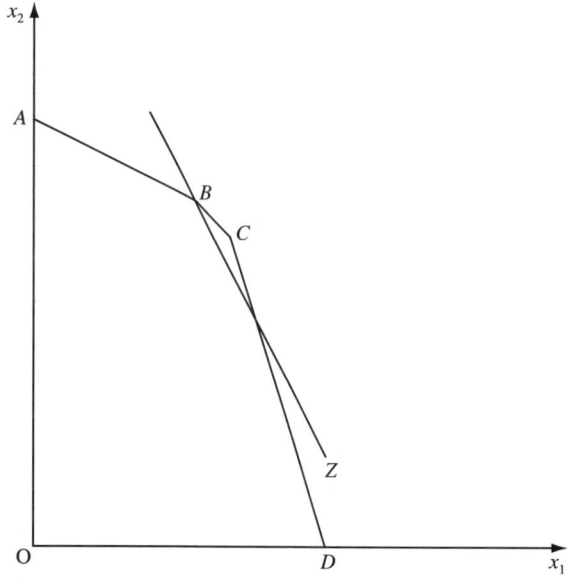

Figure 7.2 In the absence of the equality constraint, the optimal vertex would be at C. B, which is the optimal position in the presence of the equality constraint lies on a lower valued iso-revenue line. A tightening of the equality constraint which leads to a downwards parallel shift in the line segment AB would enable a higher valued iso-revenue line to be attained.

the remaining dual variables, we have:

$$3y_1 + y_2 = 8$$
$$y_1 + y_2 = 4$$
$$\text{Hence } y_1 = y_2 = 2$$

The value of the objective function is *168* when the third constraint must hold as an equality, but *176* when slack is allowed in that constraint. Note that if the value of the right-hand side of the third constraint is reduced from *54* to *52*, the vertex C would indeed constitute the optimal solution to the problem, with the value of the objective function increasing by an amount equal to the product of y_3 and $-b_3$, i.e. $(-4)(-2) = 8$. On the other hand, an increase in the right-hand side of the third constraint from *54* to *56* would mean that at the optimal solution x_1 would equal 8 and x_2 would equal 24, with the value of the objective function being reduced by 8 from *168* to *160*.

Example 7.3

(a) Use the two-phase method to find non-negative values of x which solve the following problem:

$$\text{Maximise } 16x_1 + 9x_2$$
$$\text{s.t. } 2x_1 + 3x_2 = 36$$
$$3x_1 + 2x_2 \leq 34$$
$$x_1 + 4x_2 \leq 50$$

(b) What is the optimal solution if slack is permitted in the first constraint?

In setting up the initial starting tableau, we introduce an artificial variable into the first constraint and slack variables into the other two constraints. For the first phase, we seek to maximise $-R_1$.

	x_1	x_2	R_1	S_2	S_3	solution
$z_j - c_j$	0	0	1	0	0	0
R_1	2	3	1	0	0	36
S_2	3	2	0	1	0	34
S_3	1	4	0	0	1	50

Expressing the $z_j - c_j$ row in terms of the non-basic variables, we have:

	x_1	x_2	R_1	S_2	S_3	solution
$z_j - c_j$	-2	-3	0	0	0	-36
R_1	2	3	1	0	0	36
S_2	3	2	0	1	0	34
S_3	1	4	0	0	1	50

We, therefore, introduce x_2 in place of R_1. Having carried out the necessary row operations, we arrive at the end of phase one.

	x_1	x_2	R_1	S_2	S_3	solution
$z_j - c_j$	0	0	1	0	0	0
x_2	2/3	1	1/3	0	0	12
S_2	5/3	0	−2/3	1	0	10
S_3	−5/3	0	−4/3	0	1	2

We now introduce the original objective function into the above tableau; we shall also retain the R_1 column, since this will provide us with information about the value of the dual variable attached to the equality constraint of the primal.

	x_1	x_2	R_1	S_2	S_3	solution
$z_j - c_j$	−16	−9	0	0	0	0
x_2	2/3	1	1/3	0	0	12
S_2	5/3	0	−2/3	1	0	10
S_3	−5/3	0	−4/3	0	1	2

We must first express the $z_j - c_j$ row in terms of the non-basic variables; this requires us to multiply the x_2 row by *9* and add to the $z_j - c_j$ row.

	x_1	x_2	R_1	S_2	S_3	solution
$z_j - c_j$	−10	1	3	0	0	108
x_2	2/3	1	1/3	0	0	12
S_2	5/3	0	−2/3	1	0	10
S_3	−5/3	0	−4/3	0	1	2

Introduce x_1 in place of S_2 to obtain

	x_1	x_2	R_1	S_2	S_3	solution
$z_j - c_j$	0	0	−1	6	0	168
x_2	0	1	3/5	−2/5	0	8
x_1	1	0	−2/5	3/5	0	6
S_3	0	0	−2	1	1	12

We have now reached the optimal solution with $x_1 = 6$, $x_2 = 8$, and the value of the objective function is *168*. The dual variables take the following values: $y_1 = -1$, $y_2 = 6$, $y_3 = 0$. Note that the negative value of y_1 is permissible since the first constraint must hold as an equality. To introduce R_1 into the basis would violate the first constraint. The value of the objective function would obviously be higher if slack were permitted in the first constraint, as we now show. Permitting slack in the first constraint involves replacing R_1 with S_1 in the optimal tableau above. We then introduce S_1 in place of x_2 to obtain:

	x_1	x_2	S_1	S_2	S_3	solution
$z_j - c_j$	0	5/3	0	16/3	0	544/3
S_1	0	5/3	1	−2/3	0	40/3
x_1	1	0	0	1/3	0	34/3
S_3	0	0	0	−1/3	1	116/3

7.3 THE SOLUTION TO THE DUAL

Given the primal problem:

$$\text{Maximise } c^T x \text{ s.t. } Ax \leq b, \; x \geq 0$$

we may write the dual as:

$$\text{Minimise } b^T y \text{ s.t. } A^T y \geq c, \; y \geq 0$$

By introducing slack dual variables we can convert the constraints of the dual into equalities. The coefficient on the ith slack dual variable in the objective function is zero, and the additional column of the augmented transposed matrix referring to the ith slack variable has -1 in the ith row and zeros everywhere else. To have an initial basic feasible solution, we also need to introduce artificial variables into the problem. The coefficient on the kth artificial dual variable in the objective function is M, and the additional column of the transposed matrix referring to the kth artificial variable has unity in the kth row and zeros everywhere else. Let y_D be a feasible basis for the dual and let D represent the matrix made up of the columns of the augmented transpose which refers to these basic dual variables. The basic dual variables, therefore, take on the following values:

$$y_D = D^{-1} c$$

and the value of the dual objective function is given by:

$$C = b_D^T D^{-1} c$$

where b_D^T is the subvector of b^T referring to the dual variables in the basis. If we were to introduce a non-basic variable, y_i, into the basis, then the dual constraints must continue to hold as equalities. Hence we must have:

$$D y_D + a_i^T y_i = c$$

where a_i^T is the ith column of the augmented transpose. Pre-multiplying by D^{-1} and re-arranging yields:

$$y_D = D^{-1} c - D^{-1} a_i^T y_i$$

The new value of the dual objective function is given by:

$$\tilde{C} = b_D^T y_D + b_i y_i$$
$$= b_D^T D^{-1} c - (b_D^T D^{-1} a_i^T - b_i) y_i$$
$$= C - (w_i - b_i) y_i$$
$$\text{where } w_i = b_D^T D^{-1} a_i^T$$

This will be smaller than the old value provided that

$$b_D^T D^{-1} a_i^T - b_i = w_i - b_i > 0$$

We should therefore introduce into the dual basis the non-basic variable which has the largest positive value of the above expression. If there are no non-basic dual variables for which the above condition holds, the current basis constitutes the optimal solution to the dual.

What economic interpretation can we give to the above optimality criterion? As before, we take as our representative primal problem the case of a firm maximising the value of its output subject to constraints on the availabilities of production inputs. Clearly for dual variables which are neither slack nor artificial variables, b_i tells us how much of the ith input the firm has available, but what significance attaches to $\boldsymbol{b}_D^T \boldsymbol{D}^{-1} \boldsymbol{a}_i^T$? Firstly, $\boldsymbol{b}_D^T \boldsymbol{D}^{-1}$ tells us the values that will be taken by the primal variables, and these depend upon the particular dual variables that are in the current dual basis. In particular, note that if y_k is the slack dual variable in the first dual constraint, the kth element of $\boldsymbol{b}_D^T$ is zero and the first column of $\boldsymbol{D}^{-1}$ has -1 in the kth row and zeros everywhere else. This follows from the fact that the co-factors of all the elements in the first row of $\boldsymbol{D}$ are zero apart from the co-factor of the element in column k which is equal to the negative of the determinant of the matrix. In arriving at the inverse of the matrix, we transpose the matrix of co-factors, and then divide each element through by the determinant of the matrix. Hence in the first column of the inverse we shall have zeros everywhere other than in row k where the element will equal -1. The clear implication of this is that the primal variable, x_1, is currently zero, as can be seen by pre-multiplying $\boldsymbol{D}^{-1}$ by $\boldsymbol{b}_D^T$:

$$x = (b_1 \ \ldots \ 0 \ \ldots \ b_n) \begin{bmatrix} 0 & \ldots & \delta_{1k} & \ldots & \delta_{1n} \\ \vdots & \ldots & \vdots & \ldots & \vdots \\ -1 & \ldots & \delta_{k2} & \ldots & \delta_{kn} \\ \vdots & \ldots & \vdots & \ldots & \vdots \\ 0 & \ldots & \delta_{n2} & \ldots & \delta_{nn} \end{bmatrix}$$

$$\text{and } x_1 = 0$$

where δ_{ij} is the element in row i column j of the inverse matrix.

Example 7.4

In order to reinforce understanding of the above discussion, consider the following simple example. The primal problem is:

$$\text{Maximise } c_1 x_1 + c_2 x_2$$
$$\text{s.t. } a_{11} x_1 + a_{12} x_2 \leq b_1$$
$$a_{21} x_1 + a_{22} x_2 \leq b_2$$
$$x_1, x_2 \geq 0$$

Convert the constraints of the dual of the above problem into equalities by introducing slack dual variables, y_3 and y_4. In order to have an initial basic feasible solution, we also need to introduce two artificial variables, y_5 and y_6 into the objective function and into the constraints. Each constraint will be modified by the introduction of its own artificial variable, this variable being assigned a coefficient of unity in its own constraint and of zero everywhere else. These artificial variables must obviously not appear in the optimal solution. To avoid this we attach a large positive coefficient, M, to each artificial variable in the objective function we are seeking to minimise. We may write the dual as follows:

$$\text{Minimise } b_1y_1 + b_2y_2 + 0y_3 + 0y_4 + My_5 + My_6$$
$$\text{s.t. } a_{11}y_1 + a_{21}y_2 - y_3 + y_5 = c_1$$
$$\phantom{\text{s.t. }} a_{12}y_1 + a_{22}y_2 - y_4 + y_6 = c_2$$
$$y_1,\ y_2,\ y_3,\ y_4,\ y_5,\ y_6 \geq 0$$

Let the current feasible dual basis contain y_1 and y_4. Then we have

$$D = \begin{bmatrix} a_{11} & 0 \\ a_{12} & -1 \end{bmatrix}$$

$$D^{-1} = \begin{bmatrix} 1/a_{11} & 0 \\ a_{12}/a_{11} & -1 \end{bmatrix}$$

$$b_D^T D^{-1} = (b_1\ 0) \begin{bmatrix} 1/a_{11} & 0 \\ a_{12}/a_{11} & -1 \end{bmatrix} = (b_1/a_{11}\ 0)$$

At this dual basis, the first dual constraint holds as an equality, but there is slack in the second dual constraint. Hence the second primal variable will be zero. The first dual variable is positive, hence the first primal constraint holds as an equality; given that the second primal variable is zero, the value which is taken by the first primal variable must be given by b_1/a_{11}.

Is this dual basis optimal? How much of the second input is necessary to produce b_1/a_{11} units of good one? To produce this amount, we would need $a_{21}b_1/a_{11}$ units of the second input. If this were larger than b_2, we would wish to introduce y_2 into the dual basis since there would be excess demand for the second input:

$$b_D^T D^{-1} a_2^T - b_2 = (b_1/a_{11}\ 0) \begin{bmatrix} a_{21} \\ a_{22} \end{bmatrix} - b_2$$

$$= \frac{a_{21}b_1}{a_{11}} - b_2 \geq 0$$

For the general case we may state the following: if y_i is the non-slack non-artificial dual variable associated with the ith primal constraint, then the column a_i^T is the same as the ith row of the matrix of technical coefficients, and the product of the row vector of primal variables and this column tells us what is the demand for the ith input. If there is excess demand for the ith input, then the dual variable attached to the ith primal constraint should be introduced into the basis. Note that if the current dual basis is not optimal, the primal is currently infeasible, since to produce the vector of outputs requires more of the ith input than is available.

Assume that y_i, the slack dual variable associated with the jth dual constraint, is non-basic. Assume that the current basis consists of normal (i.e. non-slack and non-artificial) dual variables. Then all the constraints of the dual hold as equalities; hence all the primal variables are produced. In this situation the value of the dual objective function can only be reduced by introducing a slack dual variable, if the corresponding primal variable is negative. In this case b_i is zero, and $b_D^T D^{-1} a_i^T$ measures the negative of the value of the primal variable, x_j. Only if this primal variable were negative, would introducing this dual variable into the basis reduce the value of the dual objective function. Note again that when the dual is not optimal, the primal is infeasible. In this example, we do not have excess demand for the input; instead the current dual basis implies a negative output of one of the goods, i.e. a negative value for one of the primal variables.

Consider the situation when the current basis contains a mixture of normal dual variables and artificial variables. Return to our example 7.4. Let the current feasible basis contain y_1 and y_5. We shall now see that introducing the slack dual variable y_4 into the basis would lead to a reduction in the value of the objective function.

$$w_4 - b_4 = (b_1 \ M) \begin{bmatrix} 0 & 1/a_{12} \\ 1 & -a_{11}/a_{12} \end{bmatrix} \begin{bmatrix} 0 \\ -1 \end{bmatrix} - 0$$

$$= \left(M \ \ \frac{b_1 - a_{11}M}{a_{12}} \right) \begin{bmatrix} 0 \\ -1 \end{bmatrix}$$

$$= \frac{a_{11}M - b_1}{a_{12}}$$

Since M is a very large positive number, the above expression is positive provided the other parameters in the expression are positive as they are indeed in our standard example. Note however that we would not wish to introduce the slack dual variable y_3 into the basis, since

$$w_3 - b_3 = (b_1 \ M) \begin{bmatrix} 0 & 1/a_{12} \\ 1 & -a_{11}/a_{12} \end{bmatrix} \begin{bmatrix} -1 \\ 0 \end{bmatrix} - 0$$

$$= \left(M \ \ \frac{b_1 - a_{11}M}{a_{12}} \right) \begin{bmatrix} -1 \\ 0 \end{bmatrix} = -M$$

Given this current basis, under what circumstances would y_2 be a candidate for entry into the basis? Economically, the answer is straightforward: if there is an excess demand for the second input, then we should introduce this dual variable. We now show this algebraically. We have:

$$w_2 - b_2 = (b_1 \ M) \begin{bmatrix} 0 & 1/a_{12} \\ 1 & -a_{11}/a_{12} \end{bmatrix} \begin{bmatrix} a_{21} \\ a_{22} \end{bmatrix} - b_2$$

$$= \left(M \ \ \frac{b_1 - a_{11}M}{a_{12}} \right) \begin{bmatrix} a_{21} \\ a_{22} \end{bmatrix} - b_2$$

$$= a_{21}M + a_{22} \frac{(b_1 - a_{11}M)}{a_{12}} - b_2$$

The first two terms in the last expression are the amount of the second input required to produce the quantities of the two goods (the primal variables) implied by this particular dual basis, and the third term is the available supply of the input. If the whole expression is positive, there is excess demand for the second input and the second dual variable is a candidate for introduction into the basis.

Given that M is a very large positive parameter, there will be definitely an excess demand for the second input if

$$a_{12}a_{21} - a_{11}a_{22} > 0.$$

Assuming that this condition is met, then we would introduce y_4 rather than y_2 provided that
$$w_2 - b_2 \geq w_4 - b_4$$

The feasibility criterion

Assume that introducing y_i into the basis will reduce the value of the dual objective function. Which of the current dual variables should be eliminated to make way for y_i? The new basis must continue to remain feasible. As we have shown above, the original basic variables as a function of y_i are given by
$$\mathbf{y}_D = \mathbf{D}^{-1}\mathbf{c} - \mathbf{D}^{-1}\mathbf{a}_i^T y_i$$

If feasibility is to be maintained, the value of none of these dual variables can be reduced below zero when we introduce y_i into the basis. Since the original basis was feasible, all the elements in the column vector $\mathbf{D}^{-1}\mathbf{c}$ are non-negative. We need therefore only concern ourselves with positive elements in the column vector $\mathbf{D}^{-1}\mathbf{a}_i^T$. To determine the leaving variable we calculate the ratios of the elements in the first vector to the corresponding elements in the second vector; the leaving variable is the one with the smallest non-negative ratio. Note that this feasibility condition is the same as for a maximisation problem.

7.4 THE DUAL SIMPLEX METHOD

In the previous chapter, we discussed how to solve minimisation problems, showing that in order to obtain an initial basic feasible solution we needed to introduce artificial variables into the problem. A solution could then be obtained by employing either the big M technique, or the two-phase method. In this section, we outline an alternative method of solving a restricted set of problems where the origin is not available as an initial basic feasible solution. The method we shall outline is known as the dual simplex method, and it is applicable for the solution of problems for which the current basis is optimal but infeasible. The method is not, therefore, a general replacement for the big M technique or the two-phase method.

Consider the following simple standard minimisation problem:

$$Minimise \ c_1 x_1 + c_2 x_2$$
$$s.t. \ a_{11} x_1 + a_{12} x_2 \geq b_1$$
$$a_{11} x_1 + a_{22} x_2 \geq b_2$$
$$x_1, \ x_2 \geq 0$$

We assume that both $\mathbf{c}$ and $\mathbf{b}$ are positive vectors. This problem may be converted into a maximisation problem by multiplying both the objective function and the two constraints by -1. This yields

$$Maximise \ -c_1 x_1 - c_2 x_2$$
$$s.t. \ -a_{11} x_1 - a_{12} x_2 \leq -b_1$$
$$-a_{21} x_1 - a_{22} x_2 \leq -b_2$$
$$x_1, \ x_2 \geq 0$$

Having converted the constraints into equalities by adding in two slack variables, we may now express this problem in tabular form:

	x_1	x_2	S_1	S_2	solution
$z_j - c_j$	c_1	c_2	0	0	0
S_1	$-a_{11}$	$-a_{12}$	1	0	$-b_1$
S_2	$-a_{21}$	$-a_{22}$	0	1	$-b_2$

Note that this basis containing S_1 and S_2 is optimal, since there are no non-basic variables for which $z_j - c_j$ is negative. However, it is infeasible with both slack variables taking on negative values. These are precisely the circumstances in which the dual simplex method can be applied.

In the simplex method, as we have already seen, we first use the optimality criterion to decide which, if any, of the current non-basic variables should be introduced into the basis, and then move on to the feasibility criterion for deciding which variable should be eliminated from the basis in order to make way for the new variable. In the dual simplex method, however, we first decide which of the current basic variables should be eliminated from the basis. In then deciding which non-basic variable should be introduced into the basis, we must ensure that the new basis continues to remain optimal. How should we, therefore, proceed?

The first stage is straightforward. We eliminate that basic variable which has the most negative value. The rationale for this is obvious: our current basis, though optimal, is infeasible. We therefore dispose of that variable which is most in breach of the non-negativity requirement. In our simple example, let us assume that b_1 is greater than b_2; we then have the choice of introducing either x_1 or x_2 in place of S_1. If we were to introduce x_1, then in performing the usual row operations we would have to multiply the S_1 row by c_1/a_{11} and add this to the $z_j - c_j$ row in order to obtain a coefficient of zero on x_1 in the new $z_j - c_j$ row. This would then yield a coefficient of $c_2 - a_{12}c_1/a_{11}$ on x_2 in the new $z_j - c_j$ row, and a coefficient of c_1/a_{11} on S_1 in the same row. If these two values are both non-negative, then the new basis will continue to be optimal. An obvious necessary condition is that a_{11} be positive.

Now consider introducing x_2, then in performing the usual row operations we would have to multiply the S_1 row by c_2/a_{12} and add this to the $z_j - c_j$ row in order to obtain a coefficient of zero on x_2 in the new $z_j - c_j$ row. This would then yield a coefficient of $c_1 - a_{11}c_2/a_{12}$ on x_1 in the new $z_j - c_j$ row, and a coefficient of c_2/a_{12} on S_1 in the same row. If these two values are both non-negative, then the new basis will continue to be optimal. A necessary condition that must be obviously met is that a_{12} be positive.

We may therefore reach our first conclusion as to which non-basic variable to introduce into the basis. A non-basic variable cannot be a candidate for entry into the basis if it has a positive coefficient on itself in the row of the leaving variable. Introducing such a variable would mean that the new basis was no longer optimal. Assume that both a_{11} and a_{12} are positive. We have seen above that the new basis will still be optimal when we introduce x_1 provided that:

$$c_2 - \frac{a_{12}c_1}{a_{11}} \geq 0$$

$$\text{i.e. } \frac{c_2}{a_{12}} \geq \frac{c_1}{a_{11}}$$

whereas the new basis will still be optimal when we introduce x_2 provided that:

$$c_1 - \frac{a_{11}c_2}{a_{12}} \geq 0$$

$$\text{i.e. } \frac{c_1}{a_{11}} \geq \frac{c_2}{a_{12}}$$

These two conditions can only be satisfied for the special case where

$$\frac{c_1}{a_{11}} = \frac{c_2}{a_{12}}$$

and in these circumstances we would be indifferent between introducing either of the non-basic variables. More generally, however, at this first iteration for our problem, we should introduce the non-basic variable which has the smaller positive ratio of c_j to a_{ij}.

We would then as before carry out elementary row operations to solve for the values of the new basic variables. If they all turn out to be non-negative, then the basis is now feasible. It has never ceased to be optimal, and hence we have reached the solution. If the new basis is still infeasible, then we continue with our procedure. The leaving variable is the one with the most negative value. The non-basic variable to be introduced into the basis is to be found by calculating the ratio for each such variable of

$$\frac{z_j - c_j}{\gamma_{ij}}$$

where γ_{ij} is the coefficient on the jth non-basic variable in the row of the leaving basic variable, x_1. Reject any non-basic variable as a candidate for entry if γ_{ij} is positive, and then choose the non-basic variable with the smallest absolute value of the above ratio for introduction into the basis. If all entries in the row are positive, there does not exist a feasible solution to the problem.

Alternatively, if we continue to treat the problem as a minimisation problem, then it will be optimal if all the elements in the $z_j - c_j$ row are negative, and it will continue to remain so if we introduce into the basis the non-basic variable with the smallest positive ratio of $z_j - c_j$ to γ_{ij}.

Example 7.5

$$\text{Minimise } 18x_1 + 28x_2 + 22x_3$$
$$\text{s.t.} \quad x_1 + 2x_2 + 3x_3 \geq 73$$
$$2x_1 + 4x_2 + 2x_3 \geq 78$$
$$x_1, x_2, x_3 \geq 0$$

Multiplying the objective function and the two constraints by -1, we then have the following tableau:

	x_1	x_2	x_3	S_1	S_2	solution
$z_j - c_j$	18	28	22	0	0	0
S_1	-1	-2	-3	1	0	-73
S_2	-2	-4	-2	0	1	-78

Applying the dual simplex method, we eliminate S_2 and introduce x_2. Having carried out the row operations, we obtain the new solution, which is still infeasible:

	x_1	x_2	x_3	S_1	S_2	solution
$z_j - c_j$	4	0	8	0	7	-546
S_1	0	0	-2	1	$-1/2$	-34
x_2	$1/2$	1	$1/2$	0	$-1/4$	$39/2$

We now eliminate S_1 from the basis and introduce x_3 to obtain:

	x_1	x_2	x_3	S_1	S_2	solution
$z_j - c_j$	4	0	0	4	5	-682
x_3	0	0	1	$-1/2$	$1/4$	17
x_2	$1/2$	1	0	$1/4$	$-3/8$	11

The basis is now feasible, and since it has always remained optimal throughout the iterations, the solution has been reached with $x_1 = 0$, $x_2 = 11$, and $x_3 = 17$; the value of the objective function is *682*, and the two dual variables are *4* and *5* respectively.

7.5 SENSITIVITY ANALYSIS

At the optimal solution to a linear program we have:

$$c_B^T B^{-1} a_j - c_j \geq 0 \ \forall j$$

and the optimal values of the primal basic variables are given by:

$$x_B^* = B^{-1} b$$

As far as the dual is concerned, then at the optimal solution we have:

$$b_D^T D^{-1} a_i^T - b_i \leq 0 \ \forall i$$

and the optimal values of the dual variables are given by:

$$y_D^* = D^{-1} c \geq 0$$

The **b** vector appears neither in the optimality criterion for the primal nor in the equation determining the values of the dual variables. We may, therefore, conclude that changes in this vector can at most affect the feasibility of the primal and the optimality of the dual; such changes have no implications for either the optimality of the primal or the feasibility of the dual.

The **c** vector, on the other hand, appears neither in the optimality criterion for the dual nor in the equation determining the values of the primal variables. Changes in this vector therefore affect neither the optimality of the dual nor the feasibility of the primal. At most they can cause the current dual basis to be no longer feasible, and the current primal basis to be no longer optimal. If there is a change in the coefficients that appear on a non-basic variable in the constraints of the primal or dual, we must also consider the effect of this.

First consider the effect of a change in the column vector a_j where x_j is a non-basic variable. This can obviously lead to a situation in which $z_j - c_j$ is no longer positive; if this were to be the case, then we would wish to introduce x_j into the basis. What are the implications for the dual if $z_j - c_j$ now becomes negative? The *j*th constraint of the dual will no longer be satisfied. If the change leads to the primal being no longer optimal, then the dual will no longer be feasible. As a consequence of such a change in the primal basis, the dual variables would also change in value, and the value of the objective function would increase.

Now turn to the case where there is a change in the coefficients on the non-basic variable y_i in the constraints of the dual. This could potentially lead $w_i - b_i$ to be no longer negative, and if this were so, the dual would be no longer optimal. It would also mean that there was excess demand for the *i*th productive input, so the primal basis would be no longer feasible.

Example 7.6

Consider the following problem:

$$\text{Maximise } c^T x \text{ s.t. } Ax \le b \text{ and } x \ge 0$$

$$\text{where } c^T = (10 \; 8 \; 17)$$

$$A = \begin{bmatrix} 2 & 2 & 3 \\ 1 & 1 & 2 \\ 4 & 3 & 1 \end{bmatrix}, \quad b = \begin{bmatrix} 50 \\ 31 \\ 45 \end{bmatrix}.$$

Let us first use the simplex method to solve the above problem. Our initial basic feasible solution contains the three slack variables.

	x_1	x_2	x_3	S_1	S_2	S_3	solution
$z_j - c_j$	−10	−8	−17	0	0	0	0
S_1	2	2	3	1	0	0	50
S_2	1	1	2	0	1	0	31
S_3	4	3	1	0	0	1	45

At the first iteration, we introduce x_3 in place of S_2. Having carried out the necessary row operations, we have:

	x_1	x_2	x_3	S_1	S_2	S_3	solution
$z_j - c_j$	−3/2	1/2	0	0	17/2	0	527/2
S_1	1/2	1/2	0	1	−3/2	0	7/2
x_3	1/2	1/2	1	0	1/2	0	31/2
S_3	7/2	5/2	0	0	−1/2	1	59/2

We now introduce x_1 in place of S_1. After carrying out the row operations, we find that this new basis is indeed the optimal one.

	x_1	x_2	x_3	S_1	S_2	S_3	solution
$z_j - c_j$	0	2	0	3	4	0	274
x_1	1	1	0	2	−3	0	7
x_3	0	0	1	−1	2	0	12
S_3	0	−1	0	−7	10	1	5

This is the optimal solution: $x_1 = 7$, $x_3 = 12$, and $S_3 = 5$, with the value of the objective function equal to 274. The values of the dual variables are as follows: $y_1 = 3$, $y_2 = 4$, and $y_3 = 0$.

Now assume the coefficient on x_3 in the objective function is reduced from 17 to 14. Carry out the necessary adjustments to the above optimal tableau, and derive the new optimal solution. This change to an element in the c vector can at most affect the optimality of the current basis, it still remains feasible. We firstly recalculate the dual variables. We must have

$$2y_1 + y_2 = 10$$
$$3y_1 + 2y_2 = 14$$
$$\text{hence } y_1 = 6, \; y_2 = -2.$$

We also need to recalculate the value of $z_2 - c_2$:

$$z_2 - c_2 = (6 \quad -2 \quad 0) \begin{bmatrix} 2 \\ 1 \\ 3 \end{bmatrix} - 8$$

$$= 2$$

The new value of the objective is *238*. So the adjusted tableau takes the following form.

	x_1	x_2	x_3	S_1	S_2	S_3	solution
$z_j - c_j$	0	2	0	6	-2	0	238
x_1	1	1	0	2	-3	0	7
x_2	0	0	1	-1	2	0	12
S_3	0	-1	0	-7	10	1	5

The current basis is no longer optimal. We therefore introduce S_2 in place of S_3. This new basis is optimal.

	x_1	x_2	x_3	S_1	S_2	S_3	solution
$z_j - c_j$	0	9/5	0	23/5	0	1/5	239
x_1	1	7/10	0	-1/10	0	3/10	17/2
x_3	0	1/5	1	2/5	0	-1/5	11
S_2	0	-1/10	0	-7/10	1	1/10	1/2

Now return to the optimal solution to the original problem, and let the parameter on the right-hand side of the third constraint be reduced from *45* to *30*. The current basis may no longer be feasible, though it will continue to be optimal. The new values of the current basic variables are given by:

$$x = \begin{bmatrix} 2 & -3 & 0 \\ -1 & 2 & 0 \\ -7 & 10 & 1 \end{bmatrix} \begin{bmatrix} 50 \\ 31 \\ 30 \end{bmatrix} = \begin{bmatrix} 7 \\ 12 \\ -10 \end{bmatrix}$$

Clearly we have $S_3 = -10$, so the basis is no longer feasible. We therefore apply the dual simplex method to find the new optimal solution.

	x_1	x_2	x_3	S_1	S_2	S_3	solution
$z_j - c_j$	0	2	0	3	4	0	274
x_1	1	1	0	2	-3	0	7
x_3	0	0	1	-1	2	0	12
S_3	0	-1	0	-7	10	1	-10

We must remove S_3 from the basis. There are two non-basic variables which have negative coefficients in the row of the leaving variable. The smaller absolute ratio of the element in the $z_j - c_j$ row to the corresponding element in the row of the leaving variable refers to S_1: 3/7 is less than 2. So S_1 is introduced into the basis. After carrying out row operations on the above tableau, we obtain the new optimal solution.

	x_1	x_2	x_3	S_1	S_2	S_3	solution
$z_j - c_j$	0	11/7	0	0	58/7	3/7	1888/7
x_1	1	5/7	0	0	−1/7	2/7	29/7
x_3	0	1/7	1	0	4/7	−1/7	94/7
S_1	0	1/7	0	1	−10/7	−1/7	10/7

Return to the original problem, and assume that the coefficient on x_2 in the first constraint is changed from 2 to 1. The current primal basis remains feasible, but it may no longer be optimal. We will, therefore need to adjust the original optimal tableau, since we now have:

$$z_2 - c_2 = (3 \ 4 \ 0) \begin{bmatrix} 1 \\ 1 \\ 3 \end{bmatrix} - 8 = -1$$

$$\text{and } \mathbf{B}^{-1}\mathbf{a}_2 = \begin{bmatrix} 2 & -3 & 0 \\ -1 & 2 & 0 \\ -7 & 10 & 1 \end{bmatrix} \begin{bmatrix} 1 \\ 1 \\ 3 \end{bmatrix} = \begin{bmatrix} -1 \\ 1 \\ 6 \end{bmatrix}$$

Hence we have:

	x_1	x_2	x_3	S_1	S_2	S_3	solution
$z_j - c_j$	0	−1	0	3	4	0	274
x_1	1	−1	0	2	−3	0	7
x_3	0	1	1	−1	2	0	12
S_3	0	6	0	−7	10	1	5

We therefore introduce x_2 in place of S_3. Having carried out elementary row operations, we obtain the new optimal basis:

	x_1	x_2	x_3	S_1	S_2	S_3	solution
$z_j - c_j$	0	0	0	11/6	17/3	1/6	1649/6
x_1	1	0	0	5/6	−4/3	1/6	47/6
x_3	0	0	1	1/6	1/3	−1/6	67/6
x_2	0	1	0	−7/6	5/3	1/6	5/6

7.6 CONCLUSION

In this chapter we have investigated the links between a linear program and its dual. The key results to be borne in mind are as follows:

1. The existence of a bounded solution to the primal requires that a feasible basis for the dual exists, and similarly for the solution to the dual to be bounded then, a feasible basis for the primal must exist.

2. As we move from one feasible primal basis to another one, the dual remains infeasible until we reach the optimal basis for the primal, and similarly for the dual.
3. At the optimal position, the value of the primal objective function equals the value of the dual objective function.
4. If a dual variable is positive, the corresponding primal constraint holds as an equality, and if there is slack in a primal constraint, then the corresponding dual variable is zero.
5. If a primal variable is positive, then the corresponding dual constraint holds as an equality, and if there is slack in a dual constraint, then the corresponding primal variable is zero.

Points 4. and 5. constitute the equilibrium theorem of linear programming. The economic intuition behind these results is clear. If a productive input is not being fully utilised, then its marginal valuation is zero; a firm would not benefit from having more of the input made available to it. Similarly, it would not be worthwhile producing a product if the imputed value of the resources embodied in a unit of the product exceeded the price that the firm would receive for the good. The resources are better used in producing something else.

In the next chapter we shall consider some special kinds of linear programming problems.

7.7 EXERCISES

7.1 (a) Write down the duals of the following problems:

(i) *Maximise* $16x_1 + 20x_2 + 23x_3$
s.t. $2x_1 + 3x_2 + x_3 \le 44$
$x_1 + x_2 + 3x_3 \le 47$
$x_1, x_2, x_3 \ge 0$

(ii) *Maximise* $14x_1 + 16x_2 + 10x_3$
s.t. $2x_1 + 3x_2 + 2x_3 \le 68$
$x_1 + 4x_2 + 3x_3 \ge 82$
$x_1 + x_2 \le 20$
$x_1, x_2, x_3 \ge 0$

(iii) *Minimise* $10x_1 + 3x_2$
s.t. $x_1 + 3x_2 \ge 30$
$2x_1 + x_2 \ge 20$
$4x_1 + 2x_2 \ge 64$
$x_1, x_2 \ge 0$

(iv) *Minimise* $11x_1 + 5x_2 + 6x_3$
s.t. $x_1 + 2x_2 + 3x_3 \ge 93$
$-2x_1 + x_2 + 2x_3 \le 57$
$x_1, x_2, x_3 \ge 0$

(v) *Maximise* $20x_1 + 5x_2 - 6x_3$
s.t. $2x_1 - x_2 + x_3 \le 16$
$x_1 + 2x_2 - 2x_3 \le 28$
$2x_1 + 3x_2 - 4x_3 \le 60$
$x_1, x_2, x_3 \ge 0$

(b) For the following problems, what can you say about the nature of the solutions to the primal and the associated dual problem:

(i) Maximise $2x_1 + 4x_2$

s.t. $-x_1 \leq -5$

$x_2 \leq 4$

$x_1, x_2 \geq 0$

(ii) Maximise $8x_1 + 3x_2$

s.t. $3x_1 + 2x_2 \leq 12$

$-2x_1 - x_2 \leq -10$

$x_1, x_2 \geq 0$

(iii) Maximise $3x_1 + 4x_2$

s.t. $x_1 - x_2 \leq -1$

$-x_1 + x_2 \leq 0$

$x_1, x_2 \geq 0$

(c) (i) Use the two-phase method to show that there exists no feasible solution to the following problem:

Maximise $x_1 + x_2$

s.t. $2x_1 + 3x_2 \leq 12$

$x_1 + x_2 \geq 8$

$x_1, x_2 \geq 0$

(ii) Use the two-phase method to show that there exists no bounded solution to the dual of the above problem.

7.2 (a) Three foodstuffs, each containing three nutrients, are available to meet the nutritional requirements of an individual. The individual's diet must contain at least *38* units of the first nutrient, *60* units of the second nutrient, and *50* units of the third nutrient. A unit of the first foodstuff contains *3, 4* and *1* unit respectively of the three nutrients and costs £*10*. A unit of the second foodstuff contains *1, 3* and *5* units respectively of the units and costs £*8*. Finally, a unit of the third foodstuff contains *2, 1* and *4* units respectively of the units and costs £*12*. Suppose the individual seeks to minimise the cost of satisfying the dietary requirements.

(i) Solve the dual of the minimisation problem.

(ii) What are the quantities of the three foodstuffs consumed in the cost-minimising diet?

7.3 (a) (i) Use the two-phase method to solve the following problem:

Maximise $x_1 + x_2$

s.t. $x_1 + 4x_2 = 36$

$x_1 + 2x_2 \leq 22$

$2x_1 + x_2 \leq 30$

$x_1, x_2 \geq 0$

(ii) What are the values of the dual variables at the optimal position?

(iii) What would happen if slack were permitted in the first constraint?

(b) (i) Use the two-phase method to solve the following problem:

Maximise $6x_1 + 18x_2 + 6x_3$

s.t. $x_1 + x_2 + 2x_3 = 24$

$2x_1 + 4x_2 + 2x_3 \leq 60$

$2x_1 + x_2 + x_3 \leq 20$

$x_1, x_2, x_3 \geq 0$

(ii) What are the values of the dual variables at the optimal solution?

7.4 (a) Assume the current feasible dual basis for the problem on p. 97 contained y_2 and y_6. Which of the current non-basic variables would be potential candidates to introduce into the basis?

7.5 (a) Use the dual simplex method to solve the following problems. What values are taken by the dual variables in each case?

(i) Minimise $18x_1 + 14x_2$

s.t. $4x_1 + 2x_2 \geq 58$

$x_1 + 3x_2 \geq 52$

$x_1, x_2 \geq 0$

(ii) Minimise $20x_1 + 17x_2 + 18x_3$

s.t. $2x_1 + 3x_2 + 2x_3 \geq 56$

$x_1 + 2x_2 + 2x_3 \geq 30$

$5x_1 + x_2 + 3x_3 \geq 62$

$x_1, x_2, x_3 \geq 0$

(iii) Minimise $17x_1 + 28x_2 + 32x_3$

s.t. $x_1 + 2x_2 + 3x_3 \geq 45$

$2x_1 + x_2 + 4x_3 \geq 55$

$2x_1 + 4x_2 + x_3 \geq 70$

$x_1, x_2, x_3 \geq 0$

7.6 (a) (i) Solve the following problem by means of the simplex method:

Maximise $5x_1 + 3x_2 + 10x_3$

s.t. $3x_1 + 2x_2 + 2x_3 \leq 45$

$x_1 + x_2 + 4x_3 \leq 40$

$x_1, x_2, x_3 \geq 0$

(ii) How large an increase in the RHS of the first constraint is possible before the optimal basis in (a) becomes infeasible?

(iii) How would the optimal solution change if the coefficient on x_2 in the objective function were increased from *3* to *5*?

(iv) The RHS of the second constraint is now reduced from *40* to *10*. Apply the dual simplex method to obtain the new optimal solution.

(v) The following additional constraint is now introduced into the original problem:

$$2x_1 + x_2 + 6x_3 \leq 53$$

Apply the dual simplex method to obtain the new optimal solution.

(b) (i) Use the two-phase method to solve the following problem:

Maximise $15x_1 + 7x_2 + 12x_3$

s.t. $3x_1 + 2x_2 + x_3 = 26$

$2x_1 + x_2 + 2x_3 \leq 16$

$x_1, x_2, x_3 \geq 0$

(ii) What would happen to the optimal solution if the coefficient on x_2 in the objective function were increased from *7* to *8*?

(iii) What would happen to the optimal solution if the first constraint were no longer required to hold as an equality?

(iv) Again permitting the possibility of slack in the first constraint, use the dual simplex algorithm to solve for the new optimal solution if the right-hand side of the first constraint is reduced from *26* to *20*.

CHAPTER
EIGHT

THE TRANSPORTATION PROBLEM

8.1 INTRODUCTION

In this chapter we examine a particular type of linear programming problem in which a firm faced with given supplies of some good at a set of locations and given demands for the same good at a different set of locations seeks to choose the shipment plan which minimises the costs of transporting the good from the sources to the destinations. Such a problem is known as a transportation problem. Its format is that of a linear programming problem. The unit costs of transporting a good from a particular source to a particular destination are taken to be constant and are independent of the amount shipped. The cost function whose value we are seeking to minimise is therefore a linear function of the amounts shipped over the available routes. The supply and demand conditions give rise to a set of linear constraints, and it goes without saying that the amount shipped over any route must be non-negative.

In Section 8.2 we analyse three alternative methods of finding an initial basic feasible solution to the transportation problem: these are the north-west corner method, the least cost method and the Vogel approximation method. Having found an initial feasible basic solution, we then check whether it would be possible by introducing one of the non-utilised routes to reduce the shipment charges. In order for the basis to remain feasible when we introduce a new route, then we must increase shipments over some of the existing routes and reduce them over others. It is one of this latter set of routes which restricts the amount that can be shipped over the new route. In Section 8.3 we discuss the dual of the transportation problem. Making use of the equilibrium theorem of linear programming (complementary/slackness conditions) we see that the structure of the transportation problem is such that it can be very conveniently solved by finding the values of the dual variables recursively.

Section 8.4 provides discussion of a highly practical approach based on tableaux for quickly checking whether a particular basic solution is indeed optimal. To date the problems we have dealt with have been balanced in the sense that the total supply available at the sources has been equal to the total demand at the destinations. In Section 8.5 we analyse how to adapt the transportation problem to accommodate a situation of either excess supply or demand. We shall see that we need to balance the problem artificially by introducing a fictitious destination to which the excess supply is shipped, or a fictitious source to which excess demand is allocated.

In Section 8.6 we turn to a restricted version of the transportation problem where only one unit is available at each source and is required at each destination. An obvious example of this problem is having a number of workers available to allocate to a set of tasks, with each worker being restricted to performing only one task and each task needing to be completed. This is the assignment problem. Two methods of solution are available. The assignment problem can be solved as a highly degenerate transportation problem which follows from the fact that at each allocation of a worker to a task the amount still available at the source and the amount still required at the destination are simultaneously zero. Alternatively, an operations research method can be judiciously applied in order to obtain the solution. Not only do we consider the solution to minimisation problems, but we also look at maximisation ones.

8.2 HOW TO SOLVE THE TRANSPORTATION PROBLEM

In this chapter we consider a special kind of linear programming problem where a firm has available at certain sources (warehouses) specified quantities of some good and has requirements for this same good at certain destinations (shops). Its objective is to choose the shipment plan which minimises the costs of transporting the good from warehouses to shops. We shall assume that the total supply of the good at the m sources is equal to the demand for the good at the n destinations. Shipments from the ith source must equal the amount available at that source; shipments to the jth destination must equal what is required at this destination. Later in this chapter, we shall demonstrate how to deal with situations where total availabilities of the good are not equal to total requirements; but for the moment we assume that we have a balanced problem with total supply equal to total demand. We may write out our representative transportation problem as:

$$\text{Minimise} \sum_{i=1}^{i=m} \sum_{j=1}^{j=n} c_{ij} x_{ij}$$

$$\text{s.t.} \sum_{j=1}^{j=n} x_{ij} = s_i \ \forall i$$

$$\sum_{i=1}^{i=m} x_{ij} = d_j \ \forall j$$

$$x_{ij} \geq 0 \ \forall i, j$$

where x_{ij} is the amount shipped from source i to destination j, c_{ij} is the cost of shipping a unit of the good from source i to destination j, s_i is the amount available at source i, and d_j is the amount required at destination j.

For a problem with two sources and two destinations, we would have:

$$\text{Minimise } c_{11}x_{11} + c_{12}x_{12} + c_{21}x_{21} + c_{22}x_{22}$$

$$\text{s.t.} \begin{bmatrix} 1 & 1 & 0 & 0 \\ 0 & 0 & 1 & 1 \\ 1 & 0 & 1 & 0 \\ 0 & 1 & 0 & 1 \end{bmatrix} \begin{bmatrix} x_{11} \\ x_{12} \\ x_{21} \\ x_{22} \end{bmatrix} = \begin{bmatrix} s_1 \\ s_2 \\ d_1 \\ d_2 \end{bmatrix}$$

$$x_{ij} \geq 0 \ \forall i, j$$

What can we say about the nature of the solution to the transportation problem? Given that the total supply is equal to the total demand, then for our simple two-source–two-destination problem, there are only three independent constraints. If we have a shipment plan which satisfies the first three equations, then the fourth equation will also be satisfied by this plan. For the general case of m sources and n destinations, there are $(m + n)$ constraints, but there are only $m + n - 1$ independent equations: a solution to these $m + n - 1$ equations will necessarily satisfy the remaining equation. The fact that there are only $m + n - 1$ independent equations means that in the solution to the transportation problem, only $m + n - 1$ routes will be utilised in the cost-minimising shipment plan; note that this can be considerably smaller than the maximum number of routes that are potentially available for consideration: mn. If there are ten sources and ten destinations, then a non-degenerate basic solution will involve the utilisation of only *19* of the *100* which are available. If the solution is degenerate, then positive quantities will be shipped over fewer than *19* routes. However, as we shall see later in this chapter, it will still be necessary to retain $m + n - 1$ routes in the basis in order to be able to effect a solution even though a zero quantity is being shipped over one or more routes.

Just as in our solution to a standard linear programming problem, we needed to find an initial basic feasible solution before we then applied the optimality and feasibility criteria of the simplex method in order to move to a more desirable basic feasible solution, the same procedures apply for the transportation problem. However, given the precise structure of the transportation problem, the choice of an initial basic feasible solution and the subsequent required set of iterations from one basic feasible solution to another basic feasible solution are quite easily found.

The choice of an initial basic feasible solution

The north-west corner method

There exist a number of alternative methods of finding an initial basic feasible solution for the transportation problem. One method which is easily applied, but which is not particularly efficient is known as the north-west corner method. The reason for its relative inefficiency is that it pays no attention to the unit shipment costs of utilising each of the available routes.

The procedure involves allocating the maximum amount possible to the route from the first source to the first destination: this amount is the smaller of the amount available at the first source and the amount required at the first destination. If we exhaust the availability at the first source, we then ship to the first destination from the second source an amount equal to the smaller of what is still required at the first destination and of what is available at the second destination. Alternatively, if we have met the requirements at the first destination, we then ship to the second destination an amount equal to the smaller of the amount still available at the first source and the amount required at the second destination. Assume that the former situation was one in which we found ourselves, and that as a result of allocations, we have now satisfied demand at the first destination. We now ship to the second destination from the second source an amount equal to the smaller of what is required at the second destination and what is still available at the second source, and so on. If when assigning some quantity to be shipped over route (i, j), we simultaneously satisfy the demand at the destination and exhaust the supply at the source, we must then introduce an adjacent route into the basis, either route $(i + 1, j)$ or route $(i, j + 1)$, over which a zero quantity is shipped. Failure to do this will mean that we have insufficient observations in order to assess whether or not the current basis is optimal. Note that because total supply and demand are equal, then the very last route chosen will be one at which we simultaneously meet the outstanding demand at some particular destination with the supply still remaining at the last source.

Consider the following problem: A retailer has available the following quantities of a good at four warehouses:

$$\begin{bmatrix} 600 \\ 400 \\ 750 \\ 250 \end{bmatrix}$$

Its requirements at four department stores are as follows:

$$(500 \quad 800 \quad 150 \quad 550)$$

The matrix of per unit shipment costs is given by:

$$\begin{bmatrix} 6 & 2 & 4 & 7 \\ 5 & 4 & 3 & 6 \\ 8 & 6 & 4 & 4 \\ 6 & 8 & 9 & 5 \end{bmatrix}$$

What is the cost-minimising shipment plan?

Applying the north-west corner method to obtain an initial basic feasible solution, we first allocate *500* units to route (*1,1*). This meets the demand at destination one, and the remaining *100* units at source one are now allocated to destination two. All *400* units of the good at source two are then shipped to destination two, and the remaining *300* units required at this destination are then met from source three. The *150* units needed at destination three are provided from the same source. This then leaves *300* units to be shipped out of source three to the final destination. The final decision is the residual one: *250* units are transported over route (*4,4*). Note that seven routes are utilised.

The initial basic feasible solution, is therefore:

$$\begin{bmatrix} 500 & 100 & & \\ & 400 & & \\ & 300 & 150 & 300 \\ & & & 250 \end{bmatrix}$$

and the total shipment costs are *9650*. One method of checking whether this basis is optimal is to calculate the changes in shipment costs of shipping one unit of the good over each of the non-utilised routes, having made consequential adjustments to the amounts shipped over other utilised routes so that the shipping plan continues to be met. This approach is known as the stepping stone algorithm, a utilised route being analogous to a stepping stone in a river. To ship one unit over route (*1,3*) requires us to reduce shipments over route (*3,3*) by one unit, increase by one unit shipments over route (*3,2*) and reduce by one unit shipments over route (*1,2*). The consequential change in shipping costs of these changes is given by:

$$c_{13} - c_{33} + c_{32} - c_{12} = 4 - 4 + 6 - 2$$
$$= 4$$

Since the change in cost is positive, it would not be optimal to introduce this route into the basis. We now perform similar calculations for all the other non-utilised routes.

$$\text{Route } (1,4): \ c_{14} - c_{34} + c_{32} - c_{12} = 7 - 4 + 6 - 2$$
$$= 7$$

$$\text{Route } (2,1): \ c_{21} - c_{11} + c_{12} - c_{22} = 5 - 6 + 2 - 4$$
$$= -3$$

$$\text{Route } (2,3): \ c_{23} - c_{33} + c_{32} - c_{22} = 3 - 4 + 6 - 4$$
$$= 1$$

$$\text{Route } (2,4): \ c_{14} - c_{34} + c_{32} - c_{12} = 6 - 4 + 6 - 4$$
$$= 4$$

$$\text{Route } (3,1): \ c_{31} - c_{11} + c_{12} - c_{32} = 8 - 6 + 2 - 6$$
$$= -2$$

$$\text{Route } (4,1): \ c_{41} - c_{11} + c_{12} - c_{32} + c_{34} - c_{44} = 6 - 6 + 2 - 6 + 4 - 5$$
$$= -5$$

$$\text{Route } (4,2): \ c_{42} - c_{32} + c_{34} - c_{44} = 8 - 6 + 4 - 5$$
$$= 1$$

$$\text{Route } (4,3): \ c_{43} - c_{33} + c_{34} - c_{44} = 9 - 4 + 4 - 5$$
$$= 4$$

The current basis is, therefore, not optimal since there are three routes for which our measure takes on a negative value. We introduce the route which has the largest negative value for the change in cost. This is route (4,1). We introduce this route into the basis, and given we seek to minimise costs, then we wish to ship the maximum possible over this route subject to the new allocation remaining feasible. Note that in order to introduce (4,1) we must reduce shipments over routes (1,1), (3,2) and (4,4). The amounts which are currently being shipped over these routes are 500, 300 and 250 respectively. The maximum that can, therefore, be shipped over the new route for feasibility to be maintained is 250. Route (4,4) leaves the basis, and shipments are reduced by 250 over routes (1,1) and (3,2). Shipments are increased by 250 over existing routes (2,1) and (3,4). The new basis is then:

$$\begin{bmatrix} 250 & 350 & & \\ & 400 & & \\ & & 50 & 150 & 550 \\ 250 & & & \end{bmatrix}$$

with total costs equal to *8400*. Again, we must check whether this basis is optimal. For all the non-utilised routes, we calculate the change in cost from shipping one unit over the route and making the necessary adjustments elsewhere. For this second basis, we have:

$$\text{Route } (1,3): \; c_{13} - c_{33} + c_{32} - c_{12} = 4 - 4 + 6 - 2$$
$$= 4$$

$$\text{Route } (1,4): \; c_{14} - c_{34} + c_{32} - c_{12} = 7 - 4 + 6 - 2$$
$$= 7$$

$$\text{Route } (2,1): \; c_{21} - c_{11} + c_{12} - c_{22} = 5 - 6 + 2 - 4$$
$$= -3$$

$$\text{Route } (2,3): \; c_{23} - c_{33} + c_{32} - c_{22} = 3 - 4 + 6 - 4$$
$$= 1$$

$$\text{Route } (2,4): \; c_{24} - c_{34} + c_{32} - c_{22} = 6 - 4 + 6 - 4$$
$$= 4$$

$$\text{Route } (3,1): \; c_{31} - c_{11} + c_{12} - c_{32} = 8 - 6 + 2 - 6$$
$$= -2$$

$$\text{Route } (4,2): \; c_{42} - c_{41} + c_{11} - c_{12} = 8 - 6 + 6 - 2$$
$$= 6$$

$$\text{Route } (4,3): \; c_{43} - c_{41} + c_{11} - c_{12} + c_{32} - c_{33} = 9 - 6 + 6 - 2 + 6 - 4$$
$$= 9$$

$$\text{Route } (4,4): \; c_{44} - c_{41} + c_{11} - c_{12} + c_{32} - c_{34} = 5 - 6 + 6 - 2 + 6 - 4$$
$$= 5$$

In this case there are two non-utilised routes which are potential candidates to be introduced into the basis: (2,1) and (3,1). The former route is the one with the larger negative value for the per unit cost change. We, therefore, introduce this route into the basis, and in order to retain feasibility, the most that can be shipped over this route is *250*. This results from the fact that we must reduce shipments over routes (1,1) and (2,2), and the smaller of the amounts which is currently being shipped over these two routes is *250*. The new basic solution is:

$$\begin{bmatrix} & 600 & & & \\ 250 & 150 & & & \\ & & 50 & 150 & 550 \\ 250 & & & & \end{bmatrix}$$

and the total transport cost is *7650*. Is this basis optimal? Once again, we calculate for all the non-utilised routes the change in cost from shipping one unit over the route and making the necessary adjustments elsewhere. For this third basis, we have:

$$\text{Route } (1,1): \quad c_{11} - c_{12} + c_{22} - c_{21} = 6 - 2 + 4 - 5$$
$$= 3$$

$$\text{Route } (1,3): \quad c_{13} - c_{33} + c_{32} - c_{12} = 4 - 4 + 6 - 2$$
$$= 4$$

$$\text{Route } (1,4): \quad c_{14} - c_{34} + c_{32} - c_{12} = 7 - 4 + 6 - 2$$
$$= 7$$

$$\text{Route } (2,3): \quad c_{23} - c_{33} + c_{32} - c_{22} = 3 - 4 + 6 - 4$$
$$= 1$$

$$\text{Route } (2,4): \quad c_{24} - c_{34} + c_{32} - c_{22} = 6 - 4 + 6 - 4$$
$$= 4$$

$$\text{Route } (3,1): \quad c_{31} - c_{21} + c_{22} - c_{32} = 8 - 5 + 4 - 6$$
$$= 1$$

$$\text{Route } (4,2): \quad c_{42} - c_{41} + c_{21} - c_{22} = 8 - 6 + 5 - 4$$
$$= 3$$

$$\text{Route } (4,3): \quad c_{43} - c_{41} + c_{21} - c_{22} + c_{32} - c_{33} = 9 - 6 + 5 - 4 + 6 - 4$$
$$= 6$$

$$\text{Route } (4,4): \quad c_{44} - c_{41} + c_{21} - c_{22} + c_{32} + c_{34} = 5 - 6 + 5 - 4 + 6 - 4$$
$$= 2$$

In this case since there are no non-utilised routes for which the change in unit cost is negative; this new basis is optimal.

The north-west corner method is easily applied to yield an initial basic feasible solution, but as a general rule, it will then require more iterations to reach the optimal solution than alternative methods which pay attention to cost information in arriving at an initial basic feasible solution.

The least-cost method

The least-cost method involves, as its name suggests, allocating the maximum amount possible to the route with the lowest unit transport cost. Then for the remaining feasible routes, repeat the exercise, allocating the maximum possible to the route of those still available with the lowest unit cost until a feasible plan has been reached. If simultaneously the supply is exhausted at the source and the demand fully met at the destination, then do not eliminate both the source and the destination, a zero quantity must be attached to the source (destination) which has not been eliminated. For our example, the least cost allocation would be as follows:

First allocation: *600* units to route (*1,2*);
Second allocation: *150* units to route (*2,3*);
Third allocation: *200* units to route (*2,2*);
Fourth allocation: *550* units to route (*3,4*);
Fifth allocation: *50* units to route (*2,1*);
Sixth allocation: *250* units to route (*4,1*);
Seventh allocation: *200* units to route (*3,1*).

In using the least-cost method to obtain an initial basic feasible solution, for our particular example we had to carry out as many iterations as for the case where the initial basis was derived from using the north-west corner method. This was somewhat unusual given that the latter method takes no account of information on costs.

The Vogel approximation method

A more sophisticated treatment of costs has been proposed to arrive at an initial basic feasible solution. This third approach is known as the Vogel approximation method (VAM), and it takes account of both differences in unit costs of shipping from a given source to different destinations, and of differences in unit costs of serving a given destination from different sources. Its main features are described below.

For each source, calculate the difference between the next smallest and the smallest unit shipment cost from this source to the various destinations. Perform a similar operation for each destination. Then choose the source or destination which has the largest value for this difference. If this figure relates to a source, then allocate the maximum amount possible to the route from this source with the lowest unit cost. If this figure relates to a destination, then in this case allocate as much as possible to the route to this destination which has the lowest unit cost. As a result of this allocation, one of three possibilities will have occurred: 1. supply will have been exhausted at a source; 2. demand will have been fully met at a destination; or 3. both supply and demand conditions will have been met. In the first case then the exhausted source plays no further role in arriving at the initial basis. In the second case the fulfilled destination is now ignored. The third case, however, is more complicated. We only eliminate either the source or the destination from further consideration; the one which is retained is assigned a remaining supply (demand) of zero.

If there remains only one source or destination that has not been eliminated, then a feasible basis has been reached. If there is only one source or destination remaining to which a positive supply or demand still attaches, then the least-cost method should be employed to choose the next basic variable, and its value can be obviously no larger than the minimum of what is available at the source and what is required at the destination. On the other hand, if in the one remaining source (destination) only a zero quantity attaches to the supply (demand), then the least-cost method should be used to determine the basic variable to which one then assigns a zero quantity.

If there remains for consideration more than one source or destination, then one repeats the procedure, calculating the differences between the next and smallest unit costs for every source and destination which have not been eliminated earlier, except for the special case of a source or destination which has been assigned a zero quantity.

Let us return to our earlier example, and derive the initial basic feasible solution, using the Vogel approximation method. Calculating the required cost differences, we have for the sources (*2 1 0 1*), and for the destinations (*1 2 1 1*), In this situation we are free to use either the first source or the second destination to obtain the first basic variable. Let us use the first source, then we ship *600* units over route (*1,2*). The first source is now eliminated.

The cost differences for the sources are now (*na 1 0 1*), and for the destinations (*1 2 0 1*). We therefore now look at the second destination for the next basic variable: we ship *200* units over route (*2,2*), and the second destination is now eliminated. We once more recalculate the cost differences: for the rows we have (*na 2 0 1*) and for the columns (*1 na 1 1*). The second row is now used to find the next basic variable: we ship *150* units over route (*2,3*). The third destination is now eliminated.

The new cost differences for the sources are (*na 1 4 1*), and for the destinations (*1 na na 1*). We therefore now turn to the third source for the next basic variable, and choose to ship *550* units over route (*3,4*). The fourth destination is now eliminated.

Now only the first destination remains. Hence we ship *50* units over route (*2,1*), *250* units over route (*3,1*) and *200* units over route (*3,1*). The initial basic feasible solution using the Vogel approximation method is given in the matrix below:

$$\begin{bmatrix} & 600 & & \\ 50 & 200 & 150 & \\ 200 & & & 550 \\ 250 & & & \end{bmatrix}$$

Note that in this particular case the initial feasible basis is the same as for the least-cost method.

8.3 THE DUAL OF THE TRANSPORTATION PROBLEM

In order to grasp the dual of the transportation problem, we must first modify the form in which the constraints appear in the primal problem. We shall therefore express the constraints as follows: shipments from the *i*th source must not exceed the amount available at that source; and shipments to the *j*th destination must be no less than what is required at that destination. Given that the problem is balanced in the sense that total supply is equal to total demand, then in practice the constraints will hold as equalities, though for purposes of interpretation, we shall express the constraints of the problem as weak inequalities. We may write out our representative transportation problem as:

$$Minimise \sum_{i=1}^{i=m} \sum_{j=1}^{j=n} c_{ij} x_{ij}$$

$$s.t. \sum_{j=1}^{j=n} x_{ij} \leq s_i \ \forall i$$

$$\sum_{i=1}^{i=m} x_{ij} \geq d_j \ \forall j$$

$$x_{ij} \geq 0 \ \forall i, j$$

where x_{ij} is the amount shipped from source *i* to destination *j*, c_{ij} is the cost of shipping a unit of the good from source *i* to destination *j*, s_i is the amount available at source *i*, and d_j is the amount required at destination *j*. We shall continue our convention of expressing the constraints of a minimisation problem in the form that the left-hand side of the constraints should be greater than or equal to the right-hand side. Hence multiplying the constraints relating to shipments from the sources by -1, we have:

$$\text{Minimise} \sum_{i=1}^{i=m} \sum_{j=1}^{j=n} c_{ij} x_{ij}$$

$$\text{s.t.} \quad -\sum_{j=1}^{j=n} x_{ij} \geq -s_i \; \forall i$$

$$\sum_{i=1}^{i=m} x_{ij} \geq d_j \; \forall j$$

$$x_{ij} \geq 0 \; \forall i, j$$

The dual of the above problem, therefore, takes the following form:

$$\text{Maximise} \sum_{j=1}^{j=n} v_j d_j - \sum_{i=1}^{i=m} u_i s_i$$

$$\text{s.t.} \; v_j - u_i \leq c_{ij} \; \forall i, j$$

$$u_i, \; v_j \geq 0$$

For the problem with two sources and two destinations, we would write the dual as follows:

$$\text{Minimise} \; v_1 d_1 + v_2 d_2 - u_1 s_1 + u_2 s_2$$

$$\text{s.t.} \begin{bmatrix} 1 & 0 & -1 & 0 \\ 0 & 1 & -1 & 0 \\ 1 & 0 & 0 & -1 \\ 0 & 1 & 0 & -1 \end{bmatrix} \begin{bmatrix} v_1 \\ v_2 \\ u_1 \\ u_2 \end{bmatrix} \leq \begin{bmatrix} c_{11} \\ c_{12} \\ c_{21} \\ c_{22} \end{bmatrix}$$

$$v_j, \; u_1 \geq 0 \; \forall i, j$$

We know from our discussion in the previous chapter of the diet problem that the dual variables there were to be interpreted as shadow prices of the nutrients. In the problem of finding the particular shipments which minimise transport costs, again the dual variables are going to be imputed or shadow prices: in this case the values to be attached to a unit of a good at a particular source or destination. We shall interpret v_j as the imputed value of a unit of the good at destination j, and u_i the imputed value of a unit of the good at source i. Note that the dual constraints are of the form:

$$c_{ij} \geq v_j - u_i$$

Furthermore we know from the complementary–slackness conditions that we must have at the optimal shipment plan:

$$[c_{ij} - (v_j^* - u_i^*)] x_{ij}^* \geq 0,$$

$$x_{ij}^* \geq 0, \quad c_{ij} \geq v_j^* - u_i^*$$

where an asterisk signifies that the values assigned to the dual and primal variables are the optimal ones.

Once again, these results have a straightforward economic interpretation. If a particular route is utilised, i.e. x_{ij} is a basic variable, then the costs of shipping a unit of the good from source i to destination j will just equal the increase in the imputed value of the good that results from shipping it from the source to the destination. Note that if the unit shipping cost from source i to destination j were greater than the increase in imputed value, then the route would not be utilised, i.e. x_{ij} would be a non-basic variable.

The dual of the transportation problem offers us an alternative, and what turns out to be a particularly speedy method of checking the optimality of a given basic feasible solution. For each utilised route, we must have: $c_{ij} = v_j - u_i$. We have already seen in this chapter that a basic feasible solution will contain $(m + n - 1)$ routes, but there are in total $(m + n)$ dual variables. At first sight, we seem to have a problem here in that we have only $(m + n - 1)$ equations to solve for $(m + n)$ unknowns. However, the difficulty is easily overcome once we recognise that the dual constraints require that the increase in the imputed value of the good should not exceed the unit shipment cost for any given route. We may arbitrarily set the value of one of the dual variables (in practice we shall adopt the convention of setting u_1 equal to zero), and then use the $(m + n - 1)$ equations to solve for the remaining dual variables. If at these computed values for the dual variables, the dual constraints are satisfied, then our primal basis is indeed optimal. If, however, the dual is infeasible the primal is not optimal; in these circumstances there will be one or more non-utilised routes for which the increase in the imputed value of the good is greater than the associated shipment cost. The costs of effecting the shipping plan would be reduced by introducing any such route into the basis. If there is more than one route for which the dual constraint is not met, then the route to be introduced is the one for which the difference between increase in imputed value and unit shipping cost is the greatest. This approach links in very neatly with the stepping-stone algorithm: when the dual constraint is not satisfied for a particular route, then the additional cost of shipping one unit over this route and making consequential adjustments elsewhere is indeed negative and equal to $c_{ij} - (v_j - u_i)$.

When we have a basic feasible solution, we solve for the dual variables by using the condition that $c_{ij} = v_j - u_i$ for each utilised route. The equations are easily solved recursively, having first set u_1 equal to zero.

$$\begin{bmatrix} & 2 & & \\ 5 & 4 & & \\ 8 & & 4 & 4 \\ 6 & & & \\ v_1 = 3 & v_2 = 2 & v_3 = -1 & v_4 = -1 \end{bmatrix} \begin{bmatrix} u_1 = 0 \\ u_2 = -2 \\ u_3 = -5 \\ u_4 = -3 \end{bmatrix}$$

In the matrix above we have included the unit shipment costs for each utilised route for the VAM initial basic feasible solution. The order in which we solve the equations is as follows:

(a) we must have $v_2 - u_1 = 2$, and since $u_1 = 0$, then $v_2 = 2$;
(b) we must have $v_2 - u_2 = 4$, and since $v_2 = 2$, then $u_2 = -2$;
(c) we must have $v_1 - u_2 = 5$, and since $u_2 = -2$, then $v_1 = 3$;
(d) we must have $v_1 - u_3 = 8$, and since $v_1 = 3$, then $u_3 = -5$;
(e) we must have $v_3 - u_3 = 4$, and since $u_3 = -5$, then $v_3 = -1$;
(f) we must have $v_4 - u_3 = 4$, and since $u_3 = -5$, then $v_4 = -1$;
(g) we must have $v_1 - u_4 = 6$, and since $v_1 = 3$, then $u_4 = -3$.

Note that in our solution to the dual, some of the dual variables take on negative values. This is because we have set u_1 equal to zero, and then solved for the remaining dual variables. Were we to add 5 to each dual variable, then all would be now non-negative, but we would still have the condition satisfied that for each utilised route the increase in the value of the good from shipping it from the source to the destination was equal to the unit shipment cost. We therefore need not worry about the occurrence of negative values for dual variables in the transportation problem.

Now consider whether the dual constraints are satisfied for the non-utilised routes:

(a) for route (1,1) $c_{11} - (v_1 - u_1) = 6 - (3 - 0) = 3$;
(b) for route (1,3) $c_{13} - (v_3 - u_1) = 4 - (-1 - 0) = 5$;
(c) for route (1,4) $c_{14} - (v_4 - u_1) = 7 - (-1 - 0) = 8$;
(d) for route (2,3) $c_{23} - (v_3 - u_2) = 3 - (-1 + 2) = 2$;
(e) for route (2,4) $c_{24} - (v_4 - u_2) = 6 - (-1 + 2) = 5$;
(f) for route (3,2) $c_{32} - (v_2 - u_3) = 6 - (2 + 5) = -1$;
(g) for route (4,2) $c_{42} - (v_2 - u_4) = 8 - (2 + 3) = 3$;
(h) for route (4,3) $c_{43} - (v_3 - u_4) = 9 - (-1 + 3) = 7$;
(i) for route (4,4) $c_{44} - (v_4 - u_4) = 5 - (-1 + 3) = 3$.

Note the dual constraints are satisfied with the exception of route (3,2). To make way for this route we must reduce shipments over routes (3,1) and (2,2); the first route will leave the basis since only *50* units are being shipped over this route compared to *200* units over the other one. The new values of the dual variables are given below:

$$\begin{bmatrix} & 2 & & & \\ 5 & 4 & & & \\ & & 6 & 4 & 4 \\ 6 & & & & \\ v_1 = 3 & v_2 = 2 & v_3 = 0 & v_4 = 0 \end{bmatrix} \begin{bmatrix} u_1 = 0 \\ u_2 = -2 \\ u_3 = -4 \\ u_4 = -3 \end{bmatrix}$$

(a) we must have $v_2 - u_1 = 2$, and since $u_1 = 0$, then $v_2 = 2$;
(b) we must have $v_2 - u_2 = 4$, and since $v_2 = 2$, then $u_2 = -2$;
(c) we must have $v_1 - u_2 = 5$, and since $u_2 = -2$, then $v_1 = 3$;
(d) we must have $v_2 - u_3 = 6$, and since $v_2 = 2$, then $u_3 = -4$;
(e) we must have $v_3 - u_3 = 4$, and since $u_3 = -4$, then $v_3 = 0$;
(f) we must have $v_4 - u_3 = 4$, and since $u_3 = -4$, then $v_4 = 0$;
(g) we must have $v_1 - u_4 = 6$, and since $v_1 = 3$, then $u_4 = -3$.

Now consider whether the dual constraints are satisfied for the non-utilised routes:

(a) for route (1,1) $c_{11} - (v_1 - u_1) = 6 - (3 - 0) = 3$;
(b) for route (1,3) $c_{13} - (v_3 - u_1) = 4 - (0 - 0) = 4$;
(c) for route (1,4) $c_{14} - (v_4 - u_1) = 7 - (0 - 0) = 7$;
(d) for route (2,3) $c_{23} - (v_3 - u_2) = 3 - (0 + 2) = 1$;
(e) for route (2,4) $c_{24} - (v_4 - u_2) = 6 - (0 + 2) = 4$;
(f) for route (3,1) $c_{31} - (v_1 - u_3) = 8 - (3 + 4) = 1$;
(g) for route (4,2) $c_{42} - (v_2 - u_4) = 8 - (2 + 3) = 3$;
(h) for route (4,3) $c_{43} - (v_3 - u_4) = 9 - (0 + 3) = 6$;
(i) for route (4,4) $c_{44} - (v_4 - u_4) = 5 - (0 + 3) = 2$.

8.4 A PRACTICAL HINT FOR SOLVING TRANSPORTATION PROBLEMS

We shall make use of the following simple problem to illustrate how transportation problems can be very conveniently solved using tableaux.

A good is available at three factories in the following quantities:

$$[20 \quad 50 \quad 30]$$

It is required at three warehouses in the following quantities:

$$[40 \quad 25 \quad 35]$$

The matrix of per unit shipments costs from the ith factory to the jth factory is given by:

$$C = \begin{bmatrix} 5 & 1 & 7 \\ 6 & 4 & 2 \\ 3 & 2 & 5 \end{bmatrix}$$

Derive the cost minimising shipment plan.

In the tableaux shown in Fig. 8.1, we present first the least-cost initial basic feasible solution. Route (i, j) appears in row i, column j of the tableau, and in the top right-hand corner of the square representing each route we have put the unit transport cost in a square box. Using the utilised routes, we solve for the dual variables, having first set u_1 equal to zero. For each non-utilised route, we then calculate $v_j - u_i$, and put this figure in a circle inside the relevant square. It is then straightforward to see whether the current basis is optimal or not. If there exists a non-utilised route where the circled figure exceeds the figure inside the square, introducing that route would reduce shipment costs. It is also easy to see what consequential changes will have to be made to shipments over other routes to accommodate this new route.

Examining the first tableau, we note that the dual constraint is not satisfied for route (2,2). Each unit over this route will reduce shipment costs by one unit; since shipments must be reduced over routes (2,1) and (3,2), the maximum that can be shipped over this route is 5. The result of introducing route (2,2) into the basis and eliminating route (3,2) is shown in the second tableau. We once more solve for the dual variables, and calculate $v_j - u_i$ for each of the non-utilised routes in order to check whether the new basis is optimal. As we can see by comparing the circled figures

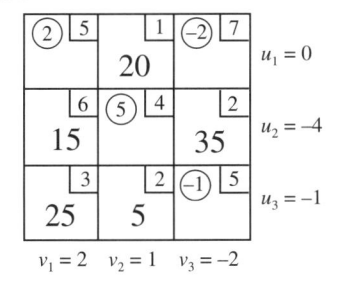

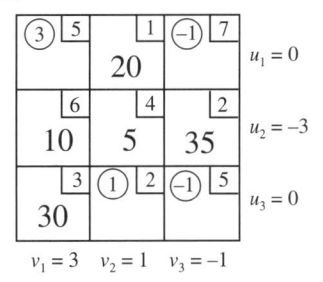

Figure 8.1

with the unit shipment costs, this new basis is indeed optimal. The total cost of shipping the goods from sources to destinations is *260*.

8.5 THE SOLUTION TO UNBALANCED PROBLEMS

We now turn to consider the procedure to be adopted when the original problem is not balanced. If the total supply exceeds the total demand, we introduce an artificial destination, with the requirement at this artificial destination being equal to the excess supply. Conversely, if total supply falls short of total demand, we introduce an artificial source to which we allocate an amount equal to the excess demand.

The question we must now address concerns the unit shipment costs to be assigned to shipments out of an artificial source, or to an artificial destination. In the simplest case, we just allocate unit shipment costs of zero to any route involving an artificial source or destination. However, there may be circumstances in which a more sophisticated approach is required. Consider a situation in which there exists an excess supply of the good. Storage capacity at one of the sources is non-existent. How should we take account of this? Clearly, if we utilise the route from this source to the artificial destination, then we have an obvious problem given the lack of storage facilities at the source. To obviate this problem, we must assign a large unit shipment cost from this source to the artificial destination. Now consider a situation of excess demand and assume that demand must be met in full at one of the destinations. This constraint will not be met if the shipment plan includes using the route from the artificial source to this destination. To prevent this event occurring, we allocate a large unit shipment cost to the route from the artificial source to the destination where demand must be met in full.

We illustrate the procedure in Fig. 8.2 by making some minor adjustments to the transportation problem we have just solved. Now assume that the availability at the second source is reduced from *50* to *30*, but the demand at the first destination must be fully satisfied. We therefore introduce a fourth source and let the unit shipment costs to the three destinations be *M*, *0* and *0* respectively. By assigning a large unit cost of shipment from the artificial source to the first destination, we shall ensure that this route is not utilised. Let us adjust the allocation that was optimal before the supply reduction; shipments over route (*2,3*) are reduced from *35* to *15*, and a hypothetical shipment of *20* units is made from the artificial source to this destination. Solving for the dual variables and checking whether the dual constraints are met for the non-utilised routes, we see in the tableau below that costs can be further reduced by introducing route

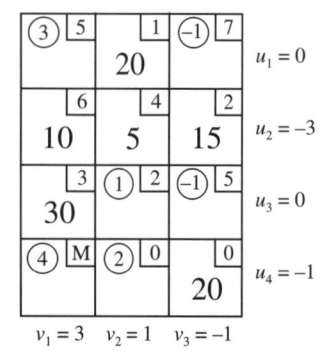

An artificial source

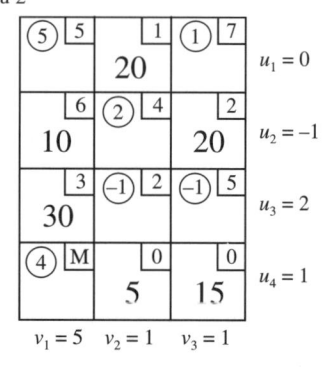

Figure 8.2

Tableau 1

An artificial destination

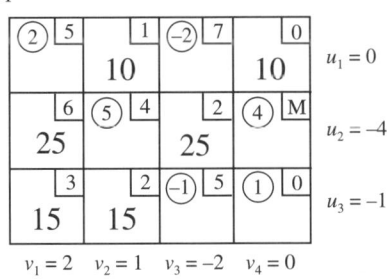

	5	1	7	0	
(2)		(-2)			$u_1 = 0$
		10		10	
	6	4	2	M	
	(5)		(4)		$u_2 = -4$
25		25			
	3	2	5	0	
			(-1)	(1)	$u_3 = -1$
15	15				

$v_1 = 2 \quad v_2 = 1 \quad v_3 = -2 \quad v_4 = 0$

Tableau 2

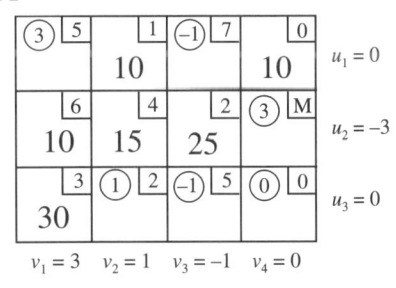

	5	1	7	0	
(3)		(-1)			$u_1 = 0$
		10		10	
	6	4	2	M	
			(3)		$u_2 = -3$
10		15	25		
	3	2	5	0	
	(1)		(-1)	(0)	$u_3 = 0$
30					

$v_1 = 3 \quad v_2 = 1 \quad v_3 = -1 \quad v_4 = 0$

Figure 8.3

(4,2) into the basis. The maximum that can be shipped over this route is 5. Having introduced this new route and solved for the new values of the dual variables, it is clear from the tableau that the optimal allocation has now been reached, though it is not unique. The non-uniqueness follows from the fact that $v_1 - u_1 = c_{11}$.

Now assume that the requirement at the third destination is reduced from 35 to 25, but there is no storage capacity at the second source. We therefore introduce an artificial destination (see Fig. 8.3), and assign unit shipment costs from the three sources to this destination of 0, M and 0 respectively. The rationale for the M parameter is to ensure that no shipments are made from the second source to the artificial destination. Whereas in the previous case of excess demand, it was straightforward to amend the optimal tableau for the original problem, for this second case, we present the least-cost initial basic feasible solution. As can be seen from the tableau, this basis is not optimal. We would now wish to introduce route (2,2) into the basis. The maximum that can be shipped over this route is 15 units with route (3,2) being eliminated from the basis. Once more, we solve for the dual variables, and check that the dual constraints are met for the non-utilised routes. We find that this allocation is optimal, though it is not unique.

8.6 THE ASSIGNMENT PROBLEM

The assignment problem is a special kind of transportation problem in which we have one unit available at each destination and one unit required at each source. An example would be a firm that has a number of workers available and a number of tasks to be performed; each worker may only be allocated to perform one task. There exists a matrix of costs of assigning each worker to each task, and the firm wishes to minimise the costs of assigning workers to tasks.

Consider a simple example of three workers and three tasks. Again, if the problem were unbalanced we can artificially balance it by introducing fictitious workers or fictitious tasks. The matrix of assignment costs is as follows.

$$\begin{bmatrix} 8 & 7 & 3 \\ 6 & 9 & 1 \\ 5 & 5 & 2 \end{bmatrix}$$

Note that the problem is going to be highly degenerate. Five allocations must be used in total, over three of them one unit is going to be assigned and over the remaining two a zero quantity must be included. Whenever a positive quantity is allocated, then the availability at the source and the requirement at the destination will be both satisfied. In arriving at an initial feasible solution using either the north-west corner method or the least-cost method, we shall adopt the convention of eliminating the row from further consideration when both availability at the source and requirement at the destination are satisfied. Now solve problem 8.3(a).

An alternative approach

The presence of degeneracy in the assignment problem means that the problems are sometimes rather messy to solve as transportation problems. An alternative approach to solving such problems is discussed below.

We may write the typical assignment problem as follows:

$$\text{Minimise } C = \sum_{i=1}^{i=n} \sum_{j=1}^{j=n} c_{ij} x_{ij}$$

$$\text{s.t. } \sum_{i=1}^{i=n} x_{ij} \geq 1 \; \forall j$$

$$\sum_{j=1}^{j=n} x_{ij} \leq 1 \; \forall i$$

$$x_{ij} = 0 \text{ or } 1$$

where c_{ij} is the cost of allocating worker i to job j, x_{ij} is equal to unity if worker i is allocated to job j, otherwise the variable is assigned to a value of zero. The other constraints ensure that a job is allocated at least one worker and that a worker is allocated to no more than one job. The problem is balanced with the number of workers equal to the number of jobs, and these constraints will indeed hold as equalities.

We now define a new cost element:

$$c_{ij}^* = c_{ij} - p_i - q_j$$

where p_i is a scalar we deduct from row i of the matrix of assignment costs and q_j is a scalar we deduct from column j of the matrix of assignment costs. We now define a new objective function to minimise:

$$C^* = \sum_{i=1}^{i=n} \sum_{j=1}^{j=n} c_{ij}^* x_{ij}$$

$$= \sum_{i=1}^{i=n} \sum_{j=1}^{j=n} (c_{ij} - p_i - q_i) x_{ij}$$

$$= \sum_{i=1}^{i=n} \sum_{j=1}^{j=n} c_{ij} x_{ij} - \sum_{i=1}^{i=n} \left(p_i \sum_{j=1}^{j=n} x_{ij} \right) - \sum_{j=1}^{j=n} \left(q_j \sum_{i=1}^{i=n} x_{ij} \right)$$

$$= C - \sum_{i=1}^{i=n} p_i - \sum_{j=1}^{j=n} q_j$$

Hence the values of the x_{ij}s which minimise C are the same as those which minimise C^*. We are now well on the way to solving the assignment problem.

The basic approach involves subtracting scalars from the rows and columns of the matrix of assignment costs. The procedure is to find the smallest element in each row and deduct this from each element in the row. If the minimum number of lines that can be drawn through the columns of the matrix of costs so as to cross out all the zero elements in the rows is less than n, then we then find the smallest element in each column of the new matrix, and deduct this from each element in the column. We now construct the minimum number of lines drawn through the rows and columns so as to cross out all the zeros. If this is less than n, we have yet to reach the optimal allocation. We then find the smallest uncrossed element in this new matrix of costs, and deduct this amount from all uncrossed elements, leaving those elements unchanged which have been crossed through by a single line. We then add this amount to those elements which are at the intersection of a line drawn through a row and a line drawn through a column. If the minimum number of lines that can now be drawn through the zero elements is n, the optimal allocation has been reached. If not, we repeat the procedure until this is the case.

The verbal discussion may sound somewhat complicated, but once the procedure is applied to an example, it will be seen to be relatively straightforward. Let us return to the example we have already solved as a transportation problem. The cost matrix is

$$\begin{bmatrix} 8 & 7 & 3 \\ 6 & 9 & 1 \\ 5 & 5 & 2 \end{bmatrix}$$

The row minima are *3*, *1* and *2* respectively. Deducting each row minimum from all the elements in the relevant row, we obtain the new cost matrix.

$$\begin{bmatrix} 5 & 4 & 0 \\ 5 & 8 & 0 \\ 3 & 3 & 0 \end{bmatrix}$$

Only one line drawn through the third column is required to cross out all the zeros. The column minima of the new matrix are *3*, *3* and *0* respectively. Performing the necessary deductions, we have

$$\begin{bmatrix} 2 & 1 & 0 \\ 2 & 5 & 0 \\ 0 & 0 & 0 \end{bmatrix}$$

We still have not reached the optimal allocation, since only two lines are needed to cross out the noughts, one drawn through the third row, and one drawn through the third column. The minimum uncrossed element is *1*. This is deducted from all the uncrossed elements, and added to the element in the third row third column, all the other elements are left unchanged. The new matrix therefore is

$$\begin{bmatrix} 1 & 0 & 0 \\ 1 & 4 & 0 \\ 0 & 0 & 1 \end{bmatrix}$$

A minimum of three lines is required to cross out all the zeros. The optimal allocation has now been reached: the second worker is allocated to the third job, the first worker to the second job, and the third worker to the first job. In terms of the redefined costs, the costs of this allocation are zero; in terms of the true costs, the total costs are $1 + 7 + 5 = 13$. The scalars that we have deducted from the rows and columns are as follows:

round one: $p_1 = 3, p_2 = 1, p_3 = 2$;
round two: $q_1 = 3, q_2 = 3, q_3 = 0$;
round three: $p_1 = 1, p_2 = 1, p_3 = 0, q_1 = 0, q_2 = 0, q_3 = -1$

Maximisation problems

The transportation and assignment problems we have discussed so far in this chapter have been minimisation problems. We now briefly turn to look at how to treat assignment problems in which we wish to make the value of the objective function as large as possible. One way to proceed would be to multiply all the coefficients in the objective function by -1, and then treat the problem as a minimisation problem. Alternatively, instead of finding row and column minima and then adjusting the original parameters of the objective function, one would instead find row and column maxima and deduct these from relevant rows and columns. Instead of finding the smallest uncrossed element, one would use the largest uncrossed element. Otherwise the procedure would be identical to that used in the minimisation problem.

Example 8.1

A firm has available three workers to assign to three tasks, with each worker being able to perform one of the three tasks. The profitability matrix of assigning worker i to task j is given below:

$$\begin{bmatrix} 75 & 80 & 60 \\ 30 & 60 & 40 \\ 30 & 20 & 25 \end{bmatrix}$$

The scalars we deduct from the three rows are: $p_1 = 80, p_2 = 60, p_3 = 30$. The new profitability matrix is then

$$\begin{bmatrix} -5 & 0 & -20 \\ -30 & 0 & -20 \\ 0 & -10 & -5 \end{bmatrix}$$

The scalars we now deduct from the columns of the new matrix are: $q_1 = 0, q_2 = 0, q_3 = -5$. The new profitability matrix is then

$$\begin{bmatrix} -5 & 0 & -15 \\ -30 & 0 & -15 \\ 0 & -10 & 0 \end{bmatrix}$$

Only two items are required to cross out the zeros, one drawn through the second column and one through the third row. The largest uncrossed element is -5. The new set of scalars, therefore, is $p_1 = -5, p_2 = -5, p_3 = 0, q_1 = 0, q_2 = 5, q_3 = 0$. This gives rise to the following adjusted profitability matrix.

$$\begin{bmatrix} 0 & 0 & -10 \\ -25 & 0 & -10 \\ 0 & -15 & 0 \end{bmatrix}$$

A minimum number of three lines must be drawn in order to cross out all the zeros. The optimal solution has, therefore, been reached: the second worker is allocated to the second task and the associated profits are 60; the first worker is allocated to the first job and the associated profits are 75; and the third worker is allocated to the third job and the associated profits are 25.

We may also consider the dual of such an assignment problem. We may write the primal problem as

$$\text{Maximise } \Pi = \sum_{i=1}^{i=n} \sum_{j=1}^{j=n} \pi_{ij} x_{ij}$$

$$\text{s.t. } -\sum_{i=1}^{i=n} x_{ij} \leq -1 \ \forall j$$

$$\sum_{j=1}^{j=n} x_{ij} \leq 1 \ \forall i$$

$$x_{ij} = 0 \text{ or } 1$$

Note that we have expressed the constraints of the maximisation problem in the standard form. The dual of the above problem is therefore given by:

$$\text{Minimise } \sum_{i=1}^{i=n} u_i - \sum_{j=1}^{j=n} v_j$$

$$\text{s.t. } u_i - v_j \geq \pi_{ij} \ \forall i, j$$

$$u_i, \ v_j \geq 0$$

What interpretation can be given to the dual variables in this case? Here, u_i is the imputed value of the ith worker, and v_j is the imputed value of the right to perform task j. By the equilibrium theorem of linear programming, we know that if $u_i - v_j > \pi_{ij}$, then $x_{ij} = 0$. In other words, if the imputed value of the ith worker net of the implicit entry charge to perform the jth task exceeds the profitability of worker i in job j, then one should not allocate that worker to that job, as they will be more profitably employed elsewhere. When $x_{ij} = 1$, then the dual constraint will hold as an equality.

8.7 CONCLUSION

The key features of the solution to a transportation problem are as follows:

1. The number of routes which are utilised in a basic solution to the problem is equal to one less the sum of the number of sources and destinations. If the basis is degenerate, then one or more of the routes in the basis will be assigned a zero quantity to be shipped.

2. For each route that is utilised, the increase in the imputed value of the good from shipping it from source *i* to destination *j* is just equal to the cost of shipping the good over this particular route. If there exist non-utilised routes for which the increase in the imputed value of the good exceeds the shipment costs, then this route should be introduced into the basis for shipment costs will thereby be reduced.
3. The current basis will be optimal provided there exist no non-utilised routes for which the increase in the imputed value of the good outweighs the unit shipment cost.
4. Since the number of utilised routes in a basic solution is one less than the number of dual variables, we arbitrarily set the value of one of the dual variables, and then solve recursively for the remaining ones. As a result of this procedure, we cannot guarantee that all the dual variables will be non-negative. An appropriate rescaling would, however, ensure, that this was the case.

8.8 EXERCISES

8.1 (a) (i) Using the least-cost initial basic feasible solution, which of the non-utilised routes should be introduced into the basis using the figures on page 112?

(ii) How much will then be shipped over this route?

(iii) Has the optimal solution now been reached? If not, which of the non-utilised routes should be introduced, and how much should be shipped over it?

8.2 (a) Derive the alternative solution to the problem on page 122 where the supply was reduced at the second source.

(b) A firm has stocks of a particular good available at each of three factories in the following quantities: *450* units at the first factory, *180* units at the second and *570* units at the third. The firm is required to ship the following quantities from its factories to four different warehouses: *300* units to the first warehouse, *225* units to the second, *480* units to the third and *195* units to the fourth. The matrix *C* of per unit shipment costs from the *i*th factory to the *j*th factory warehouse is given by:

$$C = \begin{bmatrix} 8 & 6 & 11 & 5 \\ 12 & 13 & 8 & 7 \\ 11 & 7 & 10 & 4 \end{bmatrix}$$

(i) Use the north-west corner method to obtain an initial basic feasible solution, and then derive the cost-minimising shipment plan.

(ii) Use the least-cost method to obtain an initial basic feasible solution to the above problem. How many iterations are necessary before the optimal solution is reached?

(iii) Use the Vogel approximation method to obtain an initial basic feasible solution to the above problem. How many iterations are necessary before the optimal solution is reached?

(c) A good is available at four sources in the following quantities:

$$[30 \quad 50 \quad 75 \quad 20]$$

It is required at six destinations in the following quantities:

$$[20 \quad 40 \quad 30 \quad 10 \quad 50 \quad 25]$$

The matrix of per unit shipment costs from the *i*th source to the *j*th destination is given by

$$C = \begin{bmatrix} 1 & 2 & 1 & 4 & 5 & 2 \\ 3 & 3 & 2 & 1 & 4 & 3 \\ 5 & 2 & 5 & 9 & 6 & 2 \\ 3 & 1 & 7 & 3 & 4 & 6 \end{bmatrix}$$

Use the least-cost method to obtain an initial basic feasible solution, and then derive the cost-minimising shipment plan.

(d) A good is available at three factories in the following quantities: (*150, 200, 300*); and is required at four warehouses in the following quantities (*250, 175, 125, 200*). The matrix of per unit shipment costs from factory i to warehouse j is:

$$\begin{bmatrix} 5 & 3 & 6 & 2 \\ 6 & 1 & 5 & 4 \\ 8 & 2 & 3 & 9 \end{bmatrix}$$

Demand must be met in full at the third warehouse. Derive the cost-minimising shipment plan.

(e) A firm has available at three factories the following quantities of a good:

$$\begin{bmatrix} 500 \\ 800 \\ 700 \end{bmatrix}$$

Its requirements at four destinations are:

$$[500 \quad 400 \quad 900 \quad 300]$$

The per unit penalties for not meeting the demand at the four destinations are given respectively by:

$$[6 \quad 7 \quad 4 \quad 6]$$

The matrix of per unit shipment costs is:

$$\begin{bmatrix} 5 & 7 & 3 & 8 \\ 6 & 2 & 1 & 5 \\ 3 & 9 & 6 & 4 \end{bmatrix}$$

Derive the shipping plan which minimises total costs, inclusive of penalty charges.

(f) At three oil wells, an oil company has available *4, 4* and *8* units of crude oil respectively. The crude oil is to be transported to three refineries where requirements are respectively *2, 4* and *10*. In order to transport the oil from the second oil well to the third refinery and from the third oil well to the second refinery, tankers are necessary. The company has only *6* tankers at its disposal; each tanker is able to transport one unit of crude oil. Along the other routes the oil is transported by pipeline; there is no shortage of pipeline capacity. The matrix of per unit shipment costs is given by:

$$C = \begin{bmatrix} 5 & 3 & 8 \\ 14 & 4 & 5 \\ 4 & 2 & 8 \end{bmatrix}$$

The company's objective is to minimise its transport costs subject to the constraints on availabilities, requirements and tanker capacity.

(i) Write out in full both the primal and its associated dual.
(ii) Check that the following primal basis is optimal:

$$x_{12} = 2, \ x_{13} = 2,$$
$$x_{23} = 4,$$
$$x_{31} = 2, \ x_{32} = 2, \ x_{33} = 4$$

Hint: note that six routes are used, rather than five. In addition to calculating the usual dual variables, you will also need to find the dual variables associated with the tanker constraint.

8.3 (a) (i) Check that the least-cost initial basic feasible solution is given by:

$$\begin{bmatrix} 0 & 1 & & \\ & & 1 & \\ 1 & & & 0 \end{bmatrix}$$

(ii) Show that this basis is not optimal, and proceed to obtain an optimal basis.

(iii) Check that the Vogel approximation method initial basic feasible solution is given by:

$$\begin{bmatrix} 1 & 0 & \\ & & 1 \\ 1 & 0 & \end{bmatrix}$$

(iv) Show that this basis is indeed optimal.

8.4 (a) Consider the problem of assigning four operators to four machines. The assignment costs in £ are given in the matrix below. Operator *1* cannot be assigned to machine *3*, nor can operator *3* be assigned to machine *4*. Find the cost-minimising allocation of operators to jobs.

$$\begin{bmatrix} 5 & 5 & na & 2 \\ 7 & 4 & 2 & 3 \\ 9 & 3 & 5 & na \\ 7 & 2 & 6 & 7 \end{bmatrix}$$

(b) An airline has two-way flights between London and Vienna. Crews may be based in either London or Vienna. A crew based in London (Vienna) and flying to Vienna (London) must return to London (Vienna) on a later flight on the same day or the following day. The objective is to pair the flights so as to minimise the total time the crews spend between flights at their away airport. Solve the problem as an assignment problem, using the following timetable.

Flight number	Depart London	Arrive Vienna	Flight number	Depart Vienna	Arrive London
001	08.30	10.30	101	07.00	09.00
002	12.00	14.00	102	13.00	15.15
003	18.45	20.30	103	18.15	20.30
004	21.00	23.00	104	21.45	24.00

(i) How many crews are based in Vienna?

(ii) Now assume that safety legislation is introduced whereby a crew may not return on a flight unless at least two hours have elapsed since their arrival time on the outward flight. Derive the new allocation of crews to flights which minimises stop-over time at the away airport.

8.5 (a) A racehorse owner wishes to enter four horses in four races so as to maximise her expected winnings. A horse may only be entered in one race. In the matrix P below, the element p_{ij} gives the expected winnings from entering horse i in race j:

$$P = \begin{bmatrix} 9 & 15 & 15 & 24 \\ 7 & 12 & 15 & 22.5 \\ 5 & 8 & 7.5 & 3 \\ 2 & 2 & 5 & 1.5 \end{bmatrix}$$

(i) Solve the above problem as an assignment problem.

(ii) Solve the above problem as a transportation problem, noting that it is highly degenerate.

(iii) What interpretation can be given to the dual variables of this problem? What values do they take in the optimal allocation of horses to races? (Set v_4 equal to zero.)

(iv) Using the information obtained in (iii), deduce by how much expected winnings would change if:

(1) race two were cancelled;

(2) an additional horse whose unexpected winnings were the same as those of horse two became available to be entered in a range.

CHAPTER
NINE
EIGENVALUES AND EIGENVECTORS

9.1 INTRODUCTION

In this chapter we are concerned with square matrices, and in particular with matrices which are symmetric. In Section 9.2 we introduce the concepts of eigenvalues and eigenvectors, and demonstrate how to find their values for particular square matrices. We see that in order to solve for the eigenvalues of a matrix we must find the roots of a polynomial, the degree of the polynomial being equal to the dimension of the matrix. Eigenvalues may, therefore, be real but not necessarily distinct, or on occasions we may find they come in pairs of complex conjugates. Eigenvalues are scalars, but associated with each eigenvalue is a vector known as an eigenvector. We are going to be particularly interested in those matrices whose eigenvalues are all real and distinct. In Section 9.3 we show that when the eigenvalues are all real and distinct, then the associated set of eigenvectors is a linearly independent one. This is an important result. When the eigenvectors of a matrix are linearly independent, then it is possible to diagonalise the matrix such that its eigenvalues appear along the principal diagonal, and all the other elements of this transformed matrix are equal to zero.

In Section 9.4 we restrict our discussion to symmetric matrices. The eigenvalues of such matrices are all real, and the eigenvectors of such matrices are orthogonal to each other. This means that it is particularly straightforward to transform symmetric matrices into a diagonal matrix with the eigenvalues appearing along the principal diagonal. Such diagonalisation is possible with a symmetric matrix even when we have a repeated eigenvalue. In Section 9.5, however, we briefly discuss the case where we have a repeated eigenvalue in a non-symmetric matrix. In such a situation, a strict diagonalisation is not possible.

In Section 9.6, we consider quadratic forms. These are functions of the form: $y = f(x) = x^T A x$ where A is a symmetric matrix. We show that knowledge of the numerical values of the eigenvalues of the underlying symmetric matrix enables us to determine whether or not the function will always take on a positive, non-negative, non-positive or negative value for any arbitrary non-null vector of explanatory variables. We shall find subsequently in Chapter 14 that these results are of great significance for optimisation problems where there exists more than one choice variable.

9.2 EIGENVALUES AND EIGENVECTORS

In this chapter, we introduce the concepts of an eigenvalue and an eigenvector. Alternatively an eigenvalue is sometimes referred to as a characteristic root or latent root, and an eigenvector as a characteristic vector or latent vector.

Consider the set of equations:

$$Ax = \lambda x$$

where A is a square matrix of dimension n, x is a non-null column vector with n elements in it, and λ is a scalar. The matrix A, therefore, transforms the vector x into a new vector, which is simply a scalar multiple of the original vector, so that x is an eigenvector of A, and λ is the eigenvalue associated with this eigenvector. The set of equations may alternatively be expressed as:

$$(A - \lambda I)x = 0$$

For a non-trivial solution to exist to this set of equations, it is clear that the matrix $A - \lambda I$ must be singular. Otherwise, if this is not the case, then the only solution is the one in which x is a null vector. Singularity requires the rank of $A - \lambda I$ to be less than n, which will indeed be the case if its determinant vanishes:

$$\begin{vmatrix} a_{11} - \lambda & a_{12} & \cdots & a_{1n} \\ a_{21} & a_{22} - \lambda & \cdots & a_{2n} \\ \vdots & \vdots & \cdots & \vdots \\ a_{n1} & a_{n2} & \cdots & a_{nn} - \lambda \end{vmatrix} = 0$$

A non-trivial solution to our set of equations will therefore exist for those values of λ which satisfy the above equation. By expanding the above equation, we obtain a polynomial equation in λ:

$$b_n \lambda^n + b_{n-1} \lambda^{n-1} + \cdots + b_1 \lambda + b_0 = 0$$

This is known as the characteristic polynomial, and the bs are scalars whose precise values depend upon the components of the A matrix. If A were 2×2, then the characteristic polynomial would be a quadratic:

$$(a_{11} - \lambda)(a_{22} - \lambda) - a_{12}a_{21} = \lambda^2 - (a_{11} + a_{22})\lambda + a_{11}a_{22} - a_{12}a_{21} = 0$$

and the values taken by the bs would be:

$$b_2 = 1, \quad b_1 = -(a_{11} + a_2), \quad \text{and } b_0 = a_{11}a_{22} - a_{12}a_{21}$$

For the general case, the characteristic polynomial will have n roots, which will not necessarily all be either distinct or real; some roots may be repeated, and there may also be conjugate pairs of complex roots.

We now proceed to obtain the eigenvalues and the associated eigenvectors of some 2×2 matrices

Example 9.1

Find the eigenvalues of the following matrix:

$$\text{(a) } A = \begin{bmatrix} 4 & 2 \\ 2 & 7 \end{bmatrix}$$

Then the characteristic polynomial is:
$$(4 - \lambda)(7 - \lambda) - 2(2) = 0$$
$$\lambda^2 - 11\lambda + 24 = 0$$
and on factorising, we have $(\lambda - 3)(\lambda - 8) = 0$

So the eigenvalues are *3* and *8* respectively. We now derive eigenvectors associated with these two eigenvalues. When λ is equal to *3*, we have
$$(A - 3I)x = 0$$
Hence $(4 - 3)x_1 + 2x_2 = 0$
$$x_1 = -2x_2$$
Let $x_2 = 1$, *then* $x_1 = -2$.

The eigenvector associated with this eigenvector is therefore:
$$x_1 = \begin{bmatrix} -2 \\ 1 \end{bmatrix}$$

when λ is equal to *8*, we have
$$(A - 8I)x = 0$$
Hence $(4 - 8)x_1 + 2x_2 = 0$
$$-4x_1 = -2x_2$$
Let $x_2 = 1$, *then* $x_1 = 0.5$.

The eigenvector associated with this eigenvector is, therefore:
$$x_2 = \begin{bmatrix} 0.5 \\ 1 \end{bmatrix}.$$

Note that the eigenvector is not unique. Given that $A - \lambda I$ is a singular matrix, in our 2×2 case we have a single equation relating x_1 and x_2. So we arbitrarily set the value of one of the elements of the vector, and express the other in terms of this chosen value. If x is an eigenvector of A, then so is any scalar multiple of x.

Example 9.2

Given the following matrix,
$$\text{(b) } A = \begin{bmatrix} 7 & 3 \\ -3 & 1 \end{bmatrix}$$

then its characteristic polynomial is:
$$(7 - \lambda)(1 - \lambda) + 9 = 0$$
$$\lambda^2 - 8\lambda + 16 = 0$$
Upon factorising, we have $(\lambda - 4)(\lambda - 4) = 0$

In this case, we have a repeated root with $\lambda_1 = \lambda_2 = 4$. Its eigenvector will take the following form:

$$(7-4)x_1 + 3x_2 = 0$$

$$\text{Hence } x_1 = -x_2$$

$$\text{Letting } x_2 = 1, \text{ we have}$$

$$x_1 = x_2 = \begin{bmatrix} -1 \\ 1 \end{bmatrix}$$

Example 9.3

We now turn to a case where the eigenvalues are not real. Given

$$\text{(c) } \begin{bmatrix} 1 & 2 \\ -1.25 & 2 \end{bmatrix}$$

then the characteristic polynomial is:

$$(1 - \lambda)(2 - \lambda) - 2(-1.25) = \lambda^2 - 3\lambda + 4.5 = 0$$

$$\text{Hence } \lambda = \frac{3 \pm \sqrt{(9-18)}}{2} = 1.5 \pm 1.5i$$

where i is $\sqrt{-1}$.

The eigenvalues are a conjugate pair of complex roots:

$$\lambda_1 = 1.5 + 1.5i, \quad \lambda_2 = 1.5 - 1.5i$$

To derive the eigenvectors associated with these eigenvalues, we must have for the first eigenvalue:

$$(-0.5 - 1.5i)x_1 + 2x_2 = 0$$

$$\text{Hence for } x_1 = 2, \text{ we have } x_2 = 0.5 + 1.5i$$

For the second eigenvalue, we must have:

$$(-0.5 + 1.5i)x_1 + 2x_2 = 0$$

$$\text{Hence for } x_1 = 2, \text{ we have } x_2 = 0.5 - 1.5i$$

So the two eigenvectors are:

$$x_1 = \begin{bmatrix} 2 \\ 0.5 + 1.5i \end{bmatrix}, \quad x_2 = \begin{bmatrix} 2 \\ 0.5 - 1.5i \end{bmatrix}$$

9.3 DIAGONALISATION OF A MATRIX

An interesting case arises where all the eigenvalues of A are distinct. In such a situation, the set of eigenvectors of A will be linearly independent. This is clearly so when n is 1. In fact we can show that if it is true for $(n-1)$ eigenvectors corresponding to distinct eigenvalues, then it is also true for n such eigenvectors. The outline of the proof of this proposition proceeds as follows. We start out by postulating that there are indeed n distinct roots, but that the n eigenvectors are linearly dependent. If this is so, we must have:

$$\sum_{i=1}^{i=n} \mu_i x_i = 0 \text{ not all } \mu_i = 0$$

In particular, let us assume that μ_1 is not equal to zero. By the definition of an eigenvector and an eigenvalue, we have:

$$A x_i = \lambda_i x_i \quad i = 1, \ldots, n$$

Multiply the above equation by μ_i and sum over the i equations to obtain:

$$\mu_1 A x_1 + \mu_2 A x_2 + \cdots + \mu_n A x_n = \mu_1 \lambda_1 x_1 + \mu_2 \lambda_2 x_2 + \cdots + \mu_n \lambda_n x_n = 0$$

Furthermore if we form the product

$$\lambda_n \sum_{i=1}^{i=n} \mu_i x_i$$

and subtract it from the previous equation, we obtain:

$$\mu_1(\lambda_1 - \lambda_n) x_1 + \mu_2(\lambda_2 - \lambda_n) x_2 + \cdots + \mu_{n-1}(\lambda_{n-1} - \lambda_n) x_{n-1} = 0$$

However, we assumed that the $(n-1)$ eigenvectors were linearly independent. This requires all the terms $\mu_i(\lambda_i - \lambda_n)$ to equal zero, but by assumption μ_1 is not zero. Hence, we must have λ_1 equal to λ_n, but then not all the roots are distinct. There is no way that the n eigenvectors are linearly independent if $(n-1)$ eigenvectors are linearly independent. But if we only consider one eigenvector of the n, it must be linearly independent; therefore 2 eigenvectors must be linearly independent, and so on up to all n eigenvectors.

Whenever the eigenvalues are all distinct, then A may be transformed into a diagonal matrix by using X, the matrix of eigenvectors of A in the following way:

$$D = X^{-1} A X$$

In D, the eigenvalues appear in the principal diagonal in the order which corresponds to the order in which the eigenvectors appear in the columns of X.

Let X be a matrix whose columns are eigenvectors of A. Now consider the product $X^{-1} A X$, and let the rows of X^{-1} be indexed by β_i, $i = 1, \ldots, n$. Hence

$$X^{-1} A X = \begin{bmatrix} \beta_1 A x_1 & \beta_1 A x_2 & \ldots & \beta_1 A x_n \\ \beta_2 A x_1 & \beta_2 A x_2 & \ldots & \beta_2 A x_n \\ \vdots & \vdots & & \vdots \\ \beta_n A x_1 & \beta_n A x_2 & \ldots & \beta_n A x_n \end{bmatrix}$$

But by the definition of eigenvalues and eigenvectors, we have

$$Ax_j = \lambda_j x_j$$

$$\beta_i A x_j = \lambda_j \beta_i x_j$$

$$= 0 \text{ for } i \neq j$$

$$= \lambda_j \text{ for } i = j$$

Hence $X^{-1}AX$ is a diagonal matrix whose elements are the eigenvalues of A.

However, if not all the eigenvalues are distinct, we may or may not be able to obtain a pure diagonal form. The crucial factor as to whether this is possible is whether the eigenvectors associated with the repeated eigenvalues of A are linearly independent or not. If they are linearly independent, then the matrix can be diagonalised.

We earlier defined A and B to be similar matrices if

$$B = S^{-1}AS$$

Now similar matrices have the same eigenvalues. Let x be an eigenvector of A, and λ an eigenvalue. Hence

$$Ax = \lambda x$$

Furthermore let T be a non-singular matrix, and pre-multiply the above equation by T

$$TAx = \lambda Tx$$

We may write $x = T^{-1}Tx$, and substituting for x on the left-hand side, we obtain

$$TAT^{-1}Tx = \lambda Tx$$

Now let $y = Tx$

then $TAT^{-1}y = \lambda y$

Define $S = T^{-1}$, then $S^{-1}ASy = \lambda y$

Hence $By = \lambda y$, and λ is also an eigenvalue of B

Example 9.4

Find the eigenvalues of the following matrix, and then diagonalise it so that the eigenvalues appear in the principal diagonal.

$$A = \begin{bmatrix} 4 & 1 \\ 3 & 2 \end{bmatrix}$$

$$\begin{vmatrix} 4-\lambda & 1 \\ 3 & 2-\lambda \end{vmatrix} = \lambda^2 - 6\lambda + 5 = 0$$

Hence $\lambda_1 = 1, \ \lambda_2 = 5$

EIGENVALUES AND EIGENVECTORS   **137**

To calculate the eigenvectors, we have for $\lambda_1 = 1$:

$$\begin{bmatrix} 3 & 1 \\ 3 & 1 \end{bmatrix} \begin{bmatrix} x_1 \\ x_2 \end{bmatrix} = \begin{bmatrix} 0 \\ 0 \end{bmatrix}$$

Hence $3x_1 + x_2 = 0$

Let $x_1 = 1$, then $x_2 = -3$

and for $\lambda_2 = 5$:

$$\begin{bmatrix} -1 & 1 \\ 3 & -3 \end{bmatrix} \begin{bmatrix} x_1 \\ x_2 \end{bmatrix} = \begin{bmatrix} 0 \\ 0 \end{bmatrix}$$

hence $-x_1 + x_2 = 0$

Let $x_1 = 1$, then $x_2 = 1$

The matrix of eigenvectors is, therefore, given by:

$$X = \begin{bmatrix} 1 & 1 \\ -3 & 1 \end{bmatrix}$$

The inverse of the matrix of eigenvectors is given by:

$$X^{-1} = \begin{bmatrix} 1/4 & -1/4 \\ 3/4 & 1/4 \end{bmatrix}$$

and diagonalising, we have:

$$D = \begin{bmatrix} 1/4 & -1/4 \\ 3/4 & 1/4 \end{bmatrix} \begin{bmatrix} 4 & 1 \\ 3 & 2 \end{bmatrix} \begin{bmatrix} 1 & 1 \\ -3 & 1 \end{bmatrix}$$

$$= \begin{bmatrix} 1/4 & -1/4 \\ 15/4 & 5/4 \end{bmatrix} \begin{bmatrix} 1 & 1 \\ -3 & 1 \end{bmatrix}$$

$$= \begin{bmatrix} 1 & 0 \\ 0 & 5 \end{bmatrix}$$

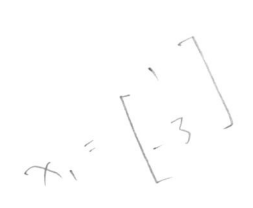

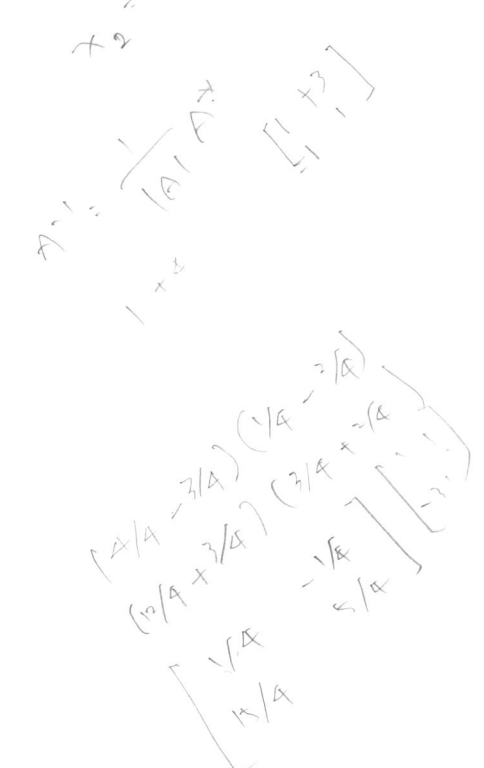

Example 9.5

Our next example is a more complicated one. We wish to find the eigenvalues of the following 3×3 matrix, and then to diagonalise it so that the eigenvalues appear in the principal diagonal.

$$A = \begin{bmatrix} 2 & -4 & 0 \\ 3 & 10 & 0 \\ 1 & 1 & 1 \end{bmatrix}$$

The characteristic polynomial is given by:

$$(1 - \lambda)[(2 - \lambda)(10 - \lambda) + 12] = (1 - \lambda)(\lambda^2 - 12\lambda + 32)$$
$$= (1 - \lambda)(\lambda - 4)(\lambda - 8) = 0$$

Hence, the three characteristic roots are all distinct:

$$\lambda_1 = 1, \quad \lambda_2 = 4, \quad \lambda_3 = 8$$

We now derive the three eigenvectors associated with these three eigenvalues. With $\lambda_1 = 1$, our three equations become:

$$x_1 - 4x_2 = 0$$
$$3x_1 + 9x_2 = 0$$
$$x_1 + x_2 = 0$$

These three equations can only be satisfied if both x_1 and x_2 are both zero. Clearly there is no restriction on the value that can be taken by x_3, and we shall set it equal to *1*.

With $\lambda_2 = 4$, our three equations become:

$$-2x_1 - 4x_2 = 0$$
$$3x_1 + 6x_2 = 0$$
$$x_1 + x_2 - 3x_3 = 0$$

If we set x_3 equal to *1*, then x_1 must equal *6* and x_2 equal *−3*.

With $\lambda_3 = 8$, our three equations become:

$$-6x_1 - 4x_2 = 0$$
$$3x_1 + 2x_2 = 0$$
$$x_1 + x_2 - 7x_3 = 0$$

If we set x_3 equal to *1*, then x_1 must equal *−14* and x_2 equal *21*. The matrix of eigenvectors is therefore given by:

$$X = \begin{bmatrix} 0 & 6 & -14 \\ 0 & -3 & 21 \\ 1 & 1 & 1 \end{bmatrix}$$

We now find the inverse of X. Its determinant and adjoint are given respectively by:

$$\det . X = 6(21) + (-14)(3) = 84$$

$$adj. X = \begin{bmatrix} -24 & -20 & 84 \\ 21 & 14 & 0 \\ 3 & 6 & 0 \end{bmatrix}$$

Multiplying the adjoint by the inverse of the determinant yields the inverse:

$$X^{-1} = \begin{bmatrix} -2/7 & -5/21 & 1 \\ 1/4 & 1/6 & 0 \\ 1/28 & 1/14 & 0 \end{bmatrix}$$

The reader should check that if we post-multiply A by X and pre-multiply A by X^{-1} we obtain a diagonal matrix with the eigenvalues appearing in the principal diagonal.

9.4 EIGENVALUES AND EIGENVECTORS OF SYMMETRIC MATRICES

There are some important properties possessed by the eigenvalues and eigenvectors of a symmetric matrix. First, the eigenvalues of a symmetric matrix are all real; and second, the eigenvectors associated with distinct eigenvalues of a symmetric matrix are orthogonal to each other. A general proof of the first proposition is beyond the scope of this volume, but it is straightforward to show for the case of a 2×2 symmetric matrix. The characteristic equation for this case is given by:

$$\begin{vmatrix} a_{11} - \lambda & a_{12} \\ a_{21} & a_{22} - \lambda \end{vmatrix} = \lambda^2 - (a_{11} + a_{22})\lambda + a_{11}a_{22} - b^2 = 0$$

where $b = a_{12} = a_{21}$. For the roots of this equation to be real, we must have

$$(a_{11} + a_{22})^2 \geq 4(a_{11}a_{22} - b^2)$$

Expanding and collecting terms, we obtain the following condition:

$$a_{11}^2 - 2a_{11}a_{22} + a_{22}^2 = (a_{11} - a_{22})^2 \geq -4b^2$$

Since the left-hand side must be non-negative, and the right-hand side must be non-positive, a symmetric 2×2 matrix will indeed have real eigenvalues.

We now outline the derivation of the second proposition. x_1 and x_2 are two eigenvectors of a symmetric matrix A, and λ_1 and λ_2 are the associated eigenvalues. Hence we have:

$$Ax_1 = \lambda_1 x_1, \text{ and } Ax_2 = \lambda_2 x_2$$

Pre-multiplying each equation by the transposes of x_2 and x_1 respectively, we obtain

$$x_2^T A x_1 = \lambda_1 x_2^T x_1, \text{ and } x_1^T A x_2 = \lambda_2 x_1^T x_2$$

If we now transpose $x_2^T A x_1$, we have

$$(x_2^T A x_1)^T = x_1^T A^T x_2$$
$$= x_1^T A x_2$$
$$= \lambda_1 x_1^T x_2$$

Hence it follows that:

$$\lambda_1 x_1^T x_2 = \lambda_2 x_1^T x_2$$

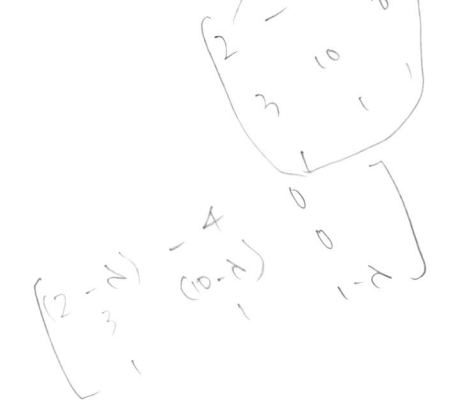

Collecting all the terms on the left-hand side of the equation yields:

$$(\lambda_1 - \lambda_2)x_1^T x_2 = 0.$$

Since by assumption the eigenvalues are distinct, the above result can only hold if the eigenvectors are orthogonal to each other. If we were to normalise the eigenvectors such that they were each of unit length, then we would have:

$$X^T X = I$$

from which it clearly follows that the transpose of the matrix of eigenvectors is equal to the inverse of the matrix of eigenvectors.

Example 9.6

Consider the following symmetric matrix:

$$A = \begin{bmatrix} 3 & \sqrt{8} \\ \sqrt{8} & 1 \end{bmatrix}$$

then $\det.(A - \lambda I) = (3 - \lambda)(1 - \lambda) - (\sqrt{8})^2$

$$= \lambda^2 - 4\lambda - 5 = 0$$

Hence $\lambda_1 = 5, \ \lambda_2 = -1$

We now derive the eigenvectors associated with these eigenvectors. For $\lambda_1 = 5$, we have

$$\begin{bmatrix} -2 & \sqrt{8} \\ \sqrt{8} & -4 \end{bmatrix} \begin{bmatrix} x_1 \\ x_2 \end{bmatrix} = \begin{bmatrix} 0 \\ 0 \end{bmatrix}$$

hence $-2x_1 + \sqrt{8}x_2 = 0$

Let $x_2 = \sqrt{8}$, then $x_1 = 4$

For $\lambda_2 = -1$, we have

$$\begin{bmatrix} 4 & \sqrt{8} \\ \sqrt{8} & 2 \end{bmatrix} \begin{bmatrix} x_1 \\ x_2 \end{bmatrix} = \begin{bmatrix} 0 \\ 0 \end{bmatrix}$$

hence $4x_1 + \sqrt{8}x_2 = 0$

Let $x_2 = \sqrt{8}$, then $x_1 = -2$

The matrix of eigenvectors is

$$X = \begin{bmatrix} 4 & -2 \\ \sqrt{8} & \sqrt{8} \end{bmatrix}$$

To normalise the two vectors so that they are both of unit length, we multiply the first by the reciprocal of $\sqrt{24}$, and the second by the reciprocal of $\sqrt{12}$. Hence

$$X = \begin{bmatrix} 4/\sqrt{24} & -2/\sqrt{12} \\ \sqrt{8}/\sqrt{24} & \sqrt{8}/\sqrt{12} \end{bmatrix}$$

The reader should check that the transpose of the above matrix is equal to its inverse.

We now diagonalise A:

$$X^{-1}AX = \begin{bmatrix} \dfrac{4}{\sqrt{24}} & \dfrac{\sqrt{8}}{\sqrt{24}} \\ -\dfrac{2}{\sqrt{12}} & \dfrac{\sqrt{8}}{\sqrt{12}} \end{bmatrix} \begin{bmatrix} 3 & \sqrt{8} \\ \sqrt{8} & 1 \end{bmatrix} \begin{bmatrix} \dfrac{4}{\sqrt{24}} & -\dfrac{2}{\sqrt{12}} \\ \dfrac{\sqrt{8}}{\sqrt{24}} & \dfrac{\sqrt{8}}{\sqrt{12}} \end{bmatrix}$$

$$= \begin{bmatrix} \dfrac{20}{\sqrt{24}} & \dfrac{5\sqrt{8}}{\sqrt{24}} \\ \dfrac{2}{\sqrt{12}} & -\dfrac{\sqrt{8}}{\sqrt{24}} \end{bmatrix} \begin{bmatrix} \dfrac{4}{\sqrt{24}} & -\dfrac{2}{\sqrt{12}} \\ \dfrac{\sqrt{8}}{\sqrt{24}} & \dfrac{\sqrt{8}}{\sqrt{12}} \end{bmatrix} = \begin{bmatrix} 5 & 0 \\ 0 & -1 \end{bmatrix}$$

A symmetric matrix with a repeated eigenvalue

We now turn to consider the case of a symmetric matrix with a repeated eigenvalue. We show that such a matrix can also be diagonalised.

Example 9.7

Given the following matrix

$$A = \begin{bmatrix} 5 & 0 & 0 \\ 0 & 4 & \sqrt{6} \\ 0 & \sqrt{6} & -1 \end{bmatrix}$$

its characteristic polynomial is given by

$$\det.(A - \lambda I) = (5 - \lambda)(\lambda^2 - 3\lambda - 10)$$

$$= (5 - \lambda)(\lambda - 5)(\lambda + 2) = 0$$

Its eigenvalues are therefore equal to 5, 5 and -2. The derivation of the associated eigenvectors is straightforward. For $\lambda_1 = 5$, we just set x_1 equal to unity, and the other two elements of the vector equal to zero. For $\lambda_2 = 5$, we let x_1 equal zero, and therefore we must have:

$$-x_2 + \sqrt{6}x_3 = 0$$

Now let $x_3 = \sqrt{6}$, then $x_2 = 6$, and normalising we have the following eigenvector:

$$\begin{bmatrix} 0 \\ \dfrac{6}{\sqrt{42}} \\ \dfrac{\sqrt{6}}{\sqrt{42}} \end{bmatrix}$$

For the eigenvector associated with $\lambda_3 = -2$, let $x_1 = 0$; then we must have:

$$6x_2 + \sqrt{6}x_3 = 0$$

Let $x_3 = \sqrt{6}$, then $x_2 = -1$, and normalising we have:

$$\begin{bmatrix} 0 \\ -\dfrac{1}{\sqrt{7}} \\ \dfrac{\sqrt{6}}{\sqrt{7}} \end{bmatrix}$$

Since the eigenvectors are orthonormal, $X^T = X^{-1}$. Hence

$$X^{-1}AX = \begin{bmatrix} 1 & 0 & 0 \\ 0 & \dfrac{6}{\sqrt{42}} & \dfrac{\sqrt{6}}{\sqrt{42}} \\ 0 & -\dfrac{1}{\sqrt{7}} & \dfrac{\sqrt{6}}{\sqrt{7}} \end{bmatrix} \begin{bmatrix} 5 & 0 & 0 \\ 0 & 4 & \sqrt{6} \\ 0 & \sqrt{6} & -1 \end{bmatrix} \begin{bmatrix} 1 & 0 & 0 \\ 0 & \dfrac{6}{\sqrt{42}} & -\dfrac{1}{\sqrt{7}} \\ 0 & \dfrac{\sqrt{6}}{\sqrt{42}} & \dfrac{\sqrt{6}}{\sqrt{7}} \end{bmatrix}$$

$$= \begin{bmatrix} 5 & 0 & 0 \\ 0 & \dfrac{30}{\sqrt{42}} & \dfrac{5\sqrt{6}}{\sqrt{42}} \\ 0 & \dfrac{2}{\sqrt{7}} & -\dfrac{2\sqrt{6}}{\sqrt{42}} \end{bmatrix} \begin{bmatrix} 1 & 0 & 0 \\ 0 & \dfrac{6}{\sqrt{42}} & -\dfrac{1}{\sqrt{7}} \\ 0 & \dfrac{\sqrt{6}}{\sqrt{42}} & \dfrac{\sqrt{6}}{\sqrt{7}} \end{bmatrix}$$

$$= \begin{bmatrix} 5 & 0 & 0 \\ 0 & 5 & 0 \\ 0 & 0 & -2 \end{bmatrix}$$

The determinant of a symmetric matrix

The determinant of a symmetric matrix is equal to the product of all its eigenvalues. Letting D represent the diagonal matrix of eigenvalues of A, then $D = X^{-1}AX$. Pre-multiplying D by X^{-1} and post-multiplying D by X, we obtain

$$A = XDX^{-1}$$

Now the determinant of a matrix which is the product of n matrices is equal to the product of the determinants of these n matrices. Hence

$$\det . A = (\det . X)(\det . D)(\det . X^{-1})$$

However $XX^{-1} = I$, and hence $\det . X \det . X^{-1} = \det . I = 1$, so $\det . A = \det . D$, but

$$\det . D = \begin{vmatrix} \lambda_1 & 0 & \cdots & 0 \\ 0 & \lambda_2 & \cdots & 0 \\ \vdots & \vdots & & \vdots \\ 0 & 0 & \cdots & \lambda_n \end{vmatrix} = \prod_{i=1}^{i=n} \lambda_i = \lambda_1 \lambda_2 \ldots \lambda_n$$

9.5 A NON-SYMMETRIC MATRIX WITH A REPEATED EIGENVALUE

Let us now consider an example of a non-symmetric matrix A with a repeated eigenvalue. We shall see that it is not possible to diagonalise this matrix since its associated eigenvectors are not linearly independent.

Example 9.8

Given

$$A = \begin{bmatrix} 2 & \frac{1}{4} \\ -1 & 1 \end{bmatrix}$$

the characteristic equation is

$$\det . (A - \lambda I) = (2 - \lambda)(1 - \lambda) + \frac{1}{4}$$

$$= \lambda^2 - 3\lambda + \frac{9}{4} = 0$$

In this case we have a repeated root:

$$\lambda_1 = \lambda_2 = 3/2$$

However, when we come to calculate the eigenvectors, we find that they are not linearly independent. We simply have one eigenvector; we must have:

$$0.5x_1 + 0.25x_2 = 0$$

Letting $x_1 = 1$, then we must have $x_2 = -2$.

Hence we cannot diagonalise A using a matrix whose columns are the eigenvectors of A since X would be a singular matrix in this case. However, it has been shown that a similarity transformation can be performed on any square matrix which will lead to the eigenvalues appearing in the principal diagonal of a matrix C. This matrix has the properties that all the elements below the principal diagonal are zero. Furthermore when $c_{ii} = c_{i+1,i+1}$, that is when a root is repeated, then $c_{i,i+1}$ takes on a value of unity if the eigenvectors associated with the repeated root are linearly dependent, and a value of zero if they are linearly independent.

In other words for our particular example, we can find a matrix B where

$$B = \begin{bmatrix} 1 & b_{12} \\ -2 & b_{22} \end{bmatrix} \text{ such that}$$

$$C = B^{-1}AB = \begin{bmatrix} \lambda & 1 \\ 0 & \lambda \end{bmatrix}$$

Note that the first column of B is the eigenvector associated with the repeated root, and the second column is to be determined from the condition that $C = B^{-1}AB$.

9.6 QUADRATIC FORMS

Consider the following function:

$$f(x) = x^T A x$$

where x is a column vector with n elements, and A is a square matrix of dimension n. Such a function is known as a quadratic form. For the 3×3 case, we have:

$$f(x) = (x_1 \quad x_2 \quad x_3) \begin{bmatrix} a_{11} & a_{12} & a_{13} \\ a_{21} & a_{22} & a_{23} \\ a_{31} & a_{32} & a_{33} \end{bmatrix} \begin{bmatrix} x_1 \\ x_2 \\ x_3 \end{bmatrix}$$

Expanding the above equation, collecting terms and simplifying, we obtain:

$$f(x) = a_{11}x_1^2 + (a_{12} + a_{21})x_1 x_2$$
$$+ (a_{13} + a_{31})x_1 x_3 + a_{22}x_2^2 + (a_{23} + a_{32})x_2 x_3 + a_{33}x_3^2$$

More generally, when A is $n \times n$, then

$$x^T A x = \sum_{i=1}^{i=n} \sum_{j=1}^{j=n} a_{ij} x_i x_j$$

We shall always take the A matrix of the quadratic form to be a symmetric matrix. This is completely innocuous and highly convenient, since we can always convert a non-symmetric matrix into a symmetric one without altering the value of $f(x)$. This is done by defining a new element:

$$\tilde{a}_{ij} = \tilde{a}_{ji} = \frac{a_{ij} + a_{ji}}{2}$$

It is clear that the above function is unchanged as a result of this manipulation.

An important question relating to quadratic forms is the following: what conditions must be imposed upon A for $f(x)$ to be strictly positive for any arbitrary non-null vector x? Before we proceed any further, we must provide some definitions.

- If $x^T A x$ is positive for all non-null x vectors, then A is said to be a positive definite matrix.
- If $x^T A x$ is non-negative for all non-null x vectors, then A is said to be a positive semi-definite matrix.
- If $x^T A x$ is negative for all non-null x vectors, then A is said to be a negative definite matrix.
- If $x^T A x$ is non-positive for all non-null x vectors, then A is said to be a negative semi-definite matrix.

We shall now see that a symmetric matrix is positive definite *iff* all its eigenvalues are positive, positive semi-definite *iff* all its eigenvalues are non-negative, negative definite *iff* all its eigenvalues are negative, and negative semi-definite *iff* all its eigenvalues are non-positive.

If we define x as being equal to Ey where E is a matrix whose columns are the normalised eigenvectors of A, and y is a column vector. Then given that A is a symmetric matrix, E is the matrix which diagonalises A, and its transpose is equal to its inverse. Hence

$$x^T A x = y^T E^T A E y$$

$$= y^T \begin{bmatrix} \lambda_1 & 0 & \cdots & 0 \\ 0 & \lambda_2 & \cdots & 0 \\ \vdots & \vdots & & \vdots \\ 0 & 0 & \cdots & \lambda_n \end{bmatrix} y$$

$$= \lambda_1 y_1^2 + \lambda_2 y_2^2 + \cdots + \lambda_n y_n^2$$

$$= \sum_{i=1}^{i=n} \lambda_i y_i^2$$

If all the eigenvalues are positive, it is clear that the quadratic form must take a positive value for any non-null y and hence for any non-null x vector, and so on.

An alternative test for positive definiteness is a determinantal test. A is a positive definite matrix *iff* all the principal minors of A are positive:

$$|a_{11}| > 0, \quad \begin{vmatrix} a_{11} & a_{12} \\ a_{21} & a_{22} \end{vmatrix} > 0,$$

$$\begin{vmatrix} a_{11} & a_{12} & a_{13} \\ a_{21} & a_{22} & a_{23} \\ a_{31} & a_{32} & a_{33} \end{vmatrix} > 0, \ldots, |A| > 0.$$

For positive semi-definiteness, some of the principal minors may be zero.

A is negative definite *iff* its principal minors alternate in sign, starting negative:

$$|a_{11}| < 0, \quad \begin{vmatrix} a_{11} & a_{12} \\ a_{21} & a_{22} \end{vmatrix} > 0,$$

$$\begin{vmatrix} a_{11} & a_{12} & a_{13} \\ a_{21} & a_{22} & a_{23} \\ a_{31} & a_{32} & a_{33} \end{vmatrix} < 0, \ldots,$$

$|A| > 0$ for *even n* and < 0 for *odd n*

For negative semi-definiteness, some of the principal minors may be zero.

Example 9.9

Let us consider whether the following function always takes on a positive value for any non-zero x vector:

$$f(x) = x_1^2 - 4x_1x_2 + 5x_2^2$$

What form does the matrix A take such that

$$f(x) = x^T A x?$$

The coefficients on the squared terms appear in the principal diagonal of the matrix, and to ensure symmetry the off-diagonal element is equal to one half the value of the coefficient on the cross-product term. Hence we have:

$$A = \begin{bmatrix} 1 & -2 \\ -2 & 5 \end{bmatrix}$$

The characteristic polynomial of this matrix is

$$\lambda^2 - 6\lambda + 1 = 0$$

and the eigenvalues are, therefore,

$$\lambda_1 = 3 + \sqrt{8}, \quad \lambda_2 = 3 - \sqrt{8}$$

Both of these roots are positive. Alternatively, calculating the principal minors, we have:

$$|a_{11}| = 1$$

$$\begin{vmatrix} a_{11} & a_{12} \\ a_{21} & a_{22} \end{vmatrix} = \begin{vmatrix} 1 & -2 \\ -2 & 5 \end{vmatrix} = 1$$

A is a positive definite matrix, and $f(x)$ is always positive for a non-null vector x.

Example 9.10

Now consider the following quadratic form:

$$f(x) = 2x_1^2 + 6x_1x_2 + 3x_2^2$$

In this case, the symmetric matrix is given by

$$A = \begin{bmatrix} 2 & 3 \\ 3 & 3 \end{bmatrix}$$

and the characteristic polynomial is
$$\lambda^2 - 5\lambda - 3 = 0$$

Solving this equation, we obtain the eigenvalues:
$$\lambda_1 = 2.5 + \sqrt{9.25}, \quad \lambda_2 = 2.5 - \sqrt{9.25}$$

The two eigenvalues are of opposite sign, and A is an indefinite matrix. The values of the principal minors are 2 and -3 respectively. It is clear that $f(x)$ will be positive if both elements of the vector are both non-negative, or both non-positive. However, when one element is positive and one negative, then we cannot rule out the possibility that the absolute value of the cross-product term will be greater than the sum of the squared terms, leading to a negative value of the function; for example, if $x_1 = 1$, $x_2 = -1$, then $f(x) = -1$.

Example 9.11

Let us consider whether the following function always takes on a positive value for any non-zero x vector:
$$f(x) = 2x_1^2 + 5x_2^2 + 13x_3^2 + 6x_1x_2 + 10x_1x_3 + 14x_2x_3$$

Then $f(x)$ is a quadratic form with
$$A = \begin{bmatrix} 2 & 3 & 5 \\ 3 & 5 & 7 \\ 5 & 7 & 13 \end{bmatrix}$$

The reader should check that for the above matrix
$$f(x) = x^T A x$$

Expanding the determinant,
$$\begin{vmatrix} 2-\lambda & 3 & 5 \\ 3 & 5-\lambda & 7 \\ 5 & 7 & 13-\lambda \end{vmatrix} = 0$$

we obtain the characteristic polynomial:
$$-\lambda^3 + 20\lambda^2 - 18\lambda = 0$$

whose roots are
$$\lambda_1 = 0, \quad \lambda_2 = 10 + \sqrt{82}, \quad \lambda_3 = 10 - \sqrt{82}$$

No root is negative, but one is zero, so A is a positive semi-definite matrix, and $f(x)$ is at most non-negative. The reader should check that the value of the function is zero for the vector: $(-4, 1, 1)$, but for any other vector which only differs from the above in the value of x_1, the function has a positive value.

We shall make great use of these results in Chapter 14 where we discuss optimisation with more than one choice variable.

9.7 SUMMARY

In this chapter we have explained the concepts of eigenvalues and eigenvectors. Eigenvalues of a symmetric matrix are always real, and such a matrix can always be transformed into a matrix where the eigenvalues appear along the principal diagonal. This result is extremely helpful in enabling us to sign quadratic forms, which are functions of the form: $y = x^T A x$. A quadratic form will have a positive value for any non-null vector x if the associated symmetric matrix is positive definite, and this will be guaranteed to be the case if all its eigenvalues are positive. The quadratic form will have a non-negative value for any non-null vector x if the associated symmetric matrix is positive semi-definite, and this will be guaranteed to be the case if all its eigenvalues are non-negative. The quadratic form will have a non-positive value for any non-null vector x if the associated symmetric matrix is negative semi-definite, and this will be guaranteed to be the case if all its eigenvalues are non-positive. The quadratic form will have a negative value for any non-null vector x if the associated symmetric matrix is negative definite, and this will be guaranteed to be the case if all its eigenvalues are negative.

9.8 EXERCISES

9.1 (a) Find the eigenvalues and hence the eigenvectors of the following 2×2 matrices:

$$\text{(i) } A = \begin{bmatrix} 4 & 3 \\ 5 & 2 \end{bmatrix}, \quad \text{(ii) } B = \begin{bmatrix} -2 & 7 \\ 4 & 1 \end{bmatrix},$$

$$\text{(iii) } C = \begin{bmatrix} 5 & 3 \\ -1 & 1 \end{bmatrix}, \quad \text{(iv) } D = \begin{bmatrix} 3 & -2 \\ 0.5 & 1 \end{bmatrix}.$$

(b) Find the eigenvalues and hence the eigenvectors of the following 3×3 matrices:

$$\text{(i) } A = \begin{bmatrix} 2 & 1 & -1 \\ 0 & 1 & 1 \\ 2 & 0 & -2 \end{bmatrix}, \quad \text{(ii) } B = \begin{bmatrix} -2 & 0 & 0 \\ 0 & 4 & 3 \\ 0 & 5 & 2 \end{bmatrix},$$

$$\text{(iii) } C = \begin{bmatrix} 3 & 1 & 0 \\ 1 & 3 & 0 \\ 0 & 0 & -2 \end{bmatrix}, \quad \text{(iv) } D = \begin{bmatrix} 2 & 1 & 1 \\ 1 & 3 & -2 \\ 1 & -2 & 3 \end{bmatrix}.$$

9.2 (a) For the three matrices below, carry out the following operations: find the matrix of eigenvectors, X; find X^{-1}; find $D = X^{-1}AX$.

$$\text{(i) } A = \begin{bmatrix} 4 & 3 \\ 16 & 6 \end{bmatrix}, \quad \text{(ii) } A = \begin{bmatrix} -1 & 3 \\ 0 & 2 \end{bmatrix},$$

$$\text{(iii) } A = \begin{bmatrix} 2 & 0 & 0 \\ 6 & 3 & 0 \\ 0 & 0 & 4 \end{bmatrix}$$

9.3 (a) (i) Find the eigenvalues of the following real symmetric matrix:

$$A = \begin{bmatrix} 2 & 1 & 1 \\ 1 & 1 & 0 \\ 1 & 0 & 1 \end{bmatrix}$$

(ii) Find and normalise each eigenvector so that each has unit length, and show that, after normalisation, the matrix of eigenvectors, X, is orthogonal. Finally, obtain the diagonal matrix:

$$D = X^{-1}AX$$

(b) (i) Show that the following matrix possesses a repeated eigenvalue.
(ii) Find the matrix of normalised eigenvectors, and show that this matrix is non-singular.
(iii) Diagonalise the A matrix.

$$A = \begin{bmatrix} 6 & 0 & -\sqrt{8} \\ 0 & 8 & 0 \\ -\sqrt{8} & 0 & 4 \end{bmatrix}$$

(c) The rank of a symmetric matrix is equal to $n - k$ where k is the number of eigenvalues of the matrix which are equal to zero. Show that this result holds for the following matrices.

$$\text{(a) } A = \begin{bmatrix} 1 & -2 & 3 \\ -2 & 4 & -6 \\ 3 & -6 & 9 \end{bmatrix}, \quad \text{(b) } B = \begin{bmatrix} 5 & 0 & 0 \\ 0 & 6 & 3 \\ 0 & 3 & 4 \end{bmatrix},$$

$$\text{(c) } C = \begin{bmatrix} 3 & -1 & 2 \\ 1 & -5 & 4 \\ 2 & 4 & -2 \end{bmatrix}.$$

9.4 (a) Show that we must have $b_{12} = b_{22} = 4/3$ for the result in example 9.8 on pages 143–144 to hold.
(b) What are the determinants of the inverses, where they exist, of the following matrices? Do not derive the inverses.

$$\text{(a) } \begin{bmatrix} 7 & 2 \\ -4 & 6 \end{bmatrix}, \quad \text{(b) } \begin{bmatrix} 0.2 & 0.25 \\ -0.04 & 0.5 \end{bmatrix}$$

$$\text{(c) } \begin{bmatrix} 3 & -1 & 4 \\ -2 & 6 & 0 \\ 2 & 1 & 3 \end{bmatrix}, \quad \text{(d) } \begin{bmatrix} 1 & -2 & 5 \\ 2 & 1 & 0 \\ -4 & -3 & 2 \end{bmatrix}$$

9.5 (a) Which of the following matrices are positive definite, positive semi-definite, negative definite, negative semi-definite, or indefinite?

$$\text{(i) } A = \begin{bmatrix} 2 & -1 & 1 \\ -1 & 3 & 0 \\ 1 & 0 & 1 \end{bmatrix}, \quad \text{(ii) } B = \begin{bmatrix} 1 & 0 & 0 \\ 0 & 5 & \sqrt{11} \\ 0 & \sqrt{11} & -5 \end{bmatrix}$$

$$\text{(iii) } C = \begin{bmatrix} -3 & -1 & 0 \\ -1 & -3 & 0 \\ 0 & 0 & -2 \end{bmatrix}, \quad \text{(iv) } D = \begin{bmatrix} 2 & 1 & 1 \\ 1 & 3 & -2 \\ 1 & -2 & 3 \end{bmatrix}$$

(b) Do the following functions always take on a positive value for any arbitrary non-null x vector?

(i) $f(x) = -2x_1^2 + 2x_1x_2 - 3x_2^2$

(ii) $f(x) = 4x_1^2 + 4x_1x_2 + 3x_2^2$

(iii) $f(x) = x_1^2 + 3x_1x_2 + 2x_2^2$

(iv) $f(x) = 2x_1^2 + 3x_2^2 + 3x_3^2 + 2x_1x_2 + 2x_1x_3 + 4x_2x_3$

(v) $f(x) = 2x_1^2 + 3x_2^2 + 3x_3^2 + 2x_1x_2 + 2x_1x_3 - 4x_2x_3$

CHAPTER
TEN
NON-NEGATIVE SQUARE MATRICES

10.1 INTRODUCTION

In this chapter we are concerned with non-negative square matrices, i.e. matrices whose elements are all non-negative in value. The analysis in this chapter follows on from the last chapter where we introduced the concepts of eigenvalues and eigenvectors. In Section 10.2 we briefly touch upon the Cayley–Hamilton Theorem, which states that a square matrix satisfies its own characteristic polynomial. As we have seen in Chapter 9, the eigenvalues of a matrix are found by solving the characteristic polynomial. The Cayley–Hamilton Theorem informs us that not only is the characteristic equation satisfied by the eigenvalues of some square matrix, but by the matrix itself.

In Section 10.3 we introduce the concept of an indecomposable matrix. Any $n \times n$ matrix may by partitioned into a set of four submatrices with the two submatrices containing any elements from the principal diagonal being square. A matrix is said to be indecomposable if it is not possible to obtain a matrix which contains a null sub-matrix in its bottom left-hand corner by interchanging the rows and columns of the matrix. We state in Section 10.3 some important properties possessed by indecomposable matrices.

An important application of non-negative square matrices in economics is provided by input–output economics. This is a planning technique which, given a linear technology in which goods are used to produce goods, enables an analyst to determine the total outputs which it will be necessary for an economy to produce in order to make available given quantities of goods for consumption or other final demand purposes. We shall see in Section 10.4 that the concept of an indecomposable matrix is useful in this context. Questions of obvious interest are the conditions that must be imposed on the nature of the fixed production coefficients technology for it to be viable. In Section 10.5, we consider non-negative matrices whose column sums are all unity. Such matrices are known as stochastic matrices, with the element in row i column j representing the probability of moving from state j to state i.

10.2 THE CAYLEY–HAMILTON THEOREM

Positive and non-negative matrices

In this chapter we are concerned with square matrices, and in particular with square matrices which are either positive or non-negative.

A positive matrix is a matrix, all of whose elements are positive: i.e. $a_{ij} > 0$ for all i, j. Note that a positive matrix is not to be confused with a positive definite matrix.

A non-negative matrix is a matrix, all of whose elements are non-negative: i.e. $a_{ij} \geq 0$ for all i, j.

A semi-positive matrix is a matrix, all of whose elements are non-negative and in which each row and column has at least one positive element:

$$a_{ij} \geq 0, \quad \sum_{i=1}^{i=n} a_{ij} > 0, \quad \sum_{j=1}^{j=n} a_{ij} > 0$$

The Cayley–Hamilton Theorem

This theorem tells us that any square matrix A satisfies its own characteristic equation. We know that in order to calculate the eigenvalues of a matrix we must solve a polynomial equation of the form:

$$\det.(A - \lambda I) = f(\lambda) = 0$$

The Cayley–Hamilton Theorem is that if $f(\lambda) = 0$, then we must also have $f(A) = \mathbf{0}$.

Example 10.1

We provide a simple illustration of the theorem. Given

$$A = \begin{bmatrix} 2 & 4 \\ -2 & 8 \end{bmatrix}$$

Then its characteristic polynomial is given by:

$$\begin{aligned} f(\lambda) = \det(A - \lambda I) &= (2 - \lambda)(8 - \lambda) + 8 \\ &= \lambda^2 - 10\lambda + 24 \\ &= (\lambda - 4)(\lambda - 6) = 0 \end{aligned}$$

and we shall also have:

$$\begin{aligned} f(A) &= (A - 4I)(A - 6I) \\ &= \begin{bmatrix} -2 & 4 \\ -2 & 4 \end{bmatrix} \begin{bmatrix} -4 & 4 \\ -2 & 2 \end{bmatrix} \\ &= \begin{bmatrix} 0 & 0 \\ 0 & 0 \end{bmatrix} \end{aligned}$$

Arising from this theorem is another important result: if a matrix B is itself a polynomial function of some other matrix A, then the eigenvalues of B will be given by the same polynomial function applied to the eigenvalues of A, the λ_i s. For example if $B = f(A) = A^2$, then the eigenvalues of B are given by $f(\lambda) = \lambda_i^2$.

Assume that we have derived the eigenvectors of some matrix A and have found them to be linearly independent. Now take a weighted average of these eigenvectors:

$$z = \sum_{i=1}^{i=n} \alpha_i x_i$$

Pre-multiplying by A and using the result that $Ax_i = \lambda_i x_i$, we have:

$$Az = \sum_{i=1}^{i=n} \alpha_i \lambda_i x_i$$

$$A^t z = \sum_{i=1}^{i=n} \alpha_i \lambda_i^t x_i$$

What will happen through time to $A^t z$ depends crucially on the eigenvalue with the largest absolute value. Convergence will only occur if all the eigenvalues of A are no greater than unity in absolute value. More generally, it can be shown that

$$\lim_{t \to \infty} A^t = \lim_{t \to \infty} \lambda_1^t x_1 y_1^T$$

where λ_1 is the eigenvalue with the largest absolute value, x_1 is the eigenvector of A associated with this eigenvalue, and y_1 is the eigenvector of A^T associated with this eigenvalue.

10.3 DECOMPOSABLE AND INDECOMPOSABLE MATRICES

Consider a square matrix A. Such a matrix is said to be decomposable if it is possible to interchange its rows and columns in such a way as to obtain a matrix of the following form:

$$\tilde{A} = \begin{bmatrix} A_{11} & A_{12} \\ 0 & A_{22} \end{bmatrix}$$

where A_{11} and A_{22} are square submatrices of order $k \times k$ and $(n-k) \times (n-k)$ respectively, A_{12} is $k \times (n-k)$, and 0 is an $(n-k) \times k$ null matrix.

Consider the following set of equations:

$$\begin{bmatrix} a_{11} & 0 & a_{13} \\ a_{21} & a_{22} & a_{23} \\ a_{31} & 0 & a_{33} \end{bmatrix} \begin{bmatrix} x_1 \\ x_2 \\ x_3 \end{bmatrix} = \begin{bmatrix} b_1 \\ b_2 \\ b_3 \end{bmatrix}$$

Now interchange rows such that the original second row becomes the new first row, the original first row becomes the new second row, and the third row stays the same:

$$\begin{bmatrix} a_{21} & a_{22} & a_{23} \\ a_{11} & 0 & a_{13} \\ a_{31} & 0 & a_{33} \end{bmatrix} \begin{bmatrix} x_1 \\ x_2 \\ x_3 \end{bmatrix} = \begin{bmatrix} b_2 \\ b_1 \\ b_3 \end{bmatrix}$$

Now perform the same set of changes on the columns of the new matrix: the second column of this matrix becomes the new first column, its first column now becomes the new second column, the third column is unchanged. We obtain:

$$\begin{bmatrix} a_{22} & a_{21} & a_{23} \\ 0 & a_{11} & a_{13} \\ 0 & a_{31} & a_{33} \end{bmatrix} \begin{bmatrix} x_2 \\ x_1 \\ x_3 \end{bmatrix} = \begin{bmatrix} b_2 \\ b_1 \\ b_3 \end{bmatrix}$$

A is, therefore, a decomposable matrix with:

$$A_{11} = [a_{22}], \quad A_{12} = [a_{21} \quad a_{23}]$$

$$A_{21} = \begin{bmatrix} 0 \\ 0 \end{bmatrix}, \quad A_{22} = \begin{bmatrix} a_{11} & a_{13} \\ a_{31} & a_{33} \end{bmatrix}$$

Basically, what we have done in the above operations is to pre-multiply A by P^{-1} and post-multiply it by P where P and P^{-1} are permutation matrices which interchange rows and columns respectively:

$$P = \begin{bmatrix} 0 & 1 & 0 \\ 1 & 0 & 0 \\ 0 & 0 & 1 \end{bmatrix}$$

$$P^T = P^{-1} = \begin{bmatrix} 0 & 1 & 0 \\ 1 & 0 & 0 \\ 0 & 0 & 1 \end{bmatrix}$$

More generally, when A is a decomposable matrix, we may express the system of equations $Ax = b$ as follows:

$$\begin{bmatrix} x_1 \\ x_2 \end{bmatrix} = \begin{bmatrix} A_{11} & A_{12} \\ 0 & A_{22} \end{bmatrix}^{-1} \begin{bmatrix} b_1 \\ b_2 \end{bmatrix}$$

Let us first evaluate the inverse in the above equation. We must have:

$$\begin{bmatrix} A_{11} & A_{12} \\ 0 & A_{22} \end{bmatrix} \begin{bmatrix} P & Q \\ R & S \end{bmatrix} = \begin{bmatrix} I & 0 \\ 0 & I \end{bmatrix}$$

Expanding the above yields:

$$A_{11}P + A_{12}R = I$$
$$A_{11}Q + A_{12}S = 0$$
$$A_{22}R = 0$$
$$A_{22}S = I$$

from which it follows that:

$$R = 0$$
$$S = A_{22}^{-1}$$
$$P = A_{11}^{-1}$$
$$Q = -A_{11}^{-1} A_{12} A_{22}^{-1}$$

We, therefore, have:

$$\begin{bmatrix} x_1 \\ x_2 \end{bmatrix} = \begin{bmatrix} A_{11}^{-1} & -A_{11}^{-1}A_{12}A_{22}^{-1} \\ 0 & A_{22}^{-1} \end{bmatrix} \begin{bmatrix} b_1 \\ b_2 \end{bmatrix}$$

It is clear from the above that x_2 only depends upon the subvector b_2, whereas x_1 depends upon both b_1 and b_2. The system would have been completely decomposable had A_{12} also been a null matrix, for then in addition to x_2 depending only upon b_2, x_1 would have only depended upon b_1.

A matrix is accordingly indecomposable if it is not possible by interchanging rows and columns to end up with square submatrices along the principal diagonal and a rectangular null matrix in the bottom left-hand corner.

Properties of indecomposable matrices

Important properties are possessed by non-negative square indecomposable matrices. We briefly describe these properties:

1. The largest positive eigenvalue of such a matrix is known as the dominant eigenvalue, and is often referred to as the Frobenius root. The dominant eigenvalue is at least as large as the absolute value of any other eigenvalue, and in fact is greater than the absolute value of any other eigenvalue if the matrix is positive.
2. The eigenvector associated with the dominant eigenvalue is positive. In fact, there are no other eigenvectors which are even non-negative.
3. The dominant eigenvalue increases in value with any increase in any component, a_{ij}, of A.
4. Furthermore, its value must be smaller than the largest of the row (column) sums of A and larger than the smallest row (column) sum of A, unless all the row (column) sums are the same, in which case the dominant eigenvalue is equal to this sum.
5. Finally, the inverse of the matrix $(\mu I - A)$ will only be positive when μ is larger than the dominant eigenvalue.

Assume that A is a semi-positive indecomposable matrix, and let x be a semi-positive vector. Now define a new vector $y = (I + A)x$. We shall show that the number of zero elements in y, $\Omega(y)$, is smaller than the number of zero elements in x, $\Omega(x)$. Given that $(I + A)$ is a semi-positive matrix, it is immediately obvious that the number of zero elements in y cannot be larger than the number of such elements in x. We now show that if the number of zero elements in the two vectors is the same, then A must be a decomposable matrix. Assume that the number of zero elements is the same in the two vectors. Partitioning the matrix $I + A$ and the vectors x and y enables us to write the equations as follows:

$$\begin{bmatrix} \hat{y} \\ 0 \end{bmatrix} = \begin{bmatrix} I + A_{11} & A_{12} \\ A_{21} & I + A_{22} \end{bmatrix} \begin{bmatrix} \hat{x} \\ 0 \end{bmatrix}$$

where $\hat{y}$ and $\hat{x}$ are positive vectors. Multiplying out, we obtain:

$$\hat{y} = (I + A_{11})\hat{x}$$
$$0 = A_{21}\hat{x}$$

But since $\hat{x}$ is a positive vector, the second equation can only be satisfied if A_{21} is a null matrix; but this is impossible given our assumption of indecomposability. Hence $\Omega(y) < \Omega(x)$, and more generally, we must have $\Omega(z) = 0$, where $z = (I + A)^{n-1}x$. In other words, z is a positive vector, whereas x need only have at a minimum one positive element with all the rest equal to zero.

Let us now consider the following series:

$$S = I + A + A^2 + A^3 + \cdots + A^{t-1}$$

Pre-multiplying by A yields:

$$AS = A + A^2 + A^3 + \cdots + A^t$$

Subtracting the second equation from the first yields:

$$S - AS = S(I - A) = I - A^t$$

Hence if the series converges, we have

$$S = (I - A)^{-1} \text{ given } \lim_{t \to \infty} A^t = 0$$

Convergence occurs provided that the Frobenius root of A is less than unity.

Let us assume that A is a semi-positive 3×3 indecomposable matrix A, and let $M = I + 2A + A^2$. Then we know from our earlier result that:

$$M = I + 2A + A^2 > 0$$

Now consider the elements of M:

$$m_{ii} = 1 + 2a_{ii} + \alpha_i \cdot a_i > 0$$
$$m_{ij} = 0 + 2a_{ij} + \alpha_i \cdot a_j > 0$$

where α_i and a_j are the ith row and jth column respectively of A. All of the terms on the right-hand side of the above expressions are non-negative, and at least one of them must be positive. Now consider the inverse of $(I - A)$, assuming that it is defined. We have shown above that

$$(I - A)^{-1} = I + A + A^2 + \cdots$$

The elements of this inverse are given by

$$\beta_{ii} = 1 + a_{ii} + \alpha_i \cdot a_i + \text{further non-negative terms}$$
$$\beta_{ij} = 0 + a_{ij} + \alpha_i \cdot a_j + \text{further non-negative terms}$$

Since in discussing the elements of M we saw that at least one of the first three terms, on the right-hand side of the above expressions, all of which are non-negative, must be positive, we may now conclude that all the elements of $(I - A)^{-1}$ are positive.

Example 10.2

The following non-negative square matrix is indecomposable:

$$A = \begin{bmatrix} 1 & 1 & 0 \\ 1 & 2 & 1 \\ 2 & 4 & 2 \end{bmatrix}$$

Let us now find its eigenvalues by solving the characteristic polynomial:

$$\det.(A - \lambda I) = \begin{vmatrix} 1-\lambda & 1 & 0 \\ 1 & 2-\lambda & 1 \\ 2 & 4 & 2-\lambda \end{vmatrix}$$

$$= (1-\lambda)(\lambda^2 - 4\lambda) + \lambda$$

$$= -\lambda(\lambda^2 - 5\lambda + 3) = 0$$

The eigenvalues are *0, 0.6972* and *4.3028*. The dominant eigenvalue is *4.3028*, and the eigenvector associated with this eigenvalue can now be shown to be positive. We must have

$$-3.3028 x_1 + x_2 = 0$$
$$x_1 - 2.3028 x_2 + x_3 = 0$$

Let $x_1 = 1$, then $x_2 = 3.3028$ and $x_3 = 6.6057$. Note also that the value of the dominant eigenvalue, *4.3028*, lies between the minimum row sum, *2*, and the maximum row sum, *8*; and between the minimum column sum, *3*, and the maximum column sum, *7*.

10.4 INPUT–OUTPUT ECONOMICS

Consider an economy in which products are produced subject to a linear constant returns to scale technology. In addition to primary factors of production, such as labour and land, production requires the use of intermediate inputs. To produce steel, we need, *inter alia*, inputs of coal, electricity, and many other products. To obtain coal, we need inputs of coal, steel, electricity etc; to produce electricity, we need inputs of coal, electricity, steel etc. The system is highly interdependent, and complex with electricity being needed to extract the coal which in turn is required to generate the electricity, and so on. A portion of the output of any particular product is used as an intermediate input in the production of products, including itself. The remainder is then used for final demand purposes: some will be consumed by either the personal sector or by the government, some may be used for investment purposes, and in an open economy, some may be exported to the rest of the world. Furthermore in the latter scenario, some of the final demand may be met by imports, and some non-competitive imports, i.e. goods which are not produced at home, may be used in the production of the various products. In this chapter, however, we shall restrict our analysis to a closed economy.

We let the production technology be characterised by the following square matrix:

$$A = \begin{bmatrix} a_{11} & a_{12} & \cdots & a_{1n} \\ a_{21} & a_{22} & \cdots & a_{2n} \\ \vdots & \vdots & & \vdots \\ a_{n1} & a_{n2} & \cdots & a_{nn} \end{bmatrix}$$

where a_{ij} is a technical input–output coefficient which measures the amount of good *i* that must be used directly to produce a unit of gross output of good *j*. The gross output vector for the economy, x, is, therefore, given by:

$$x = Ax + d$$

where Ax is the vector of intermediate inputs and d the vector of final demands.

One question we may ask ourselves is the following: what vector of gross outputs will it be necessary to produce in order to satisfy an arbitrary vector of final demands? Rearranging the above equation, we have:

$$(I - A)x = d$$

and pre-multiplying by $(I - A)^{-1}$, assuming it exists, yields:

$$x = (I - A)^{-1}d$$

Naturally, we require x to be a non-negative vector. Since any vector of final demands must be non-negative, the required vector of gross outputs will be non-negative if $(I - A)^{-1}$ (known as the Leontief inverse after Wassily Leontief, the founder of input–output economics and Nobel laureate for economics) is also a non-negative matrix. We have already seen that $(I - A)^{-1}$ will indeed be a non-negative matrix provided that the Frobenius root of A is less than unity. Furthermore, we know given this condition is satisfied that all the elements of the inverse will be positive if A is an indecomposable matrix, whereas if A is decomposable, then the Leontief inverse will be a non-negative matrix. Let the element in row i column j of this inverse be given by β_{ij}.

What interpretation can we give to the elements of the Leontief inverse? Assume we wish to make available one unit of good j for final demand purposes; in other words unity appears in the jth row of the vector and zeros everywhere else. Hence we have

$$d = \begin{bmatrix} 0 \\ \vdots \\ 1 \\ \vdots \\ 0 \end{bmatrix}$$

Pre-multiplying this vector by the Leontief inverse yields

$$x = \begin{bmatrix} \beta_{11} & \cdots & \beta_{1j} & \cdots & \beta_{1n} \\ \beta_{21} & \cdots & \beta_{2j} & \cdots & \beta_{2n} \\ \vdots & \vdots & \vdots & & \vdots \\ \beta_{n1} & \cdots & \beta_{nj} & \cdots & \beta_{nn} \end{bmatrix} \begin{bmatrix} 0 \\ \vdots \\ 1 \\ \vdots \\ 0 \end{bmatrix}$$

$$= \begin{bmatrix} \beta_{1j} \\ \beta_{2j} \\ \vdots \\ \beta_{nj} \end{bmatrix}$$

The elements in the jth column of the Leontief inverse accordingly inform us of the quantities of all the n goods which would have to be produced in order to make possible the provision of one unit of good j for say final consumption; β_{ij}, therefore, measures the total amount of good i necessary to produce unit net output of good j, and includes both the direct and indirect requirements for good i. Good i may be a direct intermediate input into the production of good j, but there will also be indirect links such as when an amount of good i is required to produce good k, which in turn is needed to produce good j, and so on. A similar interpretation naturally applies to all the other columns of the Leontief inverse. If A is an indecomposable matrix, all the elements of the Leontief inverse will be positive, and positive quantities of all goods will have to be produced in order to satisfy the simplest of all final demand vectors, i.e. one containing a unit of good j and zero quantities of all other goods. Economically, it is clear that all the elements of the Leontief inverse must be non-negative; given the above interpretation, it would be economically nonsensical for any of these elements to be negative.

Example 10.3

Consider the following simple two-sector input–output model in which the second good, steel, is a direct input into the production of the first good, corn, and the first good is a direct input into the production of the second good. To produce one unit of corn we directly require a_{21} units of steel, and to produce one unit of steel we directly require a_{12} units of corn. Corn is not a direct input into the production of corn, nor is steel a direct input into the production of steel. Then

$$A = \begin{bmatrix} 0 & a_{12} \\ a_{21} & 0 \end{bmatrix}$$

To produce one unit of net output of corn one requires the following total production of corn:

$$x_1 = 1 + a_{12}a_{21} + a_{12}^2 a_{21}^2 + a_{12}^3 a_{21}^3 + \cdots + a_{12}^{n-1} a_{21}^{n-1} + \cdots$$

where the first term in the series is unit net output of corn, the second term is the amount of corn needed to produce the steel required for the production of the corn, the third term represents the amount of corn needed to produce the steel to produce the corn to produce the steel, and so on.

To produce one unit of net output of corn one requires the following total production of steel:

$$x_2 = a_{21} + a_{21}^2 a_{12} + a_{21}^3 a_{12}^2 + a_{21}^4 a_{12}^3 + \cdots + a_{21}^{n-1} a_{12}^{n-2} + \cdots$$

where the first term in the series is the amount of steel to produce one unit of corn, the second term is the amount of steel to produce the corn to produce the steel, the third term is the amount of steel to produce the corn to produce the steel to produce the corn, and so on.

Multiplying both expressions by $a_{12}a_{21}$, subtracting the respective new equation from the relevant original one, and simplifying we have:

$$x_1 = \frac{1 - (a_{12}a_{21})^n}{1 - a_{12}a_{21}}$$

$$x_2 = \frac{a_{21} - a_{21}^n a_{12}^{n-1}}{1 - a_{12}a_{21}}$$

Then provided that

$$1 > a_{12}a_{21} > 0$$

as *n* approaches infinity, we have

$$\lim_{n\to\infty} x_1 = \frac{1}{1 - a_{12}a_{21}}$$

$$\lim_{n\to\infty} x_2 = \frac{1}{1 - a_{12}a_{21}}$$

The above condition will be met if a_{12} and a_{21} are both less than unity, given that the two coefficients are both positive. Naturally, the column sums of *A* would then all be less than unity in this case.

A diagrammatic analysis

Let us now deal with the general *2 × 2* input–output model, and provide a diagrammatic analysis of the conditions which must be met for the technology to be viable. Assume one unit of gross output of good 1 is produced, then net output of good 1 would be *1 − a_{11}*, which we take to be positive, and net output of good 2 would be negative and equal to $-a_{21}$. Assume further that there is just one primary input, labour, and the quantity available is *L**; labour requirements for unit gross output of the two goods are l_1 and l_2 respectively. If all the labour was allocated to the production of good 1, net output of good 1 would be equal to $(L^*/l_1)(1 - a_{11})$, and net output of good 2 would be equal to $-a_{21}(L^*/l_1)$. Similarly if gross output of good 2 was unity, this would imply net output of good 1 equal to $-a_{21}$ and net output of good 2 equal to *1 − a_{22}*, which we again take to be positive. With all labour allocated to the production of good 2, net outputs of goods 1 and 2 would be $-a_{12}(L^*/l_2)$ and $(L^*/l_2)(1 - a_{22})$ respectively. These two points are depicted in Fig. 10.1 in which the net output of good 1 is measured along the horizontal axis, and

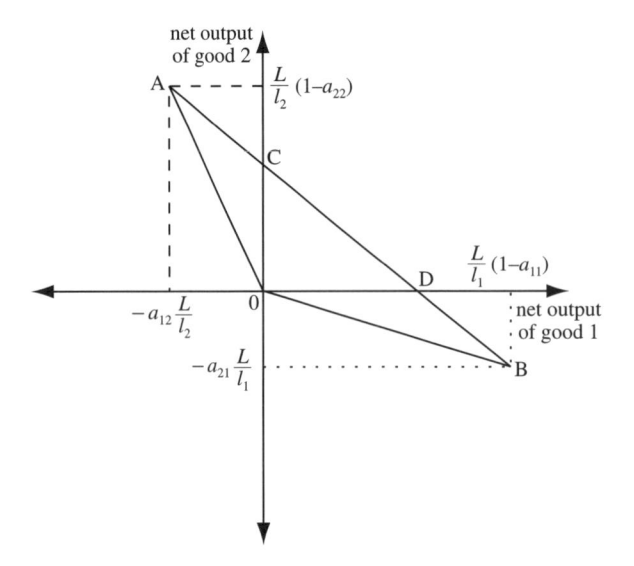

Figure 10.1 Production possibilities in a two good, one primary input (labour) economy. If all the labour were allocated to the production of good 1, then net outputs of the two goods would be given by point B. If all the labour were allocated to the production of good 2, then net outputs of the two goods would be given by point A. Negative net outputs are impossible: the production possibility frontier is CD.

the net output of good 2 along the vertical axis. Points along the straight line joining up these two points are the net outputs made possible by allocating labour to the production of the two goods. At the mid-point along AB, half the labour is utilised in each industry. Outcomes with negative net outputs are economically inefficient, and for the technology to be viable, the line joining up the two points must pass through the positive quadrant. This will indeed be the case if the absolute slope of the ray OA is steeper than the absolute slope of the ray OB. It is clear that this requires:

$$\frac{1 - a_{22}}{a_{12}} > \frac{a_{21}}{1 - a_{11}}$$

Positive net outputs of the two goods are possible if

$$(1 - a_{11}) > 0$$

$$(1 - a_{11})(1 - a_{22}) > a_{12}a_{21}$$

These conditions are known as the Hawkins–Simon conditions, and for the $n \times n$ case, they require all the principal minors of $(\boldsymbol{I} - \boldsymbol{A})$ to be positive.

$$|1 - a_{11}| > 0, \quad \begin{vmatrix} 1 - a_{11} & -a_{12} \\ -a_{21} & 1 - a_{2} \end{vmatrix} > 0$$

$$\begin{vmatrix} 1 - a_{11} & -a_{12} & -a_{13} \\ a_{21} & 1 - a_{22} & -a_{23} \\ -a_{31} & -a_{32} & 1 - a_{33} \end{vmatrix} > 0, \; \dots, \; |\boldsymbol{I} - \boldsymbol{A}| > 0$$

These conditions will in fact be met if the Frobenius root of $\boldsymbol{A}$ is less than unity.

Typically, economic statisticians when constructing input–output tables use data expressed in value terms rather than in terms of physical quantities. In other words, in arriving at estimates of the input–output coefficients, what is measured is not the kW hours of electricity required to produce a tonne of coal, but rather the value of the electricity needed in order to produce a particular value of coal, say a one pound sterling's worth. Let us now sum the elements in a given column of $\boldsymbol{A}$, our matrix of input–output coefficients. For the technology to be viable, we would expect the sum of these coefficients to be less than unity; the cost of the intermediate inputs necessary to produce gross output of the good with a value of unity must be less than unity, thereby providing positive value added out of which the primary factors of production can be recompensed. But if this is indeed the case, then the Frobenius root of $\boldsymbol{A}$ will be less than unity, and the Leontief inverse will indeed be a non-negative matrix.

Example 10.4

The table below provides information for a three-sector economy on the use to which the gross output of each sector was put. For example, the gross output of the agricultural sector

	Uses of output				
Sector	*Agriculture*	*Manufacturing*	*Services*	*Final demand*	*Gross output*
Agriculture	400	1500	600	1500	4000
Manufacturing	800	500	750	2950	5000
Services	400	1000	150	1450	3000

was £4000m, of which £400m was used as an intermediate input in agricultural production, £1500m was used as an input in the manufacturing sector, £600m was used as an input in the service sector, and the remaining £1500m was used for final demand purposes. Similar interpretations can be given to the other rows of the table.

If we now assume that the underlying technology of this economy exhibits constant returns to scale, we may easily calculate the implied technical input–output coefficients. Agricultural inputs valued at £400m were required to produce a gross agricultural output of £4000m, thereby yielding an input–output coefficient of *0.1*. Manufacturing inputs valued at £800m were used to produce a gross agricultural output of £4000m, thereby yielding an input–output coefficient of *0.2*. £400m of inputs from the service sector were needed to produce the agricultural output, implying an input–output coefficient in this case equal to *0.1*. These calculations provide us with the first column of the matrix of technical input–output coefficients. The second column can be derived by expressing the various inputs into manufacturing as a proportion of total manufacturing output, and likewise for services to obtain the third column. Hence we have:

$$A = \begin{bmatrix} 0.1 & 0.3 & 0.2 \\ 0.2 & 0.1 & 0.25 \\ 0.1 & 0.2 & 0.05 \end{bmatrix}$$

and

$$(I - A) = \begin{bmatrix} 0.9 & -0.3 & -0.2 \\ -0.2 & 0.9 & -0.25 \\ -0.1 & -0.2 & 0.95 \end{bmatrix}$$

The matrix of co-factors of $I - A$ and the determinant of $I - A$ are given respectively by:

$$C = \begin{bmatrix} 0.805 & 0.215 & 0.130 \\ 0.325 & 0.835 & 0.210 \\ 0.255 & 0.265 & 0.750 \end{bmatrix}$$

$$\det.(I - A) = 0.9(0.805) - 0.3(0.215) - 0.2(0.130) = 0.634$$

Transposing the matrix of co-factors and multiplying the adjoint by a scalar equal to the reciprocal of $\det.(I - A)$, we have the Leontief inverse:

$$(I - A)^{-1} = \frac{1}{0.634} \begin{bmatrix} 0.805 & 0.325 & 0.255 \\ 0.215 & 0.835 & 0.265 \\ 0.130 & 0.210 & 0.750 \end{bmatrix}$$

The reader should check that if the above matrix is post-multiplied by the given column of final demands we do indeed end up with the last column of our original data on sectoral gross outputs.

10.5 STOCHASTIC MATRICES

A stochastic matrix is a non-negative matrix all of whose column sums are unity, with the element in row i column j measuring the probability of moving from state j to state i. All possible transitions from one state to another are accounted for, so every column must add up to one. Its dominant eigenvalue (Frobenius root) must, therefore, be equal to unity.

Example 10.5

Assume that there are *100,000* individuals participating in a particular local labour market. If an individual is employed in the current period, there is a probability of *0.9* that he or she will still be employed in the next period, and a probability of *0.1* that he or she will have become unemployed. For an individual who is unemployed in the current period there is a probability of *0.4* that he or she will have found employment, and a probability of *0.6* that the unemployment spell will continue. The stochastic matrix, therefore, takes the following form:

$$P = \begin{bmatrix} 0.9 & 0.4 \\ 0.1 & 0.6 \end{bmatrix}$$

We wish to find the equilibrium rate of unemployment in this local labour market. This will occur when the flows into and out of unemployment are equal to each other. In such circumstances, the number of workers employed and unemployed in successive periods will be unchanging. We need to find the vector x which satisfies the following equation:

$$Px = x$$

We may obviously write the above equation as:

$$(P - I)x = 0$$

Unity is clearly an eigenvalue of P. Since $(P - I)$ is a singular matrix, there is only one independent equation, which we may express as:

$$-0.1x_1 + 0.4x_2 = 0$$

where x_1 is the equilibrium number of employed workers and x_2 the equilibrium number of unemployed workers. We must, therefore, have $x_1 = 4x_2$. However, we also know the overall size of the labour force. Since $x_1 + x_2 = 100,000$, we must have $x_1 = 80,000$ and $x_2 = 20,000$; the overall unemployment rate is, therefore *20* per cent.

We shall draw upon the concept of a stochastic matrix in Chapter 22 where we discuss simultaneous difference equations. The solution to such equations will enable us to find the numbers of employed and unemployed workers in each time period, and not just the long-run equilibrium values of these variables.

10.6 SUMMARY AND CONCLUSIONS

In this final chapter on linear algebra, we have been looking at non-negative square matrices, which are matrices whose elements are all non-negative. We have introduced the concept of an indecomposable matrix and discussed the important properties which are possessed by such matrices. Important applications of non-negative square matrices in economics include the matrix of technical input–output coefficients. We have provided a discussion of the basics of input–output economics, and have shown that, given the technology is viable, if the input–output coefficients matrix is an indecomposable matrix, then all the elements of the Leontief inverse will be positive. The implications of this are straightforward: even if we wish to meet a final demand vector which includes only one good, say bread, we shall have to produce positive quantities of all the goods the economy produces. All other goods are needed, either directly or indirectly in order for bread to be made available to consumers. Again assuming a viable technology, if the matrix of input–output coefficients is decomposable, then the Leontief inverse will be a non-negative matrix, and for some goods to be made available to consumers, it will not be necessary to produce a gross output vector which contains positive quantities of all the economy's goods.

Another important non-negative square matrix is a stochastic matrix whose elements are transition probabilities, the probabilities of moving from one state of the world to another, and whose column sums are all unity. The long-run equilibrium proportions of the relevant population falling into a particular state can easily be found by finding the eigenvector associated with the dominant eigenvalue (Frobenius root). The more difficult topic of deriving the precise time-path for the numbers in each state is a subject for discussion in the final chapter of the book.

10.7 EXERCISES

10.1 (a) (i) Calculate the eigenvalues of the following matrix:

$$A = \begin{bmatrix} 2 & 1 \\ 0 & 6 \end{bmatrix}$$

(ii) Show that A satisfies its own characteristic equation.

(iii) Calculate the eigenvalues of A^2, checking that they are indeed equal to the square of your earlier answers.

10.2 Which of the following matrices are indecomposable?

$$\text{(i)} \begin{bmatrix} 4 & 1 & 8 \\ 3 & 4 & 0 \\ 1 & 0 & 6 \end{bmatrix} \quad \text{(ii)} \begin{bmatrix} 7 & 9 & 0 \\ 2 & 1 & 0 \\ 3 & 0 & 5 \end{bmatrix}$$

$$\text{(iii)} \begin{bmatrix} 5 & 1 & 2 \\ 0 & 0 & 0 \\ 4 & 3 & 6 \end{bmatrix} \quad \text{(iv)} \begin{bmatrix} 0 & 3 & 0 \\ 0 & 0 & 8 \\ 2 & 0 & 0 \end{bmatrix}$$

10.3 (a) Complete example 10.2 on pages 156–157 by obtaining the eigenvectors associated with the other two eigenvalues, and show that they are not non-negative.

(b) Now set $\mu = 5$, and then find the inverse of $(\mu I - A)$.

(c) Set $\mu = 4$, and then find the inverse of $(\mu I - A)$.

10.4 (a) Using the above approach shown in example 10.3 on pages 159–160, write out the infinite series showing how much corn will have to be produced to make available one unit of steel for final demand purposes. What is the limiting value of the sum of the terms in this series?

(b) Obtain the infinite series showing how much steel will have to be produced to make available one unit of steel for final demand purposes. What is the limiting value of the sum of the terms in this series?

10.5 (a) Given the following matrix of input–output coefficients and vector of final demands

$$A = \begin{bmatrix} 0 & 0.25 & 0 \\ 0.1 & 0 & 0.4 \\ 0.3 & 0.15 & 0 \end{bmatrix}, \quad d = \begin{bmatrix} 500 \\ 1000 \\ 750 \end{bmatrix}$$

(i) Derive the Leontief inverse.

(ii) Obtain the gross output vector it will be necessary to produce in order to meet the final demand vector.

(iii) Explain in this case why A is an indecomposable matrix.

(iv) If one unit of the first good requires 2 hours of labour time for its production, one unit of the second good requires 5 hours of labour time for its production, and one unit of the third good requires 1 hour of labour time, how many hours of labour time are needed to meet the vector of final demands.

(b) Which of the following matrices of technical input–output coefficients are indecomposable?

$$\text{(i)} \ A = \begin{bmatrix} 0.2 & 0 \\ 0.3 & 0.15 \end{bmatrix} \quad \text{(ii)} \ A = \begin{bmatrix} 0 & 0.2 \\ 0.25 & 0 \end{bmatrix}$$

$$\text{(iii)} \ A = \begin{bmatrix} 0.2 & 0.1 & 0 \\ 0 & 0.2 & 0.25 \\ 0.05 & 0 & 0.2 \end{bmatrix} \quad \text{(iv)} \ A = \begin{bmatrix} 0.2 & 0 & 0.3 \\ 0.1 & 0.2 & 0.1 \\ 0.4 & 0 & 0 \end{bmatrix}$$

$$\text{(v)} \ A = \begin{bmatrix} 0.05 & 0 & 0.2 & 0 \\ 0.1 & 0.3 & 0.25 & 0.2 \\ 0.4 & 0 & 0.05 & 0 \\ 0.2 & 0.05 & 0.25 & 0.1 \end{bmatrix}$$

(c) For case (iv) in (b) above, calculate the Leontief inverse. Show that both x_1 and x_3 are independent of d_2.

10.6 (a) Find the eigenvector associated with the dominant eigenvalue of the following matrix:

$$P = \begin{bmatrix} 0.9 & 0.2 & 0.15 \\ 0.1 & 0.5 & 0.15 \\ 0 & 0.3 & 0.7 \end{bmatrix}$$

(b) (i) Find the eigenvalues of the matrix P.

$$P = \begin{bmatrix} 0.8 & 0.2 & 0.05 \\ 0.1 & 0.75 & 0.05 \\ 0.1 & 0.05 & 0.9 \end{bmatrix}$$

(ii) Obtain the eigenvector associated with the largest eigenvalue of P.

(iii) What is distinctive about the eigenvector associated with the largest eigenvalue of P?

CHAPTER
ELEVEN
AN INTRODUCTION TO DIFFERENTIAL CALCULUS

11.1 INTRODUCTION

This chapter provides an introduction to differential calculus. In economic analysis marginal concepts play a key role. In the theory of the consumer, the student is familiar with such concepts as the marginal utility of a good such as apples: the increase in the consumer's utility gained from consuming an additional apple; or the marginal rate of substitution between a pair of goods, say apples and bananas: the number of additional apples a consumer would require for giving up one banana in order to remain as well off as she was prior to the transaction. On the production side, one comes across the concept of the marginal product of a factor of production: the increase in output that results when a firm employs an additional unit of labour services. All economics students are aware that a necessary condition for profits to be maximised by a firm is that marginal revenue should equal marginal cost: profits will be unchanged if the production of an additional unit of output adds exactly the same amount to the firm's revenues as it does to the firm's costs. Note in each of the cases we have discussed above, we have referred to a discrete change in the variable under consideration. The consumer ate another apple or gave up one banana for a given quantity of apples; the firm employed another worker or produced another unit of output.

There are close connections between the concept of the margin and differential calculus. In the latter we are concerned with the rate of change of a variable with respect to another variable. A firm's total revenue depends upon how much output it sells; its total costs on how much it produces. What the differential calculus will enable us to do is evaluate the impact that a very small change in the quantity sold (amount produced) will have on the firm's total revenue (total cost). In the calculus we deal not with discrete changes in some variable which then impinge on a further variable, but we consider the impact of infinitesimally small changes in the variable, and evaluate the impact that such a change has on the dependent variable. We shall be defining marginal cost as the slope of the total cost function evaluated at a particular output level; similarly marginal revenue will be taken as the slope of the total revenue function, again evaluated at a particular level of output rather than as the change in cost of revenue which results from a unit change in output.

The chapter is structured as follows. In Section 11.2 we begin by showing that the derivative of a function measures the slope of the function at a point. We discuss the conditions which must be met for the slope of a function to be defined at a particular point. We shall see that this requires the function to be both smooth and continuous. Having identified the conditions under which the derivative of a function is defined, we then proceed in Section 11.3 to show by first principles how the derivatives of some simple functions can be found. In Section 11.4 we examine some basic rules of differentiation: the power rule, the sum/difference rule, the product rule, the quotient rule, the chain rule and the inverse function rule. We introduce into the discussion higher-order derivatives, and then go onto look at the concept of concavity and convexity as applied to the function of a single variable. Some further rules are dealt with in Section 11.5 where the derivatives of exponential, logarithmically and some trigonometric functions are analysed. The chapter ends with a summary of results.

11.2 THE CONCEPT OF A DERIVATIVE

Consider the following function:
$$y = f(x)$$

Let the value of x change by an amount Δx, then the new value of the function will be given by:
$$y + \Delta y = f(x + \Delta x)$$

and the increase in the value of the function is found by subtracting the first equation from the second one to obtain:
$$\Delta y = f(x + \Delta x) - f(x)$$

If we now divide both sides of the above equation by Δx, we obtain what is known as the difference quotient, the ratio of the change in y to the change in x.
$$\frac{\Delta y}{\Delta x} = \frac{f(x + \Delta x) - f(x)}{\Delta x}$$

We depict the difference quotient in Fig. 11.1. Assume the original value of x if OA and the associated value of the function is given by the vertical distance AC. Now increase x to OB, and the new value of the function is given by the vertical distance BD. The difference quotient is,

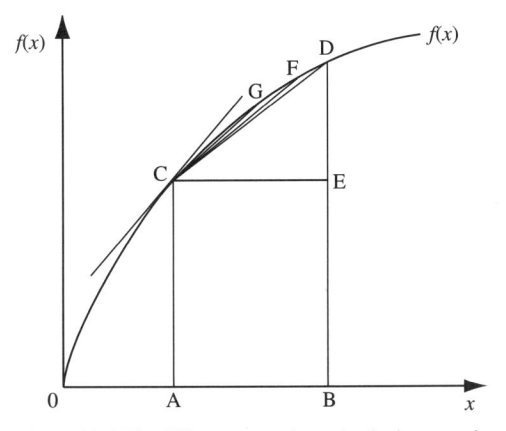

Figure 11.1 The difference quotient. As the increase in x starting from A becomes smaller and smaller, then the value of the difference quotient becomes larger. As we move from A to B, it is given by the slope of CD. but as we make the increase approach zero, then we obtain the derivative of the function with respect to x. This is given by the slope of the tangent drawn to the function at C.

therefore, given by the ratio of *BD–AC* to *OB–OA*, i.e. it is equal to the slope of the line *CD* which is given by *DE/CE*. Note that as long as the function is not linear, the value of the difference quotient will depend upon how large is the postulated change in *x*. If we now let the change in *x* become smaller and smaller, what will happen to the value of the difference quotient? Clearly in our particular example, the slope of the straight line drawn from the point *C* to points such as *F* and *G* which lie on the function will become steeper and steeper. In the limit as we make the change in *x* infinitesimally small, then the line whose slope we will have to measure in order to obtain the value of the difference quotient will be that of a tangent drawn to the function at the point *C*. We define the derivative of $y = f(x)$ with respect to *x* as the limiting value of the difference quotient as Δx approaches zero. In symbols, we have:

$$\frac{dy}{dx} = \lim_{\Delta x \to 0} \frac{\Delta y}{\Delta x}$$

The symbols for the derivative we read as *dy* by *dx*. An alternative and highly useful symbol for the derivative is $f'(x)$. The derivative we have obtained is the first derivative of the function. We shall consider the case of higher-order derivatives later in this chapter.

The first derivative of a function evaluated at a particular point measures, as we have seen in our diagrammatic analysis, the slope of the function at that point. Before we proceed any further, we must first consider the conditions which must be satisfied for us to be able to find the derivative of a function at a particular point. Basically, these conditions must be such that the slope of the function is indeed defined at the point we are interested in. Let us call it *x**. For this to be the case, the function in the neighbourhood of *x** must be both continuous and smooth. We can easily give an intuitive definition of continuity: consider depicting on a diagram how $f(x)$ varies as starting from a value of *x* which is smaller than *x** we increase *x* and move through *x** to values of *x* larger than *x**. If in plotting this function our pencil never leaves the paper, if there are no gaps anywhere, then the function is continuous in the neighbourhood of *x**.

More formally, we can say that the function will be continuous in the vicinity of *x** if the following conditions are met:

1. *x** must lie in the domain of the function;
2. the limiting value of the function should be the same whether we approach *x** from the values of *x* smaller than or larger than *x**, with the former limit being known as the left-hand-side limit, and the latter as the right-hand-side limit;
3. both the left-hand-side and right-hand-side limits should equal the value of the function at $x = x^*$.

Consider the following function:

$$y = f(x) = 0 \text{ for } x < 10$$
$$= -8 + 2x \text{ for } x \geq 10$$

We depict this function in Fig. 11.2. It is clear that this function is not continuous at the point $x = 10$, though *10* is a value of *x* for which the function applies. Consider what happens as *x* approaches *10* from values of *x* smaller than *10*. For $x = 9, f(x) = 0$, for $x = 9.9, f(x) = 0$, for $x = 9.99, f(x) = 0$ and so on. The left-hand limit is equal to *0*. Whereas if *x* approaches *10* from values larger than *10*, we have: for $x = 11, f(x) = 14$, for $x = 10.1, f(x) = 12.2$, for $x = 10.01$, $f(x) = 12.02$ and so on. The right-hand limit is equal to *12*. The function suddenly jumps in value from *0* to *12* as *x* reaches *10* starting from values less than *10*, and suddenly falls in value from *12* to *0* as the value of *x* just falls below *10*.

AN INTRODUCTION TO DIFFERENTIAL CALCULUS 169

$y = f(x) = 0$ for $x > 10$
$= -8 + 2x$ for $x \geq 10$

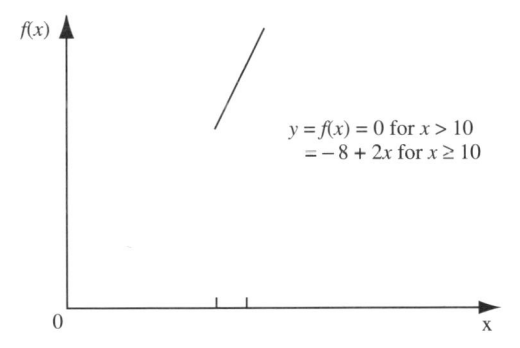

Figure 11.2 A discontinuous function. As the value of x reaches 10, there is a sudden jump in the value of the function.

An economic example of a function similar to the one we have been discussing might be that of a competitive firm's supply function. The firm is unwilling to enter the market until the price has reached a particular level, but once this level is reached, the firm is willing to supply a positive quantity. So for our example: below a price of *10*, the firm supplies nothing at all, but once the price has risen to *10*, the firm is willing to enter the market and supply *12* units of its output.

Consider the following function:

$$y = f(x) = x^2 - 12x + 50 \text{ for } x \neq 6$$
$$= 10 \text{ for } x = 6$$

which is shown in Fig. 11.3, This function is not continuous at $x = 6$, despite the fact that the left-hand side and right-hand side limits are the same. The reader should check that these two limits are both equal to *14*, but this value is not equal to the value of the function at this point which is equal to *10*. So, again if we plot the function, we would have to lift our pencil from the paper as x reached the value of 6. There would once again be a discrete jump in the value of the function as we reached the point $x = 6$, whether the direction of the move was from values smaller or larger than 6.

Continuity by itself, however, is not sufficient for us to be able to differentiate a function at a particular point. In addition, we require the function to be smooth at this point: it must not have a sharp point at x^* for us to be able to differentiate the function at this point.

Consider the following function:

$$y = f(x) = 0 \text{ for } x < 10$$
$$= -10 + 2x \text{ for } x \geq 10$$

$y = f(x)$
$= x^2 - 12x + 50$ for $x \neq 6$
$= 10$ for $x = 6$

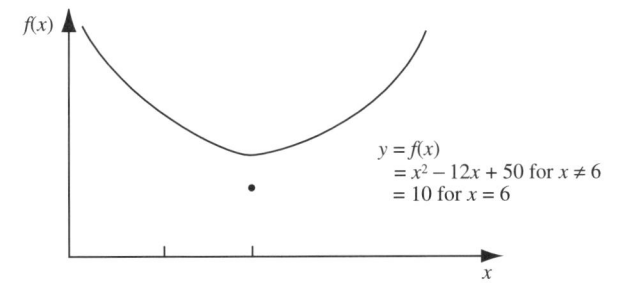

Figure 11.3 Another discontinuous function. In this case both the left-hand side and right-hand side limits as x approaches 6 are the same and equal to 14, whereas the value of the function at this point is 10.

$f(x)$

$y = f(x) = 0$ for $0 < x < 10$
     $= -10 + 2x$ for $x \geq 10$

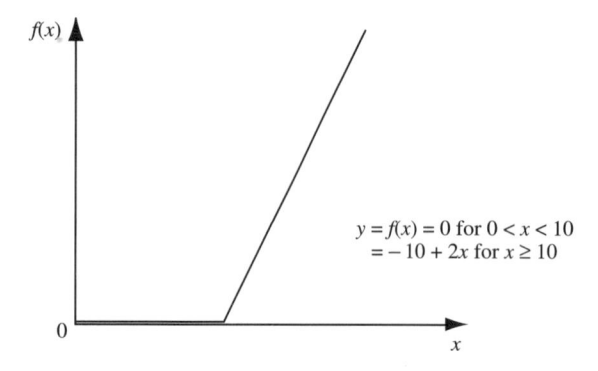

Figure 11.4 A kinked function. The function has a kink at $x = 10$. We cannot define the slope at this point and hence the derivative is not defined at this point.

We have slightly modified our first function in order to make it continuous, and it is depicted in Fig. 11.4. Note the left-hand side and right-hand side limits are both equal to *0* as x approaches the value of *10*. In addition this limiting value of the function is also equal to the value of the function when $x = 10$. However, if we were to plot the function on a diagram, we would easily see that the function has a kink in it at the point $x = 10$. The function gives rise to a horizontal line which coincides with the x axis until x exceeds *10* when we have an upward sloping straight line whose slope is equal to *2*. It is not possible to construct a unique tangent to the function at the point $x = 10$. Any line whose slope is not less than zero and not greater than *2* can be drawn such that it touches the point of the kink. The slope is, therefore, not defined at $x = 10$, even though in this case, the function is continuous at this point. The derivative of this function can be found at all other points which lie in the domain of the function except for the point $x = 10$.

Finally, consider the case of the following function:

$$y = f(x) = 100x^{-1} \text{ for } x \neq 0$$

which is depicted in Fig. 11.5. If we were to plot this function we would find that we would obtain two rectangular hyperbolas, i.e. curves in which any rectangle under the curve has the same area: one in the positive quadrant and one in the negative quadrant. The function is clearly continuous and smooth for any positive value of x and for any negative value of x, but it is not defined for $x = 0$. We can therefore differentiate the function at any value of x apart from $x = 0$. Note too that as x approaches zero, the left-hand side limit is equal to minus infinity, and the right-hand side limit is equal to plus infinity.

$f(x)$

$y = f(x) = 100x^{-1}$

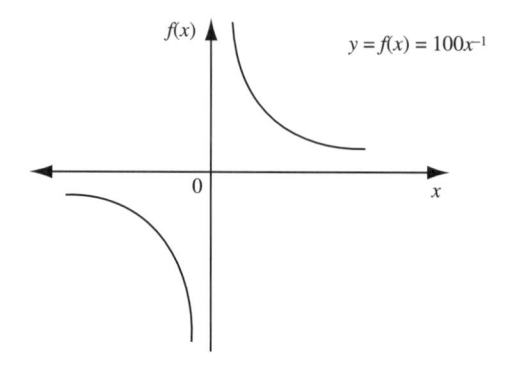

Figure 11.5 A discontinuity at $x = 0$. As x approaches 0 from values greater than 0, the value of the function approaches infinity. As x approaches 0 from values less than 0 the value of the function approaches minus infinity.

11.3 DIFFERENTIATION USING FIRST PRINCIPLES

We shall begin our discussion of the rules by first showing how to obtain the derivatives of some particular functions from first principles. We deal firstly with the case of $y = f(x) = x^2$. We allow x to change by an amount Δx and calculate the new value of the function:

$$y + \Delta y = (x + \Delta x)^2 = x^2 + 2x\Delta x + (\Delta x)^2$$

Hence the increase in the value of the function is given by:

$$\Delta y = 2x\Delta x + (\Delta x)^2$$

Dividing by Δx, we obtain the difference quotient:

$$\frac{\Delta y}{\Delta x} = 2x + \Delta x$$

and taking the limit as Δx approaches zero, we obtain the derivative of x:

$$\frac{dy}{dx} = 2x$$

Now consider the case where $y = f(x) = x^3$. Proceeding as before, we let x change by an amount Δx and then calculate the new value of the function:

$$y + \Delta y = (x + \Delta x)^3 = x^3 + 3x^2\Delta x + 3x(\Delta x)^2 + (\Delta x)^3$$

The increase in the value of the function is, therefore, given by:

$$\Delta y = 3x^2\Delta x + 3x(\Delta x)^2 + (\Delta x)^3$$

Dividing by Δx we obtain the difference quotient:

$$\frac{\Delta y}{\Delta x} = 3x^2 + 3x\Delta x + (\Delta x)^2$$

and taking the limit as Δx approaches zero yields the derivative:

$$\frac{dy}{dx} = 3x^2$$

For our third case, consider $y = f(x) = x^{-1}$. Repeating our standard procedure, we obtain the following expression for the increase in the value of the function:

$$\Delta y = \frac{1}{x + \Delta x} - \frac{1}{x}$$
$$= \frac{x - \Delta x - x}{x(x + \Delta x)} = \frac{-\Delta x}{x^2 + x\Delta x}$$

Divide by Δx to obtain the difference quotient, we have:

$$\frac{\Delta y}{\Delta x} = \frac{-1}{x^2 + x\Delta x}$$

Once again taking the limit as Δx approaches zero yields the derivative in this case:

$$\frac{dy}{dx} = \frac{-1}{x^2} = -x^{-2}$$

11.4 SOME SIMPLE RULES OF DIFFERENTIATION

The power rule of differentiation

The three examples which we looked at in Section 11.3 suggest a rule, which is known as the power rule of differentiation

$$\text{if } y = x^n, \text{ then } \frac{dy}{dx} = nx^{n-1}$$

This rule applies not only to positive and negative integer values of n, but also to fractional values of n. So if we have $y = f(x) = x^{1/2}$, then

$$\frac{dy}{dx} = \frac{1}{2}x^{-1/2}$$

Using the power rule, it is clear that the derivatives of a constant is equal to zero. Consider the case where $y = f(x) = a$. We may obviously express this as

$$y = f(x) = a = ax^0$$

and applying the power rule, we have:

$$\frac{dy}{dx} = 0ax^{-1} = 0$$

It is also the case that the derivative of a linear function of x is a constant, independent of the value of x. Given $y = f(x) = ax$. Then the exponent on x in this case is unity, and application of the power rule yields:

$$\frac{dy}{dx} = ax^1 = ax^0 = a$$

The sum/difference rule of differentiation

Our next rule is particularly straightforward: it states that the derivative of a function that is the sum(difference) of two functions is just equal to the sum(difference) of the derivatives of the two separate functions. We have:

$$\text{if } y = f(x) \pm g(x), \text{ then } \frac{dy}{dx} = f'(x) \pm g'(x)$$

For example, assume

$$y = x^4 + 6x^{-1/3}$$

$$\text{then } \frac{dy}{dx} = 4x^3 - 2x^{-4/3}$$

$$\text{if } y = 8x^{-2} - 2x^{-5/2}$$

$$\text{then } \frac{dy}{dx} = -16x^{-3} + 5x^{-7/2}$$

The product rule of differentiation

Assume we have $y = uv$ where $u = u(x)$ and $v = v(x)$; in words, y is the product of two functions which are, in turn, each functions of x. We shall derive how to differentiate functions of this form from first principles. Let the value of x change by an amount Δx, then we must have:

$$u + \Delta u = u(x + \Delta x) \quad and \quad v + \Delta v = v(x + \Delta x)$$

and the new value of y is, therefore,

$$y + \Delta y = (u + \Delta u)(v + \Delta v)$$

The increase in the value of y is

$$\Delta y = v\Delta u + u\Delta v$$

and dividing by Δx gives us the difference quotient:

$$\frac{\Delta y}{\Delta x} = v\frac{\Delta u}{\Delta x} + u\frac{\Delta v}{\Delta x}$$

We now take the limiting value of the difference quotient as Δx approaches zero and the derivative in this case is, therefore, given by:

$$\frac{dy}{dx} = v\frac{du}{dx} + u\frac{dv}{dx}$$

This is known as the product rule of differentiation. We work through some examples of this rule.

$$y = (x^6 + 2x^3)(x^{-1} - 8x^{1/2})$$

We first let

$$u = x^6 + 2x^3 \quad and \quad v = x^{-1} - 8x^{1/2}$$

Then differentiating both u and v with respect to x, we obtain by applying the power and sum(difference) rules:

$$\frac{du}{dx} = 6x^5 + 6x^2 \quad and \quad \frac{dv}{dx} = -x^{-2} - 4x^{-1/2}$$

We, then, have by the product rule:

$$\frac{dy}{dx} = (x^{-1} - 8x^{1/2})(6x^5 + 6x^2) + (x^6 + 2x^3)(-x^{-2} - 4x^{-1/2})$$

$$= 6x^4 + 6x - 48x^{11/2} - 48x^{5/2} - x^4 - 4x^{11/2} - 2x - 8x^{5/2}$$

$$= 5x^4 + 4x - 52x^{11/2} - 56x^{5/2}$$

The reader should check the solution by multiplying out the two bracketed terms in the original function, and then differentiating each term separately with respect to x. This will obviously yield the same solution for the derivative as our application of the power rule has done.

The links between price, marginal revenue and elasticity of demand

We now provide an economic application of the power rule. Let x represent output and p price or average revenue. Average revenue is a function of output: $p = p(x)$. Then the total revenue function is given by:

$$TR(x) = xp(x)$$

Let $u = x$ and $v = p(x)$, then

$$\frac{du}{dx} = 1 \quad \text{and} \quad \frac{dv}{dx} = p'(x)$$

We therefore obtain on applying the product rule of differential calculus:

$$\frac{dTR}{dx} = p(x) + xp'(x)$$

$$= p(x)\left[1 + \frac{x}{p(x)}\frac{dp}{dx}\right]$$

The derivative of total revenue with respect to output is known to economists as marginal revenue. Furthermore, the own-price elasticity of demand for the good is given by the reciprocal of the second term inside the square brackets. Remember that economists define the own-price elasticity of demand as the ratio of the proportionate change in quantity demanded to the proportionate change in price. For a discrete change in the price, we would be measuring

$$\frac{\Delta x}{x} \div \frac{\Delta p}{p} = \frac{\Delta x}{\Delta p}\frac{p}{x}$$

However, if we make the change in price infinitesimally small, then we have the point elasticity of demand:

$$\eta_d = \lim_{\Delta p \to 0} \frac{\Delta x}{\Delta p}\frac{p}{x} = \frac{dx}{dp}\frac{p}{x}$$

Hence we have the following relationship between marginal revenue, price and own-price elasticity of demand:

$$MR = p\left[1 - \frac{1}{|\eta_d|}\right]$$

where we have taken the absolute value of the elasticity of demand. Note that marginal revenue is positive if the elasticity of demand is greater than unity, zero if the elasticity is unity, and negative if the elasticity is less than unity.

The quotient rule

Assume we have $y = u/v$ where $u = u(x)$ and $v = v(x)$; in words, y is the ratio of two functions which are, in turn, each functions of x. We shall derive how to differentiate functions of this type from first principles. Let the value of x change by an amount Δx, then u will change by an amount Δu, and v by an amount Δv, then we must have:

$$y + \Delta y = \frac{u + \Delta u}{v + \Delta v}$$

and the increase in the value of y is given by:

$$\Delta y = \frac{u + \Delta u}{v + \Delta v} - \frac{u}{v}$$

$$= \frac{uv + v\Delta u - uv - u\Delta v}{v(v + \Delta v)}$$

$$= \frac{v\Delta u - u\Delta v}{v^2 + v\Delta v}$$

Dividing by Δx, we obtain the difference quotient:

$$\frac{\Delta y}{\Delta x} = \frac{v\frac{\Delta u}{\Delta x} - u\frac{\Delta v}{\Delta x}}{v^2 + v\Delta v}$$

If we now let the change in x become infinitesimally small, we obtain the derivative of this function with respect to x:

$$\frac{dy}{dx} = \lim_{\Delta x \to 0} \frac{\Delta y}{\Delta x} = \frac{v\frac{du}{dx} - u\frac{dv}{dx}}{v^2}$$

Note that as the change in x becomes infinitesimally small, then so does the change in v, thereby leaving us with simply the term in v^2 in the denominator of the expression for the derivative.

The rule we have derived here is known as the quotient rule. To illustrate the usefulness of the rule, consider the following example:

$$y = f(x) = \frac{5x^2 + 2x^{-1}}{x^3 + 2x^{1/2}}$$

We define:

$$u = 5x^2 + 2x^{-1} \quad \text{and} \quad v = x^3 + 2x^{1/2}$$

Then differentiating both u and v with respect to x, we obtain by applying the power and sum(difference) rules:

$$\frac{du}{dx} = 10x - 2x^{-2} \quad \text{and} \quad \frac{dv}{dx} = 3x^2 + x^{-1/2}$$

Making use of the quotient rule, we then obtain:

$$\frac{dy}{dx} = \frac{(x^3 + 2x^{1/2})(10x - 2x^{-2}) - (5x^2 + 2x^{-1})(3x^2 + x^{-1/2})}{(x^3 + 2x^{1/2})^2}$$

We now provide an economic application of the quotient rule. Assume that total cost (TC) is a function of output (x). Then average cost is obtained by dividing total cost by output. Hence, we have:

$$AC = \frac{TC}{x} = \frac{c(x)}{x}$$

We apply the quotient rule by first letting $u = c(x)$ and $v = x$.

Then differentiating both u and v with respect to x yields:

$$\frac{du}{dx} = c'(x) \quad \text{and} \quad \frac{dv}{dx} = 1$$

Then applying the quotient rule, we have:

$$\frac{dAC}{dx} = \frac{xc'(x) - c(x)}{x^2}$$

Now divide numerator and denominator by x to obtain:

$$\frac{dAC}{dx} = \frac{c'(x) - \frac{c(x)}{x}}{x}$$

Note, however, that the derivative of total cost with respect to output is equal to $c'(x)$, and this is what economists call marginal cost (MC). We may therefore write the derivative of average cost with respect to output as:

$$\frac{dAC}{dx} = \frac{MC - AC}{x}$$

We shall return to this result later when we have discussed maximisation and minimisation of functions of a single variable.

The function of a function or chain rule

Consider a situation in which y is a function of z and in turn z is a function of x. Then y is a function of x. Changes in the value of x lead to changes in the value of z, which in turn then lead to changes in the value of y. Given

$$y = f(z) \quad \text{and} \quad z = g(x), \quad \text{then } y = f(g(x))$$

The chain rule or function of a function rule then states that

$$\frac{dy}{dx} = \frac{dy}{dz}\frac{dz}{dx} = f'(z)g'(x)$$

This is a very useful rule, and it enables us to differentiate quite complicated functions easily. To illustrate its usefulness, let us work through a number of examples where this rule can be applied. How can we find the derivatives of the following function?

$$y = (x^3 + 10x)^7$$

One approach would be to expand the expression on the right-hand side and then differentiate each term separately, but this would be an extremely tedious and time-consuming procedure. It is much more straightforward to apply the function of a function rule. We start out by letting

$$z = x^3 + 10x$$

Hence

$$y = z^7$$

We now differentiate y with respect to z, and z with respect to x to obtain:

$$\frac{dy}{dz} = 7z^6 = 7(x^3 + 10x)^6$$

$$\frac{dz}{dx} = 3x^2 + 10$$

If we then form the product of the two derivatives, we have:

$$\frac{dy}{dx} = 7(x^3 + 10x)^6(3x^2 + 10)$$

Assume we have

$$y = f(x) = (3x^2 + x^{-1})^{1/2}$$

Then we let z equal the term inside the brackets, from which it follows that

$$y = z^{1/2} \quad \text{and} \quad z = (3x^2 + x^{-1})$$

Once again, differentiating y with respect to z and z with respect to x yields:

$$\frac{dy}{dz} = \frac{1}{2}z^{-1/2} = \frac{1}{2}(3x^2 + x^{-1})^{-1/2}$$

$$\frac{dz}{dx} = 6x - x^{-2}$$

Multiplying these two derivatives together, we obtain the derivative of y with respect to x:

$$\frac{dy}{dx} = \frac{1}{2}(3x^2 + x^{-1})^{-1/2}(6x - x^{-2})$$

Assume a firm's short-run production function and average revenue function are given respectively by:

$$x = f(N) = 100N^{3/4}$$

$$p = g(x) = 40x^{-1/2}$$

where x is output, N the input of labour services and p the price of the product. We wish to investigate how the firm's revenue will vary as it changes its employment of labour services. Multiplying price by output, we obtain total revenue (TR). We now differentiate total revenue with respect to output to obtain marginal revenue, and differentiate output with respect to the labour input in order to obtain the marginal product of labour:

$$\frac{dTR}{dx} = 20x^{-1/2}$$

$$\frac{dx}{dN} = 75N^{-1/4}$$

The marginal revenue product of labour is then given by the product of the marginal revenue of output and the marginal (physical) product of labour:

$$\frac{dTR}{dN} = \frac{dTR}{dx}\frac{dx}{dN}$$

$$= (20x^{-1/2})(75N^{-1/4})$$

$$= 1500(100N^{3/4})^{-1/2}N^{-1/4}$$

$$= 150N^{-5/8}$$

11.5 CONCAVITY AND CONVEXITY

Higher-order derivatives

Given a differentiable function

$$y = f(x)$$

Then we have seen that the first derivative of this function evaluated at some point x^* measures the slope of the function at this particular point. If we now differentiate the first derivative with respect to x, we obtain the second derivative, the symbol for which is

$$\frac{d^2y}{dx^2} = f''(x)$$

This measures the rate of change of the first derivative; if we were to plot on a diagram the first derivative of x with respect to x as a function of x, then the second derivative is measuring the slope of this function. Consider the following example:

$$y = f(x) = 100x^{1/2}$$

Then if we differentiate this function twice with respect to x, we have:

$$\frac{dy}{dx} = 50x^{-1/2}$$

$$\frac{d^2y}{dx^2} = -25x^{-3/2}$$

Taking the positive value of the square root of x, the first derivative is always positive and the second derivative is always negative for positive x. If we were to plot the function on a diagram, we would find that as x increases y increases, but at a diminishing rate.

Now consider the case where

$$y = f(x) = 50x^{-1} \text{ for } x > 0$$

Then differentiating twice with respect to x yields:

$$\frac{dy}{dx} = -50x^{-2}$$

$$\frac{d^2y}{dx} = 100x^{-3}$$

In this second example, the first derivative is always negative and the second derivative is always positive. The function gives rise to a rectangular hyperbola in the positive quadrant: the function is downward sloping, but as x increases the slope of the function becomes less steep.

Our two examples have an infinite number of non-zero higher-order derivatives. If we differentiate the two second-order derivatives, we obtain:

(a) $\dfrac{d^3y}{dx^3} = 37.5x^{-5/2}$

(b) $\dfrac{d^3y}{dx^3} = -300x^{-4}$

We may also differentiate these third-order derivatives:

$$\text{(a)} \quad \frac{d^4 y}{dx^4} = -93.75 x^{-7/2}$$

$$\text{(b)} \quad \frac{d^4 y}{dx^4} = 1200 x^{-5}$$

and so on indefinitely.

The following function, on the other hand, has only a finite number of non-zero higher-order derivatives:

$$y = f(x) = x^3$$

Differentiating this function successively with respect to x yields:

$$\frac{dy}{dx} = 3x^2$$

$$\frac{d^2 y}{dx^2} = 6x$$

$$\frac{d^3 y}{dx^3} = 6$$

$$\frac{d^4 x}{dx^4} = 0$$

The fourth and all subsequent higher-order derivatives are zero.

Concave and convex functions

Consider a function $f(x)$ and assume that x, x' and x'' all lie in the domain of this function where

$$x = \alpha x' + (1-\alpha) x'' \text{ and } 1 \geq \alpha \geq 0$$

In words, x is just a weighted average of x' and x''. The function is defined to be concave if the following condition is met:

$$f(x) \geq \alpha f(x') + (1-\alpha) f(x'')$$

The function is strictly concave if

$$f(x) > \alpha f(x') + (1-\alpha) f(x'')$$

Convexity, on the other hand, requires the inequality sign to be reversed; $f(x)$, therefore, is convex if

$$f(x) \leq \alpha f(x') + (1-\alpha) f(x'')$$

whereas strict convexity requires

$$f(x) < \alpha f(x') + (1-\alpha) f(x'')$$

Consider the following function:

$$y = f(x) = x^2$$

Then $f(3) = 9$, $f(5) = 25$, $4 = (1/2)3 + (1/2)5$, $f(4) = 16$, $0.5f(3) + 0.5f(5) = 17$; so this function is strictly convex.

Whereas if we had

$$y = f(x) = x^{1/2}$$

Then $f(36) = 6$, $f(100) = 10$, $64 = (0.5625)36 + (0.4375)100$, $f(64) = 8$, $0.5625f(36) + (0.4375)f(100) = 7.75$; hence this function is strictly concave.

When the function we are dealing with is differentiable, then we may define concavity in the following way. A differentiable function is concave if for two points, x^* and x, which lie in the domain of the function, the following inequality is satisfied:

$$f(x) \leq f(x^*) + f'(x^*)(x - x^*)$$

and for strict concavity, we require a strong inequality ($<$). A differentiable function will be convex if

$$f(x) \geq f(x^*) + f'(x^*)(x - x^*)$$

and for strict convexity, we require a strong inequality ($>$).

In Figs. 11.6 and 11.7 we depict a strictly concave differentiable function and a strictly convex differentiable function. It is clear from Fig. 11.6 that $f(x')$ is equal to the vertical distance, Bx', that $f(x^*)$ is equal to the vertical distance Dx^*, $x' - x^*$ is equal to the horizontal distance DC, and the derivative of $f(x)$ with respect to x evaluated at $x = x^*$ is equal to AC/DC. It is then clear that $f(x')$ falls short of the value of $f(x^*) + f'(x^*)(x' - x^*)$ by the vertical distance AB. The function is strictly concave, and a sufficient condition for this to be the case is that the second derivative of $f(x)$ with respect to x be negative.

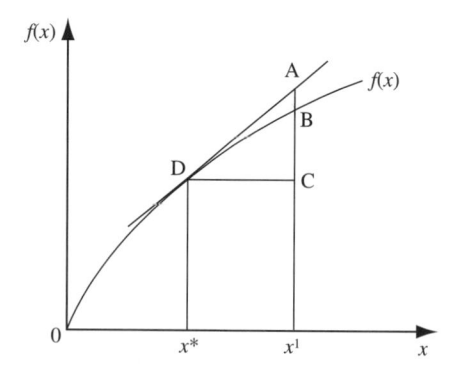

Figure 11.6 A strictly concave function $f(x')$ falls short of $f(x^*) + f'(x^*)(x' - x^*)$ by the distance AB.

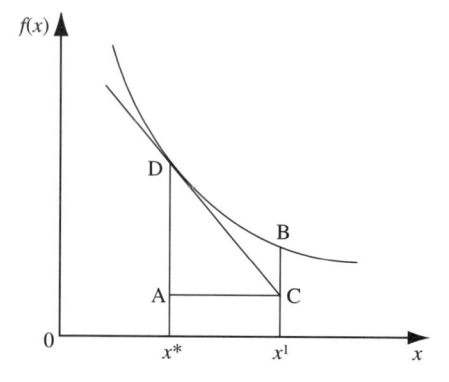

Figure 11.7 A strictly convex function $f(x')$ exceeds $f(x^*) + f'(x^*)(x' - x^*)$ by the distance BC.

Now turn to Fig. 11.7. It is clear that $f(x')$ is equal to the vertical distance, Bx', that $f(x^*)$ is equal to the vertical distance Dx^*, $x' - x^*$ is equal to the horizontal distance AC, and the derivative of $f(x)$ with respect to x evaluated at $x = x^*$ is equal to $-DA/AC$. It is then clear that $f(x)$ is larger than the value of $f(x^*) + f'(x^*)(x - x^*)$ by the vertical distance BC. The function is strictly convex, and a sufficient condition for this case to be so is that the second derivative of $f(x)$ with respect to x be positive.

11.6 SOME MORE RULES OF DIFFERENTIATION

The inverse function rule

Given a function $y = f(x)$, then if the first derivative of this function never changes its sign, i.e. is always either positive or negative, then the function is said to be monotonic. In these circumstances, we may also define the inverse function where x is a function of y. There will be a unique value of x associated with any particular value of y, given that the original function is monotonic. The inverse function rule states that the derivative of x with respect to y is simply the reciprocal of the derivative of y with respect to x.

$$x = f^{-1}(y) \quad \text{then} \quad \frac{dx}{dy} = \frac{1}{f'(x)}$$

We shall make use of this rule in our discussion of logarithmic differentiation.

The exponential rule

Let us assume that as an impecunious student, you have borrowed money from a particularly usurious moneylender, the rate of interest being *100* per cent per annum. Having borrowed an amount A, at the end of the year you will now owe an amount equal to $2A$. Now assume that instead of interest being levied once at the end of the year on the amount borrowed, interest is charged every six months at an annual rate of *100* per cent and is then compounded. How much will your debt then have accumulated to at the end of the year? In this case, you will owe $A(1 + 1/2)^2$. If interest were added to the account every four months and then compounded, then at the end of the year you would now owe $A(1 + 1/3)^3$. More generally, if interest were added n times each year and then compounded, by the end of the year your debt would have increased to $A(1 + 1/n)^n$. Let us now consider what happens to the value of $(1 + 1/n)^n$ as n becomes larger and larger:

n	$(1 + 1/n)^n$
100	2.704814
1000	2.716924
10000	2.718146
100000	2.718268
infinity	2.718281 ...

As n becomes larger and larger, we converge on the value 2.718281828... If you borrow £1 for a year at an annual rate of 100 per cent, then with the interest being continuously compounded at the end of the year you will owe almost £2.72. The limit of $(1 + 1/n)^n$ as n approaches infinity is a famous mathematical constant, the symbol for which is e.

If instead of the annual rate of interest being *100* per cent, it had been *10* per cent, then with continuous compounding, an amount A would have accumulated to $Ae^{0.1}$ after one year and to $Ae^{0.1t}$ after t years. More generally, if the interest rate is *100x*, an amount A would have accumulated to Ae^x after one year and to Ae^{xt} after t years.

We now take the opportunity to refresh the reader's memory on the rules relating to exponents.

1. The product of x to the power m and x raised to the power n is equal to x raised to the power $m + n$. To illustrate this rule, consider

$$y^4 \times y^2 = y \times y \times y \times y \times y \times y = y^6$$

2. The result of dividing x raised to the power m by x raised to the power n is x raised to the power $m - n$. To illustrate this rule, consider

$$y^4 \div y^2 = \frac{y \times y \times y \times y}{y \times y} = y^2$$

3. The result of raising x raised to the power m to the power n is x raised to the power mn. To illustrate this rule, consider

$$(y^4)^2 = (y \times y \times y \times y) \times (y \times y \times y \times y) = y^8$$

When y is an exponential function of x, then we have

$$y = f(x) = e^x$$

The derivative of this function is given by the exponential rule of differential calculus, which of all the rules of the differential calculus is the most straightforward. When $y = e^x$, then the derivative of this function is equal to the original function.

$$y = e^x, \text{ then } \frac{dy}{dx} = e^x$$

At this stage, we just state the rule, but after we have discussed the logarithmic rule of differentiation below, we shall return to it to discuss it more formally.

The chain rule can then be combined with the exponential rule in order to obtain the derivative of an exponential function where the exponent is itself a function of x. Consider the following example:

$$y = e^{x^2 + 3x + 5}$$

We adopt the standard procedure of letting

$$z = x^2 + 3x + 5$$

hence $y = e^z$

$$\frac{dy}{dz} = e^z = e^{x^2 + 3x + 5}$$

$$\frac{dz}{dx} = 2x + 3$$

and $\dfrac{dy}{dx} = (2x + 3)\, e^{x^2 + 3x + 5}$

The logarithmic rule

Assume two variables are related to each other in the following way:

$$x = b^y$$

then y is said to be the logarithm of x to base b. If b is equal to *10*, then the logarithm of *100* to base *10* is *2*. This clearly follows from the fact that the square of *10* is equal to *100*. The most useful base in analytical work is base e, logarithms to this base being known as natural logarithms or Napierian logarithms after John Napier, the famous Scottish mathematician, who first tabulated them.

Since a logarithm is an exponent, then the rules for operating on logarithms are simply those that apply to exponents. We briefly state these rules.

1. The logarithm of a product is equal to the sum of the logarithms of the components in the product:
$$\log_b(xy) = \log_b x + \log_b y$$

This follows from the fact that by the definition of a logarithm, we have:
$$x = b^{\log_b x} \text{ and } y = b^{\log_b y}$$
$$\text{hence } xy = b^{\log_b x + \log_b y}$$
$$\text{and on taking logs to base } b, \ \log_b(xy) = \log_b x + \log_b y$$

2. The logarithm of a quotient is equal to the logarithm of the variable in the numerator less the logarithm of the variable in the denominator.
$$\log_b(x/y) = \log_b x - \log_b y$$

This follows from the fact that we have:
$$x/y = \frac{b^{\log_b x}}{b^{\log_b y}} = b^{\log_b x - \log_b y}$$
$$\text{and on taking logs to base } b, \ \log_b(xy) = \log_b x - \log_b y$$

3. The logarithm of a variable raised to a power is equal to the product of the exponent and the logarithms of the variable.
$$\log_b(x^n) = n \log_b x$$

This follows from the fact that
$$x^n = (b^{\log_b x})^n = b^{n \log_b x}$$
$$\text{and on taking logs we have } \log_b x^n = n \log_b x$$

Having outlined the rules relating to operations on logarithms, we now turn to the logarithmic rule of the differential calculus. This states that
$$\text{if } y = f(x) = \log_e x, \text{ then } \frac{dy}{dx} = \frac{1}{x}$$

We may derive this result from first principles. Let x increase by an amount Δx, then the increase in the value of the function will be given by:
$$\Delta y = \log_e(x + \Delta x) - \log_e x$$

and dividing by Δx to obtain the difference quotient, we have:
$$\frac{\Delta y}{\Delta x} = \frac{\log_e(x + \Delta x) - \log_e x}{\Delta x}$$
$$= \log_e \left(\frac{x + \Delta x}{x}\right)^{\frac{1}{\Delta x}}$$
$$= \log_e \left(1 + \frac{\Delta x}{x}\right)^{\frac{1}{\Delta x}}$$

184 MATHEMATICS IN ECONOMICS

Let $n = 1/\Delta x$, then we may write the difference quotient as

$$\frac{\Delta y}{\Delta x} = \left(1 + \frac{1/x}{n}\right)^n$$

Now as Δx approaches zero, then n approaches infinity. Hence we have:

$$\frac{dy}{dx} = \lim_{n \to \infty} \log_e \left(1 + \frac{1/x}{n}\right)^n$$

$$= \log_e(e^{1/x}) = \frac{1}{x}$$

Note that the logarithmic function is only defined for positive values of x, so this derivative is always positive, and the function is said to be monotonic. Given that this is the case, then the inverse function exists and its derivative is equal to the reciprocal of the derivative of the logarithmic function. Hence

$$\text{if } y = \log_e x, \text{ then } \frac{dy}{dx} = \frac{1}{x} > 0$$

$$\text{and } x = f^{-1}(y) \text{ exists with } \frac{dx}{dy} = x$$

But what happens if we invert the logarithmic function?

$$\text{if } y = \log_e x, \text{ then } x = e^y$$

We know from our discussion of monotonicity that the derivative of x with respect to y is equal to x, but x equals e^y. This proves the exponential rule of the differential calculus.

The chain rule may also be applied along with the logarithmic rule in order to find the derivative of a function of the form:

$$y = f(x) = \log_e(g(x))$$

Assume we have

$$y = f(x) = \log_e(x^3 - 2x^{-2})$$

Then we let z equal the bracketed term. It then follows that

$$\frac{dy}{dz} = \frac{1}{z} = \frac{1}{x^3 - 2x^{-2}}$$

$$\frac{dz}{dx} = 3x^2 + 4x^{-3}$$

$$\text{hence } \frac{dy}{dx} = \frac{3x^2 + 4x^{-2}}{x^3 - 2x^{-2}}$$

Assume we have

$$y = f(x) = Ax^\alpha$$

Let us now differentiate with respect to x to obtain:

$$\frac{dy}{dx} = \alpha A x^{\alpha - 1}$$

If we now multiply the derivative by y/x, we obtain the point elasticity of y with respect to x:

$$\frac{dy}{dx}\frac{x}{y} = \frac{\alpha A x^{\alpha-1} x}{A x^{\alpha}}$$

$$= \alpha$$

This function is therefore one of constant elasticity. Alternatively, we could have taken logarithms of the original function; this would have given us

$$\log_e y = \log_e A + \alpha \log_e x$$

If we now differentiate with respect to $\log x$, we obtain:

$$\frac{d\log_e y}{d\log_e x} = \alpha$$

In other words,

$$\frac{d\log_e y}{d\log_e x} = \frac{dy}{dx}\frac{x}{y}$$

The differentiation of some trigonometric functions

Consider the case where $y = f(x) = \sin x$. Then again by first principles, we have

$$y + \Delta y = \sin(x + \Delta x)$$

$$\text{and } \Delta y = \sin(x + \Delta x) - \sin x$$

$$\text{but } \sin(x + \Delta x) = \sin x \cos \Delta x + \sin \Delta x \cos x$$

$$\text{hence } \frac{\Delta y}{\Delta x} = \frac{\sin x \cos \Delta x + \sin \Delta x \cos x - \sin x}{\Delta x}$$

If we now take the limit of this expression as Δx approaches zero, we shall have found the derivative of $\sin x$. The first thing to notice is that as Δx approaches zero, then $\cos \Delta x$ approaches unity. Hence

$$\frac{dy}{dx} = \lim_{\Delta x \to 0} \frac{\sin \Delta x}{\Delta x} \cos x$$

In order to evaluate the limiting value of $(\sin \Delta x)/\Delta x$, consider Fig. 11.8 in which we have constructed a circle whose radius is unity. Let us calculate the area of the triangle OAB. This is given by $(1/2)OA.DB$, which is equal to $(1/2)\sin x$. Remember $\sin x$ is given by the ratio of the opposite side to the hypotenuse (DB/OB), but since OB is equal to unity, then $\sin x$ is equal to DB. Since OA is also equal to unity, then the area of triangle OAB is equal to DB. Now measure the area of the triangle OAC. This is given by $(1/2)OA.AC$, and given that the circle is of unit radius, this is equal to $(1/2)\tan x$; since $\tan x$ is equal to AC/OA, and since OA is unity, we get the above result. Furthermore, since $\tan x$ is equal to $\sin x/\cos x$, the area of this second triangle is given by $(1/2)\sin x/\cos x$. Now consider the area of the segment of the circle, OAB. The unit circle has area π, so when we measure the angle in radians, the segment's area is equal to $(1/2)x$. It is clear from

186 MATHEMATICS IN ECONOMICS

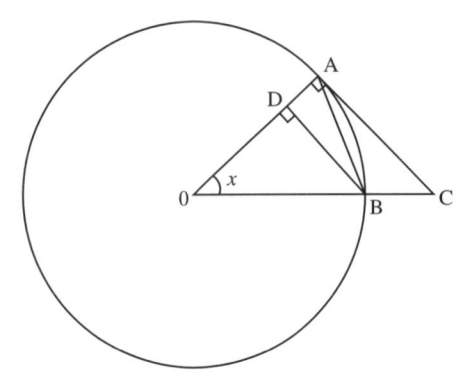

Figure 11.8 A unit circle. The radius of the circle is unity. The area of the triangle OAB equals $\frac{1}{2}\sin x$; the area of the triangle OAC equals $\frac{1}{2}\tan x$, which may also be expressed as $\frac{1}{2}(\sin x/\cos x)$; and the area of the segment of the circle OAB equals $\frac{1}{2}x$ where x is measured in radians. The area of the segment of the circle lies between that of the two triangles.

the diagram that

$$0.5\sin x \leq 0.5x \leq \frac{0.5\sin x}{\cos x}$$

Given that the angle x is positive but less than $\pi/2$ radians, then *sin x* is positive; dividing the above inequalities by *0.5sin x*, we obtain:

$$1 \leq \frac{x}{\sin x} \leq \frac{1}{\cos x}$$

Now as x approaches 0, then *cos x* approaches unity, and therefore, so must $x/\sin x$. Given that this is the case, then as Δx approaches zero, then *sin* $\Delta x/\Delta x$ must also approach unity. It follows from this that

$$\text{for } y = \sin x, \text{ then } \frac{dy}{dx} = \cos x$$

A similar procedure would enable us to show that

$$\text{for } y = \cos x, \text{ then } \frac{dy}{dx} = -\sin x$$

Let x change by an amount Δx, then the increase in the value of y is given by:

$$\Delta y = \cos(x + \Delta x) - \cos x$$
$$= \cos x \cos \Delta x - \sin x \sin \Delta x - \cos x$$

The difference quotient is therefore given by:

$$\frac{\Delta y}{\Delta x} = \frac{\cos x \cos \Delta x - \sin x \sin \Delta x - \cos x}{\Delta x}$$

and as we take the limit of this expression as Δx approaches zero, we have:

$$\frac{dy}{dx} = -\sin x$$

11.7 SUMMARY

We provide here a summary table of some standard derivatives:

$$f(x) = x^n, \quad f'(x) = nx^{n-1}$$
$$f(x) = c, \quad f'(x) = 0$$
$$f(x) = u(x) + v(x), \quad f'(x) = u'(x) + v'(x)$$
$$f(x) = u(x)\,v(x), \quad f'(x) = v\frac{du}{dx} + u\frac{dv}{dx}$$
$$f(x) = \frac{u(x)}{v(x)}, \quad f'(x) = \frac{v\dfrac{du}{dx} - u\dfrac{dv}{dx}}{v^2}$$
$$f(x) = f(g(x)), \quad f'(x) = f'(g'(x))$$
$$f(x) = e^x, \quad f'(x) = e^x$$
$$f(x) = \log_e x, \quad f'(x) = \frac{1}{x}$$
$$f(x) = \cos x, \quad f'(x) = -\sin x$$
$$f(x) = \sin x, \quad f'(x) = \cos x$$

A function of a single variable is strictly concave if $f''(x)$ is negative, concave if $f''(x)$ is non-positive, convex if $f''(x)$ is non-negative, and strictly convex if $f''(x)$ is positive.

11.8 EXERCISES

11.1 (a) The domain for each of the following functions is the set of all real numbers. Which of the functions below are differentiable at all points which lie in the domain?

(i) $f(x) = x^2 - 20x + 100$

(ii) $f(x) = |x - 10|$

(iii) $f(x) = 200 - x$ for $x \leq 40$
$= 240 - 2x$ for $x > 40$

(iv) $f(x) = 200 - 2x$ for $x \leq 40$
$= 240 - 4x$ for $x > 40$

(v) $f(x) = x^3 + 10$

(vi) $f(x) = x^3 + 10$ for $x \neq 2$
$= 12$ for $x = 2$

(b) For each of the following demand functions, where x is quantity demanded and p is price,

(i) $x = 450 p^{-1}$;

(ii) $x = 8100 p^{-2}$.

(i) calculate the ratio of the change in quantity demanded to the change in price (the difference quotient) as the price falls from *10* to *5*;

(ii) calculate the ratio of the change in quantity demanded to the change in price as the price falls from *10* to *9*;

(iii) what value does the difference quotient take as starting from an initial price of *10* the change in price approaches zero?

11.2 (a) Differentiate from first principles the following functions:

(i) $f(x) = 2 + 5x$

(ii) $f(x) = 5x^2$

(iii) $f(x) = -x^{-2}$

(iv) $f(x) = x + 4x^3$

(b) Differentiate the following functions:

(i) $f(x) = 4x^{-2}$

(ii) $f(x) = 8x^{1/2}$

(iii) $f(x) = x^{10}$

(iv) $f(x) = 120$

(v) $f(x) = 3 + 2x - 10x^{-1/2}$

(vi) $f(x) = 7x^3 - 2x + 6x^{1/3}$

(vii) $f(x) = 2 - 3x^{-4} + 3x^3$

(viii) $f(x) = 64x^{1/8} + 4x^{-1}$

11.3 (a) Differentiate the following functions:

(i) $f(x) = (x^3 + 2x^2)(2x^{-1/2} + 4x)$

(ii) $f(x) = (x^4 - 2x^{-1})(10 - 4x)$

(iii) $f(x) = (8x^{3/2} - 2x^2)(2x^4 + 6x^{-2/3})$

(iv) $f(x) = (10x - x^5)(3 + x^2)$

(b) A firm's average revenue function is given by:

$$p = 400 - 4x$$

(i) Invert the average revenue function to obtain the demand function. Then evaluate the point own-price elasticity of demand for x when (1) $p = 300$ and (2) $p = 240$.

(ii) Write down the total revenue function as a function of x, and then by differentiating this function with respect to x obtain the marginal revenue function. At what output is marginal revenue equal to zero? What is the value of the price at this output level? Check that the own-price elasticity of demand is equal to -1 at this price.

11.4 (a) Differentiate the following functions:

(i) $f(x) = \dfrac{x^4 + 2}{x^2 + 5x}$

(ii) $f(x) = \dfrac{x^{-1/4} + 6x}{8 - x^2}$

(iii) $f(x) = \dfrac{4x^5 - 2x^{-1}}{x^3 - 10}$

(iv) $f(x) = \dfrac{x^{5/2} + 12x}{4x^{1/2} + 2x}$

(b) A firm's total cost is given by

$$TC = 200 + 0.5x^2$$

(i) Obtain the firm's marginal cost function.

(ii) Write down the average cost function and then differentiate it with respect to x. What is the value of this derivative at (i) $x = 10$; (ii) $x = 20$, (iii) $x = 40$?

11.5 Differentiate the following functions:

(i) $f(x) = (2x^3 + 4x)^{1/2}$

(ii) $f(x) = (x^{-2} + 2x)^{-3}$

(iii) $f(x) = (10 + x^2)^5$

(iv) $f(x) = (7x^4 - x^{-2})^{-1/2}$

11.6 (a) Obtain the first- and second-order derivatives of the following functions:

(i) $f(x) = 10x^{-1/2}$

(ii) $f(x) = 6x^{3/4}$

(iii) $f(x) = 10 + x^2 + x^3$

(iv) $f(x) = 7 + 2x$

(v) $f(x) = 8x^{-2}$

(vi) $f(x) = x^3 - 9x^2 + 12x + 15$

(b) Which of the functions in (a) above are concave, and which are convex?

11.7 (a) What are the logarithms to base *10* of the following:

(i) *1000*; (ii) *0.1*; (iii) *0.001*; (iv) *1m*?

(b) What are the logarithms to base *2* of the following:

(i) *0.0625*; (ii) *64*; (iii) *1*; (iv) *0.25*?

11.8 (a) Differentiate the following functions:

(i) $f(x) = e^{-x^2}$

(ii) $f(x) = e^{5+x^3}$

(iii) $f(x) = (x^2 + 4x)e^{4+x}$

(iv) $f(x) = 10e^{-0.1x}$

(v) $f(x) = \dfrac{e^{x^2}}{x^3 - 10}$

(b) Differentiate the following functions:

(i) $f(x) = \log_e(3x^2 + 5x)$

(ii) $f(x) = \log_e(2x^3 + x^{-1/2})$

(iii) $f(x) = x \log_e x - x$

(iv) $f(x) = (6x^{1/2} + 2x) \log_e(x^4 - x^{-1})$

(v) $f(x) = \log_e(x^2 + 6x)^5$

(c) Calculate the point elasticity of demand for the following demand function when (i) $p = 10$ and (ii) $p = 5$:

(i) $x = f(p) = 200 - 4p$

(ii) $x = f(p) = 160 - 8p$

(iii) $x = f(p) = 1000p^{-2}$

(iv) $x = f(p) = 1250p^{-3}$

11.9 (a) Differentiate the following functions:

(i) $f(x) = \cos 2x$

(ii) $f(x) = \sin^2 x$

(iii) $f(x) = \cos^2 x$

(iv) $f(x) = \cos x \, \sin x$

(v) $f(x) = \sin(x^2 + 4)$

(vi) $f(x) = \cos(2x + 4x^{-1})$

(b) Given that *tan x* is equal to *sin x/cos x*, find the derivative of *tan x*.

(c) Differentiate the following trigonometric functions:

(i) $f(x) = \sec x = \dfrac{1}{\sin x}$

(ii) $f(x) = \operatorname{cosec} x = \dfrac{1}{\cos x}$

(iii) $f(x) = \cot x = \dfrac{1}{\tan x}$

CHAPTER TWELVE
FURTHER DIFFERENTIAL CALCULUS AND APPLICATIONS TO ECONOMICS

12.1 INTRODUCTION

In this chapter we continue our discussion of differential calculus by turning to an analysis of functions of more than one variable. We begin in Section 12.2 by introducing the concept of a partial derivative which tells us how the value of a function will be altered if we allow one of the explanatory variables to change by a very small amount, whilst holding constant the values of all the other explanatory variables. A consumer derives utility from a wide range of different commodities that he consumes: an increase in his consumption of say apples, everything else remaining unchanged, will lead to an increase in his utility. If we allow for an infinitesimally small change in his consumption of apples, then the marginal utility of apples will be measured by the partial derivative of the utility function with respect to apples. Alternatively, a firm may employ in its production process many different factors of production: the partial derivative of output with respect to, say, the input of labour services then tells us how the output would change as the employment of labour changed by a very small amount, again leaving unchanged the employment of the other factors of production. What we have measured here is the marginal product of labour, though remember we have not dealt with a discrete change in employment; the change has been an infinitesimally small one. The value of the partial derivative will also typically depend not only upon the current level of the labour input, but also upon the levels of usage of the other factors of production. The same naturally applies to the marginal utility a consumer derives from the consumption of apples or other commodities.

The extent to which the marginal utility of a good or the marginal product of a factor varies as consumption of the good or employment of the factor varies is given by what is known as the second-order partial derivative. We then go on to consider how the marginal utility of a good or the marginal product of a factor varies with an infinitesimally small change in the consumption of another good or employment of another factor, holding fixed everything else: this is given by the second-order cross-partial derivative.

Having shown how to find the first-order and second-order partial derivatives of a function, we then move on in Section 12.3 to investigate the properties of multi-variable functions. From the economic viewpoint, an important question we can ask about the nature of a firm's production function is what would happen to output if there was a proportionate expansion in the employment of all the factors of production. We introduce the concept of a homogeneous function and explain the significance of Euler's Theorem, which is a famous result which applies to homogeneous functions, and which as we shall see has important implications for marginal productivity factor pricing.

Following our discussion of homogeneous functions and Euler's Theorem, in Section 12.4 we turn to the concept of a differential and of a total derivative. We then make use of these concepts in further analysing some issues in the theory of the consumer and in the theory of production.

The final new mathematical concept that we introduce in this chapter is that of an implicit function which we discuss in Section 12.5. Knowledge of this concept then enables us to carry out comparative static analysis on a set of quite general economic models. We show how to analyse qualitatively the effects of government's fiscal and monetary policy on such key macroeconomic variables as output, the rate of interest and the exchange rate in a limited number of macroeconomic models. This comparative static analysis where we compare the effects of changes in government expenditure or in the money supply requires us to make use of some earlier techniques which we have discussed in the linear algebra chapters of the book: these include determinants and Cramer's rule.

12.2 PARTIAL DIFFERENTIATION

We now turn to consider functions of more than one variable. Assume we have:

$$y = f(\mathbf{x}) = f(x_1, x_2, \ldots, x_i, \ldots, x_n)$$

We now investigate how the value of this function will change as we make a change in one of the independent variables, holding constant the values of all the other independent variables. If we increase x_i by an amount Δx_i, then the new value of the objective function is given by

$$\Delta y = f(x_1, x_2, \ldots, x_i + \Delta x_i, \ldots, x_n) - f(x_1, x_2, \ldots, x_i, \ldots, x_n)$$

If we divide the above expression by Δx_i, we obtain the difference quotient:

$$\frac{\Delta y}{\Delta x_i} = \frac{f(x_1, x_2, \ldots, x_i + \Delta x_i, \ldots, x_n) - f(x_1, x_2, \ldots, x_i, \ldots, x_n)}{\Delta x_i}$$

If we then take the limit of this expression as Δx_i approaches zero, we have what is known as the partial derivative of the function with respect to x_i. The symbol which we use for a first-order partial derivative is

$$\frac{\partial y}{\partial x_i} \quad \text{or alternatively } f_i$$

Example: we wish to find the first-order partial derivatives of the following function:

$$y = f(x) = x_1^3 + 2x_1^2 x_2 + 6x_1 x_3^4 + 4x_2^2 - x_2 x_3^2 + x_3^{-1}$$

To find the partial derivative with respect to x_1, we treat the other xs as constants; differentiating partially with respect to x_1 then yields:

$$f_1 = 3x_1^2 + 4x_1 x_2 + 6x_3^4$$

Similarly, we also have on differentiating partially with respect first to x_2 and then with respect to x_3:

$$f_2 = 2x_1^2 + 8x_2 - x_3^2$$

$$f_3 = 24x_1 x_3^3 - 2x_2 x_3 - x_3^{-2}$$

We may then proceed to differentiate partially the first-order partial derivatives. Consider the partial derivative f_1. Then not only may we differentiate f_1 partially with respect to x_1, but we may also differentiate f_1 partially with respect to x_2 or with respect to x_3. These are known as the second-order partial derivatives. We shall symbolise these second-order partial derivatives in the following way:

$$\frac{\partial^2 y}{\partial x_i^2} = f_{ii}$$

$$\frac{\partial^2 y}{\partial x_i \partial x_j} = f_{ij}$$

Let us now find all the second-order partial derivatives of our specific function: to find f_{ii}, then we must differentiate f_i with respect to x_i, treating as constants all the other xs. To find the cross-partial derivative f_{ij}, then we must differentiate f_i with respect to x_j, holding constant all the other xs. We have:

$$f_{11} = 6x_1 + 4x_2$$
$$f_{12} = 4x_1$$
$$f_{13} = 24x_3^3$$
$$f_{21} = 4x_1$$
$$f_{22} = 8$$
$$f_{23} = -2x_3$$
$$f_{31} = 24x_3^3$$
$$f_{32} = -2x_3$$
$$f_{33} = 72x_1 x_3^2 - 2x_2 + 2x_3^{-3}$$

Notice that as far as the second-order cross-partial derivatives are concerned, it does not matter in which order we perform the differentiation. Whether we first differentiate with respect to x_i and then with respect to x_j or first differentiate with respect to x_j and then differentiate with respect to x_i, we shall obtain the same answer. The second-order cross-partial derivatives are symmetric with

$$f_{ij} = f_{ji} \quad \forall i, j$$

An economic application

A firm's production function takes the following form:

$$Q = f(K, N) = AK^\alpha N^\beta$$

where Q is output and K and N are inputs of capital services and labour services respectively, A is a positive constant and α and β are two parameters whose values are greater than zero but less than one. Such a production function is known as the Cobb–Douglas production, named after Charles Cobb who was an American engineer and Paul Douglas who was an economist and US senator for Illinois. The economic interpretation of the partial derivatives of the production function is straightforward. The partial derivative of output with respect to capital services measures the marginal product of capital, and the partial derivative of output with respect to labour services measures the marginal product of labour. Differentiating the production function partially with respect to K and N, we obtain:

$$\frac{\partial Q}{\partial K} = f_K = \alpha A K^{\alpha-1} N^\beta$$

$$\frac{\partial Q}{\partial N} = f_N = \beta A K^\alpha N^{\beta-1}$$

Both of these partial derivatives are always positive for positive levels of the two inputs. If we now partially differentiate the two marginal products with respect to K and N, we shall find the second-order partial derivatives of the production function:

$$\frac{\partial^2 Q}{\partial K^2} = f_{KK} = (\alpha - 1)\alpha A K^{\alpha-2} N^\beta$$

$$= \frac{(\alpha - 1)\alpha Q}{K^2}$$

$$\frac{\partial^2 Q}{\partial K \partial N} = f_{KN} = \alpha\beta K^{\alpha-1} N^{\beta-1}$$

$$= \frac{\alpha\beta Q}{KN}$$

$$\frac{\partial^2 Q}{\partial N^2} = f_{NN} = (\beta - 1)\beta K^\alpha N^{\beta-1}$$

$$= \frac{(\beta - 1)\beta Q}{N^2}$$

$$\frac{\partial^2 Q}{\partial N \partial K} = f_{NK} = \alpha\beta K^{\alpha-1} N^{\beta-1}$$

$$= \frac{\alpha\beta Q}{KN}$$

Given the conditions we have imposed on the exponents, α and β, the cross-partial derivatives are positive, and the other second-order partial derivatives are negative. Economically, this production function has the following properties: the marginal product of labour is positive, with the marginal product of labour falling as we employ more labour, holding fixed the amount of capital services, and the marginal product of labour increasing at a given level of the labour input as we employ more capital services. Similarly, the marginal product of capital is positive, diminishes as we increase the employment of capital services and increases as we utilise more labour services, other things being equal.

12.3 HOMOGENEOUS FUNCTIONS AND EULER'S THEOREM

A function of many variables is said to be homogeneous of degree n if

$$f(\lambda x_1, \lambda x_2, \ldots, \lambda x_n) = \lambda^n f(x_1, x_2, \ldots, x_n)$$

Otherwise, the function is non-homogeneous.

Let us see whether the following function is homogeneous:

$$f(x_1, x_2) = x^2 + 6x_1 x_2 + x_1^5 x_2^{-3}$$

Multiplying x_1 and x_2 by a scalar λ and evaluating the new value of the function, we have:

$$f(\lambda x_1, \lambda x_2) = (\lambda x_1)^2 + 6(\lambda x_1)(\lambda x_2) + (\lambda x_1)^5 (\lambda x_2)^{-3}$$
$$= \lambda^2 x_1^2 + 6\lambda^2 x_1 x_2 + \lambda^2 x_1^5 x_2^{-3}$$
$$= \lambda^2 f(x_1, x_2)$$

Hence this function is homogeneous of degree 2.

Now consider the following case:

$$f(x_1, x_2) = x_1^3 - 2x_1 x_2^2 + 8x_2^2$$

Again multiplying x_1 and x_2 by a scalar λ and evaluating the new value of the function, we have:

$$f(\lambda x_1, \lambda x_2) = (\lambda x_1)^3 - 2(\lambda x_1)(\lambda x_2)^2 + 8(\lambda x_2)^2$$
$$= \lambda^2 (\lambda x_1^3 - 2\lambda x_1 x_2 + 8x_2^2)$$
$$\neq \lambda^2 f(x_1, x_2)$$

So in this case, the function is non-homogeneous.

Now consider the Cobb–Douglas production function:

$$Q = f(K, N) = AK^\alpha N^\beta$$

We shall now show that this function is homogeneous of degree $\alpha + \beta$. Multiplying K and N by λ yields:

$$f(\lambda K, \lambda N) = A(\lambda K)^\alpha (\lambda N)^\beta = \lambda^{\alpha+\beta} K^\alpha N^\beta$$

What is the economic significance of the production function being homogeneous? Let λ equal 2; then what will happen to output as a result of doubling the employment of the two factors of production? Given that the Cobb–Douglas production function is homogeneous of degree $\alpha + \beta$, then output will be a multiple of its original level, the value of the multiplier being given by $2^{\alpha+\beta}$. The multiplier will be less than 2 for $\alpha + \beta$ less than one, equal to 2 for $\alpha + \beta$ equal to unity, and greater than 2 for $\alpha + \beta$ greater than unity. We may therefore conclude that the production function will exhibit constant returns to scale when $\alpha + \beta$ is equal to unity: a doubling of the inputs will lead to a doubling of output. The production function is homogeneous of degree one; alternatively, we may say that it is linear homogeneous. When $\alpha + \beta$ is less than one, the production function exhibits decreasing returns to scale: a doubling of the inputs leads to a less than doubling of output. Finally when $\alpha + \beta$ exceeds unity, we have increasing returns to scale: a doubling of the inputs leads to output more than doubling.

For functions which are homogeneous of degree n, Euler's Theorem states:

$$f_1 x_1 + f_2 x_2 + \cdots + f_n x_n = nf(x_1, x_2, \ldots, x_n)$$

The sum of the products of each independent variable and its partial derivative is equal to n times the value of the function.

Let us check that it holds for the following function which we earlier demonstrated was homogeneous of degree 2.

$$f(x_1, x_2) = x_1^2 + 6x_1 x_2 + x_1^5 x_2^{-3}$$

Differentiating partially with respect to x_1 and x_2, we have:
$$f_1 = 2x_1 + 6x_2 + 5x_1^4 x_2^{-3}$$
$$f_2 = 6x_1 - 3x_1^5 x_2^{-4}$$

Hence

$$\sum_{i=1}^{i=2} x_i f_i = 2x_1^2 + 6x_1 x_2 + 5x_1^5 x_2^{-3} + 6x_1 x_2 - 3x_1^5 x_2^{-3}$$
$$= 2(x_1^2 + 6x_1 x_2 + x_1^5 x_2^{-3})$$
$$= 2f(x_1, x_2)$$

In the context of our production function, Euler's Theorem states that if the production is linear homogeneous (i.e. exhibits constant returns to scale) then the total product will just be exhausted if the factors of production receive the value of their marginal products. With marginal productivity factor pricing, total payments to the factors of production are given by

$$pf_K K + pf_N N$$

where p is the price of the product and pf_K and pf_N are the values of the marginal products of capital and labour services respectively. By Euler's theorem, we have

$$pf_K K + pf_N N = (\alpha + \beta)pf(K, N) = (\alpha + \beta)pQ$$

With constant returns to scale $\alpha + \beta$ equals unity and the value of output is just sufficient to pay the factors of production the value of their marginal products. With decreasing returns to scale, there will be a surplus left over after factors have been rewarded according to the value of their marginal products. However, if there are increasing returns to scale, the value of output will be insufficient to enable factors to be paid the value of their marginal products.

When the production function is homogeneous of degree one, then we know that

$$F(\lambda K, \lambda N) = \lambda F(K, N)$$

If we now let $\lambda = 1/N$, then it must also be the case that

$$F\left(\frac{K}{N}, 1\right) = \frac{1}{N} F(K, N)$$

Hence

$$\frac{Q}{N} = F\left(\frac{K}{N}, 1\right) = f\left(\frac{K}{N}\right)$$
$$\text{and } Q = Nf\left(\frac{K}{N}\right)$$

Differentiating output partially with respect to K and N, we may express the marginal products of the two factors in the following way:

$$\frac{\partial Q}{\partial K} = f'\left(\frac{K}{N}\right) = f'(k)$$
$$\frac{\partial Q}{\partial N} = f\left(\frac{K}{N}\right) - \frac{K}{N} f'\left(\frac{K}{N}\right)$$
$$= f(k) - kf'(k)$$

where k is capital per head. In order to find the marginal product of capital, one must apply the chain rule, whereas to obtain the marginal product of labour, one must apply both the product rule and the chain rule. Note also that equating the value of the marginal product of each factor with its price, w being the wage rate and r the price of capital services, we shall have:

$$w = pf(k) - pkf'(k)$$
$$r = pf'(k)$$

With marginal productivity factor pricing we shall have:

$$wN + rK = (pf(k) - pkf'(k))N + pf'(k)K$$
$$= pNf(k)$$
$$= pF(K, N)$$

The total product is just exhausted by marginal productivity factor pricing when we have constant returns to scale.

12.4 DIFFERENTIALS AND TOTAL DERIVATIVES

Differentials

Given a function of a single variable

$$y = f(x)$$

then the first derivative of this function is

$$\frac{dy}{dx} = f'(x)$$

Multiplying both sides of the derivative by dx, we obtain what is known as the differential:

$$dy = f'(x)\,dx$$

If we now turn to a function of many variables,

$$y = f(x_1, x_2, \ldots, x_n)$$

then the total differential of this function takes the following form:

$$dy = f_1\,dx_1 + f_2\,dx_2 + \cdots + f_n\,dx_n$$
$$= \sum_{i=1}^{i=n} f_i\,dx_i$$

A consumer's preferences can be represented by the following utility function:

$$U = U(x_1, x_2) = \log_e x_1 + \log_e x_2$$

Totally differentiating the utility function yields:

$$dU = U_1\,dx_1 + U_2\,dx_2 = \frac{1}{x_1}\,dx_1 + \frac{1}{x_2}\,dx_2$$

Along an indifference curve, utility is unchanging; hence setting dU equal to zero, and rearranging we obtain the slope of the indifference curve:

$$\frac{dx_2}{dx_1} = -\frac{U_1}{U_2} = -\frac{x_2}{x_1}$$

The absolute value of the slope is the marginal rate of substitution of good 2 for good 1.

A firm's production function is given by:

$$Q = [\alpha K^{-\rho} + (1-\alpha)N^{-\rho}]^{-\nu/\rho}$$

where K represents capital services, N labour services, α, ν and ρ are all positive parameters, with α being less than unity. What is the value of the marginal rate of substitution of capital services for labour services, i.e. the absolute value of the slope of an isoquant? We must find the total differential and then set it equal to zero. First of all, differentiate partially with respect to K and N to obtain the marginal products of the two factors of production. This requires us to make use of the chain rule by letting the term inside the square brackets equal Z. Hence

$$Z = \alpha K^{-\rho} + (1-\alpha)N^{-\rho}$$
$$Q = Z^{-\nu/\rho}$$

Differentiate Q with respect to Z and Z partially with respect to K to obtain:

$$\frac{dQ}{dZ} = -(\nu/\rho)Z^{-\nu/\rho-1}$$
$$\frac{\partial Z}{\partial K} = -\alpha\rho K^{-\rho-1}$$

Multiplying these two derivatives gives us the marginal product of capital:

$$\frac{\partial Q}{\partial K} = \alpha\nu K^{-\rho-1}Z^{-\nu/\rho-1}$$

Adopting the same procedure, it is straightforward to show that the marginal product of labour is given by:

$$\frac{\partial Q}{\partial N} = (1-\alpha)\nu N^{-\rho-1}Z^{-\nu/\rho-1}$$

Along an isoquant, output is fixed. Hence

$$dQ = f_K\, dK + f_N\, dN = 0$$

So the marginal rate of substitution is given by:

$$MRS_{KN} = \frac{f_N}{f_K} = \frac{(1-\alpha)N^{-\rho-1}}{\alpha K^{-\rho-1}}$$
$$= \frac{(1-\alpha)}{\alpha}\left(\frac{K}{N}\right)^{1+\rho}$$

The marginal rate of substitution depends upon the capital–labour ratio. As we move outwards along a ray through the origin moving on to higher and higher isoquants, then the slope of all these isoquants is the same at the intersection points. The expansion path which maps out the combinations of capital and labour services which the firm would choose to employ at a given set of factor prices in order to produce different levels of output is linear.

If we invert the expression for the marginal rate of substitution in order to express the capital–labour ratio as a function of the marginal rate of substitution, we obtain:

$$\frac{K}{N} = BM^{1/1+\rho}$$

where M is the marginal rate of substitution of capital for labour and B is a constant given by:

$$B = \left(\frac{\alpha}{1-\alpha}\right)^{1/1+\rho}$$

Taking logs and then differentiating the log of the capital–labour ratio with respect to the log of the marginal rate of substitution, we obtain what is known as the elasticity of substitution, which measures the ratio of the proportionate change in the capital-ratio to the proportionate change in the marginal rate of substitution.

$$\frac{d\log(K/N)}{d\log M} = \frac{1}{1+\rho}$$

The elasticity of substitution of our particular production function is constant and independent of the capital–labour ratio. It is accordingly known as the constant elasticity of substitution (*CES*) production function.

The total derivative

Assume we have a function:

$$y = f(x_1, x_2)$$

Then its total differential is given by:

$$dy = f_1\, dx_1 + f_2\, dx_2$$

Let it also be the case that

$$x_2 = g(x_1)$$

Accordingly when x_1 changes, there will be two effects on y: a direct effect since y depends upon x_1, but also an indirect effect through the change in x_2 induced by the change in x_1. We may, therefore, define the total derivative of y with respect to x_1:

$$\frac{dy}{dx_1} = f_1 + f_2 \frac{dx_2}{dx_1}$$

The first term on the right-hand side is the direct impact of the change in x_1 and the second term is the indirect impact through the effect the change in x_1 has on x_2 and hence on y.

Consider the following example:

$$y = f(x_1, x_2) = 4x_1^{0.5} + 3x_1 x_2^2$$

$$x_2 = g(x_1) = 10 + x_1^2$$

Partially differentiating the first function with respect to x_1 and x_2, we obtain:

$$f_1 = 2x_1^{-0.5} + 3x_2^2$$
$$f_2 = 6x_1 x_2$$

Differentiating the second function with respect to x_1 yields:

$$\frac{dx_2}{dx_1} = 2x_1$$

The total derivative of y with respect to x_1 is, therefore, given by:

$$\begin{aligned}\frac{dy}{dx_1} &= (2x_1^{-0.5} + 3x_2^2) + 6x_1 x_2 (2x_1) \\ &= 2x_1^{-0.5} + 3x_2^2 + 12x_1^2 x_2 \\ &= 2x_1^{-0.5} + 3(10 + x_1^2)^2 + 12x_1^2(10 + x_1^2) \\ &= 2x_1^{-0.5} + 300 + 60x_1^2 + 3x_2^4 + 120x_1^2 + 12x_1^4 \\ &= 2x_1^{-0.5} + 300 + 180x_1^2 + 15x_1^4\end{aligned}$$

An economic example

Consider the following production function

$$Y(t) = e^{\delta t} F(K(t), N(t))$$

where output (Y) and the input of capital (K) and labour services (N) are all functions of time t, and δ is the rate of technical progress. Let us differentiate the production function totally with respect to time:

$$\frac{dY}{dt} = e^{\delta t}\left(F_K \frac{dK}{dt} + F_N \frac{dN}{dt} + \delta F(K, N)\right)$$

We now multiply and divide the first term inside the brackets on the right-hand side by K, multiply and divide the second term by N and divide both sides by Y. This yields:

$$\frac{dY}{dt}\frac{1}{Y} = \frac{KF_K}{Y}\frac{dK}{dt}\frac{1}{K} + \frac{NF_N}{Y}\frac{dN}{dt}\frac{1}{N} + \delta$$

The rate of growth of output is therefore a weighted average of the rates of growth of the two inputs plus the rate of technical progress. What can we say about the weights attached to the input growth rates? If factors are paid the value of their marginal products, then the weights are the relative income shares of the two factors.

12.5 AN INTRODUCTION TO COMPARATIVE STATIC ANALYSIS

Economic theorists are often interested in predicting the effects of some parametric change on the equilibrium in a particular model. We shall be interested in this section in carrying out such comparative static analysis on some basic macroeconomic models. The model is static in that we are not concerned with the dynamics of the movement from one position of equilibrium to

Implicit functions

A function is explicit when it can be expressed, for example, in the following way:

$$y = f(x_1, x_2) = x_1^3 + 2x_1 x_2 + x_2^2$$

It is also clear that this function has the following first-order partial derivatives:

$$f_1 = 3x_1^2 + 2x_2 \text{ and } f_2 = 2x_1 + 2x_2$$

But now consider the case where we have:

$$F(y, x_1, x_2) = 0$$

Under what circumstances is it possible to express y as an implicit function of x_1 and x_2? If we take the total differential of $F(y, x_1, x_2)$, we obtain:

$$F_y \, dy + F_1 \, dx_1 + F_2 \, dx_2 = 0$$

If we assume that the partial derivatives F_y, F_1 and F_2 are continuous, then if at a point which satisfies the equation $F(y, x_1, x_2) = 0$, F_y is not equal to zero, then we may state that in the vicinity of this point we may define y as an implicit function of x_1 and x_2, $y = f(x_1, x_2)$, and that the partial derivatives of this function are given by:

$$f_1 = \frac{-F_1}{F_y} \text{ and } f_2 = \frac{-F_2}{F_y}$$

Assume that we have

$$F(y, x_1, x_2) = 10 x_1 y + x_1^2 x_2 + y^2 x_2 = 0$$

Can we define y as an implicit function of x_1 and x_2 in the vicinity of the point ($y = 1$, $x_1 = -1$, $x_2 = 5$) which satisfies the above equation? First of all, let us find the partial derivatives of $F(y, x_1, x_2) = 0$ and evaluate them at this point:

$$F_y = 10 x_1 + 2 y x_2 = -10 + 10 = 0$$
$$F_1 = 10 y + 2 x_1 x_2 = 10 - 10 = 0$$
$$F_2 = x_1^2 + y^2 = 1 + 1 = 2$$

Since F_y is equal to zero at this point, we are unable to define y as an implicit function of the xs in the vicinity of this particular point.

Let us consider another point that satisfies the equation: ($y = 1$, $x_1 = -2$, $x_2 = 4$). At this point, we find:

$$F_y = -20 + 8 = -12$$
$$F_1 = 10 - 16 = -6$$
$$F_2 = 4 + 1 = 5$$

In this case, F_y does not vanish, and we may, therefore, define y as an implicit function of the xs in the vicinity of this particular point. The partial derivatives of the implicit function are:

$$f_1 = -\left(\frac{-6}{-12}\right) = -1/2$$

$$f_2 = -\left(\frac{5}{-12}\right) = 5/12$$

Now assume that we have a pair of simultaneous equations expressed in the form:

$$F(y_1, y_2, x_1, x_2) = 0$$
$$G(y_1, y_2, x_1, x_2) = 0$$

We are interested in the circumstances under which we may write:

$$y_1 = f(x_1, x_2)$$
$$y_2 = g(x_1, x_2)$$

As in our discussion of the single equation case, we shall assume that F and G have continuous first-order partial derivatives. Totally differentiating the two functions yields:

$$F_{y_1} dy_1 + F_{y_2} dy_2 + F_{x_1} dx_1 + F_{x_2} dx_2 = 0$$
$$G_{y_1} dy_1 + G_{y_2} dy_2 + G_{x_1} dx_1 + G_{x_2} dx_2 = 0$$

In matrix notation, we have:

$$\begin{bmatrix} F_{y_1} & F_{y_2} \\ G_{y_1} & G_{y_2} \end{bmatrix} \begin{bmatrix} dy_1 \\ dy_2 \end{bmatrix} = \begin{bmatrix} -F_{x_1} dx_1 - F_{x_2} dx_2 \\ -G_{x_1} dx_1 - G_{x_2} dx_2 \end{bmatrix}$$

If we apply Cramer's rule in order for example to solve for dy_1, the determinant we shall have to evaluate in the denominator of the expression is:

$$\begin{vmatrix} F_{y_1} & F_{y_2} \\ G_{y_1} & G_{y_2} \end{vmatrix} = F_{y_1} G_{y_2} - F_{y_2} G_{y_1}$$

This determinant, which is known as a Jacobian determinant, must not vanish; as long as it is not equal to zero at a point which satisfies the two equations, then we may define the ys as implicit functions of the xs in the vicinity of such a point. Furthermore the partial derivatives of these implicit functions are given by:

$$\frac{\partial y_1}{\partial x_1} = \frac{\begin{vmatrix} -F_{x_1} & F_{y_2} \\ -G_{x_1} & G_{y_2} \end{vmatrix}}{|J|}$$

$$\frac{\partial y_1}{\partial x_2} = \frac{\begin{vmatrix} -F_{x_2} & F_{y_2} \\ -G_{x_2} & G_{y_2} \end{vmatrix}}{|J|}$$

$$\frac{\partial y_2}{\partial x_1} = \frac{\begin{vmatrix} F_{y_1} & -F_{x_1} \\ G_{y_1} & -G_{x_1} \end{vmatrix}}{|J|}$$

$$\frac{\partial y_2}{\partial x_2} = \frac{\begin{vmatrix} F_{y_1} & -F_{x_2} \\ G_{y_1} & -G_{x_2} \end{vmatrix}}{|J|}$$

where $|J|$ is the Jacobian determinant.

The result is of general applicability. For the n equation case,

$$F^1(y_1, y_2, \ldots, y_n, x_1, x_2, \ldots, x_m) = 0$$

$$F^2(y_1, y_2, \ldots, y_n, x_1, x_2, \ldots, x_m) = 0$$

$$\vdots \qquad \qquad \vdots$$

$$F^n(y_1, y_2, \ldots, y_n, x_1, x_2, \ldots, x_m) = 0$$

we shall be able to proceed to evaluate the sign of the partial derivative:

$$\frac{\partial y_i}{\partial x_j}$$

provided that the following Jacobian determinant does not vanish:

$$\begin{vmatrix} F^1_{y_1} & F^1_{y_2} & \cdots & F^1_{y_n} \\ F^2_{y_1} & F^2_{y_2} & \cdots & F^2_{y_n} \\ \vdots & \vdots & \cdots & \vdots \\ F^n_{y_1} & F^n_{y_2} & \cdots & F^n_{y_n} \end{vmatrix} \neq 0$$

We now show how these techniques can be employed to perform some comparative statics on a variety of macroeconomic models.

A simple model of a small open economy

We assume that planned expenditure on domestically produced output has three components: consumption (C), investment (I), and net exports (NX), i.e. exports (X) less imports (M). Consumption and imports are taken to be functions of income (Y) with the marginal propensities to consume (C_Y) and import (M_Y) being positive but less than unity, whereas investment and exports are assumed to be exogenously given. In equilibrium, planned expenditure must equal income. Hence we have:

$$Y = C(Y) + I + X - M(Y)$$

$$NX = X - M(Y)$$

Totally differentiating the equilibrium condition and the equation defining the current account of the balance of payments, we obtain:

$$dY = C_Y\, dY + dI + dX - M_Y\, dY$$
$$dNX = dX - M_Y\, dY$$

Income and the balance of trade are the endogenous variables, which may be written as functions of the exogenous variables, I and X, provided that the Jacobian determinant does not vanish. Re-arranging the equations and putting them in matrix form, we obtain:

$$\begin{bmatrix} 1 - C_Y + M_Y & 0 \\ M_Y & 1 \end{bmatrix} \begin{bmatrix} dY \\ dNX \end{bmatrix} = \begin{bmatrix} dI + dX \\ dX \end{bmatrix}$$

The Jacobian determinant is equal to:

$$1 - C_Y + M_Y$$

Since the marginal propensities to consume and to import are both positive but less than unity, the Jacobian determinant is positive, and Y and NX may both be written as implicit functions of I and X. Employing Cramer's rule to solve for dY and dNX, we have:

$$dY = \frac{\begin{vmatrix} dI + dX & 0 \\ dX & 1 \end{vmatrix}}{|J|} = \frac{dI + dX}{|J|}$$

$$dNX = \frac{\begin{vmatrix} 1 - C_Y + M_Y & dI + dX \\ M_Y & dX \end{vmatrix}}{|J|} = \frac{[1 - C_Y]\, dX - M_Y\, dI}{|J|}$$

From the above equations, we can easily derive the following partial derivatives:

$$\frac{\partial Y}{\partial I} = \frac{1}{1 - C_Y + M_Y} > 0$$

$$\frac{\partial Y}{\partial X} = \frac{1}{1 - C_Y + M_Y} > 0$$

$$\frac{\partial NX}{\partial I} = \frac{-M_Y}{1 - C_Y + M_Y} < 0$$

$$\frac{\partial NX}{\partial X} = \frac{1 - C_Y}{1 - C_Y + M_Y} > 0$$

The partial derivatives of output with respect to investment and exports are identical and are equal to the Keynesian multiplier. An increase in investment increases output, but reduces the trade balance because of the induced increase in imports. An increase in exports, however, increases both output and the trade balance, though the improvement in the trade balance is less than the increase in exports because the rise in income leads to additional imports.

An *IS/LM* model for a closed economy

We assume that: planned consumption expenditure is a function of disposable income with the marginal propensity to consume out of disposable income (C_D) and the marginal tax rate (T_Y)

both being positive but less than unity; planned investment is an inverse function of the rate of interest ($I_r < 0$); and government expenditure (G) is exogenously given. The demand for money $L(Y,r)$ is positively related to income ($L_Y > 0$), and is negatively related to the rate of interest ($L_r < 0$). The supply of money (M_s) is exogenously given. In equilibrium, income must equal planned expenditure, and the demand and supply of money must be equal to each other. Hence we have:

$$Y - C(Y - T(Y)) - I(r) - G = 0$$

$$L(Y, r) = M_s$$

Totally differentiating the two equilibrium conditions, we have:

$$dY - C_D(1 - T_Y)\,dY - I_r\,dr - dG = 0$$

$$L_Y\,dY + L_r\,dr = dM_s$$

Collecting terms and rearranging in matrix form, we obtain:

$$\begin{bmatrix} 1 - C_D(1 - T_Y) & -I_r \\ L_Y & L_r \end{bmatrix} \begin{bmatrix} dY \\ dr \end{bmatrix} = \begin{bmatrix} dG \\ dM_s \end{bmatrix}$$

The slopes of the *IS* and *LM* functions are given respectively by:

$$\text{IS:} \quad \frac{dr}{dY} = \frac{1 - C_D(1 - T_Y)}{I_r} < 0$$

$$\text{LM:} \quad \frac{dr}{dY} = \frac{-L_Y}{L_r} > 0$$

Y and r are implicit functions of the exogenous variables of this model, G and M_s, provided that the Jacobian determinant does not disappear. The Jacobian determinant is given by:

$$|J| = [1 - C_D(1 - T_Y)]L_r + I_r L_Y$$

It is straightforward to check that this determinant does not vanish, but will have a negative sign: the term inside the square bracket is positive since both the marginal propensity to consume and the marginal tax rate are both positive but smaller than unity, the partial derivative of the demand for money with respect to the rate of interest is negative as is the partial derivative of investment demand with respect to the rate of interest, whereas the demand for money is increasing in income.

Employing Cramer's rule, we obtain the following set of partial derivatives:

$$\frac{\partial Y}{\partial G} = \frac{L_r}{|J|} > 0$$

$$\frac{\partial r}{\partial G} = \frac{-L_Y}{|J|} > 0$$

$$\frac{\partial Y}{\partial M_s} = \frac{I_r}{|J|} > 0$$

$$\frac{\partial r}{\partial M_s} = \frac{1 - C_D(1 - T_Y)}{|J|} < 0$$

An expansionary fiscal policy as exemplified by an increase in the level of government expenditure will raise both income and the rate of interest. Income rises as a result of the increase in demand, but with increased transactions demand for money and an unchanged money supply, the rate of interest must rise in order to equilibrate the money market. This increase in the rate of interest leads to some crowding-out of private investment expenditure. An expansionary monetary policy will increase income and cause the rate of interest to fall. Excess supply in the money market leads to a bidding-up of bond prices, the mirror image of which is a fall in the rate of interest. Aggregate demand is then stimulated by the increase in investment induced by the interest rate fall, and there is a multiplier effect on output.

We now consider some special cases.

$$\text{If } L_r = 0, \text{ then } \frac{\partial Y}{\partial G} = 0$$

$$\text{If } I_r = 0, \text{ then } \frac{\partial Y}{\partial M_s} = 0$$

In words, for our simple macroeconomic model we have that, if the demand for money is completely insensitive to the rate of interest, the fiscal multiplier will be zero; in this case the *LM* curve is vertical. The increase in government expenditure is exactly offset by an equivalent reduction in private investment. If investment is not influenced by the rate of interest, the money multiplier will be zero; in this case the *IS* curve is vertical. In this simple model, there is no channel through which a monetary expansion gets transmitted into an increase in aggregate demand.

We now move on to consider more complicated cases where we evaluate limiting values of the fiscal and money multipliers as L_r and I_r respectively approach minus infinity.

$$\lim_{L_r \to -\infty} \frac{\partial Y}{\partial M_s} = 0$$

$$\lim_{L_r \to -\infty} \frac{\partial Y}{\partial G} = \lim_{L_r \to -\infty} \frac{L_r}{[1 - C_D(1 - T_Y)]L_r + I_r L_Y}$$

$$= \lim_{L_r \to -\infty} \frac{1}{[1 - C_D(1 - T_Y)] + I_r L_Y / L_r}$$

$$= \frac{1}{1 - C_D(1 - T_Y)}$$

If the demand for money is infinitely elastic to the rate of interest, then monetary policy is impotent; there will be no change in the level of income. An increase in the money supply leaves the rate of interest unchanged, with the result that aggregate demand remains unchanged; the *LM* curve is horizontal. On the other hand, if government expenditure is increased, there will be no crowding out of private investment expenditures as the rate of interest does not change as a result of the fiscal expansion in this situation. The fiscal multiplier takes the same value it would have done in a rock-bottom model with no monetary sector.

Similarly, it can be shown that:

$$\lim_{I_r \to -\infty} \frac{\partial Y}{\partial M_s} = \frac{1}{L_Y}$$

$$\lim_{I_r \to -\infty} \frac{\partial Y}{\partial G} = 0$$

When the demand for private investment expenditure is infinitely elastic to the rate of interest, fiscal policy is impotent. The *IS* curve in these circumstances is horizontal. An increase in government expenditure leads to an equivalent reduction of private investment expenditures; there is complete crowding-out. On the other hand, the money multiplier is large and equal to the reciprocal of the partial derivative of the demand for money with respect to the level of income. Since the rate of interest is effectively fixed, following a change in the money supply the whole burden of adjustment as the economy moves to the new equilibrium position is placed upon the level of income. Hence in these circumstances monetary policy is particularly efficacious in changing output and employment levels.

An *IS/LM* model for an open economy with a floating exchange rate and capital mobility

For the development of this model, we shall assume somewhat heroically that the domestic and foreign price level are both fixed and equal to unity. We let e represent the nominal exchange rate which we define as the foreign exchange price of domestic currency with the obvious implication that an increase in e is an appreciation of the domestic currency *vis-à-vis* the foreign currency. Given the assumptions we have made about foreign and domestic prices, this is also equal to the real exchange rate. We shall assume that the home economy is small relative to the size of the world economy so that the world rate of interest is fixed and independent of any developments in the domestic economy.

Our model then takes the following form:

$$Y - C(Y) - I(r) - G - NX(Y, e) = 0$$
$$L(Y, r) - M_s = 0$$
$$NX(Y, e) + K(r) = 0$$

where the symbols are as before, but in addition NX stands for net exports and $K(r)$ are net capital flows into the domestic economy. The first equation is the condition that income should equal planned expenditure, the second equation that the demand for money should equal the supply of money, and the third equation states that the balance of payments, the sum of net exports and capital flows, should be in equilibrium. Totally differentiating these three equations, we obtain:

$$dY - C'(Y)dY - I'(r)dr - dG - NX_Y dY - NX_e de = 0$$
$$L_Y dY + L_r dr - dM_s = 0$$
$$NX_Y dY + NX_e de + K'(r) dr = 0$$

Re-arranging and expressing the equations in matrix form yields:

$$\begin{bmatrix} 1 - C'(Y) - NX_Y & -I'(r) & -NX_e \\ L_y & L_r & 0 \\ NX_Y & K'(r) & NX_e \end{bmatrix} \begin{bmatrix} dY \\ dr \\ de \end{bmatrix} = \begin{bmatrix} dG \\ dM_s \\ 0 \end{bmatrix}$$

We impose the following restrictions upon the derivatives.

$$1 > C'(Y) > 0, \quad I'(r) < 0, \quad NX_e < 0, \quad -1 < NX_Y < 0$$
$$L_Y > 0, \quad L_r < 0, \quad K'(r) > 0$$

The marginal propensity to consume is positive, but less than unity; investment is negatively related to the rate of interest, an appreciation of the exchange rate leads to a reduction in net exports; net exports fall as income increases, but by less than the rise in income, i.e. the marginal propensity to import is positive but less than unity; the demand for money is positively related to income and negatively related to the rate of interest, net capital inflows rise as the domestic rate of interest increases.

We first check whether the Jacobian determinant vanishes:

$$|J| = L_Y NX_e(I'(r) - K'(r)) + L_r NX_e(1 - C'(Y))$$

Given the conditions we have imposed on the derivatives, it is clear that the Jacobian determinant is positive.

We now consider the impact that changes in fiscal and monetary policy will have on output, the rate of interest and the nominal exchange rate. First we will examine the effect of an expansionary fiscal policy which we model by an increase in government expenditure.

$$\frac{\partial Y}{\partial G} = \frac{\begin{vmatrix} 1 & -I'(r) & -NX_e \\ 0 & L_r & 0 \\ 0 & K'(r) & NX_e \end{vmatrix}}{|J|}$$

$$= \frac{L_r NX_e}{|J|} > 0$$

$$\frac{\partial r}{\partial G} = \frac{\begin{vmatrix} 1 - C'(Y) - NX_Y & 1 & -NX_e \\ L_Y & 0 & 0 \\ NX_Y & 0 & NX_e \end{vmatrix}}{|J|}$$

$$= \frac{-L_Y NX_e}{|J|} > 0$$

$$\frac{\partial e}{\partial G} = \frac{\begin{vmatrix} 1 - C'(Y) - NX_Y & -I'(r) & 1 \\ L_Y & L_r & 0 \\ NX_Y & K'(r) & 0 \end{vmatrix}}{|J|}$$

$$= \frac{L_Y K'(r) - L_r NX_Y}{|J|}$$

Both output and the rate of interest will rise as a result of an expansionary fiscal policy, but we cannot unequivocally sign the impact that a change in government expenditure will have on the nominal exchange rate. The outcome depends crucially upon the relative slopes of the *LM* curve and the *BP* curve, the latter being a locus of points for a given exchange rate for which the balance of payments is in equilibrium. Totally differentiating the *LM* curve and then setting the total differential equal to zero and rearranging yields the slope of the *LM* curve:

$$L_Y dY + L_r dr = 0$$

$$\frac{dr}{dY} = -\frac{L_Y}{L_r}$$

Performing the same operations on the balance of payments equation, but holding the exchange rate fixed, we obtain:

$$NX_Y \, dY + K'(r) \, dr = 0$$

$$\frac{dr}{dY} = -\frac{NX_Y}{K'(r)}$$

There will, therefore, be a depreciation of the exchange rate following an increase in government expenditure if the *BP* schedule slopes upwards more steeply than the *LM* schedule does. Conversely, if the *BP* schedule is flatter than the *LM* schedule then the exchange rate will rise in response to an increase in the level of government expenditure. When the *BP* schedule is relatively steep, then capital flows are not very sensitive to interest rate differentials, and at an unchanged exchange rate the improvement in the capital account is smaller than the deterioration in the current account which results from the increase in income. The exchange rate must, therefore, depreciate. We have the converse case when the *BP* curve is relatively flat. The multiplier effect on output of the increase in government expenditure will be smaller if the *BP* schedule is flatter than the *LM* schedule than when the reverse is the case. The reason for this is simple: in the former case there will be some crowding-out of net exports resulting from the appreciation of the nominal exchange rate, whereas in the latter case, there will be a further stimulus to aggregate demand provided by the depreciation of the exchange rate.

We now investigate the effects that an increase in the domestic money supply has an output, the interest rate and the nominal exchange rate.

$$\frac{\partial Y}{\partial M} = \frac{\begin{vmatrix} 0 & -I'(r) & -NX_e \\ 1 & L_r & 0 \\ 0 & K'(r) & NX_e \end{vmatrix}}{|J|}$$

$$= \frac{NX_e(I'(r) - K'(r))}{|J|} > 0$$

$$\frac{dr}{dM} = \frac{\begin{vmatrix} 1 - C'(Y) - NX_Y & 0 & -NX_e \\ L_y & 1 & 0 \\ NX_Y & 0 & NX_e \end{vmatrix}}{|J|}$$

$$= \frac{(1 - C'(Y))NX_e}{|J|} < 0$$

$$\frac{de}{dM} = \frac{\begin{vmatrix} 1 - C'(Y) - NX_Y & -I'(r) & 0 \\ L_y & L_r & 1 \\ NX_Y & K'(r) & 0 \end{vmatrix}}{|J|}$$

$$= \frac{-NX_Y I'(r) - (1 - C'(Y) - NX_Y)K'(r)}{|J|} < 0$$

In this case, there are no ambiguities. An expansionary monetary policy raises output, reduces the rate of interest and depreciates the nominal exchange rate. The excess supply of money balances leads to an attempt by economic agents to move out of money and into bonds. Bond prices rise and the interest rate falls. This in turn leads to an increase in investment and a capital outflow. At an unchanged exchange rate, the balance of payments deteriorates on both the current and capital account. The rise in income stimulates an increase in imports, and hot money flows out of the country. A depreciation of the exchange rate is required to re-establish external balance.

An important characteristic of the model we have examined above is that foreign and domestic bonds were not perfect substitutes for each other. The small domestic economy, therefore, was enabled to have an interest rate that differed from the exogenously given world rate of interest. In terms of the parameters of the model, the derivative of net capital flows into the domestic economy was positive but finite. Had there been zero capital mobility, then this derivative would have equalled zero, whereas with perfect capital mobility, it would have approached infinity.

An *IS/LM* model for an open economy with a fixed exchange rate and capital mobility

What difference does it make to our story if instead of the exchange rate regime being one of floating exchange rates, it is one in which the exchange rate is fixed? The endogenous variables are now the level of output, the domestic interest rate and the money supply. A surplus on the balance of payments is associated with an increase in the small domestic economy's holdings of foreign exchange reserves, which then feeds through into the domestic money supply. The money supply can also change as a result of developments in the domestic economy with the monetary authorities increasing domestic credit. Our model now takes the following form:

$$Y - C(Y) - I(r) - G - NX(Y) = 0$$

$$L(Y, r) - M_s = 0$$

$$M_s - M_s(-1) - D - NX(Y) - K(r) = 0$$

where $M_s(-1)$ is the money supply of the previous period, and D is domestic credit expansion. Totally differentiating these three equations, we obtain:

$$dY - C'(Y)\,dY - I'(r)\,dr - dG - NX_Y\,dY = 0$$

$$L_Y\,dY + L_r\,dr - dM_s = 0$$

$$dM_s - dD - NX_Y\,dY - K'(r)\,dr = 0$$

Re-arranging and expressing the equations in matrix form yields:

$$\begin{bmatrix} 1 - C'(Y) - NX_Y & -I'(r) & 0 \\ L_Y & L_r & -1 \\ -NX_Y & -K'(r) & 1 \end{bmatrix} \begin{bmatrix} dY \\ dr \\ dM_s \end{bmatrix} = \begin{bmatrix} dG \\ 0 \\ dD \end{bmatrix}$$

Let us first see whether the Jacobian determinant vanishes; in this case, we have:

$$|J| = (1 - C'(Y) - NX_Y)(L_r - K'(r)) + I'(r)(L_Y - NX_Y)$$

Given the signs of the derivatives, the Jacobian determinant is unambiguously negative. We may, therefore, express Y, r and M_s as implicit functions of G and D. Applying Cramer's rule, we obtain the following partial derivatives:

$$\frac{\partial Y}{\partial G} = \frac{\begin{vmatrix} 1 & -I'(r) & 0 \\ 0 & L_r & -1 \\ 0 & -K'(r) & 1 \end{vmatrix}}{|J|} = \frac{L_r - K'(r)}{|J|} > 0$$

$$\frac{\partial Y}{\partial D} = \frac{\begin{vmatrix} 0 & -I'(r) & 0 \\ 0 & L_r & -1 \\ 1 & -K'(r) & 1 \end{vmatrix}}{|J|} = \frac{I'(r)}{|J|} > 0$$

$$\frac{\partial r}{\partial G} = \frac{\begin{vmatrix} 1 - C'(Y) - NX_Y & 1 & 0 \\ L_Y & 0 & -1 \\ -NX_Y & 0 & 1 \end{vmatrix}}{|J|} = \frac{-L_Y + NX_Y}{|J|} > 0$$

$$\frac{\partial r}{\partial D} = \frac{\begin{vmatrix} 1 - C'(Y) - NX_Y & 0 & 0 \\ L_Y & 0 & -1 \\ -NX_Y & 1 & 1 \end{vmatrix}}{|J|} = \frac{1 - C'(Y) - NX_Y}{|J|} < 0$$

$$\frac{\partial M_s}{\partial G} = \frac{\begin{vmatrix} 1 - C'(Y) - NX_Y & -I'(r) & 1 \\ L_Y & L_r & 0 \\ -NX_Y & -K'(r) & 0 \end{vmatrix}}{|J|} = \frac{-L_Y K'(r) + L_r NX_Y}{|J|}$$

$$\frac{\partial M_s}{\partial D} = \frac{\begin{vmatrix} 1 - C'(Y) - NX_Y & -I'(r) & 0 \\ L_y & L_r & 0 \\ -NX_Y & -K'(r) & 1 \end{vmatrix}}{|J|} = \frac{(1 - C'(Y) - NX_Y)L_r + I'(r)L_Y}{|J|} > 0$$

Expansionary fiscal and monetary policies both raise output, but the former is associated with a rise in the rate of interest and a consequential crowding-out of private investment expenditures. On the other hand, expansionary monetary policy reduces the rate of interest and consequently leads to an increase in private investment expenditures. An expansionary fiscal policy has an ambiguous impact on the money supply: the current account of the balance of payments will deteriorate as imports rise following the reflationary impact of the fiscal expansion, whereas the rise in the rate of interest will lead to a capital inflow. If the latter effect dominates, then the balance of payments improves, and the money supply rises. If the converse is the case, then the money supply will fall. As before in our discussion of the floating exchange rate case, the crucial factor is the relative slopes of the *LM* and *BP* curves. If the former has a steeper slope than the latter, then the balance of payments will improve following an increase in government expenditure, and the money supply will rise. Conversely, if the *BP* curve has a steeper slope than the *LM* curve, then the balance of payments will deteriorate and the money supply will fall with an increase in government expenditure. Naturally, we are assuming in this discussion that the monetary authorities do not act to offset these effects on the money supply arising from the balance of payments. For the case of a rise in domestic credit expansion, there is no ambiguity: the money supply will rise.

12.6 SUMMARY

The reader has been introduced in this chapter to the techniques of partial and total differentiation. Armed with these techniques and making use of the implicit function theorem, one is equipped to handle mathematically comparative static analysis, a technique which is widely used in economics to analyse the impact that a change in some feature of an economic model has on the properties of its equilibrium. In this chapter, we have drawn upon some well known macroeconomic models to which students are typically exposed in intermediate macroeconomics courses to illustrate the procedure. In the next two chapters, we shall look at optimisation and shall return to some comparative static analysis in some microeconomic models at the end of Chapter 14.

12.7 EXERCISES

12.1 (a) Find all the first- and second-order partial derivatives of the following functions:

(i) $f(x_1, x_2) = x_1^3 + 2x_1 x_2 - x_2^2$

(ii) $f(x_1, x_2) = x_1^{0.5} x_2^{-1}$

(iii) $f(x_1, x_2) = x_1 x_2$

(iv) $f(x_1, x_2) = \log_e x_1 + 5x_1^2 x_2$

(v) $f(x_1, x_2, x_3) = x_1^2 x_2^3 x_3$

(vi) $f(x_1, x_2, x_3) = e^{2x_1 + x_2^3 - 5x_3}$

12.2 (a) Which of the functions in Exercise 12.1 are homogeneous?
(b) For those functions which are homogeneous, check that Euler's Theorem holds.

12.3 (a) Show that the *CES* production on page 198 function is homogeneous of degree ν.
(b) Check that Euler's Theorem is satisfied for the above production function.
(c) What is the value of the elasticity of substitution for the Cobb–Douglas production function?

$$Q = AK^\alpha N^\beta$$

(d) Given that in the long run, a cost-minimising firm will equate the marginal rate of substitution of capital for labour with the price of labour relative to the price of capital services, what will happen to the ratio of the income of labour to that of capital as the wage rate rises relative to the price of capital services in the case where (i) the firm's production function is Cobb–Douglas and (ii) where the firm's production function is *CES*?

12.4 (a) For each of the following, obtain the total derivative of y with respect to x_2.

(i) $y = f(x_1, x_2) = x_1^2 + 2x_1 x_2 + x_2^3$

$x_1 = g(x_2) = x_2^{0.5}$

(ii) $y = f(x_1, x_2) = 2x_1 x_2 + x_2^{0.5}$

$x_1 = g(x_2) = \log_e x_2$

(iii) $y = f(x_1, x_2, x_3) = x_1 x_2 + x_1 x_3 + x_2 x_3$
$x_1 = g(x_2) = 5 - x_2$
$x_3 = h(x_2) = 10x_2^{-1}$

(b) For the following Cobb–Douglas production function, derive the expression for the rate of growth of output in terms of the rates of growth of the factor inputs:

$$Y(t) = F(K(t), N(t)) = e^{0.05t} 100 K(t)^{0.25} N(t)^{0.75}$$

(c) Do the same thing for the following *CES* production function:

$$Y(t) = e^{0.1t} [0.2 K(t)^{-4} + 0.8 N(t)^{-4}]^{-0.25}$$

12.5 (a) Using the model on pages 204–205, derive the limiting values of the partial derivatives of the rate of interest with rsepect to government expenditure and the money supply as L_r and I_r respectively approach minus infinity.

12.6 (a) Use the model on page 207 to consider the implications for output, the interest rate and the nominal exchange rate of expansionary fiscal and monetary policies in the case where there is perfect capital mobility in the small open economy, i.e. the domestic rate of interest must equal the world rate of interest and the derivative of net capital flows with respect to the domestic rate of interest is infinite.

12.7 (a) How are the results on pages 210–211 modified if we now assume that there is perfect capital mobility so that the domestic rate of interest cannot differ from the exogenously given world rate of interest?

CHAPTER THIRTEEN

OPTIMISATION WITH A SINGLE CHOICE VARIABLE

13.1 INTRODUCTION

The aim of this chapter is to introduce the reader to the important question of how to find maximum and minimum values of a differentiable function. We restrict ourselves to the case of functions of a single variable, leaving until the next chapter the analysis of optimisation for the case of functions of more than one variable. We shall be concerned with identifying points which are relative extrema. By this we mean a point which gives rise to a larger or smaller value of the function than neighbouring points which lie on either side of it. We shall see that in some circumstances there exists a single point which gives rise to a maximum or minimum value of the function. In these circumstances we shall have discovered a global maximum or minimum of the function. In other cases there will not be a unique maximum or minimum; and in yet other cases there will not exist a finite value of the independent variable which is associated with a relative extremum. We shall see how to identify each of these situations.

A considerable corpus of economic analysis, particularly in microeconomics, is concerned with optimisation. In the theory of the firm, firms are typically assumed to be profit maximisers. Later in this chapter we shall analyse the behaviour of profit-maximising firms in different forms of market structures. In subsequent chapters, we shall broaden the discussion of optimisation: in Chapter 14 we shall be considering the case of functions of more than one variable, and shall investigate the conditions which must be satisfied for a maximum or minimum value of a function to be reached. This will enable us to extend our analysis to consider the case of firms which produce more than one product, or sell a given product in more than one market. Many optimising problems with which the economist is concerned involve the existence of constraints. A consumer wishes to maximise his utility, but he is constrained by his limited income. Given his income and the vector of market prices, how should he allocate his expenditure over a set of commodities in order to maximise his utility? Alternatively, a firm faced with a given set of factor prices wishes to minimise the costs of producing a particular level of output. In this case, the firm is constrained in its choice of the quantities of factors of production to employ by the available production technology for converting inputs into outputs. The topic of constrained optimisation is discussed in Chapter 16, and further developed in Chapter 17 where we modify the constraints of the problem by explicitly requiring the choice variables to take on non-negative values and allow for the possibility of slack being present in the constraints.

Chapter 13 is organised as follows. We commence in Section 13.2 by discussing in a relatively informal manner the conditions under which a function will reach a maximum or minimum value. We show how we may be able to distinguish between the two cases by looking at the sign of the second derivative. In Section 13.3 we provide a more advanced discussion of the conditions which must be met in order for the function to reach an extreme point. This requires us to introduce the concept of the expansion of a function, and we discuss both the Taylor-series and Maclaurin-series expansions of a function of a single variable. Making use of the Taylor-series expansion around the point which satisfies the first-order condition for a maximum or minimum, we derive general conditions for identifying a relative extremum. This section is technically more advanced than the other parts of this chapter and can be omitted on first reading.

In Section 13.4, we make use of the mathematical analysis to analyse some simple optimisation problems in economics. We look at profit maximisation in perfect competition and monopoly from a mathematical perspective, and provide in Exercise 13.4 an extensive set of problems with an economic flavour. Finally, in Section 13.5, we show how the first- and second-order conditions for a maximum can be utilised in order to evaluate the effect that a change in a parameter of a model will have on the equilibrium of that model. We analyse how levying a tax on a good would change both the output that a representative competitive firm would wish to produce, and the price at which the output would be sold. A summary follows in Section 13.6.

13.2 OPTIMISATION

In this section we consider how to find values of x which give rise to extreme values of the differentiable function $f(x)$. Consider Fig. 13.1 in which we have depicted an inverse U-shaped function. It is clear from the diagram that when $x = x^*$, the value of the function is maximised. The slope of the function at $x = x^*$ is equal to zero; an infinitesimally small positive or negative change in x starting out from the point x^* will lead to no change in the value of the function. We may conclude, therefore, that a necessary condition for $f(x)$ to reach a maximum value is that the first derivative of $f(x)$ with respect to x should be equal to zero.

Turning to Fig. 13.2, where we have depicted a U-shaped function, it is also obvious that when $x = x^*$, the value of $f(x)$ is minimised. The slope of the function is again equal to zero. It is also, therefore, the case that a necessary condition for $f(x)$ to reach a minimum value is that its first derivative with respect to x should be equal to zero.

How are we able to distinguish between the two cases then, given that the first-order condition is the same whether we are concerned with identifying a maximum or a minimum point? We shall provide an intuitive discussion of how we might be able to distinguish between the two cases, before going on later in the chapter to provide a more formal treatment.

Consider Fig. 13.3 in which we have depicted a function which gives rise to both a maximum

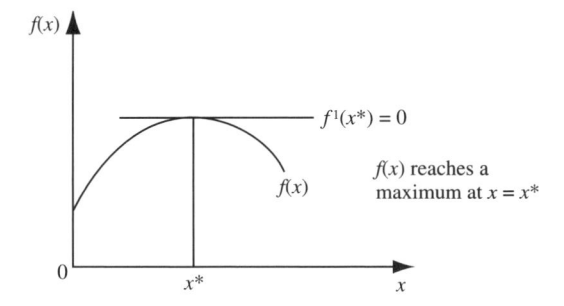

Figure 13.1 A maximum point.

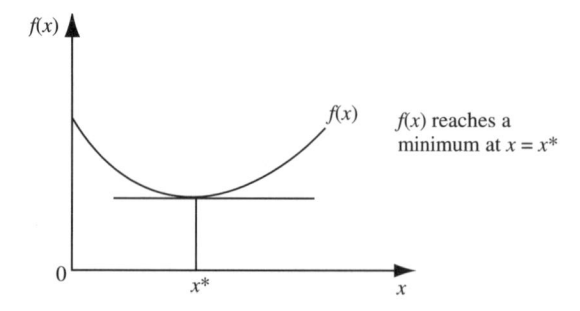

Figure 13.2 A minimum point.

and a minimum value of the function. Note that in the case of a maximum at x^*, for values of x slightly smaller than x^*, the slope of the function is positive, and for values of x slightly larger than x^*, the slope of the function is negative. The first derivative of the function is, accordingly, changing in value from being positive to being negative as x increases in value, starting out from a value of x somewhat less than x^*, and finishing up with a value of x somewhat greater than x^*. At the point x^{**}, however, where the function reaches a minimum value, the opposite situation arises. For values of x somewhat smaller then x^{**}, the function is negatively sloped, and for values of x somewhat larger than x^{**}, the function is positively sloped. The first derivative has moved from being negative to being positive as x has been increased in value, starting out from a value of x somewhat less than x^{**} and finishing up with a value somewhat larger than x^{**}. In the case of the maximum, we may conclude that in the vicinity of the point x^* the rate of change of the first derivative has been negative, whereas in the case of the minimum, the rate of change of the first derivative has been positive.

We may therefore state the following: if at a point which satisfies the first-order condition for a maximum of a function, the value of the second derivative is negative, when evaluated at this point, we shall certainly have identified a maximum value of the function; on the other hand, if at a point which satisfies the first-order condition for a minimum of a function, the value of the second derivative, when evaluated at this point, is positive, we shall certainly have identified a minimum value of the function.

The conditions that the second-order derivative be negative for a maximum and positive for a minimum are sufficient, but as we shall see below, following our discussion of Taylor-series expansions of a function, these conditions are not necessary for the particular outcomes.

Some examples

Consider the case of a quadratic function:

$$f(x) = 24 + 12x - x^2$$

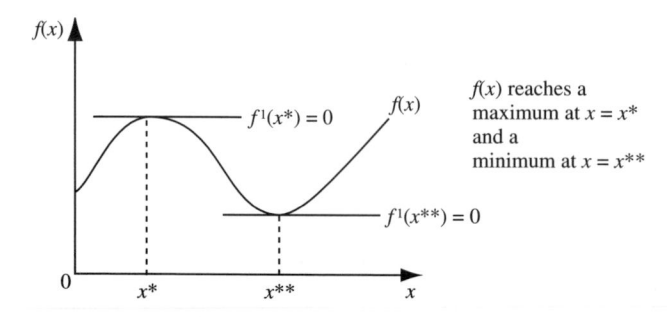

Figure 13.3 A maximum and a minimum.

Then differentiating with respect to x, setting the first derivative equal to zero, and solving for x, we obtain:
$$f'(x) = 12 - 2x = 0$$
$$\text{hence } x = 6$$

Differentiating again to obtain the second-order derivative yields:
$$f''(x) = -2$$

Since the second-order derivative is negative, regardless of the value of x, we may conclude that the function has reached a maximum value at $x = 6$, with $f(6) = 60$.

Now turn to the following quadratic function:
$$f(x) = 100 - 10x + 0.5x^2$$

Then differentiating with respect to x, setting the first derivative equal to zero, and solving for x, we obtain:
$$f'(x) = -10 + x = 0$$
$$\text{hence } x = 10$$

Differentiating again to obtain the second-order derivative yields:
$$f''(x) = 1$$

Since the second-order derivative is positive, regardless of the value of x, we may conclude that the function has reached a minimum value at $x = 10$, with $f(10) = 50$.

For the general case of a quadratic function, we would have:
$$f(x) = ax^2 + bx + c$$

whose first- and second-order derivatives are given respectively by:
$$f'(x) = 2ax + b, \quad f''(x) = 2a$$

We may, therefore, conclude that the quadratic function will reach an extreme value at $x = -b/2a$, and this point will be a global maximum if a is negative, and a global minimum if a is positive.

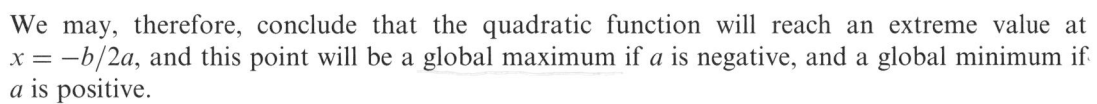

Let us now turn to a cubic function. Assume we have
$$f(x) = \tfrac{1}{3}x^3 - 6x^2 + 20x + 48$$

Then differentiating with respect to x yields:
$$f'(x) = x^2 - 12x + 20 = 0$$

from which it follows that
$$f'(x) = (x - 2)(x - 10) = 0$$

There are, therefore, two values of x for which the first derivative is equal to zero: $x = 2$, and $x = 10$. Differentiate again to obtain the second derivative:
$$f''(x) = 2x - 12$$

The second-order derivative will therefore be positive for $x > 6$, zero for $x = 6$, and negative for $x < 6$. We have therefore identified a local maximum at the point $x = 2$, and a local minimum at the point $x = 10$. The dominant term in the function is the cubed term, with the result that as x approaches infinity, so does the value of the function, and as x approaches minus infinity then so does the value of the function. The points we have identified where the first derivative is equal to zero in this case, therefore, only give rise to a local maximum at $x = 2$ with $f(2) = 66.66\ldots$, and a local minimum at $x = 2$ with $f(10) = -18.66\ldots$. Remember in the case of our quadratic functions there is just one point that satisfies the first-order condition, and this, depending on the sign of the parameter a, gives rise to either a global maximum or a global minimum.

13.3 THE GENERAL CONDITIONS FOR A RELATIVE EXTREMUM

Given a function $f(x)$, we may expand this function around some point x^* in the following way:

$$f(x) = \frac{f(x^*)}{0!} + \frac{df(x^*)}{1!\,dx}(x - x^*) + \frac{d^2f(x^*)}{2!\,dx^2}(x - x^*)^2 + \frac{d^3f(x^*)}{3!\,dx^3}(x - x^*)^3 + \frac{d^4f(x^*)}{4!\,dx^4}(x - x^*)^4 + \cdots$$

where $n!$ is $n(n-1)(n-2)\ldots(2)(1)$ and $0!$ is defined to be equal to unity. This is known as the Taylor-series (T-S) expansion of the function. If our function is a polynomial of degree n, then it will have a finite number of non-zero higher order derivatives with each derivative being evaluated at $x = x^*$. The $(n+1)$th derivative and all subsequent higher-order derivatives will equal zero, and if we expand the function up to and including the nth derivative, we will indeed find that the expansion is exactly equal to the original function. Consider the following example where the function we wish to expand is a cubic function of x.

$$f(x) = x^3 + 2x^2 - 5x + 10$$

This function has the following non-zero derivatives:

$$\frac{df}{dx} = 3x^2 + 4x - 5$$

$$\frac{d^2f}{dx^2} = 6x + 4$$

$$\frac{d^3f}{dx^3} = 6$$

Let us now expand the function around the point $x = 5$. Evaluating the value of the function and of its derivatives at this point we have:

$$f(5) = 160, \quad \frac{df}{dx}(5) = 90$$

$$\frac{d^2f}{dx^2} = 34, \quad \frac{d^3f}{dx^3} = 6$$

Substituting into the expression for the T-S expansion, we have:

$$f(x) = 160 + 90(x-5) + \frac{34}{2!}(x-5)^2 + \frac{6}{3!}(x-5)^3$$

$$= 160 + 90x - 450 + 17x^2 - 170x + 425 + x^3 - 15x^2 + 75x - 125$$

$$= x^3 + 2x^2 - 5x + 10$$

If we expand a polynomial function, but abort the process before we have included all the non-vanishing higher-order derivatives, we will not obtain an expression which is equal to the original function. What would have happened had we just taken a second-order T-S expansion of the cubic function above? Obviously, we would have omitted a non-zero third-order derivative, and we would have been left with the following expression:

$$17x^2 - 80x + 135$$

In order for this second-order expansion to have equalled the original function, it would have been necessary to include a remainder term, which would have to have taken the following form:

$$R_3 = x^3 - 15x^2 + 75x - 125$$

The value of the remainder term obviously depends upon the extent to which we have truncated the expansion. The reader should check that had we only made use of the first derivative in deriving the expansion, the remainder term would have been equal to:

$$R_2 = x^3 + 2x^2 - 95x + 300$$

For the general case, the remainder term takes the following form:

$$R_n = \frac{1}{(n+1)!} \frac{d^n f(\alpha)}{dx^n}(x - x^*)^{n+1}$$

where α lies between x and x^*. Unfortunately, the expression for the remainder does not specify the value of α other than to require it to lie between x and x^*.

Say we sought to evaluate the function when $x = 7$, having first taken a second-order T-S expansion around the point $x = 5$, then we would have:

$$f(7) = 17(7)^2 - 80(7) + 135 = 408$$

This differs somewhat from the true value of the function when $x = 7$, which is *416*. In this case, we have no real problem since the value of the third derivative is a constant, independent of the value of α, so we may let α take any value between *5* and *7*. Then the remainder is

$$R_2 = \frac{1}{3!} \frac{df^3(6)}{dx^3} 2^3 = 8$$

and our evaluation is indeed equal to its true value of *416*. Alternatively, had we just taken a first-order T-S expansion, then the remainder term would have had to have been equal to

$$R_1 = \frac{6(\alpha) + 4}{2!} 2^2 = 76$$

given that $f(7) = 416$ and that the first-order T-S expansion of $f(x)$ around *5* yields a value equal to *340*. Solving, we find that we would have required $\alpha = 17/3$.

Had we taken a zero-order T-S expansion around $x = 5$, given that $f(5) = 160$, then the remainder in this case would be given by

$$R_0 = 2(3\alpha^2 + 4\alpha - 5) = 256$$

Solving the quadratic in α, and taking the value which lies in the relevant interval, we find α must equal *6.025*.

Diagrammatically, what our procedure involves in the case of a zero-order expansion is the following. We plot the function in Fig. 13.4, marking the two values of x, the one around which the function is expanded, x^*, and the one for which we are going to evaluate the function, x. Construct the chord which joins $f(x^*)$ and $f(x)$, then shift this chord parallel to itself until it forms a tangent to the function. The value to be taken by α is then given by dropping a perpendicular from this tangency position to the x axis. Mathematically, the condition which must be satisfied by α is that

$$f(x) = f(x^*) + \frac{df}{dx}(\alpha)(x - x^*)$$

It is clear from the diagram that

$$f(x^*) = Kx^*, \quad f(x) = Lx,$$
$$\frac{df}{dx}(\alpha) = \frac{LM}{KM}, \quad f(x^*) - f(x^*) = LM$$
$$x - x^* = KM$$

and our evaluation of the function at x is correct.

A remainder term is necessary for a polynomial function when the order of the T-S expansion of the function is less than the degree of the polynomial. A remainder term is also required in functions which have an infinite number of non-zero higher-order derivatives.

In addition to a Taylor-series expansion where we expand the function around an arbitrary value of x which lies in the domain of the function, we may also expand a function around the point $x = 0$. This yields what is known as the Maclaurin-series expansion.

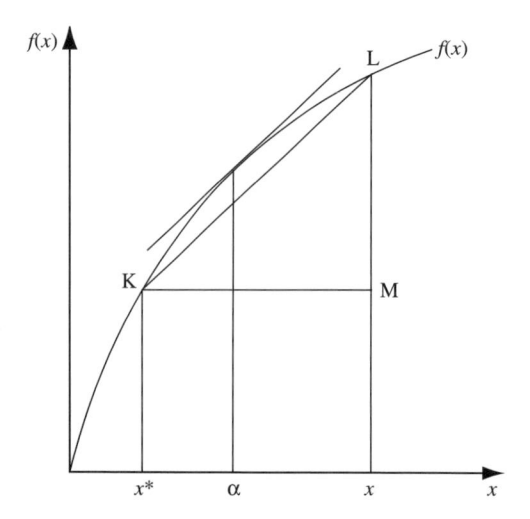

Figure 13.4 A zero-order T-S expansion. In order to obtain the remainder term in the zero-order T-S expansion around x^* the chord KL is shifted up parallel to itself until it forms a tangent to $f(x)$. The value of x at this tangency portion gives the required value of α.

$$f(x) = \frac{f(0)}{0!} + \frac{df(0)}{1!\,dx}x + \frac{d^2f(0)}{2!\,dx^2}x^2 + \frac{d^3f(0)}{3!\,dx^3}x^3$$
$$+ \frac{d^4f(0)}{4!\,dx^4}x^4 + \cdots$$

Consider the following function:
$$f(x) = x^2 + 8x + 16$$

Since this is a quadratic function, then we only need concern ourselves with the first and second derivatives; these are
$$f'(x) = 2x + 8, \text{ hence } f'(0) = 8$$
$$f''(x) = 2, \text{ hence } f''(0) = 2$$

Substituting in the expression for the Maclaurin-series expansion, we obtain:
$$f(x) = \frac{16}{0!} + \frac{8}{1!}x + \frac{2}{2!}x^2$$
$$= x^2 + 8x + 16$$

Consider a differentiable function $f(x)$ which has the property that its first derivative is equal to zero at $x = x^*$. What can we say about the nature of the point that we have identified here? In order to answer this question, let us evaluate the value of the function when $x = x^* + h$ by taking a Taylor-series expansion around the point $x = x^*$. This will give us the following expression:

$$f(x^* + h) = f(x^*) + \frac{df(x^*)}{dx}h + \frac{d^2f(x^*)}{2!\,dx^2}h^2 + \frac{d^3f(x^*)}{3!\,dx^3}h^3$$
$$+ \frac{d^4f(x^*)}{4!\,dx^4}h^4 + \cdots$$

Similarly, if we evaluate the value of the function at the point $x = x^* - h$ by taking a Taylor-series expansion around the point $x = x^*$, we would obtain:

$$f(x^* - h) = f(x^*) - \frac{df(x^*)}{dx}h + \frac{d^2f(x^*)}{2!\,dx^2}h^2 - \frac{d^3f(x^*)}{3!\,dx^3}h^3$$
$$+ \frac{d^4f(x^*)}{4!\,dx^4}h^4 - \cdots$$

Under what conditions will $f(x^*)$ be greater than both $f(x^* + h)$ and $f(x^* - h)$ as we let h approach zero? We have:

$$f(x^*) - f(x^* + h) = -\frac{d^2f}{2!\,dx^2}h^2 - \frac{d^3f}{3!\,dx^3}h^3 - \frac{d^4f}{4!\,dx^4}h^4 \cdots -$$

$$f(x^*) - f(x^* - h) = -\frac{d^2f}{2!\,dx^2}h^2 + \frac{d^3f}{3!\,dx^3}h^3 - \frac{d^4f}{4!\,dx^4}h^4 \cdots +$$

given that the first derivative when evaluated at $x = x^*$ is equal to zero. Now as h becomes smaller and smaller, then we can ignore terms containing powers of h greater than 2. It will be the case that $f(x^*)$ is greater than both $f(x^* + h)$ and $f(x^* - h)$ when

$$\frac{d^2f}{dx^2} < 0$$

Under what conditions will $f(x^*)$ be less than both $f(x^*+h)$ and $f(x^*-h)$ as we let h approach zero? We have:

$$f(x^*+h) - f(x^*) = \frac{d^2f}{2!\,dx^2}h^2 + \frac{d^3f}{3!\,dx^3}h^3 + \frac{d^4f}{4!\,dx^4}h^4 \cdots + \cdots$$

$$f(x^*-h) - f(x^*) = \frac{d^2f}{2!\,dx^2}h^2 - \frac{d^3f}{3!\,dx^3}h^3 + \frac{d^4f}{4!\,dx^4}h^4 \cdots - \cdots$$

given that the first derivative when evaluated at $x = x^*$ is equal to zero. Now as h becomes smaller and smaller, then we can ignore terms containing powers of h greater than 2. It will be the case that $f(x^*)$ is less than both $f(x^*+h)$ and $f(x^*-h)$ when

$$\frac{d^2f}{dx^2} > 0$$

The above conditions, however, are only sufficient conditions. They are not necessary, as we shall now see. Consider the case where both the first and second derivatives when evaluated at $x = x^*$ are equal to zero. Then we shall have the following result if the third derivative is positive:

$$f(x^*+h) > f(x^*) > f(x^*-h)$$

since

$$f(x^*) + \frac{d^3f}{3!\,dx^3}h^3 > f(x^*) > f(x^*) - \frac{d^3f}{3!\,dx^3}h^3$$

On the other hand, if the third derivative is negative, then

$$f(x^*+h) < f(x^*) < f(x^*-h)$$

since

$$f(x^*) + \frac{d^3f}{3!\,dx^3}h^3 < f(x^*) < f(x^*) - \frac{d^3f}{3!\,dx^3}h^3$$

the point we have identified in these two cases is neither a local maximum nor a local minimum, but instead, we have a stationary inflexion point.

However, if the first three derivatives when evaluated at $x = x^*$ are all zero, then we will have identified a local maximum if the fourth derivative is negative at this point, or a local minimum if the fourth derivative is positive at this point. The procedure in this case is to ignore all terms containing powers of h higher than four. It is then clear that for

$$f(x^*) > f(x^*+h) \text{ and } f(x^*) > f(x^*-h)$$

then we must have

$$\frac{d^4f}{dx^4} < 0$$

Furthermore, for

$$f(x^*) < f(x^*+h) \text{ and } f(x^*) < f(x^*-h)$$

then we must have

$$\frac{d^4f}{dx^4} > 0$$

We assume that the first-order derivative is equal to zero at $x = x^*$. The general second-order condition is that we will have identified a local maximum at $x = x^*$ if the first non-zero derivative we find at this point is even-numbered and takes on a negative value. We shall have identified a local minimum at $x = x^*$ if the first non-zero derivative we find at this point is even-numbered and takes on a positive value. If the first non-zero derivative is odd-numbered, then we shall have identified a stationary inflexion point.

For completeness, we have a non-stationary inflexion point at $x = x^*$, when the first derivative is non-zero, and the second derivative is zero.

Some examples

Consider the following function:

$$f(x) = x^3 - 15x^2 + 72x + 10$$

Differentiating to obtain the first- and second-order derivatives, we obtain:

$$\frac{df}{dx} = 3x^2 - 30x + 72$$

$$\frac{d^2f}{dx^2} = 6x - 30$$

Setting the first derivative equal to zero, and solving the quadratic equation, we find:

$$3(x^2 - 10x + 24) = 3(x - 4)(x - 6) = 0$$

Hence the roots of the quadratic are *4* and *6*. Let us now evaluate the second-order derivative at these two values of x. When $x = 4$, the second derivative is equal to -6, and when $x = 6$, the second derivative is equal to 6. Hence, we have identified a local maximum at $x = 4$, with $f(4) = 122$, whereas at $x = 6$, we have a local minimum with $f(6) = 118$. Note for completeness at $x = 5$, we have a non-stationary inflexion point, since the second derivative is equal to zero at this point, and $f(5) = 120$.

Now consider the following function:

$$f(x) = x^3 + 3x^2 + 25x + 10$$

Differentiating and setting the first-order derivative equal to zero, we have:

$$\frac{df}{dx} = 3x^2 + 6x + 25 = 0$$

When we apply the formula for finding the roots of a quadratic equation, we have:

$$x_1, x_2 = \frac{-6 \pm \sqrt{-264}}{6}$$

The quadratic equation does not have any real roots: in other words, there are no values of x for which the first derivative of the given function is equal to zero. If we were to plot the first derivative as a function of x, then we would have a U-shaped function. Since the second and third derivatives of the original function are given by

$$\frac{d^2f}{dx^2} = 6x + 6, \text{ and } \frac{d^3f}{dx^3} = 6$$

the first derivative reaches a minimum at $x = -1$, and the value of the first derivative at this point is 22. The first derivative of the original function is always positive, so the value of this function is always increasing as x increases. Note, however, that the second derivative is equal to zero at $x = -1$, and so this function has a non-stationary inflexion point here, with the value of the function being -13.

Consider the following function.

$$f(x) = -4x^3 + 12x^2 - 12x$$

Differentiating with respect to x and setting the derivative equal to zero, we have

$$\frac{df}{dx} = -12x^2 + 24x - 12 = 0$$

Solving the quadratic equation, we find it has a repeated root with $x = 1$. Differentiating again and evaluating the second derivative at $x = 1$, we obtain:

$$\frac{d^2f}{dx^2} = -24x + 24, \text{ and hence } \frac{d^2f}{dx^2}(1) = 0$$

Differentiating again, we find that the third derivative is the first one to have a non-zero derivative at $x = 1$, so we have a stationary inflexion point.

Consider the function

$$f(x) = (x - 2)^4$$

Differentiating with respect to x, and setting the first derivative equal to zero, we have:

$$\frac{df}{dx} = 4(x - 2)^3 = 0$$
$$\text{hence } x = 2$$

Now consider the higher-order derivatives:

$$\frac{d^2f}{dx^2} = 12(x - 2)^2$$

$$\frac{d^3f}{dx^3} = 24(x - 2)$$

$$\frac{d^4f}{dx^4} = 24$$

When $x = 2$, the fourth-order derivative is the first one not to be equal to zero, and given that it is positive, we have identified a minimum at this point.

13.4 SOME ECONOMIC APPLICATIONS OF MAXIMA AND MINIMA

Consider a firm whose total cost function is given by

$$TC = c(q) \text{ with } c'(q) > 0 \text{ and } c''(q) > 0$$

where TC is total cost and q is output. Hence, marginal cost, the derivative of total cost with respect to output, is a positive increasing function of output. Dividing the total cost function by output, we have the firm's average cost function:

$$AC = \frac{c(q)}{q}$$

Differentiating the average cost function twice with respect to output, we obtain:

$$\frac{dAC}{dq} = \frac{c'(q)q - c(q)}{q^2}$$

$$= \frac{c'(q) - c(q)/q}{q}$$

$$= \frac{MC - AC}{q}$$

$$\frac{d^2 AC}{dq^2} = \frac{c''(q)q^3 - 2q(c'(q)q - c(q))}{q^4}$$

If at some output level the first derivative of average cost with respect to output is equal to zero, then marginal and average cost are equal to each other. Assuming the first derivative is zero at $x = x^*$, then evaluating the second derivative at this point we find that

$$\frac{d^2 AC}{dq^2} = \frac{c''(q^*)}{q^*}$$

and since the second derivative is positive, we have identified a minimum point. Average cost of production is minimised at an output level at which average cost is equal to marginal cost and marginal cost is rising.

Now let the firm's inverse demand function be given by:

$$p = p(q)$$

where p is price. Multiplying through by output q, we obtain the firm's total revenue function:

$$TR = p(q)q$$

What conditions must be satisfied for the firm's total revenue to be maximised? Differentiating the total revenue function with respect to output, we have marginal revenue:

$$\frac{dTR}{dq} = p(q) + qp'(q)$$

$$= p(q)\left(1 + \frac{qp'(q)}{p(q)}\right)$$

$$= p\left(1 + \frac{1}{\eta_d}\right)$$

where η_d is the own-price elasticity of demand. Total revenue will, therefore, be maximised when marginal revenue is zero, and as can be seen from the above expression, this will be the case if the absolute value of the own-price elasticity of demand is equal to unity. If the elasticity of demand is always absolutely greater than unity, then price reductions will always increase total revenue; conversely, if the elasticity of demand is always absolutely less than unity, then price reductions will always reduce total revenue. To check that the second-order condition is satisfied, then we must differentiate marginal revenue with respect to output. If this derivative is negative at the output at which the elasticity of demand is unity, then total revenue will have been maximised.

$$\frac{d^2 TR}{dq^2} = \frac{dMR}{dq} = 2p'(q) + qp''(q) < 0$$

If the inverse demand curve is linear, then $p''(q)$ will equal zero, and there will definitely exist an output at which total revenue is maximised as long as the inverse demand curve is negatively sloped, since in this case $p'(q)$ is negative.

Profit maximisation in a competitive market

Let us now turn to consider profit maximisation. We first deal with a firm which is a price taker in the output market. Its profit's function (Π) is given by:

$$\Pi = pq - c(q) - F$$

where we have decomposed the cost function into fixed costs, F, and variable costs, $c(q)$. Differentiating the profit's function with respect to output and setting the derivative equal to zero, we obtain:

$$\frac{d\Pi}{dq} = p - c'(q) = 0$$

$$\frac{d^2\Pi}{dq^2} = -c''(q) < 0$$

Necessary conditions for the maximisation of profits, therefore, are that at the chosen output level, q^*, price should equal marginal cost, and marginal cost should be increasing. However, it must also be the case that the firm be earning greater profits by producing than by not producing. In the short run, fixed costs must be met regardless of whether the firm produces. Hence, if the firm were to shut down, its short-run profits would be equal to $-F$. For a positive level of output to be produced in the short run, it is clear that the following condition must be satisfied:

$$\Pi(q^*) \geq \Pi(0)$$

This requires that

$$pq^* - c(q^*) \geq 0$$

$$p \geq c(q^*)/q^* = AVC$$

It would still be in the firm's interest to produce a positive level of output in the short run even if this involved the firm making losses as long as it was at least covering its variable costs. In such circumstances, the losses would be smaller than if it shut down but still had to meet its fixed costs. The implications for the nature of the short-run supply curve of the competitive firm are straightforward: the firm would be unwilling to supply any output at a price below its average variable costs of production. Once, however, price is at least as high as its average variable costs, then the firm's supply schedule will be given by its marginal cost curve.

In the long run all costs become avoidable. There may be set-up costs which are independent of the firm's level of output, but if the firm closed permanently, then these costs would not have to be met. Hence, the competitive firm's long-run cost curve would take the form:

$$LRTC = 0 \text{ for } q = 0$$
$$= F + C(q) \text{ for } q > 0$$

The profit-maximising conditions now require price to equal long-run marginal cost, marginal cost to be increasing, and the price to be at least as large as long-run average total cost. In a perfectly competitive market, in the long run firms are able to expand or reduce their capacity and there is freedom of entry into and exit from the market, so that long-run equilibrium also requires only normal profits be earned. The firms are just satisfied with what they are earning and have no desire to change their level of output, while no other firms have any incentive to enter the industry.

Profit maximisation in monopoly

Let us now turn to consider the case of a firm with a monopoly. The market and the firm's demand curve, therefore, coincide with each other. We ignore the short-run/long-run distinction, and just concentrate on the long-run outcome. We write the firm's profits function as follows:

$$\Pi = p(Q)Q - C(Q)$$

where $p(Q)$ is the inverse demand function, and $C(Q)$ is the long-run total cost function, and Q is output. Differentiating with respect to output, and setting the derivative equal to zero, we obtain the first-order condition for a maximum of profit:

$$\frac{d\Pi}{dQ} = p(Q) + p'(Q)Q - C'(Q) = 0$$

The first two terms on the right-hand side of the equation equal marginal revenue, and the last term is marginal cost. We have the well known result: the monopolist must equate marginal revenue with marginal cost. Differentiating again with respect to output to obtain the second-order condition, we have:

$$\frac{d^2\Pi}{dQ^2} = \frac{d^2TR}{dQ^2} - \frac{d^2TC}{dQ^2}$$
$$= \frac{dMR}{dQ} - \frac{dMC}{dQ}$$
$$= 2p'(Q) + Qp''(Q) - C''(Q) < 0$$

The marginal cost function must cut the marginal revenue function from below. If profits were negative at the output level at which the above two conditions are satisfied, then the firm would close down.

When discussing revenue maximising, we derived a relationship between marginal revenue and price:

$$MR = p\left(1 + \frac{1}{\eta_d}\right)$$

In a perfectly competitive market, price is equal to marginal cost. We now show that in a monopolistic market, the gap between price and marginal cost will be larger the less elastic demand is for the product. Given that profit maximisation in a monopolistic market requires the equality of marginal revenue and marginal cost, we must have:

$$MC = p\left(1 + \frac{1}{\eta_d}\right)$$

from which it follows that the relative price–cost margin is given by

$$\frac{p - MC}{p} = -\frac{1}{\eta_d}$$

Note also that a profit-maximising monopolist must produce an output the demand for which is price-elastic. If this were not the case, then marginal revenue would be negative, and could not then equal marginal cost, which in any plausible world is going to be positive.

Profit maximisation in monopolistic competition

In such a market structure, firms produce differentiated products, with the implication that the demand for an individual firm's product is an inverse function of the price. Unlike perfect competition, but as in monopoly, marginal revenue is therefore a decreasing function of output. There exist a large number of firms in the industry, and there is freedom of entry into and exit from the industry. Hence, in the short run if the firms in the industry are earning greater than normal profits, then there will be an incentive both for other firms to enter the industry and for the existing firms to alter their scale of operations. In long-run equilibrium, then the existing firms must be content with their scale of operations, and no outsider would wish to enter the industry. Not only must we have for long-run profit maximisation that long-run marginal cost be equal to long-run marginal revenue, that the slope of the long-run marginal cost curve be greater than that of the long-run marginal revenue curve, but supernormal profits must also be zero.

13.5 SOME COMPARATIVE STATIC ANALYSIS

Let us consider the long-run implications of the government levying a per unit tax on a product produced by a perfectly competitive industry. The profits function of a representative firm is given by:

$$\Pi = pq - c(q) - tq$$

where t is the unit tax. Long-run equilibrium requires the following conditions to be satisfied:

$$\Pi = pq - c(q) - tq = 0$$
$$p - c'(q) - t = 0$$
$$-c''(q) < 0$$

If we now totally differentiate both the condition that profits be zero in long-run equilibrium and the first-order condition for a maximum of profit, we obtain the following two equations:

$$d\Pi = qdp + (p - c'(q) - t)dq - qdt = 0$$
$$dp - c''(q)dq - dt = 0$$

Re-arranging the equations in matrix form and taking into account the fact that the first-order condition requires $p - c'(q) - t = 0$, we obtain:

$$\begin{bmatrix} q & 0 \\ 1 & -c''(q) \end{bmatrix} \begin{bmatrix} dp \\ dq \end{bmatrix} = \begin{bmatrix} qdt \\ dt \end{bmatrix}$$

It is now a simple matter to investigate the impact of a change in the tax rate on the product price and on the output of the representative firm. Applying Cramer's rule, we have:

$$\frac{dp}{dt} = \frac{\begin{vmatrix} q & 0 \\ 1 & -c''(q) \end{vmatrix}}{\begin{vmatrix} q & 0 \\ 1 & -c''(q) \end{vmatrix}} = 1$$

$$\frac{dq}{dt} = \frac{\begin{vmatrix} q & q \\ 1 & 1 \end{vmatrix}}{\begin{vmatrix} q & 0 \\ 1 & -c''(q) \end{vmatrix}} = 0$$

The full burden of the incidence of the tax will fall upon the consumers of the product as the unit tax increase leads to an equivalent increase in the price of the good. The representative firm will produce an unchanged output. Total industry output must, however, be lower; otherwise the price of the good would not have risen, so some firms must have exited from the industry. The long-run supply curve of the industry is perfectly elastic at a price which enables the producing firms to make normal profits, so this has been shifted upwards by the full amount of the tax. The short-run industry supply curve, on the other hand, has been shifted to the left as a result of the exit of some firms from the industry.

What has been implicitly assumed throughout the above analysis is that the nature of the long-run cost function has not been changed as a result of pecuniary externalities which have led the prices of the factors of production to alter as a result of the reduced demand for factors of production. We are implicitly assuming that not only is there a perfectly elastic supply of each factor of production to an individual firm, but that the factor prices are invariant to changes in demand for factors at the level of the industry as a whole. If factor prices were to change, then the position of the representative firm's long-run cost function would also shift, and it would no longer necessarily follow that those firms that remained in the industry produced the same output as they did prior to the tax increase. The new level of output at which the long-run average cost curve was horizontal would depend upon both the technology available to the firm as embodied in its production function, and also on the change in relative factor prices. Nor would the full incidence of the tax be shifted on to consumers; some now would be shifted backwards on to factor suppliers, given a less than perfectly elastic supply at the level of the industry.

13.6 SUMMARY

Having worked through this chapter, the reader will now be familiar with the conditions which must be met for the value of a function to have reached a maximum or minimum. Necessary-and-sufficient conditions for a maximum are that the first derivative be equal to zero and the second derivative be negative. If the second derivative is always negative regardless of the value of the independent variable, x, and given that there exists a point at which the first derivative is zero, then there will be a unique point at which the function reaches a maximum value. Necessary-and-sufficient conditions for a minimum are that the first derivative be equal to zero and the second derivative be positive. If the second derivative is always positive regardless of the value of the independent variable, x, and given that there exists a point at which the first derivative is zero, then there will be a unique point at which the function reaches a minimum value. In some circumstances, we shall have to concern ourselves with the signs of higher-order derivatives. In these cases, the crucial factor for us to have identified an extreme point is that the first non-zero derivative be even-numbered. If it is negative, we shall have found a maximum; if it is positive, we shall have found a minimum. If the first non-zero derivative is odd-numbered, then we have identified a non-stationary inflexion point.

With the above mathematical background firmly in place, the reader is then in a position to apply the differential calculus to some simple optimising problems in economics. Not only can the methods be applied to simple numerical problems, but it is possible to derive some simple predictions of the effects of some policy change in models in which we do not specify the precise form of the functions, but simply impose some restrictions on the signs of some derivatives. These restrictions are such as to ensure that the second-order conditions are satisfied. In the next chapter we shall move on to look at optimisation with functions of more than one variable.

13.7 EXERCISES

13.1 Find the value(s) of x which give rise to extreme values of the following functions, commenting on whether you have identified maximum or minimum values of the function. Calculate $f(x)$ at these points.

(i) $f(x) = 42 + 24x - 3x^2$

(ii) $f(x) = 400 - 12x + 0.25x^2$

(iii) $f(x) = 300 - 64x + 4x^2$

(iv) $f(x) = 250 + 100x - 2x^2$

(v) $f(x) = x^3 - 18x^2 + 10$

(vi) $f(x) = \frac{1}{3}x^3 + 4x^2 - 48x$

(vii) $f(x) = 2x^3 + 3x^2 - 36x + 5$

(viii) $f(x) = -4x^3 + 12x^2 + 36x$

(ix) $f(x) = 3x^4 - 32x^3 + 30x^2 + 168x$

(x) $f(x) = -x^4$

13.2 (a) Approximate the following functions by writing out a third-order Taylor-series expansion around the point $x = 1$:

(i) $f(x) = 2x^3 + 6x - 100$

(ii) $f(x) = x^2 - 7x + 12$

(iii) $f(x) = \dfrac{1}{x}$

(iv) $f(x) = x^{0.5}$

(v) $f(x) = \log_e x$

(b) Approximate the following functions by writing out a third-order Maclaurin-series expansion:

(i) $f(x) = x^3 + 8$

(ii) $f(x) = \sin x$

(iii) $f(x) = \cos x$

(iv) $f(x) = e^x$

(v) $f(x) = \log_e(1+x)$

13.3 Find where they exist all the points which give rise to extreme values of the following functions as well as any inflexion points, both stationary and non-stationary ones.

(i) $f(x) = x^3 - 6x^2 + 15x + 8$

(ii) $f(x) = x^3 - 6x^2 + 12x$

(iii) $f(x) = 2x^3 + 21x^2 - 108x$

(iv) $f(x) = -x^3 + 12x^2 - 51x$

(v) $f(x) = x^3 + 10$

(vi) $f(x) = -x^4 + 2x^2 + 100$

(vii) $f(x) = 5 + x^5$

(viii) $f(x) = 256 - x^8$

(ix) $f(x) = 0.5x^{25}$

(x) $f(x) = 2x^{50}$

13.4 (a) A competitive firm's short-run average variable cost function ($SRAVC$) is given by:

$$SRAVC = q^2 - 40q + 410$$

where q is the firm's output. What is the minimum price at which this firm would be prepared to supply its output in the short run?

(b) A competitive firm's long-run total cost curve is given by:

$$LRTC = 0 \text{ for } q = 0$$
$$= 4q^2 + 10q + 100 \text{ for } q > 0$$

What is the minimum price at which this firm would be preferred to supply its output in the long run?

(c) A profit-maximising competitive firm can sell all it produces at a price of 21. Its total cost function (TC) is given by:

$$TC = q^3 - 4.5q^2 + 24q$$

How much will it produce and how large are its profits?

(d) A perfectly competitive firm's total cost function is given by:

$$TC = \tfrac{2}{3}q^3 - 10q^2 + 60q$$

where TC is total cost and q is output.

(i) If the market price is 28, how much will the firm produce? How large will its profits be?

(ii) At what output will the firm's average costs be minimised? At what price will the firm only be earning normal profits?

(e) The inverse demand function for some good is given by:

$$p = 1250 - Q$$

where p is price, and Q is quantity. The supply (marginal cost) function is given by:

$$MC = 50 + 4Q$$

(i) What would be the equilibrium output of a competitive industry? What price would be charged?

(ii) Obtain the output which would be produced by a profit-maximising monopolist faced with the same demand and cost conditions. At what price would this output be sold?

(iii) Assume that as a by-product of producing this good, a river is polluted. Let the marginal external cost (*MEC*) be given by:
$$MEC = 1.25Q.$$

What is the socially efficient level output of good?

(iv) If the government wishes to ensure the socially efficient output level is produced when the good is produced by a competitive industry, what per unit tax should it impose on the good?

(v) How should the government act to secure the socially efficient level of output if the good is produced by the monopolist?

(f) The inverse demand function for some good is given by:
$$p = 420 - 3q$$

where p is price and q is quantity. The good is supplied by a monopolist whose total cost (*TC*) function is given by
$$TC = 10\,000 + 0.5q^2$$

(i) Derive the profit-maximising level of output. What price would a profit-maximising monopolist charge, and how large would its profits be?

(ii) How much would a sales-maximising monopolist produce? What would be the own-price elasticity of demand at this output level? How large would its profits be?

(g) A publicly owned enterprise sets a price for its product equal to its marginal cost of production. The demand function for its output is given by:
$$q_d = 60 - 0.5p$$

where q_d is quantity demanded and p is price. Its total cost (*TC*) function is as follows:
$$TC = q^2$$

(i) Derive the price the enterprise will set, obtain the quantity demanded of the good, and hence calculate the value of the own-price elasticity of demand at the equilibrium position.

The enterprise is now privatised as a monopoly and follows an objective of profit maximisation. Its demand and cost functions are unchanged.

(ii) (1) Find the profit-maximising levels of output and price for the monopolist.

(2) Obtain the welfare loss from privatising the firm.

(3) How much would a revenue-maximising monopolist produce?

Assume once more that the firm is a profit maximiser, and that the firm has been able by virtue of privatisation to obtain efficiency gains such that its *TC* function is now given by:
$$TC = 0.5q^2$$

(iii) Calculate the new profit-maximising level of output. Has social welfare increased compared to the pre-privatisation position?

(h) The inverse demand function and the total cost function for a monopolistically competitive firm are given respectively by:
$$p = 100 - q$$
$$LRTC = 1000 + 1.5q^2 \text{ for } q > 0$$

Derive the profit-maximising level of output for this firm. Is the firm in long-run equilibrium when it produces this particular level of output?

(i) In a perfectly competitive market, each firm's long-run total cost function is given by:
$$C(q) = 20q^3 - 40q^2 + 30q$$

where q is the firm's output. The market demand function is:
$$Q_d(p) = 140 - 10p$$

where Q_d is quantity demanded and p is price.

(i) Derive the long-run supply function of the representative firm.
(ii) What are the long-run equilibrium values of price and quantity?
(iii) How many firms will be active in long-run equilibrium?
(iv) Suppose that due to technical progress the cost of producing q units is reduced by an amount αq. Determine the new long-run equilibrium supply of each firm and the new long-run equilibrium price, expressing both as a function of α.

(j) The inverse demand function for a monopolist is given by:

$$p = 200 - 0.5q$$

where p is price and q is output.

(i) At what price is the product sold and how large are the firm's profits?
(ii) Assume the government imposes a tax of *30* per unit on the good, how much will the monopolist now produce?
(iii) What is the value of the tax rate, t, which will maximise the government's tax revenue?
(iv) If the government desires the monopolist to produce the socially optimal level of output, what per unit subsidy should it offer on the good?

13.5 (a) Assuming the industry is perfectly competitive, analyse the effect on total industry output, the output of a representative firm, and the price of the product of the introduction of a per unit subsidy.

(b) For a monopolist, analyse the effect on output and price of (i) the imposition of a per unit tax on the good; and (ii) the imposition of a proportional sales tax. Note that in the later case, the price received by the firm is given by $p(1-t)$ where p is the price paid by the consumer, and t is the proportional rate of tax.

CHAPTER FOURTEEN

OPTIMISATION WITH MORE THAN ONE CHOICE VARIABLE

14.1 INTRODUCTION

In Chapter 14 we turn to functions of more than one variable and discuss how to identify points which give rise to a relative extremum of the function. In Section 14.2 we look first of all at the case of a function of two variables, before going on to look at the general case of a function of n variables. We shall see that the conditions which must be satisfied are a natural development of the conditions for the single variable case. Whereas in the single variable case, the first-order condition required the first derivative to be zero, in the multi-variable case we shall require all the first-order partial derivatives of the function to be zero. We also saw in Chapter 13 that given the first-order condition is satisfied, it is sufficient then to identify a maximum point for the second derivative to be negative. Correspondingly for a minimum, the sufficient condition is that the second derivative be positive. We shall see that in the multi-variable case, the sufficient condition relates to the rate of change of the total differential, which in turn requires certain conditions on the second-order partial derivatives to be met.

Having discussed the mathematical conditions for identifying an extreme point, we move on in Section 14.3 to draw some economic illustrations from the theory of the firm. We look at the case of a monopolist engaging in price discrimination, consider the output decisions of a profit-maximising multi-plant monopolist, examine the behaviour of duopolists in both a non-cooperative and a cooperative equilibrium.

In Section 14.4 we engage in some comparative static analysis of some economic models in which the relevant economic agent is assumed to be a maximiser. We are interested in ascertaining the impact which a change in a variable which is not under the control of the agent will have on the agent's optimal choices. In many cases we shall be dealing with very general functions and will be drawing upon the second-order conditions for a maximum in order to be able to measure qualitatively the impact that a change in an exogenous variable will have on the model's equilibrium. By qualitatively, we mean the direction of movement: for example, what will happen to the employment of factors of production following an increase in the price of one of the factors, or to the outputs produced by a firm following a change in an indirect tax rate or in a subsidy?

14.2 THE FIRST- AND SECOND-ORDER CONDITIONS

Assume we have the following functional relationship, showing the dependence of a firm's profits Π on its output of two products, x_1 and x_2:

$$\Pi = f(x_1, x_2)$$

Totally differentiating the profits function yields:

$$d\Pi = f_1\, dx_1 + f_2\, dx_2$$

For the firm to be maximising its profits then an infinitesimally small change in the output of either product should leave profits unchanged. We must have $d\Pi$ equal to zero, and this will only be the case where the partial derivatives are both equal to zero. We saw in Chapter 13 that a sufficient second-order condition for a maximum was that the second derivative be negative. The equivalent condition here is that the total differential of $d\Pi$ be negative. In order to proceed further, we must first differentiate $d\Pi$ totally. In carrying out this differentiation, we treat dx_1 and dx_2 as constants. We, therefore, obtain:

$$d(d\Pi) = d^2\Pi = \frac{\partial(d\Pi)}{\partial x_1} dx_1 + \frac{\partial(d\Pi)}{\partial x_2} dx_2$$

$$= (f_{11}\, dx_1 + f_{12}\, dx_2)\, dx_1 + (f_{21}\, dx_1 + f_{22}\, dx_2)\, dx_2$$

$$= f_{11}(dx_1)^2 + 2f_{12}\, dx_1\, dx_2 + f_{22}(dx_2)^2$$

In order to proceed further with the evaluation of the sign of $d^2\Pi$, note that we have here a quadratic form. We may express $d^2\Pi$ as follows:

$$d^2\Pi = (dx_1 \quad dx_2) \begin{bmatrix} f_{11} & f_{12} \\ f_{21} & f_{22} \end{bmatrix} \begin{bmatrix} dx_1 \\ dx_2 \end{bmatrix}$$

We have earlier seen that this quadratic form will be negative provided the matrix of second-order partial derivatives is negative definite, these partial derivatives being evaluated at the point which satisfies the first-order conditions. This will indeed be the case if all the eigenvalues are negative, or alternatively if the following determinantal conditions are met:

$$|H_1| = |f_{11}| < 0$$

$$|H_2| = \begin{vmatrix} f_{11} & f_{12} \\ f_{21} & f_{22} \end{vmatrix} > 0$$

The above determinants are known as Hessian determinants. If we are dealing with a minimisation problem, then the first-order conditions are unchanged: we still require all the second-order partial derivatives to be equal to zero. For the second-order condition, however, we now require $d^2\Pi$ to be positive. This will indeed be the case if the matrix of second-order partial derivatives is positive definite at the point which satisfies the first-order conditions. This matrix will be positive definite, provided that all its eigenvalues are positive. Alternatively, the Hessian determinants must be both positive.

$$|H_1| = |f_{11}| > 0$$

$$|H_2| = \begin{vmatrix} f_{11} & f_{12} \\ f_{21} & f_{22} \end{vmatrix} > 0$$

We now turn to the general case. Consider the case where the functional relationship contains a set of variables: $x_1, x_2, \ldots, x_n$, and we wish to find the conditions that must be satisfied for a point in this n-dimensional space to give rise to a maximum or minimum value of $f(x)$. Let us first totally differentiate $f(x)$ to obtain:

$$df = f_1 \, dx_1 + f_2 \, dx_2 + \cdots + f_n \, dx_n = 0$$

It is clear that for the value of the function to be invariant to an infinitesimally small change in x_j, then we must have f_j equal to zero, and this must be true for all j. The first-order conditions are, therefore, very straightforward. We shall have identified an extreme point of the function at x^* if all the first-order partial derivatives of the function when evaluated at this point are equal to zero.

How can we then determine whether the point which satisfies the first-order conditions for an extreme value of the function gives rise to a maximum or minimum value of the function? Let us first consider the case of a maximum. We are looking for the analogue of the sufficient second-order condition in the single variable case that the second-order derivative be negative. The way to proceed is as follows: totally differentiate df, but treat as constants during this differentiation the terms $dx_j, j = 1, \ldots, n$. This yields the following expression:

$$d^2 f = f_{11} \, dx_1^2 + 2f_{12} \, dx_1 \, dx_2 + \cdots + 2f_{1n} \, dx_1 \, dx_n$$
$$+ f_{22} \, dx_2^2 + \cdots + 2f_{2n} \, dx_2 \, dx_n + \cdots + f_{nn} \, dx_n^2$$

If $d^2 f$ is negative when evaluated at the point x^*, then we shall have identified a point which gives rise to a maximum of the function. Conversely, if $d^2 f$ is positive when evaluated at the point x^*, then we shall have identified a point which gives rise to a minimum of the function. However, $d^2 f$ is a quadratic form, which can be written as follows:

$$d^2 f = [dx_1 \ \ dx_2 \ \cdots \ dx_n] \begin{bmatrix} f_{11} & f_{12} & \cdots & f_{1n} \\ f_{21} & f_{22} & \cdots & f_{2n} \\ \vdots & \vdots & \cdots & \vdots \\ f_{n1} & f_{n2} & \cdots & f_{nn} \end{bmatrix} \begin{bmatrix} dx_1 \\ dx_2 \\ \vdots \\ dx_n \end{bmatrix}$$

From our earlier discussion, we know that $d^2 f$ will be negative if the matrix of second-order partial derivatives evaluated at the point that satisfies the first-order conditions is negative definite. This will be the case if all its eigenvalues are negative, or alternatively, if its principal minors alternate in sign, starting negative. On the other hand, we shall have identified a minimum value of the function if the matrix of second-order partial derivative evaluated at the point that satisfies the first-order conditions is positive definite. This will be the case if all the eigenvalues are positive, or alternatively, if all the principal minors are positive.

If we take a second-order Taylor-series expansion around the point x^*, we shall have:

$$f(x) = f(x^*) + \sum_{j=1}^{j=n} f_j(x^*)(x_j - x_j^*)$$
$$+ \sum_{i=1}^{i=n} \sum_{j=1}^{j=n} f_{ij}(x^*)(x_i - x_i^*)(x_j - x_j^*)$$

Given that all the first-order partial derivatives of $f(x)$ are zero at the point x^*, the second term on the RHS is equal to zero. Now let the difference between each x_j and x_j^* be infinitesimally small and equal to dx_j, then we can safely ignore the higher-order terms that we omitted from our Taylor-series expansion, since they will be of a very small order of magnitude. Consider the third term on the RHS of our expansion: this is a quadratic form which will be negative if the matrix of second-order partial derivatives is negative definite, and of the points in the vicinity of x^*, x^* is the one which will give rise to the largest value of $f(x)$. The function will reach a local maximum at this point.

Alternatively, the third term on the RHS will be positive if the matrix of second-order partial derivatives is positive definite, and in this case, of the points in the vicinity of x^*, x^* is the one which will give rise to the smallest value of $f(x)$. The function will reach a local minimum at this point.

If the matrix of second-order derivatives is always negative definite regardless of the point at which we evaluate the second-order partial derivatives, then if there exists a point which satisfies the first-order conditions, this point will give rise to a global maximum of the function. There will be a unique solution to the maximisation problem.

We may tie the above in with a discussion of strict concavity and convexity. Given a function $f(x)$ which has continuous first- and second-order partial derivatives, such a function is said to be strictly concave if

$$f(x) < f(x^*) + \sum_{j=1}^{j=n} f_j(x^*)(x_j - x_j^*)$$

If at the point x^* all the first-order partial derivatives are zero, it must be the case that

$$f(x) < f(x^*)$$

In other words, no other point in the domain of the function $f(x)$ regardless of whether or not it is close to x^* gives rise to as large a value of $f(x)$ as does the point x^*.

If the matrix of second-order derivatives is always positive definite regardless of the point at which we evaluate the second-order partial derivatives, then if there exists a point which satisfies the first-order conditions, this point will give rise to a global minimum of the function. There will be a unique solution to the minimisation problem. Such an outcome implies that the objective function is strictly convex. In this situation, we have:

$$f(x) > f(x^*) + \sum_{j=1}^{j=n} f_j(x^*)(x_j - x_j^*)$$

and at any other point which lies in the domain of the function, the value of the function is larger than it is at x^*.

Some examples

Assume we have the following function:

$$f(x) = 100x_1 - 2x_1^2 - 2x_1 x_2 + 150x_2 - 3x_2^2$$

Differentiating partially with respect to x_1 and x_2 and setting these derivatives equal to zero, we obtain:

$$f_1 = 100 - 4x_1 - 2x_2 = 0$$
$$f_2 = 150 - 2x_1 - 6x_2 = 0$$

Solving these two linear simultaneous equations yields:
$$x_1 = 15, \quad x_2 = 20, \quad \text{and } f(15, 20) = 2250$$

What kind of a point have we identified here? Differentiating partially the first-order derivatives, we have:
$$f_{11} = -4, \quad f_{12} = f_{21} = -2, \quad f_{22} = -6$$

Stacking these partial derivatives in a matrix and evaluating the principal minors, also known as Hessian determinants, we have:
$$|H_1| = -4, \quad |H_2| = \begin{vmatrix} -4 & -2 \\ -2 & -6 \end{vmatrix} = 20$$

Hence the principal minors alternate in sign, starting negative. We have identified a maximum, and since the matrix of partial derivatives is always negative definite, the objective function is strictly concave, and the point gives rise to a global maximum. Alternatively, we could have derived the eigenvalues of the matrix of second-order partial derivatives. Using the eigenvalue test for the negative definiteness of the matrix of second-order partial derivatives, we have:
$$\begin{vmatrix} -4-\lambda & -2 \\ -2 & -6-\lambda \end{vmatrix} = (-4-\lambda)(-6-\lambda) - (-2)^2$$
$$= \lambda^2 + 10\lambda + 20 = 0$$

Solving the quadratic equation yields the values of the two eigenvalues:
$$\lambda_1 = -5 + 0.5\sqrt{20}, \quad \lambda_2 = -5 - 0.5\sqrt{20}$$

Both eigenvalues are negative, which confirms our result that the matrix of second-order partial derivatives is negative definite.

Now consider the following function:
$$f(\mathbf{x}) = 4x_1^2 - 48x_1 + 4x_1 x_2 + 3x_2^2 - 60x_2$$

Differentiating partially with respect to x_1 and x_2 and setting these derivatives equal to zero, we obtain:
$$f_1 = 8x_1 + 4x_2 - 48 = 0$$
$$f_2 = 4x_1 + 6x_2 - 60 = 0$$

Solving these two linear simultaneous equations yields:
$$x_1 = 1.5, \quad x_2 = 9, \quad \text{and } f(1.5, 9) = -306$$

What kind of a point have we identified here? Differentiating partially the first-order derivatives, we have:
$$f_{11} = 8, \quad f_{12} = f_{21} = 4, \quad f_{22} = 6$$

Stacking these partial derivatives in a matrix and evaluating the principal minors, we have:
$$|H_1| = 8, \quad |H_2| = \begin{vmatrix} 8 & 4 \\ 4 & 6 \end{vmatrix} = 32$$

Hence the principal minors are both positive. We have identified a minimum, and since the matrix of partial derivatives is always positive definite, the objective function is strictly convex, and the point gives rise to a global minimum. Alternatively, we could have derived the eigenvalues of the matrix of second-order partial derivatives. Using the eigenvalue test to check whether the matrix of second-order partial derivatives is positive definite, we have:

$$\begin{vmatrix} 8-\lambda & 4 \\ 4 & 6-\lambda \end{vmatrix} = (8-\lambda)(6-\lambda) - (4)^2$$

$$= \lambda^2 - 14\lambda + 32 = 0$$

Solving the quadratic equation yields the values of the two eigenvalues:

$$\lambda_1 = 7 + 0.5\sqrt{68}, \quad \lambda_2 = 7 - 0.5\sqrt{68}$$

Both eigenvalues are positive, which confirms our result that the matrix of second-order partial derivatives is positive definite.

Consider the following function:

$$f(x) = 20x_1 - x_1^2 - x_1 x_2 + 2x_2^2 - 35x_2$$

Differentiating partially with respect to x_1 and x_2 and setting these derivatives equal to zero, we obtain:

$$f_1 = 20 - 2x_1 - x_2 = 0$$
$$f_2 = -x_1 + 4x_2 - 35 = 0$$

Solving these two linear simultaneous equations yields:

$$x_1 = 5, \quad x_2 = 10, \text{ and } f(5, 10) = -125$$

What kind of a point have we identified here? Differentiating partially the first-order derivatives, we have:

$$f_{11} = -2, \quad f_{12} = f_{21} = -1, \quad f_{22} = 4$$

Stacking these partial derivatives in a matrix and evaluating the principal minors, we have:

$$|H_1| = -2, \quad |H_2| = \begin{vmatrix} -2 & -1 \\ -1 & 4 \end{vmatrix} = -9$$

Hence the principal minors are both negative. We have identified neither a maximum nor a minimum. The matrix of partial derivatives is indefinite. The point we have identified is in fact a saddle point. The function has reached a maximum with respect to the variable x_1 and a minimum with respect to the variable x_2. Note f_{11} is negative and f_{22} is positive. Using the eigenvalue test, the reader should show that the two eigenvalues have opposite signs.

14.3 SOME ECONOMIC APPLICATIONS

Price discrimination in monopoly

Assume there exists a monopolist who is able to sell his product in two separate markets. Consumers are not able to transfer the good between themselves, either because the product is a service which is consumed at the point of production, for example a haircut, medical care etc. or because transport costs would make such activity on the part of consumers unprofitable, or the law may intervene to prevent parallel imports. The possibility obviously presents itself for the monopolist to engage in profit-maximising price discrimination, where prices to different consumers differ for reasons other than differences in the costs of supplying them.

Assume a monopolist can sell a product in two separate markets. Though the transfer of the product between consumers in the two markets is ruled out, it may still be possible to transfer demand between markets as for example when students travel by train using a young person's railcard, but would have still made some journeys had they been only able to travel at full fare. Let the inverse demand functions in the two markets be given respectively by:

$$p_1 = f(x_1, x_2) \text{ and } p_2 = g(x_1, x_2)$$

where p_i is the price and x_i the quantity sold in market i. The presence of x_i in the inverse demand function for market j is to allow for the transfer of demand between markets. The monopolist's total cost (TC) function is given by

$$TC = c(x_1, x_2)$$

We shall assume that the total cost function is strictly convex. Multiplying each inverse demand function by the relevant output and subtracting the total cost function from the total revenue function, we obtain the monopolist's profits function:

$$\Pi = x_1 f(x_1, x_2) + x_2 g(x_1, x_2) - c(x_1, x_2)$$

We shall assume that the total revenue function is strictly concave; given our assumption of a strictly convex cost function, then the negative of the cost function is strictly concave as is the profits function.

Differentiate the profits function partially with respect to x_1 and x_2 to obtain:

$$\Pi_1 = MR_1 - MC_1 = 0$$
$$\Pi_2 = MR_2 - MC_2 = 0$$

where MR_i and MC_i is the marginal revenue and marginal cost respectively of slightly increasing sales in market i. If the firm's total costs only depend upon its total output, and not upon the way a given output is distributed between the two markets, then

$$TC(x_1, x_2) = TC(x_1 + x_2)$$

and marginal cost in the two markets will be the same. Assume that this is the case, so that the only reason why the profit-maximising price might differ between the two markets must be the result of differences in demand conditions. For profits to be maximised, we must, therefore, have:

$$MR_1 = MC = MR_2$$

The intuition behind this condition is straightforward. Assume a given total output is distributed between the two markets such that marginal revenue in the first market is higher than marginal revenue in the second market. Given our assumption that total costs are independent of the way the total output is distributed between the two markets, slightly reducing sales in the second market and transferring this output to the first market will increase total revenue, but total costs are unchanged, and profits must, therefore, increase. Marginal revenue must be equalised between the two markets, and in order for the correct total output to be produced this equalised marginal revenue must equal marginal cost. We have also shown earlier that

$$MR = p\left[1 + \frac{1}{\eta_d}\right]$$

where η_d is the own-price elasticity of demand, and this will normally be negative. So in this case we must have:

$$p_1\left[1 + \frac{1}{\eta_{d_1}}\right] = p_2\left[1 + \frac{1}{\eta_{d_2}}\right]$$

from which it follows that the price which the monopolist will set will be higher in the market with the more inelastic demand. Assume we start out from a position in which the price charged in the two markets is the same. Then unless the elasticity of demand is the same in the two markets, then the marginal revenue must differ between the two markets. It will be lower in the market with the less elastic demand, but this means that we should reduce sales in this market and increase them in the other market until we have equalised the marginal revenues in the two markets. The price must, therefore rise in the market with the less elastic demand and fall in the market with the more elastic demand, and as a result of this price discrimination, total profits will rise.

If the cost function is not simply dependent upon total output, but is influenced by the way the sales are distributed between the two markets as a result for example of different transport costs, then we have the more general condition that we should equate marginal revenue with marginal cost in each market.

The multi-plant monopolist

Now consider the case of a monopolist who sells a product in a single market, but who possesses a number of different plants. How much should the monopolist produce, and how much output should the monopolist produce in each plant in order to maximise profit?

The monopolist's profit function is given by:

$$\Pi = R\left(\sum_{i=1}^{i=n} x_i\right) - \sum_{i=1}^{i=n} c_i(x_i)$$

where R is the total revenue function which depends upon total output (X), and c_i is the total cost function of plant i. Differentiating partially with respect to x_i yields the first-order conditions:

$$\Pi_i = \frac{dR}{dX}\frac{\partial X}{\partial x_i} - MC_i = 0$$

Since the partial derivative of total output with respect to output produced in plant i is unity, the monopolist must accordingly allocate his output between the plants so as to equalise the marginal cost of production in each plant, and ensure that this is equal to marginal revenue. The rationale for this is straightforward: assume that total output is given, and hence so is marginal revenue, but the marginal cost of production in plant j is higher than the marginal cost of production in plant k, then it is obvious that by reallocating the given output by producing a little bit more output in plant k and a little bit less in plant j then total costs of production will fall, total revenue is unchanged since total output has not altered, and profits are higher.

Duopoly

Assume there are only two firms in an industry, each producing a homogeneous product. The price which each firm will receive for its output will depend not only upon its own output, but also upon the output of the other firm. We may, therefore, write out each firm's profits function as follows:

$$\Pi_1 = p(x_1 + x_2)x_1 - c_1(x_1)$$
$$\Pi_2 = p(x_1 + x_2)x_2 - c_2(x_2)$$

If each duopolist treats its competitor's output as fixed, then the first-order conditions for a maximum of profit for each firm take the following form:

$$p(x_1 + \hat{x}_2) + p'(x_1 + \hat{x}_2)x_1 - MC_1 = 0$$
$$p(\hat{x}_1 + x_2) + p'(\hat{x}_1 + x_2)x_2 - MC_2 = 0$$

where a circumflex over a variable signifies the firm's expectation as to what the other firm will produce. For each firm marginal revenue should equal marginal cost, but the marginal revenue that each firm would receive for a very small increase in its output is also dependent upon the level of output of the other firm. The larger the output of one firm is, *ceteris paribus*, the lower will be market price and the lower will be the marginal revenue of the other firm, and hence the smaller the output it would wish to produce. Each first-order condition implicitly defines a best response for each firm, conditional upon its expectation regarding its rival's output. We can call this response the firm's reaction function. The pair of outputs x_1^* and x_2^* would constitute an equilibrium if when firm 1 produced x_1^*, firm 2's best response was x_2^*, and when firm 2 produced x_2^*, firm 1's best response was x_1^*. This is known as the Cournot–Nash equilibrium: given what the other firm is doing, neither firm can unilaterally increase its profits by changing its output. Given what the other firm is doing, each firm is maximising its profits, but as we shall now see total industry profits are not being maximised. At the total output the duopolists are producing, marginal revenue is given by:

$$p(x_1^* + x_2^*) + p'(x_1^* + x_2^*)(x_1 + x_2^*)$$

and this is smaller than the marginal cost of each duopolist since in the Cournot–Nash equilibrium, we have:

$$p(x_1^* + x_2^*) + p'(x_1^* + x_2^*)x_1 - MC_1 = 0$$
$$p(x_1^* + x_2^*) + p'(x_1^* + x_2^*)x_2 - MC_2 = 0$$

Remember the inverse demand function is downward sloping so the derivative of price with respect to output is negative. The firms are producing too much, their joint profits are not being maximised. By collaborating in a cartel in which they agreed output quotas such that their marginal costs of production were equalised and set equal to marginal revenue, total profits would be higher.

In the Cournot–Nash equilibrium, each firm is being myopic and is neglecting the strategic interdependence that exists between the two firms in the industry. If the industry consisted of a very large number of small firms, then each firm could legitimately assume that it need not worry about how the other firms might respond to anything it did. Each firm is so small in relation to the size of the market that anything that an individual firm might do is too insignificant to warrant a response by any other firm. This is not the case when the number of firms is small. If the duopolists were either to merge or to join together in a cartel, then account would indeed be taken of the interdependence of their actions.

Let us consider the case where the industry, instead of being a duopoly, consists of n identical firms, each with the same total cost function $c(x_i)$. Let us investigate the nature of the Cournot equilibrium in this case. Firm i's profits function is given by:

$$\Pi_i = p(X)x_i - c(x_i)$$

where X is total industry output. Differentiating with respect to x_i on the assumption that the outputs of all the other firms in the industry are held fixed, we obtain:

$$p(X) + p'(X)x_i - MC_i = 0$$

Since by assumption the firms are all identical, in the Cournot–Nash equilibrium, they must all produce the same output, hence we must have:

$$x_i = \frac{X}{n}$$

Substituting for x_i in the equilibrium condition, we obtain:

$$p(X) + p'(X)\frac{X}{n} = MC_i$$

$$\text{hence } p(X)\left[1 - \frac{1}{n|\eta_d|}\right] = MC_i$$

$$\text{and } \frac{p - MC_i}{p} = \frac{1}{n|\eta_d|}$$

It is then clear that as the number of firms becomes very large, the gap between price and marginal cost becomes smaller and smaller. In the limit as n approaches infinity, we have the perfectly competitive outcome with price equal to marginal cost.

We will now work through a simple numerical example of a duopoly, where we assume the duopolists have identical and constant marginal costs, and the inverse demand curve is linear.

$$c(x_i) = 40x_i \quad i = 1, 2$$
$$p = 200 - 2X$$
$$= 200 - 2(x_1 + x_2)$$

Then the profit functions of the two firms are given respectively by:

$$\Pi_1 = (200 - 2(x_1 + x_2))x_1 - 40x_1$$
$$= 160x_1 - 2x_1^2 - 2x_1x_2$$
$$\Pi_2 = (200 - 2(x_1 + x_2))x_2 - 40x_2$$
$$= 160x_2 - 2x_1x_2 - 2x_2^2$$

Differentiating each firm's profits function on the assumption that the other firm's output is fixed, we obtain the following two first-order conditions:

$$\frac{d\Pi_1}{dx_1} = 160 - 4x_1 - 2x_2 = 0$$

$$\frac{d\Pi_2}{dx_2} = 160 - 2x_1 - 4x_2 = 0$$

Firm 1's best response for a given output of firm two is, therefore, given by:
$$x_1 = 40 - 0.5x_2$$

Similarly, firm 2's best repose for a given level of output of firm 1 is given by:
$$x_2 = 40 - 0.5x_1$$

Solving these two equations simultaneously yields the outputs that the two firms would produce in the Cournot equilibrium.
$$x_1 = x_2 = \frac{80}{3} \text{ and } X = \frac{160}{3}$$

At these output levels, we would also have:
$$p = \frac{440}{3} \text{ and } \frac{p - MC}{p} = \frac{8}{11}$$

Now assume that the industry consisted of *10* identical firms. What would be the Cournot equilibrium in this situation? Differentiating firm *i*'s profits function with respect to x_i, setting the derivative equal to zero and x_i equal to $X/10$ yields
$$200 - 2X - \frac{2X}{10} - 40 = 0$$

from which it follows that
$$X = \frac{800}{11}, \quad x_i = \frac{80}{11}$$
$$p = \frac{600}{11} \text{ and } \frac{p - MC}{p} = \frac{4}{15}$$

Similarly, it can be shown that if there are *100* identical firms, then total industry output is given by *8000/101*, and if there are *1000* firms, then total industry output is given by *80 000/1001*. The reader should check that when there are *n* firms, total industry output in the Cournot equilibrium is given by *80n/n + 1*.

What happens to total industry output as *n* becomes very large? In such a situation, no firm has any market power and we end up with the perfectly competitive outcome: price is equal to marginal cost which equals *40* and total industry output is equal to *80*. Alternatively, we could have taken the limit of *80n/n + 1* as *n* approaches infinity. How may we proceed to do this? Obviously as *n* approaches infinity, both the numerator and denominator of our expression approach infinity, but what about the ratio of the two. Infinity upon infinity is not defined, so we must proceed differently to evaluate the limit in this particular case. One possibility is to make use of l'Hôpital's rule, which in this context states that
$$\lim_{n \to \infty} \frac{f(n)}{g(n)} = \lim_{n \to \infty} \frac{f'(n)}{g'(n)}$$

Since the derivative of *80n* with respect to *n* is *80*, and the derivative of *n + 1* with respect to *n* is unity, the limit is *80*. Alternatively, we may divide *n* by *n + 1*. We have
$$\frac{n}{n+1} = 1 - \frac{1}{n+1}$$
$$\text{and } \lim_{n \to \infty} 1 - \frac{1}{n+1} = 1$$

which again yields a value of *80* for output as the number of firms becomes infinitely large.

Let us now return to our original duopoly, and assume that they join together in a profit-maximising cartel. Total profits are given by:

$$\Pi = 200(x_1 + x_2) - 2(x_1 + x_2)^2 - 40(x_1 + x_2)$$
$$= 160x_1 + 160x_2 - 2x_1^2 - 4x_1 x_2 - 2x_2^2$$

Differentiating partially with respect to x_1 and x_2, we obtain the first-order conditions for a maximum:

$$\frac{\partial \Pi}{\partial x_1} = 160 - 4x_1 - 4x_2 = 0$$

$$\frac{\partial \Pi}{\partial x_2} = 160 - 4x_1 - 4x_2 = 0$$

Note that we do not have a unique solution to the joint-profit maximising problem, since because of the fact that the marginal costs of the duopolists are constant and equal to each other, the two first-order conditions are linearly independent. The solution must, therefore, take the following form:

$$x_1 = 40 - x_2 \text{ for } 0 \leq x_2 \leq 40$$

The fairest solution would obviously be to allocate a quota of *20* units to each firm.

If, however, each firm were faced with set-up costs which were independent of the amount of positive output, but which were avoidable if the firm were to produce nothing at all, then total industry profits would be maximised by having only one of the two firms producing: the one with the lower set-up costs, assuming that they differed between the firms. Otherwise, one could toss a coin to decide which firm should produce. By allocating a zero output to one of the duopolists, one would save on one set of set-up costs, and remember that variable costs depend only upon the total output produced and not on how the output is allocated between the two firms since they have equal and constant marginal costs. In either case, the non-producer would have to be compensated by receiving a side payment from the other firm, at least equal in size to its profits in the Cournot equilibrium in order to induce it to agree to the allocation.

14.4 SOME COMPARATIVE STATIC ANALYSIS

Let us now turn to examine the case of a perfectly competitive firm's choice of how many inputs to employ when faced with given prices for both its output and for its factors. The firm's production function is assumed to be one which satisfies the conventional neo-classical assumptions:

$$Q = F(K, N)$$
$$F_K > 0, \quad F_N > 0, \quad F_{KK} < 0, \quad F_{NN} < 0, \quad F_{KN} > 0$$

where Q is output, K the input of capital services and N the input of labour services. The marginal product of each factor is positive, diminishes as the use of its own factor is increased, and increases as the employment of the other factor is raised. Letting p, r and w represent respectively the product price, the price of a unit of capital services, and the wage rate, then the firm's profits function is given by:

$$\Pi = pF(K, N) - rK - wN$$

Differentiate partially with respect to K and N to obtain the first-order conditions for a maximum:

$$\Pi_K = pF_K - r = 0$$
$$\Pi_N = pF_N - w = 0$$

The firm should employ each factor of production up to the point where the value of the marginal product is equal to the factor price. The second-order partial derivatives of the profits function are:

$$\Pi_{KK} = pF_{KK}, \quad \Pi_{KN} = pF_{KN}, \quad \Pi_{NN} = pF_{NN}$$

The second-order conditions for a maximum of profits, therefore, are:

$$pF_{KK} < 0, \quad p^2(F_{KK}F_{NN} - F_{KN}^2) > 0$$

If the production function is strictly concave, then these conditions will indeed be met. Let us assume that this is indeed the case. We shall now investigate how the firm's demand for the factors of production might be expected to alter in response to changes in the product price and in the prices of the factors of production.

Totally differentiating the first-order conditions for a maximum of profit yields the following two equations:

$$pF_{KK}\,dK + pF_{KN}\,dN + F_K\,dp - dr = 0$$
$$pF_{NK}\,dK + pF_{NN}\,dN + F_N\,dp - dw = 0$$

In matrix notation, we have:

$$\begin{bmatrix} pF_{KK} & pF_{KN} \\ pF_{NK} & pF_{NN} \end{bmatrix} \begin{bmatrix} dK \\ dN \end{bmatrix} = \begin{bmatrix} -F_K\,dp + dr \\ -F_N\,dp + dw \end{bmatrix}$$

If we successively allow one of the prices to vary, holding constant the other two, then employing Cramer's rule, we can obtain the following partial derivatives:

$$\frac{\partial K}{\partial p} = \frac{\begin{vmatrix} -F_K & pF_{KN} \\ -F_N & pF_{NN} \end{vmatrix}}{|H|}$$

$$= \frac{-p(F_K F_{NN} - F_N F_{KN})}{|H|} > 0$$

where

$$H = p^2(F_{KK}F_{NN} - F_{KN}^2) > 0$$

and given that the second-order conditions for a maximum are satisfied. The numerator is also positive.

$$\frac{\partial N}{\partial p} = \frac{\begin{vmatrix} pF_{KK} & -F_K \\ pF_{NK} & -F_N \end{vmatrix}}{|H|}$$

$$= \frac{-p(F_N F_{KK} - F_K F_{NK})}{|H|} > 0$$

$$\frac{\partial K}{\partial r} = \frac{\begin{vmatrix} 1 & pF_{KN} \\ 0 & pF_{NN} \end{vmatrix}}{|H|}$$

$$= \frac{pF_{NN}}{|H|} < 0$$

$$\frac{\partial N}{\partial r} = \frac{\begin{vmatrix} pF_{KK} & 1 \\ pF_{NK} & 0 \end{vmatrix}}{|H|}$$

$$= \frac{-pF_{NK}}{|H|} < 0$$

$$\frac{\partial K}{\partial w} = \frac{\begin{vmatrix} 0 & pF_{KN} \\ 1 & pF_{NN} \end{vmatrix}}{|H|}$$

$$= \frac{-pF_{KN}}{|H|} < 0$$

$$\frac{\partial N}{\partial w} = \frac{\begin{vmatrix} pF_{KK} & 0 \\ pF_{NK} & 1 \end{vmatrix}}{|H|}$$

$$= \frac{pF_{KK}}{|H|} < 0$$

We may, therefore, conclude that the demand for both factors of production is increasing in the price of the product. As the product price rises, at the existing levels of employment of the two inputs, the value of the marginal product of each factor is now greater than the factor price, and it pays the firm to increase employment of both factors. The demand for both factors of production is decreasing in both factor prices. The factors of production in this case are gross complements. A rise in the price of labour will lead the firm to produce its output with a more capital-intensive technique of production; the substitution effect will, therefore, raise the demand for capital services. The rise in the wage rate will also raise the firm's marginal costs, and correspondingly reduce the output which the firm will be willing to supply at the given output price. This scale effect will reduce the demand for both factors of production. For the factor whose price has risen it is clear that both the substitution and the scale effects are working in the same direction to reduce demand for the factor. For the other factor, however, they have opposite implications for demand, but for the function we have specified the scale effect dominates the substitution effect, and the demand for capital (labour) will fall when the wage rate (price of capital services) rises etc.

14.5 SUMMARY

In this chapter we have investigated the conditions which must be satisfied for a function of many variables to reach a maximum or minimum value. We summarise the results here.

For a maximum, we require all the first-order partial derivatives to be zero. A sufficient second-order condition, then, is that the matrix of second-order partial derivatives when evaluated at the point which satisfies the first-order conditions be negative definite. There are two tests for negative definiteness which we can employ: the eigenvalue test which requires all the eigenvalues to be negative, or the principal minors test which requires the principal minors to alternate in sign, starting negative. If the function is strictly concave, and there exists a point which satisfies the first-order conditions for a maximum, then this point gives rise to a global maximum of the function. There is no other point which satisfies the maximum conditions.

For a minimum, we require all the first-order partial derivatives to be zero. A sufficient second-order condition, then, is that the matrix of second-order partial derivatives when evaluated at the point which satisfies the first-order conditions be positive definite. There are two tests for positive definiteness which we can employ: the eigenvalue test which requires all the eigenvalues to be positive, or the principal minors test which requires all the principal minors to be positive. If the function is strictly convex, and there exists a point which satisfies the first-order conditions for a minimum, then this point gives rise to a global minimum of the function. There is no other point which satisfies the minimum conditions.

The second-order conditions can be usefully employed in comparative static analysis. Assuming that the second-order conditions are indeed met in general function models means not only that the endogenous variables, those variables whose values are determined within the model, can be written as implicit functions of the exogenous variables, those variables whose values are given from outside the model, but also that the signing of the derivatives of the implicit function becomes relatively straightforward.

14.6 EXERCISES

14.1 (a) Find the values, if any, of x_1 and x_2 for which the following functions reach a maximum or minimum.

(i) $f(x) = 48x_1 - x_1^2 - 3x_1 x_2 + 36x_2 - 3x_2^2$

(ii) $f(x) = 6x_1^2 - 16x_1 - 4x_1 x_2 + x_2^2 - 12x_2 + 100$

(iii) $f(x) = 2x_1^2 - 14x_1 - 5x_1 x_2 + 4x_2^2 - 35x_2 + 25$

(iv) $f(x) = 2x_1^2 - 24x_1 - x_1 x_2 - x_2^2 - 12x_2$

(v) $f(x) = 100x_1 - 2x_1^2 - 6x_1 x_2 + 180x_2 - 5x_2^2$

(vi) $f(x) = 120x_1 - 0.5x_1^2 - x_1 x_2 + 150x_2 - x_2^2$

(vii) $f(x) = x_1^2 - 30x_1 - 2x_1 x_2 + 4x_2^2 - 18x_2 + 400$

(viii) $f(x) = 20x_1 - x_1^2 - 2x_1 x_2 + 1.5x^2 - 60x_2$

14.2 (a) The profits function of a firm producing three goods is given by:

$$\Pi(x) = 40x_1 - 0.5x_1^2 + 104x_2 - 3x_2^2 - 2x_1 x_2 + 80x_3 - 2x_3^2$$

(i) Find the profit maximising output bundle. How large are profits?
(ii) Check that the second-order conditions for a maximum of profits are satisfied.
(b) A firm's profit's function is given by

$$\Pi = 60x_1 - 2.5x_1^2 + 100x_2 - 2x_2^2 - 2x_2 x_3 + 110x_3 - 3.5x_3^2$$

where x_i is the amount produced of good i, $i = 1, 2, 3$.
(i) Derive the profit-maximising levels of output of the three goods.

(ii) Find the eigenvalues of the matrix of the second-order partial derivatives of the profits function.
(iii) Is the above matrix negative definite? Explain your answer.
(c) A monopolist produces three goods whose inverse demand functions are given by:

$$p_1 = 120 - 2x_1 - x_2$$
$$p_2 = 100 - x_1 - x_2$$
$$p_3 = 50 - x_3$$

where p_j and x_j are respectively the price and quantity of good $j, j = 1, \ldots, 3$.
The firm's total cost function is:

$$TC = 100 + 10x_1 + 18x_2 + 20x_3$$

(i) Obtain the profit maximising levels of output of each good.
(ii) Find the eigenvalues of the matrix of second-order partial derivatives of the profits function.
(iii) Hence, or otherwise, check that the second-order conditions for a maximum are satisfied.
(d) A monopolist firm is able to sell its output in two markets, the inverse demand functions in these two markets being given respectively by:

$$p_1 = 100x_1^{-0.5}$$
$$p_2 = 40x_2^{-0.25}$$

The firm's total cost (TC) function is

$$TC = 10x$$

where x is total output. Derive the profit-maximising levels of output in the two markets, and the associated prices at which the product will be sold.

(e) A monopolist firm can produces its output in one of two different plants. The costs of production in the two plants are given respectively by:

$$TC(x_1) = 2x_1^2$$
$$TC(x_2) = 100 + 20x_2$$

where x_i is the output produced in plant i. The inverse demand function takes the following form:

$$p = 200 - 2x$$

where x is total output. How much output should the profit-maximising monopolist produce in each plant?

(f) The inverse demand function for a product produced by a duopoly is given by:

$$p = 120 - X = 120 - x_1 - x_2$$

where X is total output and x_i is the output of firm i. The total cost functions of the two firms are given respectively by:

$$TC_1 = x_1^2$$
$$TC_2 = 20x_2$$

(i) Obtain the reaction functions for the two firms.
(ii) What outputs would the duopolists produce in the Cournot–Nash equilibrium?
(iii) If the two firms were to join together in a profit-maximising cartel, what outputs would they then produce?
(iv) What has happened to firm 1's profits as we move from the Cournet–Nash equilibrium to the position where total industry profits are maximised?
(v) How might firm 2 persuade firm 1 to join the cartel?

14.3 (a) A firm's production function is given by:

$$Q = NF(K/N) \text{ with } F'(K/N) > 0 \text{ and } F''(K/N) < 0$$

where Q is output, N the input of labour services, and K the input of capital services. The marginal product of labour is always positive.

(i) Assume the capital input is held fixed at $K = K^*$, and let r represent the price of a unit of capital services, w the wage rate and p the price of output. Show for a perfectly competitive profit-maximising firm that its demand for labour is increasing in p, and that the firm's supply of output is also an increasing function of the price.

(ii) Now assume the firm is labour-managed and that its objective is to maximise net income per worker (i.e. $pF(K/N) - r(K/N)$). Assume once more that K is held fixed at K^*. Show for this firm that the demand for labour is a decreasing function of p, and that its supply of output is also a decreasing function of the price.

(b) The price (P) at which a profit-maximising monopolist can sell its product depends inversely on the quantity sold (Q) and positively on the amount spent on advertising (A).

$$P = 8Q^{-0.75}A^{0.5}$$

Unit costs of production are constant and equal to c. The government levies a tax of t per unit on advertising expenditure.

(i) Derive the profit-maximising levels of Q and A as functions of c and t, checking that the second-order conditions for a maximum of profit are satisfied.

(ii) Show that a profit-maximising monopolist would reduce both advertising expenditure and output if the per unit tax on advertising expenditure (t) were increased.

(c) A profit-maximising monopolist sells its product in two markets; in both markets a per unit sales tax is levied on the good, the tax being t_i in market i, $i = 1, 2$. The profits function is given by:

$$\Pi = R(x_1, x_2) - C(x_1 + x_2) - t_1 x_1 - t_2 x_2$$

where R is the total revenue function, and C is the total cost function.

(i) Write down the first-order conditions for a maximum of profit.

(ii) Assuming the second-order conditions for a maximum are met, show that x_1 is a decreasing function of t_1 and an increasing function of t_2.

(d) A profit-maximising monopolist produces two goods, x_1 and x_2. A per unit subsidy of s is given on good 1, and a per unit tax of t is levied on good 2. The monopolist's profits function is given by:

$$\Pi = R(x_1, x_2) - C(x_1, x_2) + sx_1 - tx_2$$

where $R(\ )$ and $C(\ )$ are the firm's revenue and total cost functions respectively. The partial derivatives of these functions have the following signs:

$$R_1 > 0, \quad R_2 > 0, \quad R_{11} < 0, \quad R_{12} = R_{21} < 0, \quad R_{22} < 0$$
$$C_1 > 0, \quad C_2 > 0, \quad C_{11} > 0, \quad C_{12} = C_{21} > 0, \quad C_{22} > 0$$

(i) Obtain the first-order conditions for a maximum of profit.

(ii) Write out the second-order conditions for a maximum of profit.

(iii) Totally differentiate the first-order conditions for a maximum of profit, and then obtain and sign the following partial derivatives:

$$\frac{\partial x_1}{\partial s}, \quad \frac{\partial x_2}{\partial s}$$
$$\frac{\partial x_1}{\partial t}, \quad \frac{\partial x_2}{\partial t}$$

(iv) Show that

$$\frac{\partial x_1}{\partial t} = -\frac{\partial x_2}{\partial s}$$

CHAPTER FIFTEEN

AN INTRODUCTION TO INTEGRAL CALCULUS

15.1 INTRODUCTION

In this chapter we provide a discussion of techniques of integration, and present a number of economic applications of these techniques. We have discussed in great detail earlier in the book techniques of differentiation. There we started with a particular function, say $F(x)$, which we then differentiated with respect to x. The first derivative measures the slope of the original function with respect to x. In integral calculus, however, the basic procedure is the reverse of what is done in differential calculus. In integral calculus we start with a given function and seek to find the original function for which our given function is the derivative. Given the slope of the original function, what form must the original or primitive function take is the question we seek to answer. Naturally, given this relationship between differential and integral calculus, there exist close connections between the rules of integration and those of differentiation as we shall see in this chapter. In Section 15.2 we discuss some basic rules of integration. We then introduce in Section 15.3 the concepts of a definite integral and an improper integral. We see that the definite integral is the measure of the area under a curve between two values of the dependent variable. Improper integrals arise when one of the values of the variable is not finite. Having provided the basic discussion of the mathematical concepts, we then look at some applications of integral calculus in economics in Section 15.4. We consider problems which have a time dimension: here we look at such matters as the depletion of exhaustible resources and investment decisions involving human and non-human capital. We also show that the techniques can be utilised in order to examine some problems in which space rather than time is the key variable. We end the chapter by providing a summary table of some key integrals.

15.2 SOME RULES OF INTEGRATION

The convention which we shall adopt regarding notation in this chapter is the standard one in the literature, and is as follows. We shall use $f(x)$ to represent the integrand, i.e. the function that we are seeking to integrate, whilst $F(x)$ represents the integral, i.e. the function whose derivative with respect to x is equal to $f(x)$. Obviously, we have:

$$\frac{dF}{dx} = F'(x) = f(x)$$

The sign that tells us that we should find the integral of $f(x)$ is an elongated S; the significance of this will become apparent below when we introduce the concept of the definite integral.

$$\int f(x)\,dx$$

Here we have the integral sign which tells us that we should find the integral of $f(x)$, and the presence of the differential dx in the expression signifies that the integration should be performed with respect to the variable x.

Though there are close connections between the techniques of integral and differential calculus, there is one important difference that we should immediately point out. This relates to the fact that whereas the derivative of a function is unique, this is *not* the case for the integral of a function. If $F(x)$ is the integral of $f(x)$ with respect to x, then it will also be the case, given that the derivative of a constant is zero, that $F(x) + k$ will also be the integral of $f(x)$ where k is an arbitrary constant. We now turn to discuss some simple rules of integration.

The power rule

We know from our discussion of differential calculus that:

$$y = f(x) = x^n; \quad \frac{dy}{dx} = nx^{n-1}$$

We therefore have the power rule of integral calculus which states:

$$\int x^n\,dx = \frac{1}{n+1}x^{n+1} + k \text{ for } n \neq -1$$

This rule holds for all values of n, both integer and non-integer values, except for n equal to -1. The case where $n = -1$, we shall discuss below.

Let us consider some examples of this rule.

(a) $\quad \int x^4\,dx = \frac{1}{5}x^5 + k$

(b) $\quad \int x^{-3}\,dx = \frac{-1}{2}x^{-2} + k$

(c) $\quad \int x^{1.5}\,dx = \frac{2}{5}x^{2.5} + k$

(d) $\quad \int -x^{-0.5}\,dx = -2x^{0.5} + k$

(e) $\quad \int dx = x + k$

Note that example (e) is the case where $n = 0$.

The logarithmic rule

From the logarithmic rule of differential calculus, we know that

$$y = f(x) = \log_e x; \quad \frac{dy}{dx} = \frac{1}{x} = x^{-1}$$

Hence, we can now deal with the case where $n = -1$. We must have

$$\int x^{-1} \, dx = \log_e x + k$$

The exponential rule

Again from our study of differential calculus we know that

$$y = f(x) = e^x; \quad \frac{dy}{dx} = e^x$$

Hence it follows that

$$\int e^x \, dx = e^x + k$$

The integral of cox x and sin x

In Chapter 11 it was shown that

$$\text{if } y = \cos x, \text{ then } \frac{dy}{dx} = -\sin x$$

$$\text{and if } y = \sin x, \text{ then } \frac{dy}{dx} = \cos x$$

Given the above, it follows that we must have

$$\int \sin x \, dx = -\cos x + k$$

$$\text{and } \int \cos x \, dx = \sin x + k$$

The integral of the multiple of a function

The integral of the multiple of a function is equal to the multiple of the integral of the function.

$$\int a f(x) \, dx = a \int f(x) \, dx$$

We simply take the multiple outside the integral sign. To illustrate this rule, consider the following examples.

(a) $\int 3x^2 \, dx = 3 \int x^2 \, dx = 3(\frac{1}{3}x^3 + k_1) = x^3 + k$

(b) $\int 0.5x^2 \, dx = 0.5 \int x^2 \, dx = 0.5(\frac{1}{3}x^3 + k_1) = \frac{1}{6}x^3 + k$

(c) $\int 2x^{-2} \, dx = 2 \int x^{-2} = 2(-x^{-1} + k_1) = -2x^{-1} + k$

The integral of a sum or difference of two functions

The integral of a sum or difference of two functions is equal to the sum (difference) of the separate integrals.

$$\int [f(x) \pm g(x)] \, dx = \int f(x) \, dx \pm \int g(x) \, dx$$

We provide some examples of this rule

(i) $\int (3x^2 + 2e^x + 5x^{-1}) \, dx = \int 3x^2 \, dx + 2\int e^x \, dx + 5\int x^{-1} \, dx$

$$= x^3 + k_1 + 2(e^x + k_2) + 5(\log_e x + k_3)$$
$$= x^3 + 2e^x + 5\log_e x + k$$

(ii) $\int (-2x^{-3} + 4x^3 - x^{0.5}) \, dx = \int -2x^{-3} \, dx + \int 4x^3 \, dx - \int x^{0.5} \, dx$

$$= x^{-2} + k_1 + x^4 + k_2 - \tfrac{2}{3}x^{1.5} + k_3$$
$$= x^{-2} + x^4 - \tfrac{2}{3}x^{1.5} + k$$

(iii) $\int (3x^5 + x^{-0.5} + 5) \, dx = \int 3x^5 \, dx + \int x^{-0.5} \, dx + \int 5 \, dx$

$$= 0.5x^6 + k_1 + 2x^{0.5} + k_2 + 5x + k_3$$
$$= 0.5x^6 + 2x^{0.5} + 5x + k$$

The substitution rule

Consider the function $G(u)$, and assume that $u = U(x)$, then

$$G(u) = G(U(x)) = F(x)$$

On differentiating the above, we have:

$$G'(u) = G'(U'(x)) = F'(x)$$

Alternatively, using lower case letters for derivatives, we have

$$g(u) = g(u(x)) = f(x)$$

This is the function of a function, or chain rule, of differential calculus which we met earlier in Chapter 11. In terms of differentials we have:

$$g(u) \, du = g(u)u(x) \, dx = g(u) \frac{du}{dx} \, dx = f(x) \, dx$$

On taking integrals we obtain:

$$\int f(x) \, dx = \int g(u) \frac{du}{dx} \, dx$$

This is known as the substitution rule of integral calculus. Whenever, by using an appropriate substitution, we are able to express $f(x)$ as the product of some function of u and the derivative of u with respect to x, this rule may be utilised to find the integral of $f(x)$.

Let us work through some examples to illustrate the use of this rule.

(a) $\int e^{ax} \, dx$

Let $u = ax$, then $du = a\,dx$ and $dx = (1/a)\,du$. Substituting into the above integral yield:

$$\int e^{ax}\,dx = \int \frac{1}{a} e^u\,du = \frac{1}{a} \int e^u\,du$$

$$= \frac{1}{a} e^u + k = \frac{1}{a} e^{ax} + k$$

Now consider the following example:

(b) $\int (3x^2 + 5)(x^3 + 5x + 2)^n\,dx$

Note that the first bracketed term is the derivative of the second bracketed term, ignoring the power term outside the bracket. Let

$$u = x^3 + 5x + 2$$

then

$$du = (3x^2 + 5)\,dx$$

and

$$dx = \frac{1}{3x^2 + 5}\,du$$

On substituting into the above integral, we obtain:

$$\int u^n\,du = \frac{1}{n+1} u^{n+1} + k$$

$$= \frac{1}{n+1} (x^3 + 5x + 2)^{n+1} + k$$

In the next example the term in the numerator is the derivative with respect to x of the term in the denominator.

(c) $\int \dfrac{2x+3}{x^2 + 3x}\,dx$

Let

$$u = x^2 + 3x$$

then

$$du = (2x + 3)\,dx$$

and

$$dx = \frac{1}{2x+3}\,du$$

Hence we have:

$$\int \frac{2x+3}{x^2+3x}\,dx = \int \frac{1}{u}\,du$$

$$= \log_e u + k = \log_e(x^2 + 3x) + k$$

In differential calculus we can always obtain the derivative of a function with respect to x where the function is the product of two functions of x, or the ratio of two functions of x. In the first case we just apply the product rule of differential calculus, and in the second case the quotient rule. Life, however, is much more difficult for us when we seek to find the integral of a function which is the product, or ratio, of two functions of x. The substitution rule can only be made use of in the special case where one term in the expression can be expressed as the derivative of another term in the expression.

Consider the following example:

$$\int \frac{x^2 + 5x + 8}{x + 5} \, dx$$

In this example we cannot immediately apply the substitution rule since the derivative of the numerator is not equal to the denominator. However, by dividing the numerator by the denominator we can express the integrand in a form in which we can then proceed to find the integral. We may rewrite the integral as:

$$\int \left(x + \frac{8}{x+5} \right) dx = 0.5x^2 + k_1 + \int \frac{8}{x+5} \, dx$$

Letting $u = x + 5$, then $du = dx$ and hence,

$$\int \frac{8}{x+5} \, dx = \int \frac{8}{u} \, du$$

$$= 8 \log_e u + k_2 = 8 \log_e(x + 5) + k_2$$

Hence

$$\int \frac{x^2 + 5x + 8}{x + 5} \, dx = 0.5x^2 + 8 \log_e(x + 5) + k$$

Integration by parts

Assume we have two functions of x: $u = u(x)$ and $v = v(x)$. Now consider a third function which is the product of these two functions: $z(x) = u(x)v(x)$. Then the total differential of $z(x)$ is given by:

$$dz = d(uv) = v \, du + u \, dv$$

Integrating both sides, we obviously have:

$$z = uv = \int v \, du + \int u \, dv$$

Re-arranging, we obtain:

$$\int v \, du = uv - \int u \, dv$$

This is the formula for integration by parts; it is, as we have seen, the integral calculus counterpart of the product rule of differential calculus. In order to illustrate the rule let us work through some examples. Consider

(a) $\int \log_e x \, dx$

Let $v = \log_e x$ and $du = dx$. Then $dv = (1/x)\,dx$ and $u = x$. So we have:

$$\int \log_e x\, dx = x\log_e x - \int dx = x\log_e x - x + k$$

Check that this is indeed the correct answer by differentiating with respect to x.
We now turn to some trigonometric functions:

$$\text{(b)} \int (x \sin x)\, dx$$

Let $v = x$ and $du = \sin x\, dx$. Then $dv = dx$ and $u = -\cos x$. So we have:

$$\int x \sin x\, dx = -x \cos x - \int -\cos x\, dx$$
$$= -x \cos x + \sin x + k$$

Consider

$$\text{(c)} \int \cos x \sin x\, dx$$

Let $v = \cos x$ and $du = \sin x\, dx$. Then $dv = -\sin x\, dx$ and $u = -\cos x$. Hence we have:

$$\int \cos x \sin x\, dx = -\cos^2 x - \int \cos x \sin x\, dx$$

Hence

$$2 \int \cos x \sin x\, dx = -\cos^2 x$$

and

$$\int \cos x \sin x\, dx = -0.5 \cos^2 x + k$$

Finally, let us see how to find

$$\text{(d)} \int \cos^2 x\, dx$$

Let $v = \cos x$ and $du = \cos x\, dx$. Then $dv = -\sin x$ and $u = \sin x$. Substituting in the formula for integration by parts, we obtain:

$$\int \cos^2 x\, dx = \cos x \sin x + \int \sin^2 x\, dx$$

Since $\cos^2 x + \sin^2 x = 1$, we have, on substituting $\sin^2 x = 1 - \cos^2 x$ into the above expression:

$$\int \cos^2 x\, dx = \cos x \sin x + \int (1 - \cos^2 x)\, dx$$

Hence we obtain

$$2 \int \cos^2 x\, dx = \cos x \sin x + \int 1\, dx$$

and it then follows that

$$\int \cos^2 x \, dx = 0.5[\cos x \sin x + x] + k$$

Integration and partial fractions

Let us consider how we might set about finding

$$\int \frac{1}{x^2 - 8x + 12} \, dx$$

Given we have on factorising,

$$x^2 - 8x + 12 = (x - 2)(x - 6)$$

let us find values of A and B such that:

$$\frac{A}{x - 2} + \frac{B}{x - 6} = \frac{1}{x^2 - 8x + 12}$$

Cross-multiplying we have:

$$A(x - 6) + B(x - 2) = (A + B)x - 6A - 2B = 1$$

Since this must be true for all x, then it must be the case that:

$$A + B = 0 \text{ and } -6A - 2B = 1$$

from which it follows that $A = -0.25$ and $B = 0.25$. We may therefore write the integral as:

$$\int \left(\frac{-0.25}{x - 2} + \frac{0.25}{x - 6} \right) dx$$

with solution

$$-0.25 \log_e |x - 2| + 0.25 \log_e |x - 6| + k$$

The reader should check this result by differentiating the above expression with respect to x, considering outcomes where $x < 2$, $2 < x < 6$, and $x > 6$.

More generally, let us consider how to find the integral of the reciprocal of a quadratic in x with distinct real roots, r_1 and r_2. We wish to find:

$$\int \frac{1}{a(x - r_1)(x - r_2)} \, dx$$

In this case, since we must have for all x that

$$\frac{A}{x - r_1} + \frac{B}{x - r_2} = \frac{1}{(x - r_1)(x - r_2)}$$

it can be shown that we must have

$$A = \frac{-1}{r_2 - r_1}; \quad B = \frac{1}{r_2 - r_1}$$

Using the above the reader should now show that the integral we seek is given by the following expression:

$$\int \frac{1}{a(x-r_1)(x-r_2)} \, dx = \frac{1}{a(r_2-r_1)} \log_e \left| \frac{x-r_2}{x-r_1} \right| + k$$

15.3 DEFINITE AND IMPROPER INTEGRALS

The definite integral

The integrals we have been concerned with so far in this chapter are known as indefinite integrals. We now move on to consider the concept of a definite integral. Consider the following exercise: given an integrand $f(x)$, find by integration the primitive function $F(x)+k$; then taking two values of x which lie in the domain of the function, evaluate first the value of the primitive function at the higher value of x (x_h) and then at the lower value of x (x_l), and finally calculate the difference between these two values. What emerges is a numerical value which is independent of the value of the constant of integration. In symbols we have:

$$\int_{x_l}^{x_h} F(x) \, dx = F(x_h) + k - F(x_l) - k$$
$$= F(x_h) - F(x_l)$$

where x_l is the lower limit of integration, and x_h is the upper limit of integration.

Examples

Evaluate the following definite integrals.

(i) $\displaystyle\int_0^{10} 2x \, dx = x^2 \Big|_{x=0}^{x=10}$

$= 10^2 - 0^2 = 100$

(ii) $\displaystyle\int_{10}^{25} 100x^{-2} \, dx = -100x^{-1} \Big|_{x=10}^{x=25}$

$= -\dfrac{100}{25} + \dfrac{100}{10}$

$= -4 + 10 = 6$

(iii) $\displaystyle\int_0^{20} 250 e^{0.05x} \, dx = \dfrac{250}{0.05} e^{0.05x} \Big|_{x=0}^{x=20}$

$= 5000[e^1 - e^0]$

$= 5000[2.71828 - 1] = 859.41$

We now provide a geometrical interpretation of the definite integral. Given a function $f(x)$ and two values of x, x_0 and x_n, which lie in the domain of this function, calculate the area of the rectangle $f(x_0)(x_n - x_0)$. This measures the area of the rectangle $x_0 f(x_0) a x_n$ in Fig. 15.1. Now divide the distance between x_0 and x_n into n sub-divisions with sub-distances: Δx_i where $\Delta x_i = x_i - x_{i-1}$. Now calculate the sum of the products of $f(x_{i-1})\Delta x_i$. This sum

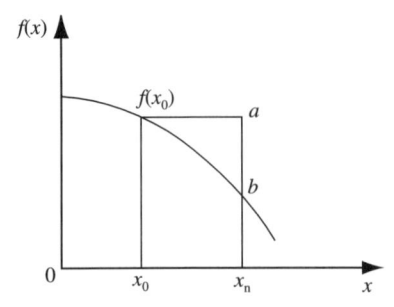

Figure 15.1 The area $f(x_0)(x_n - x_0)$ overestimates the area under the curve between x_0 and x_n by the area $f(x_0)ab$.

is given by:

$$S = \sum_{i=1}^{n} f(x_{i-1})\Delta x_i$$

Note that the sum S approximates the area under $f(x)$ between the lower value $x = x_0$ and the upper value $x = x_n$. For the function given in Fig. 15.2, S overestimates the area under the curve by the amount of the shaded areas, but this overestimation can be made smaller and smaller by making the sub-distances Δx_i smaller and smaller. Had $f(x)$ been an increasing function of x, then we would have underestimated the area under the curve. In the limit as n approaches infinity, then Δx_i approaches dx and S approaches:

$$\int_{x_0}^{x_n} f(x)\,dx$$

and the definite integral measures precisely the area under the curve between the lower and upper limits of integration.

Improper integrals

We now turn to a consideration of the definite integral where at least one of the limits of integration is not finite. Say we desire to evaluate:

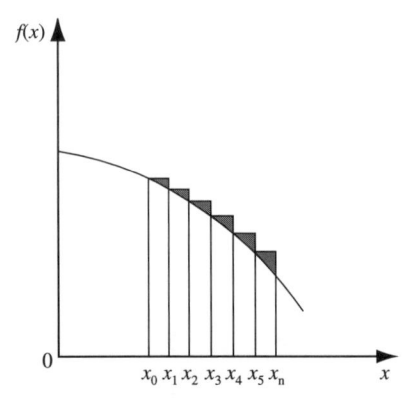

$$\int_{x_1}^{\infty} f(x)\,dx$$

Figure 15.2 The area $\sum_{i=1}^{n} f(x_{i-1})\Delta x_i$ overestimates the area under the curve between x_0 and x_n by the sum of the six shaded areas.

This is known as an improper integral, and we proceed as follows:

$$\int_{x_l}^{\infty} f(x)\,dx = \lim_{x_h \to \infty} \int_{x_l}^{x_h} f(x)\,dx$$

$$= \lim_{x_h \to \infty} [F(x_h) - F(x_l)]$$

Now, as x_h approaches infinity we may find that $F(x_h)$ converges on some finite value: in such a case the improper integral exists. However, we cannot guarantee that this will be the case. There will be cases where the limit of $F(x_h)$ as x_h approaches infinity is not finite; in such a case the improper integral does not exist.

15.4 SOME ECONOMIC APPLICATIONS OF INTEGRAL CALCULUS

From marginal cost to total cost

Assume that a firm's marginal cost (MC) function is given by

$$MC(x) = 4 + 4x^2$$

where x is output. Then if we integrate the marginal cost function with respect to output, we shall obtain the firm's total cost function:

$$\int MC(x)\,dx = \int (4 + 4x)\,dx$$

$$= 4x + 2x^2 + k$$

where in this context the constant of integration is equal to the firm's fixed costs of production. If we were asked to find by how much the firm's costs of production would rise if its output were increased from 25 to 50, then we would need to evaluate the following definite integral:

$$\int_{x=25}^{x=50} (4 + 4x)\,dx = (4x + 2x^2)\Big|_{x=25}^{x=50}$$

$$= 4(50) + 2(50)^2 - (4(25) + 2(25)^2)$$

$$= 200 + 5000 - 100 - 1250 = 3850$$

From marginal revenue to total revenue

Now consider the case of a firm whose marginal revenue function is given by:

$$MR(x) = 250x^{-0.5}$$

Integrating the marginal revenue function with respect to output x will give us the firm's total revenue function:

$$\int MR(x)\,dx = \int 250x^{-0.5}\,dx$$

$$= 500x^{0.5} + k$$

We have included a constant of integration, but let us reflect further on this. If the firm produces and sells nothing then its revenue will be zero, hence the constant of integration will be equal to zero. Again, by evaluating the following definite integral we can obtain the firm's loss of revenue if it were to reduce sales from *400* to *144*:

$$\int_{x=400}^{x=144} 250x^{-0.5} \, dx = 500x^{0.5} \Big|_{x=400}^{x=144}$$

$$= 500(12) - 500(20)$$

$$= -4000$$

It should come as no surprise that total revenue has fallen as sales were reduced, since if we were to divide the total revenue function by quantity to obtain the average revenue function, and then invert this function we would find that the demand function was one of constant elasticity of demand, with its absolute value being equal to *2*. The demand function is elastic throughout, and increases in revenue are positively associated with increases in sales.

The depletion of an exhaustible resource

At the current rate of extraction it is estimated that the known reserves of a non-renewable resource will be fully depleted in *500* years. Economists have just predicted that it is expected that the demand for this resource will grow at an exponential rate of *2.5* per cent a year. When will the reserves be finally exhausted? Letting A represent the current rate of extraction, then cumulative extraction from time $t = 0$ to time $t = T$ is given by the following definite integral:

$$\int_0^T A e^{0.025t} \, dt = \frac{A e^{0.025t}}{0.025} \Big|_{t=0}^{t=T}$$

$$= 40A(e^{0.025T} - 1)$$

Since the unexploited stock at time $t = 0$ equals $500A$, then the resource will be exhausted at the value of T which satisfies the following equation:

$$40A(e^{0.025T} - 1) = 500A$$

$$e^{0.025T} = 13.5$$

$$T = 40 \log_e 13.5$$

$$= 104.11$$

In this example, therefore, that we must solve for is not the value of the definite integral (this is known to us), but the value of the upper limit of integration which makes the cumulative amount extracted equal to the initial unexploited stock (i.e. the value of the definite integral).

The rate of return on a life assurance policy

An investor has contributed continuous payments to a life assurance policy over a *25* year period; the annual premiums as a continuous flow have been *£360* and the policy has just matured, yielding the investor a lump sum of *£57,256.61*. What is the effective rate of return on this investment? In this example we know the value of the definite integral and the value of both the limits of integration. What is to be found is the value of r which makes the accumulated value of the premiums equal to the payment on maturity. We must solve for the value of r in the following expression.

$$\int_0^{25} 360 e^{rt}\, dt = 57{,}256.61$$

$$\text{hence } \frac{360}{r} e^{rt}\Big|_{r=0}^{r=25} = 57{,}256.61$$

$$\frac{360}{r}[e^{25r} - 1] = 57{,}256.61$$

This is a non-linear equation, the solution to which can be solved by trial and error. Setting $r = 0.115$, the reader would find that the left-hand side is equal to $52{,}357.85$, whereas for $r = 0.125$ the left-hand side would equal $62{,}668.50$. The rate of return must, therefore, lie between these two values since the left-hand side is monotonically increasing in r. The value of r which actually satisfies the equation is 0.12; this is the rate then which the policyholder ultimately receives from the life assurance company.

Improper integrals and the evaluation of consumer surplus

Let the demand for a particular product be given by $f(p) = Ap^{-\alpha}$ where A and α are two positive constants. Let the current market price be p^*. How large is consumer surplus?

Since there is no finite price at which the demand for this product is reduced to zero, in order to calculate the amount of consumer surplus it is necessary to evaluate the following improper integral:

$$\int_{p^*}^{\infty} Ap^{-\alpha}\, dp = \lim_{p_h \to \infty} \int_{p^*}^{p_h} Ap^{-\alpha}\, dp$$

$$= \lim_{p_h \to \infty}\left[\frac{A}{1-\alpha}(p_h^{1-\alpha} - p^{*1-\alpha})\right]$$

$$= \frac{A}{\alpha - 1} p^{*1-\alpha} \text{ iff } \alpha > 1$$

If α (the absolute value of the own price elasticity of demand) ≤ 1, the improper integral is not defined. Note, however, in such a case the change in consumer surplus which results from a finite change in the price is measurable. For $\alpha = 1$, we would have:

$$\int_{p_1}^{p_h} Ap^{-1}\, dp = A \log_e p \Big|_{p=p_1}^{p=p_h}$$

$$= A \log_e\left(\frac{p_h}{p_1}\right)$$

Investment in human capital

An individual at time $t = 0$ has the option of entering the labour market and receiving a salary as a continuous flow at a rate of $Y(0)$ per year until retirement at time $t = T$. Alternatively, she may decide to undergo s additional years of education, which will then enable her to enter a different occupation and to receive a salary as a continuous flow at the rate of $Y(s)$ per year until retirement at time $t = T$. Assuming her objective is to maximise the present value of her earnings stream discounted back to the present at interest rate r, derive the relationship which must hold between $Y(0)$ and $Y(s)$ for her to be indifferent between the two occupations. We must, therefore, have:

$$\int_0^T Y(0) e^{-rt} dt = \int_s^T Y(s) e^{-rt}$$

$$-\frac{Y(0)}{r} e^{-rt}\Big|_{t=0}^{t=T} = -\frac{Y(s)}{r} e^{-rt}\Big|_{t=s}^{t=T}$$

$$\frac{Y(0)}{r}(1 - e^{-rT}) = \frac{Y(s)}{r}(e^{-rs} - e^{-rT})$$

$$Y(s) = \left[\frac{1 - e^{-rT}}{e^{-rs} - e^{-rT}}\right] Y(0)$$

If we assume that the individual's working life is not finite, then the integral to be evaluated will be an improper integral. As T approaches infinity we have:

$$Y(s) = Y(0) e^{rs}$$

with r being the return to an additional year of schooling.

A problem in the economics of forestry

Assuming perfect competition exists, foresters have to determine the optimal time at which to fell the trees growing on the land which they rent in order to maximise the value of the harvested timber. For the moment planting and harvesting costs are assumed to be zero. The value of cut timber of age T, $f(T)$, is an increasing, concave function of T where T is the age of the timber, and its present value discounted to time zero at rate of interest, r, is given by $f(T) e^{-rT}$. Given we are assuming a competitive market then land rents (R) will have been set at such a level that the net return from forestry is zero. We must, therefore, have:

$$f(T) e^{-rT} = \int_0^T R e^{-rt} dt$$

i.e. the present value of the timber harvested at time T equals the present value of the land rents payable over the time interval from $t = 0$ to $t = T$. The land rent must, therefore, satisfy the following condition:

$$f(T) e^{-rT} = -\frac{R}{r} e^{-rt}\Big|_{t=0}^{t=T}$$

$$= \frac{R}{r}[1 - e^{-rT}]$$

$$\text{hence } R = \frac{rf(T) e^{-rT}}{1 - e^{-rT}}$$

$$= \frac{rf(T)}{e^{rT} - 1}$$

Let us now choose the value of T which maximises the land rent. Differentiating R with respect to T, we obtain:

$$\frac{dR}{dT} = \frac{rf'(T)[e^{rT} - 1] - r^2 e^{rT} f(T)}{[e^{rT} - 1]^2} = 0$$

from which it follows that:
$$\frac{f'(T)}{f(T)} = \frac{re^{rT}}{e^{rT}-1} = \frac{r}{1-e^{-rT}}$$

Alternatively we may write this condition as
$$f'(T) = rf(T) + \frac{rf(T)}{e^{rT}-1}$$
$$= rf(T) + R$$

The optimal time to cut the timber, therefore, occurs when the rate of increase in the value of the cut timber is greater than the rate of interest. Remember we have assumed that $f(T)$ is concave in T, and hence $f'(T)/f(T)$ is decreasing in T. When the timber is of optimal age the increase in the value of the timber net of the interest forgone by not cutting the timber slightly earlier in time is equal to the competitive rent. Only if land is so plentiful that land rents are zero will it pay the forester to delay cutting the trees until the rate of increase in the value of the cut timber is just equal to the rate of interest in the economy. In such circumstances the forester will wish to choose the value of T which gives rise to a maximum of $f(T)e^{-rT}$. It is straightforward to show that this requires that $f'(T)/f(T) = r$.

The above discussion dealt solely with one timber cycle. Let us now calculate the present value of timber sales from an infinite number of cycles. This is given by:
$$PV = \lim_{n \to \infty} f(T)e^{-rT} + f(T)e^{-2rT} + \cdots + f(T)e^{-nrT}$$
$$= \frac{f(T)}{e^{rT}-1}$$

For this present value to be maximised we must have:
$$\frac{dPV}{dT} = \frac{f'(T)(e^{rT}-1) - re^{rT}f(T)}{[e^{rT}-1]^2} = 0$$

which requires
$$\frac{f'(T)}{f(T)} = \frac{r}{1-e^{-rT}}$$

This is exactly the same condition that we derived above for the single cycle case with the payment of competitive rents driving net revenue in present value terms to zero. Hence maximising R in the single cycle case leads to the same length of growing period as emerges from maximising the present value of timber sales over an infinite number of cycles.

What happens if we allow for the incurring of costs during the growing cycle in addition to the payment of rent. Assume for purposes of simplicity that these costs are constant, c, in each period. From the perspective of the forester, we have for the single cycle case the following net revenue function in terms of present value:
$$PV = f(T)e^{-rT} - \int_0^T (c+R)e^{-rT}\,dt$$
$$= f(T)e^{-rT} - \frac{(c+R)}{r}(1-e^{-rT})$$

Differentiating present value with respect to T and setting the derivative equal to zero, we obtain the first-order condition that must be satisfied by T in order to have net present value as large as possible, which is:

$$f'(T) - rf(T) = c + R$$

The increase in the value of the timber net of the interest forgone by not cutting slightly earlier should equal the sum of rent and felling cost.

Spatial analysis of a firm's market

In the two previous examples, we used the technique of integration to throw light on problems which had a time dimension to them. In this example we provide a spatial dimension and demonstrate how integration techniques can be used to analyse the behaviour of a firm which supplies consumers who are differentiated by residence.

A firm produces a good at a particular location at a constant unit cost (h), and charges a price at the factory gate of $p(0)$. Its customers are evenly distributed across space with population density d^*. The customer is responsible for meeting the delivery charges, which are proportional to distance, r, and are given by cr where c is a constant. A consumer located at distance r from the factory, therefore, pays an effective price per unit of $p(r)$ where $p(r) = p(0) + cr$. The inverse demand function for a consumer at distance r from the factory is given by:

$$p(r) = a - bq$$

where q is quantity purchased.

What value should the firm choose for $p(0)$ in order to maximise its profits?

The firm's market area is a circle of radius $r^* = (a - p(0))/c$ since at this distance from the factory $p(r)$ will equal a, and demand will be completely choked off. The population served by the firm is given by the following definite integral:

$$\int_0^{r^*} 2\pi d^* r \, dr = \pi d^* r^2 \Big|_{r=0}^{r=r^*}$$

$$= \pi d^* \left[\frac{a - p(0)}{c}\right]^2$$

The demand of an individual consumer located at distance r from the factory is given by:

$$q(r) = \frac{a - p(0)}{b} - \frac{c}{b} r$$

and at this distance from the factory there are $2\pi r d^*$ consumers. Remember the circumference of a circle is given by $2\pi r$ and at each point on the boundary of the circle there are d^* individuals. Total demand for the good (Q) is, therefore, given by:

$$\int_0^{r^*} 2\pi d^* \left[\frac{a - p(0)}{b} r - \frac{c}{b} r^2\right] dr = 2\pi d^* \left[\frac{a - p(0)}{2b} r^2 - \frac{c}{3b} r^3\right]\Big|_{r=0}^{r=r^*}$$

$$= \frac{\pi d^* [a - p(0)]^3}{3bc^2}$$

The firm's profits are, therefore, given by:

$$\Pi(p(0)) = [p(0) - h]\left[\frac{\pi d^* [a - p(0)]^3}{3bc^2}\right]$$

and differentiating with respect to $p(0)$, we obtain:
$$\Pi'(p(0)) = \frac{\pi d^*[a-p(0)]^3}{3bc^2} - \frac{3\pi d^*[p(0)-h][a-p(0)]^2}{3bc^2} = 0$$

from which it follows that
$$p(0) = \frac{a+3h}{4}$$

We now check that the second-order condition for a maximum of profits is satisfied at this factory gate price. Differentiate the first-order condition with respect to $p(0)$ to obtain:
$$\Pi''(p(0)) = \frac{1}{3bc^2}[-3\pi d^*(a-p(0))^2 - 3\pi d^*(a-p(0))^2 + 6\pi d^*(p(0)-h)(a-p(0))]$$

For the second derivative to be negative, then we must have on collecting terms and simplifying
$$(p(0) - h) < (a - p(0))$$

Substituting in the value of $p(0)$ which satisfies the first-order condition and simplifying yields the following simple condition:
$$a > h$$

The second-order condition for a maximum of profits will be satisfied provided that the choke price is greater than the firm's marginal cost of production. In any meaningful model, this will be the case; if it were not, then the firm would obviously not wish to produce anything at all.

At what distance from the factor is demand highest? Letting $Q(r)$ represent total demand at distance r from the factory, $q(r)$ the demand of a representative consumer located at distance r from the factory, and $n(r)$ the number of consumers at distance r from the factory, then
$$Q(r) = q(r)n(r)$$
$$= 2\pi d^* r \left[\frac{a - p(0) - cr}{b}\right]$$

Substituting into the above expression the optimal value of the factory gate price, we obtain
$$Q(r) = 2\pi d^* r \frac{[0.75(a-h) - cr]}{b}$$

Differentiating partially with respect to r yields:
$$\frac{\partial Q(r)}{\partial r} = \pi d^* \frac{[1.5(a-h) - 4cr]}{b} = 0$$

and solving for r we have
$$r = \frac{0.375(a-h)}{c}$$

It is a straightforward matter to check that the second-order condition for a maximum is met at this distance from the factory. As we move further away from the centre, each individual consumer buys less of the product since the price inclusive of the transport cost is higher, but there are more customers located along the boundary of a circle whose distance from the factory is greater. The two countervailing effects just offset each other at the distance given above, which

The size of a city

Consider a circular city where the distance from the city centre to the boundary of the city is r^*. The density of the population at the city centre is given by $d(0)$, and density at distance r from the centre is given by $d(r) = d(0) e^{-\alpha r}$. What is the population of the city?

The number of people who live at distance r from the centre is given by $2\pi r d(0) e^{-\alpha r}$. Once again, remember the circumference of a circle of radius r is given by $2\pi r$ and the density at distance r from the centre is given by $d(0) e^{-\alpha r}$. Hence the population of the city is given by:

$$\int_0^{r^*} 2\pi d(0) r e^{-\alpha r} \, dr$$

Let us first find the indefinite integral:

$$\int 2\pi d(0) r e^{-\alpha r} \, dr$$

This is a case for which we can find the integral by using integration by parts. Let $v = r$, and $du = e^{-\alpha r} \, dr$. Then $dv = dr$, and $u = -(1/\alpha) e^{-\alpha r}$. Hence

$$\int r e^{-\alpha r} \, dr = -(r/\alpha) e^{-\alpha r} - \int -(1/\alpha) e^{-\alpha r} \, dr$$

$$= -(r/\alpha) e^{-\alpha r} - (1/\alpha^2) e^{-\alpha r}$$

We therefore have for the definite integral:

$$\int_0^{r^*} 2\pi d(0) r e^{-\alpha r} \, dr = -2\pi d(0) [(r/\alpha) e^{-\alpha r} + (1/\alpha^2) e^{-\alpha r}]_{r=0}^{r=r^*}$$

$$= (2\pi d(0)/\alpha^2)[1 - (1 + \alpha r^*) e^{-\alpha r^*}]$$

Note that in the limit as r^* approaches ∞, the population of the city approaches $2\pi d(0)/\alpha^2$, and the proportion of the population who live within radius (r) of the centre, $P(r)$, is given by:

$$P(r) = 1 - (1 + \alpha r) e^{-\alpha r}$$

15.5 SUMMARY

We here provide a summary table of some common integrals:

$$\int x^n \, dx = \frac{1}{n+1} x^{n+1} + k$$

$$\int dx = x + k$$

$$\int a f(x) \, dx = a \int f(x) \, dx$$

$$\int (f(x) \pm g(x)) \, dx = \int f(x) \, dx \pm \int g(x) \, dx$$

$$\int e^x \, dx = e^x + k$$

$$\int \frac{1}{x} = \log_e x + k$$

$$\int \cos x \, dx = -\sin x + k$$

$$\int \sin x \, dx = \cos x + k$$

$$\int u(x) \frac{du}{dx} \, dx = \int u \, du$$

$$\int v \, du = uv - \int u \, dv$$

We shall also be making use of the techniques we have outlined in this chapter in our discussion of differential equations in Chapters 18, 19 and 22.

15.6 EXERCISES

15.1 (a) Find the following:

(i) $\int x^3 \, dx$

(ii) $\int x^{-3} \, dx$

(iii) $\int -x^{-1.5} \, dx$

(iv) $\int x^{0.25} \, dx$

(v) $\int x^{-0.75} \, dx$

15.2 (a) Find the following:

(i) $\int 5x^{-1} \, dx$

(ii) $\int 2e^x \, dx$

(iii) $\int (5x^4 + e^x - 4x^{-0.5}) \, dx$

(iv) $\int (2x^{-5} + 9x^2 + x^{0.6}) \, dx$

(v) $\int (10x^{2/3} - 0.5x^{-1}) \, dx$

15.3 (a) Find the following:

(i) $\int 100 \, e^{0.1x} \, dx$

(ii) $\int 10 \, e^{-0.05x} \, dx$

(iii) $\int (16x + 4x^{-1})(2x^2 + \log_e x)^3 \, dx$

(iv) $\int (2x^{0.5} + 6x + 5)^{0.5}(x^{-0.5} + 6)\,dx$

(v) $\int \left(\dfrac{4x^3 + 10x - 2e^x}{x^4 + 5x^2 - 2e^x}\right)dx$

(vi) $\int \left(\dfrac{3x^2 + x^{-2}}{x^3 - x^{-1}}\right)dx$

(vii) $\int \left(\dfrac{2x^2 - 4x + 12}{x - 2}\right)dx$

15.4 (a) Find the following:

(i) $\int \log_e x^2\, dx$

(ii) $\int x e^x\, dx$

(iii) $\int x e^{2x}\, dx$

(iv) $\int x^2 e^x\, dx$

(v) $\int \sin^2 x\, dx$

(vi) $\int x \cos x\, dx$

(vii) $\int x^2 \cos x\, dx$

15.5 (a) Find the following:

(i) $\int \dfrac{1}{x^2 + x - 6}\, dx$

(ii) $\int \dfrac{1}{2x^2 + 10x + 12}\, dx$

(iii) $\int \dfrac{1}{0.5x^2 - 3x + 4}\, dx$

(iv) $\int \dfrac{1}{0.1x^2 + 0.2x}\, dx$

(v) $\int \dfrac{-1}{x^2 - 2x + 1}\, dx$

15.6 (a) Evaluate the following:

(i) $\int_0^{50} (100 - 2x)\, dx$

(ii) $\int_3^9 3x^2\, dx$

(iii) $\int_{0.5}^{10} x^{-1}\, dx$

(iv) $\int_1^{49} 2x^{-0.5}\, dx$

(v) $\int_3^{12} (x^2 - 10x + 24)\, dx$

(vi) $\int_0^{20} 10 e^{-0.05x}\, dx$

(vii) $\int_{25}^{50} 5 e^{0.1x}\, dx$

(b) Evaluate, where possible, the following:

(i) $\int_5^\infty 2x\,dx$

(ii) $\int_1^\infty 25x^{-2}\,dx$

(iii) $\int_{-\infty}^0 100e^{0.1x}\,dx$

(iv) $\int_0^\infty 50e^{-0.05}\,dx$

(v) $\int_0^\infty x^{-3}\,dx$

(vi) $\int_1^\infty x^{-3}\,dx$

15.7 (a) The demand function for a firm's output is given by:
$$x = f(p) = 6400p^{-2}$$
Alternatively by inverting the above function, we obtain the inverse demand function:
$$p = 80x^{-0.5}$$
where x is quantity and p price. The firm's fixed costs are *100* and its marginal cost curve is given by
$$MC = 6 + 0.02x$$

(i) Calculate the change in consumer surplus which results when (1) the price falls from *10* to *5*, and (2) the price rises from *10* to *20*.

(ii) If the firm adopted marginal cost pricing, how much output would it produce, and what would be the amount of producer surplus?

(iii) Show that if the firm were to act as a profit-maximiser, it would produce *34.54* units of output.

(iv) Calculate the welfare loss to society in moving from the marginal cost pricing level of output to the profit-maximising level of output.

(b) The demand function for a particular good is given by:
$$q = 100p^{-0.5}$$
The current price is *4*.

(i) Show that it is impossible to calculate the amount of consumer surplus that consumers receive.

(ii) Obtain the change in consumer surplus that results from (1) the price rising from *4* to *16*, and (2) the price falling from *4* to *1*.

(c) The demand function for a good is given by:
$$q^d = 400p^{-3}$$
and the current price is *5*.

(i) Calculate the amount of consumer surplus.

(ii) What happens to the amount of consumer surprlus as (1) the price rises from *5* to *10*, and (2) falls from *5* to *2*?

(d) An irredeemable security offers an income of £*A* per period as a continuous flow. The prevailing rate of interest is *r*. At what price will this security trade on the stock market?

15.8 (a) For the model on pages 264–265, analyse the effect on the size of the salary differential of changes in *r*, *s* and *T*.

(b) If students are paid a maintenance grant for each additional year of full-time education of *G* per year again as a continuous flow, what difference will this make to the differential which is necessary to induce entry into the occupation requiring more education? Show that in the limit as *T* approaches infinity we must have:
$$Y(s) = Y(0)e^{rs} - G(e^{rs} - 1)$$

15.9 (a) (i) Given that the value of cut timber at time *T* is given by
$$f(T) = 100e^{0.3T - 0.00265T^2}$$

and the rate of interest is *0.025*, show that the optimal time to cut the timber is *50* years. How large is the annual land rent?

(ii) If land were so plentiful that rents were zero, when would be the optimal time to cut the timber?

(b) A whisky distillery is deciding on the optimal time for its products to age in the vat before being brought to market. The rate of interest is *0.05*, and storage costs as a continuous flow are *10* for each year stored. The value of a vat of whisky T years old is given by:

$$V = 250T^{0.5}$$

(i) What is the optimal age at which to sell the whisky?

(ii) How would the optimal age at which to sell be affected by (1) an increase in the annual storage costs from *10* to *20*, and (2) a fall in the rate of interest to *0.025*?

15.10 (a) Using the model on page 268, show that the population is more highly concentrated in the inner areas of the city and that the higher is the value of the parameter α.

(b) Let us now make the radius of the same city an endogenously determined variable. We shall assume that farmers are willing to pay a land rent of $R_a(r)$ at distance r from the city centre where $R_a(r)$ is given by:

$$R_a(r) = R_a(0)\,e^{-\beta r}$$

On the other hand, non-agricultural users of land are prepared to pay a land rent of $R_n(r)$ at distance r from the centre where

$$R_n(r) = R_n(0)\,e^{-\gamma r}$$

We assume that $R_n(0) > R_a(0)$, and that $\beta < \gamma$.

(i) Determine the radius of the city.

(ii) How much revenue is raised in non-agricultural land rent?

CHAPTER SIXTEEN
CONSTRAINED OPTIMISATION

16.1 INTRODUCTION

In this chapter we are concerned with constrained optimisation problems. Such problems are very common in economics. Consumers with a limited amount to spend and faced with a given set of prices seek to allocate their expenditure across a range of goods in such a way as to maximise their utility. A firm who may choose alternative techniques for producing a particular product wishes at given prices for its inputs to minimise the costs of producing a specified level of output. A policy maker constrained by the existence of a long run trade-off between inflation and unemployment desires to choose the point on the trade-off which minimises some index of social misery.

In the first case we have:

$$\text{Maximise } U(x)$$
$$\text{subject to } M - p \cdot x = 0$$

where x is a vector of consumption goods, p is a vector of their prices, M is money income and $U(x)$ is the consumer's utility function.

In the second case we have:

$$\text{Minimise } r \cdot z$$
$$\text{subject to } Q - F(z) = 0$$

where z is a vector of productive inputs, r a vector of their prices, Q output and $F(z)$ the production function.

In the third case we have:

$$\text{Minimise } M(p, u)$$
$$\text{subject to } g(p, u) = 0$$

where p is the rate of inflation, u is the unemployment rate, $M(p, u)$ is the misery index and $g(p, u)$ is the trade-off between inflation and unemployment.

Note that in each case the constraint is an equality. We do not permit consumers to leave unspent part of their income, or the firm to produce more than the specified level of output. Similarly the policy maker's choice of p and u must lie on the long-run trade-off. In the next chapter we shall drop the requirement that the constraints hold as equalities, and shall allow for the presence of slack in constraints.

In Section 16.2 we discuss how to solve some simple constrained optimisation problems. We introduce the concept of the Lagrangean multiplier and show how Lagrange's method can be employed to find the optimal value of our function whilst ensuring that the constraint is met. We shall see that the value of the Lagrangean multiplier has an important mathematical and economic interpretation: it informs us of the impact that a very small relaxation of the constraint will have on the value of the objective function. In Section 16.3 we discuss the second-order conditions for a constrained optimisation problem. This then leads us on to a more general discussion of the concepts of quasi-concavity and quasi-convexity in Section 16.4. We turn in Section 16.5 to look at some economic applications of constrained optimisation. We look at the behaviour of firms in a duopoly; this application uses various optimisation approaches, starting with some simple unconstrained maximisation before going on to bring in a profits constraint. We show how to derive demand functions for goods by solving the problem facing a consumer who is seeking to maximise utility subject to a budget constraint. We also engage in some comparative static analysis. In Section 16.6 we look in more detail at the interpretation of the Lagrangean multiplier, and develop further our discussion of consumer demand. Not only do we consider the problem of maximising utility subject to a budget constraint, but also consider the dual problem of minimising the cost of achieving a given level of utility. We shall see that this approach enables us to find Hicksian (compensated) demand functions for goods in which we see how the demand for a good varies holding utility constant. We end by showing how, given information on the production technology available to a firm, its cost function can be derived.

16.2 SOLUTION METHODS FOR CONSTRAINED OPTIMISATION PROBLEMS

Consider the following problem:

$$\text{Maximise } f(x_1, x_2)$$
$$\text{subject to } c - g(x_1, x_2) = 0$$

where c is a constant.

The substitution approach

One way of proceeding is to rearrange the constraint such that x_2 is expressed as a function of x_1 and c. This expression for x_2 can then be substituted into the objective function which will then depend only upon x_1 and the exogenous constant c. Let the expression for x_2 be given by:

$$x_2 = h(x_1, c)$$

Hence we have the reformulated problem:

$$\text{Maximise } f(x_1, h(x_2, c))$$

Differentiating with respect to x_1 yields the first-order condition for a maximum of the function subject to the constraint. We obtain

$$f_1 + f_2 \frac{\partial h}{\partial x_1} = 0$$

where f_1 and f_2 are the first-order partial derivatives of the objective function. However, by the implicit function theorem, we have

$$\frac{\partial h}{\partial x_1} = -\frac{g_1}{g_2}$$

where g_1 and g_2 are the partial derivatives of the constraint. Hence, we may write the first order condition as

$$\frac{f_1}{f_2} = \frac{g_1}{g_2}$$

The total differential approach

Another approach is to differentiate totally both the objective function and the constraint to obtain respectively:

$$df = f_1 x_1 + f_2 \, dx_2$$
$$dc = g_1 \, dx_1 + g_2 \, dx_2 = 0$$

From the total differential of the constraint we have:

$$dx_2 = -\frac{g_1}{g_2} \, dx_2$$

and substituting for dx_2 in the total differential of the objective function we have:

$$df = \left(f_1 - \frac{g_1}{g_2} f_2 \right) dx_1$$

For the first-order condition to be satisfied we must have $df = 0$, and we can see from the above that this requires:

$$\frac{f_1}{f_2} = \frac{g_1}{g_2}$$

Note that along the constraint it is the case that:

$$\frac{dx_2}{dx_1} = -\frac{g_1}{g_2}$$

Now consider combinations of x_1 and x_2 which give rise to the same value of the objective function: along an iso-value locus we must have:

$$df = f_1 \, dx_1 + f_2 \, dx_2 = 0$$

from which it follows that the slope of such a locus must be given by:

$$\frac{dx_2}{dx_1} = -\frac{f_1}{f_2}$$

The optimal position therefore involves a tangency position between the constraint and an iso-value locus of the objective function.

The Lagrangean multiplier approach

An alternative and general procedure for solving constrained optimisation problems and the one which we will concentrate on is one due to the famous French mathematician J-L Lagrange. Given the problem:

$$\text{Maximise } f(x_1, x_2)$$
$$\text{subject to } c - g(x_1, x_2) = 0$$

we set up the following Lagrangean function:

$$L = f(x_1, x_2) + y[c - g(x_1, x_2)]$$

where y is known as a Lagrangean multiplier, the precise interpretation of which we shall defer discussing until later. Let us choose the values of x_1, x_2 and y which give rise to a maximum of the Lagrangean function. Differentiating partially with respect to x_1, x_2 and y, we obtain the following set of first-order conditions:

$$\frac{\partial L}{\partial x_1} = f_1 - yg_1 = 0$$

$$\frac{\partial L}{\partial x_2} = f_2 - yg_2 = 0$$

$$\frac{\partial L}{\partial y} = c - g(x_1, x_2) = 0$$

Note that the requirement that the partial derivative with respect to the Lagrangean multiplier should equal zero ensures that the constraint of the problem does indeed hold as an equality. Maximising L with respect to x_1, x_2 and y will ensure that we maximise the objective function subject to the equality constraint. From the conditions that the partial derivatives with respect to x_1 and x_2 are both zero, it is clear that:

$$\frac{f_1}{f_2} = \frac{g_1}{g_2}$$

which is our tangency condition again.

Regarding the interpretation of the Lagrangean multiplier, let us differentiate totally the Lagrangean multiplier:

$$dL = (f_1 - yg_1)\,dx_1 + (f_2 - yg_2)\,dx_2 + [c - g(x_1, x_2)]\,dy + y\,dc$$

and evaluate this total differential at the point which satisfies the first-order conditions for a maximum, we now have:

$$dL = y\,dc, \text{ hence } \frac{dL}{dc} = y$$

The increase in the value of the Lagrangean function and hence the value of the objective function which results from a very small relaxation of the constraint is given by the Lagrangean multiplier. We discuss this result in more detail in Section 16.6.

16.3 THE SECOND-ORDER CONDITIONS

Consider a second-order Taylor-series expansion of the Lagrangean function around the point (x_1^*, x_2^*, y^*) which satisfies the first-order conditions for a maximum.

$$L(x_1, x_2, y) = f(x_1^*, x_2^*) + \sum_j L_j(x_j - x_j^*) + L_y(y - y^*)$$
$$+ \sum_i \sum_j L_{ij}(x_i - x_i^*)(x_j - x_j^*)$$
$$+ \sum_j L_{yj}(y - y^*)(x_j - x_j^*) + L_{yy}(y - y^*)^2$$

where L_j and L_y are the first order partial derivatives and L_{ij}, L_{yj} and L_{yy} are the second-order partial derivatives of the Lagrangean function evaluated at the point: x_1^*, x_2^*, y^*. The first-order partial derivatives are all equal to zero at this point. Differentiating partially the first-order partial derivatives, we obtain the second-order partial derivatives:

$$L_{11} = f_{11} - yg_{11}$$
$$L_{12} = f_{12} - yg_{12}$$
$$L_{22} = f_{22} - yg_{22}$$
$$L_{1y} = -g_1$$
$$L_{2y} = -g_2$$
$$L_{yy} = 0$$

Furthermore, let the differences between x_j and x_j^*, and between y and y^*, be very small; so we may write:

$$dx_j = x_j - x_j^* \text{ and } dy = y - y^*$$

Note also that since the constraint must continue to hold as an equality we must have

$$dx_2 = -\frac{g_1}{g_2} dx_1$$

We may therefore write the second-order Taylor-series expansion of the Lagrangean function around the point that satisfies the first-order conditions for a maximum as:

$$L(x_1, x_2, y) = L(x_1^*, x_2^*, y^*) + \left[L_{11} - 2L_{12}\left(\frac{g_1}{g_2}\right) + L_{22}\left(\frac{g_1^2}{g_2^2}\right) \right] dx_1^2$$

Hence

$$L(x_1, x_2, y) < L(x_1^*, x_2^*, y)$$

provided that

$$L_{11} - 2L_{12}(g_1/g_2) + L_{22}(g_1/g_2)^2 < 0$$

Multiplying the above inequality by $-g_2^2$, we may alternatively write the condition as:

$$-L_{11}g_2^2 + 2L_{12}g_1g_2 - L_{22}g_1^2 > 0$$

Now evaluate the following determinant:

$$\begin{vmatrix} 0 & g_1 & g_2 \\ g_1 & L_{11} & L_{12} \\ g_2 & L_{21} & L_{22} \end{vmatrix} = -L_{11}g_2^2 + 2L_{12}g_1g_2 - L_{22}g_1^2$$

It is clear that if this determinant is positive, then we will have identified a constrained maximum at the point which satisfies the first-order conditions for a maximum of the Lagrangean function. The sufficient second-order condition is that the above determinant (which is known as a bordered Hessian determinant) be positive. Note the second-order partial derivatives of the Lagrangean function with respect to the choice variables x_1 and x_2, are bordered by a row and a column, each containing the partial derivatives of the constraint function with respect to the choice variables, g_1 and g_2.

We now state the second-order conditions for a maximum of $f(x)$ subject to $c - g(x) = 0$ where x is a vector containing n components. The bordered Hessian determinant is given by:

$$|\overline{H}| = \begin{vmatrix} 0 & g_1 & g_2 & \cdots & g_n \\ g_1 & L_{11} & L_{12} & \cdots & L_{1n} \\ g_2 & L_{21} & L_{22} & \cdots & L_{2n} \\ \cdots & \cdots & \cdots & \cdots & \cdots \\ g_n & L_{n1} & L_{n2} & \cdots & L_{nn} \end{vmatrix}$$

and its principal minors are:

$$|\overline{H_2}| = \begin{vmatrix} 0 & g_1 & g_2 \\ g_1 & L_{11} & L_{12} \\ g_2 & L_{21} & L_{22} \end{vmatrix}$$

$$|\overline{H_3}| = \begin{vmatrix} 0 & g_1 & g_2 & g_3 \\ g_1 & L_{11} & L_{12} & L_{13} \\ g_2 & L_{21} & L_{22} & L_{23} \\ g_3 & L_{31} & L_{32} & L_{33} \end{vmatrix}$$

and so on up to

$$|\overline{H_n}| = |\overline{H}|$$

Sufficient second-order conditions for a maximum of $f(x)$ subject to $c - g(x) = 0$ are that these principal minors should alternate in sign, starting positive. It goes without saying that the first-order partial derivatives of the constraint and the second-order partial derivatives of the Lagrangean function are to be evaluated at the point which satisfies the first-order conditions for a maximum of the Lagrangean function. Hence, we require:

$$|\overline{H_2}| > 0, \quad |\overline{H_3}| < 0, \quad |\overline{H_4}| > 0, \ldots, (-1)^n |\overline{H}| > 0$$

For a constrained minimisation problem,

Minimise $f(x_1, x_2)$ *subject to* $c = g(x_1, x_2)$

we would again set up a Lagrangean function

$$L = f(x_1, x_2) + y[c - g(x_1, x_2)]$$

and the first-order conditions are identical to those of a maximisation problem: the first-order partial derivatives with respect to the xs and the Lagrangean multiplier should all equal zero. Regarding the second-order condition, we require that

$$-L_{11}g_2^2 + 2L_{12}g_1g_2 - L_{22}g_1^2 < 0$$

for

$$L(x_1, x_2, y) > L(x_1^*, x_2^*, y^*)$$

at the point at which all the first-order partial derivatives of the Lagrangean function are equal to zero. We will then have identified a minimum of the function subject to the constraint. The bordered Hessian determinant should, therefore, be negative.

Sufficient second-order conditions for a minimum of $f(x)$ subject to $c - g(x) = 0$ are that the principal minors of the bordered Hessian determinant should all be negative. Hence, we require:

$$|\overline{H_2}| < 0, \quad |\overline{H_3}| < 0, \quad |\overline{H_4}| < 0, \ldots, |\overline{H}| < 0$$

We defer discussion of constrained optimisation problems with more than one constraint to the next chapter in which we shall also impose non-negativity requirements on the variables and allow for the existence of slack in the constraints.

As we have seen in Chapters 13 and 14, for unconstrained extremum problems a point which satisfies the first-order conditions for a maximum (minimum) gives rise to a maximum (minimum) value of the objective function provided that the objective function is concave (convex) in the vicinity of the point that satisfies the first-order conditions. If the objective function is strictly concave (convex) everywhere in the domain of the function, then if there exists a point satisfying the first-order conditions, it will be unique and will give rise to a global maximum (minimum) of the function.

Before considering the conditions that we need to impose on the objective function to be able to make similar statements about the nature of the point which satisfies the first-order conditions for a constrained optimisation problem, in order to set the scene, we shall work through two examples of a constrained maximisation problem.

Utility maximisation

Firstly consider the case of a utility-maximising consumer whose utility function is given by:

$$U = U(x_1, x_2) = (x_1 x_2)^2$$

The consumer has an income of *400*, and the prices of the two goods are *2* and *4* respectively. The Lagrangean function is, therefore:

$$L = (x_1 x_2)^2 + y[400 - 2x_1 - 4x_2]$$

and the first-order conditions for a maximum are:

$$L_1 = 2x_1 x_2^2 - 2y = 0$$

$$L_2 = 2x_1^2 x_2 - 4y = 0$$

$$L_y = 400 - 2x_1 - 4x_2 = 0$$

Solving the above three equations we find that $x_1 = 100$, $x_2 = 50$, $y = 25(10)^4$. The second-order partial derivatives of the Lagrangean function are

$$L_{11} = 2x_2^2 = 0.5(10)^4$$
$$L_{12} = 4x_1x_2 = 2(10)^4$$
$$L_{22} = 2x_1^2 = 2(10)^4$$

From the constraint we have

$$g_1 = 2 \text{ and } g_2 = 4$$

The bordered Hessian determinant is, therefore:

$$|\overline{H}| = \begin{vmatrix} 0 & 2 & 4 \\ 2 & 0.5(10)^4 & 2(10)^4 \\ 4 & 2(10)^4 & 2(10)^4 \end{vmatrix} = 16(10)^4$$

Hence we have identified a maximum point subject to the budget constraint. Note, however, that the utility function is not concave since:

$$|U_{11}| > 0, \quad \begin{vmatrix} U_{11} & U_{12} \\ U_{21} & U_{22} \end{vmatrix} = 0$$

However as can easily be checked, the indifference curves associated with the utility function are convex to the origin, and at the point $x_1 = 100$, $x_2 = 50$, we do indeed have a tangency position between the budget constraint and a convex to the origin indifference curve.

A profit-maximising firm

Our second example concerns a firm whose profits function is given by:

$$\Pi = 12x_1 - x_1^2 + 24x_2 - 1.5x_2^2$$

where x_1 and x_2 are two goods. The firm is also subject to a constraint on the availability of a particular input which is necessary for the production of both goods. Two units of the input are required to produce a unit of the first good and one unit to produce a unit of the second good; 27 units of the input are available. Hence the Lagrangean function is:

$$L = 12x_1 - x_1^2 + 24x_2 - 1.5x_2^2 + y(27 - 2x_1 - x_2)$$

and the first-order conditions for a maximum of profit subject to the constraint are:

$$L_1 = 12 - 2x_1 - 2y = 0$$
$$L_2 = 24 - 3x_2 - y = 0$$
$$L_y = 27 - 2x_1 - x_2 = 0$$

Solving the above three equations we find that: $x_1 = 9$, $x_2 = 9$, and $y = -3$. The second-order partial derivatives of the Lagrangean function with respect to x_1 and x_2 are:

$$L_{11} = -2, \quad L_{12} = L_{21} = 0, \quad L_{22} = -3$$

Given $g_1 = 2$ and $g_2 = 1$, the bordered Hessian determinant is

$$|\overline{H}| = \begin{vmatrix} 0 & 2 & 3 \\ 2 & -2 & 0 \\ 3 & 0 & -3 \end{vmatrix} = 30$$

Hence profits in the case above are indeed maximised subject to the resource constraint when the firm produces 9 units of each good, and profits equal *121.5*. For this particular problem it is straightforward to see that in the absence of the resource constraint, the firm would make larger profits by producing smaller quantities of both goods. In the unconstrained case, we have the following first-order conditions for a maximum of profits:

$$\Pi_1 = 12 - 2x_1 = 0$$

$$\Pi_2 = 24 - 3x_2 = 0$$

$$\text{hence } x_1 = 6 \text{ and } x_2 = 8$$

Let us check that the second-order conditions for a maximum are satisfied:

$$\Pi_{11} = -2, \quad \begin{vmatrix} \Pi_{11} & \Pi_{12} \\ \Pi_{21} & \Pi_{22} \end{vmatrix} = \begin{vmatrix} -2 & 0 \\ 0 & -3 \end{vmatrix} = 6$$

The profits function is concave throughout, and the second-order conditions for a maximum are met. Note that at the constrained optimum, profits are smaller than in the unconstrained optimum, and the Lagrangean multiplier is, in fact, negative. The iso-profit contours of the profit's function are circles centred on the point $x_1 = 6$, $x_2 = 8$. This is the unconstrained maximum, and the point $x_1 = 9$, $x_2 = 9$ lies to the north-east of this point on a lower iso-profit contour. At the constrained optimum, both Π_1 and Π_2 are negative, and the iso-profit contour is concave rather than convex to the origin.

What these two simple examples hint at is that, given a convex constraint, the optimal solution to a constrained maximisation problem must occur at a tangency position either between a convex to the origin iso-value locus and the constraint or a concave to the origin iso-value locus and the constraint. We observe the former outcome when the first-order partial derivatives of the objective function are positive when evaluated at the optimal position. Note this also involves a positive value for the Lagrangean multiplier. The latter outcome arises when the first-order partial derivatives of the objective function are negative when evaluated at the optimal position. Note that this also involves a negative value for the Lagrangean multiplier.

16.4 QUASI-CONCAVITY AND QUASI-CONVEXITY

As the first example in Section 16.3 demonstrated, we do not require the objective function in a constrained maximisation problem to be concave in the vicinity of the point satisfying the first-order conditions. We can get by with a less restrictive condition on the nature of the objective function. The requirement is that the objective function be quasi-concave. Quasi-concavity may be defined in a number of different ways depending upon whether the function is or is not differentiable. Naturally, since we are using classical calculus techniques in this chapter we assume throughout that both the objective functions and the constraints of the problems in this chapter are smooth, continuous functions with continuous first- and second-order partial derivatives. But we shall begin our discussion of quasi-concavity by dealing with the more general case in which differentiability has not been imposed on the function.

A function $f(x)$ is defined as being quasi-concave iff $f(x'') \geq f(x')$ implies $f(ax'' + [1-a]x') \geq f(x')$ where x'' and x' both lie in the domain of the function and $1 > a > 0$. For quasi-concavity (strict quasi-concavity), therefore, the value of the function at a point which is a weighted average of two points which lie in the domain of the function must be no less than (greater than) the value of the function at x' given that $f(x'') \geq f(x')$; and this must be the case for all pairs of points in the domain.

Conversely, $f(x)$ is defined as being quasi-convex iff $f(x'') \geq f(x')$ implies $f(ax'' + [1-a]x') \leq f(x'')$, again with x'' and x' both lying in the domain of the function and $1 > a > 0$. For quasi-convexity (strict quasi-convexity), therefore, the value of the function at a point which is a weighted average of two points lying in the domain of the function must be no greater than (less than) the value of the function at x'' given that $f(x'') \geq f(x')$; and this must be the case for all pairs of points in the domain.

Assume now that $f(x)$ is a differentiable function. Letting $f(x'') \geq f(x')$, then for $f(x)$ to be quasi-concave requires that:

$$\sum f_j(x')(x_j'' - x_j') \geq 0$$

On the other hand, again assuming that $f(x'') \geq f(x')$, quasi-convexity of $f(x)$ requires that:

$$\sum f_j(x'')(x_j'' - x_j') \geq 0$$

When $f(x)$ possesses continuous first- and second-order partial derivatives, determinantal tests for quasi-concavity and quasi-convexity are available. $f(x)$ is quasi-concave if the principal minors of the following matrix alternate in sign, starting non-positive:

$$B = \begin{bmatrix} 0 & f_1 & f_2 & \cdots & f_n \\ f_1 & f_{11} & f_{12} & \cdots & f_{1n} \\ f_2 & f_{21} & f_{22} & \cdots & f_{2n} \\ \vdots & \vdots & \vdots & \cdots & \vdots \\ f_{n1} & f_{n2} & f_{n3} & \cdots & f_{nn} \end{bmatrix}$$

Hence, we must have:

$$|B_1| = \begin{vmatrix} 0 & f_1 \\ f_1 & f_{11} \end{vmatrix} \leq 0, \quad |B_2| = \begin{vmatrix} 0 & f_1 & f_2 \\ f_1 & f_{11} & f_{12} \\ f_2 & f_{21} & f_{22} \end{vmatrix} \geq 0, \ldots$$

$$|B_n| = \begin{vmatrix} 0 & f_1 & f_2 & \cdots & f_n \\ f_1 & f_{11} & f_{12} & \cdots & f_{1n} \\ f_2 & f_{21} & f_{22} & \cdots & f_{2n} \\ \vdots & \vdots & \vdots & \cdots & \vdots \\ f_n & f_{n1} & f_{n2} & \cdots & f_{nn} \end{vmatrix} \geq 0 \text{ for } n \text{ even, } \leq 0 \text{ for } n \text{ odd}$$

$f(\mathbf{x})$ is quasi-convex if the principal minors of the above matrix, $\mathbf{B}$, are all non-positive:

$$|B_1| = \begin{vmatrix} 0 & f_1 \\ f_1 & f_{11} \end{vmatrix} \leq 0, \quad |B_2| = \begin{vmatrix} 0 & f_1 & f_2 \\ f_1 & f_{11} & f_{12} \\ f_2 & f_{21} & f_{22} \end{vmatrix} \leq 0, \ldots$$

$$|B_n| = \begin{vmatrix} 0 & f_1 & f_2 & \cdots & f_n \\ f_1 & f_{11} & f_{12} & \cdots & f_{1n} \\ f_2 & f_{21} & f_{22} & \cdots & f_{2n} \\ \vdots & \vdots & \vdots & \cdots & \vdots \\ f_n & f_{n1} & f_{n2} & \cdots & f_{nn} \end{vmatrix} \leq 0$$

Consider the case of a differentiable function $f(x_1, x_2)$ which is strictly quasi-concave. Then we must have:

$$-f_1^2 < 0, \quad -f_{22}f_1^2 + 2f_{12}f_1f_2 - f_{11}f_2^2 > 0$$

Along an iso-value locus of $f(x_1, x_2)$ we have:

$$df = f_1\, dx_1 + f_2\, dx_2 = 0$$

$$\text{and let } S = \frac{dx_1}{dx_2}, \text{ then } S = -\frac{f_2}{f_1}$$

Differentiating S totally with respect to x_2 in order to obtain the rate of change of the slope of the iso-value locus yields:

$$\frac{dS}{dx_2} = \frac{-f_{22}f_1^2 + 2f_{12}f_1f_2 - f_{11}f_2^2}{f_1^3}$$

Since $f(x_1, x_2)$ has been assumed to be strictly quasi-concave, then the numerator of the above expression must be positive, and f_1 must be non-zero. If $f_1 > 0$, then the iso-value loci of $f(x_1, x_2)$ are convex to the origin; if $f_1 < 0$, then the iso-value loci of $f(x_1, x_2)$ are concave to the origin.

Consider our earlier example in Section 16.3 of a non-concave utility function:

$$U = (x_1 x_2)^2$$

We shall now show using the above determinantal test that this utility function is indeed quasi-concave. Differentiating partially with respect to x_1 and x_2, we have the following set of first- and second-order partial derivatives:

$$U_1 = 2x_1 x_2^2, \quad U_2 = 2x_1^2 x_2$$
$$U_{11} = 2x_2^2, \quad U_{12} = U_{21} = 4x_1 x_2, \quad U_{22} = 2x_1^2$$

Hence,

$$|B_1| = \begin{vmatrix} 0 & 2x_1 x_2^2 \\ 2x_1 x_2^2 & 2x_2^2 \end{vmatrix} = -4x_1^2 x_2^4 \leq 0$$

$$|B_2| = \begin{vmatrix} 0 & 2x_1 x_2^2 & 2x_1^2 x_2 \\ 2x_1 x_2^2 & 2x_2^2 & 4x_1 x_2 \\ 2x_1^2 x_2 & 4x_1 x_2 & 2x_1^2 \end{vmatrix} = 16x_1^4 x_2^2 \geq 0$$

For positive quantities of the two goods, it is clear that the utility function is strictly quasi-concave. Note that in general the Cobb–Douglas function in the two good case is only quasi-concave in the non-negative quadrant, though for our particular example the function is quasi-concave everywhere.

As we have just seen, quasi-concavity does not imply concavity. A concave function, however, will be quasi-concave. For a differentiable function with continuous first- and second-order derivatives, concavity requires:

$$f_{11} \leq 0 \text{ and } f_{11}f_{22} - f_{12}^2 \geq 0$$

Quasi-concavity, on the other hand, requires, *inter alia*, that:

$$-f_{22}f_1^2 + 2f_{12}f_1f_2 - f_{11}f_2^2 \geq 0$$

A sufficient, but not necessary, condition for the above quadratic form to be positive semi-definite is that:

$$f_{11} \leq 0 \text{ and } f_{11}f_{22} - f_{12}^2 \geq 0$$

which are conditions which also guarantee concavity.

In many constrained optimisation problems in economics, the constraint is linear; in this case, there exists a very straightforward connection between the principal minors of B and those of the bordered Hessian determinant, $\overline{H}$. In the latter, the second-order partial derivatives of the Lagrangean function are bordered by the first-order partial derivatives of the constraint, whilst in the former the second-order partial derivatives of the objective function, $f(x)$, are bordered by its first-order partial derivatives. However when the constraint is linear, we have:

$$L_{ij} = f_{ij} \text{ for all } i, j$$

Furthermore, from the first-order conditions we have:

$$f_j - y g_j = 0$$

Hence B only differs from $\overline{H}$ in that its first row and first column are simply scalar multiples of the first row and column of $\overline{H}$ where the scalar is the Lagrangean multiplier, y. So we must have:

$$|B| = y^2 |\overline{H}|$$

and similarly for all the principal minors. The signs of the principal minors of $\overline{H}$ and of B will, therefore, be the same in this case.

In conclusion, therefore, we may state that if the objective function is quasi-concave and the constraint is linear, then the point satisfying the first-order conditions will give rise to a global maximum of the objective function subject to the constraint; and if the objective function is strictly quasi-concave, then this global maximum will indeed be unique. Note that strict quasi-concavity rules out the possibility that an iso-value locus of the objective function has a linear segment, thereby making it impossible for there to be more than one point of tangency between the constraint and an iso-value locus.

16.5 SOME ECONOMIC APPLICATIONS OF CONSTRAINED OPTIMISATION

Duopoly

The inverse demand function for some good produced by a duopoly is given by:
$$p = 100 - x$$
where p is price and x is output. The cost functions of the two firms in the industry are:
$$C_1 = 12x_1 \text{ and } C_2 = x_2^2$$
where C_i represents the total costs and x_i is the output produced by firm i, $i = 1, 2$. Each firm is motivated to maximise its profits. The profits functions of the two firms are given respectively by:
$$\Pi_1 = (100 - x_1 - x_2)x_1 - 12x_1$$
$$= 88x_1 - x_1^2 - x_1 x_2$$
$$\Pi_2 = (100 - x_1 - x_2)x_2 - x_2^2$$
$$= 100x_2 - x_1 x_2 - 2x_2^2$$

What output should firm 1 produce in order to maximise its profits? Differentiating firm 1s profits function with respect to its own output, we have:
$$\frac{\partial \Pi_1}{\partial x_1} = 88 - 2x_1 - x_2 - x_1 \frac{\partial x_2}{\partial x_1} = 0$$

Similarly, we have for firm 2:
$$\frac{\partial \Pi}{\partial x_2} = 100 - x_1 - 4x_2 - x_2 \frac{\partial x_1}{\partial x_2} = 0$$

In the Cournot solution to the duopoly problem, each firm assumes that the other firm will not change its output in response to a change in its own output. The conjectural variation is said to be zero:
$$\frac{\partial x_i}{\partial x_j} = 0 \text{ for all } i, j$$

Hence in the Cournot solution we must have:
$$88 - 2x_1 - x_2 = 0$$
$$100 - x_1 - 4x_2 = 0$$

Solving these two equations, we find that $x_1 = 36$, $x_2 = 16$; and the associated profits are $\Pi_1 = 1296$, $\Pi_2 = 512$. Given that firm 1 is producing *36* units, firm 2 maximises its profits by producing *16* units. Given that firm 2 produces *16* units, firm 1 maximises its profits by producing *36* units. Given what the other firm is doing, neither firm would wish to alter its output. Their output decisions are mutually consistent. Note that with firm 2's (1's) output treated as fixed by firm 1 (2), we have
$$\frac{d^2\Pi_1}{dx_1^2} < 0 \text{ and } \frac{d^2\Pi_2}{dx_2^2} < 0$$
so the second-order conditions for a maximum are met.

Let the two firms now decide to collude in order to maximise their joint profits. Joint profits are given by:

$$\Pi = (100 - x_1 - x_2)(x_1 + x_2) - 12x_1 - x_2^2$$
$$= 88x_1 - x_1^2 - 2x_1x_2 + 100x_2 - 2x_2^2$$

Differentiating the profits function partially with respect to x_1 and x_2, we obtain the following first-order conditions:

$$88 - 2x_1 - 2x_2 = 0$$
$$100 - 2x_1 - 4x_2 = 0$$

from which it follows that $x_1 = 38$, $x_2 = 6$; $\Pi_1 = 1672$, $\Pi_2 = 300$. Since the second-order partial derivatives of the profits function are: $\Pi_{11} = -2$, $\Pi_{12} = -2$, $\Pi_{22} = -4$, the reader may easily check that the second-order conditions for a maximum of profits are satisfied at these output levels. Comparing this outcome with the Cournot equilibrium, we see that the profits of firm 2 have fallen; this obviously casts doubts on the willingness of firm 2 to participate in the joint profit-maximising cartel. If side payments are permitted, then it is possible for firm 2 to be compensated by receiving a payment of *212* from firm 1. If this were to occur then firm 2 would be just as well off as in the Cournot equilibrium, and firm 1 would be better off, with profits after the side-payment of *1460*, compared to *1296* in the Cournot equilibrium.

If side-payments are ruled out, then it is still possible to achieve a Pareto improvement with firm 1's profits being higher than in the non-cooperative equilibrium, but with firm 2 just being as well off as before. Mathematically we have:

$$\text{Maximise } \Pi_1 \text{ subject to } \Pi_2 = \Pi_2^c$$

For our specific numerical example, we have:

$$L = 88x_1 - x_1^2 - x_1x_2 + y(100x_2 - x_1x_2 - 2x_2^2 - 512)$$

and the first order conditions are:

$$L_1 = 88 - 2x_1 - x_2 - yx_2 = 0$$
$$L_2 = -x_1 + y(100 - x_1 - 4x_2) = 0$$
$$L_y = 100x_2 - x_1x_2 - 2x_2^2 - 512 = 0$$

Solving the above three equations, we find that $x_1 = 31.4545$, $x_2 = 11$, and $y = 1.281$. The profits of firm 1 are *1432.61*. Let us now check that the second-order conditions for a maximum are satisfied at this point. The second-order partial derivatives of the Lagrangean function are as follows:

$$L_{11} = -2,$$
$$L_{12} = L_{21} = -1 - y = -2.281,$$
$$L_{22} = -4y = -5.124$$

The derivatives of the constraint are as follows:

$$g_1 = -x_2 = -11$$
$$g_2 = 100 - x_1 - 4x_2 = 24.5455$$

Evaluating the bordered Hessian determinant at the point which satisfies the first-order conditions for a maximum we have:

$$|\overline{H}| = \begin{vmatrix} 0 & -x_2 & 100 - x_1 - 4x_2 \\ -x_2 & -2 & -1 - y \\ 100 - x_1 - 4x_2 & -1 - y & -4y \end{vmatrix} = 3056.71 > 0$$

Hence, we have identified a maximum of firm 1's profits subject to the constraint on the value of firm 2's profits.

More generally, we have:

$$\text{Maximise } \Pi_1 \text{ subject to } \Pi_2 = \Pi_2^c$$
$$\text{and hence } L = \Pi_1(x_1, x_2) + y(\Pi_2 - \Pi_2^c)$$

with first order conditions:

$$\frac{\partial L}{\partial x_1} = \frac{\partial \Pi_1}{\partial x_1} + y \frac{\partial \Pi_2}{\partial x_1} = 0$$

$$\frac{\partial L}{\partial x_2} = \frac{\partial \Pi_1}{\partial x_2} + y \frac{\partial \Pi_2}{\partial x_2} = 0$$

$$\frac{\partial L}{\partial y} = \Pi_2 - \Pi_2^c = 0$$

from which it follows that:

$$\frac{\partial \Pi_1}{\partial x_1} \bigg/ \frac{\partial \Pi_1}{\partial x_2} = \frac{\partial \Pi_2}{\partial x_1} \bigg/ \frac{\partial \Pi_2}{\partial x_2}$$

Along an iso-profit contour for firm 1, we have $d\Pi_1 = 0$. Hence, totally differentiating firm 1's profits function we have, along an iso-profit contour:

$$\frac{\partial \Pi_1}{\partial x_1} dx_1 + \frac{\partial \Pi_1}{\partial x_2} dx_2 = 0$$

Hence

$$\frac{\partial x_2}{\partial x_1} = -\frac{\partial \Pi_1}{\partial x_1} \bigg/ \frac{\partial \Pi_2}{\partial x_2}$$

The slope of an iso-profit contour is therefore given by the negative of the ratios of the partial derivatives of the profits function. Our solution obviously involves a tangency position between a pair of iso-profit contours.

Utility maximisation and the derivation of demand functions

There are two individuals, A and B, each with an identical Cobb–Douglas utility function defined over two commodities, x_1 and x_2.

$$U^A = x_{1A} x_{2A} \text{ and } U^B = x_{1B} x_{2B}$$

Their initial endowments are x_{1A}^0, x_{2A}^0 and x_{1B}^0, x_{2B}^0 respectively. Let us first of all obtain A's demand functions for x_1 and x_2, having first let x_2 be the numeraire with its price set equal to unity. Given that A's income is the value of her initial endowment, we have the following problem:

$$\text{Maximise } U^A = x_{1A} x_{2A}$$
$$\text{subject to } p_1 x_{1A}^0 + x_{2A}^0 = p_1 x_{1A} + x_{2B}$$

The Lagrangean function is, therefore,

$$L = x_{1A} x_{2A} + y(p_1 x_{1A}^0 + x_{2A}^0 - p_1 x_{1A} - x_{2A})$$

Differentiating partially with respect to x_{1A}, x_{2A} and y, we obtain the first order conditions for a maximum of A's utility subject to her budget constraint:

$$L_{1A} = x_{2A} - yp_1 = 0$$
$$L_{2A} = x_{1A} - y = 0$$
$$L_y = p_1 x_{1A}^0 + x_{2A}^0 - p_1 x_{1A} - x_{2A} = 0$$

The reader should check that for positive quantities of both goods, the utility function is quasi-concave. Given that the constraint is linear, the point which satisfies the first-order condition will give rise to a global maximum of utility subject to the constraint.

From the first-order conditions it follows that $x_{2A} = p_1 x_{1A}$. Substituting in A's budget constraint, we obtain her demand function for good 1:

$$x_{1A} = \frac{0.5(p_1 x_{1A}^0 + x_{2A}^0)}{p_1}$$

Similarly, it can be shown that A's demand function for good 2 is given by:

$$x_{2A} = 0.5(p_1 x_{1A}^0 + x_{2A}^0)$$

Given that B's utility function is identical to that of A, his demand functions take a similar form:

$$x_{1B} = \frac{0.5(p_1 x_{1B}^0 + x_{2B}^0)}{p_1}$$
$$x_{2B} = 0.5(p_1 x_{1B}^0 + x_{2B}^0)$$

Assuming rather heroically that the economy just consists of these two individuals, both of whom act as price takers, we may solve for the Walrasian equilibrium. The excess demand for good 2 must be zero. Hence

$$0.5(p_1 x_{1A}^0 + x_{2A}^0) + 0.5(p_1 x_{1B}^0 + x_{2B}^0) = x_2^0$$

where $x_2^0 = x_{2A}^0 + x_{2B}^0$. Since $x_{1A}^0 + x_{1B}^0 = x_1^0$, we have, on simplifying:

$$p_1 = \frac{x_2^0}{x_1^0}$$

Since the market for good 2 is in equilibrium at the above price, this will also be true, by Walras's Law, of the market for good 1. The reader should check that this indeed is the case.

Let us assume that the initial endowments are as follows:

$$x^0_{1A} = 40, \quad x^0_{2A} = 120, \quad x^0_{1B} = 60, \quad x^0_{2B} = 80$$

Hence at the Walrasian equilibrium $p_1 = 2$. Note that prior to trade between the two agents, $U^A = U^B = 4800$. In the post-trade position, both agents consume *50* units of good 1 and *100* units of good 2, with $U^A = U^B = 5000$.

Consumer demand and comparative static analysis

Consider the case of a consumer who consumes two goods and whose objective is to maximise his utility subject to a budget constraint. The Lagrangean function is

$$L = U(x_1, x_2) + y(M - p_1 x_1 - p_2 x_2)$$

Partially differentiating with respect to the two goods and the Lagrangean multiplier yields the first-order conditions:

$$L_1 = U_1 - yp_1 = 0$$
$$L_2 = U_2 - yp_2 = 0$$
$$L_y = M - p_1 x_1 - p_2 x_2 = 0$$

If we now totally differentiate these first-order conditions, we obtain:

$$U_{11} dx_1 + U_{12} dx_2 - p_1 dy - y dp_1 = 0$$
$$U_{21} dx_1 + U_{22} dx_2 - p_2 dy - y dp_2 = 0$$
$$-p_1 dx_1 - p_2 dx_2 - x_1 dp_1 - x_2 dp_2 + dM = 0$$

Alternatively, we may express the above three equations in matrix form:

$$\begin{bmatrix} 0 & -p_1 & -p_2 \\ -p_1 & U_{11} & U_{12} \\ -p_2 & U_{21} & U_{22} \end{bmatrix} \begin{bmatrix} dy \\ dx_1 \\ dx_2 \end{bmatrix} = \begin{bmatrix} x_1 dp_1 + x_2 dp_2 - dM \\ y dp_1 \\ y dp_2 \end{bmatrix}$$

Now, holding fixed the prices of the two goods, let there be an increase in money income. What effect will this have on the demand for good 1? Applying Cramer's rule, we have:

$$dx_1 = \frac{\begin{vmatrix} 0 & -dM & -p_2 \\ -p_1 & 0 & U_{12} \\ -p_2 & 0 & U_{22} \end{vmatrix}}{\begin{vmatrix} 0 & -p_1 & -p_2 \\ -p_1 & U_{11} & U_{12} \\ -p_2 & U_{21} & U_{22} \end{vmatrix}}$$

The determinant in the denominator (the Jacobian, $|J|$) takes the same value as the bordered Hessian determinant, $|\overline{H}|$, since the first row and the first column in this determinant simply equal minus *1* times the corresponding row and column of the bordered Hessian determinant. For the chosen consumption bundle to give rise to a maximum of utility subject to the budget constraint, this determinant must be positive. Expanding the determinant in the numerator, we have:

$$\begin{vmatrix} 0 & -dM & -p_2 \\ -p_1 & 0 & U_{12} \\ -p_2 & 0 & U_{22} \end{vmatrix} = [-p_1 U_{22} + p_2 U_{12}]\, dM$$

Hence

$$\frac{\partial x_1}{\partial M} = \frac{-p_1 U_{22} + p_2 U_{12}}{|J|}$$

Though the denominator must be positive, we cannot sign the numerator without imposing further restrictions on the utility function.

Let us now consider the implications of changing the price of good 1. Then

$$dx_1 = \frac{\begin{vmatrix} 0 & x_1\, dp_1 & -p_2 \\ -p_1 & y\, dp_1 & U_{12} \\ -p_2 & 0 & U_{22} \end{vmatrix}}{|J|} = \frac{1}{|J|}[x_1(p_1 U_{22} - p_2 U_{12}) - p_2^2 y]\, dp_1$$

and given that

$$\frac{\partial x_1}{\partial M} = \frac{-p_1 U_{22} + p_2 U_{12}}{|J|}$$

we have

$$\frac{\partial x_1}{\partial p_1} = -\frac{p_2^2 y}{|J|} - \frac{x_1 \partial x_1}{\partial M}$$

The first term on the right-hand side will be negative, assuming that the second-order conditions for a maximum are satisfied, if the Lagrangean multiplier, y, is positive. This will indeed be the case provided that the consumer's preference ordering satisfies the axiom of non-satiation, i.e. $U_j > 0$ for all j, since we must have $y = U_j/p_j$.

If we had changed the price of one good and simultaneously altered the consumer's income so that she could have still bought the original consumption bundle, then we would have had $x_1\, dp_1 - dM = 0$. What would have happened to the demand for x_1 in this special case?

$$\frac{\partial x_1}{\partial p_1} = \frac{\begin{vmatrix} 0 & 0 & -p_2 \\ -p_1 & y & U_{12} \\ -p_2 & 0 & U_{22} \end{vmatrix}}{|J|} = \frac{-p_2^2 y}{|J|}$$

This, therefore, is the substitution effect of the price change, whereas the second term on the right-hand side of the original equation is the income effect of the price change. Hence we have:

$$\frac{\partial x_1}{\partial p_1} = \frac{\partial x_1}{\partial p_1}\bigg|_{\text{utility constant}} - x_1 \frac{\partial x_1}{\partial M}$$

This is the well known Slutsky equation which we may express in elasticity form by multiplying through by p_1/x_1:

$$\frac{\partial x_1}{\partial p_1}\frac{p_1}{x_1} = \frac{\partial x_1}{\partial p_1}\frac{p_1}{x_1}\bigg|_{\text{utility constant}} - \frac{p_1 x_1}{M}\frac{\partial x_1}{\partial M}\frac{M}{x_1}$$

For any normal good (i.e. a good with a positive income effect), the income effect reinforces the substitution effect of the price change. For the theoretical curiosum of a Giffen good, not only must the good have a negative income elasticity, but it must also account for a substantial share of total expenditure for the substitution effect to be outweighed by the income effect.

What happens to the demand for good 1 if the price of good 2 changes? Applying Cramer's rule, we have:

$$dx_1 = \frac{\begin{vmatrix} 0 & x_2\,dp_2 & -p_2 \\ -p_1 & 0 & U_{12} \\ -p_2 & y\,dp_2 & U_{22} \end{vmatrix}}{|J|} = \frac{-1}{|J|}[(-p_1 U_{22} + p_2 U_{12})x_2 - p_1 p_2 y]\,dp_2$$

If we were to hold the consumer's utility constant at the original level, then $x_2\,dp_2 - dM = 0$, and in these circumstances we would have:

$$\frac{\partial x_1}{\partial p_2}\bigg|_{\text{utility constant}} = \frac{p_1 p_2 y}{|J|}$$

Remembering that

$$\frac{\partial x_1}{\partial M} = \frac{-p_1 U_{22} + p_2 U_{12}}{|J|}$$

we obtain

$$\frac{\partial x_1}{\partial p_2} = \frac{p_1 p_2 y}{|J|} - x_2 \frac{\partial x_1}{\partial M} = \frac{\partial x_1}{\partial p_2}\bigg|_{\text{utility constant}} - x_2 \frac{\partial x_1}{\partial M}$$

Similarly, it can be shown that:

$$\frac{\partial x_2}{\partial p_1} = \frac{p_1 p_2 y}{|J|} - x_1 \frac{\partial x_2}{\partial M} = \frac{\partial x_2}{\partial p_1}\bigg|_{\text{utility constant}} - x_2 \frac{\partial x_2}{\partial M}$$

Note the symmetry of the cross-price effects holding utility constant.

16.6 MORE ON THE INTERPRETATION OF THE LAGRANGEAN MULTIPLIER

Consider the case of a utility-maximising consumer whose utility function is given by $U(x)$ and whose budget constraint is $M - p \cdot x = 0$, where x is a vector of goods, p of prices and M of money income. The Lagrangean function is:

$$L = U(x) + y(M - p \cdot x)$$

The first-order conditions for a maximum of L are as follows:

$$U_j - p_j = 0 \quad j = 1, \ldots, n$$
$$M - p \cdot x = 0$$

Let x^* be the consumption vector and y^* the value of the Lagrangean multiplier which satisfy these first-order conditions. Note both x^* and y^* are functions of M and p. The maximum value function or indirect utility function is given by $V(M, p)$ where

$$V(M, p) = U(x^*) = L(x^*, y^*; M, p)$$
$$= U(x^*) + y^*(M - p \cdot x^*)$$

Let x' be the utility-maximising consumption vector when income is M' and the price vector p'. The Lagrangean multiplier will change its value as income or any product price changes. Allowing y to change its value as money income changes, but holding constant the consumption vector at x' and the price vector at p', we have the following Lagrangean function:

$$L(x', y^*; M, p') = U(x') + y^*(M - p \cdot x)$$

For $M = M'$, we have

$$V(M, p') = L(x', y^*; M', p')$$

As we allow M to vary, but keep the consumption vector unchanged, then since

$$L(x^*, y^*; M, p') \geq L(x', y^*; M, p')$$

we must have:

$$V(M, p') \geq L(x', y^*; M, p')$$

Only when $M = M'$ will the above Lagrangean function give rise to the same value as the maximum value function does. Otherwise as M diverges from M' in either direction, the value of the Lagrangean function will fall short of the value of $V(M, p')$. Given that this is the case, then the two functions must have the same slope at the point $M = M'$ where they are equal to each other. The maximum value function forms an envelope to a set of Lagrangean functions. Differentiating the Lagrangean function with respect to M, allowing for the fact that y^* depends, *inter alia*, upon M, but holding x constant at $x = x'$, we obtain:

$$\frac{\partial L}{\partial M} = y^* + \frac{\partial y^*}{\partial M}(M - p' \cdot x')$$

When $M = M'$, the utility-maximising consumer bought the bundle x' at price p', spending all their income. At $M = M'$, we have:

$$\frac{\partial L}{\partial M} = \frac{\partial V}{\partial M} = y^*$$

The Lagrangean multiplier, therefore, measures the impact on the value of the objective function of an infinitesimally small relaxation of the constraint. For the utility maximisation case, y^* measures the marginal utility of money income.

Let us now consider the implications of changing one of the elements of the price vector. As before, let the initial position be where x' is the utility-maximising consumption bundle when

income is M', and the price vector is p'. Then we have:
$$V(M',p') = L(x',y^*; M',p')$$

Now change the price of good j. It must now be the case that:
$$V(M',p) \geq L(x',y^*; M',p)$$

with equality holding when $p = p'$. At M', p', we must, therefore, have once again a tangency position between the maximum value function and the Lagrangean function:
$$\frac{\partial V}{\partial p_j} = \frac{\partial L}{\partial p_j}$$

Since $L(x',y^*; M',p) = U(x') + y^*(M' - p \cdot x')$, we have, on differentiating partially with respect to p_j,
$$\frac{\partial L}{\partial p_j} = -y^* x_j + \frac{\partial y^*}{\partial p_j}(M' - p \cdot x')$$

Evaluating this derivative at M', p', since $M' - p' \cdot x' = 0$, we have:
$$\frac{\partial L}{\partial p_j} = -y^* x_j$$

and, hence
$$\frac{\partial V}{\partial p_j} = -y^* x_j$$

Since it has already been shown that
$$\frac{\partial V}{\partial M} = y^*$$

we have now found an alternative procedure for obtaining the demand function for good j. From the indirect utility (maximum value) function we have:
$$x_j^* = -\frac{\partial V}{\partial p_j} \bigg/ \frac{\partial V}{\partial M}$$

This is known as Roy's identity, and it permits us to write the Marshallian demand function for good j as the negative of the ratio of the partial derivative of the indirect utility function with respect to good j to the partial derivative of the same function with respect to money income.

We may now pose a slightly different question: What is the minimum expenditure a consumer need incur in order to attain a specified level of utility? In this case the problem we wish to solve is:
$$\textit{Minimise } C(x) = p \cdot x$$
$$\textit{subject to } U(x) = U'$$

Setting up the Lagrangean function we have:
$$L = p \cdot x + y(U' - U(x))$$

Differentiating partially with respect to x and y, we obtain the following set of first order conditions:

$$L_j = p_j - yU_j = 0 \quad j = 1,\ldots,n$$
$$L_y = U' - U(x) = 0$$

Let x^* and y^* be the expenditure-minimising value of the consumption vector and the optimal value of the Lagrangean multiplier respectively. We may define an expenditure function which gives us the minimum expenditure which must be incurred at some price vector p in order to guarantee the consumer a specified value of utility U':

$$E(p, U') = C(x^*) = L(x^*, y^*; p, U')$$

Let the cost minimising bundle for utility level U' when the price vector is p' be x'. Now assume a change in the price vector. Let the Lagrangean multiplier move to its new optimal value, but keep the consumption bundle fixed at x'. We have in this case that:

$$E(p, U') \leq L(x', y^*; p, U')$$

with equality holding when $p = p'$. Hence, at this value of the price vector, we must have a tangency position between the expenditure function and the Lagrangean function. Differentiating the Lagrangean function partially with respect to p_j, we have:

$$\frac{\partial L}{\partial p_j} = x_j + \frac{\partial y}{\partial p_j}(U' - U(x'))$$

Since $U' = U(x')$, at the tangency position between the expenditure function and the Lagrangean function, we must have:

$$\frac{\partial E}{\partial p_j} = x_j$$

Consider the expenditure function for the case of two goods:

$$E(p, U') = p_1 x_1^* + p_2 x_2^*$$
$$= p_1 x_1(p_1, p_2, U') + p_2 x_2(p_1, p_2, U')$$

Then differentiate with respect to p_1 to obtain:

$$\frac{\partial E}{\partial p_1} = x_1^* + p_1 \frac{\partial x_1}{\partial p_1} + \frac{\partial x_2}{\partial p_1}$$

From the first order conditions we have:

$$p_1 - yU_1 = 0 \text{ and } p_1 - yU_2 = 0$$

Given that utility is held constant at U', we also have from totally differentiating the utility function that:

$$U_1 \, dx_1 + U_2 \, dx_2 = 0$$

Multiply by y and substitute in the first-order conditions to obtain:

$$p_1 \, dx_1 + p_2 \, dx_2 = 0$$

Therefore,

$$p_1 \frac{\partial x_1}{\partial p_1} + p_2 \frac{\partial x_2}{\partial p_1} = 0$$

from which it follows that

$$\frac{\partial E}{\partial p_1} = x_1^*$$

This is known as Shepherd's lemma; it gives us the compensated (Hicksian) demand function for good 1; the partial derivative of the expenditure function with respect to p_j tells us how the demand for good j will vary as its price changes, holding utility constant at the initial level, U'.

Now allow the utility level to vary, but keep both the price vector and the consumption vector fixed at their original levels, p' and x'. Note that as before we allow the Lagrangean multiplier to change in value. Then we have:

$$E(p', U) \leq L(x', y^*; p', U)$$

with equality holding when $U = U'$. Given that

$$L(x', y^*; p', U) = p' \cdot x' + y^*(U - U(x'))$$

then differentiating with respect to U, we have:

$$\frac{\partial L}{\partial U} = y^* + \frac{\partial y}{\partial U}(U - U(x'))$$

When $U = U'$, $U = U(x')$ and

$$\frac{\partial L}{\partial U} = \frac{\partial E}{\partial U} = y^*$$

The Lagrangean multiplier measures in this case the additional expenditure that must be incurred in order for the consumer to reach a slightly higher level of utility; it measures marginal cost: what must be paid for a slight relaxation of the constraint.

From the expenditure function we can calculate how much additional expenditure would be required to enable a consumer to maintain their utility at some specified level when the price of one or more products changes. From the indirect utility function it is straightforward to see how the maximum attainable level of utility would change following a change in the price vector. Increases in prices require a greater expenditure in order to leave utility unchanged, whilst such price increases are associated with a fall in utility when money income is unchanged. This provides us with an insight into how to place a monetary valuation on the welfare changes brought about by price changes.

Assume p_1 rises from p_1' to p_1''; with both money income and the prices of other goods unchanged, the consumer will now be worse off. One way of valuing this welfare loss is to ask how large an increase in money income would be required to enable the consumer to be just as well off as they were before the price of good 1 rose. For the case where the consumer just buys two commodities, the required increase in their money income is given by:

$$E(p_1'', p_2, U') - E(p_1', p_2, U')$$

Alternatively, we can pose a slightly different question. From the indirect utility function we know that, other things being unchanged, when the price of good 1 rises from p_1' to p_1'', the maximum attainable level of utility will fall from U' to U''. We may therefore ask: What is the maximum amount the consumer would be prepared to pay in order to avoid the rise in the price of good 1? This requires us to compare the costs of achieving utility level U'' when faced with alternative price vectors. For the two commodity case, this measure of the welfare loss from the rise in the price of good 1 from p_1' to p_1'' is given by:

$$E(p_1'', p_2, U'') - E(p_1', p_2, U'')$$

Note that our first measure is defined with respect to the original level of utility, whereas our second measure is defined with respect to the new level of utility following the price change. These alternative measures can be shown on a standard indifference curve diagram.

Let the original budget constraint be given by AB in Fig. 16.1. The utility maximising position occurs at the tangency position at point E between the budget line AB and $IC2$. The price of good 1 now rises, giving rise to the new budget constraint AC, and a new tangency position between AC and the lower indifference curve $IC1$ at point F. If the consumer is to achieve the utility level associated with indifference curve $IC2$ when faced with this new price vector, then their money income will have to be increased in terms of good 2 by the vertical distance AA'. With budget constraint $A'C'$, which is parallel to AC, the consumer would choose to consume at point **G** and the original level of utility would be re-established. For simplification purposes, let p_2 equal one, and this measure of the welfare loss would be given by AA'.

The second measure of the welfare loss can be depicted diagrammatically in the following way in Fig. 16.2. Shift the budget line AB inwards to the left parallel to itself until it forms a tangent to $IC1$. This tangency position occurs at point H. If the agent's income were to be reduced by the amount $A''A$ (we are still assuming a price of unity for good 2), but the goods could still be bought at the old prices, the agent would be just as well as in the new optimal position. The second measure of the welfare loss is, therefore, $A''A$. Note that AA' and $A''A$ will

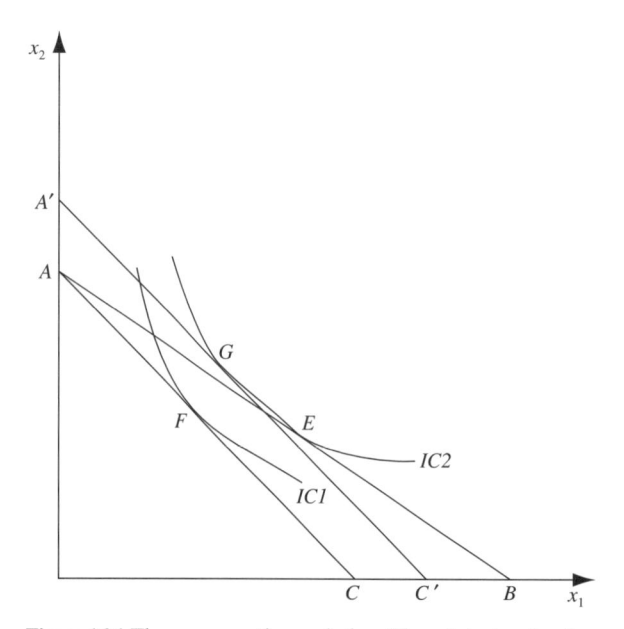

Figure 16.1 The compensating variation. The original optimal consumption bundle is the tangency position at E between AB and $IC2$. When the price of x_1 rises, the new optimal position is the tangency position at F between AC and $IC1$. If the consumer was now given an increase in income equal to AA', point G along $IC2$ is attainable and the original level of welfare is regained. AA' measures the compensating variation of the welfare loss caused by the increase in the price of x_1.

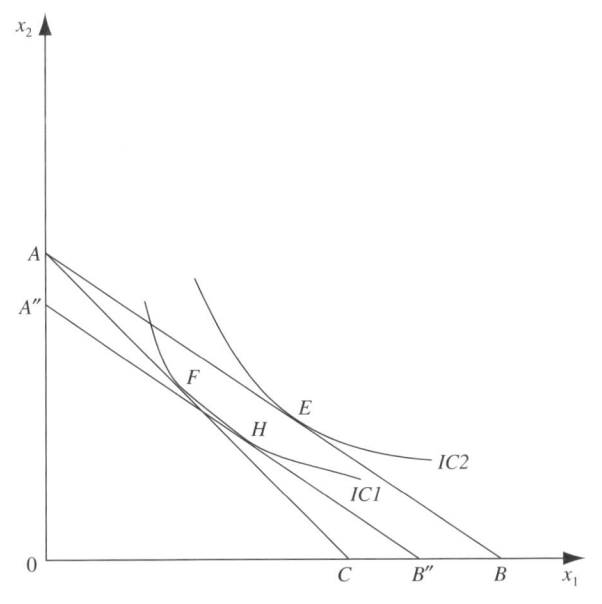

Figure 16.2 The equivalent variation. The original optimal consumption bundle is at E along AB. Following the rise in the price of x_1, the new optimal bundle is at F along AC. Had the consumer's income been reduced by AA'' but with the initial prices still in force consumption would have been at H with utility the same as with the price increase of good 1. AA'' is the equivalent variation of the welfare loss caused by the increase in the price of good 1.

not generally be equal to each other. We discuss below the circumstances under which the two measures of the welfare loss would be the same.

Economists call the first measure of the welfare loss the compensating variation (CV), and the second measure of the welfare loss the equivalent variation (EV). Hence we have:

$$CV = E(p_1'', p_2', U') - E(p_1', p_2', U')$$

Using the fundamental theorem of calculus we may write the CV measure of the loss as:

$$CV = \int_{p_1'}^{\infty} \frac{\partial E}{\partial p_1}(p_1, p_2', U') \, dp_1 - \int_{p_1''}^{\infty} \frac{\partial E}{\partial p_1}(p_1, p_2', U') \, dp_1$$

Hence

$$CV = \int_{p_1'}^{p_1''} \frac{\partial E}{\partial p_1}(p_1, p_2', U') \, dp_1$$

Similarly, we may write the EV measure of the welfare loss as:

$$EV = \int_{p_1'}^{p_1''} \frac{\partial E}{\partial p_1}(p_1, p_2', U'') \, dp_1$$

However, we know by Shepherd's lemma that:

$$\frac{\partial E}{\partial p_1} = x_1$$

The CV measure of the welfare loss is therefore given by the area under the Hicksian demand

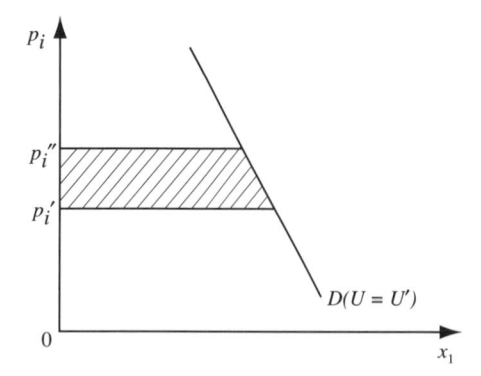

Figure 16.3 Compensating variation measure of the welfare loss due to a price increase. $D(U = U')$ shows the Hicksian (compensated) demand curve for x_1, with utility at level u'. As the price rises from p_1' to p_1'', the CV measure of the welfare loss is given by the shaded area.

function for good 1 with utility fixed at U' between the original price p_1' and the new higher price p_1''. This area is the shaded area in Fig. 16.3. The EV measure of the welfare loss, on the other hand, is given by the area under the Hicksian demand function for good 1 with utility fixed at level U'' between the original price p_1' and the new higher price p_1''. If the good is a normal good, i.e. the income effect is positive, this second Hicksian demand curve will lie to the left of the earlier one, and the EV measure of the welfare loss will be smaller than the CV measure. This outcome is shown in Fig. 16.4. If the income effect on the demand for good 1 is zero, then the demand for good 1 only changes when the price of good 1 changes due to the substitution effect. The Hicksian demand curves for different levels of utility then all coincide, and the two welfare measures give rise to the same numerical value. Returning to our earlier indifference curve diagram, if the income effect for good 1 is zero, the indifference curves are vertically parallel to each other, and AA' would then equal $A''A$. If good 1 is an inferior good, the EV measure would be greater than the CV measure.

The reader should ascertain that if the price of good 1 fell, other things being equal, the CV measure of the welfare gain would be smaller than the EV measure if good 1 is normal, larger than the EV measure if good 1 is inferior, and the same if the income effect on the demand for good 1 is zero.

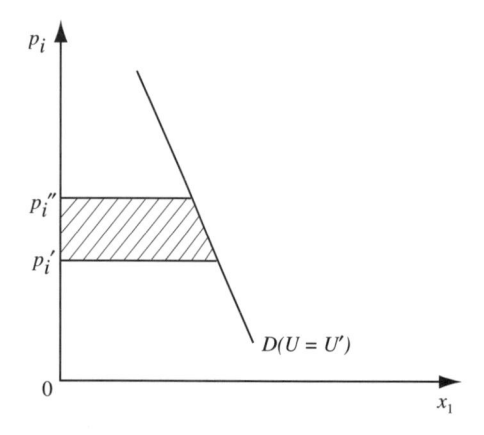

Figure 16.4 Equivalent variation measure of the welfare loss due to a price increase. $D(U = U'')$ shows the Hicksian (compensated) demand curve for x_1 with utility at level U''. U'' is less than U' and x_1 is a normal good. The EV measure of the welfare loss as the price rises from p_1' to p_1'' is given by the shaded area which is smaller than that in Fig. 16.3.

Cost minimisation and the Cobb–Douglas production function

A firm's production technology can be specified by the following Cobb–Douglas production function:

$$Q = F(K, N) = 10K^{0.5}N^{0.5}$$

What are the cost-minimising quantities of its two inputs, capital services, K, and labour services, N, if the firm wishes to produce an output, Q, of *500* units, given that the wage rate is *8* and the price of a unit of capital services is *2*?

Setting up the Lagrangian function, we have:

$$L = 2K + 8N + y(500 - 10K^{0.5}N^{0.5})$$

Differentiating partially with respect to K, N, and y gives us the first-order conditions for a minimum:

$$\frac{\partial L}{\partial K} = 2 - 5yK^{-0.5}N^{0.5} = 0$$

$$\frac{\partial L}{\partial N} = 8 - 5yK^{0.5}N^{-0.5} = 0$$

$$\frac{\partial L}{\partial y} = 500 - 10K^{0.5}N^{0.5} = 0$$

from which it follows that:

$$\frac{2}{8} = \frac{5yK^{-0.5}N^{0.5}}{5yK^{0.5}N^{-0.5}}$$

Hence $K = 4N$, and substituting for K in the production function yields:

$$500 = 10(4N)^{0.5}N^{0.5} = 20N$$

Hence $N = 25$, and, therefore, $K = 100$, and $y = 0.8$.

In order to see whether costs are indeed minimised at this input combination, we need to check whether the second-order conditions for a minimum are satisfied at the point $(100, 25, 0.8)$. The second order partial derivatives of the Lagrangean function with respect to K, N, and y are as follows:

$$\frac{\partial^2 L}{\partial K^2} = 2.5yK^{-1.5}N^{0.5}$$

$$\frac{\partial^2 L}{\partial K \partial N} = -2.5yK^{-0.5}N^{-0.5}$$

$$\frac{\partial^2 L}{\partial N^2} = 2.5yK^{0.5}N^{-1.5}$$

and the partial derivatives of the constraint with respect to K and N are:

$$\frac{\partial Q}{\partial K} = 5K^{-0.5}N^{0.5}$$

$$\frac{\partial Q}{\partial N} = 5K^{0.5}N^{-0.5}$$

Evaluating the above derivatives at the point ($100, 25, 0.8$), the bordered Hessian determinant is given by:

$$|\overline{H}| = \begin{vmatrix} 0 & 2.5 & 10 \\ 2.5 & 0.01 & -0.04 \\ 10 & -0.04 & 0.16 \end{vmatrix} = -4$$

Since the bordered Hessian determinant is negative, we have identified a minimum point. The minimum cost of producing 500 units of output is 400, with the firm employing 100 units of capital and 25 units of labour. Its marginal cost of production is given by the Lagrangean multiplier, and is equal to 0.8. At these particular values of the factor prices, it is straightforward to see that the firm's long-run total cost function takes the following simple form:

$$TC = 0.8Q$$

This results from the fact that $N = 0.05Q$ and $K = 0.2Q$.

What would happen in the short run if the capital input were held fixed at 100 units? The short-run relationship between output and the labour input is given by:

$$Q = 100N^{0.5}$$

which, when inverted, yields:

$$N = 0.0001Q^2$$

Variable costs are $wN = 8N = 0.0008Q^2$, and the fixed capital costs are $rK^* = 2K^* = 200$. Hence the short-run total cost function with capital input held fixed at 100 is:

$$SRTC = 200 + 0.0008Q^2$$

16.7 SUMMARY

This has been a long chapter in which we have considered many important aspects of constrained optimisation. The most general method of solution to such problems is to set up the relevant Lagrangean function. The Lagrangean multiplier is closely related to the concept of the dual variable in linear programming. It informs us of the effect on the value of the function we are seeking to maximise or minimise of a very small relaxation in the constraint. For the utility-maximising consumer, it measures the marginal utility of money income. For the firm seeking to minimise the costs of producing a particular level of income, it measures the marginal cost of production at that level of output. Provided that the constraint of our problem is linear or convex, then if the function we are seeking to maximise is quasi-concave, then the point which satisfies the Lagrangean conditions for a maximum will give rise to a global maximum of the function subject to the constraint. If the constraint is linear or concave then we shall have a global minimum subject to the constraint if the function whose value we are seeking to minimise is quasi-convex.

In the next chapter we shall continue our discussion of constrained optimisation by modifying the basic structure of the problems we have been discussing by allowing the possibility of slack in a constraint and by introducing the requirement that the variables under consideration be restricted to take non-negative values.

16.8 EXERCISES

16.1 (a) Find the solutions to the following constrained maximisation problems, checking that the second-order conditions for a maximum are met:

(i) Maximise $40x_1 - x_1^2 - 2x_1x_2 + 56x_2 - 2x_2^2$

subject to $5x_1 + 8x_2 = 90$

(ii) Maximise $2x_1 + x_2$

subject to $x_1^2 + x_2^2 = 180$

(iii) Maximise $x_1^2 + 10x_1x_2 + 2.5x_2^2$

subject to $x_1 + 2x_2 = 9$

(iv) Maximise $4x_1 + 12x_2 - x_2^2$

$x_1 + x_2 = 24$

(b) Find the solutions to the following constrained minimisation problems, checking that the second-order conditions for a minimum are met:

(i) Minimise $2x_1^2 - 28x_1 + x_1x_2 + 3x_2^2 - 36x_2$

subject to $x_1 + x_2 = 16$

(ii) Minimise $2x_1 + x_2$

subject to $x_1^2 + x_2^2 = 180$

(iii) Minimise $x_1^2 - 20x_1 + 4x_2^2$

subject to $x_2 = 5$

(iv) Minimise $x_1^2 - 2x_1x_2^2 + 46x_2$

$x_1 + 3x_2 = 11$

16.2 (a) Which of the following functions are quasi-concave and which are quasi-convex?

(i) $f(x) = x + x^3$

(ii) $f(x) = 48 - 4x - 2x^3$

(iii) $f(x_1, x_2) = x_1 + x_1^3 + 4x_2 + 2x_2^3 - 48 \quad (x_1 > 0, x_2 > 0)$

(b) Show that for non-negative values of x_1 and x_2, the following function is not concave, but is quasi-concave:

$f(x_1, x_2) = x_1^{0.5} + x_1x_2 \quad (x_2 > 0, x_2 > 0)$

(c) Determine which of the following functions are quasi-concave and which are quasi-convex:

(i) $f(x_1, x_2) = 10 + x_1 + x_2 + x_2^2 + x_2^4$

(ii) $f(x_1, x_2) = x_1 e^{x_2} \quad (x_1 > 0)$

(iii) $f(x_1, x_2) = -x_1^3 x_2^2 \quad (x_1 > 0, x_2 > 0)$

(iv) $f(x_1, x_2) = x_1 x_2^{-1} \quad (x_1 > 0, x_2 > 0)$

16.3 (a) Let us now assume that the two agents in the example on pages 287–289, rather than responding to externally given prices, now bargain with each other.

(i) Solve for the case where A is such a skilful bargainer that all the gains from trade accrue to her, and B is just as well off as she is in the original pre-trade position.

(ii) Check that the relevant bordered Hessian determinant is positive for the above case where all the gains from trade accrue to A.

(iii) Now let B drive such a hard bargain that all the gains from trade accrue to him, with A being indifferent between consuming her initial endowment and trading. Show that in this case that the implied price of good 1 is 2.4494.

(b) A labour supplier derives utility from income and leisure according to the following utility function:
$$U = U(Y, T - H) = AY^\alpha(T - H)^{1-\alpha}$$
where Y is income, T total time available, H hours of work, and α is a parameter lying between *0* and *1*. Time is allocated to either work or leisure.

(i) On the assumption that the individual's only source of income is earned income, and letting w represent the hourly wage rate, show that the individual's supply of hours of work is completely inelastic to changes in the wage rate.

(ii) Derive the individual's supply of labour schedule if he is also in receipt of dividend income equal to D. Is his desired supply of hours now influenced by the wage rate?

16.4 (a) A consumer's utility function is given by:
$$U = x_1 x_2$$

(i) Derive the individual's demand functions for each good as a function of the prices of the two goods, x_1 and x_2 and money income, M. Obtain the function specifying the Lagrangean multiplier as a function of the same three variables.

(ii) Obtain the maximum value function, $V(p, M)$ and obtain the partial derivatives of this function. Making use of Roy's identity, write down the Marshallian demand functions, checking that the answers are the same as you obtained in section (a).

(iii) Now consider the problem of minimising the cost of the consumer attaining a specified level of utility, U'. Obtain the cost-minimising quantities of the two goods as a function of p_1, p_2 and U'.

(iv) Write down the expenditure (minimum cost) function and then obtain the Hicksian demand functions for the two commodities.

(v) Assume that initially we have $p_1 = 2, p_2 = 5, M = 100$. The price of good 2 falls from *5* to *4*. Calculate the CV and EV measures of the welfare gain to the consumer of this price fall. What is the associated change in consumer surplus?

(b) For the following utility function
$$U = 100x_1 - 0.5x_1^2 + x_2$$

(i) Derive the Marshallian demand functions for the two goods as functions of p_1, p_2 and M.

(ii) Obtain the minimum expenditure required for the consumer to attain utility level equal to U'.

(iii) Obtain the Hicksian demand functions for the two goods and explain why the Hicksian and Marshallian demand functions for good 1 coincide.

(iv) Holding constant money income at *1000* and the price of good 2 at unity, calculate the CV and EV measures of the welfare loss that results from an increase in the price of good 1 from *10* to *20*. What can you say about the impact of this change on consumer surplus?

16.5 (a) Consider the following general Cobb–Douglas production function:
$$Q = AK^\alpha N^\beta$$
where Q is output, K the input of capital services, N the input of labour services, r the price of a unit of capital services, w the wage rate, and A, α and β are all positive parameters with α and β being both less than one.

(i) Letting r represent the price of capital services and w the wage rate, derive the firm's long-run total cost function.

(ii) Under what circumstances will marginal cost be an increasing, constant and decreasing function of output?

(iii) Differentiate the total cost function partially with respect to the price of capital services and the wage rate. Interpret your results.

(b) Now consider the following CES production function
$$Q = [0.5K^{-1} + 0.5N^{-1}]^{-1}$$
where Q is output, K the input of capital services, N the input of labour services. Again letting r represent the price of capital services and w the wage rate, derive the firm's long-run total cost function.

(c) In an economy there are two perfectly competitive industries, each producing a private good at constant marginal cost. The government wishes to spend an amount G on providing a public good, and intends to finance its provision by levying a set of *ad valorem* taxes on the consumption of the private goods. In setting these taxes the government's objective is to minimise the loss of consumer surplus net of government tax receipts.

The inverse demand functions for the two private goods are:
$$p_1 = 100 - x_1$$
$$p_2 = 100 - 0.5x_2$$

where p_1 is the price paid by the consumer for good i, and x_i is the quantity demanded of good i. Suppose that the two total cost functions are

$$TC_1 = 50x_1$$
$$TC_2 = 60x_2$$

where TC_i is the total cost of good i. The price received by the producer of good i is equal to its marginal cost, whereas the price paid by the consumer of good i is given by:

$$p_1 = 50(1 + t_1) \text{ and } p_2 = 60(1 + t_2)$$

where t_i is the tax rate on good i.

(i) Derive the tax rates which the government should set in order to finance the provision of the public good, G, costing 1197 in order to minimise the burden of the taxation.

(ii) By how much would the excess burden have been increased had the government chosen to impose the same *ad valorem* tax rate on the two goods?

CHAPTER SEVENTEEN
AN INTRODUCTION TO NON-LINEAR PROGRAMMING

17.1 INTRODUCTION

In the last chapter we dealt with optimisation problems where the values that could be taken by the independent variables were constrained by the presence of an equality constraint. Furthermore, we imposed no sign restrictions on the values that could be taken by the choice variables. In the economic problems which we investigated, the solutions invariably resulted in the choice variables taking on positive values: it would obviously have been ridiculous for a profit-maximising firm to have been required to produce negative quantities of some products, or for a utility-maximising consumer to have consumed negative quantities of some goods. We also deliberately avoided outcomes where some particular good was not produced by the profit-maximising firm, or not consumed by the utility-maximising consumer; i.e. where a choice variable was assigned a value of zero in the optimal solution.

The typical problem we wish to consider how to solve in this chapter is one in which we seek to find non-negative values for a particular set of variables which will give rise to the maximum or minimum of some function subject to a set of inequality constraints. We proceed in Section 17.2 to deal with the basic problem of maximising or minimising a function subject only to a requirement that the variable under consideration is restricted to taking a non-negative value. We then open up the discussion by dropping the requirement that a constraint hold as an inequality, and permit the presence of slack in a constraint. This leads us into a discussion of the Kuhn–Tucker conditions for a maximum and for a minimum. We show that a point which satisfies the Kuhn–Tucker (KT) maximum conditions will give rise to a global maximum value of the objective function subject to the constraints and non-negativity requirements of the problem provided that the objective function is concave and the constraints are convex. We shall see the important links between the KT conditions and the complementary/slackness conditions of linear programming.

Furthermore, we shall see that if the objective function is convex and the constraints are concave, then a point which satisfies the Kuhn–Tucker minimum conditions will give rise to a global minimum value of the objective function subject to the constraints and non-negativity requirements.

In Section 17.3 we provide some economic applications of non-linear programming. We look at some problems in public enterprise economics. We consider the case of a product the demand for which varies in some predictable manner over the course of the day. We investigate the appropriate pricing and investment decisions that the enterprise should take in order to maximise net social benefits. We then develop the model to elucidate what would happen if, for some reason, differential pricing across time periods was not permitted. The problems in Exercise 17.2 provide the reader with further opportunities to apply non-linear programming techniques in a microeconomic context.

We provide further links with our discussion of linear programming in Section 17.4 where we analyse a restricted category of non-linear programming problems in which the objective function is a quadratic and the constraints are a set of linear inequalities. We shall see here that a solution to this subset of non-linear programming problems can be achieved by making use of the Kuhn–Tucker conditions and the first phase of the two-phase method for solving linear programming problems when the origin is not available as an initial basic feasible solution.

17.2 THE SOLUTION TO A NON-LINEAR PROGRAM

We begin our discussion of non-linear programming by dealing firstly with the significance for the analysis of the requirement that the variables under consideration are restricted to take on non-negative values. Having shown how the first-order conditions for a maximum and for a minimum need to be amended to deal with this restriction, we then turn to examine the Kuhn–Tucker maximum and minimum conditions for non-linear programming problems, commenting upon their economic significance.

The significance of non-negativity requirements

We shall commence our discussion with a very simple problem. We wish to ascertain the first-order conditions which must be satisfied for a function of a single variable to reach a maximum value subject only to the choice variable being non-negative. Figure 17.1 depicts the possible solutions to our maximisation problem:

$$\text{Maximise } f(x) \text{ subject to } x \geq 0$$

In Fig. 17.1(a), it is clear that the function reaches a maximum value at $x = x^*$, with the first derivative of the function being zero at this point. In Fig. 17.1(b) we have depicted a situation where $f(x)$ is a monotonically decreasing function of x. It is obvious in this case that the value of the function is maximised when x is equal to zero, and the first derivative of the function at this point is negative. The final case is shown in Fig. 17.1(c), and this is the special case where the derivative of the function at $x = 0$ is also zero. Mathematically, we may express the first-order conditions for this problem as follows:

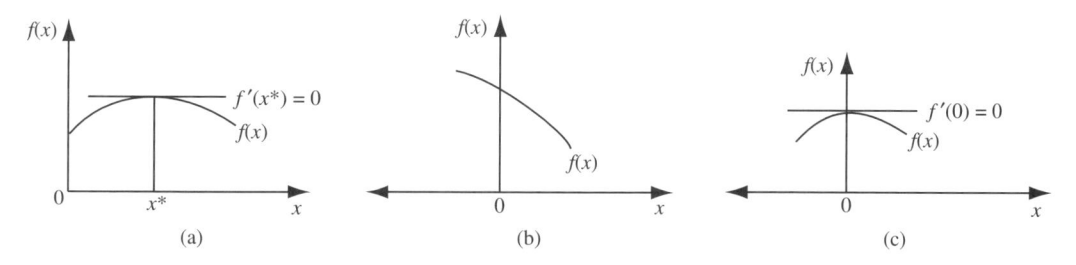

Figure 17.1 (a) Maximisation with a non-negativity requirement: $f(x)$ reaches a maximum $x = x^*$ with $f'(x^*) = 0$. (b) $f(x)$ reaches a maximum at $x = 0$ with $f'(0) < 0$. (c) $f(x)$ reaches a maximum at $x = 0$ with $f'(0) = 0$.

1. in case (a), we have $f'(x) = 0$, and $x > 0$;
2. in case (b), we have $f'(x) < 0$, and $x = 0$;
3. in case (c), we have $f'(x) = 0$, and $x = 0$.

Combining the above three results, we have:
$$f'(x) \leq 0, \quad x \geq 0, \quad xf'(x) = 0$$

In words, the first derivative must be non-positive, the variable x must be non-negative, and the product of x and the derivative $f'(x)$ must equal zero. If in the solution to our problem x is positive, then the first derivative must be zero. On the other hand, if the solution to the problem is one in which x is zero, then the first derivative must be either negative or zero. If at the solution the first derivative is zero, then x must be non-negative and will be positive other than in the special case (c), whereas if at the solution the first derivative is negative, then x must be zero.

We may carry out a similar diagrammatical analysis of the problem of minimising $f(x)$ subject to the requirement that x be non-negative. The possibilities are depicted in Fig. 17.2. In Fig. 17.2(a), it is clear that the function reaches a minimum value at $x = x^*$, with the first derivative of the function being zero at this point. In Fig. 17.2(b) we have depicted a situation where $f(x)$ is a monotonically increasing function of x. It is obvious in this case that the value of the function is minimised when x is equal to zero, and the first derivative of the function at this point is positive. The final case is shown in Fig. 17.2(c), and this is the special case where the derivative of the function at $x = 0$ is also zero. Mathematically, we may express the first-order conditions for our minimisation problem as follows:

1. in case (a), we have $f'(x) = 0$, and $x > 0$;
2. in case (b), we have $f'(x) > 0$, and $x = 0$;
3. in case (c), we have $f'(x) = 0$, and $x = 0$.

Combining the above three results, we have:
$$f'(x) \geq 0, \quad x \geq 0, \quad xf'(x) = 0$$

In words, the first derivative must be non-negative, the variable x must be non-negative, and the product of x and the derivative $f'(x)$ must equal zero. If in the solution to our problem x is positive, then the first derivative must be zero. On the other hand, if the solution to the problem is one in which x is zero, then the first derivative must be either positive or zero. If at the solution the first derivative is zero, then x must be non-negative and will be positive other than in case (c), whereas if at the solution the first derivative is positive, then x must be zero.

An alternative procedure is to set up the following Lagrangean expression for our basic

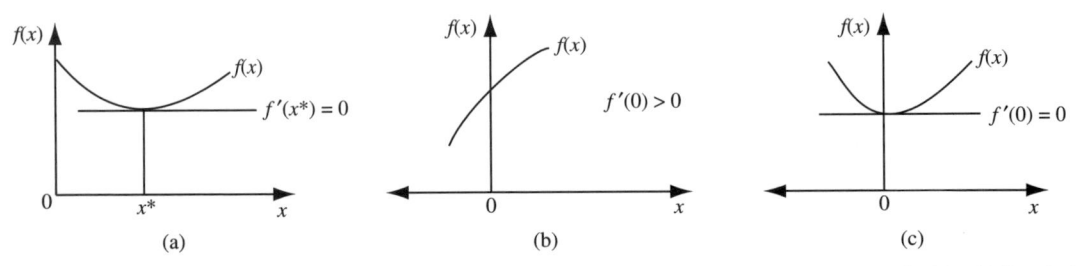

Figure 17.2 (a) Minimisation with a non-negativity requirements: $f(x)$ reaches a minimum at $x = x^*$ with $f'(x^*) = 0$. (b) $f(x)$ reaches a minimum at $x = 0$ with $f'(0) > 0$. (c) $f(x)$ reaches a minimum at $x = 0$ with $f'(0) = 0$.

maximisation problem:
$$L = f(x) + \mu x$$

Differentiate the Lagrangean partially with respect to x and μ to obtain:
$$\frac{\partial L}{\partial x} = f'(x) + \mu = 0$$
$$\frac{\partial L}{\partial \mu} = x \geq 0, \quad \mu \geq 0, \quad \mu \frac{\partial L}{\partial \mu} = 0$$

When we differentiate with respect to the Lagrangean multiplier μ, we ensure that the constraint that x be non-negative is satisfied. If x is positive, then the cross-product condition requires μ to be zero, and then from the condition that the partial derivative of the Lagrangean function with respect to x be zero, we see that in this case $f'(x)$ must equal zero. On the other hand, if μ is positive, then the cross-product term requires that the partial derivative of the Lagrangean function with respect to μ be zero; in other words, x must be zero. With μ being positive, then from the condition that the partial derivative of the Lagrangean function with respect to x equal zero, $f'(x)$ must be negative.

For the basic minimisation problem, we may also proceed as follows. The Lagrangean function in this case is:
$$L = f(x) - \mu x$$

Differentiate the Lagrangean partially with respect to x and μ to obtain:
$$\frac{\partial L}{\partial x} = f'(x) - \mu = 0$$
$$\frac{\partial L}{\partial \mu} = -x \leq 0, \quad \mu \geq 0, \quad \mu \frac{\partial L}{\partial \mu} = 0$$

When we differentiate with respect to the Lagrangean multiplier μ, we ensure that the constraint that x be non-negative is satisfied. If x is positive, then the cross-product condition requires μ to be zero, and then from the condition that the partial derivative of the Lagrangean function with respect to x be zero, we see that in this case $f'(x)$ must equal zero. On the other hand, if μ is positive, then the cross-product term requires that the partial derivative of the Lagrangean function with respect to μ be zero; in other words, x must be zero. With μ being positive, then from the condition that the partial derivative of the Lagrangean function with respect to x equal zero, then $f'(x)$ must be positive.

The Kuhn–Tucker conditions for a maximum

Having outlined the significance of a non-negativity requirement for a simple maximisation or minimisation problem, we now turn to the more general problem in which we have not only non-negativity requirements, but also inequality constraints. Consider the following problem:
$$\text{Maximise } f(x_1, x_2, \ldots, x_n)$$
$$\text{s.t. } g^i(x_1, x_2, \ldots, x_n) \leq c_i \quad i = 1, \ldots, m$$
$$x_j \geq 0 \text{ for all } j$$

The Lagrangean function for the above problem is

$$L = f(x_1, x_2, \ldots, x_n) + \sum_{i=1}^{i=m} y_i(c_i - g^i(x_1, x_2, \ldots, x_n))$$

It is important in writing out the Lagrangean function for a maximisation problem that we collect all the non-zero terms in each constraint together on the one side of the inequality such that this particular side of the inequality is required to be non-negative. If we differentiate the Lagrangean function with respect to x_j and y_i, we obtain the following set of first-order conditions for our constrained maximisation problem:

$$\frac{\partial L}{\partial x_j} = f_j - \sum_{i=1}^{i=m} y_i g^i_j \leq 0, \quad x_j \geq 0, \quad x_j \frac{\partial L}{\partial x_j} = 0$$

$$\frac{\partial L}{\partial y_i} = c_i - g^i(x_1, x_2, \ldots, x_n) \geq 0, \quad y_i \geq 0, \quad y_i \frac{\partial L}{\partial y_i} = 0$$

where f_j is the partial derivative of the objective function with respect to x_j, and g^i_j is the partial derivative of the ith constraint with respect to x_j. These conditions are known as the Kuhn–Tucker (KT) maximum conditions. Provided certain other conditions to be discussed later in this chapter are met, if there exists a point which satisfies the KT maximum conditions, then this point will give rise to a constrained global maximum of the problem.

Let us provide an intuitive discussion of these conditions. Those relating to x_j are straightforward given our earlier discussion of the significance of the non-negativity requirements. If the partial derivative with respect to x_j is negative, then x_j must be zero; if x_j is positive, then the partial derivative with respect to x_j must be zero. Turning to the conditions relating to the Lagrangean multipliers, note the similarity with the complementary/slackness conditions of linear programming. If there is slack in the ith constraint, then the corresponding Lagrangean multiplier y_i is zero; if the Lagrangean multiplier y_i is positive, then the corresponding constraint must hold as an equality. Finally, we cannot rule out the possibility that the constraint holds with equality and the Lagrangian multiplier is also zero. The Lagrangean multiplier attached to a particular constraint, like the dual variable of linear programming, measures the impact on the objective function of marginally relaxing the constraint. If there is slack already in the constraint then relaxing the constraint will not enable a higher value of the objective function to be achieved: for example, by allocating additional quantities of an input that a firm is not fully utilising in the original situation will not enable the firm to produce a more valuable bundle of outputs; the unutilised stockpile of the input would just increase. At the margin, the input is of no value to the firm, and its shadow price (marginal profitability) to the firm will be zero. However, if the input is currently being fully utilised, only in very special circumstances will it not be possible to produce a more valuable bundle of outputs, and one would expect the Lagrangean multiplier to be positive.

Consider the following problem:

$$\text{Maximise } 100x_1 - x_1^2 + 12x_2 - 6x_2^2 - 4x_1 x_2$$
$$\text{s.t. } x_1 + x_2 \leq 40$$
$$2x_1 + 3x_2 \leq 90$$
$$x_1, x_2 \geq 0$$

Setting up the Lagrangean function yields:

$$L = 100x_1 - x_1^2 + 12x_2 - 6x_2^2 - 4x_1 x_2 + y_1(40 - x_1 - x_2) + y_2(90 - 2x_1 - 3x_2)$$

The Kuhn–Tucker maximum conditions for this problem are as follows:

$$\frac{\partial L}{\partial x_1} = 100 - 2x_1 - 4x_2 - y_1 - 2y_2 \leq 0, \quad x_1 \geq 0, \quad x_1 \frac{\partial L}{\partial x_1} = 0$$

$$\frac{\partial L}{\partial x_2} = 12 - 4x_1 - 12x_2 - y_1 - 3y_2 \leq 0, \quad x_2 \geq 0, \quad x_2 \frac{\partial L}{\partial x_2} = 0$$

$$\frac{\partial L}{\partial y_1} = 40 - x_1 - x_2 \geq 0, \quad y_1 \geq 0, \quad y_1 \frac{\partial L}{\partial y_1} = 0$$

$$\frac{\partial L}{\partial y_2} = 90 - 2x_1 - 3x_2 \geq 0, \quad y_2 \geq 0, \quad y_2 \frac{\partial L}{\partial y_2} = 0$$

In Fig. 17.3 we have depicted the feasible region for our example. If this were a linear program, then the solution would occur at one of the four vertices. Non-linear programming problems however are more complicated. Not only might the solution occur at a vertex, but it could also involve a point of tangency between an iso-value contour of the objective function and the boundary of the feasible region. If this tangency position lay somewhere along the line segment AB, then there would be slack in the first constraint, whereas if the tangency position occurred somewhere along the line segment BC, then there would be slack in the second constraint. It may even be the case that the solution to the problem involves slack in both constraints, which would be the outcome if the unconstrained maximum of the function lay in the interior of the feasible region $OABC$.

How might we proceed to find the point that satisfies the Kuhn–Tucker maximum conditions? Let us first see whether the solution occurs at the vertex B. Here both constraints hold as equalities. Hence, setting the partial derivatives of the Lagrangean function with respect to y_1 and y_2 equal to zero, we obtain two equations to solve for x_1 and x_2.

$$x_1 + x_2 = 40$$
$$2x_1 + 3x_2 = 90$$

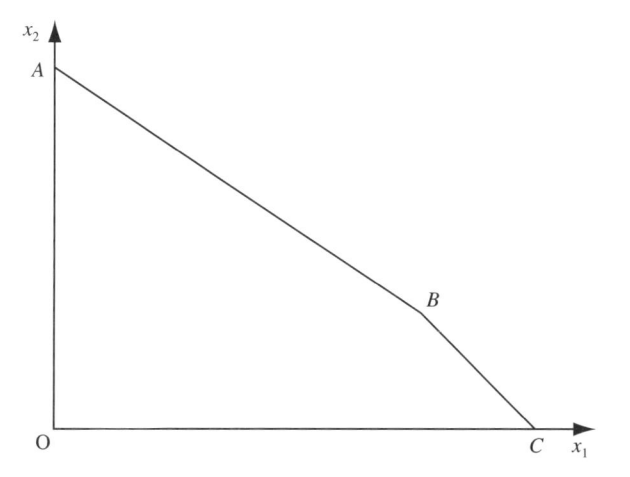

Figure 17.3 The feasible region and the potential optimum point. The feasible region for the maximisation problem is $OABC$. Depending on the precise nature of the function we are seeking to maximise, the solution could occur at a vertex, at a tangency position along one of the linear segments on the boundary of the feasible region, or at an interior point.

from which it follows that $x_1 = 30$ and $x_2 = 10$. Given that x_1 and x_2 are both positive, then we now set the partial derivatives of the Lagrangean function with respect to x_1 and x_2 equal to zero. Substituting in the above values of the xs, we obtain two equations in y_1 and y_2:

$$y_1 + 2y_2 = 0$$
$$y_1 + 3y_2 = -228$$

from which it follows that $y_1 = 456$ and $y_2 = -228$. This point does not satisfy the Kuhn–Tucker maximum conditions.

In which direction should we now move? The fact that the Lagrangean multiplier attached to the second constraint was negative informs us that we would be able to improve the value of the objective function by introducing slack into the second constraint. Remember our discussion of classical optimisation theory. The Lagrangean multiplier measures the impact on the objective function of slightly relaxing the relevant constraint. Given that in this case, y_2 was negative, we would be better off if this were a classical optimisation problem with a tightening of the second constraint. In the context of a problem in which slack is permitted in a constraint, then we should move away from vertex B and consider the possibility of a tangency position along BC with slack in the second constraint. Setting the partial derivatives of the Lagrangean with respect to x_1, x_2 and y_1 all equal to zero, and y_2 also equal to zero because of slack in the second constraint, we have the following three equations:

$$2x_1 + 4x_2 + y_1 = 100$$
$$4x_1 + 12x_2 + y_1 = 12$$
$$x_1 + x_2 = 40$$

Solving these three equations, we find $x_1 = 68$, $x_2 = -28$, $y_1 = 76$. Check the second constraint to see that there is indeed slack in the second constraint. The tangency position, therefore, does not occur along the line segment BC, but in the SE quadrant. This point, therefore, does not satisfy the Kuhn–Tucker maximum conditions. We have gone too far; we therefore next see whether the vertex C is the optimal position. Since there is slack in the second constraint then y_2 must be zero, and since x_2 is zero, then the partial derivative with respect to x_2 is likely to be negative. The two equations to solve for the two unknowns, x_1 and y_1 are obtained by setting the partial derivatives of the Lagrangean with respect to x_1 and y_1 both equal to zero:

$$2x_1 + y_1 = 100$$
$$x_1 = 40$$

Hence $x_1 = 40$, $y_1 = 20$. The Kuhn–Tucker maximum conditions are indeed satisfied at the point: $x_1 = 40$, $x_2 = 0$, $y_1 = 20$, $y_2 = 0$.

Closer inspection of the objective function might have enabled us to have homed in more quickly on the optimal point. Setting x_2 equal to zero, and finding the value of x_1 which maximises the objective function, we find x_1 must equal 50, which is outside the feasible region. Doing likewise for x_2, we find that x_2 equal to 1 would give rise to a maximum. These results would then suggest to us that given the presence of the term $-4x_1x_2$ in the objective function, the strong likelihood that in the optimal solution to the problem x_2 is going to be zero and x_1 as large as possible. That does in fact prove to be the case.

The Kuhn–Tucker conditions for a minimum

Consider the following minimisation problem:

$$\text{Minimise } f(x_1, x_2, \ldots, x_n)$$
$$\text{s.t. } g^i(x_1, x_2, \ldots, x_n) \geq c_i \quad i = 1, \ldots, m$$
$$x_j \geq 0 \text{ for all } j$$

The Lagrangean for the above problem is

$$L = f(x_1, x_2, \ldots, x_n) + \sum_{i=1}^{i=m} y_i(c_i - g(x_1, x_2, \ldots, x_n))$$

It is important in writing out the Lagrangean function for a minimisation problem that we collect all the non-zero terms in each constraint together on the one side of the inequality such that this particular side of the inequality is required to be non-positive. If we differentiate the Lagrangean function with respect to x_j and y_i, we obtain the following set of first-order conditions for our constrained minimisation problem:

$$\frac{\partial L}{\partial x_j} = f_j - \sum_{i=1}^{i=m} y_i g_j^i \geq 0, \quad x_j \geq 0, \quad x_j \frac{\partial L}{\partial x_j} = 0$$

$$\frac{\partial L}{\partial y_i} = c_i - g^i(x_1, x_2, \ldots, x_n) \leq 0, \quad y_i \geq 0, \quad y_i \frac{\partial L}{\partial y_i} = 0$$

where f_j is the partial derivative of the objective function with respect to x_j, and g_j^i is the partial derivative of the ith constraint with respect to x_j. These conditions are known as the Kuhn–Tucker minimum conditions. Under certain circumstances to be discussed later in this chapter, if there exists a point which satisfies the Kuhn–Tucker minimum conditions, then this will give rise to a constrained global minimum to the problem.

Let us provide an intuitive discussion of these conditions. Those relating to x_j are straightforward given our earlier discussion of the significance of the non-negativity requirements. If the partial derivative with respect to x_j is positive, then x_j must be zero; if x_j is positive, then the partial derivative with respect to x_j must be zero. Turning to the conditions relating to the Lagrangean multipliers, and note the similarity with the complementary/slackness conditions of linear programming. If there is slack in the ith constraint, then the corresponding Lagrangean multiplier y_i is zero; if the Lagrangean multiplier y_i is positive, then the corresponding constraint must hold as an equality. Finally, we cannot rule out the possibility that the constraint holds with equality and the Lagrangean multiplier is also zero.

Consider the following example:

$$\text{Minimise } 2x_1^2 - 32x_1 + x_2^2 - 20x_2$$
$$\text{s.t. } x_1 + 2x_2 \geq 36$$
$$3x_1 + x_2 \geq 43$$
$$x_1, x_2 \geq 0$$

Then the Lagrangean function is given by:

$$L = 2x_1^2 - 32x_1 + x_2^2 - 20x_2 + y_1(36 - x_1 - 2x_2) + y_2(43 - 3x_1 - x_2)$$

The Kuhn–Tucker minimum conditions are:

$$\frac{\partial L}{\partial x_1} = 4x_1 - 32 - y_1 - 3y_2 \geq 0, \quad x_1 \geq 0, \quad x_1 \frac{\partial L}{\partial x_1} = 0$$

$$\frac{\partial L}{\partial x_2} = 2x_2 - 20 - 2y_1 - y_2 \geq 0, \quad x_2 \geq 0, \quad x_2 \frac{\partial L}{\partial x_2} = 0$$

$$\frac{\partial L}{\partial y_1} = 36 - x_1 - 2x_2 \leq 0, \quad y_1 \geq 0, \quad y_1 \frac{\partial L}{\partial y_1} = 0$$

$$\frac{\partial L}{\partial y_2} = 43 - 3x_1 - x_2 \leq 0, \quad y_2 \geq 0, \quad y_2 \frac{\partial L}{\partial y_2} = 0$$

Let us first see whether at the optimal solution both constraints hold as equalities. Solving the two equations:

$$x_1 + 2x_2 = 36$$
$$3x_1 + x_2 = 43$$

we find $x_1 = 10$, $x_2 = 13$. Since both x_1 and x_2 are positive, then setting the partial derivatives of the Lagrangean function with respect to x_1 and x_2 equal to zero, and substituting in the above two values for the xs, we have two equations in the Lagrangean multipliers:

$$y_1 + 3y_2 = 8$$
$$2y_1 + y_2 = 6$$

from which it follows that $y_1 = 2$ and $y_2 = 2$. The Kuhn–Tucker minimum conditions are indeed satisfied at this point.

A warning

Unfortunately, it is not always the case that the solution to a non-linear maximisation problem occurs at a point which satisfies the Kuhn–Tucker maximum conditions. Consider the following example:

$$\text{Maximise } 24x_1 - x_1^2 - x_1 x_2 - x_2^2$$
$$\text{s.t. } -(5 - x_1)^3 + x_2 \leq 0$$
$$x_1, x_2 \geq 0$$

The Lagrangean function is

$$L = 24x_1 - x_1^2 - x_1 x_2 - x_2^2 + y[(5 - x_1)^3 - x_2]$$

The KT maximum conditions are

$$\frac{\partial L}{\partial x_1} = 24 - 2x_1 - x_2 - 3y(5 - x_1)^2 \leq 0, \quad x_1 \geq 0, \quad x_1 \frac{\partial L}{\partial x_1} = 0$$

$$\frac{\partial L}{\partial x_2} = -x_1 - 2x_2 - y \leq 0, \quad x_2 \geq 0, \quad x_2 \frac{\partial L}{\partial x_2} = 0$$

$$\frac{\partial L}{\partial y} = (5 - x_1)^3 - x_2 \geq 0, \quad y \geq 0, \quad y \frac{\partial L}{\partial y} = 0$$

In solving this problem, note that the unconstrained maximum of the objective function requires x_1 to equal *16* and x_2 to equal *−8*. We therefore wish x_1 to be as large as possible: given the constraint it cannot exceed *5*. However, the partial derivative with respect to x_1 evaluated at the point $x_1 = 5$, $x_2 = 0$ is not equal to zero, but equals *14*. So the KT conditions are not met at the point which does indeed give rise to a constrained maximum of the function. Basically, what is happening at the optimal point is there is a sharp point known as a cusp, where there is a change in the direction of the boundary of the feasible region, yet the slope of the boundary of the region is the same on either side of the point. Note it is equal to zero whether we approach the point along the x_1 axis from values of x_1 slightly smaller than *5* or down the curve from values of x_1 slightly smaller than *5* and values of x_2 slightly larger than *0*.

Another example in which the optimal solution does not occur at a point which satisfies the KT maximum conditions is as follows:

$$\text{Maximise } 4x_1 - x_1^2 + 100x_2 - 2x_2^2$$
$$\text{s.t. } (x_1^2 + x_2^2 - 100)^2 \leq 0$$
$$-x_1 \leq -8$$
$$x_1, x_2 \geq 0$$

The Lagrangean function, therefore, is given by:

$$L = 4x_1 - x_1^2 + 100x_2 - 2x_2^2 - y_1(x_1^2 + x_2^2 - 100)^2 + y_2(x_1 - 8)$$

The Kuhn–Tucker maximum conditions are

$$\frac{\partial L}{\partial x_1} = 4 - 2x_1 - 4y_1 x_1(x_1^2 + x_2^2 - 100) + y_2 \leq 0, \quad x_1 \geq 0, \quad x_1 \frac{\partial L}{\partial x_1} = 0$$

$$\frac{\partial L}{\partial x_2} = 100 - 4x_2 - 4y_1 x_2(x_1^2 + x_2^2 - 100) \leq 0, \quad x_2 \geq 0, \quad x_2 \frac{\partial L}{\partial x_2} = 0$$

$$\frac{\partial L}{\partial y_1} = -(x_1^2 + x_2^2 - 100)^2 \geq 0, \quad y_1 \geq 0, \quad y_1 \frac{\partial L}{\partial y_1} = 0$$

$$\frac{\partial L}{\partial y_2} = x_1 - 8 \geq 0, \quad y_2 \geq 0, \quad y_2 \frac{\partial L}{\partial y_2} = 0$$

Note the unconstrained maximum for this objective function is $x_1 = 2$ and $x_2 = 25$. In the light of this and given the constraints, we shall require x_1 to equal *8*, which in turn implies that x_2 equals *6*. Note that for the partial derivative of the Lagrangean with respect to x_1 to equal zero, then y_2 must equal *12*, but y_1 can take on any non-negative value. However, when we turn to the partial derivative with respect to x_2, we note that this will not equal zero, but will be positive and equal to *76*. The constrained optimum does indeed occur at the point $x_1 = 8$, $x_2 = 6$, y_1 is any non-negative number and $y_2 = 12$, even though the Kuhn–Tucker maximum conditions are not satisfied at this point. The optimal point in this case is not a cusp, since the slopes on either side of the point are not equal to each other.

Irregularities on the boundaries of the feasible region can therefore cause us problems. Mathematicians have developed results to show what conditions must be imposed for such boundary irregularities to be ruled out. This is not of particular interest to economists, and we eschew discussion of these issues here.

The Kuhn–Tucker sufficiency theorem

However, by imposing certain conditions on the nature of the objective function and of the constraints, we can be certain that in non-linear programming problems where these conditions are indeed met that, if there exists a point that satisfies the Kuhn–Tucker maximum (minimum) conditions, then the solution to the problem will be given by this point. Furthermore, this point will in fact give rise to a global maximum or minimum of the function subject to the constraints and the non-negativity requirements.

For a maximum problem, we require the objective function $f(x)$ to be a concave differentiable function for non-negative values of the choice variables, and the constraint functions, the $g^i(x)$s, to be convex differentiable functions for non-negative values of the choice variables. In these circumstances, if there exists a point which satisfies the Kuhn–Tucker maximum conditions, then this point will give rise to a global maximum of the objective function: there will be no other point which satisfies the constraints and the non-negativity requirements which will give rise to a larger value of the objective function than the point which satisfies the Kuhn–Tucker maximum conditions.

Regarding constrained minimisation problems, then if the objective function is a convex differentiable function for non-negative values of the choice variables, and the constraint functions, the $g^i(x)$s, are concave differentiable functions for non-negative values of the choice variables, and there is a point which satisfies the Kuhn–Tucker minimum conditions, then that point will give rise to a global minimum of the objective function: there will be no other point which satisfies the constraints and the non-negativity requirements which will give rise to a smaller value of the objective function than the point which satisfies the Kuhn–Tucker minimum conditions. This is known as the Kuhn–Tucker sufficiency theorem.

Let us return to the four examples we examined above. In the first case, we had the following objective function:

$$f(x) = 100x_1 - x_1^2 + 12x_2 - 6x_2^2 - 4x_1 x_2$$

The first-order partial derivatives of this function are

$$f_1 = 100 - 2x_1 - 4x_2$$
$$f_2 = 12 - 4x_1 - 12x_2$$

and the second-order partial derivatives are

$$f_{11} = -2, \quad f_{12} = f_{21} = -4, \quad f_{22} = -12$$

We can easily see that this function is concave, since the Hessian determinants alternate in sign starting negative:

$$|f_{11}| = -2, \quad \begin{vmatrix} f_{11} & f_{12} \\ f_{21} & f_{22} \end{vmatrix} = \begin{vmatrix} -2 & -4 \\ -4 & -12 \end{vmatrix} = 8$$

The two constraints of the first problem are both linear, and hence the two constraints are both convex functions, though they are not strictly convex. Furthermore, as we saw earlier there is a point which satisfies the Kuhn–Tucker maximum conditions.

In the minimisation problem, then we had the following objective function:

$$f(x) = 2x_1^2 - 32x_1 + x_2^2 - 20x_2$$

Its first- and second-order partial derivatives are as follows:

$$f_1 = 4x_1 - 32, \quad f_2 = 2x_2 - 20$$
$$f_{11} = 4, \quad f_{12} = f_{21} = 0, \quad f_{22} = 2$$

The Hessian determinants are both positive, equalling *4* and *8* respectively, so the function is convex. Again the two constraints are linear, so they are concave functions, but they are not strictly concave. In this case too, there exists a point that satisfies the Kuhn–Tucker minimum conditions, and this point gives rise to a global minimum of the objective function subject to the constraints.

In the third example, it is easy to check that the objective function is concave, and the constraint is convex, but there is no point that satisfies the KT maximum conditions. However, if we were to increase the value of the constant in the constraint, we would find that the KT maximum conditions are indeed met once the constant were equal to at least *12*. The point $x_1 = 12$, $x_2 = 0$ is the solution to the problem if we dispense with the constraint, but maintain the non-negativity requirements. If the constant were equal to or greater than *12*, then the Lagrangean multiplier would be zero. If the constant were *12*, then there would be no slack in the constraint, but a relaxation of the constraint would not make possible a higher value of the objective function; hence *y* must be zero in this case. If the constant were greater than *12*, then there would be slack in the constraint, which obviously requires a zero value for the Lagrangean multiplier. If the constant in the constraint were smaller than *12*, then at the optimal point the slope of the iso-value contour of the objective function would be positive, whereas that of the constraint would be zero. The value of the Lagrangean multiplier would then have to be positive, but a unique value cannot be assigned to it from the KT maximum conditions, which we have seen are not satisfied anyway. However, a slight relaxation of the constraint would holding x_2 constant at zero increase the value of the objective function by $24 - 2x_1$, which must then equal *y*. With the constant equal to *12*, there would be a tangency position between the constraint and an iso-value contour of the objective function, the slopes of both being zero at this point. If the constant were greater than *12*, then the optimal point would lie in the interior of the feasible region.

In the fourth case, the solution to the problem occurred at a point which did not satisfy the Kuhn–Tucker maximum conditions. It is a straightforward matter to check that the objective function is indeed concave in this case. But what about the constraints? One is linear and hence convex; the other constraint requires us to be on that part of the boundary of a circle centred on the origin with radius *10* which lies in the non-negative quadrant. We may write this constraint as:

$$x_2 = (100 - x_1^2)^{1/2}$$

Differentiating this function twice, we have:

$$\frac{dx_2}{dx_1} = -x_1(100 - x_1^2)^{-1/2}$$

$$\frac{d^2x_2}{dx_1^2} = -(100 - x_1^2)^{-1/2} - x_1^2(100 - x_1^2)^{-3/2}$$

and since x_1 may not exceed *10*, the second derivative is negative, and the function is convex. Taking the two constraints together, the feasible region collapses to a single point: $x_1 = 8$ and $x_2 = 6$, and as we have already seen, the Kuhn–Tucker maximum conditions are not satisfied at this point. So the third condition for the KT sufficiency theorem to hold is not met.

A saddle point

Consider a non-linear programming maximisation problem, where the objective function is concave and the constraints of the problem are convex. Since if we multiply a convex function by minus one we convert it into a concave function, then the Lagrangean function is concave in the choice variables, the xs, and linear in the Lagrangean multipliers, the ys.

$$L(x, y) = f(x) + \sum_{i=1}^{i=m} y_i(c_i - g^i(x))$$

Assume the point (x^*, y^*) satisfies the KT maximum conditions. Then given that the Lagrangean function is concave in x, then it must be the case that

$$L(x, y^*) \leq L(x^*, y^*) + \sum_{j=1}^{j=n} \frac{\partial L}{\partial x_j}(x_j - x_j^*)$$

where the partial derivatives of the Lagrangean are to be evaluated at the point which satisfies the KT maximum conditions. Given that the KT maximum conditions are satisfied, we know that

$$x_j^* \frac{\partial L}{\partial x_j} = 0 \text{ for all } j$$

$$\text{and } x_j \frac{\partial L}{\partial x_j} \leq 0 \text{ for all } j$$

The first set of conditions follows directly from the KT maximum conditions, and the second set from the fact that x_j must be non-negative, and the partial derivative evaluated at the point which satisfies the KT maximum conditions must be non-positive, yielding a product which must be non-positive. Given the above, it is clear that

$$L(x, y^*) \leq L(x^*, y^*)$$

Given the vector y^*, there is no other x vector which gives a larger value of the Lagrangean function than x^*.

Now since the Lagrangean function is linear in y, then it is also convex in y. Now assume as before that the KT maximum conditions are satisfied at the point (x^*, y^*), then it follows from the definition of convexity that

$$L(x^*, y) \geq L(x^*, y^*) + \sum_{i=1}^{i=m} \frac{\partial L}{\partial y_i}(y_i - y_1^*)$$

As before, the partial derivatives of the Lagrangean function are to be evaluated at the point which satisfies the KT maximum conditions. In this case, given that the KT maximum conditions are met, we must have

$$y_i^* \frac{\partial L}{\partial y_i} = 0 \text{ for all } i$$

$$\text{and } y_i \frac{\partial L}{\partial y_i} \geq 0 \text{ for all } i$$

The first set of conditions follows directly from the KT maximum conditions, and the second set from the fact that y_i must be non-negative, and the partial derivative evaluated at the point which satisfies the KT maximum conditions must be non-negative, yielding a product which must be non-negative. Given the above, it is clear that

$$L(x, y^*) \geq L(x^*, y^*)$$

Given the vector x^*, there is no other y vector which gives a smaller value of the Lagrangean function than y^*.

Putting the two results together, we have:

$$L(x^*, y) \geq L(x^*, y^*) \geq L(x, y^*)$$

The point which satisfies the KT maximum conditions, therefore, is a saddle point. The Lagrangean function has been maximised with respect to the vector of choice variables and has been minimised with respect to the Lagrangean multipliers.

An economic example

A utility-maximising consumer's utility function takes the following form:

$$U(x) = 20x_1 - 2x_1^2 + 100x_2 - x_2^2$$

where x_i is the amount consumed of good i, $i = 1, 2$. Throughout, the prices of the two goods are held constant with the price of good 1 being *10* and the price of good 2 being unity. The consumer's money income is M.

The Lagrangean function is

$$L = 20x_1 - 2x_1^2 + 100x_1 - x_2^2 + y(M - 10x_1 - x_2)$$

Differentiating partially with respect to x_1, x_2 and y, we obtain the KT maximum conditions:

$$\frac{\partial L}{\partial x_1} = 20 - 4x_1 - 10y \leq 0, \quad x_1 \geq 0, \quad x_1 \frac{\partial L}{\partial x_1} = 0$$

$$\frac{\partial L}{\partial x_2} = 100 - 2x_2 - y \leq 0, \quad x_2 \geq 0, \quad x_2 \frac{\partial L}{\partial x_2} = 0$$

$$\frac{\partial L}{\partial y} = M - 10x_1 - x_2 \geq 0, \quad y \geq 0, \quad y \frac{\partial L}{\partial y} = 0$$

Let us now see how consumption of the two goods will vary as the consumer's income changes.

We first consider the circumstances under which the consumer will not consume the first good. If $x_1 = 0$, then $y \geq 2$. If the marginal utility of spending a pound on good 1 when zero units of the good are consumed is less than the marginal utility of money income as measured by the Lagrangean multiplier, it is not in the consumer's interests to consume good 1. The Lagrangean multiplier can only be positive if all the income is spent. To satisfy the inequality on y, then x_2 must be positive and not greater than *49*. Given the price of the second good is unity, we may conclude that

$$x_1 = 0, \quad x_2 = M \text{ for } 0 \leq M \leq 49$$

If both goods are consumed and there is no slack in the budget constraint then we must have

$$20 - 4x_1 - 10y = 0$$
$$100 - 2x_2 - y = 0$$
$$M - 10x_1 - x_2 = 0$$

Solving for x_1 and x_2, we have

$$x_1 = \frac{20M - 980}{204} \text{ and } x_2 = \frac{4M + 9800}{204}$$

However, y cannot be negative, which imposes upper limits on the values of x_1 and x_2 for which the above equations must hold. Since

$$y = 20 - 4x_1 = 100 - 2x_2$$

then x_1 cannot exceed 5 and x_2 cannot exceed 50. The above two equations, therefore define the demand for the two commodities for M being greater than 49 and no greater than 100.

For $M = 100$, then y is zero, and increases in income beyond this point lead to no changes in the quantities consumed of the two goods; there is slack in the budget constraint and the Lagrangean multiplier remains at zero. We have reached the unconstrained maximum, the point of satiation. Hence

$$x_1 = 5 \text{ and } x_2 = 50 \text{ for } M \geq 100$$

We may also investigate how the value of the Lagrangean multiplier varies as income increases.

1. For $0 \leq M \leq 49$, only the second good is consumed with $x_2 = M$. Hence $y = 100 - 2M$.
2. For $49 < M \leq 100$, then $x_2 = (4M + 9800)/204$ and $y = 100 - 2x_2$. Hence we must have $y = (800 - 8M)/204$.
3. For $M > 100$, then $x_2 = 50$ and $y = 0$.

What is the maximum utility that the consumer can attain at different levels of income? This is given by the maximum value function:

$$V(M) = U(x_1^*, x_2^*)$$

where x_1^* and x_2^* are the values of x_1 and x_2 satisfy the KT maximum conditions. For this particular example, we have:

$$V(M) = 100M - M^2 \text{ for } 0 < M \leq 49$$

$$= \frac{480\,200 + 800M - 4M^2}{204} \text{ for } 49 < M \leq 100$$

$$= 2550 \text{ for } M > 100$$

If we differentiate V with respect to M, we obtain the impact on utility of marginally relaxing the constraint. The derivative will give us the value of the Langrangean multiplier:

$$\frac{dV}{dM} = 100 - 2M \text{ for } 0 < M \leq 49$$

$$= \frac{800 - 8M}{204} \text{ for } 49 < M \leq 100$$

$$= 0 \text{ for } M > 100$$

Just compare the above results with the ones we have derived above for y.

17.3 NON-LINEAR PROGRAMMING AND PUBLIC ENTERPRISE ECONOMICS

The optimal outcome with differential pricing

A public utility produces a non-storable good, the demand for which varies systematically over the course of the day. To make the analysis simple, let us assume that the day can be divided into two equal periods, with demand at any price being higher in period one than in period two. The inverse demand functions for the good in the two time periods are given respectively by:

$$p_1 = p_1(x_1)$$
$$p_2 = p_2(x_2)$$

The gross benefits to consumers in each time period is the area under the relevant inverse demand function. Hence

$$B_i = B_i(x_i) = \int_{x_i=0}^{x_i=x_i'} p_i(x_i)\,dx_i$$

The utility has sufficient capacity installed to be able to produce x_c units per half day. The variable cost functions are the same in each time period and are given by $c(x_i)$. The fixed costs on a daily basis are given by $f(x_c)$.

If the aim of the utility is to maximise net social benefits, what pricing policy should it adopt?

The Lagrangean function in this case is given by:

$$L = B_1(x_1) + B_2(x_2) - c_1(x_1) - c_2(x_2) - f(x_c) + y_1(x_c - x_1) + y_2(x_c - x_2)$$

Differentiating partially with respect to the xs and the ys, we obtain the KT conditions for a maximum:

$$\frac{\partial L}{\partial x_1} = p_1 - MC_1 - y_1 \leq 0, \quad x_1 \geq 0, \quad x_1 \frac{\partial L}{\partial x_1} = 0$$

$$\frac{\partial L}{\partial x_2} = p_2 - MC_2 - y_2 \leq 0, \quad x_2 \geq 0, \quad x_2 \frac{\partial L}{\partial x_2} = 0$$

$$\frac{\partial L}{\partial y_1} = x_c - x_1 \geq 0, \quad y_1 \geq 0, \quad y_1 \frac{\partial L}{\partial y_1} = 0$$

$$\frac{\partial L}{\partial y_2} = x_c - x_2 \geq 0, \quad y_2 \geq 0, \quad y_2 \frac{\partial L}{\partial y_2} = 0$$

If we assume that the capacity is only fully utilised in the first period, then the utility must set a price for the off-peak period which is just equal to marginal operating costs if the good is to be supplied in the off-peak period. There may obviously be circumstances in which the choke price (the maximum price the consumer would be prepared to pay) in the off-peak period is less than marginal cost at zero output; in this case it is not efficient to produce anything in the off-peak period. The price in the peak period will typically be higher than marginal operating cost by an amount sufficient to ration demand to capacity, this amount being equal to the value of the Lagrangean multiplier, y_1.

If capacity is fully utilised in both the peak and off-peak periods, then the price will typically be higher than marginal operating cost in the off-peak period as well.

In the long run, we allow the installed level of capacity to become a choice variable. We must therefore add the additional condition to the above set of KT maximum conditions:

$$\frac{\partial L}{\partial x_c} = y_1 + y_1 - MC(x_c) \leq 0, \quad x_c \geq 0, \quad x_c \frac{\partial L}{\partial x_c} = 0$$

where $MC(x_c)$ is the marginal cost of expanding capacity. The interpretation of this condition is straightforward: y_1 measures the valuation consumers place on having a little bit more capacity available in the peak period, and similarly y_2 measures the valuation consumers place on having a little bit more capacity in the off-peak period. Capacity should, therefore, be expanded as long as the sum of these valuations is greater than the cost of expanding capacity.

To clarify the above discussion, we will work through a simple numerical example. The peak period and off-peak period inverse demand functions are as follows:

$$p_1 = 200 - 2x_1$$
$$p_2 = 160 - 4x_2$$

Let us further assume that the installed level of capacity is such that *75* units can be produced in each period. The marginal operating cost is the same in each period and is equal to *10*, marginal capacity cost is constant and equal to *40*. What prices should be charged in each period in order to maximise net social benefits?

The Lagrangean function is

$$L = B_1(x_1) + B_2(x_2) - 10(x_1 + x_2) + y_1(75 - x_1) + y_2(75 - x_2)$$

where $B_i(x_i)$ is the gross benefit function in period i. The gross benefits are simply given by the area under the demand curve, and, hence, when we differentiate partially the relevant gross benefit function with respect to output we just get p_i. The Kuhn–Tucker maximum conditions, therefore, are

$$\frac{\partial L}{\partial x_1} = p_1 - 10 - y_1 \leq 0, \quad x_1 \geq 0, \quad x_1 \frac{\partial L}{\partial x_1} = 0$$

$$\frac{\partial L}{\partial x_2} = p_2 - 10 - y_2 \leq 0, \quad x_2 \geq 0, \quad x_2 \frac{\partial L}{\partial x_2} = 0$$

$$\frac{\partial L}{\partial y_1} = 75 - x_1 \geq 0, \quad y_1 \geq 0, \quad y_1 \frac{\partial L}{\partial y_1} = 0$$

$$\frac{\partial L}{\partial y_2} = 75 - x_2 \geq 0, \quad y_2 \geq 0, \quad y_2 \frac{\partial L}{\partial y_2} = 0$$

It is clear that in order to ration demand to capacity in the peak period the price must equal *50*, with the obvious implication that y_i is equal to *40*. In the off-peak period, however, capacity is not going to be fully utilised, and the price must just cover marginal operating cost. Hence, we have $p_2 = 10$ and $x_2 = 37.5$. Note that the installed level of capacity is at the optimal level since y_1 is equal to marginal capacity cost.

Let us now consider what would happen if there was an increase in demand in the two periods. Assume the new inverse demand functions are now given by:

$$p_1 = 210 - 2x_1$$
$$p_2 = 190 - 2x_2$$

Now, in order to ration demand to capacity in the peak period, p_1 would have to rise from *50* to *60*; the new value of y_1 would now be equal to *50* rather than *40*. In the off-peak period, we would now require p_2 to equal *40*, with y_2 having increased in value from *0* to *30*. In the long run, the level of installed capacity should be increased, since $y_1 + y_2$ exceeds marginal capacity cost of *40*. Capacity would be at its new optimal level when

$$y_1 + y_2 = 40$$
$$\text{but } y_1 = p_1 - 10 \text{ and } y_2 = p_2 - 10$$
$$\text{hence } 210 - 2x_c - 10 + 190 - 2x_c - 10 = 40$$
$$x_c = 85 \text{ with } p_1 = 40, y_1 = 30, p_2 = 20 \text{ and } y_2 = 10$$

The optimal outcome with uniform pricing

Let us now consider what would happen if a uniform price was required to be charged in each time period. We are then interested in choosing the optimal uniform price and the optimal level of capacity. We then wish to compare how this equilibrium would differ from that in which differential pricing was permitted. Assume that with differential pricing capacity is only fully utilised in the peak period, so price in the off-peak period just reflects marginal operating costs. Furthermore assume that capacity is at the optimal level; hence the peak period price is equal to the sum of marginal operating and capacity cost.

For the moment, assume installed capacity is at the level which is optimal in the differential pricing regime. If we were to choose as the uniform price the peak period price, then there would be a loss of consumer surplus in the off-peak period, which would only be partially offset by the increased profitability of the public enterprise. The welfare loss in the off-peak period is depicted in Fig. 17.4(a) in which it has been assumed that marginal operating and capacity costs are both constant. If on the other hand, the uniform price were to be the previous off-peak period price, then though there would be no welfare loss in the off-peak period, the increase in consumer surplus of the peak period consumers would just be offset by the failure to cover capacity costs, and given the excess demand there would now be rationing costs to be borne. This situation is depicted in Fig. 17.4(b). Intuitively, then it would seem that the uniform price must lie somewhere between the two previous prices.

Let us analyse this problem more formally. First we must explicitly introduce the costs of rationing into the analysis. We shall assume that rationing costs are a positive function of demand in the peak period, which will depend upon the uniform price which is set, and a negative function of the installed level of capacity. We may express the net social benefit function as follows:

$$B_1(x_1) - c(x_1) - R(x_1(p), x_c) - f(x_c) + B_2(x_2(p)) - c(x_2)$$

where $R(x_1(p), x_c)$ is the rationing cost function which is increasing in the demand for x_1 and decreasing in x_c. We shall also assume that marginal operating and capacity costs are both constant. Output in either period may not exceed the installed level of capacity. The long-run equilibrium is going to involve a situation in which capacity is fully utilised in the peak period, but there is unused capacity in the off-peak period. If we substitute $x_1 = x_c$ in the net benefit function, we obtain:

$$B_1(x_c) - c(x_c) - R(x_1(p), x_c) - f(x_c) + B_2(x_2(p)) - c(x_2)$$

Differentiating partially with respect to p and x_c, we obtain the first-order conditions for a

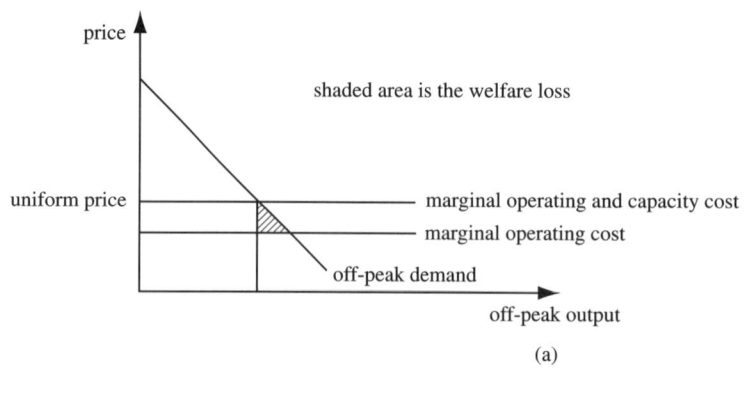

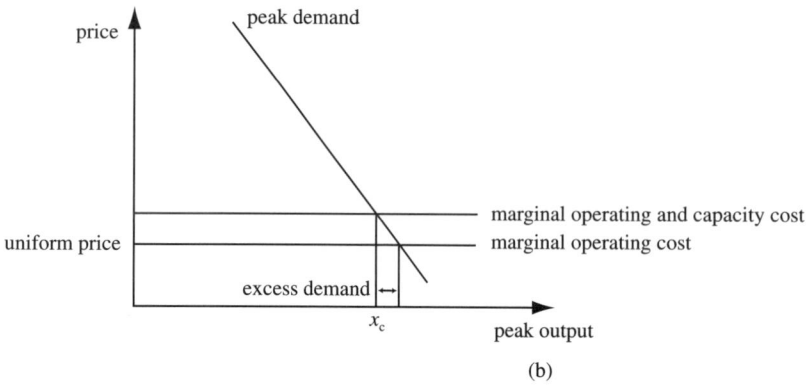

Figure 17.4 (a) The off-peak period. With the uniform price set equal to the sum of marginal operating and capacity costs, a welfare loss equal to the shaded area is borne by off-peak period consumers. (b) The peak period. The position shown is one of excess demand with the uniform price set equal to marginal operating cost. Some consumers will be rationed.

maximum:

$$\frac{\partial NSB}{\partial p} = (p - MOC)\frac{dx_2}{dp} - \frac{\partial R}{\partial x_1}\frac{dx_1}{dp} = 0$$

$$\frac{\partial NSB}{\partial x_c} = p_v - MOC - \frac{\partial R}{\partial x_c} - MCC = 0$$

where MOC and MCC are marginal operating and marginal capacity costs respectively, and p_v is the valuation placed on the last unit consumed in the peak period.

What interpretation can we put on these conditions? Regarding price, then the uniform price will be at its optimal level if the marginal benefit in the off-peak period from cutting the price is just equal to the marginal costs of the increased amount of rationing that is now incurred in the peak period as a result of the increase in excess demand. Regarding capacity, then capacity will be at its optimal level if the marginal cost (both operating and capacity) of output in the peak period is just equal to its marginal benefit. The marginal benefit has two components: there will be the marginal benefit of consumption which will be valued more highly than the price which is charged, and secondly as capacity output increases at an unchanged price then rationing costs will fall as excess demand falls. Regarding the marginal benefit of consumption in the peak period, we could somewhat heroically assume that p_v is the price which would clear the market in the peak period with the supply equal to x_c. This is an heroic assumption since it implicitly assumes that in the rationing process, those with the lowest marginal valuations are the ones who are denied the good, or equivalently that all consumers have identical demand functions and are then rationed equally. Given this assumption, it is easy to see that installed capacity will be larger than with differential pricing. With differential pricing, the peak period price is equal to the sum of marginal operating and marginal capacity costs; with a uniform price, then the price at which the market would clear in the peak falls short of the sum of marginal operating and capacity costs by an amount that reflects the fall in rationing costs from having a slightly larger level of installed capacity. Given that marginal operating and capacity costs are both constant, then p_v must be lower than p_1, but then the installed level of capacity must be higher with a uniform price than with a differential price. A consequence of the uniform pricing regime then is that capacity costs are higher. Is it possible that the uniform price could be equal to p_v with the implication that there would be no rationing costs incurred in the peak period? For this to be the case would require

$$\left(MCC + \frac{\partial R}{\partial x_1}\right)\frac{dx_2}{dp} = \frac{\partial R}{\partial x_1}\frac{dx_1}{dp}$$

A necessary, but not sufficient, condition for this to hold is that

$$\left|\frac{dx_1}{dp}\right| > \left|\frac{dx_2}{dp}\right|$$

In the off-peak period, there is a loss of consumer surplus as compared to the differential pricing regime. As can be seen from the first-order condition on the price, the uniform price is higher than marginal operating cost by an amount that reflects the effect a small change in price has on peak period demand and hence on rationing costs.

The greater capacity costs, likely rationing costs and the loss of consumer surplus in the off-peak period which result from a uniform pricing regime then have then to be compared with the greater costs associated with operating a differential pricing scheme which have been ignored in the above discussion.

17.4 QUADRATIC PROGRAMMING

For the set of non-linear programming problems where the objective function is a quadratic function of the choice variables and the constraints are a set of linear inequalities, then we may solve the problem using the first phase of the two-phase method which we have earlier outlined in our discussion of linear programming techniques in Chapter 6. This method is known as the quadratic programming algorithm.

The basic procedure can be best explained by means of an example. Consider the following problem:

$$Maximise\ 48x_1 - x_1^2 - 2x_1x_2 + 72x_2 - 2x_2^2$$
$$s.t.\ x_1 + 2x_2 \leq 32$$
$$x_1,\ x_2 \geq 0$$

The Lagrangean function, therefore, is given by:

$$L = 48x_1 - x_1^2 - 2x_1x_2 + 72x_2 - 2x_2^2 + y_1(32 - x_1 - 2x_2) + \mu_1 x_1 + \mu_2 x_2$$

where we have explicitly introduced the non-negativity requirements on the xs into the function.

The KT conditions for a maximum are as follows:

$$\frac{\partial L}{\partial x_1} = 48 - 2x_1 - 2x_2 - y_1 + \mu_1 = 0$$

$$\frac{\partial L}{\partial x_2} = 72 - 2x_1 - 4x_2 - 2y_1 + \mu_2 = 0$$

$$\frac{\partial L}{\partial \mu_1} = x_1 \geq 0, \quad \mu_1 \geq 0, \quad \mu_1 \frac{\partial L}{\partial \mu_1} = 0$$

$$\frac{\partial L}{\partial \mu_2} = x_2 \geq 0, \quad \mu_2 \geq 0, \quad \mu_2 \frac{\partial L}{\partial \mu_2} = 0$$

$$\frac{\partial L}{\partial y_1} = 32 - x_1 - 2x_2 \geq 0, \quad y_1 \geq 0, \quad y_1 \frac{\partial L}{\partial y_1} = 0$$

We may then utilise these conditions in setting up the following artificial problem, the solution to which will yield the optimal values of the choice variables and the Lagrangean multiplier.

$$\text{Maximise } -R_1 - R_2$$
$$\text{s.t. } 2x_1 + 2x_2 + y_1 - \mu_1 + R_1 = 48$$
$$2x_1 + 4x_2 + 2y - \mu_2 + R_2 = 72$$
$$x_1 + 2x_2 + S_1 = 32$$
$$x_j \geq 0, \quad \mu_j \geq 0, \quad \mu_j x_j = 0, \quad j = 1, 2$$
$$y_1 \geq 0, \quad S_1 \geq 0, \quad y_1 S_1 = 0$$

where R_1 and R_2 are two artificial variables and S_1 is the slack variable in the constraint. An initial basic feasible solution for our problem is one that contains the two artificial variables and the slack variable. We then have the following tableau.

	x_1	x_2	μ_1	μ_2	R_1	R_2	S_1	y_1	solution
$z_j - c_j$	0	0	0	0	1	1	0	0	0
R_1	2	2	-1	0	1	0	0	1	48
R_2	2	4	0	-1	0	1	0	2	72
S_1	1	2	0	0	0	0	1	0	32

The row operations we perform are as follows. We must adjust the first tableau by expressing the $z_j - c_j$ row in terms of the non-basic variables. To do this we multiply both the R_1 and R_2 rows by -1 and add to the $z_j - c_j$ row.

	x_1	x_2	μ_1	μ_2	R_1	R_2	S_1	y_1	solution
$z_j - c_j$	-4	-6	1	1	0	0	0	-3	-120
R_1	2	2	-1	0	1	0	0	1	48
R_2	2	4	0	-1	0	1	0	2	72
S_1	1	2	0	0	0	0	1	0	32

We are now in a position to apply the simplex method for a maximisation problem. We wish to enter the non-basic variable with the largest negative value subject to the KT conditions continuing to hold. The non-basic variable with the largest negative value is x_2, and given that μ_2 is a non-basic variable, we may introduce this variable into the basis. For the new basis to remain feasible, we eliminate S_1. The row operations we carry out to derive the third tableau are:

1. multiply the S_1 row by *1/2*;
2. multiply the S_1 row by *−1* and add to the R_1 row;
3. multiply the S_1 row by *−2* and add to the R_2 row;
4. multiply the S_1 row by *3* and add to the $z_j - c_j$ row.

	x_1	x_2	μ_1	μ_2	R_1	R_2	S_1	y_1	solution
$z_j - c_j$	−1	0	1	1	0	0	3	−3	−24
R_1	1	0	−1	0	1	0	−1	1	16
R_2	0	0	0	−1	0	1	−2	2	8
x_2	1/2	1	0	0	0	0	1/2	0	16

Applying the optimality criterion, we now introduce y_1; this is permissible since S_1 is no longer a basic variable. To retain feasibility R_2 must leave the basis. The row operations we perform in order to obtain the next tableau are:

1. multiply the R_2 row by *1/2*;
2. multiply the R_2 row by *−1/2* and add to the R_1 row;
3. multiply the R_2 row by *3/2* and add to the $z_j - c_j$ row.

	x_1	x_2	μ_1	μ_2	R_1	R_2	S_1	y_1	solution
$z_j - c_j$	−1	0	1	−1/2	0	3/2	0	0	−12
R_1	1	0	−1	1/2	1	−1/2	0	0	12
y_1	0	0	0	−1/2	0	1/2	−1	1	4
x_2	1/2	1	0	0	0	0	1/2	0	16

At the next iteration, we introduce x_1 in place of R_1; this is permissible since μ_1 is not a basic variable. The row operations we now perform in order to obtain the new tableau are:

1. multiply the R_1 row by *−1/2* and add to the x_2 row;
2. add the R_1 to the $z_j - c_j$ row.

	x_1	x_2	μ_1	μ_2	R_1	R_2	S_1	y_1	solution
$z_j - c_j$	0	0	0	0	1	1	0	0	0
x_1	1	0	−1	1/2	1	−1/2	0	0	12
y_1	0	0	0	−1/2	0	1/2	−1	1	4
x_2	0	1	1/2	−1/4	−1/2	1/4	0	0	10

We have now eliminated the two artificial variables. The KT maximum conditions are met at the point: $x_1 = 12$, $x_2 = 10$ and $y_1 = 4$. To obtain the value of the objective function, we simply substitute the above values of x_1 and x_2 into the objective function. We find its value at this point is *716*.

Let us now turn to a minimisation problem, which can be solved in a similar manner.

$$\text{Minimise } 3x_1^2 - 12x_1 + x_2^2 - 18x_2 + 2x_1x_2$$
$$\text{s.t. } 0.5x_1 + 2x_2 \geq 20$$
$$x_1, x_2 \geq 0$$

Then explicitly introducing the non-negativity requirements into the Lagrangean function yields

$$L = 3x_1^2 - 12x_1 + x_2^2 - 18x_2 + 2x_1x_2 + y_1(20 - 0.5x_1 - 2x_2) - \mu_1 x_1 - \mu_2 x_2$$

The KT minimum conditions are, therefore, as follows:

$$\frac{\partial L}{\partial x_1} = 6x_1 - 12 + 2x_2 - 0.5y_1 - \mu_1 = 0$$

$$\frac{\partial L}{\partial x_2} = 2x_2 - 18 + 2x_1 - 2y_1 - \mu_2 = 0$$

$$\frac{\partial L}{\partial \mu_1} = -x_1 \leq 0, \quad \mu_1 \geq 0, \quad \mu_1 \frac{\partial L}{\partial \mu_1} = 0$$

$$\frac{\partial L}{\partial \mu_2} = -x_2 \leq 0, \quad \mu_2 \geq 0, \quad \mu_2 \frac{\partial L}{\partial \mu_2} = 0$$

$$\frac{\partial L}{\partial y_1} = 20 - 0.5x_1 - 2x_2 \leq 0, \quad y_1 \geq 0, \quad y_1 \frac{\partial L}{\partial y_1} = 0$$

We now formulate the following problem which takes into account the above KT minimum conditions.

$$\text{Minimise } R_1 + R_2 + R_3$$
$$\text{s.t. } 6x_1 + 2x_1 - \mu_1 + R_1 - 0.5y_1 = 12$$
$$2x_1 + 2x_2 - \mu_2 + R_2 - 2y_1 = 18$$
$$0.5x_1 + 2x_2 + R_3 - S_1 = 20$$
$$x_j \geq 0, \quad \mu_j \geq 0, \quad \mu_j x_j = 0, \quad j = 1, 2$$
$$y_1 \geq 0, \quad S_1 \geq 0, \quad y_1 S_1 = 0$$

An initial basic feasible solution for our problem is one that contains the three artificial variables. We then have the following tableau.

	x_1	x_2	μ_1	μ_2	R_1	R_2	R_3	S_1	y_1	solution
$z_j - c_j$	0	0	0	0	-1	-1	-1	0	0	0
R_1	6	2	-1	0	1	0	0	0	$-1/2$	12
R_2	2	2	0	-1	0	1	0	0	-2	18
R_3	1/2	2	0	0	0	0	1	-1	0	20

The row operations we perform are as follows. We must adjust the first tableau by expressing the $z_j - c_j$ row in terms of the non-basic variables. To do this we add the R_1, R_2 and R_3 rows to the $z_j - c_j$ row.

	x_1	x_2	μ_1	μ_2	R_1	R_2	R_3	S_1	y_1	solution
$z_j - c_j$	17/2	6	−1	−1	0	0	0	−1	−5/2	50
R_1	6	2	−1	0	1	0	0	0	−1/2	12
R_2	2	2	0	−1	0	1	0	0	−2	18
R_3	1/2	2	0	0	0	0	1	−1	0	20

We are now in a position to apply the simplex method for a minimisation problem. We wish to enter the non-basic variable with the largest positive value subject to the KT conditions continuing to hold. The non-basic variable with the largest positive value is x_1, and given that μ_1 is a non-basic variable, we may introduce this variable into the basis. For the new basis to remain feasible, we eliminate R_1. The row operations we carry out to derive the third tableau are:

1. multiply the R_1 row by *1/6*;
2. multiply the R_1 row by −1/3 and add to the R_2 row;
3. multiply the R_1 row by −1/12 and add to the R_3 row;
4. multiply the R_1 row by −17/12 and add to the $z_j - c_j$ row.

	x_1	x_2	μ_1	μ_2	R_1	R_2	R_3	S_1	y_1	solution
$z_j - c_j$	0	19/6	5/12	−1	−17/12	0	0	−1	−43/24	33
x_1	1	1/3	−1/6	0	1/6	0	0	0	−1/12	2
R_2	0	4/3	1/3	−1	−1/3	1	0	0	−11/6	14
R_3	0	11/6	1/12	0	−1/12	0	1	−1	1/24	19

Applying the optimality criterion, we now introduce x_2; this is permissible since μ_2 is not a basic variable. To retain feasibility x_1 must leave the basis. The row operations we perform in order to obtain the next tableau are:

1. multiply the x_1 row by *3*;
2. multiply the x_1 row by −4 and add to the R_2 row;
3. multiply the x_1 row by −11/2 and add to the R_3 row;
4. multiply the x_1 row by −19/2 and add to the $z_j - c_j$ row.

	x_1	x_2	μ_1	μ_2	R_1	R_2	R_3	S_1	y_1	solution
$z_j - c_j$	−19/2	0	2	−1	3	0	0	−1	−1	14
x_2	3	1	−1/2	0	1/2	0	0	0	−1/4	6
R_2	−4	0	1	−1	−1	1	0	0	−3/2	6
R_3	−11/2	0	1	0	−1	0	1	−1	1/2	8

At the next iteration, we introduce μ_1 in place of R_2; this is permissible since x_1 is not a basic variable. The row operations we now perform in order to obtain the new tableau are:

1. multiply the R_2 row by 1/2 and add to the x_2 row;
2. multiply the R_2 row by −1 and add to the R_3 row;
3. multiply the R_2 row by −1 and add to the $z_j - c_j$ row.

	x_1	x_2	μ_1	μ_2	R_1	R_2	R_3	S_1	y_1	solution
$z_j - c_j$	−3/2	0	0	1	−1	−2	0	−1	2	2
x_2	1	1	0	−1/2	0	1/2	0	0	−1	9
μ_1	−4	0	1	−1	−1	1	0	0	−3/2	6
R_3	−3/2	0	0	1	0	−1	1	−1	2	2

We now introduce y_1; this is permissible since S_1 is not a basic variable, and y_1 is introduced in place of R_3. The row operations are as follows:

1. multiply the R_3 row by $1/2$;
2. multiply the R_3 row by $1/2$ and add to the x_2 row;
3. multiply the R_3 row by $3/4$ and add to the μ_1 row;
4. multiply the R_3 by -1 and add to the $z_j - c_j$ row.

	x_1	x_2	μ_1	μ_2	R_1	R_2	R_3	S_1	y_1	solution
$z_j - c_j$	0	0	0	0	-1	-1	-1	0	0	0
x_2	1/4	1	0	0	0	0	1/2	$-1/2$	0	10
μ_1	$-23/4$	0	1	$-1/4$	-1	1/4	3/4	$-3/4$	0	15/2
y_3	$-3/4$	0	0	1/2	0	$-1/2$	1/2	$-1/2$	1	1

We have now eliminated the three artificial variables. The KT minimum conditions are met at the point: $x_2 = 10$, $\mu_1 = 15/2$ and $y_1 = 1$. To obtain the value of the objective function, we just substitute the above value of x_2 into the objective function. We find its value at this point is -80.

The above procedure can be applied to solve non-linear programming problems whenever the objective function is a quadratic function of the choice variables and the constraints are a set of linear inequalities. In comparison with more heuristic approaches we have outlined earlier, it may have seemed that we have used a sledgehammer to crack a nut. Certainly, the amount of effort required to obtain the solution was possibly excessive, and this for numerical problems in which there was only one constraint in addition to the non-negativity requirements. However, where the approach would clearly come into its own would be as the basis for a computing algorithm to solve such problems.

17.5 SUMMARY

The key features of this chapter are the Kuhn–Tucker maximum and minimum conditions. Provided the objective function is concave and differentiable for non-negative values of the choice variables, and the constraints are similarly convex and differentiable, then the solution to our non-linear programming problem will be given by a point which satisfies the Kuhn–Tucker maximum conditions. The form which these conditions take are as follows:

$$\frac{\partial L}{\partial x_j} = f_j - \sum_{i=1}^{i=m} y_i g_j^i \leq 0, \quad x_j \geq 0, \quad x_j \frac{\partial L}{\partial x_j} = 0$$

$$\frac{\partial L}{\partial y_i} = c_i - g^i(x_1, x_2, \ldots, x_n) \geq 0, \quad y_i \geq 0, \quad y_i \frac{\partial L}{\partial y_i} = 0$$

If our problem is a minimisation one, then given that the objective function is differentiable and convex for non-negative values of the choice variables, and the constraints differentiable and concave for non-negative values of the choice variables, then the solution to our non-linear programming problem will be given by a point which satisfies the Kuhn–Tucker minimum conditions. The form which these conditions take are as follows:

$$\frac{\partial L}{\partial x_j} = f_j - \sum_{i=1}^{i=m} y_i g_j^i \geq 0, \quad x_j \geq 0, \quad x_j \frac{\partial L}{\partial x_j} = 0$$

$$\frac{\partial L}{\partial y_i} = c_i - g^i(x_1, x_2, \ldots, x_n) \leq 0, \quad y_i \geq 0, \quad y_i \frac{\partial L}{\partial y_i} = 0$$

A differentiable function is strictly concave if all the eigenvalues of the matrix of second-order partial derivatives are negative, and is concave if all the above eigenvalues are non-positive. Alternatively, strict concavity is guaranteed if the principal minors of the matrix of second-order partial derivatives alternate in sign, starting negative; whereas concavity requires that the weak inequality of the minors should reverse, starting non-positive.

Regarding convexity, a differentiable function is strictly convex if all the eigenvalues of the matrix of second-order partial derivatives are positive, and is convex if all the above eigenvalues are non-negative. Alternatively, strict convexity is guaranteed if the principal minors of the matrix of second-order partial derivatives are all positive, whereas convexity requires that they all be non-negative.

17.6 EXERCISES

17.1 (a) Solve the following problems:

(i) *Maximise* $36x_1 - 1.5x_1^2 + 30x_2 - x_2^2$

s.t. $2x_1 + x_2 \leq 28$

$2x_1 + 3x_2 \leq 60$

$x_1, x_2 \geq 0$

(ii) *Maximise* $200x_1 + 150x_2 - 2x_1^2 - 3x_2^2 - 2x_1 x_2$

s.t. $4x_1 + 3x_2 \leq 26$

$2x_1 + 6x_2 \leq 25$

$x_1, x_2 \geq 0$

(iii) *Minimise* $2x_1^2 - 32x_1 + 1.5x_2^2 - 36x_2$

s.t. $2x_1 + 3x_2 \geq 50$

$2x_1 + x_2 \geq 32$

$x_1, x_2 \geq 0$

(iv) *Minimise* $2x_1^2 - 30x_1 + 8x_2^2 - 16x_2 + 5x_1 x_2$

s.t. $2x_1 + 4x_2 \geq 24$

$4x_1 + 3x_2 \geq 36$

$x_1, x_2 \geq 0$

(b) Find the solution to the following two problems:

(i) *Minimise* $x_1^2 + 2x_2^2$

s.t. $x_1 x_2 \geq 36$

$x_1, x_2 \geq 0$

(ii) *Minimise* $x_1^2 - 2x_1x_2 + 2x_2^2$

$$\text{s.t. } x_1x_2 \geq 24$$
$$x_1 + x_2 \geq 10$$
$$x_1, x_2 \geq 0$$

(c) Consider the following problem:

$$\text{Maximise } 2x_1^2 + x_2^2$$
$$\text{s.t. } x_1^{1/2} + x_2 \leq 8$$
$$x_1, x_2 \geq 0$$

(i) Show that the Kuhn–Tucker maximum conditions are met at $x_1 = 1.42525$, $x_2 = 6.80616$.
(ii) Explain why the above point is not the optimal solution.
(iii) Find the optimal solution and check that the KT conditions are indeed also met here.

(d) A firm can produce two goods, and has available limited supplies of two inputs, steel and electricity. In order to produce one unit of the first good it requires 5 tonnes of steel and 8 MW of electricity; to produce a unit of the second good 7 tonnes of steel and 3 MW of electricity are required. The firm has available 87 tonnes of steel and 100 MW of electricity. Its profits function is given by:

$$\Pi = 40x_1 - x_1^2 + 56x_2 - 2x_2^2 - 2x_1x_2$$

where x_1 and x_2 are the quantities produced of the two goods.
(i) Write out the Lagrangean function and derive the Kuhn–Tucker conditions for a maximum.
(ii) Obtain the profit-maximising output bundle and the values of the Lagrangean multipliers.
(iii) Have you identified a global maximum of profits subject to the constraints?

(e) Given the problem:

$$\text{Maximise } ax_1 - x_1^2 + cx_2 - x_2^2$$
$$\text{s.t. } x_1 + 2x_2 \leq 20$$
$$3x_1 + 2x_2 \leq 27$$
$$x_1, x_2 \geq 0$$

where a and c are both positive parameters.
(i) Write out the Kuhn–Tucker conditions for a maximum.
(ii) Discuss the conditions which must be imposed upon the parameters, a and c, for a global maximum of the function subject to the above constraints to occur at:

(1) $x_1 = 0, \quad x_2 = 10$
(2) $x_1 = 9, \quad x_2 = 0$

(f) A firm has a limited amount of two inputs which are required for the manufacture of the two goods it produces. In order to produce a unit of the first good, the firm must employ two units of the first input and three units of the second input, whereas unit production of the second good requires five units of the first input and one unit of the second input. The firm has available 250 units of the first input and 300 units of the second input. The firm's profits function is given by:

$$\Pi = 50x_1 - 2x_1^2 - x_1x_2 + 120x_2 - x_2^2$$

(i) Derive the firm's profit-maximising output bundle.
(ii) What would happen to the optimal solution if there were a marginal increase in the availability of the first input?
(iii) What would happen to the optimal solution if the coefficient on x_1 in the profits function were increased from 50 to 70?

(g) An individual has undertaken a risky investment which has three possible outcomes:

- a loss of *19* with probability p;
- a profit of *44* with probability q; and
- to break even with probability $1 - p - q$.

Depending on which outcome occurs, the investor's total income is *81, 144* or *100* respectively. The following constraints are placed on the values that may be taken by the probabilities:
$$p \geq 0, \quad q \geq 0, \quad 1 - p - q \geq 0, \quad pq \geq c, \quad c \geq 0$$

(i) Plot the constraints on a diagram in p, q space. For what values of c is the feasible region non-empty?

(ii) Show that the constraints define a convex set of pairs of probabilities.

Assume the individual's utility is a function of their income and is given by:
$$U(y) = y^{0.5}$$

where y is income.

(iii) Write out the Kuhn–Tucker conditions for a maximum of expected utility with respect to p and q which must still satisfy the above constraints.

(iv) Show how p and q will vary as c varies.

17.2 (a) (i) A profit-maximising monopolist sells its product in two markets. The inverse demand functions are given respectively by:
$$p_1 = 120 - 2x_1$$
$$p_2 = 150 - 0.5x_2$$

where p_i is price, and x_i is quantity demanded, in market i. The monopolist's total cost function (TC) is given by:
$$TC = x^2$$

where x is total output. Derive the profit-maximising levels of sales in the two markets.

(ii) Now assume the demand falls in the first market such that the inverse demand function in that market is now given by:
$$p_1 = 90 - 2x_1$$

Obtain the new profit-maximising quantities sold in each of the two markets.

(iii) Now assume that the inverse demand functions are as follows:
$$p_1 = 120 - x_1$$
$$p_2 = 150 - x_2$$

and that the total cost function is given by
$$TC = 3125 + 30x$$

If the firm has been nationalised, and is required to maximise net social benefits subject to its profits being non-negative:

(1) show that the firm will set x_1 equal to *75*, and x_2 equal to *100*;

(2) obtain the value of the Lagrangean multiplier and provide an interpretation of it.

(b) A public enterprise produces two products, whose inverse demand functions are given respectively by:
$$p_1 = 100 - x_1$$
$$p_2 = 120 - x_2$$

The total cost schedules for the two functions are given respectively by:
$$TC_1 = 250 + 20x_1$$
$$TC_2 = 500 + 40x_2$$

(i) If the public enterprise is to maximise net social benefits, what prices should it set for the two products? How large will be the enterprise's profits?

(ii) Now assume that the public enterprise must break even. What prices will it set in order to maximise net social benefits subject to the break-even constraint?

(iii) Show that the ratio of price to marginal cost is lower for the good with the more elastic demand.

(c) The inverse demand functions for a good in the peak and off-peak periods are given respectively by:
$$p_1 = 100 - x_1$$
$$p_2 = 60 - x_2$$

Unit operating costs are the same in the two periods, are constant and equal to *20*. Unit capacity costs are constant and equal to *30*; a unit of capacity can produce a unit of output per half-day. Installed capacity is sufficient to produce *60* units per period.

(i) What prices should be charged in the peak and off-peak periods in order for net social benefits to be maximised?

(ii) What difference would it make if the off-peak inverse demand curve now became:

$$\text{(i) } p_2 = 18 - 0.1x_2$$
$$\text{(ii) } p_2 = 80 - 0.5x_2$$

(iii) Assuming that the inverse demand functions are those initially given, what is the long-run equilibrium level of installed capacity?

(d) An airport has sufficient runway capacity to enable it to handle *300* aircraft movements in period one (between *06:30* hrs and *22:30* hrs), and *150* aircraft movements in period two (between *22:30* hrs and *06:30* hrs). Unit operating costs of the airport authority are £*250* per aircraft movement in period one, and £*300* per aircraft movement in period two. The inverse demand functions of the airlines for aircraft movements are given respectively by:

$$p_1 = 1000 - 0.4x_1$$
$$p_2 = 800 - 2.5x_2$$

where p_i is the price in period i, and x_i is the number of aircraft movements in period i. The airport authority is regulated, and is required to maximise net social benefits.

(i) What prices will it set for aircraft movements in the two periods? What interpretation can be given to the Lagrangean multipliers of this problem, and what values do they take in the welfare-maximising solution?

(ii) What additional information would you require in order to be able to advise on whether runway capacity should be expanded?

(iii) If residents in the vicinity of the airport are adversely affected by noise where the external costs, EC, of this noise nuisance are given by:

$$EC(x_1) = 0.5x_1^2$$
$$EC(x_2) = 1.25x_2^2$$

derive the welfare-maximising prices for period one and period two aircraft movements.

(e) A nationalised industry produces a good which can either be sold in the current period, or stored and then sold in the next period. Demand alternates between low and high in successive time periods. In period one demand is low and in period two demand is high. Actual consumption is x_1 and x_2 respectively, and the actual amount stored is s. Unit costs of producing and storing the good are given respectively by c and d. Available productive capacity is x_c per period; a period is of *12* hours' duration. Similarly, available storage capacity is x_s. Total capital cost on a daily basis is ex_c for production and fx_s for storage.

(i) Write out the Kuhn–Tucker conditions for the maximisation of net social benefits.

(ii) What conditions must be satisfied for productive capacity and storage capacity to be at their optimal levels?

(iii) Under what circumstances would the industry not wish to store output?

17.3 (a) Use the quadratic programming algorithm to solve the following problems:

(i) *Minimise* $2x_1^2 - 32x_1 + 1.5x_2^2 - 36x_2$
s.t. $2x_1 + x_2 \geq 32$
$x_1, x_2 \geq 0$

(ii) *Maximise* $36x_1 - 1.5x_1^2 + 30x_2 - x_2^2$
s.t. $2x_1 + x_2 \leq 28$
$x_1 + 2x_2 \leq 35$
$x_1, x_2 \geq 0$

(iii) *Maximise* $16x_1 - x_1^2 + 24x_2 - x_2^2$
s.t. $2x_1 + 4x_2 \leq 34$
$x_1, x_2 \geq 0$

CHAPTER
EIGHTEEN
FIRST-ORDER DIFFERENTIAL EQUATIONS

18.1 INTRODUCTION

In this chapter we apply the techniques of calculus to solve for the time-path of economic variables. Time in this and the next chapter is treated as a continuous variable so calculus techniques can be used. We may have information on the instantaneous rate of change through time of a variable such as income, consumption, ownership of a consumer durable, number of firms who have adopted an innovation, and we wish to solve such a differential equation in order to find the underlying function which describes the evolution through time of the variable itself. In Chapters 20 and 21, we shall look at dynamic problems where time is treated as a discrete variable and shall show how the technique of difference equations can be employed to find the time-path of variables when time, instead of being a continuous variable, is now restricted to integer values only.

In Section 18.2 we start out by analysing the simplest case of a linear first-order differential equation. In such an equation the derivative with respect to time of the variable, y, whose time-path we are interested in obtaining is a simple linear function of the variable itself. We show that the solution to each differential equation can be decomposed into two parts: a part known as the complementary function and a part known as the particular integral. If there is absent from the differential equation a term which is independent of y, then the solution to the equation will just consist of the complementary function. In discussing the nature of the complementary function, we shall start with the most basic model and then move on to examine the general case. The nature of the particular integral we shall see depends upon whether the term in the differential equation which is independent of y is itself a constant or a function of time.

In Section 18.3 we look at the topic of non-linear first-order differential equations. We see that some non-linear equations can be quite easily solved by separating the equation into a part containing y and a part containing time. Other non-linear equations can be converted by means of a simple substitution into a linear form, and then the methods outlined in Section 18.2 can be used to find the time-path of the variable under investigation. Finally we look at the case where the variable enters the differential equation quadratically. We shall see that the logistic function, which has important applications in areas such as the diffusion of innovations and epidemiology, is a subset of this case. The chapter ends with a brief summary in Section 18.4.

18.2 THE SOLUTION TO SIMPLE FIRST-ORDER LINEAR DIFFERENTIAL EQUATIONS

The homogeneous case

Assume we are given the following information about the rate of change of an economy's output:

$$\frac{dy}{dt} = 0.1y$$

where y is output and t is time. Given the above, we wish to find the function which defines the time-path of output in this particular economy. How should we proceed? Multiplying the above equation through by dt and dividing by y, we obtain:

$$\frac{1}{y} dy = 0.1 dt$$

Now find the integral of the left-hand side with respect to y, and the integral of the right-hand side with respect to t:

$$\int \frac{1}{y} dy = \log_e y + c_1$$

$$\int 0.1 \, dt = 0.1t + c_2$$

where c_1 and c_2 are constants of integration.

Taking anti-logs of the two integrals and setting them equal to each other yields:

$$y(t) = Ae^{0.1t} \text{ where } A = e^{c_2 - c_1}$$

This is the general solution to our differential equation. If we are further informed that the value of the economy's output at time $t = 0$ was *100*, then we can find the value of the arbitrary constant A. In this case, we would simply have $A = 100$, and the time-path of output would be given by:

$$y(t) = 100e^{0.1t}$$

This is the particular solution to our differential equation.

What we have solved here is what is known as a differential equation. In particular, the equation whose solution we have found is a first-order, homogeneous, linear differential equation. It is described as being of the first-order, since the only derivative which appears in the equation is the first-order derivative of output with respect to time. It is homogeneous because it does not contain a constant term. It is a linear equation since the variable y appears in the equation in a linear form. Later in this chapter we shall consider first-order differential equations which are non-linear in y, and in the next chapter we shall consider differential equations of the second order (i.e. equations which contain as the highest-order derivative the second derivative of y with respect to time).

We shall write the linear, homogeneous, first-order equation in the form:

$$\frac{dy}{dt} + \alpha y = 0$$

and its solution is given by:

$$y(t) = Ay^{-\alpha t} = y(0)\,e^{-\alpha t}$$

If α is positive, then $y(t)$ will approach *0* as *t* approaches infinity. On the other hand, if α is negative, then $y(t)$ will increase or decrease without limit as *t* increases depending upon whether the initial value of y is positive or negative.

The non-homogeneous case

Now consider the non-homogeneous case:

$$\frac{dy}{dt} + \alpha y = \beta$$

where β is a constant. The solution to a first-order, non-homogeneous, linear differential equation has two components to it: (a) a complementary function, and (b) a particular integral. The complementary function is just the solution to the homogeneous case. Hence

$$y^c(t) = Ae^{-\alpha t}$$

Regarding the particular integral, we first try a solution of the form that y is a constant. If y is constant, then clearly the first derivative with respect to time must equal zero. Setting the derivative equal to zero, it follows that

$$y^p(t) = \frac{\beta}{\alpha} \quad \text{for } \alpha \neq 0$$

As long as α is not equal to zero, then the general solution in the non-homogeneous case is given by:

$$y(t) = y^c(t) + y^P(t) = Ae^{-\alpha t} + \frac{\beta}{\alpha}$$

We make A definite by using the initial condition on y. We must have:

$$y(0) = A + \frac{\beta}{\alpha}$$

from which it follows that

$$A = y(0) - \frac{\beta}{\alpha}$$

Hence the particular solution to the non-homogeneous case is given by:

$$y(t) = \left(y(0) - \frac{\beta}{\alpha}\right)e^{-\alpha t} + \frac{\beta}{\alpha} \quad \text{for } \alpha \neq 0$$

Note that $y(t)$ will converge on β/α provided that α is positive, otherwise $y(t)$ will increasingly diverge through time away from β/α.

The case where α is zero

We now turn to consider the case where α is equal to zero. In this case our differential equation is given by:

$$\frac{dy}{dt} = \beta$$

Hence

$$dy = \beta \, dt$$

and upon integrating both sides we have:

$$y(t) = \beta t + c$$

where c is the constant of integration. Making use of the initial condition, it is clear that:

$$c = y(0)$$

and hence the particular solution in this case is given by:

$$y(t) = y(0) + \beta t$$

The time-path of y is just a linear function of time in this case.

The general case

We now turn to deal with the most general case of a first-order linear differential equation. This occurs where α and β, instead of being parameters, are now themselves both functions of time. The differential equation now takes the form:

$$\frac{dy}{dt} + \alpha(t) y = \beta(t)$$

Before we seek to solve the above equation, we shall first consider some less general cases. First, let us deal with the case where $\beta(t) = 0$. Then

$$\frac{1}{y} dy = -\alpha(t) \, dt$$

Integrating both sides and then taking antilogs yields:

$$y(t) = A e^{\int -\alpha(t) \, dt}$$

Without knowing the form of the function $\alpha(t)$, we can go no further.

Example 18.1

$$\frac{dy}{dt} + 2ty = 0$$

Hence we have

$$\frac{1}{y} dy = -2t \, dt$$

Upon integrating we obtain

$$\log_e y + c_1 = -t^2 + c_2$$

and after taking antilogs, we have

$$y(t) = Ae^{-t^2}$$

We may check that we have obtained the correct answer by differentiating the solution with respect to time, and then substituting this derivative and the solution into the original differential equation.

$$\frac{dy}{dt} = -2tAe^{-t^2}$$

and

$$\frac{dy}{dt} + 2ty = -2tAe^{-t^2} + 2tAe^{-t^2} = 0$$

The second case we turn to is where $\alpha(t)$ is a non-zero constant, and $\beta(t)$ is a function whose derivatives take a finite number of different forms. We may for example consider cases where $\beta(t)$ is an nth degree polynomial function of time, for in such a case all higher-order derivatives after the nth one will be zero. The method we are about to outline, which is known as the method of undetermined coefficients, will not work if this condition is not met. To illustrate the procedure, we turn to a specific example.

Example 18.2

$$\frac{dy}{dt} + y = 5 + 5t + 2t^2$$

The complementary function is as in the simplest case we dealt with at the start of this chapter:

$$y^c(t) = Ae^{-t}$$

To find the particular integral, we note that $\beta(t)$ is a quadratic function of time, and hence the first and second derivatives are non-zero, and all higher-order derivatives are zero. For the particular integral we therefore try a solution of the form:

$$y^p(t) = B_0 + B_1 t + B_2 t^2$$

On differentiating, we have:

$$\frac{dy^p}{dt} = B_1 + 2B_2 t$$

$$\frac{d^2 y^p}{dt^2} = 2B_2$$

$$\frac{d^n y^p}{dt^n} = 0, \quad n > 2$$

Substituting for $y^p(t)$ and its first derivative in the differential equation yields:

$$B_1 + 2B_2 t + B_0 + B_1 t + B_2 t^2 = 5 + 5t + 2t^2$$

from which it follows that:
$$B_0 + B_1 = 5$$
$$(B_1 + 2B_2)t = 5t$$
$$B_2 t^2 = 2t^2$$

We may then solve recursively for the coefficients, the Bs.
$$B_2 = 2$$
$$B_1 = 5 - 2B_2 = 1$$
$$B_0 = 5 - B_1 = 4$$

The particular integral is, therefore, given by:
$$y^p(t) = 4 + t + 2t^2$$

and the general solution to our equation is given by:
$$y(t) = y^c(t) + y^p(t) = Ae^{-t} + 4 + t + 2t^2$$

If $y(0) = 6$, then $A = 2$, and the particular solution is given by:
$$y(t) = 2e^{-t} + 4 + t + 2t^2.$$

Again we may check that this is correct by differentiating, and substituting the derivative and the solution in the differential equation. The first derivative is:
$$\frac{dy}{dt} = -2e^{-t} + 1 + 4t$$

Hence we have
$$\frac{dy}{dt} + y = -2e^{-t} + 1 + 4t + 2e^{-t} + 4 + t + 2t^2$$
$$= 5 + 5t + 2t^2$$

Now consider what would have happened had $\beta(t)$ been given by $1/t$. We would have been unable to apply the method of undetermined coefficients since there does not exist a finite number of forms for the derivatives in this case. We have the following set of derivatives:
$$-t^{-2}, 2t^{-3}, -6t^{-4}, 24t^{-5}, -120t^{-6}, etc$$

The derivatives never become equal to zero, and they are all different from each other. However, had $\beta(t)$ been equal to, say, $\sin t$, though the derivatives never become equal to zero, they take one of four forms:
$$\cos t, -\sin t, -\cos t, \text{ and } \sin t$$

So the method of undetermined coefficients can be applied in such a case, and we would try a solution for the particular integral of the form:
$$y^p(t) = B_1 \sin t + B_2 \cos t$$

Finally, we turn to the general case of a linear, first-order differential equation, where both α and β are both functions of time. In this case the solution to the differential equation

$$\frac{dy}{dt} + \alpha(t)y = \beta(t)$$

is given by:

$$y(t) = e^{\int -\alpha(t)\,dt}\left(A + \int \beta(t) e^{\int \alpha(t)\,dt}\,dt\right)$$

The derivation of this result is complicated, and we will not derive it here. What we shall do is check that the result is indeed correct by using the standard procedure of first obtaining dy/dt by differentiating the above equation with respect to time, and then by substituting the derivative and the solution into the original differential equation.

We first let

$$e^{\int -\alpha(t)\,dt} = e^{-\Phi(t)}$$

We may then write the solution as

$$y(t) = e^{-\Phi(t)}\left(A + \int \beta(t) e^{\Phi(t)}\,dt\right)$$

and now differentiating with respect to time, we obtain:

$$\frac{dy}{dt} = -\alpha(t) e^{-\Phi(t)}\left(A + \int \beta(t) e^{\Phi(t)}\,dt\right) + e^{-\Phi(t)}\beta(t) e^{\Phi(t)}$$

Hence

$$\frac{dy}{dt} + \alpha(t)y = -\alpha(t) e^{-\Phi(t)}\left(A + \int \beta(t) e^{\Phi(t)}\,dt\right)$$

$$+ \beta(t) + \alpha(t)A e^{-\Phi(t)} + \alpha(t) e^{-\Phi(t)} \int \beta(t) e^{\Phi(t)}\,dt$$

$$= \beta(t)$$

We will now work through some examples to illustrate the procedure.

Example 18.3

$$\frac{dy}{dt} - 3y = -e^t, \quad y(0) = 2.5$$

In this case, $\alpha(t) = -3$, and $\beta(t) = -e^t$. So we have

$$e^{\int \alpha(t)\,dt} = e^{\int -3\,dt} = e^{-3t}$$

$$\int \beta(t) e^{\int \alpha(t)\,dt}\,dt = \int -e^t e^{-3t}\,dt = \int -e^{-2t}\,dt$$

$$= 0.5 e^{-2t}$$

Hence the general solution takes the form:
$$y(t) = e^{3t}(A + 0.5e^{-2t})$$

To make definite the arbitrary constant, we have:
$$2.5 = A + 0.5$$
$$A = 2$$

The particular solution, therefore, is given by:
$$y(t) = 2e^{3t} + 0.5e^{t}.$$

The reader should check that the answer is indeed correct.

Example 18.4
$$\frac{dy}{dt} + 2ty = t, \quad y(0) = 1.5$$

Then $\alpha(t) = 2t$ and $\beta(t) = t$. Hence
$$\int \alpha(t)\,dt = \int 2t\,dt = t^2$$
$$\int \beta(t)\,e^{\int \alpha(t)\,dt}\,dt = \int t e^{t^2}\,dt$$

To find the second integral, let
$$z = t^2$$

Differentiating z with respect to t yields:
$$dz = 2t\,dt, \text{ and } dt = \frac{1}{2t}\,dz$$

On substituting it is clear that
$$\int t^2 e^{t^2}\,dt = \int t e^z \frac{1}{2t}\,dz$$
$$= \int 0.5 e^z\,dz = 0.5 e^z$$
$$= 0.5 e^{t^2}$$

Hence we have:
$$y(t) = e^{-t^2}(A + 0.5e^{t^2})$$

Given $y(0) = 1.5$, we have
$$1.5 = A + 0.5$$
$$A = 1$$

So the particular solution is:

$$y(t) = e^{-t^2}(1 + 0.5e^{t^2}) = e^{-t^2} + 0.5$$

Again the standard approach can be employed to check that the solution is correct.

Finally we look at an example that requires us to use integration by parts to arrive at the solution to the differential equation.

Example 18.5

$$\frac{dy}{dt} + t^{-1}y = e^{-0.1t}$$

Here we have:

$$\alpha(t) = t^{-1}, \text{ and } \int \alpha(t)\, dt = \int t^{-1}\, dt = \log_e t$$

$$\int \beta(t) e^{\int \alpha(t)\, dt}\, dt = \int e^{-0.1t} e^{\log_e t}\, dt = \int t e^{-0.1t}\, dt$$

To evaluate the second integral, we must employ integration by parts. Let

$$v = t \text{ and } du = e^{-0.1t}\, dt$$
$$\text{Hence } dv = dt \text{ and } u = -10e^{-0.1t}$$

The formula for integration by parts is

$$\int v\, du = uv - \int u\, dv$$

Substituting into the formula for integration by parts, we obtain:

$$\int t e^{-0.1t}\, dt = -10te^{-0.1t} + \int 10e^{-0.1t}\, dt$$
$$= -10te^{-0.1t} - 100e^{-0.1t}$$

Hence the solution is

$$y(t) = \frac{1}{t}(A - 10te^{-0.1t} - 100e^{-0.1t})$$

18.3 FIRST-ORDER NON-LINEAR DIFFERENTIAL EQUATIONS

In this section, we look at how to solve some simple first-order non-linear differential equations, these being equations in which y does not simply enter in the form $\alpha(t)y$. We may have y raised to some power n entering the equation, or the product of $y\, dy/dt$ being included. The introduction of either of these two possibilities introduces non-linearities into the equation. We first consider equations which are separable in y and time. Second, we deal with cases where, as a result of a suitable substitution, the original non-linear equation can be converted into a linear equation. Finally, as a development of the second set of problems, we consider cases where the first derivative of y with respect to time is a quadratic function of time. In these last problems, we shall be interested in the solution of differential equations where the variable is not allowed to take on negative values.

Separable variables

Consider the following first-order differential equation:

$$\frac{dy}{dt} = y^{0.5} t^3$$

This may be alternatively expressed as:

$$y^{-0.5} dy = t^3 dt$$

The term on dy does not depend upon t, and the term on dt does not depend upon y. This is an example of a non-linear equation which is separable in y and t. We shall now see that it is a straightforward matter to solve the equation. We integrate the function on the left-hand side with respect to y, and the function on the right-hand side with respect to t. Hence we have:

$$\int y^{-0.5} dy = 2y^{0.5} + c_1$$

$$\int t^3 dt = 0.25 t^4 + c_2$$

Equating the two integrals yields:

$$y^{0.5} = 0.125 t^4 + c \text{ where } c = \frac{c_1 - c_2}{2}$$

We may, therefore, write the general solution as:

$$y(t) = (0.125 t^4 + c)^2$$

If $y(0)$ is known, then we can make definite the arbitrary constant. Assume $y(0) = 9$, then the particular solution is

$$y(t) = (0.125 t^4 + 3)^2$$

Even where the term on dy contains t, or the term on dt contains y, it may still be possible to convert the differential equation into a separable form.

Example 18.6

As an example of this, consider the following equation:

$$e^{rt} dy = -t y^{-1} dt$$

Multiplying through by $y e^{-rt}$, we find that the equation is now indeed separable.

$$y \, dy = -t e^{-rt} dt$$

$$\int y \, dy = 0.5 y^2$$

Using integration by parts, we find that

$$\int -te^{-rt}\,dt = \frac{t}{r}e^{-rt} + \frac{1}{r^2}e^{-rt}$$

It, therefore, follows that the solution takes the following form:

$$0.5y^2 + c_1 = \frac{t}{r}e^{-rt} + \frac{1}{r^2}e^{-rt} + c_2$$

$$y(t) = \left(\frac{2te^{-rt}}{r} + \frac{2e^{-rt}}{r^2} + c\right)^{0.5}$$

Conversion of a non-linear differential equation into a linear differential equation

Assume we have the following differential equation:

$$\frac{dy}{dt} + \alpha(t)y = \beta(t)y^n$$

If we now multiply this equation through by y^{-n}, we obtain:

$$y^{-n}\frac{dy}{dt} + \alpha(t)y^{1-n} = \beta(t)$$

Now define a new variable:

$$x = y^{1-n}$$

$$\text{Therefore } \frac{dx}{dt} = (1-n)y^{-n}\frac{dy}{dt}$$

$$\text{Hence we have on substituting } \frac{1}{1-n}\frac{dx}{dt} + \alpha(t)x = \beta(t)$$

$$\text{Multiplying by } (1-n) \text{ yields } \frac{dx}{dt} + (1-n)\alpha(t) = (1-n)\beta(t)$$

Hence we have converted our original non-linear equation in y into a linear equation in x, which in this chapter we can now solve using the techniques discussed. Having found the equation defining the time-path of x, we can then find the equation that defines the time-path of y, given that $y = x^{1/(1-n)}$.

Example 18.7

$$\frac{dy}{dt} + 4y = y^2, \quad y(0) = 2$$

Multiply by y^{-2} to obtain:

$$y^{-2}\frac{dy}{dt} + 4y^{-1} = 1$$

Let $x = y^{-1}$; we therefore have on differentiating with respect to time:

$$\frac{dx}{dt} = -y^{-2}\frac{dy}{dt}$$

Substituting into the original differential equation, and multiplying by -1 yields:

$$\frac{dx}{dt} - 4x = -1$$

This is a simple linear differential equation, whose solution is easily obtained:

$$x(t) = Ae^{4t} + 0.25$$

Given that y is just the reciprocal of x, we can quickly obtain the time-path of y:

$$y(t) = \frac{1}{Ae^{4t} + 0.25}$$

Given the initial condition that $y(0) = 2$, then the arbitrary constant $A = 0.25$. The particular solution is therefore given by:

$$y(t) = \frac{1}{0.25e^{4t} + 0.25}$$

The logistic and other functions

Consider the following first-order non-linear differential equation in y where y is a non-negative variable:

$$\frac{dy}{dt} = ay^2 + by + c \text{ for } y > 0$$

$$\frac{dy}{dt} = 0 \text{ for } y = 0$$

Let us further assume that the quadratic on the right-hand side of the above differential equation has two distinct real roots. Let these two roots be A and B respectively. Hence we have:

$$ay^2 + by + c = a(A - y)(B - y)$$

and we may write the differential equation as follows:

$$\frac{1}{(y - A)(y - B)} dy = a\, dt$$

Let

$$\frac{1}{(y - A)(y - B)} = \frac{\alpha}{y - A} + \frac{\beta}{y - B}$$

We now wish to find the values of α and β which satisfy the above equation. Obviously, we must have:

$$\alpha(y - B) + \beta(y - A) = 1$$

and this must be true for all values of y. Setting $y = 0$, and then equal to 1, we obtain two equations to solve for α and β:

$$-B\alpha - A\beta = 1$$

$$(1 - B)\alpha + (1 - A)\beta = 1$$

Using Cramer's rule, or some other method, we have:

$$\alpha = \frac{1}{A-B}, \quad \beta = \frac{-1}{A-B}$$

Hence, we may write:

$$\frac{1}{(y-A)(y-B)} = \frac{1}{A-B}\left[\frac{1}{(y-A)} - \frac{1}{(y-B)}\right]$$

and our differential equation becomes:

$$\left[\frac{1}{y-A} - \frac{1}{y-B}\right]dy = a(A-B)\,dt$$

The integral of the function on the right-hand side is straightforward. But what about the integral of the function on the left-hand side. Let us consider a number of possibilities. First of all, assume that $y > A$, $y > B$. We have on integrating both sides:

$$\log_e(y-A) - \log_e(y-B) = a(A-B)t + c$$

Taking antilogs, we obtain:

$$\frac{y-A}{y-B} = -ke^{a(A-B)t} \text{ where } k = -e^c$$

Cross-multiplying and simplifying, we obtain:

$$y(t) = \frac{A + kBe^{a(A-B)t}}{1 + ke^{a(A-B)t}}$$

$$= B + \frac{A-B}{1 + ke^{a(A-B)t}}$$

If we assume that $a < 0$ and $B > A$, then $y(t)$ will converge on B provided that it has not been driven to zero in finite time.

By employing the same procedure, it can also be shown that the solution to the differential equation is the same as above for both $B > y > A$, and for $B > A > y$.

Example 18.8

$$\frac{dy}{dt} = -y^2 + 5y - 6, \text{ for } y > 0$$

$$otherwise \quad \frac{dy}{dt} = 0$$

Hence

$$a(y-A)(y-B) = -1(y-2)(y-3)$$

Given that $a = -1$, $A = 2$, $B = 3$, the solution is given by:

$$y(t) = 3 - \frac{1}{1 + ke^t}$$

To make k definite we need an initial condition. Let $y(0) = 2$, then

$$2 = 3 - \frac{1}{1+k}$$

hence $k = 0$ and $y(t) = 2$

Now assume that $y(0) = 4$, then

$$4 = 3 - \frac{1}{1+k}, \text{ hence } k = -2$$

and $y(t) = 3 + \dfrac{1}{2e^t - 1}$

Finally let $y(0) = 1$, then

$$1 = 3 - \frac{1}{1+k}, \text{ hence } k = -0.5$$

and $y(t) = 3 + \dfrac{1}{0.5e^t - 1}$

Note, however, in this last case that y is driven to zero at $t = 0.28768$, and y will therefore continue to be zero for all subsequent values of t.

We now consider two other cases: (a) where the roots of the quadratic are repeated and positive; (b) where one of the roots of the quadratic is zero and the other is positive.

In case (a), the differential equation takes the following form:

$$\frac{dy}{dt} = a(y - A)^2$$

$$\text{Hence } \int \frac{1}{(y - A)^2} \, dy = \int a \, dt$$

On integrating both sides we obtain:

$$-\frac{1}{y - A} = at + k$$

which, on re-arrangement, yields

$$y(t) = A - \frac{1}{at + k}$$

What will happen to y through time depends crucially upon whether the initial value of y is less than or greater than A, and whether the parameter a is positive or negative. The reader should check that convergence on A will occur if $y(0)$ is less than A and a is positive, or if $y(0)$ is greater than A and a is negative. Otherwise, y will either fall to zero, or increase without limit. If a is positive, then we have the situation depicted in Fig. 18.1(a), whereas if a is negative we have the situation depicted in Fig. 18.1(b). In Fig. 18.1(a) it is clear that if y is greater than A, then y will increase through time without limit, whereas if y is less than A, we will converge on A. On the other hand, Fig. 18.1(b)

FIRST-ORDER DIFFERENTIAL EQUATIONS 347

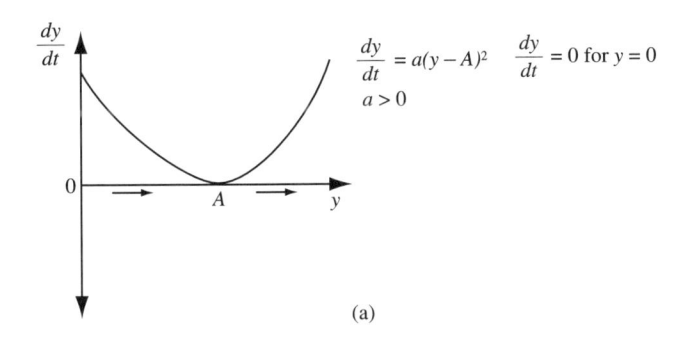

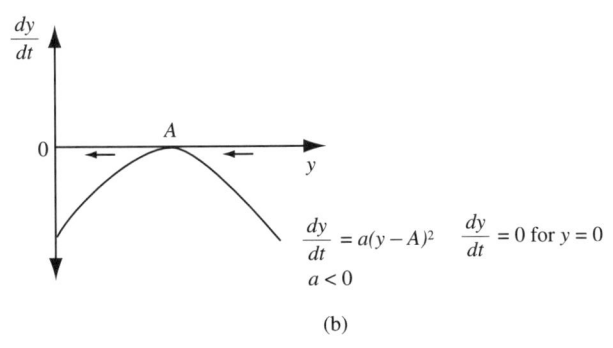

Figure 18.1 The importance of the initial condition. (a) Given that $a > 0$, then dy/dt is positive other than when $y = A$. If the initial value of y is less than A then convergence on A will occur; otherwise y will increase without limit. (b) Given that $a < 0$, then dy/dt is negative other than when $y = A$. If the initial value of y is less than A, then y will be driven to zero. Convergence on A will occur if the initial value of y is greater than A.

reveals that if y is less than A, then y will be driven to zero in finite time, but we will converge on A if y is greater than A.

Example 18.9

$$\frac{dy}{dt} = y^2 - 4y + 4 = (y-2)^2, \quad y(0) = 1$$

Given that $A = 2$, the general solution is given by:

$$y(t) = 2 - \frac{1}{t+k}$$

To find the particular solution, given that $y(0) = 1$, we must have:

$$1 = 2 - \frac{1}{k}, \text{ hence } k = 1$$

and $y(t) = 2 - \dfrac{1}{t+1}$

We now turn to case (b), where one of the roots is zero and the other is positive. Let $A = 0$, and $B > 0$; we shall also be assuming in this case that a is negative. We may therefore write the solution to the differential equation in this case as follows:

$$y(t) = \frac{B}{1 + ke^{aBt}}$$

Given the assumptions that we have made about a and B, $y(t)$ will converge through time on the value B. The above function is known as the logistic function. What other properties does it possess? By differentiating the function twice with respect to time, we can show that the function is increasing in t, but that it possesses a non-stationary inflexion point.

$$\frac{dy}{dt} = \frac{-kaB^2 e^{aBt}}{D^2} \quad \text{where } D = 1 + ke^{aBt} > 0$$

$$\frac{d^2y}{dt^2} = \frac{-ka^2 B^3 e^{aBt} D^2 + 2DkaBe^{aBt} kaB^2 e^{aBt}}{D^4}$$

Since $a < 0$, then the first derivative is always positive. Regarding the second derivative, it will be equal to zero and, therefore, we shall have a non-stationary inflexion point when

$$ka^2 B^3 e^{aBt} D^2 = 2Dk^2 a^2 B^3 e^{2aBt}$$

Simplifying, we obtain

$$D = 2ke^{aBt}$$

$$1 + ke^{aBt} = 2ke^{aBt}$$

$$ke^{aBt} = 1$$

Taking logs and solving for t, we find

$$t = \frac{1}{aB} \log_e \left(\frac{1}{k}\right)$$

Another important feature of the logistic function is that the point of inflexion occurs at the time when y has reached *50* per cent of its long-run value. We have

$$\frac{y\left(\frac{1}{aB} \log_e \frac{1}{k}\right)}{B} = \frac{B}{B(1 + ke^{\log_e(1/k)})}$$

$$= \frac{1}{1 + k\frac{1}{k}} = 0.5$$

Example 18.10

$$\frac{dy}{dt} = -0.2y^2 + 1.6y$$

We may write the differential equation in the following form:

$$\frac{dy}{dt} = -0.2y(y - 8)$$

It is clear that the roots of the quadratic in this case are $A = 0$, and $B = 8$, with $a = -0.2$. Hence the solution takes the following form:

$$y(t) = \frac{8}{1 + ke^{-1.6t}}$$

If $y(0) = 1$, then

$$1 = \frac{8}{1+k}, \quad \text{hence } k = 7$$

$$\text{and } y(t) = \frac{8}{1 + 7e^{-1.6t}}$$

The value of t at which this particular logistic function has its non-stationary inflexion point is given by

$$t = \frac{1}{-1.6} \log_e 0.125 = 1.3$$

Note that we could also have solved this equation by transforming the original non-linear equation into a linear one, as discussed earlier in this chapter.

18.4 SUMMARY

In this chapter we have worked our way through a number of simple first-order differential equations. We started out by looking at the simplest version of the linear case, and then moved on to look at more general formulations. In the second major section of the chapter, we looked at some first-order non-linear equations and demonstrated how the solution could be obtained for various particular forms of the equation. We found that non-linearities do not cause major problems if the equation is separable in the variable under consideration and time; if the equation can be converted into a linear form by means of a suitable substitution; or if the non-linearity takes the form of a quadratic.

Economic applications of these techniques include such areas as the neo-classical model of economic growth, diffusion of innovations and the growth of renewable resources. In Chapter 19 we move on to an analysis of second-order linear differential equations.

18.5 EXERCISES

18.1 (a) Find the particular solutions to the following first-order, homogeneous, linear differential equations:

(i) $\dfrac{dy}{dt} + y = 0, \quad y(0) = 10$

(ii) $\dfrac{dy}{dt} - 2y = 0, \quad y(0) = 2$

(iii) $\dfrac{dy}{dt} = 0, \quad y(0) = 8$

18.2 (a) Find the particular solutions to the following first-order, non-homogeneous, linear differential equations:

(i) $\dfrac{dy}{dt} + 2y = 10, \quad y(0) = 1$

(ii) $\dfrac{dy}{dt} - 0.5y = 4, \quad y(0) = 5$

(iii) $\dfrac{dy}{dt} + 0.05y = 50, \quad y(0) = 1000$

(iv) $\dfrac{dy}{dt} + 3y = 12, \quad y(0) = 5$

18.3 (a) Find the particular solutions to the following first-order differential equations:

(i) $\dfrac{dy}{dt} = 2, \quad y(0) = 25$

(ii) $\dfrac{dy}{dt} = -0.5, \quad y(0) = 12$

(iii) $\dfrac{dy}{dt} = 9, \quad y(0) = 25$

18.4 (a) Find the general solutions to the following differential equations:

(i) $\dfrac{dy}{dt} + ty = 0$

(ii) $\dfrac{dy}{dt} - 3t^2 y = 0$

(iii) $\dfrac{dy}{dt} + t^{-2} y = 0$

18.5 (a) Find the general solutions to the following differential equations:

(i) $\dfrac{dy}{dt} - y = 2 + 4t$

(ii) $\dfrac{dy}{dt} + 2y = \cos t$

(iii) $\dfrac{dy}{dt} - 0.5y = 10e^t$

18.6 (a) Find the general solution to the following first-order linear differential equations:

(i) $\dfrac{dy}{dt} + 2y = e^{0.5t}$

(ii) $\dfrac{dy}{dt} + t^2 y = 3t^2$

(iii) $\dfrac{dy}{dt} + t^{-1} y = 5 + 2t$

(b) A consumer has adopted a 40-year consumption plan which has the property that along it, consumption, c, will be growing at an exponential rate of 2.5 per cent. The consumer receives an earned income as a continuous flow at a rate of £10,000 per year, initial and end-period wealth are both zero, the rate of interest is 5 per cent and unearned income at time t is given by $0.05k(t)$, where $k(t)$ is wealth at time t. The evolution of the consumer's wealth is, therefore, described by the following differential equation:

$$\dfrac{dk}{dt} = 0.05k + 10{,}000 - c(0)e^{0.025t}$$

(i) Obtain the general solution to the differential equation.

(ii) Given that both initial and terminal wealth are both zero, find the particular solution, and the initial value of consumption, $c(0)$.

(iii) If the consumer decides to make a bequest of £50,000 at time $t = 40$, what difference will this make to the consumption plan?

18.7 (a) Use the method of separation of variables to find the particular solutions to the following first-order non-linear differential equations.

(i) $\dfrac{dy}{dt} = \dfrac{2t}{5y}, \quad y(0) = 5$

(ii) $\dfrac{dy}{dt} = -y^4 t^{1.5}, \quad y(0) = 1$

(iii) $\dfrac{dy}{dt} = y^{-1} \cos t, \quad y(0) = 1$

(iv) $\dfrac{dy}{dt} = yt, \quad y(0) = 42$

(b) The price of a motor car (p) is related to its age t by the differential equation:
$$\frac{dp}{dt} = \frac{-2p}{10+t}$$

(i) Solve this equation to obtain $p(t)$ given that the price of the car when new is £15,000. At what age will the price of the car be £7500?

18.8 (a) Convert the following first-order non-linear differential equations into a linear form and then solve:

(i) $\dfrac{dy}{dt} + y = 2y^3$

(ii) $\dfrac{dy}{dt} - 0.2y = 100y^{0.25}$

(iii) $\dfrac{dy}{dt} + 2y = -5y^2 t$

(b) Consider the following model of an economy:
$$y(t) = Ak(t)^\alpha, \quad A > 0, \quad 1 > \alpha > 0$$
$$\frac{dk}{dt} = sy - nk$$

where y is output per head, k capital per head, s the savings ratio, n the rate of growth of the labour force, A and α are constants.

(i) Given $A = 2$, $\alpha = 0.2$, $s = 0.2$, $n = 0.05$ and $k(0) = 1$, find the particular solution to the first-order differential equation in k. How long does it take for k to come within 90 per cent of its long-run equilibrium value?

(ii) Now assume that disembodied technical progress is occurring such that
$$y(t) = Ae^{\beta t} k(t)^\alpha$$

If $\beta = 0.04$ and the values of the other parameters are as given in (a) above, find the particular solution to the first-order differential equation in k. Comment on the nature of the long-run equilibrium.

18.9 (a) Officers of an agricultural extension service have been promoting the adoption of a new high-yielding variety of wheat in an Indian village consisting of 1000 peasant farmers. The rate of change in the number adopting the new variety is proportional to the total possible number of contacts between farmers who have already adopted the new variety and those who have not:
$$\frac{dy}{dt} = 0.001 y(t)[1000 - y(t)]$$

where $y(t)$ is the number of farmers who have adopted the new variety by time t.

(i) Assuming at time $t = 0$ the new variety has already been adopted by 100 farmers, find the time-path of $y(t)$ and comment on its properties.

(ii) How long does it take before (1) 50 per cent and (2) 95 per cent of the farmers are growing the new variety?

(b) In another part of the country, however, experience has suggested that the rate of change in the number adopting the new variety is given by the following differential equation:
$$\frac{dy}{dt} = 0.001 t^{-1} y(t)[1000 - y(t)] \text{ for } t \geq 1$$

(i) If at time $t = 1$, 100 farmers have adopted the new variety, find the particular solution to the above differential equation. How does the time-path differ from that in part (a)?

(ii) How long does it take before (1) 50 per cent and (2) 95 per cent of the farmers have adopted the new variety?

(c) No fishing has taken place for many years in a Scottish loch, and biologists have calculated that the rate of increase of its trout population is given by the following first-order differential equation:
$$\frac{dy}{dt} = f(t) = 0.1y\left[1 - \frac{y}{100}\right] \text{ for } y > 0$$
$$= 0 \text{ for } y = 0$$

where y is the trout population, measured in millions, and t is time.

(i) Find the particular solution to the above first-order differential equation given that $y(0) = 20$.

(ii) What is the long-run equilibrium trout population in the absence of fishing? When will the population reach half its long-run level?

(iii) Assume the fishery is first exploited at time $t = 0$, with a constant rate of harvesting, h, being permitted. Letting $h = 2.1$, solve the following first-order differential equation:

$$\frac{dy}{dt} = f(t) - h = 0.1y\left[1 - \frac{y}{100}\right] - 2.1 \text{ for } y > 0$$
$$= 0 \text{ for } y = 0$$

(iv) If $y(0) = 20$ and $h = 2.1$, show that the trout would be fished to extinction in finite time.

(v) If $y(0) = 40$ and $h = 2.1$, what would be the long-run equilibrium trout population?

CHAPTER NINETEEN

SECOND-ORDER LINEAR DIFFERENTIAL EQUATIONS

19.1 INTRODUCTION

In the last chapter, we discussed the subject of first-order differential equations, and demonstrated how to find the time-path of a variable given information on the first derivative of the variable with respect to time. We now move on to investigate how to solve equations which contain both the first and second derivatives with respect to time of the variable whose time-path we are interested in deriving. Whereas in the last chapter, we broadened the discussion to consider some simple non-linear first-order equations, we restrict our discussion of second-order differential equations to linear ones.

As with first-order differential equations, the solution to a second-order differential equation involves both finding a complementary function and a particular integral. In Section 19.2 we show that the solution to the complementary function requires us to find the roots of a quadratic equation. Three possibilities, therefore, arise: (1) the roots are real and distinct; (2) the root is repeated; and (3) the roots are a pair of complex conjugates. We consider each of these three cases in turn. Regarding the particular integral, we restrict the discussion in Section 19.2 to the simple case where the second-order linear differential equation contains a constant term. We develop the discussion of the particular integral further in Section 19.3 where we apply the method of undetermined coefficients, introduced in Chapter 18, to deal with some cases where the constant in the differential equation is replaced by a function of time. In Section 19.4 we touch upon higher-order linear differential equations, and comment on the conditions required for convergence to be guaranteed. The chapter ends with a summary.

19.2 HOW TO SOLVE SECOND-ORDER LINEAR DIFFERENTIAL EQUATIONS

In this chapter we consider how to solve equations of the form:

$$\frac{d^2y}{dt^2} + \alpha_1 \frac{dy}{dt} + \alpha_2 y = 0$$

This equation is linear in y; and given that it contains as its highest derivative the second derivative of y with respect to t, it is a second-order differential equation. Since the term on the right-hand side of the equation is zero, we have the homogeneous case. To proceed, we try a solution of the form:

$$y(t) = Ae^{rt}$$

If the solution takes this form, then it must be the case that the first and second derivatives are given by:

$$\frac{dY}{dt} = rAe^{rt}, \text{ and } \frac{d^2y}{dt^2} = r^2 Ae^{rt}$$

and substituting back into the original differential equation will then yield:

$$r^2 Ae^{rt} + \alpha_1 r Ae^{rt} + \alpha_2 Ae^{rt} = 0$$

Dividing the above equation through by Ae^{rt} on the assumption that A is not equal to zero, we obtain the following characteristic equation:

$$r^2 + \alpha_1 r + \alpha_2 = 0$$

This equation must be satisfied by r for our postulated solution to the differential equation to hold true. The roots of this quadratic equation are given by;

$$r_1, r_2 = \frac{-\alpha_1 \pm \sqrt{\alpha_1^2 - 4\alpha_2}}{2}$$

There are, therefore, three possibilities that we need to consider. The first case is where the roots of the quadratic equation are real and distinct. This requires that:

$$\alpha_1^2 > 4\alpha_2$$

We shall have a repeated real root when

$$\alpha_1^2 = 4\alpha_2$$

The third possibility arises when

$$\alpha_1 < 4\alpha_2$$

In this last case, we shall have a pair of complex conjugates. We turn to consider each of these three cases in turn.

Distinct real roots

To illustrate the method of solution, consider the following example:

Example 19.1

$$\frac{d^2y}{dt^2} - 5\frac{dy}{dt} + 6 = 0$$

The associated characteristic equation is:

$$r^2 - 5r + 6r = 0$$

This quadratic is easily factorised:

$$(r-2)(r-3) = 0$$
$$\text{Hence } r_1 = 2, \text{ and } r_2 = 3$$

We suggested a trial solution of the form: $y(t) = Ae^{rt}$, but we obviously have a situation above where the characteristic equation is satisfied by two values of r. How should we proceed? In order to find a particular solution to the differential equation, we will be provided with two initial conditions, one relating to the value of y and the other to the value of the first derivative with respect to time at $t = 0$. If we suppress one of the roots, then though the characteristic equation will obviously continue to be satisfied by the other root, it will not normally be the case that this solution will be compatible with the initial conditions. It would, therefore, be illegitimate to ignore one of the two roots; rather we must combine them in the following way:

$$y(t) = A_1 e^{r_1 t} + A_2 e^{r_2 t}$$

The rationale for this procedure is that in seeking to find the equation which defines the time-path of y we are effectively having to integrate twice. On each integration, a constant of integration results; hence the necessity for both combining the two roots in the specified way, and for being provided with two initial conditions. Only if we take a linear combination of the roots will the solution to our differential equation be compatible with these two initial conditions.

It is straightforward to show that the differential equation is indeed satisfied by our combined function. This follows from the obvious fact that

$$A_1 e^{r_1 t}(r_1^2 + \alpha_1 r_1 + \alpha_2) = 0$$
$$A_2 e^{r_2 t}(r_2^2 + \alpha_1 r_2 + \alpha_2) = 0$$

Assume we were given the following initial conditions for our example:

$$y(0) = 1 \text{ and } \frac{dy(0)}{dt} = 1$$

Then we must have

$$A_1 e^0 + A_2 e^0 = 1$$
$$2A_1 e^0 + 3A_2 e^0 = 1$$

from which it follows that $A_1 = 2$ and $A_2 = -1$. Hence the particular solution is given by:

$$y(t) = 2e^{2t} - e^{3t}$$

The non-homogeneous case

We now turn to deal with the simplest non-homogeneous case where we have a constant term, β, on the right-hand side of the differential equation. As with the first-order case, the solution to the non-homogeneous equation consists of the sum of the complementary function and the particular integral. We have addressed the solution to the complementary function above. For the particular integral, we first try a constant as a solution. For this to be the case, then both the first and second derivatives must be zero. If this is so, then

$$y^p(t) = \frac{\beta}{\alpha_2}$$

This will be the solution to the particular integral provided that α_2 is not equal to zero. If $\alpha_2 = 0$, then we must instead try a solution for the particular integral of the form:

$$y^P(t) = ct$$

It would then follow that

$$\frac{d^2 y^P(t)}{dt^2} = 0 \text{ and } \frac{dy^P}{dt} = c$$

Substituting in the differential equation, and remembering that $\alpha_2 = 0$, we have

$$\alpha_1 c = \beta$$

$$\text{Hence } c = \frac{\beta}{\alpha_1}$$

The solution to the particular integral will therefore be given by

$$y^P(t) = \frac{\beta}{\alpha_1} t \text{ for } \alpha_1 \neq 0$$

If α_1 and α_2 are both zero, then for the particular integral we try a solution of the form:

$$y^P(t) = ct^2$$

And in this case, the reader should show that we must have

$$c = \frac{\beta}{2}$$

$$\text{Hence } y^P(t) = \frac{\beta}{2} t^2$$

The time-path of $y(t)$

What happens to $y(t)$ through time depends crucially upon the values of the roots of the characteristic equation. If both roots are negative, then for the homogeneous case, the limiting value of $y(t)$ will be zero. In the non-homogeneous case, then $y(t)$ will converge on the solution given by the particular integral.

Again dealing with the homogeneous case, consider the case where at least one of the roots, r_1, is positive and r_1 is greater than r_2. Then differentiating the solution to the second-order differential equation with respect to time, we obtain:

$$\frac{dy}{dt} = r_1 A_1 e^{r_1 t} + r_2 A_2 e^{r_2 t}$$

Now divide by $y(t)$ to obtain the rate of growth:

$$\frac{1}{y} \frac{dy}{dt} = \frac{r_1 A_1 e^{r_1 t} + r_2 A_2 e^{r_2 t}}{A_1 e^{r_1 t} + A_2 e^{r_2 t}}$$

Multiply numerator and denominator by $\exp(-r_1 t)$

$$\frac{1}{y}\frac{dy}{dt} = \frac{r_1 A_1 + r_2 A_2 e^{(r_2-r_1)t}}{A_1 + A_2 e^{(r_2-r_1)t}}$$

As t approaches ∞, $e^{(r_2-r_1)t}$ approaches 0

and $\dfrac{1}{y}\dfrac{dy}{dt}$ approaches r_1

Here, r_1 is the dominant root, and in the long run, $y(t)$ will grow at an exponential rate equal to the value of the dominant root.

For the non-homogeneous case, where the particular integral is a constant, the reader should show that the growth rate will also converge upon r.

Repeated real roots

This case arises when

$$\alpha_1^2 - 4\alpha_2 = 0, \text{ and } r = r_1 = r_2 = \frac{-\alpha_1}{2}$$

In order for the solution to be compatible with both the characteristic equation and the two initial conditions, it must take the following form:

$$y(t) = A_1 e^{rt} + tA_2 e^{rt} + y^P(t)$$

Assuming that the particular integral is a constant, then the first and second derivatives with respect to time are given by:

$$\frac{dy}{dt} = rA_1 e^{rt} + rtA_2 e^{rt} + A_2 e^{rt}$$

$$\frac{d^2 y}{dt^2} = r^2 A_1 e^{rt} + r^2 tA_2 e^{rt} + 2rA_2 e^{rt}$$

Substituting the two derivatives and the solution to the differential equation into the original equation, if the solution is correct, we must have:

$$e^{rt}(r^2 A_1 + r^2 tA_2 + 2rA_2 + \alpha_1 rA_1 + \alpha_1 rtA_2 + \alpha_1 A_2 + \alpha_2 A_1 + \alpha_2 tA_2) + \alpha_2 y^P(t) = \beta$$

Remembering that in the case of the repeated real root and a constant for the particular integral, we have:

$$r = \frac{-\alpha_1}{2}, \text{ and } y^P(t) = \frac{\beta}{\alpha_2}$$

We have on substituting into the left-hand side of the above and collecting terms:

$$e^{rt}\left(A_1\left[\frac{-\alpha_1^2}{4} + \alpha_2\right] + tA_2\left[\frac{-\alpha_1^2}{4} + \alpha_2\right]\right)$$

The above expression will indeed equal zero in the repeated root case since we have $\alpha_1^2 - 4\alpha_2 = 0$. The solution is, therefore, correct.

Example 19.2

Find the particular solution to:
$$\frac{d^2y}{dt^2} + 2\frac{dy}{dt} + y = 2, \quad y(0) = 4, \quad y'(0) = -1.$$

For the complementary function, try a solution of the form: $y(t) = Ae^{rt}$. Substituting into the homogeneous part of the differential equation, and simplifying gives us the characteristic equation:
$$r^2 + 2r + 1 = 0,$$
$$\text{hence } (r+1)(r+1) = 0$$

The particular integral is equal to 2, and the general solution is, therefore,
$$y(t) = A_1 e^{-t} + tA_2 e^{-t} + 2$$

To make definite the arbitrary constants, we employ the initial conditions; setting $t = 0$, we must have:
$$A_1 + 2 = 4$$
$$-A_1 + A_2 = -1$$
$$\text{Hence } A_1 = 2, \; A_2 = 1$$

The particular solution is, therefore,
$$y(t) = 2e^{-t} + te^{-t} + 2$$

Since both e^{-t} and te^{-t} become smaller and smaller through time, in the long run $y(t)$ converges on the value 2.

Example 19.3

Solve the following:
$$\frac{d^2y}{dt^2} - 0.2\frac{dy}{dt} + 0.01y = 2, \quad y(0) = 202, \quad y'(0) = 0.2.$$

As before for the complementary function, we try a solution of the form: $y(t) = Ae^{rt}$. Substituting into the homogeneous part of the differential equation, and simplifying gives us the characteristic equation:
$$r^2 - 0.2r + 0.01 = 0$$
$$(r - 0.1)(r - 0.1) = 0$$
$$\text{Hence } r = 0.1$$

The particular integral is a constant, equal to 200. The general solution is:
$$y(t) = A_1 e^{0.1t} + tA_2 e^{0.1t} + 200$$

From the initial conditions, we must have at $t = 0$:
$$A_1 + 200 = 202$$
$$0.1A_1 + A_2 = 0.2$$
$$\text{Hence } A_1 = 2, \; A_2 = 0$$

The particular solution to our differential equation, therefore, is given by:
$$y(t) = 2e^{0.1t} + 200.$$
and $y(t)$ increases without limit through time.

The complex root case

As we have seen earlier in this chapter, the solution to the characteristic equation will be a pair of complex roots when
$$\alpha_1^2 - 4\alpha_2 < 0$$
To find the roots of the quadratic, we shall have to take the square root of a negative number. In mathematics, the symbol i is used to represent the square root of the number -1. Adopting this convention, the roots in the complex case are given by the following expression:
$$\frac{-\alpha_1 \pm i\sqrt{4\alpha_2 - \alpha^2}}{2}$$

Furthermore, let
$$h = \frac{-\alpha_1}{2}, \text{ and } v = \frac{\sqrt{4\alpha_2 - \alpha_1}}{2}$$

Then we may write the roots of the characteristic equation in this third case as:
$$r_1 = h + vi, \quad r_2 = h - vi$$

The complementary function, therefore, is of the form:
$$y^c(t) = A_1 e^{(h+vi)t} + A_2 e^{(h-vi)t}$$
$$= e^{ht}(A_1 e^{vit} + A_2 e^{-vit})$$

What interpretation can we now give to e^{vit} and e^{-vit}? In order to develop the analysis further, we need to make use of the Mcclaurin-series expansion of a function. Given that $y = f(x)$, then it can be approximated by the following expansion, where the function is to be expanded around the point $x = 0$.
$$f(x) = \frac{f(0)}{0!} + \frac{1}{1!}\frac{df(0)}{dx}x + \frac{1}{2!}\frac{d^2f(0)}{dx^2}x^2 + \frac{1}{3!}\frac{d^3f(0)}{dx^3}x^3 + \frac{1}{4!}\frac{d^4f(0)}{dx^4}x^4 + \cdots$$

Now let us consider the Maclaurin-series expansion of two trigonometric functions: $y = \cos x$, and $y = \sin x$. The derivatives of the first function repeat themselves in the following cycle: $-\sin x, -\cos x, \sin x, \cos x$. Evaluating each derivative at the point $x = 0$, we have the following set of repeating values: $0, -1, 0, 1$. The derivatives of the second function also repeat themselves in a four-component cycle: $\cos x, -\sin x, -\cos x, \sin x$. Again evaluating these derivatives at $x = 0$, we have the following set of repeating values: $1, 0, -1, 0$. From the Maclaurin-series expansion, we, therefore, have:
$$\cos x = \frac{1}{0!} - \frac{1}{2!}x^2 + \frac{1}{4!}x^4 - \frac{1}{6!}x^6 + \frac{1}{8!}x^8 - \cdots$$
$$\sin x = \frac{0}{0!} + \frac{1}{1!}x - \frac{1}{3!}x^3 + \frac{1}{5!}x^5 - \frac{1}{7!}x^7 + \cdots$$

Let us now turn to consider the Maclaurin-series expansion of e^{vi}

$$e^{vi} = \frac{1}{0!} + \frac{i}{1!}v + \frac{i^2}{2!}v^2 + \frac{i^3}{3!}v^3 + \frac{i^4}{4!}v^4 + \frac{i^5}{5!}v^5 + \frac{i^6}{6!}v^6 + \frac{i^7}{7!}v^7 + \frac{i^8}{8!}v^8 + \cdots$$

Now since we also have

$$i^2 = -1, \quad i^3 = -i, \quad i^4 = 1, \quad i^5 = i, \quad i^6 = -1, \quad i^7 = -i, \quad i^8 = 1$$

it follows that

$$e^{vi} = \frac{1}{0!} + \frac{i}{1!}v - \frac{1}{2!}v^2 - \frac{i}{3!}v^3 + \frac{1}{4!}v^4 + \frac{i}{5!}v^5 - \frac{1}{6!}v^6 - \frac{i}{7!}v^7 + \frac{1}{8!}v^8 + \cdots$$

But we have shown above that

$$\cos v = \frac{1}{0!} - \frac{1}{2!}v^2 + \frac{1}{4!}v^4 - \frac{1}{6!}v^6 + \frac{1}{8!}v^8 - \cdots$$

$$\text{and } i\sin v = \frac{i}{1!}v - \frac{i}{3!}v^3 + \frac{i}{5!}v^5 - \frac{i}{7!}v^7 + \cdots$$

Substituting the expressions for $\cos v$ and $i\sin v$ in the Maclaurin-series expansion of e^{vi} yields:

$$e^{vi} = \cos v + i\sin v$$

It can be similarly shown that

$$e^{-vi} = \cos v - i\sin v$$

Given these results, it is also follows that

$$e^{\pm vit} = (\cos v \pm i\sin v)^t$$

Furthermore, if we let $\phi = vt$, then

$$e^{\pm \phi i} = \cos \phi \pm i\sin \phi$$
$$= \cos vt \pm i\sin vt$$

and hence we have

$$e^{\pm vit} = (\cos vt \pm i\sin vt)$$

In the complex root case, it follows, therefore, that the complementary function which is given by:

$$y^c(t) = A_1 e^{(h+vi)t} + A_2 e^{(h-vi)t}$$

may be expressed in the following way:

$$y^c(t) = e^{ht}(A_1[\cos vt + i\sin vt] + A_2[\cos vt - i\sin vt])$$
$$= e^{ht}(A_3 \cos vt + A_4 \sin vt)$$

where $A_3 = A_1 + A_2$ and $A_4 = i(A_1 - A_2)$. Note that though the imaginary number i appears in the solution to the complementary function, this is not going to cause us any problems. Given the

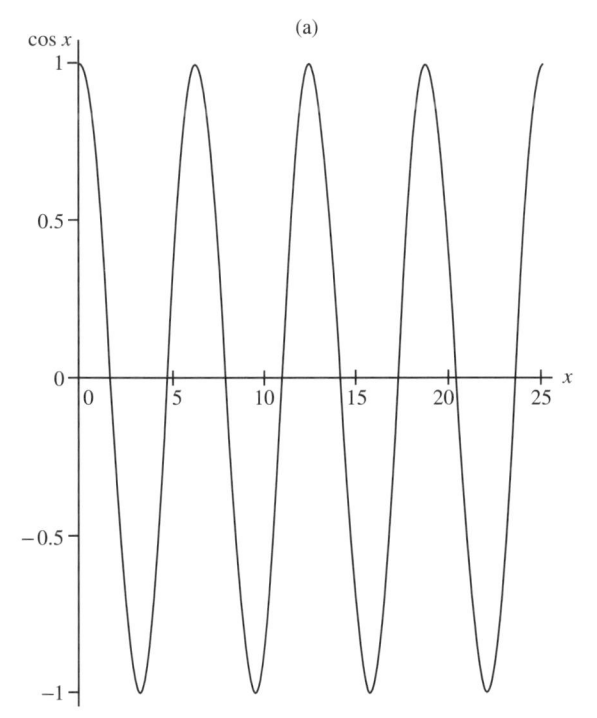

Figure 19.1 (a) The plot of cos x. The figure shows the plot of cos x as x varies from 0 to 8π.

two initial conditions, we shall be able to make definite the two arbitrary constants, and i will have disappeared.

What can we say about the time-path of $y(t)$? First of all, consider the impact of the term, e^{ht}. If h is positive, then this term will become larger and larger through time. Remember that $h = -\alpha_1/2$, so that e^{ht} will go to zero as t increases provided that α_1 is positive, will be constant for α_1 equal to zero, and will increase without limit for α_1 less than zero.

Further, what can we say about the trigonometric expression? The two functions, $f(x) = \cos x$, and $g(x) = \sin x$, are depicted in Fig. 19.1. Both functions give rise to regular cycles, with the value of both functions fluctuating between an upper limit of unity and a lower limit of minus unity, as shown in the table below, where the angle is measured in radians.

x	0	$\pi/2$	π	$3\pi/2$	2π	$5\pi/2$	3π	$7\pi/2$	4π
cos x	1	0	-1	0	1	0	-1	0	1
sin x	0	1	0	-1	0	1	0	-1	0

What we have in the solution to the complex root case, then, is a linear combination of a cosine and a sine function. This will naturally give rise to a regular cycle, the duration of which from peak to peak, or from trough to trough, will depend upon v. Whereas for the simple cosine or sine function given in the diagram and the table, the length of the cycle is equal to 2π, the length of the cycle in $y(t)$ is given by:

$$\frac{2\pi}{v} = \frac{2\pi}{0.5\sqrt{4\alpha_2 - \alpha_1}}$$

The significance of the combination of e^{ht} and the trigonometric function may now be seen.

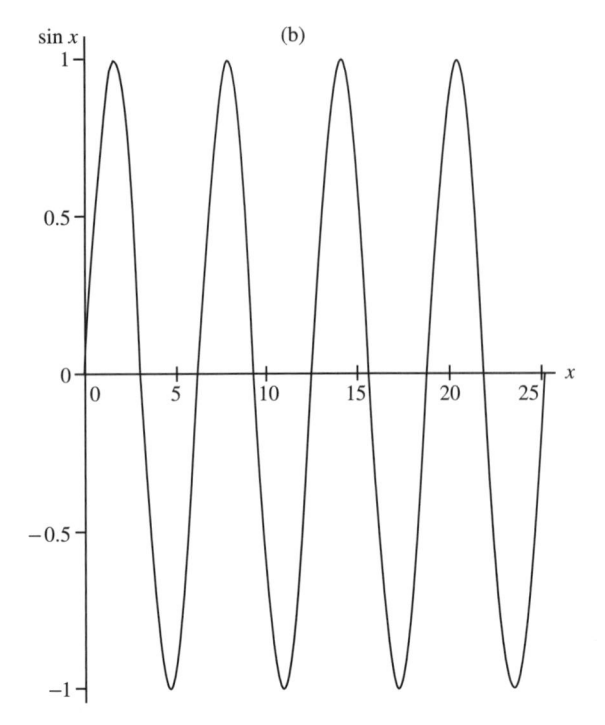

Figure 19.1 (b) The plot of sin x. The figure shows the plot of sin x as x varies from 0 to 8π.

By itself the trigonometric function gives rise to fluctuations of constant amplitude; but when multiplied by the exponential term, the amplitude of the fluctuations will increase through time if h is positive, and decrease through time if h is negative. Clearly the cycles will continue to be of constant amplitude if h is zero.

Example 19.4

$$\frac{d^2y}{dt^2} + \frac{dy}{dt} + 1.25y(t) = 12.5, \quad y(0) = 12, \quad y'(0) = 4$$

Regarding the particular integral, we set both the first and second derivatives equal to zero, this yields:

$$y^p(t) = 10$$

For the complementary function, we try a solution of the form:

$$y^c(t) = Ae^{rt}$$

hence $\dfrac{dy}{dt} = rAe^{rt}$ and $\dfrac{d^2y}{dt^2} = r^2Ae^{rt}$

The characteristic equation is, therefore, given by:

$$r^2 + r + 1.25 = 0$$
$$\text{Then } r = \frac{-1 \pm \sqrt{-4}}{2}$$
$$= -0.5 \pm i$$

In this case, we have: $h = -0.5$, $v = 1$. The complementary function is given by:

$$y^c t = A_1 e^{(-0.5+i)t} + A_2 e^{(-0.5-i)t}$$
$$= e^{-0.5t}(A_1 e^{it} + A_2 e^{-it})$$
$$= e^{-0.5t}(A_1[\cos t + i \sin t] + A_2[\cos t - i \sin t])$$
$$= e^{-0.5t}(A_3 \cos t + A_4 \sin t)$$

The general solution to our problem is:

$$y(t) = e^{-0.5t}(A_3 \cos t + A_4 \sin t) + 10$$

Differentiating the general solution with respect to time, we obtain:

$$\frac{dy}{dt} = -0.5 e^{-0.5t}(A_3 \cos t + A_4 \sin t) + e^{-0.5t}(-A_3 \sin t + A_4 \cos t)$$

Setting $t = 0$, and given the initial conditions, we have:

$$A_3 + 10 = 12$$
$$-0.5 A_3 + A_4 = 4$$

Solving these two equations, we find that

$$A_3 = 2, \quad A_4 = 5$$

So the particular solution is given by:

$$y(t) = e^{-0.5t}(2 \cos t + 5 \sin t) + 10$$

An alternative formulation for the solution in the complex root case is also available. We have seen above that the general solution takes the form:

$$y(t) = e^{ht}(A_3 \cos vt + A_4 \sin vt) + y^P(t)$$

Let us now let

$$A_3 = A \cos \phi, \text{ and } A_4 = A \sin \phi$$

This then enables us to write:

$$A_3 \cos vt + A_4 \sin vt = A(\cos vt \cos \phi - \sin vt \sin \phi)$$
$$= A(\cos(vt + \phi))$$

How may we proceed in order to find the values of A and ϕ? First of all, we use the initial conditions to obtain the values of the arbitrary constants, A_3 and A_4. We then first find the value of ϕ. Given that we have let

$$A_3 = A \cos \phi, \text{ and } A_4 = -A \sin \phi$$

then it must be the case that

$$\frac{A_4}{A_3} = \frac{-\sin \phi}{\cos \phi} = -\tan \phi$$

Having obtained ϕ by taking the inverse tan of $-A_4/A_3$, we then proceed to find A, which is given by $A_3/\cos\phi$. Returning to our numerical example, we have

$$\tan\phi = \frac{-5}{2} = -2.5$$

$$\text{Hence } \phi = -1.1903$$

$$\text{and } A = \frac{2}{\cos\phi} = \frac{2}{0.3714} = 5.3852$$

The solution is:

$$y(t) = 5.3852 e^{-0.5t} \cos(t - 1.1903) + 10$$

The time-path of $y(t)$ exhibits damped fluctuations around the value 10, with the length of the cycle being 2π. We can always check that the solution we have obtained is correct by adopting the standard procedure of first obtaining the first and second derivatives with respect to time, and then substituting them along with our solution into the second-order differential equation with which we started. We leave it as an exercise for the reader to check that the above solution is correct.

Example 19.5

$$\frac{d^2 y}{dt^2} + 0.25 y = 4, \quad y(0) = 16, \quad y'(0) = 2$$

The particular integral is a constant:

$$y^P(t) = \frac{4}{0.25} = 16$$

The characteristic equation is easily found:

$$r^2 + 0.25 = 0$$

$$\text{Hence } r = \pm 0.5i$$

So the general solution is given by:

$$y(t) = A_3 \cos 0.5t + A_4 \sin 0.5t + 16$$

Differentiate the general solution with respect to time:

$$\frac{dy}{dt} = -0.5 A_3 \sin 0.5t + 0.5 A_4 \cos 0.5t$$

Setting $t = 0$, and using the initial conditions, we have:

$$A_3 + 16 = 16$$

$$0.5 A_4 = 2$$

$$\text{Hence } A_3 = 0, \ A_4 = 4$$

The particular solution is, therefore:

$$y(t) = 4 \sin 0.5t + 16$$

The cycles are of constant amplitude, with $y(t)$ fluctuating between a maximum value of 20, and a minimum value of 12. The length of the cycle from peak to peak is 4π. In this case, $y(t)$ reaches its maximum value at values of t for which the first derivative is zero, and the second derivative is negative; minimum values of $y(t)$ occur at values of t for which the first derivative is zero, and the second derivative is positive.

$$\frac{dy}{dt} = 2\cos 0.5t, \quad \frac{d^2y}{dt^2} = -\sin 0.5t$$

It is a straightforward matter to check that maxima occur when $t = \pi$, $t = 5\pi$, $t = 9\pi$ etc; minima occur at $t = 3\pi$, $t = 7\pi$, $t = 11\pi$ etc.

19.3 MORE ON THE PARTICULAR INTEGRAL

So far in this chapter, we have dealt with second-order differential equations with a constant term on the right-hand side of the equation. In this section, we briefly touch upon cases where the right-hand side term is itself a function of time. In the previous chapter, we introduced the method of undetermined coefficients to deal with cases where there was a finite number of different forms for the derivatives of this function. The same method can be applied in similar circumstances for the case of second- and higher-order differential equations.

To reinforce our earlier discussion, we work through some examples which will bring out the main features of the analysis.

Example 19.6

$$\frac{d^2y}{dt^2} + 2\frac{dy}{dt} + 2y = \cos t, \quad y(0) = 2, \quad y'(0) = -1$$

To obtain the complementary function, we first find the roots of the characteristic equation:

$$r^2 + 2r + 2 = 0$$
$$\text{hence } r = \frac{-2 \pm \sqrt{4-8}}{2}$$
$$= -1 \pm i$$

The complementary function is, therefore, given by:

$$y^c(t) = e^{-t}(A_3 \cos t + A_4 \sin t)$$

To find the particular integral, we use the method of undetermined coefficients. Given that successive derivatives of $\cos t$ are of the form: $-\sin t$, $-\cos t$, $\sin t$, $\cos t$, we try a solution of the form:

$$y^p(t) = B_1 \cos t + B_2 \sin t$$

The first and second derivatives of this proposed solution are:

$$\frac{dy}{dt} = -B_1 \sin t + B_2 \cos t$$

$$\frac{d^2y}{dt^2} = -B_1 \cos t - B_2 \sin t$$

Substituting for the two derivatives in the differential equation, we have:
$$-B_1 \cos t - B_2 \sin t - 2B_1 \sin t + 2B_2 \cos t + 2B_1 \cos t + 2B_2 \sin t = \cos t$$

from which it follows that
$$B_1 + 2B_2 = 1$$
$$-2B_1 + B_2 = 0$$
hence $B_1 = 0.2$, $B_2 = 0.4$
and $y^p(t) = 0.2 \cos t + 0.4 \sin t$

So the general solution is:
$$y(t) = e^{-t}(A_3 \cos t + A_4 \sin t) + 0.2 \cos t + 0.4 \sin t$$
and $\dfrac{dy}{dt} = -e^{-t}(A_3 \cos t + A_4 \sin t)$
$$+ e^{-t}(-A_3 \sin t + A_4 \cos t) - 0.2 \sin t + 0.4 \cos t$$

From the initial conditions, we have:
$$y(0) = A_3 + 0.2 = 2$$
$$y'(0) = -A_3 + A_4 + 0.4 = -1$$
Hence $A_3 = 1.8$, and $A_4 = 0.4$

The particular solution is, therefore, given by:
$$y(t) = e^{-t}(1.8 \cos t + 0.4 \sin t) + 0.2 \cos t + 0.4 \sin t$$

Example 19.7
$$\frac{d^2y}{dt^2} + \frac{dy}{dt} = 10e^t$$

It is straightforward to show that the complementary function is given by:
$$y^c(t) = A_1 + A_2 e^{-t}$$

For the particular integral, we try a solution of the form:
$$y^p(t) = Be^t$$

Since all the derivatives of the term on the right-hand side of the differential equation are given by $10e^t$, the method of undetermined coefficients can again be applied. Substituting these first and second derivatives into the original differential equation yields
$$Be^t + Be^t = 10e^t$$
Hence $2B = 10$, therefore $B = 5$

So, the general solution is
$$y(t) = A_1 + A_2 e^{-t} + 5e^t$$

We may check that this solution is correct by differentiating it twice and substituting the derivatives into the original equation.

$$\frac{dy}{dt} = -A_2 e^{-t} + 5e^t$$

$$\frac{d^2y}{dt^2} = A_2 e^{-t} + 5e^t$$

$$\text{Clearly } \frac{d^2y}{dt^2} + \frac{dy}{dt} = 10e^t$$

In the example we have just solved, there was no term containing y in the differential equation. When this happens, it may be necessary to adjust the standard procedure for finding the particular integral. Indeed, we have already seen this when dealing with the simpler case of a constant term on the right-hand side of the equation. Assume the variable term on the right-hand side is a polynomial function of time, but that y does not appear on the left-hand side. Then it will be necessary for us to try as solution for the particular integral a polynomial function which is one degree higher than the right-hand side function. If we have originally a quadratic function of time, then we must try a cubic function of time as our particular integral; if we have a linear function of time, then the particular integral must be a quadratic. In fact, the outcome is completely analogous to that in the constant term case when y is excluded from the differential equation.

Example 19.8

We deal with a simple case where the right-hand side is a linear function of time, and y is excluded from the differential equation. Since our interest is in the particular integral, we have not changed the left-hand side of the previous example.

$$\frac{d^2y}{dt^2} + \frac{dy}{dt} = \beta_0 + \beta_1 t$$

We can quickly see that we shall get nowhere by trying a solution for the particular integral of the form:

$$y^p t = B_0 + B_1 t$$

In this case the second derivative vanishes, and having performed the usual substitution, we are just left with

$$B_1 = \beta_0 + \beta_1 t$$

Rather, what we should do is try a solution for the particular integral of the form:

$$y^p(t) = B_1 t + B_2 t^2$$

The derivatives of this proposed solution are:

$$\frac{dy}{dt} = B_1 + 2B_2$$

$$\frac{d^2y}{dt^2} = 2B_2$$

On substituting into the original equation, we obtain:

$$2B_2 + B_1 + 2B_2 t = \beta_0 + \beta_1 t$$

From which it follows that

$$B_2 = \frac{\beta_1}{2}, \text{ and } B_1 = \beta_0 - \beta_1$$

19.4 HIGHER-ORDER LINEAR DIFFERENTIAL EQUATIONS

We now briefly address the question of how to solve higher-order linear differential equations. By trying as before a solution for the complementary function of the form:

$$y(t)^c = A e^{rt}$$

we end up with a polynomial of degree n to solve:

$$\alpha_0 r^n + \alpha_1 r^{n-1} + \alpha_2 r^{n-2} + \cdots + \alpha_{n-1} r + \alpha_n = 0$$

In our earlier discussion of second-order linear differential equations, we have seen that convergence is guaranteed, regardless of the initial conditions, for the case of real roots if both are negative, or for the case where the solution is a pair of complex roots if the real part of the root is negative. The more general nth order equation similarly requires the real parts of all the roots to be negative for convergence to be independent of the initial conditions.

Example 19.9

Let us consider the following example:

$$\frac{d^3 y}{dr^3} + 7 \frac{d^2 y}{dt^2} + 14 \frac{dy}{dt} + 8y = 0$$

Then the characteristic equation is

$$r^3 + 7r^2 + 14r + 8 = 0$$

This may be written as

$$(r+1)(r^2 + 6r + 8) = (r+1)(r+2)(r+4) = 0$$

All the roots are negative and convergence is clearly guaranteed. The general solution is

$$y(t) = A_1 e^{-t} + A_2 e^{-2} + A_3 e^{-4t}$$

Example 19.10

If, instead, we had the following differential equation:

$$\frac{d^3 y}{dr^3} + 5 \frac{d^2 y}{dt^2} + 2 \frac{dy}{dt} - 8y = 0$$

then the characteristic equation is

$$r^3 + 5r^2 + 2r - 8 = 0$$

This may be written as

$$(r-1)(r^2 + 6r + 8) = (r-1)(r+2)(r+4) = 0$$

Only two of the roots are negative and convergence will only occur if the initial conditions are such that A_1 is zero. The general solution is

$$y(t) = A_1 e^t + A_2 e^{-2} + A_3 e^{-4t}$$

It is often difficult to obtain the roots of polynomials in order to check whether all their real parts are indeed negative. A determinantal test, known as the Routh theorem, which eschews the need to actually calculate the roots of the polynomial may be used. The Routh theorem gives necessary and sufficient conditions for all the real parts of the polynomial to be negative. For the nth order equation, we require that the following n determinants all be positive:

$$|\alpha_1|, \quad \begin{vmatrix} \alpha_1 & \alpha_3 \\ \alpha_0 & \alpha_2 \end{vmatrix}, \quad \begin{vmatrix} \alpha_1 & \alpha_3 & \alpha_5 \\ \alpha_0 & \alpha_2 & \alpha_4 \\ 0 & \alpha_1 & \alpha_3 \end{vmatrix}$$

$$\begin{vmatrix} \alpha_1 & \alpha_3 & \alpha_5 & \alpha_7 \\ \alpha_0 & \alpha_2 & \alpha_4 & \alpha_6 \\ 0 & \alpha_1 & \alpha_3 & \alpha_5 \\ 0 & \alpha_0 & \alpha_2 & \alpha_4 \end{vmatrix}, \ldots$$

Note that we must always have normalised our equation so that α_0 is equal to unity. For a third-order equation, we must evaluate three determinants. For example 19.9 above we have:

$$|7| = 7, \quad \begin{vmatrix} 7 & 8 \\ 1 & 14 \end{vmatrix} = 90$$

$$\begin{vmatrix} 7 & 8 & 0 \\ 1 & 14 & 0 \\ 0 & 7 & 8 \end{vmatrix} = 8(90) = 720$$

Hence all the three determinants are positive, and convergence is ensured. And, as we already know from having solved the problem, all three roots are indeed real and negative. For example 19.10, however, we have:

$$|5| = 5, \quad \begin{vmatrix} 5 & -8 \\ 1 & 2 \end{vmatrix} = 18$$

$$\begin{vmatrix} 5 & -8 & 0 \\ 1 & 2 & 0 \\ 0 & 5 & -8 \end{vmatrix} = -8(18) = -144$$

Convergence will not occur in this case, since only two of the three determinants are positive. And, as we already know from having solved the problem, one of the three roots is positive.

19.5 SUMMARY

In this chapter we have shown how to solve some relatively simple second-order linear differential equations. Regarding the solution to the complementary function, we must find the roots of a quadratic equation. If the roots of the quadratic are real, then convergence will occur from any arbitrary initial position provided that the roots are both negative. In the case where the solution to the quadratic equation involves a pair of complex conjugates, then the variable will follow a cyclical time-path. The amplitude of the fluctuations around the equilibrium will diminish through time provided that the real part of the root is negative. The fluctuations will be of constant amplitude if the real part of the root is zero, and will be of increasing amplitude if the real part of the root is positive.

Regarding the particular integral, if the second-order linear differential equation contains a constant, then typically the particular integral will be a constant, unless the variable itself is absent from the equation. In these circumstances, we will find that the particular integral contains a term in t. If both y and its first derivative with respect to time are absent from the differential equation, then we will find that the particular integral contains a term in t^2. If the original equation contains terms in t, then provided there exists a finite number of forms for the derivatives of this function of t, then the method of undetermined coefficients can be employed to solve for the particular integral.

The solution of higher-order differential equations involves solving a polynomial to find the roots of the characteristic equation. This may be difficult to do in practice, but as long as we are only concerned with whether convergence occurs, Routh's theorem can be used to test for whether the real parts of all the roots are negative, which is necessary-and-sufficient for convergence to occur from any arbitrary initial position.

19.6 EXERCISES

19.1 (a) Find the general solutions to the following homogeneous linear second-order differential equations:

(i) $\dfrac{d^2y}{dt^2} + 7\dfrac{dy}{dt} + 6y = 0$

(ii) $\dfrac{d^2y}{dt^2} - 6\dfrac{dy}{dt} + 8y = 0$

(iii) $\dfrac{d^2y}{dt^2} - 6\dfrac{dy}{dt} - 16y = 0$

(iv) $\dfrac{d^2y}{dt^2} + 2\dfrac{dy}{dt} - 8y = 0$

(b) Find the particular solutions to the following homogeneous linear second-order differential equations:

(i) $\dfrac{d^2y}{dt^2} - 3\dfrac{dy}{dt} - 4y = 0, \quad y(0) = 5, \quad y'(0) = 5$

(ii) $\dfrac{d^2y}{dt^2} + 5\dfrac{dy}{dt} + 4y = 0, \quad y(0) = 2, \quad y'(0) = 4$

(iii) $\dfrac{d^2y}{dt^2} - \dfrac{dy}{dt} - 6y = 0, \quad y(0) = 3, \quad y'(0) = -1$

(iv) $\dfrac{d^2y}{dt^2} - y = 0, \quad y(0) = 8, \quad y'(0) = 0$

(c) Find the particular solutions to the following non-homogeneous linear second-order differential equations:

(i) $\dfrac{d^2y}{dt^2} + 5\dfrac{dy}{dt} + 6y = 30, \quad y(0) = 4, \quad y'(0) = -4$

(ii) $\dfrac{d^2y}{dt^2} + 10\dfrac{dy}{dt} + 24y = 96, \quad y(0) = 5, \quad y'(0) = -4$

(iii) $\dfrac{d^2y}{dt^2} - 4y = 16, \quad y(0) = 0, \quad y'(0) = 4.$

19.2 (a) Solve the following equations, commenting upon the nature of the time path of the variable.

(i) $\dfrac{d^2y}{dt^2} - 0.8\dfrac{dy}{dt} - 0.2y = 0, \quad y(0) = 2.5, \quad y'(0) = -1.9$

(ii) $\dfrac{d^2y}{dt^2} + 0.5\dfrac{dy}{dt} = 0.1, \quad y(0) = 5, \quad y'(0) = 0.2$

(iii) $\dfrac{d^2y}{dt^2} - y = -4, \quad y(0) = 5, \quad y'(0) = -1$

19.3 (a) Find the particular solutions to the following differential equations

(i) $\dfrac{d^2y}{dt^2} + 10\dfrac{dy}{dt} + 25y = 750, \quad y(0) = 30, \quad y'(0) = 2$

(ii) $\dfrac{d^2y}{dt^2} - 2\dfrac{dy}{dt} + y = 7, \quad y(0) = 5, \quad y'(0) = 3$

(iii) $\dfrac{d^2y}{dt^2} = 0.5, \quad y(0) = 25, \quad y'(0) = 6$

19.4 (a) Find the particular solutions to the following homogeneous linear second-order differential equations:

(i) $\dfrac{d^2y}{dt^2} + 2\dfrac{dy}{dt} + 10y = 0, \quad y(0) = 5, \quad y'(0) = 1$

(ii) $\dfrac{d^2y}{dt^2} - 6\dfrac{dy}{dt} + 13y = 0, \quad y(0) = 4, \quad y'(0) = -4$

(iii) $\dfrac{d^2y}{dt^2} - 2\dfrac{dy}{dt} + 5y = 0, \quad y(0) = 1, \quad y'(0) = 3$

(b) Find the particular solutions to the following non-homogeneous linear second-order differential equations:

(i) $\dfrac{d^2y}{dt^2} - 2\dfrac{dy}{dt} + 2y = 4, \quad y(0) = 5, \quad y'(0) = 2$

(ii) $\dfrac{d^2y}{dt^2} + 4\dfrac{dy}{dt} + 6.25y = 50, \quad y(0) = 5, \quad y'(0) = 3$

(iii) $\dfrac{d^2y}{dt^2} + 0.16y = 8, \quad y(0) = 54, \quad y'(0) = 2$

19.5 (a) Find the particular solutions to the following second-order differential equations:

(i) $\dfrac{d^2y}{dt^2} + 7\dfrac{dy}{dt} + 12y = 6.355\, e^{0.1t}$

$y(0) = 1, \quad y'(0) = -3.95$

(ii) $\dfrac{d^2y}{dt^2} - y = 0.5t^2$

$y(0) = 4, \quad y'(0) = -5$

(iii) $\dfrac{d^2y}{dt^2} + 2\dfrac{dy}{dt} + y = 4\sin t$

$y(0) = 6, \quad y'(0) = -4$

(iv) $\dfrac{d^2y}{dt^2} + 4y = e^t$

$y(0) = 1, \quad y'(0) = 1$

19.6 (a) Solve the following third-order linear differential equations, commenting on whether convergence occurs:

(i) $\dfrac{d^3y}{dt^3} + \dfrac{d^2y}{dt^2} + 4\dfrac{dy}{dt} + 4y = 0$

(ii) $\dfrac{d^3y}{dt^3} + 4\dfrac{d^2y}{dt^2} + 5\dfrac{dy}{dt} + 2y = 0$

(iii) $\dfrac{d^3y}{dt^3} - 3\dfrac{d^2y}{dt^2} + 3\dfrac{dy}{dt} - y = 0$

(iv) $\dfrac{d^3y}{dt^3} + 3\dfrac{d^2y}{dt^2} + 3.25\dfrac{dy}{dt} + 2.5y = 0$

(b) Confirm your results regarding convergence for the above differential equations by using the Routh theorem.

(c) For the following higher-order differential equations, check for convergence by applying the Routh theorem.

(i) $\dfrac{d^3y}{dt^3} + 5\dfrac{d^2y}{dt^2} + 2\dfrac{dy}{dt} - 6y = 0$

(ii) $\dfrac{d^4y}{dt^4} + 2.5\dfrac{d^3y}{dt^3} + 3.25\dfrac{d^2y}{dt^2} + 2.375\dfrac{dy}{dt} + 0.625y = 0$

(d) Consider the following model of the market for some commodity:

$$q(t)^d = 60 - 3p(t) + \beta_1 \dfrac{dp}{dt} + \beta_2 \dfrac{d^2p}{dt^2}$$

$$q(t)^s = -10 + 2p(t) + \gamma_1 \dfrac{dp}{dt} + \gamma_2 \dfrac{d^2p}{dt^2}$$

$$q(t)^d = q(t)^s$$

where $q(t)^d$ is quantity demanded at time t, $q(t)^s$ quantity supplied at time t, and $p(t)$ price at time t. The Greek letters are parameters, which reflect the influence that expected changes in price are likely to have on quantity demanded and quantity supplied. Positive values for the βs imply that if prices are rising at an increasing rate, consumers increase their demand in the present because they expect prices to continue to rise in the future, and vice versa for negative values. A similar argument can be made regarding the γ coefficients in the supply equation.

(i) What are the long-run equilibrium values of price and quantity?

(ii) Use the Routh theorem to derive the conditions which must be imposed upon the parameters of the model for convergence to these long-run equilibrium values to occur. Comment on the economic significance of these conditions.

CHAPTER
TWENTY
FIRST-ORDER DIFFERENCE EQUATIONS

20.1 INTRODUCTION

In the previous two chapters, we have shown how to solve differential equations of the first and second order. We continue our dynamic analysis by now treating time as a discrete rather than a continuous variable and seek to derive the solution to equations where the current value of some variable depends upon the value of the same variable in earlier time periods. Hence, we are dealing with equations of the following form:

$$y_t = a + by_{t-1}$$

This is an example of a first-order linear difference equation: the equation is linear in y with the current value of the variable depending upon the value of the variable in the immediately previous period. A second-order linear difference equation takes the following form:

$$y_t = a + b_1 y_{t-1} + b_2 y_{t-2}$$

The current value of the variable depends linearly upon its value in the two immediately previous periods. Higher-order linear difference equations similarly take the form:

$$y_t = a + b_1 y_{t-1} + b_2 y_{t-2} + \cdots + b_n y_{t-n}$$

In this chapter we shall concern ourselves with the solution to first-order linear difference equations, before turning our attention to higher-order linear difference equations in the next chapter. In Section 20.2 we show how to solve first-order difference equations. One of the issues in which we are particularly interested is the nature of the time-path of the variable we are considering. Does the variable converge upon some long-run equilibrium value regardless of its initial value? Alternatively, is the equilibrium unstable in the sense that any slight perturbation away from the equilibrium will lead to the value of the variable increasingly diverging away from the equilibrium value? Do oscillations around the equilibrium occur, and if so, does the amplitude of these oscillations increase or decrease through time?

In Section 20.3 we investigate some economic applications of first-order difference equations. We look at the famous cobweb model which gives rise to an oscillating time-path for the price of an agricultural product when there exists a lagged response of the supply to the price of the

20.2 HOW TO SOLVE FIRST-ORDER LINEAR DIFFERENTIAL EQUATIONS

One method of obtaining the solution to the first-order linear difference equation is to proceed as follows. Given

$$y_t = a + by_{t-1}$$

and lagging this equation by one period, we have:

$$y_{t-1} = a + by_{t-2}$$

Substituting this equation into the earlier one yields:

$$y_t = a + ab + b^2 y_{t-2}$$

However, it must also be the case that

$$y_{t-2} = a + by_{t-3}$$

so, on further substitution, we obtain:

$$y_t = a + ab + ab^2 + b^3 y_{t-3}$$

Successively eliminating y_{t-3}, y_{t-4} and so on, we end up with the following expression:

$$y_t = a + ab + ab^2 + ab^3 + \cdots + ab^{t-1} + b^t y_{t-t}$$

Obviously, $y_{t-t} = y_0$. Now let

$$S = a + ab + ab^2 + ab^3 + \cdots + ab^{t-1}$$

Multiplying the above equation by b yields:

$$bS = ab + ab^2 + ab^3 + ab^4 + \cdots + ab^t$$

Subtracting this equation from the previous equation, we have:

$$S(1-b) = a - ab^t$$

Provided that b is not equal to unity, then

$$S = \frac{a - ab^t}{1-b}$$

We may, therefore, write the solution to our first-order linear difference equation as:

$$y_t = b^t y_0 + \frac{a - ab^t}{1-b}$$

$$= b^t \left[y_0 - \frac{a}{1-b} \right] + \frac{a}{1-b}$$

Note that in the case where b is equal to unity, then we have:
$$y_t = a + y_{t-1}$$
$$= 2a + y_{t-2}$$
$$= 3a + y_{t-3}$$
$$\ldots$$
$$= at + y_0$$

A more general approach to the solution is as follows. Let us try as the solution to the first-order linear difference equation:
$$y_t = k + Am^t$$

For this to be the solution to our equation, then it must satisfy the original difference equation. Hence substituting
$$y_t = k + Am^t \quad \text{and} \quad y_{t-1} = k + Am^{t-1}$$
into the equation we obtain:
$$k + Am^t = a + bk + bAm^{t-1}$$
from which we may write the following two equations in the two unknowns, k and m:
$$k = a + bk$$
$$Am^t = bAm^{t-1}$$

Solving these two equations is straightforward provided that b is not equal to unity. If this is the case, we have:
$$k = \frac{a}{1-b}$$
$$\text{and } m = b$$

The solution to the first-order difference equation is therefore given by:
$$y_t = \frac{a}{1-b} + Ab^t$$

One final problem needs to be resolved, and that is assigning a value to the arbitrary constant A. Note that at time $t = 0$, we must have:
$$y_0 = \frac{a}{1-b} + Ab^0$$
it follows that
$$A = y_0 - \frac{a}{1-b}$$
and the solution to the first-order difference equation is given by:
$$y_t = \frac{a}{1-b} + \left[y_0 - \frac{a}{1-b}\right]b^t$$

Just as the solution to a differential equation has two parts: a complementary function and a particular integral, so does the solution to a difference equation. For the simple case we are dealing with when b is not unity, then the particular integral is found by setting y_p equal to a constant, which then yields the solution $y_t^p = a/(1-b)$. We shall consider in the next chapter how to find the particular integral for the case where the difference equation contains instead of a constant term a time-dependent expression on the right-hand side. The complementary function is of the form: $y_t^c = Am^t$, and we have already seen above that $m = b$. Hence, we have:

$$y_t = y_t^c + y_t^p$$

$$= Ab^t + \frac{a}{1-b}$$

What can we say about the time-path of the variable y? The crucial parameter is b. If b is negative, then b^t will alternate in sign, taking a positive value for even values of t, and a negative value for odd values of t. The variable y will therefore oscillate around the value $a/(1-b)$ when b is negative. These oscillations will be damped if b lies between 0 and -1 so that in the long run y will converge on $a/(1-b)$. However, if b is less than -1, the oscillations around $a/(1-b)$ will be explosive with the absolute magnitude of the difference between y and $a/(1-b)$ increasing through time.

What happens if b is positive? In this case, there are no oscillations. Convergence on the value $a/(1-b)$ will occur if b lies between 0 and 1, whereas if b is greater than unity, then y will increase or decrease without limit depending upon whether the initial value of y was larger or smaller than $a/(1-b)$.

Clearly, the above procedure cannot be applied when b is equal to unity since it is illegitimate to divide through by zero. In such circumstances, we simply try a solution of the form:

$$y_t = A + kt$$

from which it must be the case that

$$A + kt = a + A + k(t-1)$$

Solving for the unknowns yields

$$k = a \text{ and } A = y_0$$

The solution in this case is, therefore, given by:

$$y_t = y_0 + at$$

In this latter case, the time-path of the variable is particularly straightforward: y is a simple linear function of time, increasing for positive a, and decreasing for negative a.

Example 20.1

$$y_t = 3 - 0.5y_{t-1}, \quad y_0 = 4$$

Note that in this case we have $a = 3$, and $b = 0.5$. To find the particular integral, we try a constant as the solution, and setting $y_t = y_{t-1}$ yields $y_t^p = a/(1-b) = 2$. The complementary function can be found by setting $y_t^c = Am^t$ in the homogeneous part of the equation:

$$Am^t + 0.5Am^{t-1} = 0$$

hence $m = 0.5$ and $y_t^c = 0.5^t A$

The general solution to the difference equation is therefore given by:
$$y_t = (-0.5)^t A + 2$$

Given that the initial value of y is known, we may make definite the arbitrary constant A. We must have
$$y_0 = (-0.5)^0 A + 2 = 4$$
$$\text{hence } A = 2$$

Hence the particular solution is:
$$y_t = 2(-0.5)^t + 2$$

Regarding the time-path of y it is straightforward to see that we observe damped oscillations around the long-run equilibrium value of 2. Substituting into the equation values of t running from say 0 to 7 yields the following:
$$y_0 = 4, \quad y_1 = 1, \quad y_2 = 2.5, \quad y_3 = 1.75, \quad y_4 = 2.125,$$
$$y_5 = 1.9375, \quad y_6 = 2.03125, \quad y_7 = 1.984375 \text{ etc.}$$

Example 20.2

We now consider an example where we have convergence without oscillating around the long-run equilibrium value.
$$y_t = 0.8 y_{t-1} + 2$$

For the particular integral, we have
$$y_t^p = \frac{2}{1 - 0.8} = 10$$

and for the complementary function, we have
$$y_t^c = Ab^t = A(0.8)^t$$

Hence, the general solution takes the form:
$$y_t = A(0.8)^t + 10$$

To make definite the arbitrary constant, we need information on the initial value of y. If $y_0 = 15$, then $A = 5$, and y_t will be falling through time, converging in the limit without oscillation on the value 10. On the other hand, had the initial value of y been less than 10, then A would have taken a negative value and y would have been increasing through time, converging once more without oscillation on the value 10. Had the initial value of y been 10, then A would have equalled 0, and y would have been unchanging through time.

Example 20.3

Our third example yields a time-path for y with explosive oscillations.
$$y_t = 16 + 3 y_{t-1}$$

In this case, since $a = 16$, and $b = -3$, the particular integral and complementary function are given respectively by:

$$y_t^p = \frac{16}{1-(-3)} = 4$$

$$y_t^c = A(-3)^t$$

The general solution is:

$$y_t = A(-3)^t + 4$$

If $y_0 = 5$, then $A = 1$, and the particular solution is

$$y_t = (-3)^t + 4$$

Through time y oscillates explosively around the value 4 with the first five values of y being 5, 1, 13, −23, 85 and −239.

20.3 SOME ECONOMIC APPLICATIONS

Price dynamics in an agricultural market

We will now provide an economic application of the usefulness of the first-order linear difference equation. Let us consider a market for some agricultural product where because of the gestation lag between decisions to plant and the subsequent harvest, supply decisions are conditioned by the price which is expected to rule at the time the crop is harvested; so the supply at time t depends upon the expected price at time t, and for the time being we shall adopt the simplifying assumption that the expected price at time t is equal to the actual price at time $t - 1$. The demand for the crop at time t depends upon the actual price at time t. The actual price moves to clear the market in each time period, so the market is always in short-run equilibrium. However, long-run equilibrium is only reached when expectations are realised and the expected price at time t is equal to the price which is actually observed at time t. We may, therefore, express our basic model as follows:

$$Q_t^d = a - bP_t$$

$$Q_t^s = -c + dEP_t$$

$$EP_t = P_{t-1}$$

$$Q_t^d = Q_t^s$$

where Q^d is quantity demanded, Q^s is quantity supplied, P is price, EP is expected price, and a, b, c, and d are all positive parameters. Substituting for expected price in the supply function and setting demand equal to supply, we obtain after simplification the following first-order linear difference equation in the price:

$$P_t = -\frac{d}{b}P_{t-1} + \frac{a+c}{b}$$

The particular integral is obtained by setting the current price equal to the last period's price. Note that this will give us the long-run equilibrium price, P^*, since at this value of the current price, farmers' expectations regarding the current price are realised. When $P_t = P_{t-1}$, we have

$$P_t^p = \frac{a+c}{b+d} = P^*$$

The complementary function takes the form:

$$y_t^c = A\left[\frac{-d}{b}\right]^t$$

The general solution is, therefore,

$$P_t = A\left[\frac{-d}{b}\right]^t + \frac{a+c}{b+d}$$

The particular solution depends upon the initial value of the price, and is given by

$$P_t = \left[\frac{-d}{b}\right]^t [P_0 - P^*] + P^*$$

We have oscillations around the long-run equilibrium value of the price: these oscillations are damped if $b > d$, and explosive if the inequality sign is reversed. Note that b is the absolute slope of the demand curve (i.e. minus the derivative of quantity demanded with respect to price), and d is the slope of the supply curve (i.e. the derivative of quantity supplied with respect to expected price). Convergence on the long-run equilibrium price will only occur if the absolute slope of the demand schedule is greater than that of the supply schedule.

What we have been discussing above is the well known cobweb theorem. We have shown for our simple-minded specification of the way in which expectations are formed that demand must be more elastic than supply for the market to converge on the long-run equilibrium. In Fig. 20.1, we depict three possible outcomes: a convergent cobweb; a divergent cobweb; and, for completeness, the case where the oscillations around the equilibrium are of constant amplitude.

In Fig. 20.1(a), given an initial price of P_0, Q_1 will be supplied in period one, which for the market to clear will require a price of P_1. From the supply function, we can read off the amount that will be supplied in period two. Given a quantity supplied of Q_2, then market clearing requires a price of P_2, which will generate a quantity supplied of Q_3 and a market-clearing price of P_3, and so on. Note that the price is successively below and above its long-run equilibrium value, but the absolute difference between the current price and the long-run equilibrium value is getting smaller and smaller through time.

In Fig. 20.1(b), however, we have a situation where the demand is less elastic than the supply curve. Given an initial price of P_0, Q_1 will be supply in period one, which for the market to clear will require a price of P_1. From the supply function, we can read off the amount that will be supplied in period two. Given a quantity supplied of Q_2, then market clearing requires a price of P_2, which will generate a quantity supplied of Q_3 and a market-clearing price of P_3, and so on. Note that the price is successively below and above its long-run equilibrium value, but the absolute difference between the current price and the long-run equilibrium value is getting larger and larger through time.

In Fig. 20.1(c) we have the special case where the slopes of the two functions are equal, with the result that $P_0 = P_2 = P_4$ etc, and $P_1 = P_3 = P_5$ etc. The oscillations are of constant amplitude in this special case.

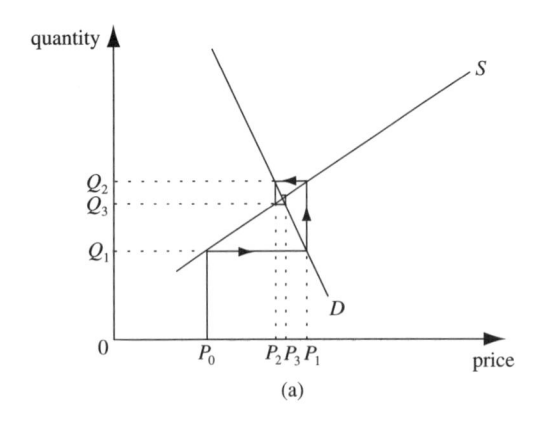

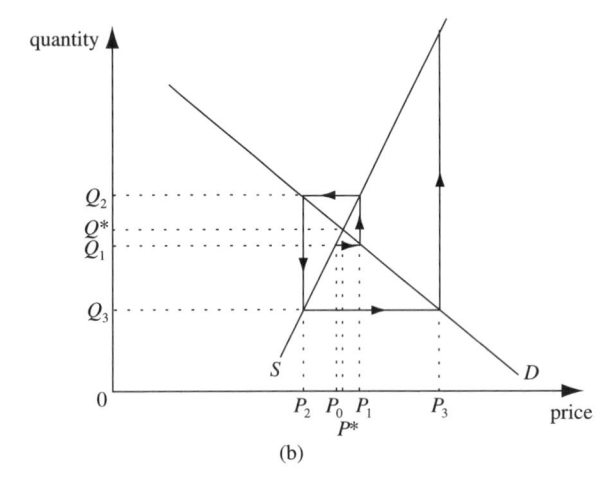

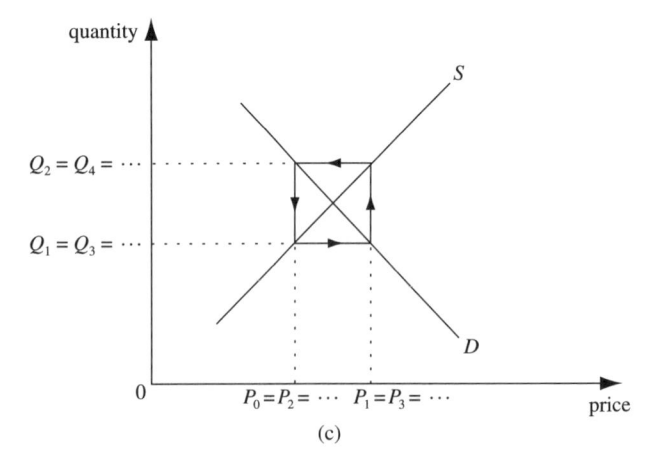

Figure 20.1 (a) A convergent cobweb. Given an initial price of P_0, Q_1 will be supplied in period one and in order to clear the market the price must rise to P_1. In period 2, Q_2 will now be supplied so the price must fall to P_2 which will lead Q_3 to be supplied in the next period with the price then rising to P_3. The oscillations around the long-run equilibrium are damped. (b) A divergent cobweb. In this case the oscillations around the long-run equilibrium are explosive. Starting with an initial price of P_0, the gap between the current price and the long-run equilibrium price P^* increases through time. (c) Oscillations of constant amplitude around the long-run equilibrium. Given an initial price of P_0, then in odd-numbered periods, the price is P_1 and in even numbered periods the price is P_0. The price and quantity repeat themselves indefinitely.

The mortgage problem

A financial institution such as a building society lends an individual a certain amount of money, L_0, at a fixed rate of interest r. Interest is added at the beginning of each year on the outstanding loan. The borrower contracts to pay off the loan by constant repayment of M each month over a term of T years. How large should the monthly repayment be?

First of all, note that the amount of the loan outstanding at the beginning of each year is given by the following expression, which is nothing more than a familiar first-order difference equation. Let P represent the annual repayment made by the borrower: this is obviously equal to $12M$. The amount of the loan outstanding at the start of year t is equal to the amount outstanding at the start of year $t-1$ plus the interest levied on that less the amount repaid during year $t-1$. Hence we have:

$$L_t = (1+r)L_{t-1} - P$$

In order to calculate the monthly repayment which must be paid in order to repay the loan, we must first obtain the solution to the difference equation. The particular integral is obtained by setting L_t equal to L_{t-1}. This yields:

$$L_t^p = \frac{P}{r}$$

The complementary function takes the following form:

$$L_t^c = A(1+r)^t$$

Hence we have the general solution:

$$L_t = A(1+r)^t + \frac{P}{r}$$

Given that the initial loan is L_0, then we have:

$$L_0 = A + \frac{P}{r}$$

$$\text{and hence } A = L_0 - \frac{P}{r}$$

The particular solution is, therefore, given by

$$L_t = \left[L_0 - \frac{P}{r}\right](1+r)^t + \frac{P}{r}$$

Having solved the difference equation, we can now derive the monthly repayment that is necessary to pay off an initial loan of L_0 at a rate of interest r over a period of T years. We must have:

$$0 = \left[L_0 - \frac{P}{r}\right](1+r)^T + \frac{P}{r}$$

$$\text{hence } \frac{P}{r}[(1+r)^T - 1] = L_0(1+r)^T$$

$$\text{and } P = \frac{rL_0(1+r)^T}{(1+r)^T - 1}$$

$$= \frac{rL_0}{1 - (1+r)^{-T}}$$

The monthly repayment is then found by dividing the above expression by 12.

Consider the case where an individual borrows £50 000 at a rate of interest of 8 per cent, and the term of the loan is 25 years. The monthly payment can then be easily calculated:

$$M = \frac{0.08(50\,000)}{12[1 - (1.08)^{-25}]}$$

$$= 390.33$$

Let us also consider the present value of the flow of annual mortgage repayments, S.

$$S = \frac{P}{1+r} + \frac{P}{(1+r)^2} + \cdots + \frac{P}{(1+r)^T}$$

Multiply the above equation by $(1+r)$ to obtain:

$$S(1+r) = P + \frac{P}{1+r} + \cdots + \frac{P}{(1+r)^{T-1}}$$

Subtracting S from $S(1+r)$ and dividing through by r, we have

$$S = \frac{P}{r}[1 - (1+r)^{-t}]$$

The annual repayments must be such that the present value of them, when discounted at the rate charged on the loan, should equal the initial amount borrowed. Setting $S = L_0$, we have

$$P = \frac{rL_0}{1 - (1+r)^{-T}}$$

which is precisely the answer we obtained from solving the difference equation.

20.4 SUMMARY

In this chapter we have shown how to solve simple linear first-order difference equations. Given

$$y_t = a + by_{t-1}$$

then as long as b is not equal to unity, then the solution to the equation is given by:

$$y_t = Ab^t + \frac{a}{1-b}$$

where A is an arbitrary constant which can be made definite if we are provided with an initial value of y. Letting y_0 be the value of y at time t, then the solution takes the following form:

$$y_t = \left(y_0 - \frac{a}{1-b}\right)b^t + \frac{a}{1-b}$$

We shall converge on the long-run equilibrium value of y, which is equal to $a/(1-b)$, provided that the absolute value of b is less than unity. Given that this is the case, there will be damped oscillations around the long-run equilibrium value if b is negative. If b is greater than unity, then we shall move further and further away through time from the long-run equilibrium, whereas if b is less than minus one, then the oscillations around $a/(1-b)$ are explosive. In the special case where b is equal to unity, then y follows a linear trend with the solution being given by:

$$y_t = y_0 + at$$

20.5 EXERCISES

20.1 (a) Solve the following homogeneous first-order difference equations and comment on the nature of the time path of y.

(i) $y_t - 3y_{t-1} = 0, \quad y_0 = 6$

(ii) $y_t + 0.5y_{t-1} = 0, \quad y_0 = 1$

(iii) $y_t - 0.4y_{t-1} = 0, \quad y_0 = 2$

(iv) $y_t + 2y_{t-1} = 0, \quad y_0 = 4$

(v) $y_t - 1.5y_{t-1} = 0, \quad y_0 = 2$

(b) Solve the following non-homogeneous first-order difference equations and comment on the nature of the time path of y.

(i) $y_t - 4y_{t-1} = 21, \quad y_0 = 8$

(ii) $y_t + 0.4y_{t-1} = 28, \quad y_0 = 5$

(iii) $y_t - y_{t-1} = 6, \quad y_0 = 7$

(iv) $y_t + 4y_{t-1} = 15, \quad y_0 = 4$

(v) $y_t - 0.5y_{t-1} = 3, \quad y_0 = 9$

20.2 (a) The demand for some agricultural product at time t is given by:

$$Q_t^d = 120 - 4P_t$$

where Q^d is quantity demanded and P is price. The supply of the product at time t is given by:

$$Q_t^s = -20 + 3EP_t$$

where Q^s is quantity supplied and EP is expected price. Assume that $EP_t = P_{t-1}$, and that the market clears period by period.
(i) Derive the equilibrium price and quantity.
(ii) If $P_0 = 25$, obtain the time path of the price and comment on its nature.
(iii) Assume the coefficient on the expected price in the supply function rises from 3 to 5. Solve the first-order difference equation in the price. Does the market converge to the long-run equilibrium?

(b) The following set of equations describe behaviour in the market for a particular commodity:

$$Q_t^d = 120 - 0.5P_t$$

$$Q_t^s = -30 + 0.3P_t$$

$$P_t = P_{t-1} - \alpha(Q_{t-1}^s - Q_{t-1}^d)$$

where Q_d is quantity demanded, Q_s is quantity supplied, P is price, and α is a positive parameter.
(i) Solve for the long-run equilibrium price.
(ii) Solve the first-order difference equation in the price and find the particular solution if P_0 is 200.
(iii) For what values of α will there be no oscillations in the price? For what values of α will there be damped oscillations in the price? For what values of α will there be explosive oscillations in the price?

20.3 (a) A household borrows £60 000 from a building society at time $t = 0$ to purchase a house at a rate of interest of *10* per cent. The loan is to be paid off by means of constant monthly repayments, M, over a period of *20* years. Interest is added to the amount of the loan outstanding at the start of each year.
(i) Find the particular solution to the first-order difference equation in the outstanding loan.
(ii) How large will be the monthly repayment to the building society?
(iii) What is the amount of the outstanding loan after *12* years have elapsed?
(iv) If after *12* years have elapsed, the interest rate were to be reduced from *10* per cent to *7.5* per cent, how large would the new monthly repayment have to be to pay off the loan in the stated period?

(v) If the household continued to make monthly repayments at the old rate, by what date would they have discharged their debt to the building society?

(vi) If after *10* years have elapsed, the interest rate were to be increased from *10* per cent to *12* per cent, how large would the new monthly repayments have to be to pay off the loan in the stated period?

(vii) If the household continued to make monthly repayments at the old rate, by what date would they have discharged their debt to the building society?

CHAPTER
TWENTY-ONE
SECOND-ORDER LINEAR DIFFERENCE EQUATIONS

21.1 INTRODUCTION

In this chapter we extend our discussion of difference equations by looking at second-order linear difference equations. In Section 21.2 we see, just as in the case of second-order linear differential equations, that in order to find the solution to a second-order linear difference equation, we must obtain the roots of a quadratic equation. Such an equation is known as the characteristic equation, and its solution will take one of three forms: (1) distinct real roots; (2) a repeated real root; and (3) a pair of complex conjugates. The solution to the second-order difference equation has two parts: a complementary function and a particular integral. To find the complementary function, we find the roots of the characteristic equation. Regarding the particular integral, in Section 21.2 we deal with the simplest case of a non-homogeneous equation where the right-hand side of the equation is just a constant. An important economic application of second-order linear difference equations arises in multiplier–accelerator models of the trade cycle. We consider this model in Section 21.3, and analyse the significance of alternative values of the multiplier and accelerator for the precise nature of the time-path of aggregate output. More complicated forms which the particular integral might take are discussed in Section 21.4. We briefly touch upon third-order linear difference equations in Section 21.4. A summary is provided in Section 21.5.

21.2 THE CHARACTERISTIC EQUATION

In this chapter we shall demonstrate how to solve for the time-path of the variable y in equations of the following type:

$$y_t = a + b_1 y_{t-1} + b_2 y_{t-2}$$

The current value of y depends linearly upon the value of y in the two most recent past periods. As in the case of the first-order linear difference equation, the solution to the second-order linear difference equation has also two parts: a complementary function and a particular integral. Before proceeding any further, we shall re-arrange our equation by collecting all the terms

containing y on the left-hand side of the equation; this yields:
$$y_t + \beta_1 y_{t-1} + \beta_2 y_{t-2} = \alpha$$
where β_i is equal to the negative of b_i, and $\alpha = a$.

Regarding the complementary function, we consider the homogeneous part of the equation: i.e. we set the constant term on the right-hand side of our equation equal to zero. We then try as the solution to the homogeneous part of the equation: $y_t = Am^t$. If this does indeed constitute the solution to the homogeneous part of the difference equation, then substituting for the current and lagged values of y, we must have:
$$Am^t + \beta_1 Am^{t-1} + \beta_2 Am^{t-2} = 0$$

Dividing the above equation by Am^{t-2}, we obtain the following quadratic equation, which is known as the characteristic equation:
$$m^2 + \beta_1 m + \beta_2 = 0$$

Applying the standard formula for finding the roots of a quadratic equation, we have:
$$m = \frac{-\beta_1 \pm \sqrt{\beta_1^2 - 4\beta_2}}{2}$$

The general form for the solution is, therefore, given by:
$$y_t^c = A_1 m_1^t + A_2 m_2^t$$

where m_1 and m_2 are the roots of the characteristic equation. The solution to the above quadratic equation may take three possible forms. The roots may be real but distinct; this case will occur when $\beta_1^2 > 4\beta_2$. The second possibility is for the solution to the root to be repeated; this occurs when $\beta_1^2 = 4\beta_2$. The third and final possibility is when the initial inequality is reversed, i.e. $\beta_1^2 < 4\beta_2$ and the roots of the quadratic equation will then be a pair of complex conjugates. We shall deal with each of these three possibilities in turn.

The case of distinct real roots

Example 21.1

Consider the following example:
$$y_t - 5y_{t-1} - 6y_{t-2} = 0$$

We try a solution of the form $y_t = Am^t$. Lagging this equation twice and then substituting into the homogeneous difference equation, we obtain after simplification the characteristic equation. In this case it is given by:
$$m^2 - 5m - 6 = 0$$

Its roots may be easily found by factorisation.
$$(m-6)(m+1) = 0$$

Hence, we have $m_1 = 6$, and $m_2 = -1$. The general solution is, therefore, given by:
$$y_t = A_1 6^t + A_2 (-1)^t$$

SECOND-ORDER LINEAR DIFFERENCE EQUATIONS

The arbitrary constants, A_1 and A_2, can be made definite if we have available two initial conditions. Assume that we are informed that $y_0 = 6$, and $y_1 = 8$, then we must have:

$$6 = A_1 6^0 + A_2(-1)^0 = A_1 + A_2$$
$$8 = A_1 6^1 + A_2(-1)^1 = 6A_1 - A_2$$

Solving the two simultaneous equations we find: $A_1 = 2$, $A_2 = 4$. Hence the particular solution is given by:

$$y_t = 2(6)^t + 4(-1)^t$$

If we set $t = 2$ and $t = 3$ for example, we can then find the values of y_2 and y_3 by substituting into the above equation. This yields $y_2 = 76$, and $y_3 = 428$. We may check that our solution is correct by returning to the original difference equation and noting that:

$$y_2 = 5y_1 + 6y_0 = 5(8) + 6(6) = 76$$
$$y_3 = 5y_2 + 6y_1 = 5(76) + 6(8) = 428$$

Note also that the second term on the right-hand side of the solution to the difference equation is equal to 4 when t is even, and -4 when t is odd, whereas the first term increases without limit.

If we now assume that the constant term is no longer zero, then we must also consider the solution to the particular integral. Returning to the general formulation of the second-order linear difference equation with a constant term, we have:

$$y_t + \beta_1 y_{t-1} + \beta_2 y_{t-2} = \alpha$$

We try as a solution to the particular integral that

$$y_t^p = y_t = y_{t-1} = y_{t-2}$$

Substituting into the difference equation and simplifying, we obtain:

$$y_t^p = \frac{\alpha}{1 + \beta_1 + \beta_2}$$

This is legitimate provided that $1 + \beta_1 + \beta_2$ is not equal to zero.

Example 21.2

$$y_t - 5y_{t-1} + 6y_{t-2} = 14$$

The characteristic equation is

$$m^2 - 5m + 6 = 0$$

Factorising, we have

$$(m - 2)(m - 3) = 0$$
$$\text{hence } m_1 = 2, \quad m_2 = 3$$

The complementary function is therefore given by:

$$y_t^c = A_1 2^t + A_2 3^t$$

To find the particular integral, we note that in this case that $1 + \beta_1 + \beta_2$ is not equal to zero. The particular integral will, therefore, be a constant:

$$(1 - 5 + 6)y_t^p = 14$$
$$\text{hence } y_t^p = 7$$

The general solution is, therefore, given by:

$$y_t = A_1 2^t + A_2 3^t + 7$$

Given values for y_0 and y_1, we may make definite the arbitrary constants. Assume $y_0 = 5$, and $y_1 = 4$, then

$$5 = A_1 + A_2 + 7$$
$$4 = 2A_1 + 3A_2 + 7$$

from which it follows that $A_1 = -3$, and $A_2 = 1$. The particular solution is, therefore,

$$y_t = -3(2)^t + 3^t + 7$$

Since both roots are positive, there will be no oscillations, and since the larger of the two roots appears with a positive coefficient, the time-path is such that the variable, after initially falling in value, will become larger and larger through time.

If the condition that $1 + \beta_1 + \beta_2$ is not equal to zero is not satisfied, then instead we must try a solution of the form: $y_t^p = kt$. Lagging twice and substituting into the difference equation, we have:

$$kt + \beta_1 k(t-1) + \beta_2 k(t-2) = \alpha$$
$$\text{hence } (1 + \beta_1 + \beta_2)kt - \beta_1 k - 2\beta_2 k = \alpha$$
$$\text{given } 1 + \beta_1 + \beta_2 = 0, \text{ then } k = \frac{-\alpha}{\beta_1 + 2\beta_2}$$
$$\text{provided that } \beta_1 + 2\beta_2 \neq 0$$

If the above condition is not met, then we try a solution of the form:

$$y_t^p = kt^2$$

Example 21.3

Now consider the following difference equation:

$$y_t + 5y_{t-1} - 6y_{t-2} = 14$$

The characteristic equation is:

$$m^2 + 5m - 6 = 0$$
$$\text{with roots } m_1 = -6, \; m_2 = 1$$

The complementary function is

$$y_t^c = A_1(-6)^t + A_2$$

Regarding the particular integral, we cannot adopt the procedure we used for solving our last example since in this case $1 + \beta_1 + \beta_2$ is indeed equal to zero. We therefore try a solution of the form: $y_t^p = kt$. Lagging the above expression twice and substituting into the difference equation yields:

$$kt + 5k(t-1) - 6k(t-2) = 14$$
$$\text{hence } 7k = 14$$
$$k = 2$$

The general solution is:

$$y_t = A_1(-6)^t + A_2 + 2t$$

Assume $y_0 = 10$, and $y_1 = 5$, then we have:

$$A_1 + A_2 = 10$$
$$-6A_1 + A_2 + 2 = 5$$
$$\text{from which it follows that } A_1 = 1, \; A_2 = 9$$

So the particular solution is:

$$y_t = (-6)^t + 9 + 2t$$

The time-path is one of explosive oscillations around a rising trend. Once again, we may check that the solution is correct. From the solution we have:

$$y_2 = (-6)^2 + 9 + 2(2) = 49$$
$$y_3 = (-6)^3 + 9 + 2(3) = -201$$

Checking from the difference equation, we have:

$$y_2 = -5y_1 + 6y_0 + 14 = -5(5) + 6(10) + 14 = 49$$
$$y_3 = -5y_2 + 6y_1 + 14 = -5(49) + 6(5) + 14 = -201$$

The case of repeated roots

We now turn to a consideration of the case where the solution to the characteristic equation of the second-order difference equation has a repeated root. It is immediately apparent that the procedure we have adopted for dealing with the case where the roots are distinct will not work. Consider the following different equation:

$$y_t - 0.8y_{t-1} + 0.16y_{t-2} = 0$$

Then we must find the roots of the following quadratic equation:

$$m^2 - 0.8m + 0.16 = 0$$
$$(m - 0.4)(m - 0.4) = 0$$
$$\text{hence } m_1 = m_2 = 0.4$$

Let us assume that the solution takes the same form as in the previous case:

$$y_t = A_1(0.4)^t + A_2(0.4)^t$$

To make definite the arbitrary constants, we would then have the following two equations:

$$A_1 + A_2 = y_0$$
$$0.4A_1 + 0.4A_2 = y_1$$

The matrix of coefficients on the As is singular, and hence the two equations will be inconsistent with each other, except in the special case when $y_1 = 0.4y_0$, when there will be an infinite number of solutions.

In the repeated root case, therefore, the complementary function takes the following form:

$$y_t^c = A_1 m^t + tA_2 m^t$$

For the homogeneous case, there is now no inconsistency when we seek to make definite the arbitrary constants. We have:

$$A_1 = y_0$$
$$mA_1 + mA_2 = y_1$$

from which it follows that

$$A_1 = y_0, \quad A_2 = \frac{y_1 - my_0}{m}$$

The particular solution is, therefore,

$$y_t = y_0 m^t + \frac{t(y_1 - my_0)}{m} m^t$$

Returning to the specific numerical example and assuming that $y_0 = 2$ and $y_1 = 2$, we have:

$$y_t = A_1 (0.4)^t + tA_2 (0.4)^t$$

Using the initial conditions, we can make definite the arbitrary constants:

$$A_1 = 2$$
$$0.4A_1 + 0.4A_2 = 2$$
$$\text{hence } A_1 = 2 \text{ and } A_2 = 3$$

The particular solution is

$$y_t = 2(0.4)^t + 3t(0.4)^t$$

The case of complex roots

The solution to the characteristic equation of the second-order linear difference equation is a pair of complex conjugates when

$$\beta_1^2 < 4\beta_2$$

We may write the roots of the quadratic in this case as:

$$m_1 = h + vi \text{ and } m_2 = h - vi$$

$$\text{where } h = \frac{-\beta_1}{2}, \quad v = \frac{\sqrt{4\beta_2 - \beta_1^2}}{2} \text{ and } i = \sqrt{-1}$$

The complementary function then is:
$$y_t^c = A_1(h+vi)^t + A_2(h-vi)^t$$

We may proceed further by defining
$$R = \sqrt{h^2 + v^2}$$

from which it then follows that
$$h = R\cos\theta \text{ and } v = R\sin\theta$$

We may therefore write the roots in our third case as:
$$m_1 = R[\cos\theta + i\sin\theta] \text{ and } m_2 = R[\cos\theta - i\sin\theta]$$
$$\text{and hence } m_1^t = R^t[\cos\theta + i\sin\theta]^t$$
$$\text{and } m_2^t = R^t[\cos\theta - i\sin\theta]^t$$

In discussing the complex root case in the solution to second-order differential equations in Chapter 19, we demonstrated that:
$$[\cos\theta \pm i\sin\theta] = e^{\pm i\theta}$$
$$\text{hence } [\cos\theta \pm i\sin\theta]^t = e^{\pm i\theta t}$$
$$\text{from which it follows that}$$
$$[\cos\theta \pm i\sin\theta]^t = [\cos\theta t \pm i\sin\theta t]$$

We may, therefore, write the complementary function as:
$$y_t^c = A_1 R^t[\cos\theta t + i\sin\theta t] + A_2 R^t[\cos\theta t - i\sin\theta t]$$
$$= R^t[(A_1 + A_2)\cos\theta t + (A_1 - A_2)i\sin\theta t]$$
$$= R^t[A_3 \cos\theta t + A_4 \sin\theta t]$$
$$\text{where } A_3 = A_1 + A_2 \text{ and } A_4 = (A_1 - A_2)i$$

We may proceed further by making use of the definition of R.
$$R = \sqrt{h^2 + v^2} = \sqrt{\frac{\beta_1^2 + 4\beta_2 - \beta_1^2}{4}}$$
$$= \sqrt{\beta_2}$$

Given that $\cos\theta = h/R$, then
$$\cos\theta = \frac{-\beta_1}{2\sqrt{\beta_2}}$$

Similarly, it can be shown that
$$\sin\theta = \sqrt{1 - \frac{\beta_1^2}{4\beta_2}}$$

Given the values of β_1 and β_2, we may find θ by taking the inverse of the cosine function, i.e. we

find the angle measured in radians whose cosine is given by
$$\frac{-\beta_1}{2\sqrt{\beta_2}}$$

Example 21.4

To illustrate the above procedure, we will work through the following example:
$$y_t - 0.8y_{t-1} + 0.25y_{t-2} = 4.5, \quad y_0 = 4, \quad y_1 = 5$$

The particular integral is easily obtained:
$$y_t^p = 10$$

The quadratic equation we must solve is
$$m^2 - 0.8m + 0.25 = 0$$

Its roots are
$$m_1, m_2 = \frac{0.8 \pm \sqrt{0.8^2 - 1}}{2}$$
$$= 0.4 \pm 0.3i$$

Since
$$\beta_1 = -0.8 \text{ and } \beta_2 = 0.25,$$
$$\text{then } \cos\theta = \frac{0.8}{2\sqrt{0.25}} = 0.8$$
$$\text{hence } \theta = 0.6435 \text{ and } R = \sqrt{0.25} = 0.5$$

The general solution, therefore, takes the form:
$$y_t = 0.5^t[A_3 \cos 0.6435t + A_4 \sin 0.6435t] + 10$$

We may now make definite the arbitrary constants by making use of the initial conditions. Note that though i appears in the definition of A_4, this is not going to cause us any problems. We simply have:
$$0.5^0[A_3 \cos 0 + A_4 \sin 0] + 10 = 4$$
$$\text{hence } A_3 = -6$$
$$\text{and } 0.5[-6 \cos 0.6435 + A_4 \sin 0.6435] + 10 = 5$$
$$-2.4 + 0.3A_4 + 10 = 5$$
$$A_4 = -26/3$$

The particular solution is, therefore,
$$y_t = 0.5^t[-6 \cos 0.6435t - \tfrac{26}{3} \sin 0.6435t] + 10$$

R is always taken to be positive and since in this case it is less than unity, R^t gets smaller and smaller through time. Regarding the term inside the square brackets, a further simplification is possible since we may write:

$$-6\cos 0.6435t - \tfrac{26}{3}\sin 0.6435t = A\cos\epsilon\cos 0.6435t - A\sin\epsilon\sin 0.6435t$$
$$= A\cos(0.6435t + \epsilon)$$

It follows from the above that

$$A\cos\epsilon = -6, \text{ and } A\sin\epsilon = 26/3$$
$$\text{since } \tan\epsilon = \frac{\sin\epsilon}{\cos\epsilon},$$
$$\text{then } \tan\epsilon = -26/18 \text{ and } \epsilon = -0.96525$$
$$\text{and } A = -10.540926$$

We may alternatively write the solution as:

$$y_t = 0.5^t[-10.540926\cos(0.6435t - 0.96525)]$$

The term inside the square brackets reaches a maximum value when t is such that the value of the cosine of the angle is -1, and the term inside the square brackets reaches a minimum value when the value of the cosine of the angle is 1. Peaks occur at $t = 6.38204$, $6.38204 + 9.76048$, $6.38204 + 2(9.76048)$, *etc.* Troughs occur at $1.5 + 9.76048$, $1.5 + 2(9.76048)$, *etc.* Since $\cos 0 = \cos 2\pi$, then the cycle repeats itself every 9.76048 periods. Strictly speaking, since this is a discrete time model, then t is confined to integer values, and we are not allowed to set t equal to non-integer values. So in practice, the periodicity of the cycles will be slightly different. There are damped fluctuations around the long-run equilibrium value of *10*, and given that R is only equal to *0.5*, convergence will occur rapidly.

21.3 AN ECONOMIC APPLICATION OF SECOND-ORDER DIFFERENCE EQUATIONS: A MODEL OF THE TRADE CYCLE

One of the most famous applications in economics of a second-order difference equation is a macroeconomic model in which the multiplier and accelerator interact under certain conditions to produce a cyclical time-path for an economy's output. This simple model has the following components. Typically, the economy is closed to international trade, and there are three categories of planned expenditure: consumption, investment, and government expenditure. Whereas the rock-bottom Keynesian income determination model treats investment as exogenous and consumption as being dependent upon current income, lags are now introduced into the model and investment is endogenous, being assumed to depend upon the rate of change of output lagged one period. The consumption and investment functions, therefore, take the following form:

$$C_t = cY_{t-1}$$
$$I_t = v(Y_{t-1} - Y_{t-2})$$

where C is consumption, I investment, Y income, c is the marginal propensity to consume which lies between zero and unity, and v is the accelerator which is positive.

Our specification differs somewhat from that originally proposed in a famous paper by Paul Samuelson in the *Review of Economics and Statistics*, 1938 in which investment was assumed to depend upon the rate of change of consumption ($C_t - C_{t-1}$). Equilibrium requires the equality of

planned expenditure and income. Hence, we have:
$$Y_t = C_t + I_t + G_t$$
where G is government expenditure, which for the time being we treat as exogenous. Substituting the consumption and investment functions into the equilibrium conditions, we obtain:
$$Y_t = cY_{t-1} + v(Y_{t-1} - Y_{t-2}) + G_t$$
Collecting the terms containing Y on the left-hand side of the equation, we have
$$Y_t - (c+v)Y_{t-1} + vY_{t-2} = G$$
where G is the exogenous level of government expenditure. The particular integral is found by setting income of the three periods equal to each other. This yields:
$$Y_t^P = \frac{G}{1-c}$$
where $(1/1-c)$ is the Keynesian multiplier. The complementary function can be found by solving the characteristic equation:
$$m^2 - (c+v)m + v = 0$$
$$\text{hence } m_1 = \frac{c+v+\sqrt{(c+v)^2 - 4v}}{2}$$
$$\text{and } m_2 = \frac{c+v-\sqrt{(c+v)^2 - 4v}}{2}$$
Note that the two roots must satisfy the following two conditions:
$$m_1 + m_2 = c+v, \text{ and } m_1 m_2 = v$$
For the solution to the characteristic equation to yield complex roots, we must have:
$$(c+v)^2 - 4v < 0$$

With complex roots, then the time-path of output will exhibit cyclical fluctuations, and these fluctuations will be explosive if the accelerator is greater than unity, of constant amplitude if it is unity, and damped if it is less than unity. This follows from the fact that in the complex root case, we have
$$R = \sqrt{v}$$

Let us now assume that the parameter values are such that the roots of the characteristic equation are real. We deal first with the case where the root is repeated. In this case, we have:
$$m_1 = m_2 = \frac{c+v}{2} = \sqrt{v}$$
The repeated root must be positive; there will therefore be no oscillations in this case. Long-run convergence requires that the accelerator be less than unity. When we have a repeated root, the solution to the difference equation is:
$$Y_t = A_1(\sqrt{v})^t + tA_2(\sqrt{v})^t + \frac{G}{1-c}$$
$$\text{with } \sqrt{v} = \frac{c+v}{2}$$

Now turn to the case where the roots are distinct. We can immediately see that both the roots will be positive. The larger of the two roots is clearly positive:

$$m_1 = \frac{c + v + \sqrt{c^2 + 2cv + v^2 - 4v}}{2}$$

Since the product of the two roots is equal to v, then the smaller root must also be positive. The time-path will therefore not involve oscillations when we have distinct real roots. What can we say about convergence in this case? Convergence will fail to occur if the larger root is greater than unity. Clearly this is possible, since the product of the two roots must equal v. If v is greater than unity, then one root at least must have a value greater than unity, and provided that v is sufficiently large, $(c+v)^2$ will exceed $4v$, and the root will indeed be real.

We may therefore summarise the situations in which convergence will occur. A necessary condition is that the accelerator have a value smaller than unity. Given this, if $(c+v)^2 < 4v$, then the roots are complex and we shall observe a time-path for the variable which converges with fluctuations; if $(c+v)^2 = 4v$, then the root is repeated and there will be convergence without oscillation; finally, if $(c+v)^2 > 4v$, we have distinct real roots and convergence without oscillation. In the above three cases, if v exceeds unity, then the time-paths will exhibit divergent behaviour, with fluctuations in the first case and without oscillations in the last two cases.

Example 21.5

Consider the following macroeconomic model:

$$Y_t = C_t + I_t + G_t$$
$$C_t = 0.6 Y_{t-1}$$
$$I_t = (Y_{t-1} - Y_{t-2})$$
$$G_t = 1000$$

Let us now solve for the time-path of Y. Given the above information, the difference equation is:

$$Y_t - 1.6 Y_{t-1} + Y_{t-2} = 1000$$

First, we can easily find the particular integral by setting $Y_t = Y_{t-1} = Y_{t-2}$. We obtain

$$Y_t^p = 2500$$

The characteristic equation is

$$m^2 - 1.6m + 1 = 0$$

$$\text{hence } m = \frac{1.6 \pm \sqrt{1.6^2 - 4}}{2}$$

$$= 0.8 \pm 0.6i$$

Given $h = 0.8$ and $v = 0.6$, then $R = 1$ and $\theta = 0.6435$ and the general solution is given by:

$$Y_t = A_3 \cos 0.6435t + A_4 \sin 0.6435t + 2500$$

If we are informed that $Y_0 = 2510$, and $Y_1 = 2526$, then we must have
$$A_3 + 2500 = 2510$$
$$A_3 \cos 0.6435 + A_4 \sin 0.6435 + 2500 = 2526$$
$$\text{hence } A_3 = 10$$
$$\text{and } 10(0.8) + A_4(0.6) + 2500 = 2526$$
$$\text{so } A_4 = 30$$

The particular solution is, therefore,
$$Y_t = 10 \cos 0.6435t + 30 \sin 0.6435t + 2500$$

The time-path of output is such that fluctuations of constant amplitude occur around the long-run equilibrium value of *2500*.

21.4 MORE ON THE PARTICULAR INTEGRAL

In this section, we consider cases where, instead of having a constant term on the right-hand side of our second-order linear difference equation, we now have a term which depends upon t.
$$y_t + \beta_1 y_{t-1} + \beta_2 y_{t-2} = f(t)$$

In Chapters 18 and 19 we examined the case of differential equations which included a variable term on the right-hand side of the equation. We saw in that discussion that provided that the derivatives of the variable term with respect to time possessed a finite number of forms we could solve for the particular integral by employing the method of undetermined coefficients. Analogously, in the difference equation case, the same procedure may be adopted when there exists a finite number of forms for the differences of the variable term. We shall use three simple examples to illustrate the procedure for the case of difference equations.

Example 21.6

Assume we have the following variable term:
$$f(t) = \alpha + \gamma t$$
Then
$$\Delta f(t) = \alpha + \gamma(t+1) - \alpha - \gamma t$$
$$= \gamma$$
$$\Delta^2 f(t) = 0$$

so we would try a solution for the particular integral of the form:
$$y_t^p = B_0 + B_1 t$$

Example 21.7

Consider the following second-order difference equation:
$$y_t + \beta_1 y_{t-1} + \beta_2 y_{t-2} = \alpha + \gamma t$$

If we now substitute into the above equation our proposed solution to the particular integral, we obtain:
$$B_0 + B_1 t + \beta_1 B_0 + \beta_1 B_1(t-1) + \beta_2 B_0 + \beta_2 B_1(t-2) = \alpha + \gamma t$$

Collecting terms and simplifying yields
$$(1 + \beta_1 + \beta_2)B_0 - (\beta_1 + 2\beta_2)B_1 = \alpha$$
$$(1 + \beta_1 + \beta_2)B_1 = \gamma$$

Provided that $(1 + \beta_1 + \beta_2)$ is not equal to zero, then we may solve the above two equations recursively for B_1 and B_0. If $(1 + \beta_1 + \beta_2)$ is equal to zero, then instead we must try a solution of the form:
$$y_t^p = \alpha t + \gamma t^2$$

Example 21.8

Now assume that
$$f(t) = \alpha + \gamma_1 t + \gamma_2 t^2$$

Then
$$\Delta f(t) = \alpha + \gamma_1(t+1) + \gamma_2(t+1)^2 - (\alpha + \gamma_1 t + \gamma_2 t^2)$$
$$= \gamma_1 + 2\gamma_2 t + \gamma_2$$

hence $\Delta^2 f(t) = \gamma_1 + 2\gamma_2(t+1) + \gamma_2 - (\gamma_1 + 2\gamma_2 t + \gamma_2)$
$$= 2\gamma_2$$

and $\Delta^3 f(t) = 0$

In this case, we would try a solution for the particular integral of the form:
$$y_t^p = B_0 + B_1 t + B_2 t^2$$

The method of undetermined coefficients can then be applied in order to obtain the values of the Bs.

Example 21.9

Our final example refers to variable terms of the form:
$$f(t) = \alpha \gamma^t$$

Writing out the difference equation
$$y_t + \beta_1 y_{t-1} + \beta_2 y_{t-2} = \alpha \gamma^t$$

We try a solution of the form:
$$y_t^p = B \gamma^t$$

Substituting our trial solution into the difference equation yields:
$$B\gamma^t + \beta_1 B\gamma^{t-1} + \beta_2 B\gamma^{t-2} = \alpha\gamma^t$$
$$\text{hence } B\gamma^t[1 + \beta_1\gamma^{-1} + \beta_2\gamma^{-2}] = \alpha\gamma^t$$
$$\text{and } B = \frac{\alpha\gamma^2}{\gamma^2 + \beta_1\gamma + \beta_2}$$
$$\text{provided that } \gamma^2 + \beta_1\gamma + \beta_2 \neq 0$$

In other words as long as γ is not a root of the characteristic equation, then we can determine the value of the unknown coefficient B in the above way. When γ is equal to one of the roots of the characteristic equation, then we must try a solution of the form:
$$y_t^p = Bt\gamma^t$$

If this also fails to work because the denominator in the expression for B is again zero, then we would have to try a solution of the form:
$$y_t^p = Bt^2\gamma^t$$

21.5 A BRIEF NOTE ON HIGHER-ORDER DIFFERENCE EQUATIONS

In solving higher-order difference equations, the complementary function is found as before by solving the characteristic equation. For the nth order linear difference equation, then this equation will be a polynomial of degree n. The roots of such an equation can, in principle, involve a combination of distinct real roots, repeated real roots and pairs of complex conjugates.

Consider the following third-order equation:
$$y_t - 2.2y_{t-1} + 1.55y_{t-2} - 0.35y_{t-3} = 0$$

The characteristic equation is, therefore, a cubic:
$$m^3 - 2.2m^2 + 1.55m - 0.35 = 0$$

It is apparent that in this case one of the roots of the cubic is unity, since the sum of the coefficients on the ms is 0.35. Dividing the cubic by $(m - 1)$, we obtain the following quadratic
$$m^2 - 1.2m + 0.35$$
whose roots are 0.5 and 0.7 respectively. The general solution therefore is:
$$y_t = A_1 + A_2(0.5)^t + A_3(0.7)^t$$

with y_t converging on A_1 in the long run.

Conditions have been derived which, if satisfied, will guarantee that the time-path of the variable will converge on that given by the solution to the particular integral. A discussion of these conditions, known as Schurr's theorem, is beyond the scope of this volume. The interested reader will find a detailed discussion of this subject in Baumol's *Economic Dynamics*, or Samuelson's *Foundations of Economic Analysis*.

21.6 SUMMARY

In this chapter, we have provided a discussion of second-order linear difference equations. If the roots of the characteristic equation are both real, then convergence will occur if both roots are absolutely less than unity. If both roots are positive but less than unity, then convergence on the long-run equilibrium value will occur without oscillations. Damped oscillations will result around the long-run equilibrium if at least one of the roots lies between zero and minus one, and the other root is absolutely less than unity. If the solution to the characteristic equation involves a pair of complex conjugates, then convergence will be guaranteed provided that the real part of the root is less than one. The complex root case gives rise to fluctuations around the long-run equilibrium value, but these fluctuations will be damped provided that the above condition is met. In the final chapter of the book we turn to consider simultaneous differential and difference equations, where the techniques which have been discussed in Chapters 19 and 21 will be employed in order to obtain solutions to simultaneous differential and difference equation models.

21.7 EXERCISES

21.1 (a) Solve the following second-order difference equations:

(i) $y_t + 5y_{t-1} + 4y_{t-2} = 0$

(ii) $y_t - y_{t-1} - 12y_{t-2} = 0$

(iii) $y_t - 4y_{t-2} = 6$

(iv) $y_t - 1.2y_{t-1} + 0.2y_{t-2} = 1.2$

(v) $y_t + 0.3y_{t-1} - 0.1y_{t-2} = 2.4$

(b) Find the particular solutions to the following second-order difference equations:

(i) $y_t + 8y_{t-1} + 12y_{t-2} = 0$, $y_0 = 1$, $y_1 = 2$

(ii) $y_t - 5y_{t-1} + 4y_{t-2} = 6$, $y_0 = 5$, $y_1 = 9$

(iii) $y_t + 6y_{t-1} + 8y_{t-2} = 75$, $y_0 = 5$, $y_1 = 1$

(iv) $y_t - 0.9y_{t-1} + 0.2y_{t-2} = 24$, $y_0 = 89$, $y_1 = 84$

(v) $y_t - 0.8y_{t-1} - 0.2y_{t-2} = -3.6$, $y_0 = 7$, $y_1 = 4$

21.2 (a) Find the general solutions to the following second-order difference equations:

(i) $y_t + 2y_{t-1} + y_{t-2} = 0$

(ii) $y_t - 0.6y_{t-1} + 0.09y_{t-2} = 0$

(iii) $y_t + 8y_{t-1} + 16y_{t-2} = 100$

(iv) $y_t - y_{t-1} + 0.25y_{t-2} = 4$

(b) Find the particular solutions to the following second-order difference equations:

(i) $y_t + 0.14y_{t-1} + 0.49y_{t-2} = 3.26$, $y_0 = 5$, $y_1 = 2$

(ii) $y_t - 6y_{t-1} + 9y_{t-2} = 16$, $y_0 = 4$, $y_1 = 7$

(iii) $y_t - 2y_{t-1} + y_{t-2} = 4$, $y_0 = 10$, $y_1 = 13$

(iv) $y_t + 1.2y_{t-1} + 0.36y_{t-2} = 7.68$, $y_0 = 2$, $y_1 = 6$

21.3 (a) Find the general solutions to the following second-order linear difference equations:

(i) $y_t - 6y_{t-1} + 10y_{t-2} = 0$

(ii) $y_t - y_{t-1} + 2.5y_{t-2} = 0$

(iii) $y_t - 4y_{t-1} + 4.25y_{t-2} = 5$

(iv) $y_t - 2y_{t-1} + 2y_{t-2} = 8$

(v) $y_t + 0.6y_{t-1} + 0.25y_{t-2} = 7.4$

(b) Find the particular solutions to the following second-order linear difference equations:

(i) $y_t - 2y_{t-1} + 5y_{t-2} = 0$, $y_0 = 5$, $y_1 = 6$

(ii) $y_t + y_{t-1} + y_{t-2} = 9$, $y_0 = 11$, $y_1 = 13$

(iii) $y_t - 2y_{t-1} + 2y_{t-2} = 4$, $y_0 = 4$, $y_1 = 6$

(iv) $y_t - 3y_{t-1} + 3.25y_{t-2} = 10$, $y_0 = 7$, $y_1 = 8$

(v) $y_t - y_{t-1} + 0.5y_2 = 5$, $y_0 = 12$, $y_1 = 11$

(c) The demand for and the supply of hogs are given respectively by:
$$Q_t^d = 160 - P_t$$
$$Q_t^s = -40 + 1.5EP_t$$

where Q_t^d is quantity demanded at time t, Q_t^s is quantity supplied at time t, P_t is price at time t, and EP_t is expected price at time t. The market clears in each period.

(i) If $EP_t = P_{t-1}$, and $P_0 = 120$, solve the first-order difference equation in the price; and comment upon its properties.

(ii) If $EP_t = 0.75P_{t-1} + 0.25P_{t-2}$, $P_0 = 120$, and $P_1 = 100$, find the equation defining the time-path of price, and comment on its properties.

(iii) Comment on the plausibility from the economic point of view of the expectations formation process in parts (a) and (b).

(d) The demand for and supply of corn at time t are given respectively by:
$$Q_t^d = 240 - 4P_t$$
$$Q_t^s = -60 + 2EP_t$$

where Q_t^d is quantity demanded at time t, Q_t^s is quantity supplied at time t, P_t is the actual price at time t, and EP_t is the expected price at time t. The market clears in each period, and $EP_t = P_{t-2}$.

(i) Solve the second-order difference equation in the price, given the following initial conditions: $P_0 = 40$, $P_1 = 45$.

(ii) What is the price at time $t = 10$? Does the price converge on its long-run equilibrium value?

21.4 (a) (i) Consider the following simple income determination model:
$$Y_t = C_t + I_t + G_t$$
$$C_t = 0.8Y_{t-1}$$
$$I_t = I = 100$$
$$G_t = G = 200$$
$$Y_0 = 500$$

where Y is national income, C consumption, I investment, and G government expenditure. Obtain the equation defining the time-path of national income.

(ii) Now assume that rather than investment being fixed, it is endogenously determined with:
$$I_t = 0.6(Y_t - Y_{t-1})$$

Derive the equation for the time-path of income.

(iii) Assume the investment function is as in (b) above, but the consumption function is now given by:
$$C_t = 0.8Y_t$$

Solve for the time-path of income, and compare the properties of this equation with that in (b) above.

(iv) Now assume that
$$C_t = 0.8Y_{t-1}$$
$$I_t = 0.6(Y_{t-1} - Y_{t-2}).$$

Obtain the general solution to the second-order difference equation in national income, commenting on the nature of the time-path.

(b) consider the following multiplier–accelerator model of the trade cycle:
$$Y_t = C_t + I_t + G_t$$
$$C_t = 0.8Y_{t-1}$$
$$I_t = v(Y_{t-1} - Y_{t-2})$$
$$G_t = G$$

where Y is national income, C is consumption, I is investment, G is government expenditure, and v is a positive parameter.

(i) Under what conditions are the roots of the characteristic equation complex?

(ii) When the roots of the characteristic equation are complex, what further conditions must be satisfied for the amplitude of the fluctuations in Y to be (i) increasing through time, and (ii) decreasing through time?

(iii) Are there any circumstances under which Y will converge to its long-run value without overshooting this value?

21.5 (a) Find the solutions to the following difference equations:

(i) $y_t + y_{t-1} + 0.24 y_{t-2} = 2 + 0.56t$

$y_0 = \frac{177}{224}, \quad y_1 = \frac{317}{224}$

(ii) $y_t + 0.5 y_{t-1} = 4.5 t^2, \quad y_0 = 1$

(iii) $y_t + 5 y_{t-1} + 6 y_{t-2} = 2^t, \quad y_0 = 0.2, \; y_1 = 0.4$

(iv) $y_t - 5 y_{t-1} + 6 y_{t-2} = 3^t, \quad y_0 = 1, \; y_1 = 7$

(v) $y_t - y_{t-1} + 0.25 y_{t-2} = 0.5^t, \quad y_0 = 100, \; y_1 = 80.25$

(b) The following equations describe the behaviour of an economy:
$$C_t = 0.75 Y_{t-1}$$
$$I_t = 100(1.05)^t + 0.9(Y_{t-1} - Y_{t-2})$$
$$Y_t = C_t + I_t$$

where Y is national income, C consumption and I investment.

(i) Find the general solution to the second-order difference equation in national income, and comment on the time-path of national income.

(ii) Obtain the particular solution for the case where $Y_0 = 400$ and $Y_1 = 440$.

CHAPTER TWENTY-TWO
SIMULTANEOUS DIFFERENTIAL AND DIFFERENCE EQUATIONS

22.1 INTRODUCTION

In this final chapter of the book we provide a brief discussion of how to solve some simple linear first-order simultaneous differential and difference equations. We shall begin in Section 22.2 by looking at simultaneous differential equations and show that the procedure for finding the solution to a set of first-order linear differential equations can be shown to require us to solve second-order differential equations in each of the unknowns. As we have seen in Chapter 19, the solution will, therefore, take one of three forms, with the roots of the characteristic equations being: (1) real and distinct; or (2) repeated; or (3) a pair of complex roots. To motivate the discussion we analyse the case of two economies in which the rate of change of output in each economy depends not only on the level of its own output but is also influenced by the output of its trading partner. The reader can then apply the methodology to analyse the dynamics of inflation and unemployment and price dynamics in linked microeconomic markets.

One question of interest is whether our model converges on the long-run equilibrium values of the variables under consideration. In Section 22.3 we introduce the concept of a phase diagram to illustrate the likely movement in the values of the variables from arbitrary starting positions.

In Section 22.4 we turn to consider the case of simultaneous first-order linear difference equations. Here too we shall find that in order to find the time paths of the variables we shall end up solving a second-order linear difference equation in each variable. We then provide some problems for the reader to analyse which make use of these techniques. We investigate how the number of agents in a particular category varies discretely through time. One can think of decisions by consumers to choose a particular retailer being determined in some probabilistic fashion, with the probabilities being dependent upon which store they used last period. Alternatively, one can look at the development of an industrial structure, investigating again in a probabilistic way how firms might move from one period to the next into a different size category.

22.2 SIMULTANEOUS DIFFERENTIAL EQUATIONS

Consider the following scenario. Anglia and Northumbria are two closed economies in which output in growing at an exponential rate; the growth rate in Anglia is α and that of Northumbria δ.

Opening up these two economies to trade with each other leads to an enhancement of growth such that we now have:

$$\frac{dx}{dt} = \alpha x + \beta y \tag{1a}$$

$$\frac{dy}{dt} = \gamma x + \delta y \tag{1b}$$

where x is output in Anglia and y is output in Northumbria and the Greek letters are positive parameters.

What we have here is a system of first-order linear differential equations in which the rate at which output changes in each economy depends linearly upon the level of output in both economies. How can we set out to obtain the solution to such a system of equations?

One way of proceeding is as follows: From equation (1a) we have:

$$y = \frac{1}{\beta}\frac{dx}{dt} - \frac{\alpha}{\beta}x \tag{2}$$

Substitute equation (2) into equation (1b) to obtain:

$$\frac{dy}{dt} = \gamma x + \frac{\delta}{\beta}\frac{dx}{dt} - \frac{\alpha\delta}{\beta}x \tag{3}$$

Totally differentiating equation (1a) yields:

$$\frac{d^2x}{dt^2} = \alpha\frac{dx}{dt} + \beta\frac{dy}{dt} \tag{4}$$

Substitute equation (3) into equation (4) to obtain

$$\frac{d^2x}{dt^2} = \alpha\frac{dx}{dt} + \beta\gamma x + \delta\frac{dx}{dt} - \alpha\delta x \tag{5}$$

Re-arranging equation (5), we have

$$\frac{d^2x}{dt^2} - (\alpha + \delta)\frac{dx}{dt} + (\alpha\delta - \beta\gamma)x = 0 \tag{6}$$

We now have a second-order linear differential equation in x, whose characteristic equation is given by:

$$r^2 - (\alpha + \delta)r + (\alpha\delta - \beta\gamma) = 0 \tag{7}$$

By adopting a similar procedure, we can also show that

$$\frac{d^2y}{dt^2} - (\alpha + \delta)\frac{dy}{dt} + (\alpha\delta - \beta\gamma)y = 0 \tag{8}$$

which obviously has the same characteristic equation as the second-order linear differential equation in x.

We may, therefore, write the solution to our system of equations as:

$$x(t) = A_1 e^{r_1 t} + A_2 e^{r_2 t} \tag{9a}$$

$$y(t) = B_1 e^{r_1 t} + B_2 e^{r_2 t} \tag{9b}$$

where r_1 and r_2 are the roots of the characteristic equation. So far, so good; but when we turn to consider making definite the arbitrary constants, there appears at first sight to be a problem since, given the values of the two variables in period zero, we have two equations in four unknowns:

$$A_1 + A_2 = x(0) \tag{10a}$$

$$B_1 + B_2 = y(0) \tag{10b}$$

However, this problem can soon be settled. Given that we know the values of x and y at time $t = 0$, then we can use the original system of equations to obtain two further equations. Differentiating the solution with respect to t and evaluating the derivatives at time $t = 0$, we have, on equating these derivatives with the two original equations:

$$\frac{dx(0)}{dt} = r_1 A_1 + r_2 A_2 = \alpha x(0) + \beta y(0) \tag{11a}$$

$$\frac{dy(0)}{dt} = r_1 B_1 + r_2 B_2 = \gamma x(0) + \delta y(0) \tag{11b}$$

These two equations along with 10(a) and 10(b) enable us to make definite the arbitrary constants.

An alternative approach is to try a solution to our equations of the form:

$$x(t) = A e^{rt} \tag{12a}$$

$$y(t) = B e^{rt} \tag{12b}$$

Differentiate equations (12a) and (12b) with respect to time: we, therefore, have:

$$\frac{dx}{dt} = rAe^{rt} \quad \text{and} \quad \frac{dy}{dt} = rBe^{rt} \tag{13}$$

If we then substitute equations (12) and (13) into equations (1a) and (1b), we obtain after some simplification the following set of equations:

$$\begin{bmatrix} \alpha - r & \beta \\ \gamma & \delta - r \end{bmatrix} \begin{bmatrix} A \\ B \end{bmatrix} = \begin{bmatrix} 0 \\ 0 \end{bmatrix} \tag{14}$$

Note that there only exists a non-trivial solution to the above set of equations if the determinant vanishes. This requires that

$$r^2 - (\alpha + \delta)r + (\alpha\delta - \beta\gamma) = 0 \tag{15}$$

but this is just our characteristic equation. Our set of equations are indeed linearly dependent, and we shall be able to solve for our four arbitrary constants, since in addition to equations (10a) and (10b), we now have:

$$(\alpha - r_1)A_1 + \beta B_1 = 0 \tag{16a}$$

$$(\alpha - r_2)A_2 + \beta B_2 = 0 \tag{16b}$$

We now work through a numerical example. Assume we have the following parameter values: $\alpha = 0.08$, $\beta = 0.01$, $\gamma = 0.005$, $\delta = 0.1$. Then the characteristic equation is

$$r^2 - 0.18r + 0.00795 = 0$$

hence $r_1 = 0.10225, \quad r_2 = 0.07775$

and the general solution to the simultaneous differential equations is given by:
$$x(t) = A_1 e^{0.10225t} + A_2 e^{0.07775t}$$
$$y(t) = B_1 e^{0.10225t} + B_2 e^{0.07775t}$$

We must also have
$$(0.08 - 0.10225)A_1 + 0.01 B_1 = 0$$
$$(0.08 - 0.07775)A_2 + 0.01 B_2 = 0$$
$$\text{hence } B_1 = 2.225 A_1$$
$$\text{and } B_2 = -0.225 A_2$$

If we are given initial values of the two variables, say $x(0) = 200$ and $y(0) = 200$, then we may now find the particular solution. We must have
$$A_1 + A_2 = 200$$
$$B_1 + B_2 = 120$$
$$-2.225 A_1 + B_1 = 0$$
$$0.225 A_2 + B_2 = 0$$

Solving these four equations, we find
$$A_1 = \frac{3300}{49}, \quad A_2 = \frac{6500}{49}$$
$$B_1 = \frac{14685}{98}, \quad B_2 = -\frac{2925}{98}$$

The particular solution is therefore
$$x(t) = \frac{3300}{49} e^{0.10225t} + \frac{6500}{49} e^{0.07775t}$$
$$y(t) = \frac{14685}{98} e^{0.10225t} - \frac{2925}{98} e^{0.0775t}$$

Let us now obtain the long-run equilibrium growth rate of the two economies. Consider first of all the general solution:
$$x(t) = A_1 e^{r_1 t} + A_2 e^{r_2 t}$$
$$\text{then } \frac{dx}{dt} = r_1 A_1 e^{r_1 t} + r_2 A_2 e^{r_2 t}$$
$$\text{and } \frac{1}{x} \frac{dx}{dt} = \frac{r_1 A_1 e^{r_1 t} + r_2 A_2 e^{r_2 t}}{A_1 e^{r_1 t} + A_2 e^{r_2 t}}$$

multiplying top and bottom by $e^{-r_1 t}$ yields
$$\frac{1}{x} \frac{dx}{dt} = \frac{r_1 A_1 + r_2 A_2 e^{(r_2 - r_1)t}}{A_1 + A_2 e^{(r_2 - r_1)t}}$$

If r_1 is positive and greater than r_2, then in the limit as t becomes very large, the growth rate will approach r_1. We may also calculate the ratio of the output in Northumbria to that in Anglia in long-run equilibrium. Since

$$\frac{1}{x}\frac{dx}{dt} = 0.08 + 0.01\frac{y}{x} = 0.10225$$

hence $y = 2.225x$ in long-run equilibrium

The non-homogeneous case

Our discussion to date has concerned itself with the homogeneous case of a simultaneous differential equations, and we have shown how to obtain the complementary function. If there are also constant terms in our equations or variable terms in t, then we must also find the particular integral since as in our earlier discussion of single differential equations, the solution will consist of the sum of the complementary function and the particular integral. In Chapters 18 and 19, we have discussed extensively the form that the particular integral may take. We shall limit our discussion here to the single case where we have constant terms in the equations defining the rates of change of x and y. We then try a constant value of both x and y for the particular integral. If we have

$$\frac{dx}{dt} = \alpha x + \beta y + \lambda$$

$$\frac{dy}{dt} = \gamma x + \delta y + \mu$$

where λ and μ are both constants, then setting the two derivatives equal to zero, and solving we obtain

$$x^p = \frac{\beta\mu - \delta\lambda}{\alpha\delta - \beta\gamma}$$

$$y^p = \frac{\gamma\lambda - \alpha\mu}{\alpha\delta - \beta\gamma}$$

Example 22.1

$$\frac{dx}{dt} = -5x - 0.5y + 12$$

$$\frac{dy}{dt} = 6x - y - 8$$

$$x(0) = 3, \quad y(0) = 6$$

To find the particular integral, we set the two derivatives equal to zero. Hence we have

$$\begin{bmatrix} -5 & -0.5 \\ 6 & -1 \end{bmatrix} \begin{bmatrix} x^p \\ y^p \end{bmatrix} = \begin{bmatrix} -12 \\ 8 \end{bmatrix}$$

$$x^p = \frac{\begin{vmatrix} -12 & 0.5 \\ 8 & -1 \end{vmatrix}}{\begin{vmatrix} -5 & -0.5 \\ 6 & -1 \end{vmatrix}} = \frac{16}{8} = 2$$

$$y^p = \frac{\begin{vmatrix} -5 & -12 \\ 6 & 8 \end{vmatrix}}{\begin{vmatrix} -5 & -0.5 \\ 6 & -1 \end{vmatrix}} = \frac{32}{8} = 4$$

For the complementary function, we try a solution of the form:
$$x(t) = Ae^{rt} \text{ and } y(t) = Be^{rt}$$

If the solution takes this form, then we must have
$$\frac{dx}{dt} = rAe^{rt} \text{ and } \frac{dy}{dt} = rBe^{rt}$$

Substituting the proposed solution and the derivatives into the original expressions defining dx/dt and dy/dt, we have:
$$\begin{bmatrix} r+5 & 0.5 \\ -6 & r+1 \end{bmatrix} \begin{bmatrix} A \\ B \end{bmatrix} = \begin{bmatrix} 0 \\ 0 \end{bmatrix}$$

The characteristic equation is, therefore,
$$(r+5)(r+1) - (0.5)(-6) = r^2 + 6r + 8 = 0$$
$$\text{hence } r_1 = -4, \quad r_2 = -2$$

The complementary functions are accordingly
$$x(t)^c = A_1 e^{-4t} + A_2 e^{-2t}$$
$$y(t)^c = B_1 e^{-4t} + B_2 e^{-2t}$$

Because of the linear dependence, we must also have
$$(r+5)A = -0.5B$$
$$\text{hence for } r_1 = -4, \quad A_1 = -0.5B_1$$
$$\text{and for } r_2 = -2, \quad 3A_2 = -0.5B_2$$

The general solution is given by
$$x(t) = A_1 e^{-4t} + A_2 e^{-2t} + 2$$
$$y(t) = B_1 e^{-4t} + B_2 e^{-2t} + 4$$

Given the initial conditions and the linear relationship between A and B, we have the following four equations to solve for the arbitrary constants:
$$A_1 + A_2 + 2 = 3$$
$$B_1 + B_2 + 4 = 6$$
$$A_1 + 0.5B_1 = 0$$
$$3A_2 + 0.5B_2 = 0$$

Solving these equations, we have:
$$A_1 = 2, \quad A_2 = -1, \quad B_1 = -4, \quad B_2 = 6$$

The particular solution, therefore, is given by:
$$x(t) = 2e^{-4t} - e^{-2t} + 2$$
$$y(t) = -4e^{-4t} + 6e^{-2t} + 4$$

In the long run x converges on the value 2, and y on the value 4.

The case of repeated roots

We now turn to consider how to deal with a simultaneous differential equation where the characteristic equation gives rise to a repeated root. We shall also see that in this case the procedure for making definite the arbitrary constants must be amended slightly.

Consider the following system of equations:
$$\frac{dx}{dt} = 1.5x - 0.25y$$
$$\frac{dy}{dt} = x + 0.5y$$

The reader should check that the characteristic equation in this case is
$$r^2 - 2r + 1 = 0$$

We obviously have a repeated root with $r_1 = r_2 = 1$. The solution will, therefore, take the form:
$$x(t) = A_1 e^t + tA_2 e^t$$
$$y(t) = B_1 e^t + tB_2 e^t$$

It is straightforward to obtain the values of A_1 and B_1. We must have
$$A_1 = x(0) \quad \text{and} \quad B_1 = y(0)$$

Furthermore, given that the following matrix is singular when $r = 1$
$$\begin{bmatrix} r - 1.5 & 0.25 \\ -1 & r - 0.5 \end{bmatrix}$$

we must have
$$A_2 = 0.5 B_2$$

Differentiating the solution with respect to time yields:
$$\frac{dx}{dt} = (A_1 + A_2)e^t + tA_2 e^t$$
$$\frac{dy}{dt} = (B_1 + B_2)e^t + tB_2 e^t$$

Substituting these derivatives and the proposed solution into the original system of equations, we obtain:

$$(A_1 + A_2)e^t + tA_2e^t = (1.5A_1 - 0.25B_1)e^t + (1.5A_2 - 0.25B_2)te^t$$
$$(B_1 + B_2)e^t + tB_2e^t = (A_1 + 0.5B_1)e^t + (A_2 + 0.5B_2)te^t$$

from which it follows that

$$A_1 + A_2 = 1.5A_1 - 0.25B_1$$
$$A_2 = 1.5A_2 - 0.25B_2$$
$$B_1 + B_2 = A_1 + 0.5B_1$$
$$B_2 = A_2 + 0.5B_2$$

Note that the second and fourth of these equations are identical, and require $A_2 = 0.5B_2$. Since it must be the case that $A_1 = x(0)$ and $B_1 = y(0)$, then we must have:

$$A_2 = 0.5x(0) - 0.25y(0)$$
$$B_2 = x(0) - 0.5y(0)$$

Note that the above results do indeed imply that the condition $A_2 = 0.5B_2$ is satisfied. The particular solution to our problem is therefore given by:

$$x(t) = [x(0) + t(0.5x(0) - 0.25y(0))]e^t$$
$$y(t) = [y(0) + t(x(0) - 0.5y(0))]e^t$$

The complex root case

We now turn to a system of equations whose solution involves complex roots. We have

$$\frac{dx}{dt} = -x + 2y - 8$$

$$\frac{dy}{dt} = -0.5x - y + 6$$

The reader should check that the characteristic equation is

$$r^2 + 2r + 2 = 0$$

with roots $r_1 = -1 + i$ and $r_2 = -1 - i$

The singularity of the matrix of coefficients when r equals either $-1 + i$ or $-1 - i$ implies the following:

$$B_1 = 0.5iA_1 \quad \text{and} \quad B_2 = -0.5iA_2$$

We may, therefore, write the complementary functions as

$$x(t)^c = e^{-t}[A_1 e^{it} + A_2 e^{-it}]$$
$$y(t)^c = e^{-t}[0.5iA_1 e^{it} - 0.5iA_2 e^{-it}]$$

We may express the complementary function for x as follows

$$x(t)^c = [A_1(\cos t + i \sin t) + A_2(\cos t - i \sin t)]$$
$$= [(A_1 + A_2)\cos t + i(A_1 - A_2)\sin t]$$

Similarly, we have

$$y(t)^c = [0.5iA_1(\cos t + i \sin t) - 0.5iA_2(\cos t - i \sin t)]$$
$$= [0.5i(A_1 - A_2)\cos t + 0.5i^2(A_1 + A_2)\sin t]$$
$$= e^{-t}[0.5i(A_1 - A_2)\cos t - 0.5(A_1 + A_2)\sin t]$$

If we now let

$$A_3 = A_1 + A_2 \quad \text{and} \quad A_4 = i(A_1 - A_2)$$

the complementary functions are

$$x(t) = e^{-t}[A_3 \cos t + A_4 \sin t]$$
$$y(t) = e^{-t}[0.5A_4 \cos t - 0.5A_3 \sin t]$$

The particular integral can be found by setting both derivatives equal to zero. This yields

$$x(t)^p = 2 \quad \text{and} \quad y(t)^p = 5$$

The general solution is

$$x(t) = e^{-t}[A_3 \cos t + A_4 \sin t] + 2$$
$$y(t) = e^{-t}[0.5A_4 \cos t - 0.5A_3 \sin t] + 5$$

Given $x(0) = 6$ and $y(0) = 10$, we can make definite the arbitrary constants:

$$A_3 + 2 = 6$$
$$0.5A_4 + 5 = 10$$
$$\text{hence } A_3 = 4 \quad \text{and} \quad A_4 = 10$$

The particular solution then is

$$x(t) = e^{-t}[4\cos t + 10 \sin t] + 2$$
$$y(t) = e^{-t}[5\cos t - 2 \sin t] + 5$$

Both variables exhibit fluctuations of diminishing amplitude around their long-run equilibrium values.

22.3 THE PHASE DIAGRAM

In this section we provide a diagrammatic analysis which will aid us in ascertaining whether the solution to our problem will converge on the long-run equilibrium values of the two variables. Mathematically, we know that if the roots of the characteristic equation are both real and negative, then regardless of the initial conditions, convergence will occur since terms of the form Ae^{rt} will approach zero as t becomes very large as long as r is negative. If the root is repeated and

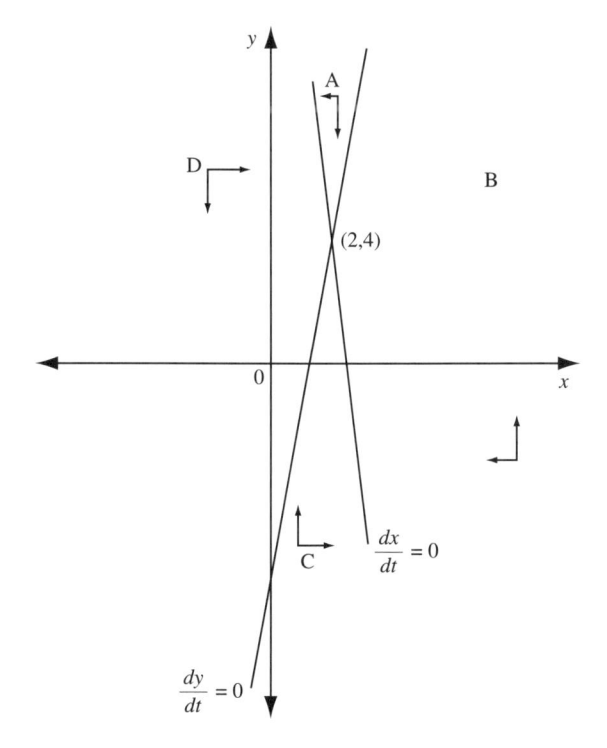

Figure 22.1 Phase diagram: Stable case, both roots negative. The figure depicts the phase diagram for the following problem: $dx/dt = -5x - 0.5y + 12$, $dy/dt = 6x - y - 8$. Regardless of the initial conditions, convergence on $x = 2, y = 4$ will result.

negative, then tAe^{rt} will also approach zero as t becomes very large. However, if both roots are real and positive, then we shall diverge away from the long-run equilibrium except in the very unlikely circumstances that the initial position actually coincided with the long-run equilibrium. A more interesting case arises when one root is positive and one is negative. We shall see below that there exists a restricted set of initial conditions for which convergence would occur, though the general conclusion is still that the long-run equilibrium will generally be unstable.

In Fig. 22.1, we plot in x, y space two linear functions from example 22.1: along the one labelled $dx/dt = 0$ the rate of change of x has been set equal to zero, and along the one labelled $dy/dt = 0$ the rate of change of y has been similarly equated to zero. Where the two loci intersect determines the long-run equilibrium values of the two variables. Since we have

$$\frac{dx}{dt} \gtreqless 0 \quad for \quad 24 - 10x \gtreqless y$$

$$\frac{dy}{dt} \gtreqless 0 \quad for \quad 6x - 8 \gtreqless y$$

then points which lie to the left of the $dx/dt = 0$ locus involve x increasing, and points to its right involve x decreasing, whereas points which lie to the left of the $dy/dt = 0$ locus involve y decreasing and points lying to its right involve y increasing. The diagram has been labelled to this effect, and arrows giving the direction of the two variables have been included in each of the four quadrants. The numerical solution we have derived for our system of equations was based upon a given initial position with $x(0) = 3$, $y(0) = 6$. This point lies to the NE of the equilibrium in quadrant B, so we would, therefore, observe that y would first of all be increasing until the $dy/dt = 0$ locus is reached, and then it would continue to fall towards its long-run value, whereas

x would initially be falling until it crossed the $dx/dt = 0$ locus when it would then be increasing up to its equilibrium value.

Differentiating the particular solution with respect to time, we have:

$$\frac{dx}{dt} = -8e^{-4t} + 2e^{-2t} \lessgtr 0 \quad \text{for} \quad t \lessgtr 0.5 \log_e 4$$

$$\frac{dy}{dt} = 16e^{-4t} - 12e^{-2t} \gtrless 0 \quad \text{for} \quad t \lessgtr 0.5 \log_e 1.33\ldots$$

The diagram, which is known as a phase diagram, enables us to say something about the qualitative nature of the time-path of the two variables starting from any arbitrary initial position. The reader should check their understanding of the diagram by tracing the direction of movement from an initial position in each of the four quadrants. Remember that whenever a locus is crossed, the direction of movement for the relevant variable is reversed.

If we differentiate the general solution with respect to time, we obtain:

$$\frac{dx}{dt} = -4A_1 e^{-4t} - 2A_2 e^{-2t}$$

$$\frac{dy}{dt} = 2A_1 e^{-4t} + 12A_2 e^{-2t}$$

$$\text{given } B_1 = 0.5 A_1 \quad \text{and} \quad B_2 = -6 A_2$$

$$\frac{dx}{dt} = 0 \quad \text{at} \quad t = 0.5 \log_e \left(\frac{-2A_1}{A_2} \right)$$

$$\frac{dy}{dt} = 0 \quad \text{at} \quad t = 0.5 \log_e \left(\frac{-A_1}{6 A_2} \right)$$

Hence a necessary condition for a change in the direction of movement of either variable is that A_1 be of opposite sign to A_2. If this is the case then we further require that the time at which the reversal takes place be positive. This will be the case for x if $-2A_1/A_2 > 1$, and for y if $-A_1/6A_2 > 1$.

If one of the roots of the characteristic equation is positive and one negative, then in the general case the system will not converge upon the long-run equilibrium values. Only if the initial conditions are such that the arbitrary constant associated with the positive root turns out to be equal to zero will convergence occur. Given the following general solution to a system of equations:

$$x(t) = A_1 e^{r_1 t} + A_2 e^{-r_2 t} + x^p$$

$$y(t) = \alpha_1 A_1 e^{r_1 t} + \alpha_2 A_2 e^{-r_2 t} + y^p$$

Making use of the initial conditions and solving for A_1, we may find the condition which must be satisfied for this variable to equal zero, and hence for convergence to occur:

$$A_1 = \frac{\begin{vmatrix} x(0) - x^p & 1 \\ y(0) - y^p & \alpha_2 \end{vmatrix}}{\begin{vmatrix} 1 & 1 \\ \alpha_1 & \alpha_2 \end{vmatrix}}$$

$$= 0 \quad \text{for} \quad \alpha = \frac{y(0) - y^p}{x(0) - x^p}$$

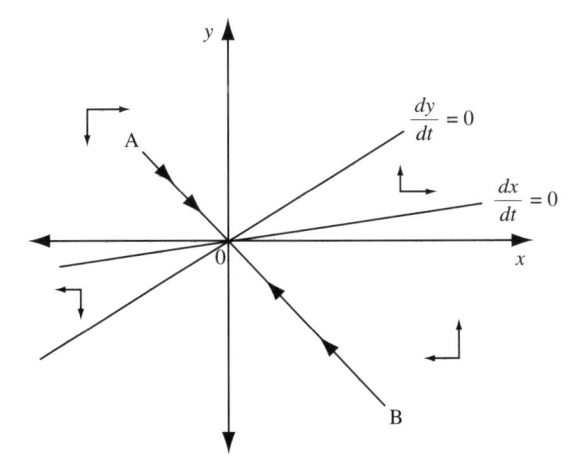

Figure 22.2 Phase diagram: one root positive, the other negative. The figure depicts the phase diagram for the following problem:
$$\frac{dx}{dt} = -\frac{1}{4}x + \frac{7}{4}x, \quad \frac{dy}{dt} = \frac{5}{4}x - \frac{3}{4}y$$

Only if the initial conditions lie on the line AB will convergence on the origin result.

Hence convergence will occur in this case if the initial conditions are such that
$$y(0) = [y^p - \alpha_2 x^p] + \alpha_2 x(0)$$

otherwise the system will move through time further and further away from the long-run equilibrium position.

The phase diagram for question (a)(ii) in Exercise 22.1 is given in Fig. 22.2. In this case, the problem was:
$$\frac{dx}{dt} = \frac{-1}{4}x + \frac{7}{4}y$$
$$\frac{dy}{dt} = \frac{5}{4}x - \frac{3}{4}y$$
$$x(0) = 4, \quad y(0) = -4$$

To the right of the locus labelled $dx/dt = 0$, x is falling in value, and to the left of the locus x is increasing in value. To the right of the locus labelled $dy/dt = 0$, y is rising in value, and to the left of the locus y is falling in value. The two loci intersect at the origin; only if the initial position lay somewhere along the downward sloping line AB with slope equal to minus one and which passes through the origin would convergence on the long-run equilibrium result. The initial conditions given in the question did indeed lie on this line, and convergence was achieved. However for the general case, this will not be the case, and we shall typically move further and further away from the origin.

Let us return to question (a)(i) of Exercise 22.1.

(a) $\dfrac{dx}{dt} = 3x + 2y$

$\dfrac{dy}{dt} = x + 2y$

$x(0) = 1, \quad y(0) = 1$

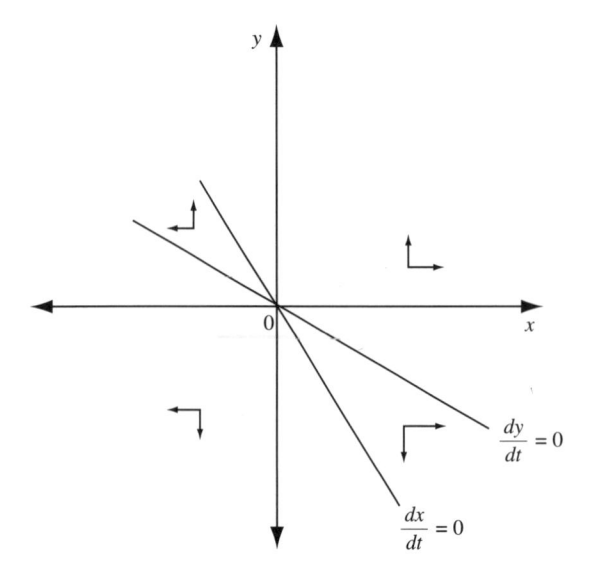

Figure 22.3 Phase diagram: unstable case, both roots positive. The figure depicts the phase diagram for the following problem:

$$\frac{dx}{dt} = 3x + 2y, \quad \frac{dy}{dt} = x + 2y$$

The origin will not be reached from any other initial position.

In this case both roots of the characteristic equation are positive. The phase diagram will take the following typical form as shown in Fig. 22.3. If the initial position is not where the two loci intersect, then we shall move further and further away from this point through time. To the left of the $dx/dt = 0$ locus, x is falling in value, and to the right of the locus x is increasing in value. To the left of the $dy/dt = 0$ locus, y is falling in value, and to the right of the locus y is increasing in value. In all four regions, the arrows are pointing away from the equilibrium point.

22.4 SIMULTANEOUS LINEAR DIFFERENCE EQUATIONS

We now turn to examine how to find the solution to a pair of simultaneous linear difference equations. The method of solution is remarkably similar to the one we have already outlined in our discussion of simultaneous differential equations. Consider the following homogeneous system of equations:

$$x_t = ax_{t-1} + by_{t-1}$$
$$y_t = cx_{t-1} + dy_{t-1}$$

We now try a solution of the form:

$$x_t = Am^t \quad \text{and} \quad y_t = Bm^t$$

After carrying out the appropriate lags, we have on substituting into our system of equations:

$$Am^t - aAm^{t-1} - bBm^{t-1} = 0$$
$$Bm^t - cAm^{t-1} - dBm^{t-1} = 0$$

from which it follows that

$$\begin{bmatrix} m-a & -b \\ -c & m-d \end{bmatrix} \begin{bmatrix} A \\ B \end{bmatrix} = \begin{bmatrix} 0 \\ 0 \end{bmatrix}$$

As before, the matrix must be singular for a non-trivial solution to exist. Hence we have the following characteristic equation:

$$m^2 - (a+d)m + (ad - bc) = 0$$

whose roots are

$$m = \frac{a + d \pm \sqrt{(a+d)^2 - 4(ad - bc)}}{2}$$

Given the singularity of the matrix, we also have

$$(m_1 - a)A_1 = bB_1$$
$$(m_2 - a)A_2 = bB_2$$

For the non-homogeneous case, then the time-path for each variable is given as expected by the sum of the complementary function and the particular integral.

Example 22.2

Assume we have the following system of equations:

$$x_t = 2x_{t-1} - 2y_{t-1} + 9$$
$$y_t = -2x_{t-1} - y_{t-1} + 24$$
$$x_0 = 9 \quad \text{and} \quad y_0 = 10$$

To find the particular integral, we set x_t equal to x_{t-1}, and y_t equal to y_{t-1}. This gives us

$$x_t^p = 5 \quad \text{and} \quad y_t^p = 7$$

For the complementary function, we try solutions of the form:

$$x_t^c = Am^t \quad \text{and} \quad y_t^c = Bm^t$$

After lagging and substituting into the homogeneous part of the system of equations, we obtain:

$$Am^t - 2Am^{t-1} + 2Bm^{t-1} = 0$$
$$Bm^t + 2Am^{t-1} + Bm^{t-1} = 0$$

from which it follows that

$$\begin{bmatrix} m-2 & 2 \\ 2 & m+1 \end{bmatrix} \begin{bmatrix} A \\ B \end{bmatrix} = \begin{bmatrix} 0 \\ 0 \end{bmatrix}$$

The characteristic equation, therefore, is

$$m^2 - m - 6 = 0$$

hence $m_1 = 3$ and $m_2 = -2$

The relationship between A and B is such that

$$A_1 + 2B_1 = 0 \quad \text{and} \quad -4A_2 + 2B_2 = 0$$

hence $B_1 = -0.5A_1$ and $B_2 = 2A_2$

The general solution, therefore, is

$$x_t = A_1(3)^t + A_2(-2)^t + 5$$
$$y_t = -0.5A_1(3)^t + 2A_2(-2)^t + 7$$

Given the initial conditions, we must also have

$$A_1 + A_2 + 5 = 9$$
$$-0.5A_1 + 2A_2 + 7 = 10$$

hence $A_1 = 2$ and $A_2 = 2$

So the particular solution is

$$x_t = 2(3)^t + 2(-2)^t + 5$$
$$y_t = -(3)^t + 4(-2)^t + 7$$

Repeat buying

10,000 households live in Lake Wobegon, Minnesota and each household shops at one of its two stores each week. If a household shops at Garrison's one week, the probability that it will return to shop there the next week is 0.9; on the other hand, if it shops at Keillor's one week the probability that it will return to shop there the next week is 0.7. In the initial week, 5000 households shop at each store.

If we let x represent the number of households who shop at Garrison's and y the number who shop at Keillor's, then we have the following system of equations:

$$x_t = 0.9x_{t-1} + 0.3y_{t-1}$$
$$y_t = 0.1x_{t-1} + 0.7y_{t-1}$$

Trying as the solution $x_t = Am^t$ and $y_t = Bm^t$ yields the following

$$\begin{bmatrix} m - 0.9 & -0.3 \\ -0.1 & m - 0.7 \end{bmatrix} \begin{bmatrix} A \\ B \end{bmatrix} = \begin{bmatrix} 0 \\ 0 \end{bmatrix}$$

and the characteristic equation is

$$m^2 - 1.6m + 0.6 = 0$$

and hence $m_1 = 1$ and $m_2 = 0.6$

The general solution then is

$$x_t = A_1 + A_2(0.6)^t$$
$$y_t = B_1 + B_2(0.6)^t$$

Given the singularity of the matrix of coefficients when $m = 1$ or 0.6, we must also have

$$0.1A_1 - 0.3B_1 = 0 \quad \text{and} \quad -0.3A_2 - 0.3B_2 = 0$$
$$\text{hence } A_1 = 3B_1 \quad \text{and} \quad A_2 = -B_2$$

Given the initial conditions and making use of the above relationships, we have

$$3B_1 - B_2 = 5000$$
$$B_1 + B_2 = 5000$$
$$\text{hence } B_1 = B_2 = 2500$$
$$\text{and } A_1 = 7500, \quad A_2 = -2500$$

The particular solution, therefore, is

$$x_t = 7500 - 2500(0.6)^t$$
$$y_t = 2500 + 2500(0.6)^t$$

In the long run, *7500* households shop at Garrison's and *2500* households at Keillor's.

We have simply dealt with the case where the characteristic equation gives rise to two real distinct roots. In principle, one can obtain solutions with a repeated root or a pair of complex roots. We have dealt with such outcomes in Chapter 21 in our discussion of second-order linear difference equations, and have touched upon them in Section 22.2 earlier in this chapter. We eschew further discussion here.

22.5 SUMMARY

In this concluding chapter of the book, we have briefly outlined how to solve some simple simultaneous linear differential and difference equations. The techniques we acquired for solving second-order linear differential and difference equations are applicable in this context too. In both cases, two first-order linear simultaneous differential or difference equations give rise to a second-order linear differential or difference equation in each variable, which can then be solved by the standard methods. Given initial conditions on the variables under consideration, we are also able to make definite the arbitrary constants.

22.6 EXERCISES

22.1 (a) Solve the following system of equations:

(i) $\dfrac{dx}{dt} = 3x + 2y$

$\dfrac{dy}{dt} = x + 2y$

$x(0) = 1, \quad y(0) = 1$

(ii) $\dfrac{dx}{dt} = \dfrac{-1}{4}x + \dfrac{7}{4}y$

$\dfrac{dy}{dt} = \dfrac{5}{4}x - \dfrac{3}{4}y$

$x(0) = 4, \quad y(0) = -4$

(iii) $\dfrac{dx}{dt} = -0.7x - 0.2y + 62$

$\dfrac{dy}{dt} = 0.2x - 0.3y + 18$

$x(0) = 68, \quad y(0) = 100$

(iii) $\dfrac{dx}{dt} = x - 4y$

$\dfrac{dy}{dt} = x + y$

$x(0) = 8, \quad y(0) = 6$

(b) The demand functions for two goods, x and y, at time t are given respectively by:

$$x^d(t) = 100 - 2p(t) + q(t)$$

$$y^d(t) = 90 + p(t) - 3q(t)$$

and the supply functions take the following form:

$$x^s(t) = -20 + p(t)$$

$$y^s(t) = -10 + 2q(t)$$

where p is the price of x, and q the price of y.

(i) What are the equilibrium prices and quantities of the two goods?

The price of each good rises in the presence of excess demand for that good. Assume:

$$\dfrac{dp(t)}{dt} = 0.2E[x(t)]$$

$$\dfrac{dq(t)}{dt} = 0.1E[y(t)]$$

where $E[x(t)]$ and $E[y(t)]$ are respectively the excess demands for x and y at time t.

(ii) Obtain the particular solution to the simultaneous first-order differential equations in the two prices, given $p(0) = 40$ and $q(0) = 40$.

(iii) Comment on the stability of the equilibrium.

(c) Consider the following macroeconomic model of output and inflation:

$$p = 0.5(y - y^n) + p^e$$

$$\dfrac{dp^e}{dt} = p - p^e$$

$$\dfrac{dy}{dt} = 0.5(m - p)$$

where p is the rate of inflation, p^e the expected rate of inflation, y is output, y^n the natural rate of output, and m the rate of growth of the money supply.

(i) By finding the particular integral, obtain the long-run equilibrium values for the rate of output and the expected rate of inflation.

(ii) Substituting out the actual rate of inflation, obtain the general solution to the system of equations defining the rate of change of output and the rate of change of the expected inflation rate.

(iii) What can you say about the nature of the time-path of output and the expected rate of inflation?

(iv) What will happen to the actual inflation rate through time?

22.2 (a) Each week *600* Norwich sixthformers visit one of two discotheques in the city, Ritzy's or Peppermint Park. Ritzy's clientele is more loyal than that of Peppermint Park, with *90* per cent of those who visit Ritzy's in a particular week returning there the following week; the corresponding figure for Peppermint Park is *80* per cent.

(i) Set up the matrix describing the loyalty transitions between the night clubs.

(ii) How many sixthformers will visit Ritzy's in the long run?

(iii) If initially Ritzy's is patronised by *200* sixthformers, and Peppermint Park by *400* such students, solve for the number of students each night club has n weeks later.

(b) Firms in a particular industry fall into one of three size categories: large, medium and small. If a firm is large in one period, the probabilities that in the next period it will remain large, fall into the medium-size category or become small are respectively *0.7*, *0.2* and *0.1*. For a firm of medium size, the probabilities that in the next period it will become large, stay medium-sized or become small are respectively *0.1*, *0.8* and *0.1*. For a small firm, the probabilities that in the next period it will become large, medium-sized or remain small are respectively *0*, *0.1* and *0.9*.

(i) Find the general solution to the simultaneous linear difference equations implied by the above information.

(ii) If the number of firms in the industry remain fixed at *4000*, how many firms will fall into each size category in long-run equilibrium?

ANSWERS TO EXERCISES

CHAPTER 2

Exercise 2.1

(a)

(i) $\sqrt{130}$, (ii) 20, (iii) $\sqrt{450}$, (iv) $\sqrt{125}$,

(v) $\sqrt{62}$, (vi) $\sqrt{186}$, (vii) $\sqrt{200}$, (viii) $\sqrt{33}$

(b) (i) 1, (ii) 0, (iii) 6, (iv) 0, (v) 0, (vi) -6.

(c) The vectors in (ii), (iv) and (v) are orthogonal to each other. The pairs of orthonormal, vectors are as follows:

$$(ii)\ \frac{1}{\sqrt{80}}\begin{bmatrix}8\\4\end{bmatrix},\ \text{and}\ \frac{1}{\sqrt{45}}\begin{bmatrix}3\\-6\end{bmatrix}$$

$$(iv)\ \frac{1}{\sqrt{174}}\begin{bmatrix}5\\-7\\10\end{bmatrix}\ \text{and}\ \frac{1}{\sqrt{59}}\begin{bmatrix}3\\-5\\-5\end{bmatrix}$$

$$(v)\ \frac{1}{\sqrt{110}}\begin{bmatrix}-4\\2\\9\\3\end{bmatrix}\ \text{and}\ \frac{1}{\sqrt{152}}\begin{bmatrix}6\\6\\4\\-8\end{bmatrix}$$

Exercise 2.2

(a) (i) The two vectors are *L.I.*
 (ii) The third vector is equal to the sum of (2/3) times the first vector and (1/3) times the second vector.
 (iii) The vectors are *L.D.*; the third vector may be expressed as 6 times the first vector plus one half of the second vector.
 (iv) The vectors are *L.D.*; the third vector may be expressed as twice the first vector plus one half of the second vector.
 (v) The vectors are *L.D.*; the third vector is equal to the second vector minus the first vector.

(b) Since the original three vectors are said to be the L.I., then

$$\lambda_1 a + \lambda_2 b + \lambda_3 c = \mathbf{0}\ \textit{iff}\ \lambda_i = 0\ \ \forall i$$

Let us first assume that $a+b$, $b+c$, $a+c$ are indeed L.D. Then for this to be the case we must have:

$$\lambda_4(a+b) + \lambda_5(b+c) + \lambda_6(a+c)$$

with not all the lambdas equal to zero. Rearranging, we have:

$$(\lambda_4 + \lambda_6)a + (\lambda_4 + \lambda_5)b + (\lambda_5 + \lambda_6)c = 0$$

Given the linear independence of the original three vectors, however, we must have:

$$\lambda_4 = -\lambda_6, \quad \lambda_4 = -\lambda_5, \quad \lambda_5 = -\lambda_6$$

but these three equations can only hold if all the lambdas are equal to zero. Contrary to our initial assumption then, the three vectors, $a+b$, $b+c$, $a+c$, are indeed L.I.

Now consider the case of the second set of vectors, $a-b$, $b+c$, $a+c$. It is immediately apparent that we must have L.D. since

$$a + c = (a - b) + (b + c)$$

(c) (i) The length of a is $\sqrt{230}$, and of b is $\sqrt{35}$.

(ii) For c and b to be orthogonal to each other, we must have

$$c \cdot b = a \cdot b + k b \cdot b = 0$$

given $a \cdot b = -70$, and $b \cdot b = 35$,

then $k = 2$ and $c = \begin{bmatrix} 7 \\ -5 \\ 4 \end{bmatrix}$

(iii) No, since the three vectors are L.D.

(iv) For d to be orthonormal to both b and c, we must have:

$$3d_1 + 5d_2 + \ d_3 = 0$$

$$7d_1 - 5d_2 + 4d_3 = 0$$

Setting d_2 equal to unity and solving for the two unknowns we have:

$$d = \begin{bmatrix} -5 \\ 1 \\ 10 \end{bmatrix}$$

(v) The orthonormal set of vectors is:

$$\frac{1}{\sqrt{35}} \begin{bmatrix} 3 \\ 5 \\ 1 \end{bmatrix}, \quad \frac{1}{\sqrt{90}} \begin{bmatrix} 7 \\ -5 \\ 4 \end{bmatrix}, \quad \frac{1}{\sqrt{126}} \begin{bmatrix} -5 \\ 1 \\ 10 \end{bmatrix}.$$

CHAPTER 3

Exercise 3.1

(a)

$$(a)\ A + B = \begin{bmatrix} 4 & 1 & 3 \\ -2 & 5 & 3 \\ 14 & 5 & 10 \end{bmatrix}, \quad (b)\ B - A = \begin{bmatrix} -2 & -7 & 1 \\ 2 & 5 & -5 \\ 4 & 7 & -4 \end{bmatrix},$$

(c) $\lambda A - \mu B = \begin{bmatrix} 7 & 31 & -6 \\ -8 & -25 & 21 \\ -25 & -34 & 13 \end{bmatrix}$, (d) $AB = \begin{bmatrix} 12 & 17 & 5 \\ 34 & 30 & 8 \\ 68 & 22 & 32 \end{bmatrix}$

(e) $BA = \begin{bmatrix} 19 & 2 & 3 \\ -15 & 1 & 13 \\ 30 & 33 & 54 \end{bmatrix}$, (f) $\mu BA = \begin{bmatrix} 95 & 10 & 15 \\ -75 & 5 & 65 \\ 150 & 165 & 270 \end{bmatrix}$

(b)

(a) $Bx = \begin{bmatrix} 52 \\ -18 \end{bmatrix}$, (b) $Ay = \begin{bmatrix} 39 \\ -1 \\ -50 \end{bmatrix}$

(c) $x^T A = (17 \ -121)$, (d) $y^T B = (12 \ -23 \ 2)$

(e) $AB = \begin{bmatrix} -88 & -60 & 18 \\ 12 & 5 & -2 \\ -8 & 34 & 4 \end{bmatrix}$, (f) $BA = \begin{bmatrix} -107 & 76 \\ -39 & 20 \end{bmatrix}$

Exercise 3.2

(a)

(i) $AB = \begin{bmatrix} 26 & 48 & 34 \\ 21 & 40 & 26 \end{bmatrix}$

(ii) $A^T B = \begin{bmatrix} 17 & 24 & 31 \\ 27 & 40 & 47 \end{bmatrix}$

(iii) BA^T is not defined,

(iv) $B^T A = (A^T B)^T = \begin{bmatrix} 17 & 27 \\ 24 & 40 \\ 31 & 47 \end{bmatrix}$

(v) $C^T - B = \begin{bmatrix} 2 & 3 & -6 \\ -2 & -8 & 4 \end{bmatrix}$

(vi) $AC^T B^T = \begin{bmatrix} 282 & 196 \\ 230 & 151 \end{bmatrix}$

and $A^T - AC^T B^T = \begin{bmatrix} -278 & -193 \\ -224 & -146 \end{bmatrix}$

(b) (i) The first matrix is an example of what is known as an idempotent matrix, since we have

$$A^2 = A = \begin{bmatrix} 0.25 & \sqrt{0.1875} \\ \sqrt{0.1875} & 0.75 \end{bmatrix}$$

Clearly, we must also have

$$A = A^2 = A^3 = A^4 = \cdots = A^n$$

(ii)

$$A^2 = \begin{bmatrix} -17 & 19 & -9 \\ 0 & 1 & 0 \\ 18 & 21 & -14 \end{bmatrix}, \quad A^3 = \begin{bmatrix} -71 & -39 & 33 \\ 0 & 1 & 0 \\ -66 & 153 & -82 \end{bmatrix},$$

$$A^4 = \begin{bmatrix} 127 & -493 & 279 \\ 0 & 1 & 0 \\ -558 & 69 & 34 \end{bmatrix}$$

(c)

(i) $\begin{bmatrix} 5 & 10 \\ -4 & 3 \end{bmatrix} = \begin{bmatrix} 5 & 3 \\ 3 & 3 \end{bmatrix} + \begin{bmatrix} 0 & 7 \\ -7 & 0 \end{bmatrix}$

(ii) $\begin{bmatrix} -2 & 8 \\ 6 & 9 \end{bmatrix} = \begin{bmatrix} -2 & 7 \\ 7 & 9 \end{bmatrix} + \begin{bmatrix} 0 & 1 \\ -1 & 0 \end{bmatrix}$

(iii) $\begin{bmatrix} 1 & 7 & 4 \\ 2 & 5 & -8 \\ 3 & -4 & 6 \end{bmatrix} = \begin{bmatrix} 1 & 4.5 & 3.5 \\ 4.5 & 5 & -6 \\ 3.5 & -6 & 6 \end{bmatrix} + \begin{bmatrix} 0 & 2.5 & 0.5 \\ -2.5 & 0 & -2 \\ -0.5 & 2 & 0 \end{bmatrix}$

(iv) $\begin{bmatrix} 2 & 4 & -6 & 3 \\ 8 & -1 & 7 & -2 \\ 1 & 11 & 0 & 5 \\ 2 & 6 & 9 & 4 \end{bmatrix} = \begin{bmatrix} 2 & 6 & -2.5 & 2.5 \\ 6 & -1 & 9 & 2 \\ -2.5 & 9 & 0 & 7 \\ 2.5 & 2 & 7 & 4 \end{bmatrix} + \begin{bmatrix} 0 & -2 & -3.5 & 0.5 \\ 2 & 0 & -2 & -4 \\ 3.5 & 2 & 0 & -2 \\ -0.5 & 4 & 2 & 0 \end{bmatrix}$

CHAPTER 4

Exercise 4.1

(a) (i) *4*

(ii) *−39*

(iii) *−39*. The matrix in (iii) only differs from that in (ii) in that the first row of (iii) is equal to the first row of (ii) minus the second row of (ii). Hence, the determinant is unchanged.

(iv) Each element in the matrix in (iii) has been multiplied by −2. Hence its determinant is equal to $-8(-39) = 312$.

(v) The matrix in (v) was obtained by transposing the matrix in (ii), and then interchanging the first and second rows. Hence, the value of the determinant is *39*.

(vi) The first row of the matrix in (vi) is equal to the first row of the matrix in (v) less the sum of the second and third rows of the matrix in (v). So the value of the determinant is still *39*.

(vii) It is straightforward to evaluate this determinant once you have defined a new third column equal to the original third column less the second column. The value of the determinant is *−240*.

(viii) The first row of this matrix is equal to the sum of twice the second row plus the third row. The determinant, therefore, vanishes.

Exercise 4.2

(a) The inverses are as follows:

$$\text{(i)} \begin{bmatrix} -2 & 5/4 \\ -1 & 1/2 \end{bmatrix}, \quad \text{(ii)} \begin{bmatrix} -49/39 & 38/39 & 17/39 \\ 34/39 & -20/39 & -11/39 \\ 8/39 & -7/39 & 2/39 \end{bmatrix}$$

$$\text{(iii)} \begin{bmatrix} -49/39 & -11/39 & 17/39 \\ 34/39 & 14/39 & -11/39 \\ 8/39 & 1/39 & 2/39 \end{bmatrix}, \quad \text{(iv)} \begin{bmatrix} 49/78 & 11/78 & -17/78 \\ -17/39 & -7/39 & 11/78 \\ -4/39 & -1/78 & -1/39 \end{bmatrix}$$

$$\text{(v)} \begin{bmatrix} 34/39 & -49/39 & 8/39 \\ -20/39 & 38/39 & -7/39 \\ -11/39 & 17/39 & 2/39 \end{bmatrix}, \quad \text{(vi)} \begin{bmatrix} 34/39 & -5/13 & 14/13 \\ -20/39 & 6/13 & -9/13 \\ -11/39 & 2/13 & -3/13 \end{bmatrix}$$

$$\text{(vii)} \begin{bmatrix} 3/80 & 17/80 & 0 & 9/80 \\ 17/80 & 289/240 & -1 & -7/240 \\ 0 & -1 & 1 & 0 \\ 9/80 & -7/240 & 0 & 1/240 \end{bmatrix}$$

Note that the matrices in (ii) and (iii) only differ in their first rows, so the co-factors of the first row of the two matrices are the same. Given that the determinants of the two matrices are equal, the first columns of the two inverses are identical. The same also applies for the matrices in (v) and (vi). It is also the case that the co-factors of the third rows of (ii) and (iii) are also identical, hence the two inverses have identical column threes. Though in (vii) we have to invert a *4 × 4* matrix, the matrix is symmetric, so we have to find *10* separate co-factors rather than the full *16*.

Exercise 4.3

(a)

$$\text{(i)} \ x_1 = \frac{\begin{vmatrix} 44 & 1 \\ 72 & 3 \end{vmatrix}}{\begin{vmatrix} 2 & 1 \\ 1 & 3 \end{vmatrix}} = \frac{60}{5} = 12$$

$$x_2 = \frac{\begin{vmatrix} 2 & 44 \\ 1 & 72 \end{vmatrix}}{5} = \frac{100}{5} = 20$$

$$\text{(ii)} \ x_1 = \frac{\begin{vmatrix} 41 & 2 \\ 53 & 5 \end{vmatrix}}{\begin{vmatrix} 3 & 2 \\ 2 & 5 \end{vmatrix}} = \frac{99}{11} = 9$$

$$x_2 = \frac{\begin{vmatrix} 3 & 41 \\ 2 & 53 \end{vmatrix}}{11} = \frac{77}{11} = 7$$

ANSWERS TO EXERCISES **425**

(iii) $x_1 = \dfrac{\begin{vmatrix} 69 & 0 & 5 \\ 46 & 2 & 4 \\ 30 & 1 & 1 \end{vmatrix}}{\begin{vmatrix} 3 & 0 & 5 \\ 0 & 2 & 4 \\ 1 & 1 & 1 \end{vmatrix}} = \dfrac{-208}{-16} = 13$

$x_2 = \dfrac{\begin{vmatrix} 3 & 69 & 5 \\ 0 & 46 & 4 \\ 1 & 30 & 1 \end{vmatrix}}{-16} = \dfrac{-176}{-16} = 11$

$x_3 = \dfrac{\begin{vmatrix} 3 & 0 & 69 \\ 0 & 2 & 46 \\ 1 & 1 & 30 \end{vmatrix}}{-16} = \dfrac{-96}{-16} = 6$

(iv) $x_1 = \dfrac{\begin{vmatrix} 76 & 2 & 3 \\ 34 & 1 & 2 \\ 20 & 5 & 0 \end{vmatrix}}{\begin{vmatrix} 5 & 2 & 3 \\ 0 & 1 & 2 \\ 4 & 5 & 0 \end{vmatrix}} = \dfrac{-230}{-46} = 5$

$x_2 = \dfrac{\begin{vmatrix} 5 & 76 & 3 \\ 0 & 34 & 2 \\ 4 & 20 & 0 \end{vmatrix}}{-46} = \dfrac{0}{-46} = 0$

$x_3 = \dfrac{\begin{vmatrix} 5 & 2 & 76 \\ 0 & 1 & 34 \\ 4 & 5 & 20 \end{vmatrix}}{-46} = \dfrac{-782}{-46} = 17$

(b)

(i) $x = \begin{bmatrix} 5/13 & 3/13 \\ -1/13 & 2/13 \end{bmatrix} \begin{bmatrix} 4 \\ 54 \end{bmatrix} = \begin{bmatrix} 14 \\ 8 \end{bmatrix}$

(ii) $x = \begin{bmatrix} 1/5 & -3/5 \\ 1/10 & 1/5 \end{bmatrix} \begin{bmatrix} 18 \\ 21 \end{bmatrix} = \begin{bmatrix} -9 \\ 6 \end{bmatrix}$

(iii) $x = \begin{bmatrix} 2/31 & -4/31 & 7/31 \\ 0 & 1 & 0 \\ 3/31 & -6/31 & -5/31 \end{bmatrix} \begin{bmatrix} 0 \\ 25 \\ 32 \end{bmatrix} = \begin{bmatrix} 4 \\ 25 \\ -10 \end{bmatrix}$

$$(iv)\ x = \begin{bmatrix} 12/5 & -4/5 & 3/5 \\ 3/5 & -1/5 & 2/5 \\ -16/5 & 7/5 & -4/5 \end{bmatrix} \begin{bmatrix} 10 \\ 45 \\ 30 \end{bmatrix} = \begin{bmatrix} 6 \\ 9 \\ 7 \end{bmatrix}$$

Exercise 4.4

(a) (i) The equations for the *IS* and *LM* curves are given respectively by:

$$0.6Y + 20R = 850$$
$$-Y + 50R = 1000$$

from which it follows that $Y = 1250$, $R = 5$.

(ii) The value of the fiscal multiplier is *1*, and of the money multiplier is *0.4*.

(iii) Since full employment output is *1400*, and the value of the fiscal multiplier is unity, then to achieve full employment output must rise by *150*, and so must government expenditure. The associated value of the rate of interest is *8*.

(iv) Using monetary policy to raise output by *150* units requires the money supply to rise by *375*, given the value of the money multiplier is *0.4*. The associated value of the rate of interest is *0.5*.

(v) The combinations of government expenditure and the money supply which yield full employment are given by the following equation:

$$G + 0.4M = 1250$$

with *G* being non-negative and *M* being positive. Furthermore, we cannot plausibly drive *R* below zero. So we must have:

$$G - 0.6M + 1150 \geq 0 \quad \text{or} \quad G \geq 0.6M - 1150$$

Hence the maximum value of *M* is 2400 and correspondingly the minimum value of government expenditure is 290 to have full employment with a non-negative rate of interest.

The greater the reliance on monetary policy then the lower will be the rate of interest and the higher will be the value of private investment expenditures. The converse will be the case if the government adopts strongly expansionary fiscal policies.

CHAPTER 5

Exercise 5.1

(a) (i) rank(A) is 2; (ii) rank(B) is 3; (iii) rank(C) is 2; (iv) rank(D) is *1*; (v) rank(E) is *3*; (vi) rank(F) is *3*

(b) (i) 2; (ii) 3; (iii) *1*; (iv) *1*; (v) 2; (vi) 3

Exercise 5.2

(a)

(i) $x_1 = -1 - 5x_3$, $x_2 = 5 + 4x_3$;

(ii) $x_1 = 5.25 - 1.25x_2$, $x_3 = -1.25 + 0.25x_2$

(b) (i)

$$x_1 = \frac{143 - 7x_3}{11}, \quad x_2 = \frac{-22 - 6x_3}{11}$$

(ii) The set of equations would be inconsistent with each other.

Exercise 5.3

(a) The inverses are respectively:

$$(i) \begin{bmatrix} 4/5 & -1/5 \\ -3/5 & 2/5 \end{bmatrix}, \quad (ii) \begin{bmatrix} -1/12 & 2/3 & 1/8 \\ 1/6 & -4/3 & 1/4 \\ 1/12 & 1/3 & -1/8 \end{bmatrix}$$

(iii) $\begin{bmatrix} 0 & -2 & -3 \\ -1/3 & 0 & 1/3 \\ 2/3 & -5 & 22/3 \end{bmatrix}$

(iv) $\begin{bmatrix} 2 & 0 & 2 & -3/2 \\ 0 & 1/5 & 0 & 0 \\ -1/3 & 0 & 0 & 1/6 \\ -13/3 & 0 & -5 & 11/3 \end{bmatrix}$

(b) (i) The elementary matrices for (a)(i) are as follows:

$$E_1 = \begin{bmatrix} 0.5 & 0 \\ 0 & 1 \end{bmatrix}, \quad E_2 = \begin{bmatrix} 1 & 0 \\ -3 & 1 \end{bmatrix}$$

$$E_3 = \begin{bmatrix} 1 & 0 \\ 0 & 2/5 \end{bmatrix}, \quad E_4 = \begin{bmatrix} 1 & -1/2 \\ 0 & 1 \end{bmatrix}$$

$$A^{-1} = E_4 E_3 E_2 E_1$$

The elementary matrices for (b)(i) are follows:

$$E_1 = \begin{bmatrix} 1/2 & 0 & 0 \\ 0 & 1 & 0 \\ 0 & 0 & 1 \end{bmatrix}, \quad E_2 = \begin{bmatrix} 1 & 0 & 0 \\ -1 & 1 & 0 \\ 0 & 0 & 1 \end{bmatrix}, \quad E_3 = \begin{bmatrix} 1 & 0 & 0 \\ 0 & 1 & 0 \\ -4 & 0 & 1 \end{bmatrix}$$

$$E_4 = \begin{bmatrix} 1 & 0 & 0 \\ 0 & -2/3 & 0 \\ 0 & 0 & 1 \end{bmatrix}, \quad E_5 = \begin{bmatrix} 1 & -3/2 & 0 \\ 0 & 1 & 0 \\ 0 & 0 & 1 \end{bmatrix}, \quad E_6 = \begin{bmatrix} 1 & 0 & 0 \\ 0 & 1 & 0 \\ 0 & 4 & 1 \end{bmatrix}$$

$$E_7 = \begin{bmatrix} 1 & 0 & 0 \\ 0 & 1 & 0 \\ 0 & 0 & -1/8 \end{bmatrix}, \quad E_8 = \begin{bmatrix} 1 & 0 & -1 \\ 0 & 1 & 0 \\ 0 & 0 & 1 \end{bmatrix}, \quad E_9 = \begin{bmatrix} 1 & 0 & 0 \\ 0 & 1 & -2 \\ 0 & 0 & 1 \end{bmatrix}$$

$$A^{-1} = E_9 E_8 \ldots E_2 E_1$$

(ii) In the first case the product of the determinants of the elementary matrices equals $(1/2)(1)(2/5)(1) = 1/5$. In the second case, we have $(1/2)(1)(1)(-2/3)(1)(1)(-1/8)(1)(1) = 1/24$. The determinants of the original matrices are 5 and 24 respectively.

(iii) We need to find the inverses of the elementary matrices we found in answering question 2(a)(i). They are:

$$E_1^{-1} = \begin{bmatrix} 2 & 0 \\ 0 & 1 \end{bmatrix}, \quad E_2^{-1} = \begin{bmatrix} 1 & 0 \\ 3 & 1 \end{bmatrix}$$

$$E_3^{-1} = \begin{bmatrix} 1 & 0 \\ 0 & 5/2 \end{bmatrix}, \quad E_4^{-1} = \begin{bmatrix} 1 & 1/2 \\ 0 & 1 \end{bmatrix}$$

$$A = E_1^{-1} E_2^{-1} E_3^{-1} E_4^{-1}$$

428 MATHEMATICS IN ECONOMICS

(iv) The product of the determinants of the elementary matrices in (iii) above is given by $(2)(1)(5/2)(1)$, which equals 5.

Exercise 5.4

(a)

$$\text{(i)} \begin{bmatrix} 4 & -1 & 2 \\ 0 & \frac{9}{4} & \frac{-5}{2} \\ 0 & 0 & \frac{-31}{9} \end{bmatrix}, \quad \text{(ii)} \begin{bmatrix} 4 & -1 & 2 \\ 0 & \frac{9}{4} & \frac{-5}{2} \\ 0 & 0 & 0 \end{bmatrix}$$

$$\text{(iii)} \begin{bmatrix} 2 & 3 & 0 & 1 \\ 0 & -7 & 2 & -2 \\ 0 & 0 & \frac{3}{7} & \frac{71}{4} \\ 0 & 0 & 0 & \frac{23}{6} \end{bmatrix}, \quad \text{(iv)} \begin{bmatrix} 2 & 3 & 0 & -1 \\ 0 & -7 & 2 & -2 \\ 0 & 0 & 0 & 0 \\ 0 & 0 & 0 & 0 \end{bmatrix}$$

(b) (i) $x_1 = 6$, $x_2 = -4$, $x_3 = 2$;
(ii) $x_1 = 10 + 0.6x_3$, $x_1 = 8 - 0.2x_3$;
(iii) $x_1 = 5$, $x_2 = 2$, $x_3 = 6$, $x_4 = 10$;
(iv) $x_1 = 4 + 2x_3 - x_4$, $x_2 = 2 - 1.5x_3 + 0.5x_4$.

CHAPTER 6

Exercise 6.1

(a) (i) There are four extreme points: (1) $S_1 = 36$, $S_2 = 34$; (2) $x_2 = 9$, $S_2 = 16$; (3) $x_1 = 8$, $x_2 = 5$; (4) $x_1 = 34/3$, $S_1 = 40/3$. The optimal position occurs at point (3) and the value of the objective function is *31*.

(ii) There are three extreme points: (1) $x_2 = 22$, $S_1 = 20$; (2) $x_1 = 4$, $x_2 = 10$; (3) $x_1 = 24$, $S_2 = 38$. The optimal position occurs at point (1) and the value of the objective function is *22*.

(iii) There are three extreme points: (1) $x_2 = 28$, $S_2 = 8$; (2) $x_2 = 32$, $S_1 = 4$; (3) $x_1 = 8$, $x_2 = 12$. The optimal position occurs at point (3) and the value of the objective function is *36*.

(iv) The feasible set of points is empty.

(b) First eliminate x_3, then the extreme points are (1) $S_1 = 48$, $S_2 = 56$; (2) $x_2 = 28$, $S_1 = 10$; (3) $x_1 = 14$, $S_1 = 20$. The optimal point is (3) and the value of the objective function is *140*.

Second, eliminate x_2, then the extreme points are (1) $S_1 = 48$, $S_2 = 56$; (2) $x_3 = 16$, $S_2 = 40$; (3) $x_1 = 12$, $x_3 = 8$; (4) $x_1 = 14$, $S_1 = 20$. The optimal point is (3) and the value of the objective function is *160*.

Third, eliminate x_1, then the extreme points are (1) $S_1 = 48$, $S_2 = 56$; (2) $x_3 = 16$, $S_2 = 40$; (3) $x_2 = 24$, $x_3 = 8$; (4) $x_2 = 28$, $S_1 = 20$. The optimal point is (3) and the value of the objective function is *136*.

The highest value of the objective function occurs when we eliminate x_2. The solution, therefore, is $x_1 = 12$, $x_3 = 8$.

(ii) Since there are only two constraints, then a basic feasible solution will only contain two basic variables. At most, therefore, two goods will be produced.

Exercise 6.2

(a) (i) $x_1 = 15$, $x_2 = 10$, $x_3 = 8$, and the value of the objective function is *444*.
(ii) $x_1 = 5$, $x_2 = 8$, $x_3 = 4$, and the value of the objective function is *151*.
(iii) $x_1 = 3$, $x_2 = 12$, $x_3 = 6$, and the value of the objective function is *390*.
(iv) $x_1 = 6$, $x_3 = 12$, $S_2 = 4$, and the value of the objective function is *324*.
(v) $x_2 = 7$, $x_3 = 8$, $S_1 = 10$, and the value of the objective function is *200*.

(b) At the proposed basis we have

$$x_B = \begin{bmatrix} 16 \\ 12 \\ 20 \end{bmatrix}$$

$$c_B B^{-1} = (0 \ 0 \ 7)$$

$$z_2 - c_2 = -10, \quad z_4 - c_4 = 0, \quad c_6 - c_6 = 0$$

Hence the basis is not optimal, and we would wish to introduce x_2 into the basis. To determine which of the basic variables is to be eliminated, we first obtain $B^{-1} a_2$

$$B^{-1} a_2 = \begin{bmatrix} 1 \\ -1 \\ 5 \end{bmatrix}, \quad \text{and} \quad B^{-1} b = \begin{bmatrix} 16 \\ 12 \\ 20 \end{bmatrix}$$

Hence the leaving variable is x_5 (the second slack variable). The new basis matrix is

$$\begin{bmatrix} 2 & 1 & 1 \\ 1 & 2 & 4 \\ 4 & 3 & 1 \end{bmatrix}$$

Its inverse is

$$\begin{bmatrix} 1 & -1/5 & -1/5 \\ -3/2 & 1/5 & 7/10 \\ 1/2 & 1/5 & -3/10 \end{bmatrix}$$

The values taken by the variables in this basis are then found by pre-multiplying b by this inverse. This yields: $x_1 = 12$, $x_3 = 16$, $x_2 = 4$. If all the elements in the new vector $c_B B^{-1}$ are positive, then we have reached the optimal solution.

$$c_B B^{-1} = (28 \ 21 \ 17) \begin{bmatrix} 1 & -1/5 & -1/5 \\ -3/2 & 1/5 & 7/10 \\ 1/2 & 1/5 & -3/10 \end{bmatrix}$$

$$= (5 \ 2 \ 4)$$

This is the optimal basis, and the value of the objective function is 740.

Exercise 6.3

(a) (i) Using the big M method the optimal tableau is

	x_1	x_2	R_1	R_2	S_1	S_2	solution
$z_j - c_j$	0	0	$2/11 - M$	$5/11 - M$	$-2/11$	$-5/11$	22
x_2	0	1	4/11	$-1/11$	$-4/11$	1/11	10
x_1	1	0	$-1/11$	3/11	1/11	$-3/11$	6

(ii) The tableau at the end of the first phase is

	x_1	x_2	R_1	R_2	S_1	S_2	solution
$z_j - c_j$	0	0	-1	-1	0	0	0
x_2	0	1	$4/11$	$-1/11$	$-4/11$	$1/11$	10
x_1	1	0	$-1/11$	$3/11$	$1/11$	$-3/11$	6

It is then a straightforward matter to substitute in the original objective function to obtain the solution.

(b) The optimal basis contains x_2, x_1 and S_3 in that order. The numerical values taken by these basic variables are 7, 8 and 7 respectively. The value of the objective function is 15.

(c) It is obvious from visual inspection that the two constraints are mutually inconsistent. However, if one applies the two-phase method, at the end of the first phase, one has the following tableau:

	x_1	x_2	S_1	R_2	S_2	solution
$z_j - c_j$	0	$1/2$	$3/2$	0	1	-6
x_1	1	$1/2$	$1/2$	0	0	4
R_2	0	$-1/2$	$-3/2$	1	-1	6

It has not been possible to eliminate the artificial variable R_2 from the basis, hence there exists no feasible solution to the problem.

CHAPTER 7

Exercise 7.1

(a) The duals are as follows:

(i) Maximise $44y_1 + 47y_2$

s.t. $2y_1 + y_2 \geq 16$
$3y_1 + y_2 \geq 20$
$y_1 + 3y_2 \geq 23$
$y_1, y_2 \geq 0$

(ii) Minimise $68y_1 - 82y_2 + 20y_3$

s.t. $2y_1 - y_2 + y_3 \geq 14$
$3y_1 - 4y_2 + y_3 \geq 16$
$2y_1 - 3y_2 \geq 10$
$y_1, y_2, y_3 \geq 0$

(iii) Maximise $30y_1 + 20y_2 + 64y_3$

s.t. $y_1 + 2y_2 + 4y_3 \leq 10$
$3y_1 + y_2 + 2y_3 \leq 3$
$y_1, y_2, y_3 \geq 0$

(iv) Maximise $93y_1 - 57y_2$

s.t. $y_1 + 2y_2 \leq 11$
$2y_1 - y_2 \leq 5$
$3y_1 - 2y_2 \leq 6$
$y_1, y_2 \geq 0$

(v) *Minimise* $16y_1 + 28y_2 + 60y_3$

$$\begin{aligned} s.t. \quad 2y_1 + y_2 + 2y_3 &\geq 20 \\ -y_1 + 2y_2 + 3y_3 &\geq 5 \\ y_1 - 2y_2 - 4y_3 &\geq -6 \\ y_1, y_2, y_3 &\geq 0 \end{aligned}$$

(b) (i) primal unbounded, dual infeasible;

(ii) primal infeasible, dual unbounded;

(iii) both primal and dual infeasible.

(c) (i) We are unable to eliminate the artificial variable in the first phase. At the end of the first phase, we have the following tableau

	x_1	x_2	S_1	R	S_2	solution
$z_j - c_j$	0	1/2	1/2	0	1	-2
x_1	1	3/2	1/2	0	0	6
R	0	$-1/2$	$-1/2$	1	-1	2

(ii) The dual of the above problem is:

Minimise $12y_1 - 8y_2$

$$\begin{aligned} s.t. \quad 2y_1 - y_2 &\geq 1 \\ 3y_1 - y_2 &\geq 1 \\ y_1, y_2 &\geq 0 \end{aligned}$$

In the first phase, we do eliminate the two artificial variables in this case, but our final tableau in the second phase is

	y_1	y_2	S_1	S_2	solution
$z_j - c_j$	0	2	-6	0	6
S_1	0	$-1/2$	$-3/2$	1	1/2
y_1	1	$-1/2$	$-1/2$	0	1/2

Since this is a minimisation problem, y_2 should enter the basis given the positive coefficient on y_2 in the $z_j - c_j$ row, but all the elements in the column of the entering variable are negative. Hence the solution is unbounded, y_2 can be made infinitely large.

Exercise 7.2

(a) (i) $y_1 = 3, y_2 = 0, y_3 = 1$

(ii) $x_1 = 10, x_2 = 8, x_3 = 0$ Note the value of the nutrients in a unit of the third foodstuff is only £10, whereas the price of the foodstuff is £12, hence it is not consumed.

Exercise 7.3

(a) (i) $x_1 = 8, x_2 = 7, S_3 = 7$, and the value of the objective function is 15.

(ii) $y_1 = -0.5, y_2 = 1.5, y_3 = 0$

(iii) Given the negative value of the first dual variable, we would wish to have slack in the first primal constraint. With slack, the optimal solution would be: $x_1 = 38/3, x_2 = 14/3, S_1 = 14/3; y_1 = 0, y_2 = 1/3, y_3 = 1/3$, and the value of the objective function is $52/3$.

(b) (i) The optimal solution is $x_2 = 12, x_3 = 6, S_3 = 2$, and the value of the objective function is 252.

(ii) the dual variables take the following values: $y_1 = -2, y_2 = 5$, and $y_3 = 0$

Exercise 7.4

(a) When the current basis consists of y_2 and y_6, then

$$b_D^T D^{-1} = \left(\frac{b_2 - M}{a_{21}} \; M \right)$$

$$w_1 - b_1 = \frac{a_{11}b_2 + (a_{12}a_{21} - a_{11}a_{22})M}{a_{21}} - b_1$$

$$w_3 - b_3 = \frac{a_{22}M - b_2}{a_{21}}$$

$$w_4 - b_4 = -M$$

Hence the potential non-basic variables to be introduced into the dual basis are y_1 and y_3.

Exercise 7.5

(a) (i) $x_1 = 7$, $x_2 = 15$; $y_1 = 4$, $y_2 = 2$
 (ii) $x_1 = 10$, $x_2 = 12$, $x_3 = 0$; $y_1 = 5$, $y_2 = 0$, $y_3 = 2$
 (iii) $x_1 = 15$, $x_2 = 9$, $x_3 = 4$; $y_1 = 7$, $y_2 = 2$, $y_3 = 3$

Exercise 7.6

(a) (i) The optimal basis contains x_1 and x_3, with $x_1 = 10$, $x_3 = 7.5$, the value of the objective function is 65.

 (ii) We have

$$\Delta x_B = \begin{bmatrix} 2/5 & -1/5 \\ -1/10 & 3/10 \end{bmatrix} \begin{bmatrix} \Delta b_1 \\ 0 \end{bmatrix}$$

Hence $\Delta x_1 = 0.4\Delta b_1$ and $\Delta x_3 = -0.1\Delta b_1$

So, if the right-hand side of the first constraint is increased by more than 75, x_3 will be driven below zero.

 (iii) If c_2 were 5, then $z_2 - c_2$ would equal -1, and we would wish to introduce x_2 into the basis in place of x_1. The new solution would be $x_2 = 50/3$, $x_3 = 35/6$. The new values of the dual variables are: $y_1 = 5/3$, and $y_2 = 5/3$.

 (iv) The original optimal basis would no longer be feasible, since we would now have $x_1 = 16$, and $x_3 = -3/2$. We, therefore, eliminate x_3 and bring S_1 into the basis in its place. The new solution is: $x_1 = 10$, $S_1 = 15$, and the value of the objective function is 50.

 (v) Note that the original optimal solution will no longer be feasible, since it requires the slack variable in the new constraint to take on a negative value. Introducing the new constraint into the original optimal tableau, and expressing the S_3 row in terms of the non-basic variables, we have:

$$-4/5x_2 - 1/5S_1 - -7/5S_2 + S_3 = -12$$

Applying dual simplex, S_3 is eliminated, and x_2 comes in to replace it. The new value of the objective function is 110, with $x_1 = 1$, $x_2 = 15$, and $x_3 = 6$; the values taken by the dual variables are 3/4, 1/4 and 5/4 respectively.

(b) (i) The value of the objective function is 118, with $x_1 = 6$, $x_2 = 4$; the dual variables are -1 and 9 respectively.

 (ii) The above primal basis is still feasible, but is it optimal? Solving for the new values of the dual variables, we find that $y_1 = 1$, $y_2 = 6$, and $z_3 - c_3 = 1$. Hence the basis is still optimal.

 (iii) When slack is permitted in the first constraint, given that the first dual variable was negative, we would now wish to introduce S_1 into the basis. We eliminate x_2. In the new basis, we have $x_1 = 8$, and $S_1 = 2$. At this basis, we find that $y_1 = 0$, and $y_2 = 7.5$; at these values of the dual variables, both $z_2 - c_2$ and $z_3 - c_3$ are positive, so the basis is indeed optimal.

 (iv) The above basis is no longer optimal, since S_1 is now equal to -4. We, therefore, eliminate S_1 and bring in x_3. This new basis is optimal with $x_1 = 6$ and $x_3 = 2$, the values of the dual variables are 3/2 and 21/4 respectively.

CHAPTER 8

Exercise 8.1
(a) (i) Introduce route (3,3).

(ii) The maximum that can be shipped over this route is *150*.

(iii) The new basis is still not optimal. One would wish to introduce route (3,2) into the basis; the maximum that can be shipped over this route is *50*. The new basis is the optimal one.

Exercise 8.2
(a) $x_{11} = 10$, $x_{12} = 10$, $x_{23} = 30$, $x_{33} = 30$, $x_{42} = 15$, $x_{43} = 5$.

(b) (i) The initial basic feasible solution by the north-west corner method is

$$\begin{bmatrix} 300 & 150 & & \\ & 75 & 105 & \\ & & 375 & 195 \end{bmatrix}$$

Total costs are *9645*, and the values of the dual variables are $u_1 = 0$, $u_2 = -7$, $u_3 = -9$, $v_1 = 8$, $v_2 = 6$, $v_3 = 1$, $v_4 = -5$. Routes (2,1), (3,1) and (3,2) are all candidates to be introduced into the basis, but the unit savings are greatest for route (3,2). To accommodate this route, shipments must be reduced over routes (2,2) and (3,3); the maximum that can be shipped over this route, therefore, is *75*. The new allocation is the optimal one.

$$\begin{bmatrix} 300 & 150 & & \\ & & 180 & \\ & 75 & 300 & 195 \end{bmatrix}$$

Total costs are *9045*, and the values of the dual variables are $u_1 = 0$, $u_2 = 1$, $u_3 = -1$, $v_1 = 8$, $v_2 = 6$, $v_3 = 9$, $v_4 = 3$. The dual constraints hold for all non-utilised routes.

(ii) Using the least-cost method, the order in which the variables are entered is as follows: $x_{34} = 195$, $x_{12} = 225$, $x_{11} = 225$, $x_{23} = 180$, $x_{33} = 300$, $x_{31} = 75$. This basis is not optimal; we must introduce route (3,2), and the maximum that can be shipped is *75*. We have, then, reached the optimal solution.

(iii) Using the Vogel approximation method, the order in which the variables is introduced is as follows: $x_{34} = 195$, $x_{11} = 300$, $x_{12} = 150$, $x_{32} = 75$, $x_{23} = 180$, $x_{33} = 300$. This initial basic feasible solution is, indeed, the optimal allocation.

(c) The optimal shipping plan is: $x_{11} = 20$, $x_{13} = 10$, $x_{23} = 20$, $x_{24} = 10$, $x_{25} = 20$, $x_{32} = 40$, $x_{35} = 10$, $x_{36} = 25$, $x_{45} = 20$. Total costs are *430*. The dual variables take on the following values: $u_1 = 0$, $u_2 = -1$, $u_3 = -3$, $u_4 = -1$, $v_1 = 1$, $v_2 = -1$, $v_3 = 1$, $v_4 = 0$, $v_5 = 3$, $v_6 = -1$.

(d) The optimal solution is degenerate, the allocation being $x_{14} = 150$, $x_{21} = 150$, $x_{23} = 0$, $x_{24} = 50$, $x_{32} = 175$, $x_{33} = 125$, $x_{41} = 100$. x_{41} is the amount shipped from the fictitious source. Total costs are *2125*.

(e) The optimal basis, which is also degenerate, is: $x_{13} = 500$, $x_{22} = 400$, $x_{23} = 400$, $x_{31} = 500$, $x_{34} = 200$, x_{43} (artificial route) $= 0$, x_{44} (artificial route) $= 100$. Total costs are *5600*, of which *600* are penalty costs.

(f) (i) The objective function we seek to minimise is:

$$5x_{11} + 3x_{12} + 8x_{13} + 14x_{21} + 4x_{22} + 5x_{23} + 4x_{31} + 2x_{32} + 8x_{33}$$

The constraints regarding the requirements may be expressed as:

$$x_{11} + x_{21} + x_{31} \geq 2$$
$$x_{12} + x_{22} + x_{32} \geq 4$$
$$x_{13} + x_{23} + x_{33} \geq 10$$

The constraints regarding the availabilities may be expressed as:

$$-x_{11} - x_{12} - x_{13} \geq -4$$
$$-x_{21} - x_{22} - x_{23} \geq -4$$
$$-x_{31} - x_{32} - x_{33} \geq -8$$

The tanker constraint can be written as:

$$-x_{23} - x_{32} \geq -6$$

The dual objective function is

$$2v_1 + 4v_2 + 10v_3 - 4u_1 - 4u_2 - 8u_3 - 6\mu$$

where μ is the dual variable attached to the tanker constraint.
The constraints of the dual are as follows:

$$v_1 - u_1 \leq 5$$
$$v_2 - u_1 \leq 3$$
$$v_3 - u_1 \leq 8$$
$$v_1 - u_2 \leq 14$$
$$v_2 - u_2 \leq 4$$
$$v_3 - u_2 - \mu \leq 5$$
$$v_1 - u_3 \leq 4$$
$$v_2 - u_3 - \mu \leq 2$$
$$v_3 - u_3 \leq 8$$

(ii) For the proposed primal basis, we can find the dual variables by solving the following set of equations:

$$v_2 - u_1 = 3$$
$$v_3 - u_1 = 8$$
$$v_3 - u_2 - \mu = 5$$
$$v_1 - u_3 = 4$$
$$v_2 - u_3 - \mu = 2$$
$$v_3 - u_3 = 8$$

We obtain, having set u_1 equal to zero, $u_2 = 2$, $u_3 = 0$, $v_1 = 4$, $v_2 = 3$, $v_3 = 8$, $\mu = 1$. We would not wish to make use of any of the non-utilised routes since

$$v_1 - u_1 \leq c_{11}$$
$$v_1 - u_2 \leq c_{21}$$
$$v_2 - u_2 \leq c_{22}$$

Hence, the allocation is, indeed, optimal.

Exercise 8.3

(a) (i) The order in which the basic variables are entered is as follows: $x_{23} = 1$, $x_{33} = 0$, $x_{31} = 1$, $x_{12} = 1$, $x_{11} = 0$.

(ii) Since $v_3 - u_1 > c_{13}$, then we must introduce x_{13} into the basis at zero level, x_{33} leaves, and this basis is, then, optimal but it is not unique since $v_1 - u_2 = c_{21}$.

(iii) The order in which the basic variables are introduced in the Vogel approximation method case is as follows: $x_{23} = 1$, $x_{13} = 0$, $x_{31} = 1$, $x_{32} = 0$, $x_{12} = 1$.

(iv) The values of the dual variables are: $u_1 = 0$, $u_2 = 2$, $u_3 = 2$, $v_1 = 7$, $v_2 = 7$, $v_3 = 4$. The dual constraints are satisfied for all the non-utilised routes, hence this allocation is optimal.

Exercise 8.4

(a) Operator *1* is allocated to machine *4* at a cost of *2*; operator *4* is allocated to machine *1* at a cost of *7*; operator *3* is allocated to machine *2* at a cost of *3*; operator *2* is allocated to machine *1* at a cost of *2*. The total cost is *14*.

(b) The stop-over times in hours for pairings of London-based crews are given in the tableau below:

	101	102	103	104
001	20.5	2.5	7.75	11.25
002	17	23	4.25	7.75
003	10.5	16.5	21.75	1.25
004	8	14	19.25	22.75

The corresponding information for Vienna-based crews is:

	101	102	103	104
001	23.5	17.25	12	8.5
002	3	20.75	15.5	12
003	9.75	3.5	22.25	18.75
004	12	5.75	0.5	21

Combining the information given in the previous two tableaux, by taking the smaller observation of each pair yields:

	101	102	103	104
001	20.5	2.5	7.75	8.5*
002	3*	20.75*	4.25	7.75
003	9.75*	3.5*	21.75	1.25
004	8	5.75*	0.5*	21*

The entries marked with an asterisk refer to Vienna-based crews.

(i) The optimal allocation is to have two crews based in London and two based in Vienna. The first London-based crew is allocated to flights *001* and *102*, and the second London-based crew to flights *003* and *104*. The first Vienna-based crew is allocated to flights *101* and *002*, and the second such crew to flights *103* and *004*. The total stop-over time is *7.75* hours.

(ii) When the safety legislation is introduced, the new tableau is:

	101	102	103	104
001	20.5	2.5	7.75	8.5*
002	3*	20.75*	4.25	7.75
003	9.75*	3.5*	21.75	18.75*
004	8	5.75*	19.25	21*

We still have two crews based in each city, but the pairings now are as follows: for the London-based crews we pair flights *002* and *103*, and flights *004* and *101*, and for the Vienna-based crew, we pair flights *102* and *003*, and flights *104* and *001*. The total stop-over time has now been increased to *23.75* hours.

Exercise 8.5

(a) (i) Horse *1* is allocated to race *4*, horse *2* to race *3*, horse *3* to race *2*, and horse *4* to race *1*. Expected winnings are *49*.

(ii) In addition to the allocation given in (a), a zero quantity is allocated to the following three routes: (*1,2*), (*2,4*) and (*3,1*).

(iii) The imputed value of horse i is u_i, and v_j is the imputed entry fee for race j. In solving recursively for the dual variables, it is convenient to set v_4 equal to zero. The dual variables take the following values:

$$u = \begin{bmatrix} 24 \\ 22.5 \\ 17 \\ 14 \end{bmatrix}, \quad v = \begin{bmatrix} 12 \\ 9 \\ 7.5 \\ 0 \end{bmatrix}$$

(iv) (1) If race 2 is cancelled, then the least valuable horse will not be raced; hence the imputed value of horse 4 will fall from *14* to *0*, but there will be a saving of *9* (the imputed entry fee for race 2). So, expected winnings will fall by *5*. The new allocation will be horse *1* to race *4*, horse *2* to race *3*, horse *3* to race *1*, and horse *4* is not raced. Expected winnings are now *44*, a reduction of *5*.

(2) The new horse has an imputed value of *22.5*; it will replace horse *4*, whose original imputed value is *14*. Hence expected winnings will rise by *8.5*, the difference between these imputed values. The new allocation will be horse *1* to race *2*, horse *2* to race *4*, horse *5* (the new one) to race *3*, horse *3* to race *1* and horse *4* is not raced. Expected winnings are now *57.5*, an increase of *8.5*.

CHAPTER 9

Exercise 9.1

(a)

(i) $\lambda_1 = 7$, $\lambda_2 = -1$

$$x_1 = \begin{bmatrix} 1 \\ 1 \end{bmatrix}, \quad x_2 = \begin{bmatrix} -3/5 \\ 1 \end{bmatrix}$$

(ii) $\lambda_1 = -6$, $\lambda_2 = 5$

$$x_1 = \begin{bmatrix} -7/4 \\ 1 \end{bmatrix}, \quad x_2 = \begin{bmatrix} 1 \\ 1 \end{bmatrix}$$

(iii) $\lambda_1 = 2$, $\lambda_2 = 4$

$$x_1 = \begin{bmatrix} 1 \\ -1 \end{bmatrix}, \quad x_2 = \begin{bmatrix} 3 \\ -1 \end{bmatrix}$$

(iv) $\lambda_1 = 2$, $\lambda_2 = 2$

$$x_1 = x_2 = \begin{bmatrix} 2 \\ 1 \end{bmatrix}$$

(b)

(i) $\lambda_1 = 0$, $\lambda_2 = -1$, $\lambda_3 = 2$

$$x_1 = \begin{bmatrix} 1 \\ -1 \\ 1 \end{bmatrix}, \quad x_2 = \begin{bmatrix} 1 \\ -1 \\ 2 \end{bmatrix}, \quad x_3 = \begin{bmatrix} 2 \\ 1 \\ 1 \end{bmatrix}$$

(ii) $\lambda_1 = -2$, $\lambda_2 = -1$, $\lambda_3 = 7$

$$x_1 = \begin{bmatrix} 1 \\ 0 \\ 0 \end{bmatrix}, \quad x_2 = \begin{bmatrix} 0 \\ -0.6 \\ 1 \end{bmatrix}, \quad x_3 = \begin{bmatrix} 0 \\ 1 \\ 1 \end{bmatrix}$$

(iii) $\lambda_1 = 4$, $\lambda_2 = 2$, $\lambda_3 = -2$

$$x_1 = \begin{bmatrix} 1 \\ 1 \\ 0 \end{bmatrix}, \quad x_2 = \begin{bmatrix} -1 \\ 1 \\ 0 \end{bmatrix}, \quad x_3 = \begin{bmatrix} 0 \\ 0 \\ 1 \end{bmatrix}$$

ANSWERS TO EXERCISES **437**

(iv) $\lambda_1 = 0, \quad \lambda_2 = 3, \quad \lambda_3 = 5$

$$x_1 = \begin{bmatrix} -1 \\ 1 \\ 1 \end{bmatrix}, \quad x_2 = \begin{bmatrix} 2 \\ 1 \\ 1 \end{bmatrix}, \quad x_3 = \begin{bmatrix} 0 \\ -1 \\ 1 \end{bmatrix}$$

Exercise 9.2

(a)

(i) $\lambda_1 = 12, \quad \lambda_2 = -2$

$$X = \begin{bmatrix} 3 & -1 \\ 8 & 2 \end{bmatrix}$$

(ii) $X^{-1} = \begin{bmatrix} \dfrac{2}{14} & \dfrac{1}{14} \\ \dfrac{-8}{14} & \dfrac{3}{14} \end{bmatrix}$

(iii) $D = \begin{bmatrix} 12 & 0 \\ 0 & -2 \end{bmatrix}$

(b)

(i) $\lambda_1 = -1, \quad \lambda_2 = 2$

$$X = \begin{bmatrix} 1 & 1 \\ 0 & 1 \end{bmatrix}$$

(ii) $X^{-1} = \begin{bmatrix} 1 & -1 \\ 0 & 1 \end{bmatrix}$

(iii) $D = \begin{bmatrix} -1 & 0 \\ 0 & 2 \end{bmatrix}$

(c)

(i) $\lambda_1 = 2, \quad \lambda_2 = 3, \quad \lambda_3 = 4$

$$X = \begin{bmatrix} 1 & 0 & 0 \\ -6 & 1 & 0 \\ 0 & 0 & 1 \end{bmatrix}$$

(ii) $X^{-1} = \begin{bmatrix} 1 & 0 & 0 \\ 6 & 1 & 0 \\ 0 & 0 & 1 \end{bmatrix}$

(iii) $D = \begin{bmatrix} 2 & 0 & 0 \\ 0 & 3 & 0 \\ 0 & 0 & 4 \end{bmatrix}$

Exercise 9.3

(a)

(i) $\lambda_1 = 0, \quad \lambda_2 = 1, \quad \lambda_3 = 3$

(ii) $X = \begin{bmatrix} -\frac{1}{\sqrt{3}} & 0 & \frac{2}{\sqrt{6}} \\ \frac{1}{\sqrt{3}} & \frac{1}{\sqrt{2}} & \frac{1}{\sqrt{6}} \\ \frac{1}{\sqrt{3}} & \frac{-1}{\sqrt{2}} & \frac{1}{\sqrt{6}} \end{bmatrix}, \quad X^T X = I$.

$$D = X^T A T = \begin{bmatrix} 0 & 0 & 0 \\ 0 & 1 & 0 \\ 0 & 0 & 3 \end{bmatrix}$$

(b) (i)
$$\lambda_1 = 8, \quad \lambda_2 = 8, \quad \lambda_3 = 2$$

(ii) The matrix of normalised eigenvectors is:

$$X = \begin{bmatrix} 0 & -\sqrt{\frac{2}{3}} & \frac{1}{\sqrt{3}} \\ 1 & 0 & 0 \\ 0 & \frac{1}{\sqrt{3}} & \sqrt{\frac{2}{3}} \end{bmatrix}$$

The inverse of this matrix is equal to its transpose, and A is then easily diagonalised.

(c) (i) The matrix has rank *1*, with the second row being minus twice the first row, and the third row being three times the first row. The three eigenvalues are *0, 0* and *14* respectively.

(ii) The matrix has full rank, with its determinant being equal to *75*. The three eigenvalues are $5, 5 + \sqrt{10}, 5 - \sqrt{10}$.

(iii) The matrix has rank *2*, with the first row being given by the sum of the other two rows. The eigenvalues are as follows:

$$\lambda_1 = 0, \quad \lambda_2 = -2 + \sqrt{34}, \quad \lambda_3 = -2 - \sqrt{34}$$

Exercise 9.4

(a) It is straightforward to check that

$$B^{-1}AB = \begin{bmatrix} \frac{1}{3} & -\frac{1}{3} \\ \frac{1}{2} & \frac{1}{4} \end{bmatrix} \begin{bmatrix} 2 & \frac{1}{4} \\ -1 & 1 \end{bmatrix} \begin{bmatrix} 1 & \frac{4}{3} \\ -2 & \frac{4}{3} \end{bmatrix}$$

$$= \begin{bmatrix} \frac{3}{2} & 1 \\ 0 & \frac{3}{2} \end{bmatrix}$$

(b) (i) *0.02*, (ii) *9.091*, (iii) *−0.125*, (iv) the inverse does not exist.

Exercise 9.5

(a) (i) The eigenvalues are all positive: $2 - \sqrt{3}, 2, 2 + \sqrt{3}$. Alternatively, one could calculate the principal minors: they have the following values: *2, 5, 2*. Hence the matrix is positive definite.

(ii) The eigenvalues do not all have the same sign: their values are *1, 6, −6*. Alternatively, one could calculate the principal minors: they have the following values: *1, 5, −36*. Hence the matrix is indefinite.

(iii) In this case, the eigenvalues are all negative: $-4, -2, -2$. The principal minors alternate in sign starting negative; their values are: $-3, 8, -16$. The matrix is negative definite.

(iv) In this case the matrix is positive semi-definite: the eigenvalues are $0, 3, 5$, and the principal minors are $2, 5, 0$.

(b) (i)
$$A = \begin{bmatrix} -2 & 1 \\ 1 & -3 \end{bmatrix}$$
$$\lambda_1, \lambda_2 = -2.5 \pm \sqrt{1.25}$$

Hence both eigenvalues are negative: the principal minors alternate in sign, starting negative: their values are $-2, 5$. A is negative definite and $f(x)$ is always negative for non-zero x.

(ii)
$$A = \begin{bmatrix} 4 & 2 \\ 2 & 3 \end{bmatrix}$$
$$\lambda_1, \lambda_2 = 3.5 \pm 0.5\sqrt{17}$$

Hence both eigenvalues are positive; the principal minors are both positive, their values being $4, 8$. A is positive definite, and $f(x)$ is always positive for non-zero x.

(iii)
$$A = \begin{bmatrix} 1 & 1.5 \\ 1.5 & 2 \end{bmatrix},$$
$$\lambda_1, \lambda_2 = 1.5 \pm \sqrt{2.5}$$

The eigenvalues are of different sign; the principal minors change sign: $1, -0.25$. A is an indefinite matrix, and $f(x)$ is neither always positive or always negative.

(iv)
$$A = \begin{bmatrix} 2 & 1 & 1 \\ 1 & 3 & 2 \\ 1 & 2 & 3 \end{bmatrix}$$

The principal minors are all positive: $2, 5, 8$. Hence, A is positive definite, and $f(x)$ is always positive.

(v)
$$A = \begin{bmatrix} 2 & 1 & 1 \\ 1 & 3 & -2 \\ 1 & -2 & 3 \end{bmatrix}$$

The principal minors are all non-negative: $2, 5, 0$. A is positive semi-definite, and $f(x)$ is not always positive, it could be zero.

CHAPTER 10

Exercise 10.1

(a) (i) The characteristic equation is given by:
$$\lambda^2 - 8\lambda + 12 = 0$$
$$\text{with roots } \lambda_1 = 2, \lambda_2 = 6$$

(ii) We must have
$$A^2 - 8A + 12I = 0$$
Given that $A^2 = \begin{bmatrix} 4 & 8 \\ 0 & 36 \end{bmatrix}$, it is easy to see that the equation holds

(iii) The characteristic equation is given by:
$$\lambda^2 - 40\lambda + 144 = 0$$
with roots $\lambda_1 = 4$, $\lambda_2 = 36$

Exercise 10.2

(a) (i) indecomposable;

(ii) decomposable, $1 \to 3$, $2 \to 2$, $3 \to 1$;

(iii) decomposable, any matrix with a row or column of zeros is decomposable, $1 \to 1$, $2 \to 3$, $3 \to 2$;

(iv) indecomposable despite the large number of zero elements; none of the five other orderings of the rows and columns yield a null two-component sub-vector.

Exercise 10.3

(a) for $\lambda = 0$, we have $x = \begin{bmatrix} 1 \\ -1 \\ 1 \end{bmatrix}$

and for $\lambda = 0.6972$ we have $x = \begin{bmatrix} 1 \\ -0.3028 \\ -0.6055 \end{bmatrix}$

(b) $(5I - A)^{-1} = \dfrac{1}{15} \begin{bmatrix} 5 & 3 & 1 \\ 5 & 12 & 4 \\ 10 & 18 & 11 \end{bmatrix}$

(c) $(4I - A)^{-1} = -\dfrac{1}{4} \begin{bmatrix} 0 & 2 & 1 \\ 4 & 6 & 3 \\ 8 & 14 & 5 \end{bmatrix}$

Exercise 10.4

(a) $a_{12} + a_{12}^2 a_{21} + a_{12}^3 a_{21}^2 + \cdots + a_{12}^{n-1} a_{21}^{n-2} + \cdots$

The limiting value is $\dfrac{a_{12}}{1 - a_{12} a_{21}}$

(b) $1 + a_{12} a_{21} + a_{12}^2 a_{21}^2 + \cdots + a_{12}^{n-1} a_{21}^{n-1} + \cdots$

The limiting value is $\dfrac{1}{1 - a_{12} a_{21}}$

The results of the above exercise on total steel production along with the earlier results on total corn production are, as we would have expected, just equal to the elements of the Leontief inverse.

$$(I - A) = \begin{bmatrix} 1 & -a_{12} \\ -a_{21} & 1 \end{bmatrix}$$

$$\det.(I - A) = 1 - a_{12}a_{21}$$

$$(I - A)^{-1} = \frac{1}{1 - a_{12}a_{21}} \begin{bmatrix} 1 & a_{12} \\ a_{21} & 1 \end{bmatrix}$$

Exercise 10.5

(a)

(i) $(I - A)^{-1} = \dfrac{1}{0.885} \begin{bmatrix} 0.94 & 0.25 & 0.1 \\ 0.22 & 1 & 0.4 \\ 0.315 & 0.225 & 0.975 \end{bmatrix}$

(ii) $x = \dfrac{1}{0.885} \begin{bmatrix} 795 \\ 1410 \\ 1113.75 \end{bmatrix}$

(iii) It is impossible to permute rows and columns of A such that we end up with a rectangular null sub-matrix in the bottom left-hand corner. Note all the elements of the Leontief inverse are positive.

(iv) Total required labour hours are $(1/0.885)(9753.75) = 11021.19$.

(b) (i) decomposable: $2 \to 1, 1 \to 2$;

(ii) indecomposable;

(iii) indecomposable;

(iv) decomposable: $2 \to 1, 3 \to 2, 1 \to 3$;

(v) decomposable: $4 \to 1, 2 \to 2, 3 \to 3, 1 \to 4$.

(c)

$$(I - A)^{-1} = \frac{1}{0.544} \begin{bmatrix} 0.8 & 0 & 0.24 \\ 0.14 & 0.68 & 0.11 \\ 0.32 & 0 & 0.64 \end{bmatrix}$$

from which it follows that d_2 is absent from the equations defining x_1 and x_2.

Exercise 10.6

(a) Given that the dominant eigenvalue is unity, the eigenvector associated with this eigenvalue can be easily found:

$$-0.1x_1 + 0.2x_2 + 0.15x_3 = 0$$
$$0.3x_2 - 0.3x_3 = 0$$

from which it follows that

$$x_2 = x_3$$
$$x_1 = 3.5x_3$$

(b) (i) Since all the column sums are unity, one of the eigenvalues is equal to unity. The characteristic equation is

$$-\lambda^3 + 2.45\lambda^2 - 1.9675\lambda + 0.5175 = 0$$

with $\lambda_1 = 1$, $\lambda_2 = 0.6349$, $\lambda_3 = 0.8151$

(ii) The eigenvector associated with the dominant eigenvalue is: $x_1 = 0.75$, $x_2 = 0.5$, $x_3 = 1$.

(iii) It is the only positive eigenvector.

CHAPTER 11

Exercise 11.1

(a) (i) is both continuous and smooth, so it is differentiable everywhere;

(ii) is continuous, but is not smooth at $x = 10$. The function is V-shaped with the point of the V at $x = 10$, so it is not differentiable at this point;

(iii) is continuous, but is kinked at $x = 40$, and is, therefore, not smooth and cannot be differentiated at this point;

(iv) there is a discontinuity at $x = 40$; the value of the left-hand side limit is 120, whereas the value of the right-hand side limit is 80. The function is not differentiable at this point.

(v) is continuous and smooth everywhere, and therefore, is differentiable everywhere;

(vi) there is a discontinuity at $x = 2$, both the left-hand side and right-hand side limits are the same and equal to 18, but the value of the function at $x = 2$ is 12, so we cannot differentiate at this point.

(b) (i) When $p = 10$, $x = 45$, and when $p = 5$, $x = 90$.
Hence $\Delta x/\Delta p = -45/5 = -9$.

When $p = 10$, $x = 45$, and when $p = 9$, $x = 50$.
Hence $\Delta x/\Delta p = -5/1 = -5$.

If the price is increased from 10 to 10.01, the difference quotient is equal to -4.4955; if the price is increased from 10 to 10.001, the difference quotient is equal to -4.49951. As the change in price approaches zero, the value of the difference quotient approaches -4.5.

(ii) When $p = 10$, $x = 81$, and when $p = 5$, $x = 324$.
Hence $\Delta x/\Delta p = -243/5 = -48.6$.

When $p = 10$, $x = 81$, and when $p = 9$, $x = 100$.
Hence $\Delta x/\Delta p = -19/1 = -19$.

(iii) If the price is increased from 10 to 10.01 the difference quotient is equal to -16.1757; if the price is increased from 10 to 10.001, the difference quotient is equal to -16.1975. As the change in price approaches zero, the value of the difference quotient approaches -16.2.

Exercise 11.2

(a) (i)

$$\Delta y = 2 + 5(x + \Delta x) - (2 + 5x)$$
$$= 5\Delta x$$
$$\frac{\Delta y}{\Delta x} = 5$$
$$\text{hence } \lim_{\Delta x \to 0} \frac{\Delta y}{\Delta x} = 5$$

(ii)

$$\Delta y = 5(x + \Delta x)^2 - 5x^2$$
$$= 10x\Delta x + 5(\Delta x)^2$$
$$\frac{\Delta y}{\Delta x} = 10x + 5\Delta x$$
$$\lim_{\Delta x \to 0} \frac{\Delta y}{\Delta x} = 10x$$

(iii)
$$\Delta y = \frac{-1}{(x+\Delta x)^2} + \frac{1}{x^2}$$
$$= \frac{-x^2 + (x+\Delta x)^2}{x^2(x+\Delta x)^2}$$
$$= \frac{2x\Delta x + (\Delta x)^2}{x^2(x+\Delta x)^2}$$
$$\frac{\Delta y}{\Delta x} = \frac{2x+\Delta x}{x^2(x+\Delta x)^2}$$
$$\lim_{\Delta x \to 0} \frac{\Delta y}{\Delta x} = 2x^{-3}$$

(iv)
$$\Delta y = (x+\Delta x) + 4(x+\Delta x)^3 - x - 4x^3$$
$$= \Delta x + 12x^2 \Delta x + 12x(\Delta x)^2 + 4(\Delta x)^3$$
$$\frac{\Delta y}{\Delta x} = 1 + 12x^2 + 12x\Delta x + 4(\Delta x)^2$$
$$\lim_{\Delta x \to 0} \frac{\Delta y}{\Delta x} = 1 + 12x^2$$

(b)

(i) $-8x^{-3}$, (ii) $4x^{-1/2}$, (iii) $10x^9$

(iv) 0, (v) $2 + 5x^{-3/2}$, (vi) $21x^2 - 2 + 2x^{-2/3}$

(vii) $12x^{-5} + 9x^2$, (viii) $8x^{-7/8} - 4x^{-2}$

Exercise 11.3

(a)

(i) $f'(x) = (2x^{-1/2} + 4x)(3x^2 + 4x) + (x^3 + 2x^2)(-x^{-3/2} + 4)$

(ii) $f'(x) = (10 - 4x)(4x^3 + 2x^{-2}) - 4(x^4 - 2x^{-1})$

(iii) $f'(x) = (2x^4 + 6x^{-2/3})(12x^{1/2} - 4x) + (8x^{3/2} - 2x^2)(8x^3 - 4x^{-5/3})$

(iv) $f'(x) = (3 + x^2)(10 - 5x^4) + 2x(10x - x^5)$

(b) (i) The demand function is
$$x = 100 - 0.25p$$

Own-price elasticity of demand for x will be: $p = 300, -3; p = 240, -1.5$

(ii) The total revenue and marginal revenue functions are respectively given by:
$$TR = 400x - 4x^2$$
$$\frac{dTR}{dx} = MR = 400 - 8x$$

Marginal revenue is zero when output is *50*; the price at this output level is *200*, and the elasticity of demand is $-0.25(200)/50 = -1$.

Exercise 11.4

(a)

(i) $f'(x) = \dfrac{4x^3(x^2+5x) - (x^4+2)(2x+5)}{(x^2+5x)^2}$

(ii) $f'(x) = \dfrac{(8-x^2)(6 - 0.25x^{-5/4}) + 2x(x^{-1/4} + 6x)}{(8-x^2)^2}$

(iii) $f'(x) = \dfrac{(x^3-10)(20x^4 + 2x^{-2}) - 3x^2(4x^5 - 2x^{-1})}{(x^3-10)^2}$

(iv) $f'(x) = \dfrac{(4x^{1/2} + 2x)(2.5x^{3/2} + 12) - (x^{5/2} + 12x)(2x^{-1/2} + 2)}{(4x^{1/2} + 2x)^2}$

(b) (i)
$$\dfrac{dTC}{dx} = x$$

(ii)
$$AC = 200x^{-1} + 0.5x$$
$$\dfrac{dAC}{dx} = -200x^{-2} + 0.5$$

$x = 10$, ACF derivative $= -1.5$; $x = 20$, ACF derivative $= 0$; and $x = 40$, ACF derivative $= 0.375$.

Exercise 11.5

(a)

(i) $f'(x) = 0.5(6x^2 + 4)(2x^3 + 4x)^{-1/2}$

(ii) $f'(x) = -3(-2x^{-3} + 2)(x^{-2} + 2x)^{-4}$

(iii) $f'(x) = 10x(10 + x^2)^4$

(iv) $f'(x) = -0.5(28x^3 + 2x^{-3})(7x^4 - x^{-2})^{-3/2}$

Exercise 11.6

(a)

(i) $f'(x) = -5x^{-3/2}$, $f''(x) = 7.5x^{-5/2}$

(ii) $f'(x) = 4.5x^{-1/4}$, $f''(x) = -1.125x^{-5/4}$

(iii) $f'(x) = 2x + 3x^2$, $f''(x) = 2 + 6x$

(iv) $f'(x) = 2$, $f''(x) = 0$

(v) $f'(x) = -16x^{-3}$, $f''(x) = 48x^{-4}$

(vi) $f'(x) = 3x^2 - 18x + 12$, $f''(x) = 6x - 18$

(b) (i) strictly convex; (ii) strictly concave; (iii) strictly convex; (iv) a linear function, linear functions are both concave and convex, but are clearly neither strictly concave nor strictly convex; (v) convex; (vi) neither since the second derivative is positive for x greater than 3, zero for x equal to 3 and negative for x less than 3.

Exercise 11.7

(a)

(i) 3 *since* $10^3 = 1000$

(ii) -1 *since* $10^{-1} = 0.1$

(iii) -3 *since* $10^{-3} = 0.001$

(iv) 6 *since* $10^6 = 1m$

(b)

(i) -4 *since* $2^{-4} = 0.0625$

(ii) 6 *since* $2^6 = 64$

(iii) 0 *since* $2^0 = 1$

(iv) -2 *since* $2^{-2} = 0.25$

Exercise 11.8

(a)

(i) $f'(x) = -2xe^{-x^2}$

(ii) $f'(x) = 3x^2 e^{5+x^3}$

(iii) $f'(x) = (x^2 + 6x + 4)e^{4+x}$

(iv) $f'(x) = -e^{-0.1x}$

(v) $f'(x) = \dfrac{(2x^4 - 3x^2 - 20x)e^{x^2}}{(x^3 - 10)^2}$

(b)

(i) $f'(x) = \dfrac{6x + 5}{3x^2 + 5x}$

(ii) $f'(x) = \dfrac{6x^2 - 0.5x^{-3/2}}{2x^3 + x^{-1/2}}$

(iii) $f'(x) = \log_e x$

(iv) $f'(x) = \dfrac{(6x^{1/2} + 2x)(4x^3 + x^{-2})}{x^4 - x^{-1}} + (3x^{-1/2} + 2)\log_e(x^4 - x^{-1})$

(v) $f'(x) = \dfrac{10x + 30}{x^2 + 6x}$

(c) (i) $-1/4$ and $-1/9$.

(ii) -1 and $-1/3$.

(iii) The elasticity is always -2 regardless of the value of the price.

(iv) The elasticity is always -3 regardless of the value of the price.

Exercise 11.9

(a)

(i) $f'(x) = -2\sin 2x$

(ii) $f'(x) = 2\cos x \sin x$

(iii) $f'(x) = -2\cos x \sin x$

(iv) $f'(x) = \cos^2 x - \sin^2 x$

(v) $f'(x) = 2x \cos(x^2 + 4)$

(vi) $f'(x) = (4x^{-2} - 2)\sin(2x + 4x^{-1})$

(b)
$$f'(x) = \frac{\cos^2 x + \sin^2 x}{\cos^2 x} = \frac{1}{\cos^2 x}$$

Remember by Pythogoras's theorem that
$$\cos^2 x + \sin^2 x = 1$$

(c)
$$\text{(i) } f'(x) = \frac{-\cos x}{\sin^2 x} = \frac{-\cos x}{1 - \cos^2 x}$$
$$\text{(ii) } f'(x) = \frac{\sin x}{\cos^2 x} = \frac{\sin x}{1 - \sin^2 x}$$
$$\text{(iii) } f'(x) = \frac{-\sin^2 x - \cos^2 x}{\sin^2 x} = \frac{-1}{\sin^2 x}$$

CHAPTER 12

Exercise 12.1

(i) $f_1 = 3x_1^2 + 2x_2$, $f_2 = 2x_1 - 2x_2$
$f_{11} = 6x_1$, $f_{12} = f_{21} = 2$, $f_{22} = -2$

(ii) $f_1 = 0.5x_1^{-0.5}x_2^{-1}$, $f_2 = -x_1^{0.5}x_2^{-2}$
$f_{11} = -0.25x_1^{-1.5}x_2^{-1}$, $f_{12} = f_{21} = -0.5x_1^{-0.5}x_2^{-2}$
$f_{22} = 2x_1^{0.5}x_2^{-3}$

(iii) $f_1 = x_2$, $f_2 = x_1$, $f_{11} = 0$, $f_{12} = f_{21} = 1$, $f_{22} = 0$

(iv) $f_1 = \dfrac{1}{x_1} + 10x_1 x_2$, $f_2 = 5x_1^2$, $f_{11} = -x_1^{-2} + 10x_2$, $f_{12} = f_{21} = 10x_1$, $f_{22} = 0$

(v) $f_1 = 2x_1 x_2^3 x_3$, $f_2 = 3x_1^2 x_2^2 x_3$, $f_3 = x_1^2 x_2^3$, $f_{11} = 2x_2^3 x_3$, $f_{12} = 6x_1 x_2^2 x_3$, $f_{13} = 2x_1 x_2^3$
$f_{22} = 6x_1^2 x_2 x_3$, $f_{23} = 3x_1^2 x_2^2$, $f_{33} = 0$

(vi) let $z = 2x_1 + x_2^3 - 5x_3$, then $f_1 = 2e^z$, $f_2 = 3x_2^2 e^z$
$f_3 = -5e^z$, $f_{11} = 4e^z$, $f_{12} = 6x_2^2 e^z$, $f_{13} = -10e^z$
$f_{22} = (6x_2 + 9x_2^4)e^z$, $f_{23} = -15x_2^2 e^z$, $f_{33} = 25e^z$

Exercise 12.2
(a) (i) non-homogeneous; (ii) homogeneous of degree -0.5; (iii) homogeneous of degree 2; (iv) non-homogeneous; (v) homogeneous of degree 6; (vi) non-homogeneous.

(b)
$$\text{(ii) } x_1 f_1 + x_2 f_2 = 0.5x_1^{0.5}x_2^{-1} - x_1^{0.5}x_2^{-1}$$
$$= -0.5f(x_1, x_2)$$
$$\text{(iii) } x_1 f_1 + x_2 f_2 = x_1 x_2 + x_2 x_1 = 2f(x_1, x_2)$$
$$\text{(v) } x_1 f_1 + x_2 f_2 + x_3 f_3 = 2x_1^2 x_2^3 x_3 + 3x_1^2 x_2^3 x_3 + x_1^2 x_2^3 x_3$$
$$= 6f(x_1, x_2, x_3)$$

Exercise 12.3
(a)
$$F(\lambda K, \lambda N) = [\alpha(\lambda K)^{-\rho} + (1-\alpha)(\lambda N)^{-\rho}]^{-\nu/\rho}$$
$$= (\lambda^{-\rho})^{-\nu/\rho}[\alpha K^{-\rho} + (1-\alpha)N^{-\rho}]^{-\nu/\rho}$$
$$= \lambda^\nu F(K, N)$$

(b)
$$F_K = \nu\alpha K^{-\rho-1}Z^{-\nu/\rho-1}$$
$$F_N = \nu(1-\alpha)N^{-\rho-1}Z^{-\nu/\rho-1}$$
$$\text{hence } KF_K + NF_N = \nu(\alpha K^{-\rho} + (1-\alpha)N^{-\rho})Z^{-\nu/\rho-1}$$
$$= \nu Z^{-\nu/\rho} = \nu F(K,N)$$

(c)
$$F_K = \alpha AK^{\alpha-1}N^\beta \text{ and } F_N = \beta AK^\alpha N^{\beta-1}$$
$$\text{hence } \frac{F_N}{F_K} = \frac{\beta}{\alpha}\frac{K}{N}$$
$$\log\frac{K}{N} = \log\frac{\alpha}{\beta} + \log M$$
$$\text{where } M = F_N/F_K$$
$$d\log\frac{K}{N} = d\log M$$
$$\text{hence } \frac{d\log\frac{K}{N}}{d\log M} = 1$$

(d)
$$\text{Let } S = \frac{NF_N}{KF_K}$$

(i) In the Cobb–Douglas case, we have
$$S = \frac{\beta}{\alpha}$$

This is a constant and, therefore, independent of the wage–rental ratio and capital–labour ratio.

(ii) In the CES case, we have
$$S = \frac{1-\alpha}{\alpha}\left(\frac{K}{N}\right)^\rho$$
$$\text{and } \frac{dS}{d(K/N)} = \rho\frac{1-\alpha}{\alpha}\left(\frac{K}{N}\right)^{\rho-1}$$

The crucial factor then is the sign of the parameter ρ. Given that the elasticity of substitution is equal to $1/(1+\rho)$, then ρ is negative, zero, positive for the elasticity of substitution being greater than, equal to, less than unity. We may, therefore conclude that as the wage–rental ratio rises, the capital–labour ratio will increase and the relative share of labour will then rise, stay the same, fall as the elasticity of substitution is less than, equal to or greater than unity.

Exercise 12.4

(a) (i)
$$f_1 = 2x_1 + 2x_2, \quad f_2 = 2x_1 + 3x_2^2$$
$$\frac{dx_1}{dx_2} = 0.5x_2^{-0.5}$$
$$\text{hence } \frac{dy}{dx_2} = (2x_1 + 2x_2)0.5x_2^{-0.5} + 2x_1 + 3x_2^2$$
$$= (2x_2^{0.5} + 2x_2)0.5x_2^{-0.5} + 2x_2^{0.5} + 3x_2^2$$
$$= 1 + 3x_2^{0.5} + 3x_2^2$$

(ii)
$$f_1 = 2x_2, \quad f_2 = 2x_1 + 0.5x_2^{-0.5}$$
$$\frac{dx_1}{dx_2} = \frac{1}{x_2}$$
hence $$\frac{dy}{dx_2} = 2x_2\frac{1}{x_2} + 2x_1 + 0.5x_2^{-0.5}$$
$$= 2 + 2\log_e x_2 + 0.5x_2^{-0.5}$$

(iii)
$$f_1 = x_2 + x_3, \quad f_2 = x_1 + x_3, \quad f_3 = x_1 + x_2$$
$$\frac{dx_1}{dx_2} = -1, \quad \frac{dx_3}{dx_2} = -10x_2^{-2}$$
hence $$\frac{dy}{dx_2} = -(x_2 + x_3) + (x_1 + x_3) - (x_1 + x_2)10x_2^{-2}$$
$$= -x_2 - 10x_2^{-1} + 5 - x_2 + 10x_2^{-1} - (5 - x_2 + x_2)10x_2^{-2}$$
$$= -2x_2 - 50x_2^{-2} + 5$$

(b)
$$\frac{dY}{dt}\frac{1}{Y} = 0.25\frac{dK}{dt}\frac{1}{K} + 0.75\frac{dN}{dt}\frac{1}{N} + 0.05$$

(c)
$$\frac{dY}{dt}\frac{1}{Y} = \frac{0.2K^{-4}}{0.2K^{-4} + 0.8N^{-4}}\frac{dK}{dt}\frac{1}{K} + \frac{0.8N^{-4}}{0.2K^{-4} + 0.8N^{-4}}\frac{dN}{dt}\frac{1}{N} + 0.1$$

Exercise 12.5
(a) Since neither $I'(r)$ nor L_r appear in the numerator of the two partial derivatives but only in the Jacobian determinant, as either of the derivatives approach minus infinity, the Jacobian determinant will approach minus infinity, and the rate of interest will be independent of both the level of government expenditure and the money supply. As $I'(r)$ approaches minus infinity, then the *IS* curve becomes horizontal, whereas as L_r approaches minus infinity, then the *LM* curve becomes horizontal.

Exercise 12.6
(a) The limiting values of the partial derivatives as $K'(r)$ approaches infinity are:
$$\frac{\partial Y}{\partial G} = 0$$
$$\frac{\partial Y}{\partial M} = \frac{1}{L_Y} > 0$$
$$\frac{\partial r}{\partial G} = 0$$
$$\frac{\partial r}{\partial M} = 0$$
$$\frac{\partial e}{\partial G} = \frac{-1}{NX_e} > 0$$
$$\frac{\partial e}{\partial M} = \frac{1 - C'(Y) - NX_Y}{L_y NX_e} < 0$$

Fiscal policy has no effect on output, but the exchange rate appreciates as a result of the capital inflow. Demand is stimulated by the increase in government expenditure, but an equivalent crowding-out of net exports resulting from the appreciation of the exchange rate leaves output unchanged. Monetary policy, on the other hand, has a strong impact on output, with the stimulus to demand being provided by the depreciation of the exchange rate which follows the monetary stimulus.

Exercise 12.7

(a) The limiting values of the partial derivatives as $K'(r)$ approaches infinity are:

$$\frac{\partial Y}{\partial G} = \frac{1}{1 - C'(Y) - NX_Y}$$

$$\frac{\partial Y}{\partial D} = 0$$

$$\frac{\partial r}{\partial G} = 0$$

$$\frac{\partial r}{\partial D} = 0$$

$$\frac{\partial M_s}{\partial G} = \frac{L_Y}{1 - C'(Y) - NX_Y}$$

Monetary policy is impotent in these circumstances, whereas the government expenditure multiplier is the same as in a rock-bottom Keynesian income-determination model with no monetary sector. The rationale for these results is straightforward: the rate of interest cannot differ from the fixed world rate, so with expansionary fiscal policy there is no crowding-out of private investment expenditures. Expansionary monetary policy, on the other hand, by putting downward pressure on the rate of interest leads to a loss of foreign exchange reserves, and in the final analysis there is no change in the money supply and no reflationary stimulus.

CHAPTER 13

Exercise 13.1

(i) We have a maximum at $x = 4$, with $f(4) = 90$.
(ii) We have a minimum at $x = 24$, with $f(24) = 256$.
(iii) We have a minimum at $x = 8$, with $f(8) = 44$.
(iv) We have a maximum at $x = 25$, with $f(25) = 1500$.
(v) We have a maximum at $x = 0$, with $f(0) = 10$, and a minimum at $x = 12$, with $f(12) = -854$.
(vi) We have a maximum at $x = -12$, with $f(-12) = 576$, and a minimum at $x = 4$, with $f(4) = -106.66\ldots$.
(vii) We have a maximum at $x = -3$, with $f(-3) = 86$ and a minimum at $x = 2$, with $f(2) = -39$.
(viii) We have a minimum at $x = -1$, with $f(-1) = -20$, and a maximum at $x = 3$, with $f(3) = 108$.
(ix) The first derivative is zero at $x = -1$, 2 and 7. The function reaches a minimum value at both $x = -1$, and $x = 7$, with $f(-1) = -103$ and $f(7) = -1127$. A maximum value of the function is reached at $x = 2$, with $f(2) = 248$.
(x) The function reaches a maximum value at $x = 0$, with $f(0) = 0$, but note the function's second derivative is also equal to zero at this point.

Exercise 13.2

(a) (i) Since the fourth and subsequent derivatives are all zero, the third-order T-S gives the precise function.
  (ii) Again, we obtain the precise function.

  (iii) $1 - (x-1) + (x-1)^2 - (x-1)^3$

  (iv) $1 + 0.5(x-1) - 0.125(x-1)^2 + 0.0625(x-1)^3$

  (v) $(x-1) - \frac{(x-1)^2}{2} + \frac{(x-1)^3}{3}$

(b) (i) The third-order expansion yields the precise function

  (ii) $x - \frac{x^3}{6}$

(iii) $1 - \dfrac{x^2}{2}$

(iv) $1 + x + \dfrac{x^2}{2} + \dfrac{x^3}{6}$

(v) $x - \dfrac{x^2}{2} + \dfrac{x^3}{3}$

Exercise 13.3

(i) The first derivative is always positive; there is a non-stationary inflexion point at $x = 2$.

(ii) Stationary inflexion point at $x = 2$.

(iii) Maximum at $x = -9$, minimum at $x = 2$, and non-stationary inflexion point at $x = -3.5$.

(iv) The first derivative is always negative; there is a non-stationary inflexion point at $x = 4$.

(v) Stationary inflexion point at $x = 0$.

(vi) Maximum at $x = -1$ and $x = 1$, minimum at $x = 0$, and non-stationary inflexion points at $x = -1/\sqrt{3}$ and $1/\sqrt{3}$.

(vii) Stationary inflexion point at $x = 0$.

(viii) Maximum at $x = 0$.

(ix) Stationary inflexion point at $x = 0$.

(x) Maximum at $x = 0$.

Exercise 13.4

(a) $SRAVC$ is minimised at $q = 20$. $SRAVC(20) = 10$. Hence, the firm would not wish to supply anything below a price of *10*.

(b) $LRAC$ is minimised at $q = 5$. $LRAC(5) = 50$. Hence, the firm would not be prepared to supply below a price of *50*.

(c) There are two levels of output at which marginal cost is equal to marginal revenue: *0.382* and *2.618*. At the former output, the marginal cost curve cuts the horizontal marginal revenue schedule from below, so the second-order condition for a maximum of profit is not satisfied. The condition is met when $q = 2.618$, and the firm makes a profit of *5.0451*.

(d) (i) There are two output levels at which marginal revenue is equal to marginal cost: *2* and *8*. Only at the higher output level is the second-order condition for a maximum satisfied, with the firm earning a profit equal to *42.66*....

(ii) Average costs are minimised when output is *7.5*, and $AC(7.5)$ is *22.5*.

(e) (i) In the competitive industry, equilibrium output is *240*, and the price is *1010*.

(ii) The monopolist would produce *200* units, which would then imply a price of *1050*.

(iii) The socially efficient output level is the one at which price is equal to marginal social cost. We must, therefore, have output equal to *192*.

(iv) A per unit tax of *240* ensure that the externality is taken into account, and the competitive industry would produce the correct output.

(v) With a monopoly producer, output is closer to the efficient level than with perfect competition. A per unit tax of *48* will ensure that when the monopolist now equates marginal revenue net of the tax and marginal cost, output of *192* is produced.

(f) (i) The profit-maximising monopolist would produce an output of *60*, and earn profits of *2600*.

(ii) The sales-maximising monopolist would produce where marginal revenue is zero, i.e. where the own-price elasticity of demand is equal to -1. The sales maximiser's output would be *70*, and the associated profits would be *2250*.

(g) (i) Inverting the demand curve, and setting price equal to marginal cost we find $q = 30$, and $p = 60$. The own-price elasticity of demand at this point is (minus) unity.

(ii) (1) The monopolist will equate marginal cost with marginal revenue; this occurs at an output of *20*, and the associated price is *80*.

(2) The welfare loss from monopolisation is given by $-0.5(30 - 20)(60 - 80) = 200$.

(3) The revenue-maximising monopolist produces where marginal revenue is zero, i.e. where the own-price elasticity of demand is equal to -1. So the same output will be produced by a revenue-maximising monopolist as by the public enterprise.

(iii) The firm will produce *24* units of output at a price of *72*. Under marginal cost pricing in the original situation, consumer surplus is *900*, and producer surplus is also *900*, yielding social welfare of *1800*. Under a profit-maximising monopoly, but with lower costs, consumer surplus is *576* and producer surplus is *1440*, giving social welfare of *2016*. Social welfare has accordingly increased, even though price is higher than marginal cost.

(h) The profit-maximising level of output is *20*, and at this price profits are zero, so there is no incentive for firms to leave or enter the industry. The firm is in long-run equilibrium selling *20* units at a price of *80*.

(i) (i) The inverse supply function is given by:

$$p = 60q^2 - 80q + 30 \text{ for } q \geq 1$$

The inverse supply function is only valid for $q \geq 1$ because average cost is above marginal cost for smaller outputs. Inverting the above function, we have:

$$q = \frac{80 + \sqrt{240p - 800}}{120} \text{ for } p \geq 10$$

(ii) In long-run equilibrium, price must equal average cost (which equals marginal cost). So the long-run equilibrium price is *10*, and the quantity demanded at this price is *40*.

(iii) Since each firm will supply one unit in equilibrium, there will be *40* firms in the industry.

(iv) With the cost reduction from technological progress, we still have average cost minimised at $q = 1$. The long-run equilibrium price is $10 - \alpha$, and the inverse supply function is

$$p = 60q^2 - 80q + 30 - \alpha \text{ for } q \geq 1$$

and the supply function is

$$q = \frac{80 + \sqrt{240(p + \alpha) - 800}}{120} \text{ for } p \geq 10 - \alpha$$

(j) (i) Profits are maximised at $q = 60$, the associated price is *170*, and total profits are *5200*.

(ii) The profit-maximising level of output is now *50*.

(iii) The profit-maximising level of output as a function of the unit tax is given by:

$$q = 60 - \frac{t}{3}$$

and total tax expenditure is

$$T = tq = 60t - \frac{t^2}{3}$$

This is maximised when $t = 90$, and q is then equal to *30*.

Exercise 13.5
(a) The price will fall by the full amount of the subsidy, the output produced by a representative firm will remain unchanged. Total output increases, thus giving a fall in the market price as a result of the entry of new firms into the industry.

(b) (i) The per unit tax will lead the monopolist to reduce output. We have on totally differentiating the first-order condition of a maximum of profit and rearranging:

$$\frac{dq}{dt} = \frac{1}{f''(q)q + 2f'(q) - c''(q)}$$

The second-order condition for a maximum of profits requires the denominator to be negative, and hence output will fall as a result of an increase in the per unit tax.

(ii) Output will also fall as a result of the imposition of a proportional tax on the good. On totally differentiating the first-order condition for a maximum of profit and rearranging:

$$\frac{dq}{dt} = \frac{p(q) + p'(q)q}{(1-t)(2p'(q) + p''(q)q) - c''(q)} < 0$$

The term in the numerator is marginal revenue, which must be positive, and the denominator will be negative as long as the second-order condition for a maximum of profits is met.

CHAPTER 14

Exercise 14.1
(i) Maximum at $x_1 = 60$, $x_2 = -24$.
(ii) Minimum at $x_1 = 10$, $x_2 = 26$.
(iii) Minimum at $x_1 = 41$, $x_2 = 30$.
(iv) Saddle point at $x_1 = 4$, $x_2 = -8$.
(v) Maximum at $x_1 = -20$, $x_2 = 30$.
(vi) Maximum at $x_1 = 90$, $x_2 = 30$.
(vii) Minimum at $x_1 = 23$, $x_2 = 8$.
(viii) Saddle point at $x_1 = -6$, $x_2 = 16$.

Exercise 14.2
(a) (i) The profit-maximising levels of output of the three goods are: $x_1 = 16$, $x_2 = 12$, $x_3 = 20$.

(ii) The principal minors are -1, 2 and -8 respectively, and since they alternate in sign, starting negative, we have indeed identified a maximum.

(b) (i) The profit-maximising levels of output of the three goods are: $x_1 = 12$, $x_2 = 20$, $x_3 = 10$.

(ii) The eigenvalues of the matrix of second-order partial derivatives are -3, -5, -8.

(iii) Since all the eigenvalues are negative, the matrix of second-order partial derivatives is negative definite. We have again identified a maximum. Alternatively, we could have obtained the principal minors: their values are -5, 20, -120, and this confirms our earlier finding.

(c) (i) The profit-maximising levels of output of the three goods are: $x_1 = 14$, $x_2 = 27$, $x_3 = 15$.

(ii) The eigenvalues of the matrix of second-order partial derivatives are -2, $-3 + \sqrt{5}$, $-3 - \sqrt{5}$. They are all negative.

(iii) The matrix of second-order partial derivatives is negative definite, with the principal minors being equal to -4, 4, and -8 respectively. Once more, we have a maximum.

(d) The profit-maximising output levels and prices are: $x_1 = 25$, $x_2 = 81$, $p_1 = 20$, $p_2 = 13.33\ldots$

(e) The monopolist should produce 5 units in the first plant, and 40 units in the second plant. When this is done, the marginal cost in each plant is the same and equal to 20, and the marginal revenue is $200 - 4(5 + 40) = 20$.

(f) (i) The profits of firm 1 are given by:

$$\Pi_1 = 120x_1 - 2x_1^2 - x_1 x_2$$

Holding x_2 constant and differentiating with respect to x_1, we have

$$\frac{d\Pi_1}{dx_1} = 120 - 4x_1 - x_2$$

Setting this derivative equal to zero and solving for x_1, we obtain the reaction function of firm 1:

$$RF_1: x_1 = 30 - 0.25x_2$$

The profits of firm 2 are given by:

$$\Pi_2 = 100x_1 - x_1 x_2 - x_2^2$$

Holding x_1 constant and differentiating with respect to x_2 yields

$$\frac{d\Pi_2}{dx_1} = 100 - x_1 - 2x_2$$

Setting this derivative equal to zero and solving for x_2, we obtain the reaction function of firm 2:

$$RF_2: x_2 = 50 - 0.5x_2$$

(ii) From RF_1, $x_1 = 20$ when $x_2 = 40$. From RF_2, $x_2 = 40$ when $x_1 = 20$.

(iii) $MC_1 = 2x_1$, so $MC_1 = 20$ at $x_1 = 10$; $MC_2 = 20$ regardless of the value of x_2. So at these two outputs, the marginal costs of the two firms are equalised. What about marginal revenue?

$$MR = 120 - 2X = 120 - 2(10 + 40) = 20$$

So, industry profits are maximised, and the price is *70*.

(iv) In the Cournot–Nash equilibrium, firm 1's profits are *800*, and firm 2's profits are *1600*. With joint profit maximising, then firm 1's profits are *600* and firm 2's profits are *2000*.

(v) Firm 2 would have to agree to pay firm 1 at least *200* so that firm 1's profits were at least as large in the cartel as they were in the Cournot–Nash equilibrium. Note that firm 2 would still be better off doing this than staying in the non-cooperative equilibrium.

Exercise 14.3

(a) (i) The firm's profits function is given by:

$$\Pi = pNF(K^*/N) - rK^* - wN$$

Differentiating with respect to N yields:

$$\frac{\partial \Pi}{\partial N} = pF(K^*/N) - \frac{pK^*}{N}F'(K^*/N) - w = 0$$

Totally differentiating the first-order condition, but treating K^* as a constant, we have:

$$\left(F(K^*/N) - \frac{K^*}{N}F'(K^*/N)\right)dp + \left(-p\frac{K^*}{N^2}F'(K^*/N) + p\frac{K^*}{N}F'(K^*/N) + p\frac{K^{*2}}{N^3}F''(K^*/N)\right)dN - dw = 0$$

from which we can then derive the impact on the demand for labour of a change in the product price.

$$\frac{\partial N}{\partial p} = \frac{F(K^*/N) - \frac{K^*}{N}F'(K^*/N)}{-p\frac{K^{*2}}{N^3}F''(K^*/N)}$$

The numerator of the above derivative is equal to the real wage (w/p), which is clearly positive, and the denominator is positive, given the concavity of the production function. Hence, the demand for labour will rise when the price of the product increases. Since the marginal product of labour is assumed always to be positive, then output will increase *pari passu* with the increase in the employment of labour.

(ii) Net income per worker is given by:

$$y = pF(K^*/N) - rK^*/N$$

Differentiate with respect to L and set this derivative equal to zero. We obtain after simplifying the following first-order condition:

$$-pK^*F'(K^*/N) + rK^*/N = 0$$

Totally differentiating the above condition with respect to p and N, but treating both K^* and r as given, we have:

$$-K^*F'(K^*/N)dp + \left[p\frac{K^{*2}}{N^2}F''(K^*/N) - \frac{rK^*}{N^2}\right]dN = 0$$

with the implication that

$$\frac{\partial N}{\partial p} = \frac{F'(K^*/N)}{\dfrac{K^*}{N^2}(F''(K^*/N)p - r)}$$

The numerator of the derivative is positive, and the denominator is negative. We may, therefore, conclude that the worker-managed firm will in the short run when the amount of capital it has available is fixed employ less labour, and correspondingly produce a smaller output, as the price of the product increases. This is the exact opposite of the response of the profit-maximising competitive firm.

(b) (i) The profit-maximising levels of Q and A are given respectively by:

$$Q = \frac{64}{(1+t)^2 c^2}$$

$$A = \frac{128}{(1+t)^3 c}$$

The principal minors of the matrix of second-order partial derivatives of the profits function are given respectively by:

$$|\Pi_{QQ}| = -1.5 Q^{-1.75} A^{0.5} < 0$$

$$\begin{vmatrix} \Pi_{QQ} & \Pi_{QA} \\ \Pi_{AQ} & \Pi_{AA} \end{vmatrix} = \begin{vmatrix} -1.5 Q^{-1.75} A^{0.5} & Q^{-0.75} A^{-0.5} \\ Q^{-0.75} A^{-0.5} & -2 Q^{0.25} A^{-1.5} \end{vmatrix}$$

$$= 2 Q^{-1.5} A^{-1} > 0$$

Hence, profits are indeed being maximised.

(ii) We have

$$\frac{\partial Q}{\partial t} = \frac{-128}{(1+t)^3 c^2} < 0$$

$$\frac{\partial A}{\partial t} = \frac{-384}{(1+t)^4 c} < 0$$

(c) (i) The first-order conditions for a maximum of profit are:

$$R_1 - C'(x_1 + x_2) - t_1 = 0$$
$$R_2 - C'(x_1 + x_2) - t_2 = 0$$

Totally differentiating the first-order conditions, we obtain:

$$[R_{11} - C''(x_1 + x_2)] dx_1 + [R_{12} - C''(x_1 + x_2)] dx_2 - dt_1 = 0$$
$$[R_{21} - C''(x_1 + x_2)] dx_1 + [R_{22} - C''(x_1 + x_2)] dx_2 - dt_2 = 0$$

We may, therefore, write the equations as:

$$\begin{bmatrix} R_{11} - C''(x) & R_{12} - C''(x) \\ R_{21} - C''(x) & R_{22} - C''(x) \end{bmatrix} \begin{bmatrix} dx_1 \\ dx_2 \end{bmatrix} = \begin{bmatrix} dt_1 \\ dt_2 \end{bmatrix}$$

where x is total output. The entries in the matrix are the second-order partial derivatives of the profits function, and the second-order conditions will be satisfied if in addition to Π_{11} being negative, the determinant of the above matrix is positive. Assuming this to be the case, then we can solve for and sign the following partial derivatives:

$$\frac{\partial x_1}{\partial t_1} = \frac{R_{22} - C''(x)}{|H|} < 0$$

$$\frac{\partial x_1}{\partial t_2} = \frac{C''(x) - R_{12}}{|H|} > 0$$

(d) (i) The first-order conditions for a maximum of profit are:
$$\Pi_1 = R_1 - C_1 + s = 0$$
$$\Pi_2 = R_2 - C_2 - t = 0$$

(ii) The second-order conditions are
$$R_{11} - C_{11} < 0$$
$$(R_{11} - C_{11})(R_{22} - C_{22}) - (R_{12} - C_{12})^2 > 0$$

(iii) Totally differentiating the first-order conditions, we have:
$$\begin{bmatrix} R_{11} - C_{11} & R_{12} - C_{12} \\ R_{21} - C_{21} & R_{22} - C_{22} \end{bmatrix} \begin{bmatrix} dx_1 \\ dx_2 \end{bmatrix} = \begin{bmatrix} -ds \\ dt \end{bmatrix}$$

from which it follows that if the second-order conditions are met
$$\frac{\partial x_1}{\partial s} = \frac{C_{22} - R_{22}}{|H|} > 0, \quad \frac{\partial x_2}{\partial s} = \frac{R_{21} - C_{21}}{|H|} < 0$$
$$\frac{\partial x_1}{\partial t} = \frac{C_{12} - R_{12}}{|H|} > 0, \quad \frac{\partial x_2}{\partial t} = \frac{R_{11} - C_{11}}{|H|} < 0$$

(iv) Given the symmetry of the cross-partial derivatives, it is clear that
$$\frac{\partial x_1}{\partial t} = -\frac{\partial x_2}{\partial s}$$

CHAPTER 15

Exercise 15.1

(a)
(i) $\frac{1}{4}x^4 + k$
(ii) $-0.5x^{-2} + k$
(iii) $2x^{-0.5} + k$
(iv) $0.8x^{1.25} + k$
(v) $4x^{0.25} + k$

Exercise 15.2

(a)
(i) $5 \log_e x + k$
(ii) $2e^x + k$
(iii) $x^5 + e^x - 8x^{0.5} + k$
(iv) $-0.5x^{-4} + 3x^3 + 0.625x^{1.6} + k$
(v) $6x^{5/3} - 0.5 \log_e x + k$

Exercise 15.3

(a)
(i) $1000e^{0.1x} + k$
(ii) $-200e^{-0.05x} + k$
(iii) $(2x^2 + \log_e x)^4 + k$
(iv) $\frac{2}{3}(x^{0.5} + 6x + 5)^{3/2} + k$

(v) $\log_e(x^4 + 5x^2 - 2e^x) + k$

(vi) $\log_e(x^3 - x^{-1}) + k$

(vii) $x^2 + 12 \log_e(x - 2) + k$

Exercise 15.4

(a)

(i) $x \log_e x^2 - 2x + k$

(ii) $xe^x - e^x + k$

(iii) $0.5xe^{2x} - 0.25e^{2x} + k$

(iv) $e^x[2 + x^2 - 2x] + k$

(v) $0.5x - 0.5 \cos x \sin x + k$

(vi) $x \sin x + \cos x + k$

(vii) $x^2 \sin x + 2x \cos x - 2 \sin x + k$

Exercise 15.5

(a)

(i) $0.2 \log_e \left[\dfrac{x-2}{x+3}\right] + k$

(ii) $0.5 \log_e \left[\dfrac{x+2}{x+3}\right] + k$

(iii) $\log_e \left[\dfrac{x-4}{x-2}\right] + k$

(iv) $5 \log_e \left[\dfrac{x}{x+2}\right] + k$

(v) $\dfrac{1}{x-1} + k$

Exercise 15.6

(a) (i) *2500*; (ii) *702*; (iii) *2.9957*; (iv) *24*; (v) *108*; (vi) *126.4241*; (vii) *6811.5333*.

(b) (i) diverges; (ii) *25*; (iii) *1000*; (vi) *1000*; (v) diverges; (vi) *0.5*.

Exercise 15.7

(a) (i) consumer surplus rises by *640*, (ii) consumer surplus falls by *320*.

(ii) the firm produces *100* units of output, the price is *8*, and producer surplus is *100*, which is the same as the firm's fixed costs. Hence the firm would break even with marginal cost pricing.

(iii) the marginal revenue function is $MR = 40x^{-0.5}$, and setting marginal revenue equal to marginal cost, we find that $x = 35.54$.

(iv) In order to evaluate the welfare loss, we must evaluate the following definite integral:

$$\int_{35.54}^{100} (80x^{-0.5} - 6 - 0.02x)\, dx$$

This is equal to *172.024*.

(b) (i) the improper integral does not converge. We have

$$\int_4^\infty 100p^{-0.5}\, dp = \lim_{p_h \to \infty} 200p^{0.5}\big|_{p=4}^{p=p_h}$$

(ii) (1) consumer surplus falls by *400*, and (2) consumer surplus rises by *200*.

(c) (i) total consumer surplus is *8*; (ii) (1) consumer surplus falls by *6*, and (2) consumer surplus rises by *42*.

(d) The value of the security is the present value of the infinite flow of interest payments. We need to evaluate the following improper integral:

$$\int_0^\infty Ae^{-rt}dt = \lim_{t_h\to\infty} -\frac{A}{r}e^{-rt}\Big|_{t=0}^{t=t_h}$$

$$= \frac{A}{r}$$

Exercise 15.8

(a) Let $D = Y(s)/Y(0)$, then

$$D = \frac{1-e^{-rT}}{e^{-rs}-e^{-rT}}$$

$$= \frac{e^{rT}-1}{e^{r(T-s)}-1}$$

from which it is straightforward to show that

$$\frac{dD}{dr} > 0, \quad \frac{dD}{ds} > 0, \quad \frac{dD}{dT} < 0$$

(b) If an individual undergoes additional years of education, then the present value of the income stream inclusive of the grant payments is

$$Y(s)(e^{-rs} - e^{-rT}) + G(1-e^{-rs})$$

Equating this with the present value of the earnings stream in the occupation requiring no additional years of education, we have on re-arranging:

$$Y(s) = \frac{Y(0)(1-e^{-rT}) - G(1-e^{-rs})}{e^{-rs} - e^{-rT}}$$

As we take the limit of the above expression as T approaches infinity, we obtain the expression given in the question.

Exercise 15.9

(a) (i) We must find the value of T which satisfies the following equation:

$$0.3 - 0.0053T = \frac{0.025}{1-e^{-0.025T}}$$

When $T = 50$, the left-hand side is equal to 0.035, and the right-hand side is equal to 0.03504. The level of the land rent is given by

$$R = \frac{0.025f(T)}{e^{0.025T}-1}$$

$$\text{for } T = 50, \text{ we have } R = \frac{0.025(433726.83)}{2.4903}$$

$$= 4354.09$$

The present value of the flow of rents is 124264.82, as is the present value of the timber cut when 50 years old.

(ii) In the absence of rent to be paid, it is now optimal to fell the timber when the increase in its value is just equal to the rate of interest. If the value of the timber is growing more rapidly than the proceeds from its sale invested at the prevailing rate of interest, it is more profitable to hold one's wealth in the form of growing timber than in financial assets, and vice versa if the rate of interest is above the rate of growth of the value of the timber. We must, therefore, have:

$$0.3 - 0.0053T = 0.025$$

from which it follows that $T = 51.9$ years. The trees are felled later when there are no rents to be paid.

(b) (i) We need to find the value of T which gives rise to a maximum of the following function:

$$250T^{0.5}e^{-0.05T} - \int_0^T 10e^{-0.05T}\,dt$$

where the first term is the present value of selling the whisky at time T and the second term is the present value of the storage costs. Having carried out the definite integration and then having differentiated with respect to T, we obtain the first-order condition for a maximum:

$$125T^{-0.5}e^{-0.05T} - 12.5T^{0.5}e^{-0.05T} - 10e^{-0.05T} = 0$$

from which we then obtain the following quadratic in T:

$$T^2 - 20.64T + 100 = 0$$

whose positive root is equal to *7.77*. The whisky should be allowed to mature for this length of time. The second-order condition is met at this point.

(ii) (1) Adopting the same procedure, we obtain the following quadratic in T:

$$T^2 - 22.56T + 100 = 0$$

whose positive root is equal to *6.06*. Because of the increased costs of storage, it is no longer optimal to store the whisky for as long as before.

(2) In this case, the quadratic that we end up with is:

$$T^2 - 42.56T + 400 = 0$$

whose positive root is equal to *14.01* years; we now have a good well-matured malt given that the opportunity cost of forgoing sales and leaving it to mature is now lower as a result of the fall in the rate of interest.

Exercise 15.10

(a) Assuming the radius of the city is infinite, then

$$P(r) = 1 - (1 + \alpha r)e^{-\alpha r}$$

$$\text{and} \quad \frac{dP(r)}{d\alpha} = \alpha r^2 e^{-\alpha r} > 0$$

(b) (i) The radius of the city will be determined by the value of r which satisfies the following equation:

$$R_2(0)e^{-\beta r} = R_n(0)e^{-\gamma r}$$

If the left-hand side of the above equation is greater than the right-hand side, then agriculturists will be able to bid land away from non-agricultural users, and conversely if the inequality is reversed, farmers will not be able to prevent the land being put to a non-agricultural use. Solving the above equation we find that the city boundary occurs at:

$$r^* = \frac{1}{\gamma - \beta}\log_e\left[\frac{R_n(0)}{R_a(0)}\right]$$

(ii) To determine the size of non-agricultural land rents, we must evaluate the following definite integral:

$$\int_0^{r^*} 2\pi r R_n(0)e^{-\gamma r}\,dr$$

Using integration by parts it can be shown that total non-agricultural rents ($TNAR$) are given by:

$$TNAR = \frac{2\pi R_n(0)}{\gamma^2}[1 + (1 + \gamma r^*)e^{-\gamma r^*}]$$

CHAPTER 16

Exercise 16.1
(a) (i) $x_1 = 10$, $x_2 = 5$, $y = 2$; and $H = 4$;
   (ii) $x_1 = 12$, $x_2 = 6$, $y = 1/12$; and $H = 120$;
   (iii) $x_1 = 5$, $x_2 = 2$, $y = 30$; and $H = 27$;
   (iv) $x_1 = 20$, $x_2 = 4$, $y = 2$; and $H = 2$.

(b) (i) $x_1 = 9$, $x_2 = 7$, $y = 15$; and $H = -8$;
   (ii) $x_1 = -12$, $x_2 = -6$, $y = -1/12$; and $H = -120$;
   (iii) $x_1 = 10$, $x_2 = 4$, $y = 40$; and $H = -2$;
   (iv) $x_1 = 5$, $x_2 = 2$, $y = 2$; and $H = -46$.

Exercise 16.2
(a) (i) Since the first derivative is always positive, the function is strictly quasi-concave.
(ii) Since the first derivative is always negative, the function is strictly quasi-concave.
(iii) Though this function is the sum of two strictly quasi-concave functions, it is in fact a strictly quasi-convex function.

(b) The function is not concave since
$$f_{11} = -0.5x_1^{-0.5} < 0$$
$$\text{but } f_{11}f_{12} - f_{12}f_{21} = -1$$

It is, however, strictly quasi-concave since
$$-f_1^2 = -(0.5x_1^{-0.5})^2 < 0$$

$$\text{and } \begin{vmatrix} 0 & f_1 & f_2 \\ f_1 & f_{11} & f_{12} \\ f_2 & f_{21} & f_{22} \end{vmatrix} = x_1^{0.5} > 0$$

(c) (i) strictly quasi-convex; (ii) strictly quasi-concave; (iii) strictly quasi-convex; (iv) strictly quasi-convex.

Exercise 16.3
(a) (i) Our problem therefore is:
$$\text{Maximise } U^A = x_{1A}x_{2A}$$
$$\text{subject to } (100 - x_{1A})(200 - x_{2A}) = 4800$$

The Lagrangean function takes the following form:
$$L = U^A = x_{1A}x_{2A} + y[(100 - x_{1A})(200 - x_{2A}) - 4800]$$

and the first-order conditions are:
$$L_{1A} = x_{2A} - y(200 - x_{2A}) = 0$$
$$L_{2A} = x_{1A} - y(100 - x_{1A}) = 0$$
$$L_y = (100 - x_{1A})(200 - x_{2A}) - 4800 = 0$$

From the first-order conditions we have
$$\frac{x_{2A}}{x_{1A}} = \frac{(200 - x_{2A})}{(100 - x_{1A})}$$

Hence
$$x_{2A} = 2x_{1A}$$

Substituting in the constraint we obtain the following quadratic equation in x_{1A}:

$$2x_{1A}^2 - 400x_{1A} + 15200 = 0$$

with roots: $x_{1A} = 51.01$ or 148.99. The larger value is infeasible since the total initial endowment is only 100. Hence, the solution is $x_{1A} = 51.01$, $x_{2A} = 102.02$ with max $U^A = 5204.04$. A buys 11.01 units of good 1 in exchange for 17.98 units of good 2; the implied price of good 1 is, therefore, 1.6331.

(ii) The value of the bordered Hessian determinant in 19595.84, so we have identified a constrained maximum.

(iii) B sells 8.99 units of good one in exchange for 22.02 units of good 2; the implied price of good 2 is therefore 2.4494.

(b) (i) The desired supply of hours in the absence of any unearned income is given by αT which is clearly independent of w. The utility function is quasi-concave and the constraint is linear, so we have a constrained maximum of utility subject to the budget constraint.

(ii) The supply of hours function is now given by:

$$H = \alpha T - \frac{(1-\alpha)D}{\alpha w}$$

and $\quad \dfrac{\partial H}{\partial w} = \dfrac{(1-\alpha)D}{\alpha w^2} > 0 \quad \text{for } D > 0$

Exercise 16.4

(a) (i) The Marshallian demand functions and the Lagrangean multiplier are given by:

$$x_1 = \frac{0.5M}{p_1} \quad \text{and} \quad x_2 = \frac{0.5M}{p_2}$$

$$y = \frac{0.5M}{p_1 p_2}$$

(ii) The maximum value function and its partial derivatives are:

$$V(\mathbf{p}, M) = \frac{0.25M^2}{p_1 p_2}$$

$$\frac{\partial V}{\partial p_1} = \frac{-0.25M^2}{p_1^2 p_2}, \quad \frac{\partial V}{\partial p_2} = \frac{-0.25M^2}{p_1 p_2^2}$$

$$\frac{\partial V}{\partial M} = \frac{0.5M}{p_1 p_2}$$

It is then straightforward to check that

$$x_1 = -\frac{\partial V}{\partial p_1} \bigg/ \frac{\partial V}{\partial M}$$

$$x_2 = -\frac{\partial V}{\partial p_2} \bigg/ \frac{\partial V}{\partial M}$$

(iii) The cost-minimising levels of the two goods are given by:

$$x_1 = \left(\frac{p_2 U'}{p_1}\right)^{0.5} \quad \text{and} \quad x_2 = \left(\frac{p_1 U'}{p_2}\right)^{0.5}$$

The expenditure function and its partial derivatives with respect to the prices are

$$E(\mathbf{p}, U') = 2(p_1 p_2 U')^{0.5}$$

$$\frac{\partial E}{\partial p_1} = \left(\frac{p_2 U'}{p_1}\right)^{0.5} \quad \text{and} \quad \frac{\partial E}{\partial p_2} = \left(\frac{p_1 U'}{p_2}\right)^{0.5}$$

(iv) The CV measure of the welfare gain is 10.56, the EV measure is 11.8, and the change in consumer surplus is 11.16.

(b) (i) The Marshallian demand curves are:

$$x_1 = 100 - \frac{p_1}{p_2}$$

$$x_2 = \frac{M - 100p_1}{p_2} + \left(\frac{p_1}{p_2}\right)^2$$

(ii) The expenditure function is

$$E = 100p_1 - \frac{0.5p_1^2}{p_2} + (U' - 5000)p_2$$

(iii) The income effect on the demand for x_1 is zero, so the Hicksian and Marshallian demand functions for good 1 coincide. The Hicksian demand function for good 2 is given by:

$$x_2 = (U' - 5000) + \frac{0.5p_1^2}{p_2^2}$$

(iv) Since the Hicksian and Marshallian demand functions for good 1 coincide, we have $CV = EV =$ the change in consumer surplus. The welfare loss is *10*.

Exercise 16.5

(a) (i) Differentiating partially with respect to K, N, and y, we obtain the following set of first-order conditions:

$$\frac{\partial L}{\partial K} = r - \alpha y A K^{\alpha-1} N^\beta = 0$$

$$\frac{\partial L}{\partial N} = w - \beta y A K^\alpha N^{\beta-1} = 0$$

$$\frac{\partial L}{\partial y} = Q - A K^\alpha N^\beta = 0$$

from which it follows that:

$$\frac{w}{r} = \frac{\beta A K^\alpha N^{\beta-1}}{\alpha A K^{\alpha-1} N^\beta} = \frac{\beta K}{\alpha N}$$

Hence $K = (\alpha w N)/\beta r$ and substituting in the production function, we obtain:

$$Q = A(\alpha/\beta)^\alpha (w/r)^\alpha N^{\alpha+\beta}$$

which we may then invert to obtain

$$N = M(w/r)^{-\alpha/(\alpha+\beta)} Q^{1/(\alpha+\beta)}$$

where

$$M = A^{-1/(\alpha+\beta)} (\alpha/\beta)^{-\alpha/(\alpha+\beta)}$$

Substituting the above expression for N in the equation yields

$$K = \frac{\alpha}{\beta} M \left(\frac{w}{r}\right)^{\beta/(\alpha+\beta)}$$

we may, therefore, write the total cost function as:

$$C = rK + wN$$

$$= \left(\frac{\alpha}{\beta} w^{\beta/(\alpha+\beta)} r^{\alpha/(\alpha+\beta)} + w^{\beta/(\alpha+\beta)} r^{\alpha/(\alpha+\beta)}\right) MQ^{1/(\alpha+\beta)}$$

Hence for given factor prices

$$C = constant \cdot Q^{1/(\alpha+\beta)}$$

(ii) Average costs will be decreasing, constant or increasing as output increases depending upon whether $\alpha + \beta$ is greater than, equal to or less than one. Note the Cobb–Douglas production function is homogeneous of degree $\alpha + \beta$. If there are constant returns to scale, then $\alpha + \beta$ is equal to one and total costs are proportional to output. If $\alpha + \beta$ is greater than one, we have increasing returns to scale: average cost falls as output increases. If $\alpha + \beta$ is less than one, we have decreasing returns to scale: average cost increases as output increases.

(iii) If we differentiate the cost function partially with respect to the wage rate, we obtain the compensated demand function for labour services:

$$N = \frac{\partial C}{\partial w} = (w/r)^{-\alpha/(\alpha+\beta)} M Q^{1/(\alpha+\beta)}$$

The compensated demand function for capital services can be similarly obtained by differentiating the cost function partially with respect to the capital services price.

$$K = \frac{\partial C}{\partial r} = \left(\frac{\alpha}{\beta}\right)\left(\frac{w}{r}\right)^{\beta/(\alpha+\beta)} M Q^{1/(\alpha+\beta)}$$

(b) From the first-order conditions, we find that

$$K = N\left(\frac{w}{r}\right)^{0.5}$$

If we then substitute this expression for K in the production function we obtain:

$$N = 0.5Q[w^{-0.5}r^{0.5} + 1]$$

from which it then follows that

$$K = 0.5Q[1 + w^{0.5}r^{-0.5}]$$

and the total cost function is, therefore,

$$TC = 0.5Q[2w^{0.5}r^{0.5} + w + r]$$

(c) (i) When *ad valorem* tax rates t_1 and t_2 are imposed, the corresponding quantities and prices are: $50(1 - t_1)$, $50(1 + t_1)$ and $80(1 - 1.5t_2)$, $60(1 + t_2)$ respectively. At these tax rates, government tax receipts, R, are as follows:

$$R = 50t_1(50 - 50t_1) + 60t_2(80 - 120t_2)$$
$$= 2500t_1 - 2500t_1^2 + 4800t_2 - 7200t_2^2$$

and this revenue must equal the cost of providing the public good. The excess burden, B, which we are seeking to minimise is given by:

$$B = 1250t_1^2 + 3600t_2^2$$

The Lagrangean expression we seek to minimise is therefore

$$L = 1250t_1^2 + 3600t_2^2 + y(G - 2500t_1 + 2500t_1^2 - 4800t_2 + 7200t_2^2)$$

On differentiating partially with respect to t_1, t_2, and y, we obtain the first-order conditions for minimising the excess burden of taxation subject to the government's budget constraint:

$$\frac{\partial L}{\partial t_1} = 2500t_1 + y(-2500 + 5000t_1) = 0$$

$$\frac{\partial L}{\partial t_2} = 7200t_2 + y(-4800 + 14400t_2) = 0$$

$$\frac{\partial L}{\partial y} = G - 2500t_1 + 2500t_1^2 - 4800t_2 + 7200t_2^2 = 0$$

from which it follows that:

$$\frac{7200t_2}{2500t_1} = \frac{14400t_2 - 4800}{5000t_1 - 2500}$$

and after cross-multiplying and simplifying, we obtain:

$$t_1 = 1.5t_2$$

Substituting the above expression into the budget constraint and then dividing by 100 yields:

$$37.5t_2^2 - 56.25t_2^2 + 48t_2 - 72t_2^2 = 0.1G$$

Collecting terms enables us to write the following quadratic equation in t_2:

$$128.25t_2^2 - 85.5t_2 + 0.01G = 0$$

Applying the formula for finding the roots of a quadratic equation we have:

$$t_2 = \frac{85.5 \pm \sqrt{(7310.25 - 5.13G)}}{265.5}$$

Given $G = 1197$, it then follows that

$$t_2 = 0.2 \quad or \quad 0.46 \ldots$$
$$and \quad t_1 = 0.3 \quad or \quad 0.7$$

whilst the Lagrangean multipliers can be found by solving the following equation:

$$y = \frac{2500t_1}{2500 - 5000t_1} = \frac{t_1}{1 - 2t_1}$$

Hence $y = 0.75$ or $-0.26\ldots$. In order to determine which of these two vectors that satisfy the first-order conditions does indeed give rise to a minimum excess burden, we must sign the Hessian bordered determinant, though the fact that in the second vector the Lagrangean multiplier takes on a negative value, and the two tax rates are higher than in the first vector obviously means that the loss is going to be greater in this second case.

Differentiating the first-order conditions partially with respect to t_1 and t_2 gives us the following second-order partial derivatives:

$$L_{11} = 2500 - 5000y$$
$$L_{12} = L_{21} = 0$$
$$L_{22} = 7200 - 14400y$$

whilst the partial derivatives of the budget constraint with respect to t_1 and t_2 are

$$g_1 = 2500 - 5000t_1, \quad g_2 = 4800 - 14400t_2$$

The bordered Hessian determinant is, therefore, as follows:

$$|\bar{H}| = \begin{vmatrix} 0 & 2500 - 5000t_1 & 4800 - 14400t_2 \\ 2500 - 5000t_1 & 2500 + 5000y & 0 \\ 4800 - 14400t_1 & 0 & 7200 + 14400y \end{vmatrix}$$

Evaluating the determinant at the point $(0.3, 0.2, 0.75)$, we find that it is equal to -4.104^{10}. Hence, the second-order conditions for a minimum are satisfied at this point. The bordered Hessian determinant evaluated at the point $(0.7, 0.46\ldots, -0.26\ldots)$ is positive. Hence, at this second point, we would indeed be maximising the excess burden of taxes subject to the government budget constraint.

(ii) Setting $t_1 - t_2 = t$, the Lagrangean function would now be

$$L = 4850t^2 + y(1197 - 7300t + 9700t^2)$$

and the first-order conditions for a maximum are:

$$9700t - y(7300 - 19400t) = 0$$

$$1197 - 7300t + 9700t^2 = 0$$

Solving the quadratic equation in t and taking the root with the smaller value, we have: $t = 0.2414$, and hence $y = 0.8948$. The excess burden is 282.66. This compares with an excess burden of 256.5 in part (a) where the government was free to set differential tax rates.

CHAPTER 17

Exercise 17.1

(a) (i) $x_1 = 8$, $x_2 = 12$, $y_1 = 6$, $y_2 = 0$;
   (ii) $x_1 = 117/21$, $x_2 = 26/21$, $y_1 = 920/21$, $y_2 = 0$;
   (iii) $x_1 = 19/2$, $x_2 = 13$, $y_1 = 0$, $y_2 = 3$;
   (iv) $x_1 = 12$, $x_2 = 0$, $y_1 = 9$, $y_2 = 0$.

(b) (i) $x_1 = 7.13524$, $x_2 = 5.04538$, $y_1 = 2.82843$;
   (ii) $x_1 = 6$, $x_2 = 4$, $y_1 = 0$, $y_2 = 4$.

(c) (i) The KT maximum conditions are:

$$\frac{\partial L}{\partial x_1} = 4x_1 - \frac{1}{2}yx_1^{-\frac{1}{2}} \le 0, \quad x_1 \ge 0, \quad x_1\frac{\partial L}{\partial x_1} = 0$$

$$\frac{\partial L}{\partial x_2} = 2x_2 - y \le 0, \quad x_2 \ge 0, \quad x_2\frac{\partial L}{\partial x_2} = 0$$

$$\frac{\partial L}{\partial y} = 8 - x_1^{\frac{1}{2}} - x_2 \ge 0, \quad y \ge 0, \quad y\frac{\partial L}{\partial y} = 0$$

If we substitute, the values given into the above conditions, we see that they are all satisfied.

(ii) The objective function is convex, and the constraint is also convex. The above point gives rise to a minimum of the function subject to the constraint holding as an equality.

(iii) The KT conditions are also met at the point: $x_1 = 64$, $x_2 = 0$, $y = 4096$. This is the optimal position.

(d) (i) The Lagrangean function is:

$$L = 40x_1 - x_1^2 + 56x_2 - 2x_2^2 - 2x_1x_2 + y_1(87 - 5x_1 - 7x_2) + y_2(100 - 8x_1 - 3x_2)$$

and the KT maximum conditions are:

$$\frac{\partial L}{\partial x_1} = 40 - 2x_1 - 2x_2 - 5y_1 - 8y_2 \le 0, \quad x_1 \ge 0, \quad x_1\frac{\partial L}{\partial x_1} = 0$$

$$\frac{\partial L}{\partial x_2} = 56 - 2x_1 - 4x_2 - 7y_1 - 3y_2 \le 0, \quad x_2 \ge 0, \quad x_2\frac{\partial L}{\partial x_2} = 0$$

$$\frac{\partial L}{\partial y_1} = 87 - 5x_1 - 7x_2 \ge 0, \quad y_1 \ge 0, \quad y_1\frac{\partial L}{\partial y_1} = 0$$

$$\frac{\partial L}{\partial y_2} = 100 - 8x_1 - 3x_2 \ge 0, \quad y_2 \ge 0, \quad y_2\frac{\partial L}{\partial y_2} = 0$$

(ii) The firm should produce 9 units of the first good and 6 units of the second; the shadow price of a tonne of steel is 2, and since there is surplus electricity allocated to the firm, its shadow price is zero.

(iii) The objective function is concave, the constraints are linear and hence convex, and there exists a point which satisfies the KT maximum conditions. We do, therefore, have a global optimum subject to the constraints.

(e) (i) The KT maximum conditions for this problem are:

$$\frac{\partial L}{\partial x_1} = a - 2x_1 - y_1 - 3y_2 \le 0, \quad x_1 \ge 0, \quad x_1 \frac{\partial L}{\partial x_1} = 0$$

$$\frac{\partial L}{\partial x_2} = c - 2x_2 - 2y_1 - 2y_2 \le 0, \quad x_2 \ge 0, \quad x_2 \frac{\partial L}{\partial x_2} = 0$$

$$\frac{\partial L}{\partial y_1} = 20 - x_1 - 2x_2 \ge 0, \quad y_1 \ge 0, \quad y_1 \frac{\partial L}{\partial y_1} = 0$$

$$\frac{\partial L}{\partial y_2} = 27 - 3x_1 - 2x_2 \ge 0, \quad y_2 \ge 0, \quad y_2 \frac{\partial L}{\partial y_2} = 0$$

(ii) (1) For $x_1 = 0$, $x_2 = 10$, then $y_2 = 0$, $y_1 = (c - 20)/2$ and $a - y_1 \le 0$. Hence, $c \ge 2a + 20$.

(2) For $x_1 = 9$, $x_2 = 0$, then $y_1 = 0$, $y_2 = (a - 18)/3$ and $c - 2y_2 \le 0$. Hence, $a \ge 1.5c + 18$.

(f) (i) The KT maximum conditions are:

$$\frac{\partial L}{\partial x_1} = 50 - 4x_1 - x_2 - 2y_1 - 3y_2 \le 0, \quad x_1 \ge 0, \quad x_1 \frac{\partial L}{\partial x_1} = 0$$

$$\frac{\partial L}{\partial x_2} = 120 - x_1 - 2x_2 - 5y_1 - y_2 \le 0, \quad x_2 \ge 0, \quad x_2 \frac{\partial L}{\partial x_2} = 0$$

$$\frac{\partial L}{\partial y_1} = 250 - 2x_1 - 5x_2 \ge 0, \quad y_1 \ge 0, \quad y_1 \frac{\partial L}{\partial y_1} = 0$$

$$\frac{\partial L}{\partial y_2} = 300 - 3x_1 - x_2 \ge 0, \quad y_2 \ge 0, \quad y_2 \frac{\partial L}{\partial y_2} = 0$$

Given the nature of the profits function, it makes sense to check first whether at the optimal solution x_1 is zero. If this is the case, then there will be slack in the second constraint, y_2 will equal zero, x_2 will equal 50, and hence the partial derivative with respect to x_2 must equal 0. This requires y_1 to equal 4, and given these values of the choice variables and the Lagrangean multipliers, the partial derivative with respect to x_1 is negative and equal to -8. Hence the KT maximum conditions are met at this point.

(ii) Since y_1 equals 4, a marginal relaxation of the first constraint would increase profits by 4.

(iii) We now have

$$\frac{\partial L}{\partial x_1} = 70 - 4x_1 - x_2 - 2y_1 - 3y_2$$

and at the original optimal solution this derivative is now positive. We therefore try as the solution the tangency position between the first constraint and an iso-profit contour.
This requires us to solve the following three equations:

$$70 - 4x_1 - x_2 - 2y_1 = 0$$

$$120 - x_1 - 2x_2 - 5y_1 = 0$$

$$250 - 2x_1 - 5x_2 = 0$$

The solution is: $x_1 = 75/22$, $x_2 = 1070/22$, $y_1 = 85/22$. At this output bundle, there is slack in the second constraint, so we are justified in having y_2 equal to zero, and this new point satisfies the KT maximum conditions.

(g) (i) If c is zero, then the feasible region is just a triangular area in the non-negative quadrant, the sides being the two axes and the line $q = 1 - p$. For positive c there are three possibilities: one where the rectangular hyperbola $q = c/p$ intersects the downward sloping line $q = 1 - p$ twice, secondly where it forms a tangent to the line and thirdly where the rectangular hyperbola lies wholly to the right of the line. In order to find the points of intersection, then solve the following

two equations:
$$pq = c \quad \text{and} \quad q = 1 - p$$

The two equations give rise to the following quadratic in q:
$$q^2 - q + c = 0$$

For the feasible region to be non-empty, the roots of this quadratic must be real; its roots are
$$r_1, r_2 = 0.5 \pm 0.5\sqrt{1 - 4c}$$

Hence they will be real for $c \leq 1/4$; the feasible region will shrink to a single point, $p = 1/2$, $q = 1/2$, for $c = 1/4$.

(ii) Given the existence of a feasible region, it will be convex, but not strictly so, since part of the boundary of the feasible region is linear.

(iii) The agent's expected utility is given by:
$$E(u) = p\sqrt{81} + q\sqrt{144} + (1 - p - q)\sqrt{100}$$
$$= 10 + 2q - p$$

Obviously the agent would like q to be as large as possible subject to the constraints. The Lagrangean function is
$$L = 10 + 2q - p + y_1(1 - p - q) + y_2(pq - c)$$

The Kuhn-Tucker maximum conditions are:

$$\frac{\partial L}{\partial p} = -1 - y_1 + y_2 q \leq 0, \quad p \geq 0, \quad p\frac{\partial L}{\partial p} = 0$$

$$\frac{\partial L}{\partial q} = 2 - y_1 + y_2 p \leq 0, \quad q \geq 0, \quad q\frac{\partial L}{\partial q} = 0$$

$$\frac{\partial L}{\partial y_1} = 1 - p - q \geq 0, \quad y_1 \geq 0, \quad y_1\frac{\partial L}{\partial y_1} = 0$$

$$\frac{\partial L}{\partial y_2} = pq - c \geq 0, \quad y_2 \geq 0, \quad y_2\frac{\partial L}{\partial y_2} = 0$$

Assume $c > 0$, then both p and q must be positive, and the partial derivatives with respect to p and q must equal zero. This can only be the case then if both Lagrangean multipliers are positive. But then the two constraints must hold as equalities. If c is zero, then p will be zero, and q unity; once again the Lagrangean multipliers will both be positive.

(iv) Provided that c does not exceed $1/4$, then we shall have:
$$q = 0.5 + 0.5\sqrt{1 - 4c}$$
$$p = 0.5 - 0.5\sqrt{1 - 4c}$$

Why do we take the larger value of q? The most straightforward explanation is that $E(U) = 10 + 2q - p$. More rigorously, the KT maximum conditions will not be satisfied at the smaller value of q. Both Lagrangean multipliers would be negative. Assume for simplicity that c is zero, then the smaller value of q which satisfies the equality constraints is zero, and p is then unity. In which case, y_1 must equal -1, and y_2 then must be no larger than -3.

Exercise 17.2

(a) (i) $x_1 = 30/7$, $x_2 = 330/7$;

(ii) $x_1 = 0$, $x_2 = 50$;

(iii) (1) Assuming that positive quantities of both goods are supplied to the two markets, from the KT maximum conditions, we end up with the following quadratic equation in x_2:
$$1.5625x_2^2 - 187.5x_2 + 3125 = 0$$

Solving this equation, we find that $x_2 = 20$ or 100. The larger value is the one that will lead to the constrained optimum. The KT maximum conditions also require $x_1 = 0.75x_2$, so we must have $x_1 = 75$.

(2) The value of the Lagrangean multiplier is equal to 0.25. This measures the cost in terms of forgone welfare of a marginal increase in the amount of profit the nationalised enterprise must earn.

(b) (i) Net social benefits are maximised when price is equal to marginal cost. Hence $p_1 = 20$ and $p_2 = 40$. The associated output levels are $x_1 = 80$ and $x_2 = 80$. Profits are negative because of the presence of fixed costs and equal to -750.

(ii) From the KT maximum conditions it follows that x_1 must equal x_2. We also obtain the following quadratic equation in x_1:

$$2x_1^2 - 160x_1 + 750 = 0$$

whose roots are 5 and 75 respectively. The higher value is the one at which social welfare is optimised.

(iii) The associated prices are: $p_1 = 25$, and $p_2 = 45$, yielding a ratio of price to marginal cost for the two goods at 1.25 and 1.125 respectively. The own-price elasticities of demand for the two goods are $-1/3$ and $-9/25$.

(c) (i) The optimal prices and quantities are as follows: $p_1 = 40$, $p_2 = 20$, $x_1 = 60$, $x_2 = 40$.

(ii) (1) No change in the peak period; the good should not be supplied in the off-peak period since the marginal operating cost is greater than the choke price at which demand falls to zero.

(2) No change in the peak period; $p_2 = 50$ and $x_2 = 60$.

(iii) The long-run equilibrium level of installed capacity is 50. In part (a) y_1 is 20 and y_2 zero since capacity is not fully utilised in the off-peak period, whereas d is 30. Capacity must therefore not be replaced as it wears out until it is reduced to 50.

(d) (i) The Lagrangean function is

$$L = B_1(x_1) + B_2(x_2) - 250x_1 - 300x_2 + y_1(300 - x_1) + y_2(150 - x_2)$$

and the KT maximum conditions are:

$$\frac{\partial L}{\partial x_1} = p_1 - 250 - y_1 \leq 0, \quad x_1 \geq 0, \quad x_1 \frac{\partial L}{\partial x_1} = 0$$

$$\frac{\partial L}{\partial x_2} = p_2 - 300 - y_2 \leq 0, \quad x_2 \geq 0, \quad x_2 \frac{\partial L}{\partial x_2} = 0$$

$$\frac{\partial L}{\partial y_1} = 300 - x_1 \geq 0, \quad y_1 \geq 0, \quad y_1 \frac{\partial L}{\partial y_1} = 0$$

$$\frac{\partial L}{\partial y_2} = 150 - x_2 \geq 0, \quad y_2 \geq 0, \quad y_2 \frac{\partial L}{\partial y_2} = 0$$

Assume capacity is fully utilised in both periods. Then with $x_1 = 300$, it follows that $p_1 = 880$ and $y_1 = 630$; and with $x_2 = 150$, then $p_2 = 425$ and $y_2 = 125$. The KT conditions are met, and this is the optimal point.

(ii) y_i is the value of having a little bit more capacity available in period i. Hence, if $y_1 + y_2$ is greater than the cost of expanding runway capacity at the margin, then it is in the interests of society that it be expanded.

(iii) The KT maximum conditions now become:

$$\frac{\partial L}{\partial x_1} = p_1 - 250 - x_1 - y_1 \leq 0, \quad x_1 \geq 0, \quad x_1 \frac{\partial L}{\partial x_1} = 0$$

$$\frac{\partial L}{\partial x_2} = p_2 - 300 - 2.5x_2 - y_2 \leq 0, \quad x_2 \geq 0, \quad x_2 \frac{\partial L}{\partial x_2} = 0$$

$$\frac{\partial L}{\partial y_1} = 300 - x_1 \geq 0, \quad y_1 \geq 0, \quad y_1 \frac{\partial L}{\partial y_1} = 0$$

$$\frac{\partial L}{\partial y_2} = 150 - x_2 \geq 0, \quad y_2 \geq 0, \quad y_2 \frac{\partial L}{\partial y_2} = 0$$

If we assume x_1 is still equal to 300, then we must have y_1 equal to 330, obviously p_1 is still equal to 880. However, for x_2 still to equal 150, it is necessary that y_2 equal -250. This violates the KT conditions. Hence demand in the off-peak period must fall short of capacity, and y_1 must be zero. We must have

$$800 - 2.5x_2 - 300 - 2.5x_2 = 0$$

$$\text{hence } x_2 = 100 \quad \text{and} \quad p_2 = 550$$

(e) (i) The Lagrangean function takes the following form:

$$L = B_1(x_1) + B_2(x_2) - c(x_1 + x_2) - ds - ex_c - fx_s + y_1(x_c - s - x_1) + y_2(x_c + s - x_2) + y_s(x_s - s)$$

Holding fixed the installed levels of productive and storage capacity, we have the following Kuhn–Tucker maximum conditions:

$$\frac{\partial L}{\partial x_1} = p_1 - c - y_1 \le 0, \quad x_1 \ge 0, \quad x_1 \frac{\partial L}{\partial x_1} = 0$$

$$\frac{\partial L}{\partial x_2} = p_2 - c - y_2 \le 0, \quad x_2 \ge 0, \quad x_2 \frac{\partial L}{\partial x_2} = 0$$

$$\frac{\partial L}{\partial s} = -d - y_1 + y_2 - y_s \le 0, \quad s \ge 0, \quad s\frac{\partial L}{\partial s} = 0$$

$$\frac{\partial L}{\partial y_1} = x_c - x_1 - s \ge 0, \quad y_1 \ge 0, \quad y_1 \frac{\partial L}{\partial y_1} = 0$$

$$\frac{\partial L}{\partial y_2} = x_c + s - x_2 \ge 0, \quad y_2 \ge 0, \quad y_2 \frac{\partial L}{\partial y_2} = 0$$

$$\frac{\partial L}{\partial y_s} = x_s - s \ge 0, \quad y_s \ge 0, \quad y_s \frac{\partial L}{\partial y_s} = 0$$

(ii) Once we allow the installed levels of productive and storage capacity to become variables, we have:

$$\frac{\partial L}{\partial x_c} = c - y_1 - y_2 \le 0, \quad x_c \ge 0, \quad x_c \frac{\partial L}{\partial x_s} = 0$$

$$\frac{\partial L}{\partial x_s} = y_s - f \le 0, \quad x_s \ge 0, \quad x_s \frac{\partial L}{\partial x_s} = 0$$

Productive capacity will be positive and at its optimum level if $e = y_1 + y_2$; willingness to pay for a little bit more capacity on the part of peak and off-peak period consumers is just equal to the marginal cost of expanding capacity. Storage capacity will be positive and optimal if y_s is equal to f.

(iii) It is straightforward to check that the long-run equilibrium condition for no storage to take place is that $f > y_s$. Furthermore, if productive capacity is only fully utilised in the peak period, then $e < d + f$. It always pays to expand productive capacity rather than to use storage: to produce a unit in the off-peak period, then store it and make it available in the peak period requires expenditure equal to $c + d + f$, whereas to make a further unit of the good available in the peak period by expanding productive capacity incurs a cost of $c + e$. It should be apparent that again assuming capacity is only fully utilised in the peak that storage capacity will be utilised if $e = d + f$. Finally storage will take place and productive capacity will be fully utilised in both periods if $e > d + f$. It is cheaper to make available a further unit for consumption in the peak period by producing more in the off-peak period and then storing it and making it available in the peak period than by expanding productive capacity.

Exercise 17.3

(a) (i) At the first iteration x_1 is introduced in place of R_1, at the next iteration x_2 is introduced and R_2 is eliminated, and finally y_1 is brought in to replace R_3, the artificial variable in the constraint. The solution is $x_1 = 19/2$, $x_2 = 13$, $y_1 = 3$. The value of the objective function is -338.

(ii) At the first iteration, x_1 is introduced in place of R_1; at the next iteration, x_2 enters in place of S_1, and finally y_1 is introduced in place of R_2. We have at the optimal solution: $x_1 = 8$, $x_2 = 12$, $y_1 = 6$, $y_2 = 0$. The value of the objective function is 408.

(iii) At the first iteration x_1 is introduced and R_1 is eliminated, then x_2 is introduced into the basis and S_1 is discarded, finally y_1 is brought into the basis in place of R_2. We have at the optimal solution: $x_1 = 5, x_2 = 6, y_1 = 3$. The value of the objective function is *163*.

(iv) At the first iteration x_2 is introduced and R_2 is eliminated, then x_1 is introduced into the basis and R_1 is removed, finally y_1 is brought into the basis in place of R_2. We have at the optimal solution: $x_1 = 7, x_2 = 9, y_1 = 4$. The value of the objective function is *−45*.

CHAPTER 18

Exercise 18.1
(a)
$$\text{(i) } y(t) = 10e^{-t}$$
$$\text{(ii) } y(t) = 2e^{2t}$$
$$\text{(iii) } y(t) = 8$$

Exercise 18.2
(a)
$$\text{(i) } y(t) = -4e^{-2t} + 5$$
$$\text{(ii) } y(t) = 13e^{0.5t} - 8$$
$$\text{(iii) } y(t) = 1000$$
$$\text{(iv) } y(t) = e^{-3t} + 4$$

Exercise 18.3
(a)
$$\text{(i) } y(t) = 25 + 2t$$
$$\text{(ii) } y(t) = 12 - 0.5t$$
$$\text{(iii) } y(t) = 25 + 9t$$

Exercise 18.4
(a)
$$\text{(i) } y(t) = Ae^{-0.5t^2}$$
$$\text{(ii) } y(t) = Ae^{t^3}$$
$$\text{(iii) } y(t) = Ae^{t^{-1}}$$

Exercise 18.5
(a)
$$\text{(i) } y(t) = Ae^t - 6 - 4t$$
$$\text{(ii) } y(t) = Ae^{-2t} + 0.2\sin t + 0.4\cos t$$
$$\text{(iii) } y(t) = Ae^{0.5t} + 20e^t$$

Exercise 18.6
(a)
$$\text{(i) } y(t) = Ae^{-2t} + 0.4e^{0.5t}$$
$$\text{(ii) } y(t) = Ae^{-\frac{1}{3}t^3} + 3$$
$$\text{(iii) } y(t) = At^{-1} + \frac{5}{2}t + \frac{2}{3}t^2$$

(b)

(i) $k(t) = Ae^{0.05t} - 200,000 + 40c(0)e^{0.025t}$

(ii) $A = -73576.372, \quad c(0) = £6839.41$

(iii) $c(0) = £6571.76$, consumption continues to grow at 2.5 per cent per annum

Exercise 18.7

(a)

(i) $y(t) = (0.4t^2 + 25)^{0.5}$

(ii) $y(t) = (1.2t^{2.5} + 1)^{-\frac{1}{3}}$

(iii) $y(t) = (2\sin t + 1)^{0.5}$

(iv) $y(t) = 42e^{0.5t^2}$

(b)

(i) $p(t) = \dfrac{1,500,000}{(10+t)^2}$

$p = 7,500$ when $t = 4.142$

Exercise 18.8

(a)

(i) $y(t) = (Ae^{2t} + 2)^{-0.5}$

(ii) $y(t) = (Ae^{0.15t} - 500)^{\frac{4}{3}}$

(iii) $y(t) = (Ae^{2t} - 2.5t - 1.25)^{-1}$

(b)

(i) $k(t) = (8 - 7e^{-0.04t})^{1.25}$

The long-run equilibrium value of $k(t)$ is $8^{1.25} = 13.4543$

90 per cent of LRE value is reached at $t = 59.546$

(ii) $k(t) = (4e^{0.04t} - 3e^{-0.04t})^{1.25}$

In LRE k is growing exponentially at a rate of 5 per cent

Exercise 18.9

(a)

(i) $y(t) = \dfrac{1000}{1 + 9e^{-t}}$

(ii) 1) $y(t) = 500$ at $t = 2.197$

(iii) 2) $y(t) = 900$ at $t = 4.394$

(b)

(a) $y(t) = \dfrac{1000}{1 + 9t^{-1}}$

there is no point of inflexion.

(i) $y(t) = 500$ at $t = 9$

(ii) $y(t) = 900$ at $t = 81$

(c)

(i) $y(t) = \dfrac{100}{1+4e^{-0.1t}}$

(ii) *Long-run equilibrium value of y is* 100

$y = 50$ *at* $t = 13.86$

(iii) $y(t) = 70 - \dfrac{40}{1+ke^{0.04t}}$

(iv) $y(t) = 70 - \dfrac{40}{1-0.2e^{0.04t}}$

$y = 0$ *at* $t = 19.05$

(v) $y(t) = 70 - \dfrac{40}{1+\frac{1}{3}e^{0.4t}}$

y converges on the value 70

CHAPTER 19

Exercise 19.1

(a)

(i) $y(t) = A_1 e^{-6t} + A_2 e^{-t}$

(ii) $y(t) = A_1 e^{4t} + A_2 e^{2t}$

(iii) $y(t) = A_1 e^{-2t} + A_2 e^{8t}$

(iv) $y(t) = A_1 e^{-4t} + A_2 e^{2t}$

(b)

(i) $y(t) = 3e^{-t} + 2e^{4t}$

(ii) $y(t) = -2e^{-4t} + 4e^{-t}$

(iii) $y(t) = 2e^{-2t} + e^{3t}$

(iv) $y(t) = 4e^{-t} + 4e^{t}$

(c)

(i) $y(t) = 6e^{-3t} - 7e^{-2t} + 5$

(ii) $y(t) = e^{-4t} + 4$

(iii) $y(t) = e^{-2t} + 3e^{2t} - 4$

Exercise 19.2

(i) $y(t) = 2e^{-t} + 0.5e^{0.2t}$

In the long run, $y(t)$ grows at an exponential rate of *20* per cent.

(ii) $y(t) = 5 + 0.2t$

$y(t)$ follows a linear trend.

(iii) $y(t) = e^{-t} + 4$

In the long run $y(t)$ converges on the value *4*.

Exercise 19.3

(i) $y(t) = 2te^{-5t} + 30$

(ii) $y(t) = -2e^t + 5te^t + 7$

(iii) $y(t) = 25 + 6t + 0.25t^2$

Exercise 19.4

(a)

(i) $y(t) = e^{-t}[5\cos 3t + 2\sin 3t]$

(ii) $y(t) = e^{3t}[4\cos 2t - 8\sin 2t]$

(iii) $y(t) = e^t[\cos 2t + \sin 2t]$

(b)

(i) $y(t) = e^t(3\cos t - \sin t) + 2$

Hence $\frac{1}{3} = \tan \phi$, $\phi = 0.3218$

$$A = \frac{3}{\cos \phi} = 3.1623$$

$y(t) = 3.1623 e^t \cos(t + 0.3218) + 2$

(ii) $y(t) = e^{-2t}(-3\cos 1.5t - 2\sin 1.5t) + 8$

Hence $\tan \phi = \frac{-2}{3}$, $\phi = -0.588$

$$A = \frac{-3}{\cos \phi} = -3.6055$$

$y(t) = -3.6055 e^{-2t} \cos(1.5t - 0.588) + 8$

(iii) $y(t) = (4\cos 0.4t + 5\sin 0.4t) + 50$

Hence $\frac{5}{4} = -\tan \phi$, $\phi = -0.8961$

$$A = \frac{4}{\cos \phi} = 6.4031$$

$y(t) = 6.4031 \cos(0.4t - 0.8961) + 50$

Exercise 19.5

(i) $y(t) = -2e^{-3t} + 2.5e^{-4t} + 0.5e^{0.1t}$

(ii) $y(t) = 5.5e^{-t} - 1 - 0.5t^2$

(iii) $y(t) = 8e^{-t} + 4te^{-t} - 2\cos t$

(iv) $y(t) = 0.8\cos 2t + 0.4\sin 2t + 0.2e^t$

Exercise 19.6

(a)

(i) $y(t) = A_1 e^{-t} + A_2 \cos t + A_3 \sin t$
regular cycles

(ii) $y(t) = A_1 e^{-2t} + A_2 e^{-t} + A_2 t e^{-t}$
converges

(iii) $y(t) = A_1 e^t + A_2 t e^t + A_3 t^2 e^t$
diverges

(iv) $y(t) = A_1 e^{-2t} + e^{-0.5t}[A_2 \cos t + A_3 \sin t]$
converges

ANSWERS TO EXERCISES 473

(b) (i) The values of the three determinants are *1, 0, 0* respectively. Hence it does not converge.
   (ii) The values of the three determinants are *4, 18, 36* respectively. So we have convergence.
   (iii) The values of the three determinants are *−3, −8, 8* respectively. Hence we do not have convergence.
   (iv) The values of the three determinants are *3, 7.25, 18.125* respectively. Hence we have convergence.
(c) (i) The values of the three determinants are *5, 16, −96*. Hence it does not converge.
   (ii) The values of the four determinants are *2.5, 5.75, 9.75, 6.09375*. Hence it does converge.
(d) (i) The long-run equilibrium values of price and quantity are *14* and *18* respectively.
   (ii) Having set quantity demanded equal to quantity supplied, rearranged the equation and normalised, we have:

$$\frac{d^2p}{dt^2} + \frac{\gamma_1 - \beta_1}{\gamma_2 - \beta_2}\frac{dp}{dt} + \frac{5}{\gamma_2 - \beta_2}p = \frac{70}{\gamma_2 - \beta_2}$$

By the Routh theorem, convergence requires the following two conditions to be met:

$$\frac{\gamma_1 - \beta_1}{\gamma_2 - \beta_2} > 0$$

$$\frac{5(\gamma_1 - \beta_1)}{(\gamma_2 - \beta_2)^2} > 0$$

If current demand responds negatively to the first and second derivatives of price with respect to time, and current supply responds positively to these same two derivatives, then these conditions will certainly be satisfied, and we will indeed converge on the long-run equilibrium price and quantity.

CHAPTER 20

Exercise 20.1

(i) $y_t = 6(3)^t$
   y increases without limit

(ii) $y_t = (-0.5)^t$
   y converges on zero with oscillations

(iii) $y_t = 2(0.4)^t$
   y converges on zero without oscillations

(iv) $y_t = 4(-2)^t$
   explosive oscillations around zero

(v) $y_t = 2(1.5)^t$
   y increases without limit

(i) $y_t = 15(4)^t - 7$
   y increases without limit

(ii) $y_t = -15(-0.4)^t + 20$
   y converges on 20 with oscillations

(iii) $y_t = 7 + 6t$
   y is a positive linear function of time

(iv) $y_t = (-4)^t + 3$
   explosive oscillations around 3

(v) $y_t = 3(0.5)^t + 6$
   y converges on 6 without oscillations

Exercise 20.2

(a) (i) $P^* = 20$, $Q^* = 40$

(ii) $P_t = 5(-0.75)^t + 20$
convergent cobweb

(iii) $P_t = \frac{85}{9}(-1.25)^t + \frac{140}{9}$
divergent cobweb

(b) (i) The long-run equilibrium price, P^*, equals 187.5.

(ii) The general solution takes the following form:

$$p_t = A[1 - 0.8\alpha]^t + 187.5$$

And since $p(0) = 200$, the particular solution is

$$p_t = 12.5[1 - 0.8\alpha]^t + 187.5$$

(iii) There will be no oscillations in the price if $1.25 > \alpha > 0$ since $1 - 0.8\alpha$ will be positive.
If $\alpha = 1.25$, then the price will always be at the long-run equilibrium value.
If $2.5 > \alpha > 1.25$, then there will be damped oscillations since $0 > 1 - 0.8\alpha > -1$.
If $\alpha = 2.5$, then there will be constant oscillations since $1 - 0.8\alpha = -1$.
If $\alpha > 2.5$, then there will be explosive oscillations since $1 - 0.8\alpha < -1$.

Exercise 20.3

(a) (i) The particular solution is

$$L_t = \left[60000 - \frac{P}{0.1}\right](1.1)^t + \frac{P}{0.1}$$

(ii) P, the annual repayment, must be £7047.58, hence the monthly repayment, M, equals £587.30.

(iii) $L_{12} = £37,598.25$.

(iv) The new monthly repayment is £534.92.

(v) If the household continue to make repayments at the old rate, then the present value of these payments when 7 additional years' payments are made is £$37,328.22$. When 8 additional years' payments are made, then the corresponding figure is £$41,279.82$. Hence the loan will be paid off in slightly more than 19 years in total.

(vi) $L_{10} = £43,304.27$. The new monthly repayment is £638.68.

(vii) If the household continue to make repayments at the old rate, then the present value of these payments when 11 additional years' payments are made is £$41,846.11$. When 12 additional years' payments are made, then the corresponding figure is £$43,655.35$. Hence the loan will be paid off in slightly less than 22 years in total.

CHAPTER 21

Exercise 21.1

(a)

(i) $y_t = A_1(-1)^t + A_2(-4)^t$

(ii) $y_t = A_1(4)^t + A_2(-3)^t$

(iii) $y_t = A_1(2)^t + A_2(-2)^t - 2$

(iv) $y_t = A_1 + A_2(0.2)^t + 1.5t$

(v) $y_t = A_1(0.2)^t + A_2(-0.5)^t + 2$

(b)

(i) $y_t = 2(-2)^t - (-6)^t$

(ii) $y_t = 2(4)^t + 3 - 2t$

(iii) $y_t = -2(-2)^t + 2(-4)^t + 5$

(iv) $y_t = 4(0.5)^t + 5(0.4)^t + 80$

(v) $y_t = 7 - 3t$

Exercise 21.2

(a)

(i) $y_t = A_1(-1)^t + A_2 t(-1)^t$

(ii) $y_t = A_1(0.3)^t + A_2 t(0.3)^t$

(iii) $y_t = A_1(-4)^t + A_2 t(-4)^t + 4$

(iv) $y_t = A_1(0.5)^t + A_2 t(0.5)^t + 16$

(b)

(i) $y_t = 3(-0.7)^t - 3t(-0.7)^t + 2$

(ii) $y_t = 4 + t3^t$

(iii) $y_t = 10 + t + 2t^2$

(iv) $y_t = -(-0.6)^t - 4t(-0.6)^t + 3$

Exercise 21.3

(a)

(i) $y_t = (\sqrt{10})^t [A_3 \cos 0.32175t + A_4 \sin 0.32175t]$

(ii) $y_t = (\sqrt{2.5})^t [A_3 \cos 1.24905t + A_4 \sin 1.24905t]$

(iii) $y_t = (\sqrt{4.25})^t [A_3 \cos 0.245t + A_4 \sin 0.245] + 4$

(iv) $y_t = (\sqrt{2})^t \left[A_3 \cos \frac{\pi}{4} t + A_4 \sin \frac{\pi}{4} t \right] + 8$

(v) $y_t = 0.5^t [A_3 \cos 2.2143t + A_4 \sin 2.2143t] + 4$

(b)

(i) $y_t = (\sqrt{5})^t [5 \cos 1.10715t + 0.5 \sin 1.10175t]$

(ii) $y_t = 8 \cos 2.0944t + 16.16585 \sin 2.0944t + 3$

(iii) $y_t = (\sqrt{2})^t \left[2 \sin \frac{\pi}{4} t \right] + 4$

(iv) $y_t = (\sqrt{3.25})^t [-\cos 0.588t + 1.5 \sin 0.588] + 8$

(v) $y_t = (\sqrt{0.5})^t \left[2 \cos \frac{\pi}{4} t \right] + 10$

(c) (i) The time-path of price exhibits explosive oscillations. The particular solution to the first-order difference equation is given by:

$$P_t = 40(-1.5)^t + 80$$

(ii) The characteristic equation of the second-order difference equation has complex roots. The particular solution is:

$$P_t = (\sqrt{0.375})^t [40 \cos 2.7352t + 175.573 \sin 2.735t] + 80$$

The price will converge on the long-run equilibrium value of *80*.

(iii) Expectations are formed adaptively in both parts (i) and (ii) rather than rationally. The speed with which the discrepancy between actual and expected outcomes is filled is greater in case (i) than in case (ii).

476 MATHEMATICS IN ECONOMICS

(d) (i) Again the solution to the second-order difference equation has complex roots. The particular solution is given by:

$$P_t = (\sqrt{0.5})^t \left[-10\cos\frac{\pi}{2}t - 7.071068\sin\frac{\pi}{2}t \right] + 50$$

(ii) In the long run the price converges on *50*. $P(10) = 50.3125$.

Exercise 21.4

(a)
(i) $Y_t = -1000(0.8)^t + 1500$
converges without oscillations

(ii) $Y_t = -500(0.5)^t + 1000$
converges without oscillations

(iii) $Y_t = -500(1.5)^t + 1000$
diverges without oscillations

(iv) $Y_t = (\sqrt{0.6})^t [A_3 \cos 0.4425t + A_4 \sin 0.4425t] + 1000$
damped fluctuations around 1000

(b) (i) The roots of the characteristic equation are given by:

$$(0.4 + 0.5v) \pm 0.5\sqrt{v^2 - 2.4v + 0.64}$$

For the roots to be complex, then

$$v^2 - 2.4v + 0.64 < 0$$

This requires v to lie in the following interval: *0.3056 < v < 2.0944*.

(ii) For v lying in the following interval $1 < v < 2.094$, the time-path will not converge, and the amplitude of the fluctuations will increase through time. For v lying in the following interval: $0.3056 < v < 1$, the time-path will converge, with the amplitude of the fluctuations becoming smaller and smaller through time. For $v = 1$, then the fluctuations will be of constant amplitude.

(iii) There will be convergence without oscillation if both roots are positive, but smaller than unity. The roots are real if either v is less than or equal to 0.3056, or greater than or equal to 2.094. If one root is positive, then both roots must be positive if v is positive, since their product is equal to v. Hence we shall have convergence without oscillation for $0 < v \le 0.3056$. If $v \ge 2.094$, then the roots will again be real, but the time-path will now be divergent.

Exercise 21.5

(a)
(i) $y_t = -\dfrac{15}{56}(-0.4)^t + \dfrac{237}{224} + \dfrac{1}{4}t$

(ii) $y_t = \dfrac{4}{3}(-0.5)^t - \dfrac{1}{3} + 2t + 3t^2$

(iii) $y_t = 0.2(2)^t$

(iv) $y_t = -4(3)^t + 5(2)^t + t(3)^{t+1}$

(v) $y_t = 100(0.5)^t + 60t(0.5)^t + t^2(0.5)^{t+1}$

(b) (i) The complementary function is given by:

$$Y_t^c = (\sqrt{0.9})^t [A_3 \cos 0.51635t + \sin 0.51635t]$$

To find the particular integral, we try a solution of the form:

$$Y_t^p = B(1.05)^t$$

hence $B(1.05)^t - 1.65B(1.05)^{t-1} + 0.9B(1.05)^{t-2} = 100(1.05)^t$

Multiplying by $(1.05)^{2-t}$, we obtain:
$$B[1.05^2 - 1.65(1.05) + 0.9] = 100(1.05)^2$$
$$\text{hence } B = \frac{100.25}{0.27} = 408.33\ldots$$

The general solution then is:
$$Y_t = (\sqrt{0.9})^t[A_3 \cos 0.51635t + A_4 \sin 0.51635t] + 408.33(1.05)^t$$

(ii) Given the initial conditions, we must have:
$$A_3 + 408.33 = 400$$
$$0.825A_3 + 0.46837A_4 + 428.75 = 440$$
$$\text{hence } A_3 = -8.33\ldots, \quad A_4 = 38.968$$

The particular solution is, therefore, given by:
$$Y_t = (\sqrt{0.9})^t[-8.33 \cos 0.51635t + 38.698 \sin 0.51635t] + 408.33(1.05)^t$$

CHAPTER 22

Exercise 22.1

(a)
$$\text{(i) } x(t) = \frac{16}{3}e^{4t} - \frac{1}{3}e^t$$
$$y(t) = \frac{8}{3}e^{4t} + \frac{1}{3}e^t$$
$$\text{(ii) } x(t) = 4e^{-2t}$$
$$y(t) = -4e^{-2t}$$
$$\text{(iii) } x(t) = 8e^{-0.5t} - 1.6te^{-0.5t} + 60$$
$$y(t) = 1.6te^{-0.5t} + 100$$
$$\text{(iv) } x(t) = e^t[8 \cos 2t - 12 \sin 2t]$$
$$y(t) = e^t[6 \cos 2t + 4 \sin 2t]$$

(b) (i) The equilibrium values are: $p^* = 50$, $q^* = 30$, $x^* = 30$, $y^* = 50$.

(ii) The particular solution is
$$p(t) = \frac{-40}{3}e^{-0.7t} + \frac{10}{3}e^{-0.4t} + 50$$
$$q(t) = \frac{20}{3}e^{-0.7t} + \frac{10}{3}e^{-0.4t} + 30$$

(iii) The equilibrium is stable: $p(t)$ rises through time and approaches 50, and $q(t)$ falls through time and approaches 30.

(c) (i) $y = y^n$, $p^n = m$.

(ii) The general solution is
$$y(t) = e^{-0.125t}[A_1 \cos \sqrt{0.9375}t + A_2 \sin \sqrt{0.9375}t] + y^n$$
$$p(t)^e = e^{-0.125t}[B_1 \cos \sqrt{0.9375}t + B_2 \sin \sqrt{0.9375}t] + m$$

(iii) Fluctuations of diminishing amplitude will occur in the two variables. Output and the expected rate of inflation will therefore converge on their long-run equilibrium values.

(iv) A similar time-path will be experienced by the actual rate of inflation and in long-run equilibrium prices will rise at a rate equal to the rate of growth of the money supply.

Exercise 22.2

(a) (i) Let R stand for Ritzy's and P for Peppermint Park. Then we have

$$\begin{bmatrix} R_t \\ P_t \end{bmatrix} = \begin{bmatrix} 0.9 & 0.2 \\ 0.1 & 0.8 \end{bmatrix} \begin{bmatrix} R_{t-1} \\ P_{t-1} \end{bmatrix}$$

(ii) Set $R_t = R_{t-1}$ and $P_t = P_{t-1}$ to obtain $R^* = 400$, $P^* = 200$.

(iii) The particular solution is

$$R_t = -200(0.7)^t + 400$$
$$P_t = 200(0.7)^t + 200$$

(b) (i) The matrix of transition probabilities is

$$\begin{bmatrix} 0.7 & 0.1 & 0 \\ 0.2 & 0.8 & 0.1 \\ 0.1 & 0.1 & 0.9 \end{bmatrix}$$

and the characteristic equation can be obtained by setting the following determinant equal to zero:

$$\begin{vmatrix} m-0.7 & -0.1 & 0 \\ -0.2 & m-0.8 & -0.1 \\ -0.1 & -0.1 & m-0.9 \end{vmatrix} = 0$$

Expanding and simplifying we obtain the following cubic

$$m^3 - 2.4m^2 + 1.88m - 0.48 = 0$$

By the Frobenius–Perron theorem, one of the roots is unity since all the column sums are one. Dividing the cubic by $(m - 1)$, we obtain the following quadratic equation:

$$m^2 - 1.4m + 0.48 = 0$$

whose roots 0.8 and 0.6. The three roots are $1, 0.8$ and 0.6. Letting L, M and S represent the number of firms in the large-, medium- and small-size categories respectively, then we have

$$L_t = A_1 + A_2(0.8)^t + A_3(0.6)^t$$
$$M_t = B_1 + B_2(0.8)^t + B_3(0.6)^t$$
$$S_t = C_1 + C_2(0.8)^t + C_3(0.6)^t$$

(ii) In long-run equilibrium, then $(P - mI)x = 0$, and the only positive eigenvector is the one associated with the dominant eigenvalue, $m_1 = 1$. Hence we have

$$\begin{bmatrix} -0.3 & 0.1 & 0 \\ 0.2 & -0.2 & 0.1 \\ 1 & 1 & 1 \end{bmatrix} \begin{bmatrix} L \\ M \\ S \end{bmatrix} = \begin{bmatrix} 0 \\ 0 \\ 4000 \end{bmatrix}$$

Solving these three equations we find

$$L^* = 500, \quad M^* = 1500, \quad S^* = 2000$$

If we had been given initial values for the number of firms in each of the three categories, then we could have used this information to find all the arbitrary constants, having taken account of the linear dependence amongst the As, Bs and Cs.

Index

artificial variables, 95, 98
assignment problem, 123–7
   alternative approach, 124–6
   basic approach, 125
   dual, 127
   presence of degeneracy, 124
   simple example, 123–4
associative property, 12
associative rule, 23
average cost function, 225

balance of payments, 204, 209
balance of trade, 204
basic variables, 100
big M technique, 75–6

capital–labour ratio, 198, 199
capital mobility, 207–12
Cayley–Hamilton theorem, 151–3
chain rule, 176–7, 182, 197, 198, 254
closed economy, IS/LM model for, 204–7
Cobb–Douglas production function, 195, 299–300
Cobb–Douglas utility function, 287
cobweb theorem, 379
co-factors, 33, 36, 38, 39
column vectors, 10
commutative property, 12
commutative rule, 23
comparative static analysis, 200–12, 228–9, 245–7, 289–91

compensating variation, 296–8
complementary function, 358, 359, 363, 365, 379, 391, 406, 407, 409–10, 415
complementary–slackness conditions, 118
concave functions, 179–80
concavity, 178–80
constant elasticity, 185
constant elasticity of substitution (CES): production function, 199
constrained minimisation problems, 278
constrained optimisation problems, 273–303
   economic applications, 285–91
   solution methods, 274–6
consumer demand, 289–91
consumer surplus, 263
consumption vector, 295
continuous function, 168, 170
convergent cobweb, 379, 380
convex functions, 179–80
convexity, 178–80
cost matrix, 125
cost minimisation, 299–300
Cournot equilibrium, 286
Cournot–Nash equilibrium, 242
Cournot solution to duopoly problem, 285
Cramer's rule, 40–2, 202, 204, 205, 229, 246, 289, 291, 345
cross-partial derivatives, 193, 194
   second-order, 193

decomposable matrix, 153–7

definite integral, 252, 259–60, 266, 268
demand functions, derivation, 287–9
depletion of exhaustible resource, 262
derivatives, 171
   first-order, 223
   second-order, 178, 216–18, 223
   third-order, 179
   fourth-order, 224
   higher-order, 178–9, 224
   concept of, 167–70
   of a function, 184
   of total revenue with respect to output, 174
   symbols for, 168
determinants, 31–45, 235, 278
   and inverse of a matrix, 38–9
   calculation, 34
   evaluation, 31–7
   of matrix of dimension n, 33
   properties of, 34–7
   symmetric matrix, 143
diagonal matrix, 26, 135–6
diagonalisation of matrix, 134–9
difference equations:
   first-order, 373–84
   second-order linear, 373, 385–401, 403
   third-order linear, 398
   higher-order, 398
difference quotient, 167, 168, 171, 175, 183–4, 186
differentiable function, 180
   extreme values, 215
differential calculus:
   analysis of functions of more than one variable, 191
   applications to economics, 191–213
   introduction, 166–90
differential equations. (*See* first-order; second-order; higher-order)
differentials, 197–9
differentiation:
   further rules of, 181–6
   of trigonometric functions, 185–6
   power rule of, 172
   product rule of, 173
   simple rules, 172–7
   sum/difference rule of, 172
   using first principles, 171
discontinuity, 170
discontinuous function, 168, 169
distributive property, 12

divergent cobweb, 379, 380
dual:
   assignment problem, 127
   constraints, 84, 85, 87, 90, 91, 97, 120, 121
   feasibility criterion, 99
   linear program, 83–94
   maximisation problems, 88–90
   minimisation problems, 90
   negative variables, 90–3
   optimal solution, 102
   problem, 84
   solution, 95
   transportation problem, 117–21
dual simplex method, 99–102
   minimisation problems, 101–2
dual variables, 87–9, 91, 93, 98, 99
   negative values, 120
duality, 82–108
   application in economics, 88
duopoly, 242–5, 285–7

echelon matrix, 54–8
eigenvalues, 131–50
   concept of, 132–4
   repeated, 141–3
   symmetric matrix, 139–43
eigenvectors, 131–50
   concept of, 132–4
   inverse of matrix of, 137, 140
   matrix of, 137–8, 140
   orthonormal, 142
   symmetric matrix, 139–43
   transpose of matrix of, 140
elasticity of demand, 173–4
elasticity of substitution, 199
elementary matrices, 50, 52, 54
endogenous variables, 204
equality constraint, 91, 92, 94
equivalent variation, 297, 298
Euclidean norm, 13, 16
Euclidean space, n-dimensional, 19
Euler's theorem, 194–7
exhaustible resource, depletion of, 262
exogenous variables, 204
expenditure function, 294, 295
explicit functions, 201
exponential function, 182
exponential rule, 181–2, 253

feasibility criterion, 99

first-order conditions, 235–9, 287, 292
first-order derivative, 223
first-order difference equations, 373–84
first-order differential equations, 333–52
first-order linear difference equations, 373
first-order linear differential equations:
    case where α is zero, 336
    economic applications, 378–82
    general case, 336–41
    homogeneous case, 334–5
    non-homogeneous case, 335
    solution, 374–8
first-order non-linear differential equations, 341–9
    conversion into linear differential equation, 343–4
    separable variables, 342–3
first-order partial derivatives, 202, 236
fixed exchange rate, 210–12
floating exchange rate, 207–10
forestry, economics, 264–6
fourth-order derivative, 224
Frobenius root, 156, 161
function, 167
    economic example, 169
    negative slope, 216
    of a function, 176–7, 254
    of more than one variable, 192, 234
    of two variables, 234
    positive slope, 216

Gaussian elimination, 55

Hessian determinant, 235, 238, 278–81, 284, 289, 300
Hicksian demand function, 295, 297–8
higher-order derivatives, 178–9, 224
higher-order difference equations, 398
higher-order linear difference equations, 373
higher-order linear differential equations, 368–9
homogeneous functions, 194–7
human capital, investment in, 263–4

identity matrix, 25–6, 50, 52, 54
implicit functions, 201–3
improper integrals, 260–1, 263
indecomposable matrices, 153–7
    properties of, 155–7
indefinite integral, 268

indifference curves, 198, 280
input–output economics:
    diagrammatic analysis, 160–2
    non-negative square matrices, 151, 157–63
integral:
    of $\cos x$ and $\sin x$, 253
    of multiple of a function, 253
    of sum or difference of two functions, 253–4
integral calculus:
    economic applications, 261–8
    introduction, 251–72
    power rule, 252
    substitution rule, 254–6
integration:
    and partial fractions, 258–9
    by parts, 256–8
    rules of, 251–9
    techniques, 251–72
inverse demand function, 225, 227, 266, 319, 320
inverse function rule, 181
inverse of matrix of eigenvectors, 140
investment in human capital, 263–4
IS/LM model:
    for closed economy, 204–7
    for open economy
        with fixed exchange rate and capital mobility, 210–12
        with floating exchange rate and capital mobility, 207–10
iso-profit contour, 287
isoquant, 198
iso-value locus, 283, 284

Jacobian determinant, 202–5, 208, 210, 289

Keynesian income determination model, 393
kinked function, 170
Kuhn–Tucker maximum conditions, 307–10, 312–17, 320, 324, 325
Kuhn–Tucker minimum conditions, 311–14, 326, 328
Kuhn–Tucker sufficiency theorem, 314–15

Lagrangean function, 276, 278–80, 284, 286, 288, 289, 291–4, 299, 307, 308, 310, 311, 316, 317, 319, 323
Lagrangean multiplier, 276, 281, 290–300, 307, 308, 310, 311, 316–19, 324
Laplace expansion, 34, 36, 40

least-cost method, 115–16
Leontief inverse, 158–9, 162
l'Hopital's rule, 244
life assurance policy, rate of return on, 262–3
linear algebra, 62
linear combinations, 16–21
linear equations, solution to set of, 48–50
linear programming, 61–81
   basic feasible solutions, 65–7
   basic features, 61
   constraints, 63, 65, 66, 70, 75
   feasible region, 64
   graphical treatment, 62–5
   initial basic feasible solution, 70–5
   no feasible solution, 63
   optimal solution, 102
   simplex method, 67–70
   tabular approach, 73–4
   three-dimensional problem, 64
   two-dimensional problem, 64
   see also duality
linear simultaneous equations, 17–19, 39–41, 238, 239
logarithm, 182–5
logarithmic function, 184
logarithmic rule, 182–5, 252–3
logistic functions, 344–9
long-run equilibrium, 228
   of two variables, 410–14
long-run total cost function, 227

Maclaurin-series expansion, 220, 359, 360
macroeconomic models, 42–3, 200, 203–12
marginal cost, 176, 261
marginal cost function, 227
marginal product of capital, 197
marginal product of labour, 198
marginal productivity factor pricing, 197
marginal rate of substitution, 198, 199
marginal revenue, 173–4, 240–1, 261–2
   and price, 227
marginal revenue product of labour, 177
Marshallian demand function, 293
matrices, 22–30
   addition, 23
   diagonalisation, 134–9
   elementary operations, 50–4
   elementary row operations, 52–3
   inverse, 38–9, 52–4, 71, 72, 137

multiplication, 24–5
   by scalar, 24
operations on, 22–5
rank, 47–8
special types, 25–8
subtraction, 23
transpose of, 26, 27
transpose of product of, 27
transpose of sum (difference) of, 27
transpose of transpose of, 27
maxima, economic applications, 224–8
maximisation problems, 61
   dual, 88–90
   dual simplex method, 99–101
   non-negativity requirements, 305
   simplex method, 324
   transportation problems, 126–7
   see also profit maximisation
maximum value, 215–16
maximum value function, 293
minima, economic applications, 224–8
minimisation problems, 75–8
   dual, 90
   dual simplex method, 101–2
   non-negativity requirements, 306, 326
   simplex method, 76, 327
   transportation problem, 118
minimum value, 216
minors, 33
monotonicity, 184
mortgage problem, 381–2
multi-plant monopolist, 241

non-basic non-slack variables, 88
non-basic variables, 89, 100, 102
non-linear programming, 304–32
   economic example, 317–18
   maximisation problem, 316
   non-negativity requirements, 305–7
non-negative matrix, 152
non-negative square indecomposable matrices, 155–7
non-negative square matrices, 151–65
   input–output economics, 151, 157–63
non-negativity requirements, 305–7, 323
non-singular matrix, 52, 54, 136
non-stationary inflexion point, 223, 348–9
non-symmetric matrix with repeated eigenvalue, 143–4

north-west corner method, 111–15
null matrix, 26

objective function, 61 4, 67–9, 71, 84, 91, 93–5, 99, 126, 275, 309, 310, 313, 314, 323, 325
open economy:
    model, 203–4
    with fixed exchange rate and capital mobility, 210–12
    with floating exchange rate and capital mobility, 207–10
optimal outcome:
    with differential pricing, 319–21
    with uniform pricing, 321–3
optimality criterion, 77, 102, 327
optimisation:
    basic theory, 215–18
    examples, 216–18
    problems, 61
    with more than one choice variable, 234–50
    with more than one variable, economic applications, 239–45
    with single choice variable, 214–33
    see also constrained optimisation problems
orthogonal vectors, 14–15
    conversion of orthonormal vectors to, 15–16
orthonormal vectors, 15–16
    conversion of orthogonal vectors to, 15–16
oscillations of constant amplitude around long-run equilibrium, 380
own-price elasticity of demand, 225

partial derivatives, 201, 202, 204, 205
    continuous first-order, 202
    first-order, 236
    second-order, 193, 194, 236, 238, 239
partial differentiation, 192–4
partial fractions and integration, 258–9
particular integral, 355–8, 365–8, 387, 388, 396–8, 406
permutation matrices, 154
phase diagram, 410–14
point of inflexion, 348
population of a city, 268
positive matrix, 152
power rule of differentiation, 172
    economic application, 173–4

power rule of integral calculus, 252
price:
    and marginal revenue, 227
    link with marginal revenue and elasticity of demand, 173–4
price discrimination in monopoly, 239–41
price dynamics in agricultural market, 378–9
primal constraints, 87
primal problems, 84, 87, 89, 96
primal variables, 88
product rule of differentiation, 173
production function, 200, 246
profit maximisation:
    in competitive market, 226–7
    in monopolistic competition, 228
    in monopoly, 227–8
profit-maximising cartel, 245
profit-maximising firm, 214, 280–1
profits function, 235
public enterprise economics, 319–23

quadratic equations, 238, 239
    roots of, 223
quadratic forms, 144–7
    important question relating to, 145
quadratic function, 216
quadratic programming, 323–8
quasi-concavity, 281–4
quasi-convexity, 281–4
quotient rule, 174–6
    economic application, 175–6

rate of return on life assurance policy, 262–3
rectangular matrix, 50
relative extremum, general conditions for, 218–24
relative price–cost margin, 228
repeat buying, 416–17
Routh theorem, 369
Roy's identity, 293

saddle point, 316–17
scalars, 9
    multiplication of matrix, 24
    multiplication of vector, 10–11
Schurr's theorem, 398
second-order conditions, 235–9, 267, 277–81, 286
second-order derivatives, 178, 216–18, 223

second-order linear difference equations, 373, 385–401, 403
   case of complex roots, 390–3
   case of distinct real roots, 386–9
   case of repeated roots, 389–90
   characteristic equation, 385–93
   economic application, 393–6
second-order linear differential equations, 353–73
   complex root case, 359–65
   distinct real roots, 354–5
   homogeneous case, 356
   non-homogeneous case, 355–7
   repeated real roots, 357
   solution of, 353–63
   time-path of $y(t)$, 356–7
second-order partial derivatives, 193, 194, 236, 238, 239
semi-positive indecomposable matrix, 155
semi-positive matrix, 152
sensitivity analysis, 102–5
Shepherd's lemma, 297
similar matrices, 52
simplex method, 67–70
   feasibility criteria, 68, 70
   maximisation problems, 324
   minimisation problems, 76, 327
   optimality, 68, 70
   see also dual simplex method
simultaneous differential equations, 402–10
   case of repeated roots, 408–9
   complex root case, 409–10
   non-homogeneous case, 406–8
simultaneous equations, 202
simultaneous linear difference equations, 414–17
   non-homogeneous case, 415
simultaneous linear equations, 46–60
singular matrix, 38
skew-symmetric matrix, 27–8
slack dual variables, 95, 97
slack variables, 87, 88, 103
Slutsky equation, 291
spatial analysis, 266–8
square matrices, 26, 28, 38, 48, 50, 52, 144
   non-negative, 151–2
   positive, 151–2
standard derivatives, 187
stationary inflexion point, 224
stochastic matrix, 163

strictly concave differentiable function, 180
strictly convex differentiable function, 180
subdeterminants, 33
substitution approach, 274–5
substitution rule of integral calculus, 254–6
sum/difference rule of differentiation, 172
supply function, 169
symmetric matrix, 27, 144, 146
   determinants, 143
   eigenvalues, 139–43
   eigenvectors, 139–43
   negative semi-definite, 145
   positive definite, 145
   positive semi-definite, 145
   with repeated eigenvalue, 141–2

Taylor-series (T-S) expansion, 218–21, 236
theory of the firm, 214
third-order derivative, 179
third-order linear difference equations, 398
total cost, 261
total cost function, 224–8, 240
total derivative, 199–200
total differential approach, 275–6
total revenue, 177, 226, 261–2
total revenue function, 225
trade cycle model, 393–6
transportation method, least-cost method, 115–16
transportation problems, 109–30
   choice of initial basic feasible solution, 111–17
   dual, 117–21
   economic interpretation, 119
   maximisation problems, 126–7
   minimisation problems, 118
   north-west corner method, 111–15
   practical hint for solving, 121–2
   solution, 110–17
   unbalanced problems, 122–3
   using tableaux, 121
   Vogel approximation method (VAM), 116–17
   see also assignment problem
transpose of matrix of eigenvectors, 140
trigonometric functions, 257–8
   differentiation of, 185–6
two-phase method, 76–8, 93

unit circle, 186
U-shaped function, 215, 223
utility function, 197, 280, 291, 317
utility maximisation, 279–80, 287–9

vector spaces, 12–13
vectors, 9–21
    addition, 11
    arithmetical operations, 10
    forming basis for *n*-dimensional Euclidean space, 19–20
    inner product, 13
    length, 14
    linear combinations, 16–21
    linearly independent, 18
    multiplication by scalar, 10–11
    operations on, 9–16
    spanning *n*-dimensional Euclidean space, 19
    subtraction, 11
    summation, 11
    two-component, 18
    two-dimensional, 10, 13
Vogel approximation method (VAM), 116–17
    initial basic feasible solution, 119

Walrasian equilibrium, 288–9
welfare loss, 298

zero-order expansion, 220

religious groups 165
responding to an environmental issue 145–147
river 133, 134, 140, 155
RSPB 133

sacral centre 33, 58, *82*, 88, 92, 104, 111, 138, 140, 182
sacred 184
    manner 143, 150, 155, 186
    unity 135
safety 87
San Gimignano 4
sea 134, 142, 155
seasonal affective disorder 94
seasons 142
self (see personality)
    -defence 87
    -discovery 15
    -healing 44
sending
    Distant Healing to the plant world 152–153
    healing to a dying animal 161–162
sending Light
    into a locality 167–168
    to a disaster situation 169–171
sending out to
    a project 188
    the injured and dying 172–174
senses 87
sensing 75
    energy field 30–32, *31*
    hand–heart energy circuit 97–98
    information in energy field 32
    skeletal energy circuits 75–78
sensing energies 52
    Earth 96–97
    hands' energies 21–22, *22*
    of partner's hands 22–23
sensing the location of base centre 86
    brow centre *85*
    centres 83–86
    crown centre *84*
sensuality 87
separation 113, 142, 165–166
seven
    breaths of greeting 184–186
    directions 184

main energy centres *33*, 39–40, 58, 72, 81, *82*, 86, 91, 95, 183
sex 87
    glands 88, 105
sexuality 88, 105, 165
shamanic 134, 137, 179
shoulders 17, 74, 75, 185
sick animal 158
signals 6, 26, 48, 82, 90, 104, 107, 143,
silver light 37, 57
sitting posture 18
situations 49, 51, 60, 102, 167, 171, 172, 175, 187
skeletal energy circuits 74, *74*, 78
skeleton 73–78, *74*
sleep 73, 112, 114, 115, 148, 191
    state 114
snow 133, 140
societal issues 7, 14, 164
'soft-belly' breathing 44
solar plexus centre 33, 58, *82*, 88, 89–90, 91, 93, 100, 101, 103, 104, 111, 138, 141, 182
sole of the foot centre *82*, 95–97, 98, 139
Source 1, 3, 5, 11, 12, 13, 16, 17, 18, 27, 36, 47, 55, 91, 94, 105, 106, 113, 135, 193, 194, 195
soul 16, 17, 27, 29, 30, 73, 80, 81, 90, 95, 180, 189, 194
    choice 138
    energy zone 115, *116*
    journey 13, 14, 16, 27
    level 52, 134
sound 156, 157
South (direction) 184
space–time 1, 13, 52, 114
spectrum 87
speed of light 27, 28, 195
Sphere of Protection *59,* 59–60,
    in astral level healing 119, *120*
spheres, light 39
spine 17, 34, 73, 75, 81, 87, 88, 139, 185
spirit 13, 27, 193
    body 180
spiritual
    being 13, 49
    core 15, 82
    development 113
    energy 194

spiritual – *continued*
   force 180, 194
   intention 180
   level 13, 28, 35, 135
   problems 105
   reality 113
Spiritual Healing Handbook, The 6
spirituality 95, 100
stomach 74
subtle
   body 28, 40
   level 13, 28, 30, 49, 179
   senses 28, 30
   vision 87
subtle energy 3, 23, 26, 28, 34, 36, 49, 71, 73, 80, 194, 195
   centres (chakras) 17, 34, 67, 80, 81–98
   circuits 67, 71–80,
   medicine 3, 195
   system 49, 110, 115, 137, 148, 191, 194, 195
sun 133, 140, 149, 184
   sign 138
survival 87, 91
sweat lodge 138
Symbiotic Planet, The 137
synchronicity 36

teaching 149
telephone 52
telling your Earth story 163–164
template, body 72, 93
   etheric 93, 180
terminal illness 14, 128, 160
therapeutic procedure 128, 179
thanking 142, 155, 188
   food 186–187
Thich Nhat Hanh 164
third challenge 187
Third Eye 94
Tiller, Professor William A. 114, 195
thought 52, 53, 89, 167
throat 92, 93, 95

throat centre 33, 58, *82*, 88, 92–93
thymus gland 87, 90, 103, 105
thyroid gland 92, 105
To Honor the Earth 134
trees 142, 144, 150, 151–152
truth 92, 105
tuning out 102, 164

unconditionality 13, 27, 35, 51, 52, 53, 102, 167, 172, 188, 189
unified field theory 166–167
universal energy field 12, 36
universe 166, 167
uterus 88

veterinary surgeons 157
vibration 28, 49, 52, 93, 180, 186
Vibrational Medicine 115
violence 129, 164, 166
violet 39–40, 58, 95, 183
visualisation 23, 39, 58, 138

waste disposal 155
water 88, 133, 135, 138, 140, 142, 149
West (direction) 184
will 28
Winkler, Gershon 50
Within (direction) 184
woodpecker 155
work space
   addressing the 47–49
   energy field 47
working with
   animals 155–163
   environment 133–148
   feelings 109–112
   injured and dying 171
   plants 149–155
world 106, 112, 113, 137

yellow, golden 39, 58, 89, 182
Yeshua 11
yongquan point 96
Your Healing Power 3, 6, 7

ENGINEERING DRAWING AND MATE[RIALS]
FOR MECHANICAL ENGINEERING TECHNI[CIANS]

VOLUME II
(In SI Units)

GENERAL TECHNICAL SERIES

General Editor:
AIR COMMODORE J. R. MORGAN, O.B.E.
B.Sc. (Eng.), C.Eng., F.I.Mech.E., F.R.Ae.S., R.A.F. (Ret'd.)
*Formerly
Director of Studies,
Royal Air Force Technical College,
and
Deputy Director, Educational Services, Air Ministry*

METRIC EXAMPLES IN ENGINEERING DRAWING AND MATERIALS
(*in four volumes*)
H. ORD, M.I.E.D., M.I.Plant.E., A.R.Ae.S.

ENGINEERING DRAWING AND MATERIALS
FOR MECHANICAL ENGINEERING TECHNICIANS
(*in four volumes*)
H. ORD, M.I.E.D., M.I.Plant.E., A.R.Ae.S.

ENGINEERING DRAWING
FOR G1 AND G2 COURSES
H. ORD, M.I.E.D., M.I.Plant.E., A.R.Ae.S.

WORKSHOP PROCESSES
FOR MECHANICAL ENGINEERING TECHNICIANS
(*in two volumes*)
R. T. PRITCHARD, C.Eng., M.I.Prod.E.

Other books of interest

T3 WORKSHOP TECHNOLOGY
FOR MECHANICAL ENGINEERING TECHNICIANS

T4 WORKSHOP TECHNOLOGY
FOR MECHANICAL ENGINEERING TECHNICIANS
R. T. PRITCHARD, C.Eng., M.I.Prod.E.

MANUFACTURING TECHNOLOGY
M. HASLEHURST, D.I.C., C.Eng., M.I.Mech.E., M.I.Prod.E.

PRINCIPLES OF JIG AND TOOL DESIGN
M. H. A. KEMPSTER, C.Eng., M.I.Mech.E., A.R.Ae.S., M.I.Prod.E.

ENGINEERING DRAWING AND MATERIALS

FOR MECHANICAL ENGINEERING TECHNICIANS

VOLUME II
(In SI Units)

H. ORD
M.I.E.D., M.I.Plant.E., A.R.Ae.S.

THE ENGLISH UNIVERSITIES PRESS LIMITED

ST PAUL'S HOUSE   WARWICK LANE

LONDON EC4

First Printed 1963
Second Edition 1965
Third Edition 1971

Copyright © 1971 H. ORD

All rights reserved. No part of this publication may be reproduced or transmitted in any form or by any means, electronic or mechanical, including photocopy, recording, or by any information storage and retrieval system, without permission in writing from the publisher.

Boards Edition ISBN 0 340 15151 X
Paperback Edition ISBN 0 340 14818 7

Printed in Great Britain for The English Universities Press Ltd
by Fletcher & Son Ltd, Norwich and bound
by Richard Clay (The Chaucer Press) Ltd, Bungay, Suffolk

EDITOR'S INTRODUCTION

The new awareness of the imperative need to make the very most of our technical potential makes a foreword to this General Technical Series almost unnecessary, for it aims directly at encouraging young men—and women—to extend their interests, widen their knowledge, and improve their technical skills.

The City and Guilds of London Institute makes special provision for the technician to acquire a qualification appropriate to his Craft. The wide range of examinations now held under its auspices is ample evidence not merely of the need to cater for the technician but also of the growing desire of the Craftsman to improve his knowledge of his Craft. Many of the books in the present series will be related to syllabuses of the City and Guilds of London Institute, but this will not limit their use merely to preparation for the examinations held by that body. The aim is to encourage students to study those technical subjects which are closely related to their daily work and, by so doing, to obtain a better understanding of basic principles. Any study of this kind cannot fail to stimulate interest in the subject and should produce a technician with a clearer understanding of what he is doing and how best it should be done.

But although the series is intended to appeal, in the first instance, to students who are interested in the certificates offered by the City and Guilds of London Institute that must be regarded as only the immediate aim. Those students who, as a result of their initial endeavours, find that they are capable of going further should aim at obtaining either a National Certificate in an appropriate field of engineering or, alternatively, a General Certificate of Education at a level appropriate to their potential attainment.

All the books in the Series will be written by experienced and well qualified teachers who are thoroughly conversant with the problems encountered by young men and women in studying the subjects with which their books deal.

J.R.M.

PREFACE TO FIRST EDITION

This volume, together with Volume I, completes the work required for the subject 'Engineering Drawing and Materials' in Part I of the Mechanical Engineering Technician's Certificate which is contained in Syllabus No. 293 of the City and Guilds of London Institute. The aim of the course is to develop the ability of the student to interpret and construct working drawings for use in the workshop, together with a facility in sketching and visualising objects at various stages of manufacture. Volume I covered the work which is required of students during the first year of the Mechanical Engineering Technician's Course. This volume is concerned with the work required of second-year students.

I have again aimed at producing a practical book for the practical man. No extensive knowledge of formal geometry has been assumed, and I have indicated, by a series of logical steps, how each drawing should be attempted. It should be possible for those students who wish to do so, to develop a facility for making and understanding workshop drawings by attempting the drawings and exercises in this book while working at home.

PREFACE TO SECOND EDITION

I have taken the opportunity of making some additions and amendments to bring the book more up to date. Additional material has been added to the sections on Tools, Jig and Fixture Design, and Materials. The drawing exercises now include examination questions recently set by the Union of Educational Institutes (by their kind permission), and it is hoped that these latest examination questions will prove helpful to all readers. In its revised form I trust that it will continue to be of help and interest to many more students.

PREFACE TO THIRD EDITION

By 1972 the Metric System (SI Units) will be in general use in Great Britain. In anticipation of this I have now revised my existing books so that all dimensions are in these new units. This volume is intended for use as a class-book in conjunction with my book of *Metric Examples in Engineering Drawing* which has recently been published. Both these books aim at introducing students to the new units in good time.

I would like to take this opportunity to thank Messrs W. and T. Avery Ltd, and Samuel Denison and Son Ltd, for their kind permission to reproduce information on, and drawings of, their testing machines and to thank the City and Guilds of London Institute for permitting me to use questions set in recent examination papers. Due acknowledgement is made in the text. I am indebted, also, to Mr P. G. W. Astley, M.I.Plant.E., A.M.I.E.D. for his help in checking the contents of this book. The drawings of the Charpy impact testing machine and specimens are taken from BS 131 by permission of the British Standards Institution, 2 Park Lane, London W1Y 4AA, from whom copies of the complete standard may be obtained.

Again I have pleasure in recording my thanks to the General Editor for help and guidance given to me in the preparation of this book and to my wife, Tessa, for her patience, encouragement, and secretarial help, without which this book could not have been completed.

Wall Heath, 1970
H. O.

CONTENTS

PART ONE: ENGINEERING DRAWING

1 Dimensioning — 3
2 Drawing Sheets, Scales, and Schedules — 13
3 Machining Symbols — 16
4 Lubrication — 18
5 Bearings — 22
6 Tools — 28
7 Marking-off Equipment — 37
8 Limit Gauges — 41
9 Clamping Devices — 46
10 Jigs and Fixtures — 50
11 Development of Surfaces — 56

PART TWO: MATERIALS

12 Cast Irons — 79
13 Steels — 83
14 Non-ferrous Metals and Alloys — 88
15 Bearing Metals — 97
16 Plastics — 99
17 Testing of Materials — 103

PART THREE: EXERCISES

Test Questions — 113
Exercises on Developments — 116
Drawing Exercises — 120

PART ONE
ENGINEERING DRAWING

CHAPTER ONE
DIMENSIONING

The dimensions shown on an engineering drawing are of fundamental importance for without them the component or part cannot be made. They must define the component completely, must be correct, and must be so positioned on the drawing that they can be clearly seen and correctly interpreted. The following general rules for dimensioning a drawing in SI units (i.e. metric units) are those recommended by the British Standards Institution in their standard BS 308. Students should make themselves familiar with the rules contained in this standard so that they will be able to apply them to their drawings correctly from memory.

1. Dimensions in metric units on mechanical engineering drawings are usually expressed in millimetres irrespective of their magnitude.
2. When drawings are dimensioned entirely or mainly in one unit, e.g. millimetres, the abbreviations for that unit need NOT be shown in the individual dimensions provided that there is placed prominently on the drawings an appropriate note such as:

    ALL DIMENSIONS ARE IN MILLIMETRES *or* ALL DIMENSIONS ARE IN CENTIMETRES
    UNLESS OTHERWISE STATED

3. If a drawing is dimensioned mainly in one unit, dimensions in any other unit should include the abbreviated form of the other unit, e.g.

    4 mm   12 cm   1·5 m.

4. On the Continent the decimal sign is a COMMA on the line through the base of the numerals, and, in the 1964 edition of BS 308, BSI recommended that this convention be used on drawings dimensioned in metric units. This recommendation has recently been reviewed, however, and in this book a POINT is used as the decimal sign. Students may expect to come across drawings using either convention.
5. When a dimension is LESS than unity it is recommended that the decimal sign be preceded by the cipher 0, e.g.

    0·5 NOT ·5

6. Dimensions involving a sequence of more than four figures not broken by a decimal point should be divided by a space between every THREE digits counting from the decimal point, e.g.

    12 000·5
    10·001 75
    1500·0

7. Dimensions should be placed so that they may be read EITHER from the bottom or from the right-hand side of the drawing.
8. Where there are several parallel dimension lines, the dimensions should be staggered as shown in Fig. 1.1 to avoid confusion.

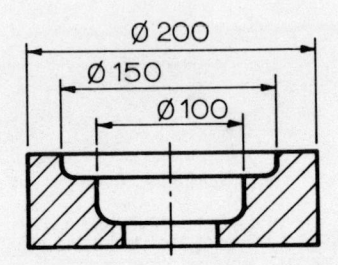

Fig. 1.1. Dimensions Staggered to Avoid Confusion

9. Overall dimensions should be placed OUTSIDE the intermediate dimensions as shown in Fig. 1.2.

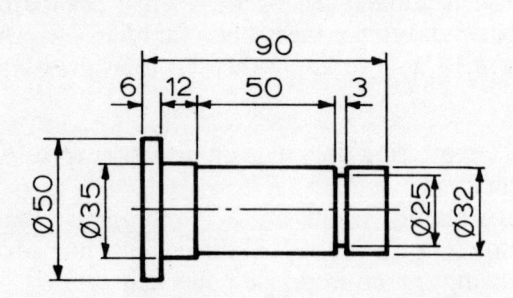

Fig. 1.2. Overall Dimensions Placed Outside Intermediate Dimensions

Fig. 1.3. Overall Length Added as an Auxiliary Dimension

10. Where an overall dimension is shown, one of the intermediate distances is redundant and SHOULD NOT be dimensioned (see Fig. 1.2). Exceptions may be made where redundant dimensions would provide useful information, in which case they should be given as 'auxiliary' dimensions. Where all the intermediate dimensions are shown, the overall distance should generally be given as an auxiliary dimension (see Fig. 1.3). Auxiliary dimensions should NOT be toleranced but should be included in brackets (see Figs. 1.3 and 1.4). Auxiliary dimensions relating to position should be based on the dimensions which define the true theoretical position of the features concerned; where they relate to size, they should normally be based on the mean sizes of the features concerned. In other cases, the basis of calculation should be clearly stated on the drawing. Auxiliary dimensions do NOT govern machining operations in any way.
11. As a general rule, tolerances for decimal dimensions should be expressed as decimals.
12. Tolerancing should be applied EITHER to individual dimensions or by a general note assigning uniform or graded tolerances to specified classes of dimensions. The use of general tolerancing notes greatly simplifies the drawing and saves much labour in its preparation. Two examples of the types of tolerancing notes are:

TOLERANCE EXCEPT WHERE OTHERWISE STATED $0 \cdot 5$	TOLERANCE ON CAST THICKNESS $\pm 12\frac{1}{2}\%$

N.B. All dimensions in this book are given in MILLIMETRES.

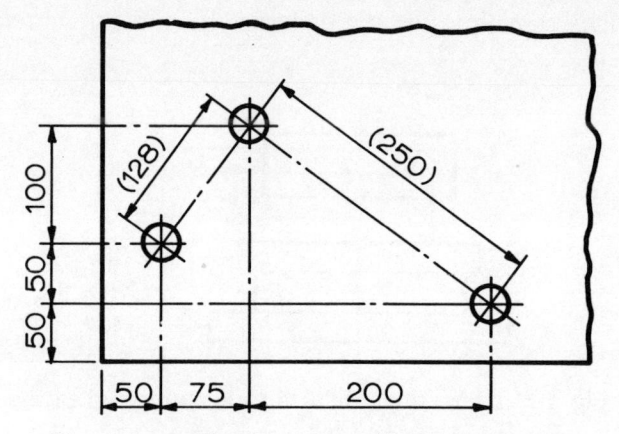

Fig. 1.4. Application of Auxiliary Dimensions

METHODS OF DIMENSIONING COMMON FEATURES

(a) Diameters

A dimension indicating the diameter of a circle or cylinder should be shown as in Fig. 1.5.

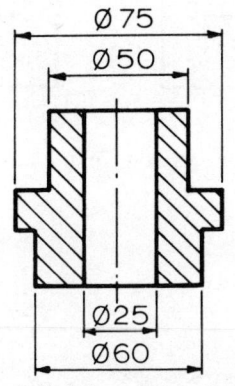

Fig. 1.5. Use of Symbol ϕ

The abbreviation DIA should be used ONLY in notes.

Dimensions of diameters should be placed on the most appropriate view to ensure clarity; for example on a longitudinal view in preference to an end view consisting of a number of concentric circles (see Fig. 1.6).

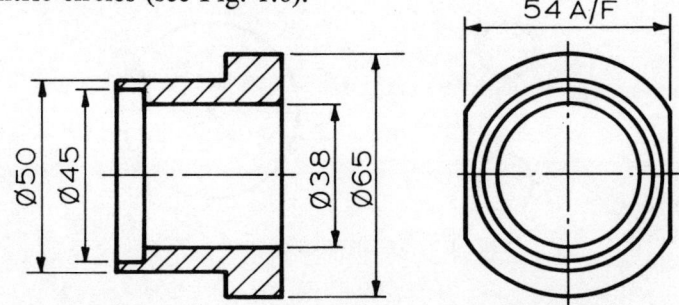

Fig. 1.6. Dimensions of Diameters Placed to Ensure Clarity

Dimension lines may sometimes be omitted and the dimensions related to features by leaders (see Fig. 1.7).

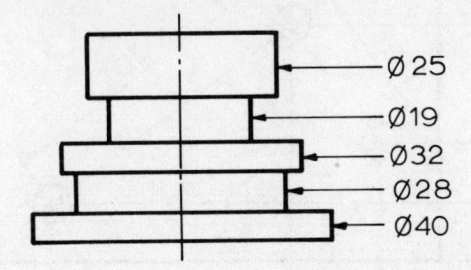

Fig. 1.7. Dimensions Related to Features by Leaders

Where space is restricted one of the methods shown in Fig. 1.8 (*a*) and (*b*) may be used.

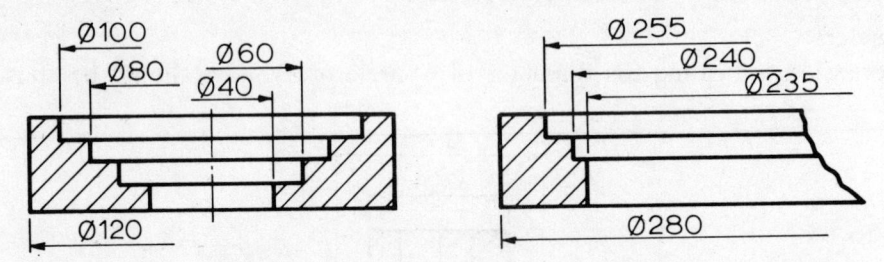

Fig. 1.8 (*a*) and (*b*). Dimensioning Diameters where Space is Restricted

(*b*) **Circles**
Circles should be dimensioned by one of the methods illustrated in Fig. 1.9.

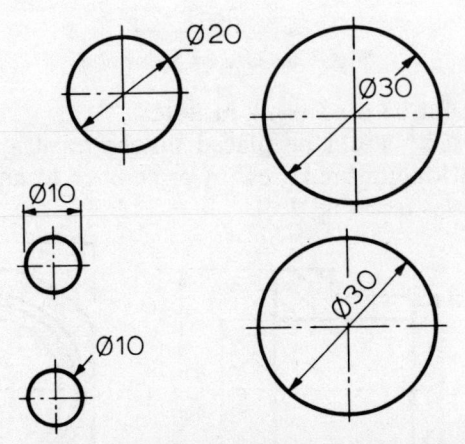

Fig. 1.9. Dimensioning of Circles

The diameter of a spherical surface should be dimensioned as shown in Fig. 1.10.

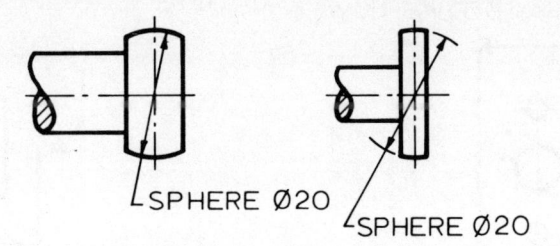

Fig. 1.10. Spherical Diameters

(c) **Radii**

Radii should be dimensioned by one of the methods shown in Fig. 1.11 (a) to (d).

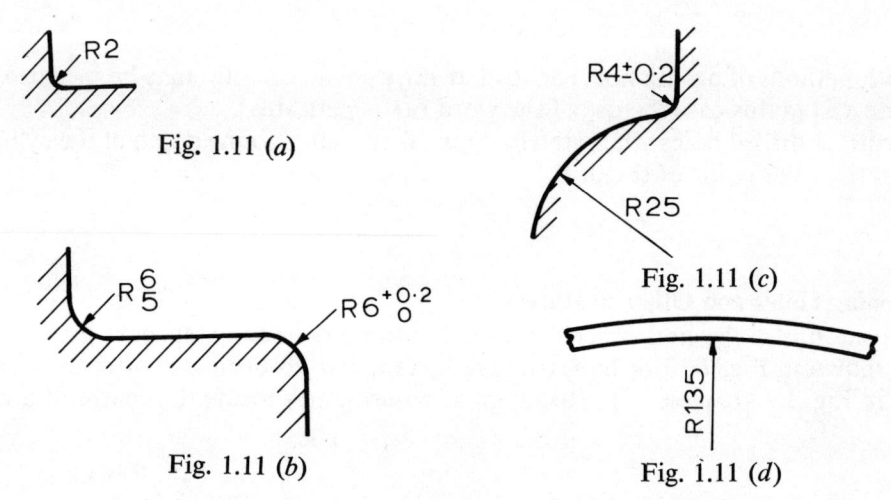

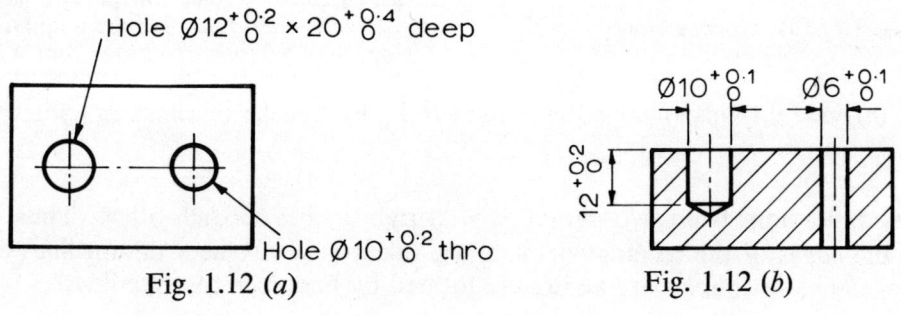

Fig. 1.11 (a)

Fig. 1.11 (c)

Fig. 1.11 (b)

Fig. 1.11 (d)

Fig. 1.11 (a), (b), (c) and (d). Dimensioning of Radii

Note that ONLY the symbol R is used and it is a CAPITAL letter and MUST PRECEDE the dimension.

(d) **Holes**

Typical methods of dimensioning holes are shown in Fig. 1.12 (a) to (d).

Fig. 1.12 (a)

Fig. 1.12 (b)

Fig. 1.12 (c)

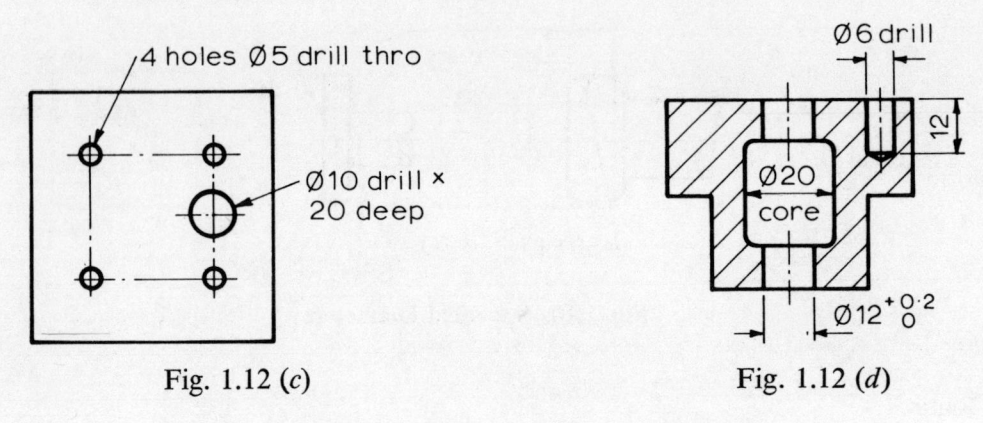

Fig. 1.12 (d)

Fig. 1.12. (a), (b), (c) and (d). Dimensioning Holes

Suitable methods of production, e.g. drill, ream, punch, core, etc., may be specified where appropriate and in this case the use of the word DIA is permitted.

The depth of drilled holes when stated in note form refers to the depth of the cylindrical hole and NOT to the point of the drill.

(e) Positioning Holes and Other Features

The position of holes and other features should be defined by spacing them on pitch circles as shown in Fig. 1.13 or by giving the rectangular co-ordinates or centre distances as shown in Fig. 1.14 (a) and (b). Rectangular co-ordinates locate the centre of a hole by

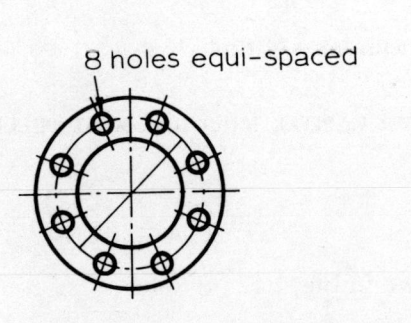

Fig. 1.13 (a). Holes Equally Spaced

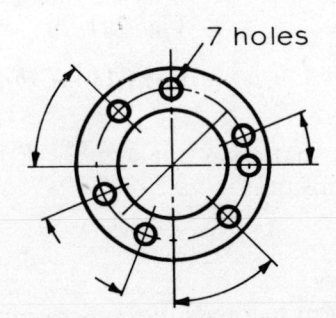

Fig. 1.13 (b). Holes Unequally Spaced. Alternatively several or all of the angular dimensions may be given from one centre line

Fig. 1.13 (a) and (b). Dimensioning Positions of Holes by Angular Spacings on a Pitch Circle

giving its dimensions from two datum lines at right angles to each other. Thus, in Fig. 1.14 (d) the edges of the rectangular plate are taken as convenient datum lines and the centres of the various holes are accurately located by reference to these lines.

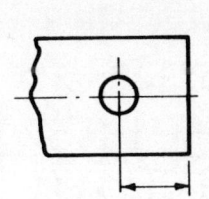

Fig. 1.14 (a). Symmetry of Hole with Edges of Plate Implied

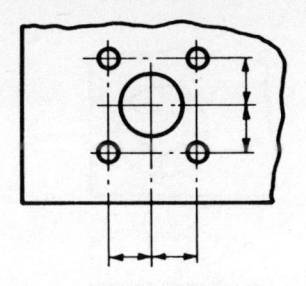

Fig. 1.14 (b). Symmetry of Holes Defined

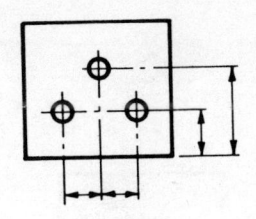

Fig. 1.14 (c). Relation to Lower Edge Important

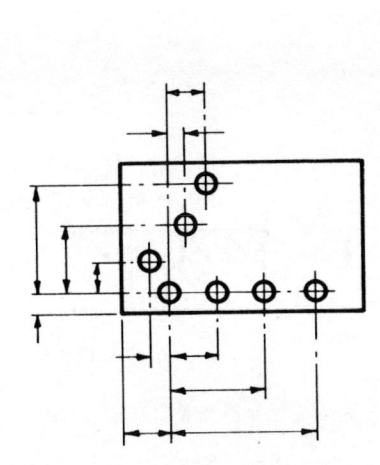

Fig. 1.14 (d). Use of Ordinates in Preference to Angular Dimensions

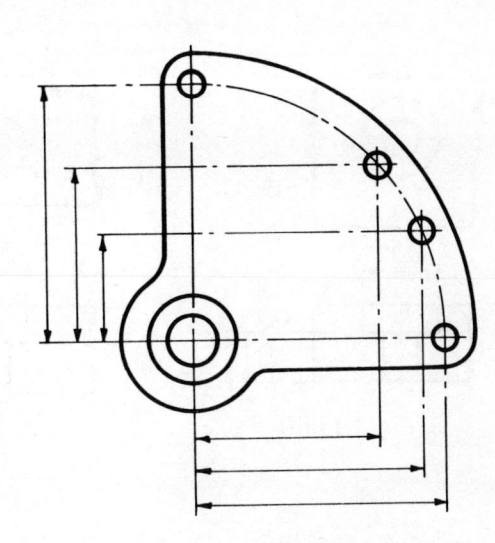

Fig. 1.14 (e). Use of Ordinates for Holes Lying on a Pitch Circle

Fig. 1.14 (a) to (e). Dimensioning Positions of Holes by Ordinates

(f) Dimensioning on Curved Surfaces

In dimensioning the spacing of holes and other features on a curved surface, care should be taken to indicate clearly the surface on which the dimensioned points are to be measured and whether the dimensions are chordal or circumferential.

(g) Countersinks, Counterbores, and Spotfaces

When dimensioning a countersink, counterbore, or spotface, the required dimensions should be given as shown in Fig. 1.15 (a) to (j).

9

Fig. 1.15 (a)

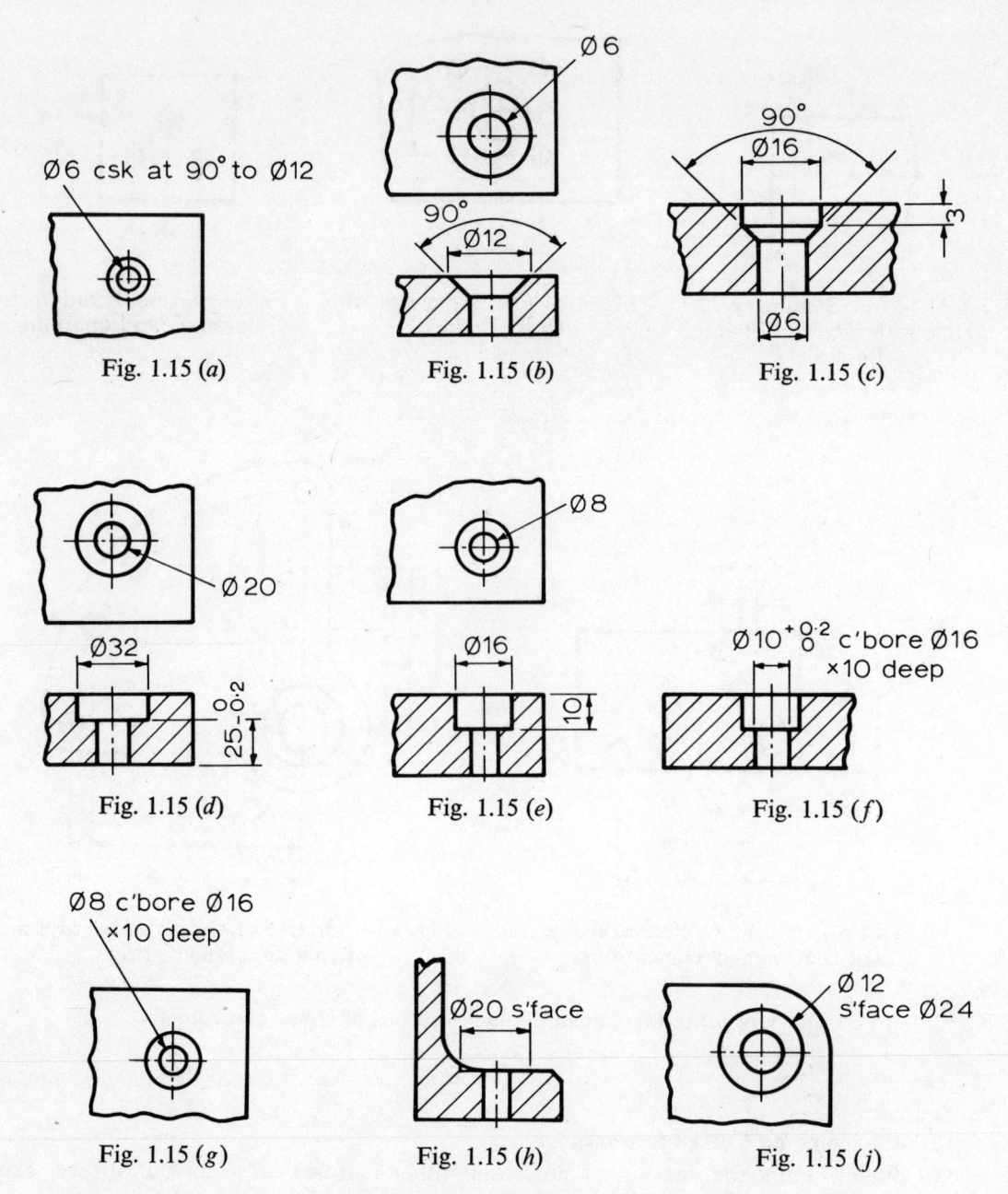

Fig. 1.15 (b)

Fig. 1.15 (c)

Fig. 1.15 (d)

Fig. 1.15 (e)

Fig. 1.15 (f)

Fig. 1.15 (g)

Fig. 1.15 (h)

Fig. 1.15 (j)

Fig. 1.15 (a) to (j). Dimensioning Countersinks, Counterbores, and Spotfaces

(h) Chamfers

To avoid any misinterpretation of dimensions of 45° chamfers, they should be specified by one of the methods shown in Fig. 1.16. Notes and leaders should NOT be used. Chamfers at angles other than 45° should be dimensioned as shown in Fig. 1.17 and should NOT be shown as a note.

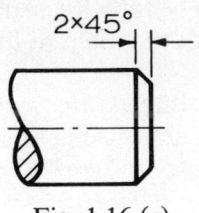

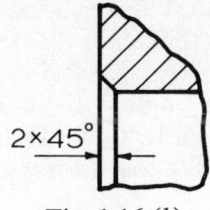

Fig. 1.16 (a)   Fig. 1.16 (b)   Fig. 1.16 (c)

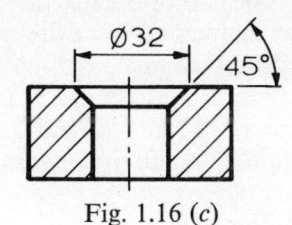

Fig. 1.16 (a) to (c). Chamfers at 45°

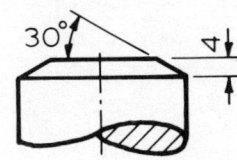

Fig. 1.17. Chamfers at Angles other than 45°

(j) Screw Threads

(i) Designation

Screw threads should be specified by using the designations recommended in the appropriate British Standard. When specifying special screw threads, the tolerances of which NEED to be calculated, the dimensions for the major, effective, and minor diameters should be given as in Fig. 1.18.

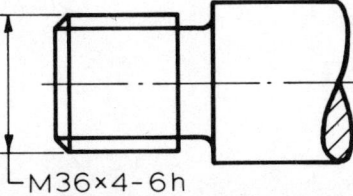

Fig. 1.18. Dimensioning a Special Screw Thread

(ii) Undercut

Where an undercut is necessary, it should be dimensioned on the drawing in accordance with the recommendations of the current British Standard *Undercuts and Runouts for Screw Threads*.

(iii) Length of Thread (Parallel Threads)

The length of full thread, or the distance to the end of the full thread should be stated where necessary using one of the methods shown in Figs. 1.19, 1.20, and 1.21.

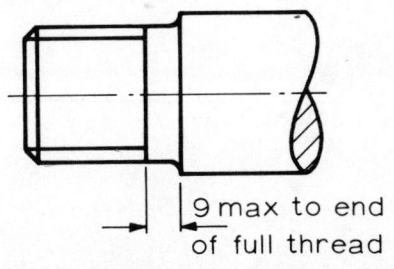

Fig. 1.19. Dimensioning to End of Full Thread

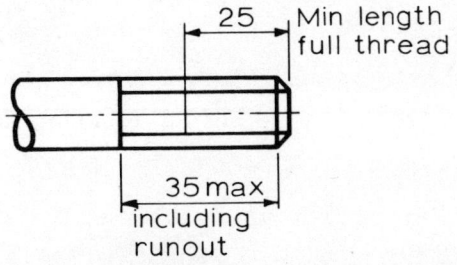

Fig. 1.20. Dimensioning to Ends of Full and Imperfect Threads

The end of the full thread is the point at which the root ceases to be fully formed. The root diameter of an external thread is the minor diameter, and that of the internal thread, the major diameter.

Where it is necessary to limit the lengths of full and imperfect threads the methods shown in Figs. 1.20 and 1.21 (*d*) should be used. In deciding these dimensions reference should be made to the current British Standard *Undercuts and Runouts for Screw Threads*.

(*iv*) *Threaded Holes*

Threaded holes should be dimensioned by one of the methods shown in Fig. 1.21 (*a*) to (*e*).

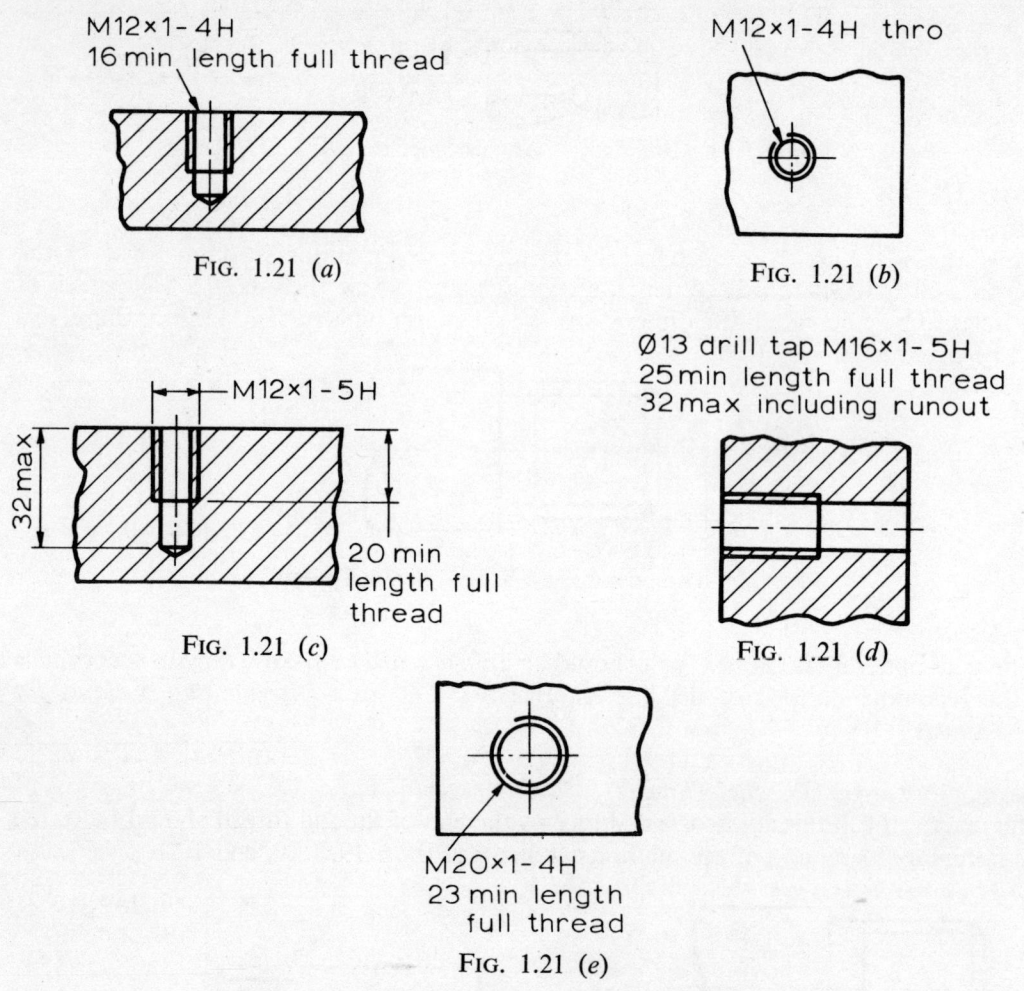

FIG. 1.21 (*a*) — M12×1-4H, 16 min length full thread

FIG. 1.21 (*b*) — M12×1-4H thro

FIG. 1.21 (*c*) — M12×1-5H, 32 max, 20 min length full thread

FIG. 1.21 (*d*) — Ø13 drill tap M16×1-5H, 25 min length full thread, 32 max including runout

FIG. 1.21 (*e*) — M20×1-4H, 23 min length full thread

Fig. 1.21 (*a*) to (*e*). Dimensioning Threaded Holes

CHAPTER TWO

DRAWING SHEETS, SCALES AND SCHEDULES

The choice of paper and drawing board to be used in a drawing office will depend largely on what has to be drawn and the scale which would be appropriate. The guiding principle should always be that the drawing sheet must be large enough to enable the component to be adequately defined. This should ensure that the drawing sheet chosen is well filled, that sufficient views of the component are provided, that all essential dimensions are clearly shown and readily seen, and that the sheet is correctly titled.

With the changeover to metric dimensions, the sizes of drawing sheets and the scale ratios have had to be revised. The British Standards Institution (BSI) has recommended that the drawing sheet sizes should be the International Standards Organisation (ISO) 'A' series. This series is based on a rectangle whose area is 1 square metre.

The range of sizes which are considered adequate for most purposes are as follows:

DESIGNATION	SIZE IN mm
A0	841 × 1189
A1	594 × 841
A2	420 × 594
A3	297 × 420
A4	210 × 297

The size which students will use most is A2.

Title Blocks

There must be a certain latitude allowed in the position and arrangement of the title blocks on a drawing sheet, but the most important requirement is that they are so arranged that the reading of the drawing is made as easy as possible.

The title-block should be located at the BOTTOM RIGHT-HAND CORNER of the sheet, and it usually contains the following information:

>   Name of firm
>   Drawing number
>   Title of drawing
>   Scale
>   Date
>   Signature of a responsible person.

It is important that the drawing number MUST be visible when the drawing is filed; it may have to be printed again so the drawing number must be in a suitable position for easy reference.

Wherever necessary the drawing sheet should include or provide for:

(*a*) Materials or parts list, which should include:
    (i) Item or part number
    (ii) Description of part
    (iii) Quantity required
    (iv) Cross reference to other drawings if used
    (v) Material, giving the British Standard or other accepted information

(*b*) Job or order number
(*c*) Treatment and finish required
(*d*) Machining symbols key
(*e*) Tolerances on dimensions if these have not been given
(*f*) Tool and gauge references
(*g*) Any general notes required.

Other information may also be given if applicable to a particular component.

Types of Drawing Sheets

There are several types of standard drawing sheets recommended by the British Standards Institution. These are:

(*a*) Sheets suitable for detail drawings and particularly where one part only is shown.
(*b*) Sheets for assembly drawings and for detail drawings which show a number of parts on the same sheet.
(*c*) Sheets for drawings of shop equipment such as jigs and tools where quantity is not involved.

Drawings and Schedules

Engineering drawings can be broadly divided into TWO main categories, namely, drawings of a general arrangement, and drawings showing details of one or more components. A general arrangement (G.A.), as its name implies, shows the various components arranged together to form the complete and finished product. Usually a G.A. drawing gives only overall dimensions; the remainder are left for the detail drawings.

The detail drawings give appropriate views of the individual components which the craftsman will need in order to produce them. All the essential dimensions must be shown, and it is usual to include also any machining instructions. Sometimes a number of components are themselves part of an assembly, or sub-assembly, of a much larger engineering component. In these circumstances it might be convenient to show on one sheet the details of the individual components and an assembly drawing showing how they are fitted together to become part of the larger component. An obvious case for drawings of this kind occurs when various parts of a larger component are manufactured under contract by a firm other than that responsible for the large component. The components are usually shown on a G.A. assembly or sub-assembly drawing by means of a distinguishing circle with the identity of the component printed neatly in the circle, usually in the form of a reference number, e.g. ①, ②, ③, etc. This is generally referred to as balloon referencing, and facilitates the cross-referencing of drawings.

Separate Material or Parts Lists

It is sometimes found more convenient to group a number of component parts on a separate sheet, distinct from the drawing sheet. This sheet is called a material or parts list. It may apply to a number of parts which are detailed on one large drawing or, alternatively, it may be used to group a number of single-part drawings, or even several multi-part drawings, into an assembly or sub-assembly. Further information can be obtained by reference to the latest British Standard No. BS 308.

Drawing List

It is often necessary, particularly with a large project, to compile a list of all drawings and assembly and sub-assembly lists.

The latest BS 308 gives detailed information on this and the student is advised to read this Standard carefully.

CHAPTER THREE
MACHINING SYMBOLS

General

Particular machining processes should not normally be specified on other than process drawings, except in special circumstances. Machining and surface texture symbols should only be shown ONCE on each surface, and should be placed on the same view as the dimensions which give the size or location of the surface concerned.

Machining Symbol

Where it is required to indicate that a surface is to be machined without defining either the surface texture grade or process to be used, a symbol as shown in Fig. 3.1 should be used.

Fig. 3.1. Machining Symbol

The symbol should be applied normal to the line representing the surface as shown in Fig. 3.2 (*a*) and (*b*). The symbol may be applied to a leader or extension line.

Fig. 3.2 (*a*) and (*b*). Form and Application of Machining Symbol

Where all the surfaces are to be machined, a general note such as shown in Fig. 3.3 may be used.

Fig. 3.3. Machining All Over

Where it is necessary to indicate a particular quality of surface texture and the surface is to be machined, the notation shown in Fig. 3.4 should be used. The notation is that recommended in BS 1134.

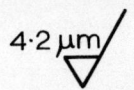

Fig. 3.4. Form of Surface Texture Symbol

Note that the figures $4 \cdot 2 \mu$m represents $4 \cdot 2$ MICROMETRES where a micrometre $= 0 \cdot 001$ mm.

If both the maximum and minimum values have to be specified, they should be shown as in Fig. 3.5.

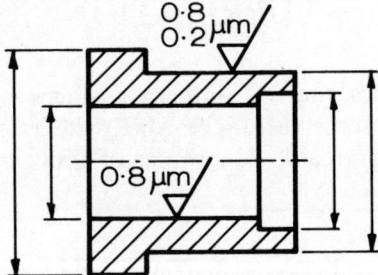

Fig. 3.5. Maximum and Minimum Values

Surface texture values may also be shown by the use of letters, provided that the meaning of the letter is clearly defined as shown in Fig. 3.6.

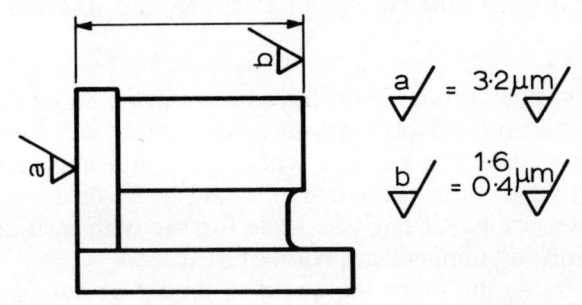

Fig. 3.6. Application of Surface Texture Symbol

17

CHAPTER FOUR

LUBRICATION

Lubrication means the maintaining of slippery surfaces between moving parts or the keeping of surfaces apart by some substance which shears easily. A lubricant can range from a very light oil to a heavy grease. The choice of a lubricant is governed by the following factors:

(a) the velocity of the shaft;
(b) the coefficient of friction between shaft and bush;
(c) the temperature conditions;
(d) the pressure;
(e) the atmospheric conditions under which the bearing is working.

Lubricants can be divided into TWO groups, namely GREASES and OILS.

Greases

Greases are mainly mineral oils which have been thickened by the addition of soaps, graphite, or other ingredients to provide particular qualities. They are important as lubricants because they can often be used where oil is not a practical proposition, for example in motor-car wheel bearings where oil could be washed out by water thrown up from the road. Greases are particularly suitable for use with medium or slow speeds of rubbing and with a working temperature below 120 °C.

When choosing a grease the following qualities should be considered.

(a) It must have the correct VISCOSITY to ensure complete distribution, and form the necessary protecting film.
(b) It must be able to resist the formation of deposits.
(c) It MUST NOT thicken like paste.
(d) It must have good heat-carrying properties.
(e) If possible it should contain graphite, as the graphite flakes break down and are caught in the 'rough spots', while remaining flakes form a highly polished surface.

When comparing it with oil, grease has a minor, yet important, position in the field of lubrication. Greasing methods can be usually placed in one of three categories:

(a) Compression cups.
(b) A one-shot system where the grease is piped to various points by intermittent pressure from a reservoir.
(c) As (b) but with a constant feed.

Grease is often used for the lubrication of machine tool parts and the simple compression cup system is often used on conveyor systems and plummer blocks. The pressure grease gun fitting, or grease nipple, is also familiar on machine tools and automobiles. Ball and roller bearings are suitable for grease lubrication.

Oil

It is usual to adopt oil lubrication when working speeds and temperatures are high. Modern machinery often uses a centralised lubricating system in order to simplify the lubrication tasks, and oil is conveyed under pressure from a central reservoir along pipe runs to individual bearings. Oil used as a lubricant can be successfully used for lubricators, oil rings, and pressure feed systems and can be filtered and used over again for as long as it retains its lubricating properties.

Viscosity

The viscosity of a lubricant can be thought of as its resistance to motion. For small viscosities the resistance to motion is low, and so movement takes place easily. High viscosities make movement difficult. As the temperature increases the viscosity decreases. A lubricant with high viscosity does not 'flow' easily, and may therefore produce dry patches. A lubricant with low viscosity may 'flow' so easily that it is squeezed out from the parts in contact. Every lubricant, therefore, must be carefully selected to ensure that it has the correct qualities for the conditions under which it is to be used. The 'oiliness' of a lubricant may be described as its ability to maintain a film between surfaces even when subjected to pressure.

LUBRICATORS

Fig. 4.1 (*a*) shows a 'Stauffer' lubricator for use with a heavy grease. It consists of a cap (a) which screws on the body (b) pushing down grease through the hole (c) and on to the shaft. The lubricator is screwed into position by the threaded portion (d) and is tightened by using a spanner on the hexagonal part (e).

Fig. 4.1 (*b*) shows a 'drop sight-feed' oil lubricator. The oil supply is contained in a glass cylinder (a) and passes through the gauze filter (b) to enter a narrow orifice leading to the lower tube (c). The size of the orifice can be controlled by raising or lowering the taper

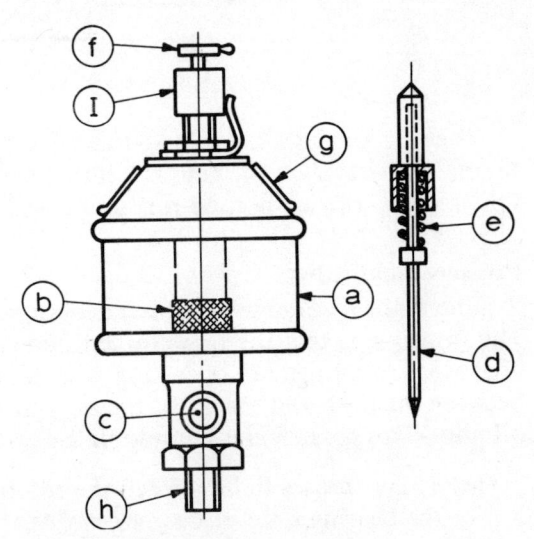

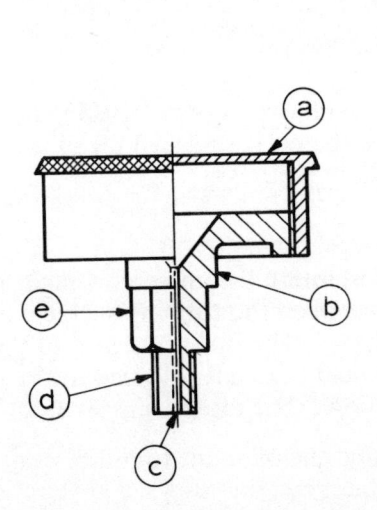

Fig. 4.1 (*a*). A 'Stauffer' Lubricator   Fig. 4.1 (*b*). A Drop Sight-feed Lubricator

Fig. 4.1 (*a*) and (*b*). Types of Lubricator

needle *d* by means of an adjusting nut *I*. Increasing the size of the orifice results in an increased oil flow and the rate of flow can be observed through the window in the lower tube. The taper needle is normally held closed by a spring *e* and is opened by operation of the snap lever *f*. The glass cylinder *a* can be refilled with oil through the sliding cover *g* in the top cap. The lubricator is fastened to the bearing housing by means of the screwed piece *h*.

There are many other kinds of lubricators in use, but in all cases the principle of operation is the same, whether oil or grease is used as the lubricant.

Fig. 4.2 shows an example of a ring oiled bearing. The points to notice are that this type requires:

(*a*) A surplus of oil to keep the level at the correct height.
(*b*) To be dustproof and waterproof.
(*c*) To have oil seals fitted at both ends of the bearing to prevent the oil creeping along the shaft.

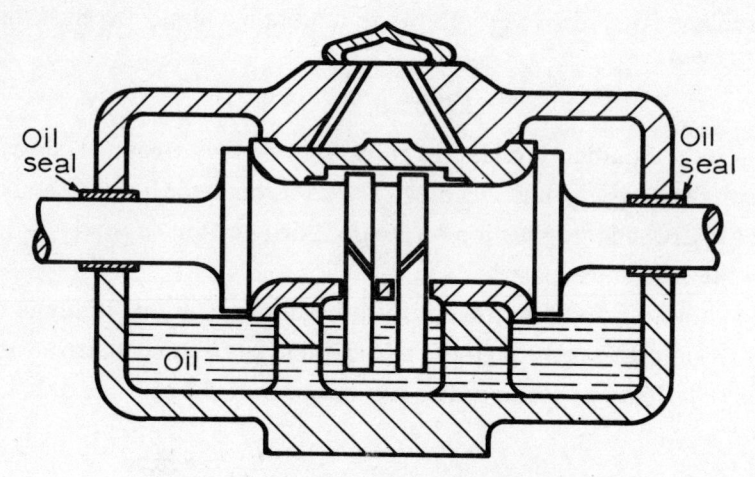

Fig. 4.2. A Typical Ring Oiled Bearing

The ring, or rings, are split so that they can be fitted on the shaft in its working position. As the shaft revolves the ring is whirled around it and the oil is splashed on to the shaft. This method is usually used for high speeds and medium loads.

Pressure Lubrication

This is the method used a great deal in machine tools, internal-combustion engines, etc. The principle is that the oil is forced under pressure between the rubbing surfaces and is used where bearings are operating with high-speed shafts. The oil is forced into the gap between the bush and the shaft, the pressure increases, and the shaft is forced to rise on an oil film. This condition is commonly called 'fully floating'. The disadvantages are:

(*a*) The oil ceases to flow when the rotation stops and the oil tends to drain away from the bearing.
(*b*) It takes time for the oil pressure to build up when starting, so the rate of wear is greatly increased during this period.

(*c*) If the oil is cold the viscosity is greater, and so extra power is required to overcome this extra friction.

Precautions to be Observed in the Use of Lubricants

It is essential that correct lubrication is used for a particular task or service. Equally important is the method of applying the lubricant. There are specialist companies both for lubricants and lubrication fittings and they should be consulted whenever particular lubrication problems arise. The following comments may serve as a useful guide to initial selection:

(*a*) High speeds and low pressures require a rather light oil.
(*b*) Low speeds and high pressure require enough 'body' in the lubricant to prevent 'starting wear'.

It is important also to remember that power loss can occur from friction within the lubricant itself if it is too viscous, and that too light an oil will not keep the surfaces apart and this causes undue wear.

CHAPTER FIVE
BEARINGS

Bearings are classified into the following TWO main groups:

(*a*) JOURNAL BEARINGS.
(*b*) THRUST BEARINGS.

Journal bearings—often referred to simply as 'journals'—are those bearings which support shafts in such a way that the pressure on the bearing is at RIGHT ANGLES to the axis of the shaft.

Thrust bearings are those bearings which support shafts in such a way that the pressure on the bearing acts in an axial direction ALONG the axis of the shaft.

Pressure

The pressure on any bearing can be obtained from the following formula:

$$\text{PRESSURE (in N/m}^2) = \frac{\text{Total load on bearing (in N)}}{\text{Projected area (in m}^2)}$$

The projected area means the area of the projection on a plane which is at right angles to the direction of the load. Orthographic projection is an ideal means of illustrating what is meant by the term 'projected area'.

Fig. 5.1 shows a sectional view through a journal bearing.

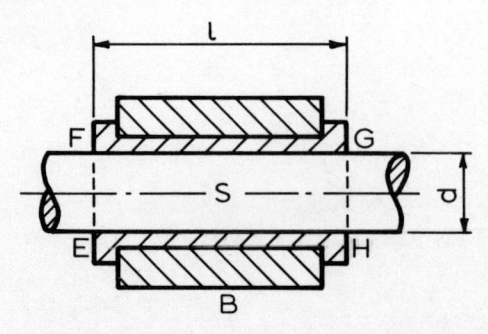

Fig. 5.1. Calculation of Projected Area of a Journal Bearing

Suppose a shaft S of diameter d is rotating in a journal bearing B of length l. Then the 'projected area' is the rectangle EFGH in the plan view shown. This area is clearly $d \times l$.

When a shaft is revolving in a bearing there will be friction and, if the friction is high, it is possible for the shaft to 'seize' in the bearing. To prevent this occurring, the friction must be reduced to as small a value as possible. This is achieved by:

(*a*) fitting bushes made from a material with a low coefficient of friction, and
(*b*) lubricating the bearing.

Simple Journal Bearing

Fig. 5.2 shows a simple journal bearing made from cast iron, which is a self-lubricating material. This bearing is used for light pressures and slow speeds. It can be lubricated either by a simple lubricator or by hand with an oil can.

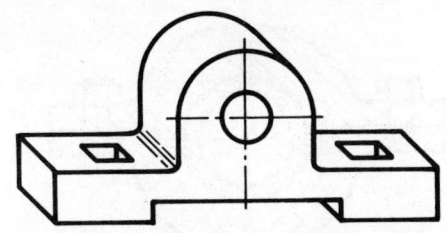

Fig. 5.2. Simple Journal Bearing

A disadvantage of this type of simple bearing is that its bore size cannot be renewed when worn. Because of this, bushes are usually used and, when these are worn they can be replaced by new ones. Bushes are cylindrical pieces of metal fitted into the bore of the bearing, which is machined to receive them. To enable the bushes to be renewed without dismantling the bearing they can be made in two parts, but there is a possibility of the bushes being turned around in the bearing housing due to the friction between themselves and the shaft. To prevent this occurring some provision must be made to secure them. Three simple methods of doing this are shown in Fig. 5.3 (*a*), (*b*) and (*c*).

Use of Round Pin or 'Snug' (Fig. 5.3 (*a*))

In this method a round pin or 'snug' is fixed to either the top or bottom half of the bush. This pin fits into a recess which is provided in the bearing housing to receive it.

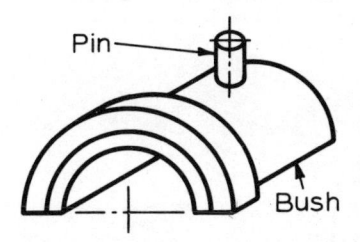

Fig. 5.3 (*a*). Use of a Round Pin

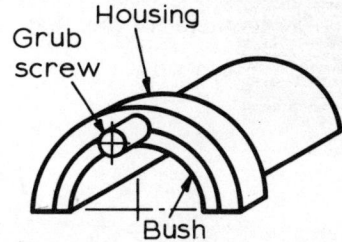

Fig. 5.3 (*b*). Use of a Grub Screw

Grub Screw Tapped into a Bush and Bearing (Fig. 5.3 (*b*))

In this method the bush is placed into position in the housing and a hole is drilled and tapped as shown. A grub screw or Allen screw is then screwed into position.

Hexagonal or Octagonal Shape at Ends of a Bush (Fig. 5.3 (*c*))

The bushes are manufactured to a specified shape, as shown. The bearing housing is made to receive this special shape.

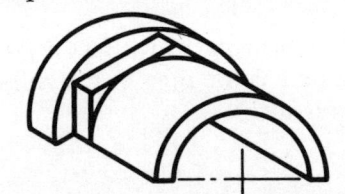

Fig. 5.3 (*c*). Use of a Hexagon

Fig. 5.3 (*a*), (*b*) and (*c*). Methods to Prevent Rotation of Bearing Bushes

Split-bush Journal Bearing

Fig. 5.4 shows a typical split-bush bearing. The bush is made in two parts to facilitate maintenance, so that when the bushes become worn they can be quickly removed and replaced. This type of journal bearing is used for high speeds and large diameters. The

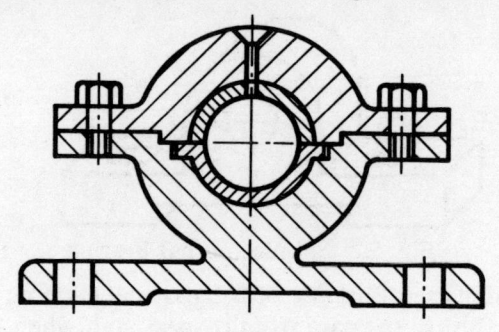

Fig. 5.4. Split-bush Journal Bearing

bushes are usually made of brass, phosphor-bronze, or gunmetal, and lubrication by some approved method is ESSENTIAL. The projected area is obtained by multiplying the length of the bush by the diameter of the shaft, as shown in Fig. 5.1.

Footstep Bearings

Fig. 5.5 shows an example of a footstep bearing, which is used for supporting the ends of shafts. The projected area here is given by the expression:

$$A = \frac{\pi}{4} d^2$$

where d is the diameter of the shaft.

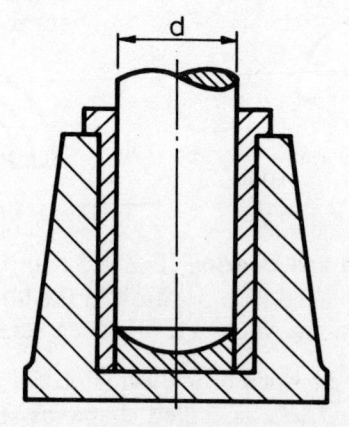

Fig. 5.5. A Footstep Bearing

Thrust Bearings

Fig. 5.6 shows a typical thrust bearing which has a particular application to marine engineering. The projected area here is the area of the collar on the shaft which takes the thrust. This is given by the expression:

$$A = \frac{\pi}{4}(D^2 - d^2)$$

where D = diameter of collar or end, and d = diameter of shaft.

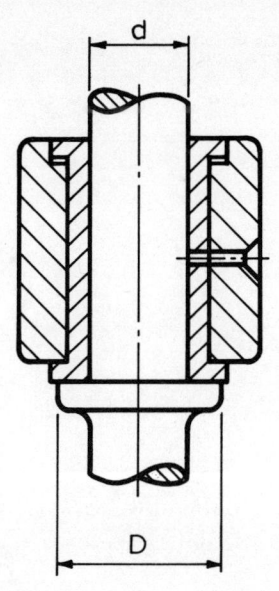

Fig. 5.6. Thrust Bearing

| | TYPES OF BEARING ||
	JOURNAL	THRUST
USES	(a) Supporting shafting which has no end thrust (b) Big-end bearings for connecting-rods	(a) Supporting shafts which have considerable end thrust
MATERIAL USED FOR BUSHES	(a) Gunmetal (b) Phosphor-bronze (c) Steel-backed white-metal shells (d) Lead-base alloys	(a) Gunmetal (b) Phosphor-bronze (c) Steel-backed white-metal shells (d) Lead-base alloys
METHODS TO PREVENT ROTATION OF BUSHES	(a) Round Pin or 'Snug' (b) Grub screw tapped into Bush and Bearing (c) Octagonal or Hexagonal shape at ends of bush	(a) Round Pin or 'Snug' (b) Grub screw tapped into Bush and Bearing (c) Octagonal or Hexagonal shape at ends of bush
LUBRICATION	(a) Oil, by hand or in Lubricator (b) Pressure Oil Feed (c) Grease	(a) Oil, by hand or in Lubricator (b) Pressure Oil Feed (c) Grease (d) Use of oil rings

Table I. Usual Uses of Journal and Thrust Bearings

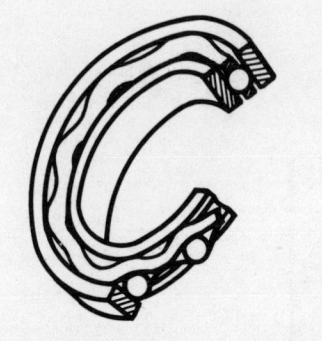

Fig. 5.7 (*a*). Ball Journal Bearing

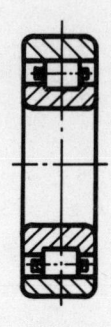

Fig. 5.7 (*b*). Roller Bearing

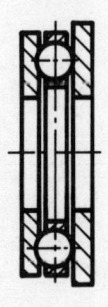

Fig. 5.7 (*c*). Ball Thrust Bearing

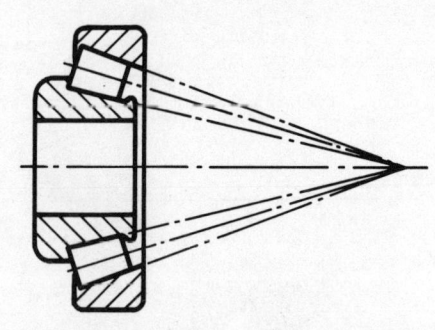

Fig. 5.7 (*d*). Tapered Roller Bearing

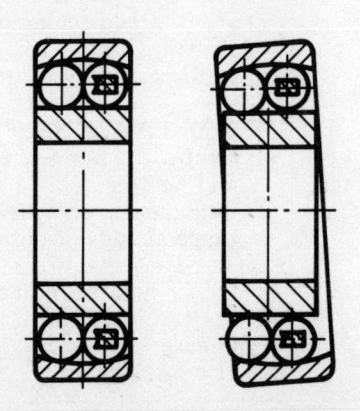

Fig. 5.7 (*e*). Self-aligning Ball Bearing

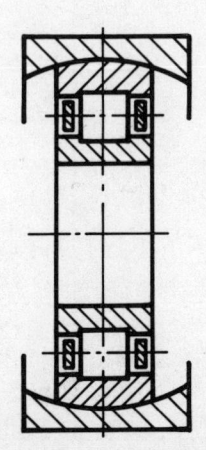

Fig. 5.7 (*f*). Self-aligning Roller Bearing

Ball and Roller Bearings

Ball or roller bearings are now increasingly used for high-speed shafts and are replacing bushes. The advantages of ball and roller bearings over journal and thrust-type bearings are:

(*a*) Less friction, because rolling friction is considerably less than sliding friction.
(*b*) Increased life due to less friction.

Fig. 5.7 (*a*) shows a BALL JOURNAL BEARING. These bearings will also carry end thrust if required, and so are widely used.

Fig. 5.7 (*b*) shows a ROLLER BEARING. These bearings are able to support heavier loads than the equivalent size ball bearing, and are used for heavy duty work.

Fig. 5.7 (*c*) shows a BALL THRUST BEARING which can support only axial loads.

Fig. 5.7 (*d*) shows a TAPERED ROLLER BEARING which is very efficient and will support axial as well as journal loads. Adjustment for wear may be effected by moving the inner and outer races toward each other.

Fig. 5.7 (*e*) shows a SELF-ALIGNING BALL BEARING. The self-alignment is effected by having an outer track of spherical form, thus allowing the inner race to have a small degree of angular movement. Alternatively, the outside of the outer race may be of spherical form, the bearing being located in a housing with a spherical bore. This enables the whole bearing to have a degree of angular movement. Fig. 5.7 (*f*) shows this method applied to a roller bearing.

Ball and Roller Bearing Construction

The basic construction consists of two hardened steel rings, between which are located one or more sets of hardened steel balls or rollers. A cage, or separator, keeps the rolling elements at the correct spacing from each other. They are manufactured to a controlled, high degree of accuracy, and are thus readily interchangeable.

CHAPTER SIX
TOOLS

DRILLS AND REAMERS

Combination Centre Drill (Fig. 6.1 (*a*))

This is a double-ended tool, with a parallel, central body, and a short fluted pilot drill, with a countersink portion, at each end. Although the smaller sizes are often used for 'opening out' a centre punch mark prior to drilling, they are mainly used to centre the ends of components prior to turning between centres on the lathe. Seven sizes ranging from 3 mm to 19 mm in diameter are available.

Twist Drills (Fig. 6.1 (*b*))

There is a wide range of these drills available in sizes from approximately 0·3 mm to 101 mm. The smaller drills are made with a parallel shank to fit in a drill chuck, while the larger drills have a morse taper shank, into which can be fitted morse taper sleeves (Fig. 6.1 (*c*)), enabling varying sizes of drill to be fitted into the drilling machine spindle. Various types of drills are available to suit the type of material to be drilled. Variations in the number of flutes, flute widths, web sections, and point angles are dictated by the increasing range of materials now used in engineering.

Reamers (Fig. 6.1 (*d*))

The purpose of a reamer is to produce a well finished and accurate hole. To achieve this, minimum metal must be removed and it is usual to use a drill size of approximately 0·2 mm LESS than the reamer size. Hand reamers have straight flutes, i.e. they are parallel with the centre line of the reamer. A square end is provided for fitting a tap wrench for hand rotation and the opposite end is provided with a taper start to allow a suitable start to the operation. Machine reamers fit into the morse taper of the machine and the flutes are left-hand spiral, as this prevents any tendency of the reamer to draw itself into the hole. High-speed steel (HSS) is used for the manufacture of drills and reamers.

Fig. 6.1 (*a*). Combination Centre Drill

Fig. 6.1 (*b*). Taper-shank Twist Drill

Fig. 6.1 (*c*). Morse-taper Sleeve

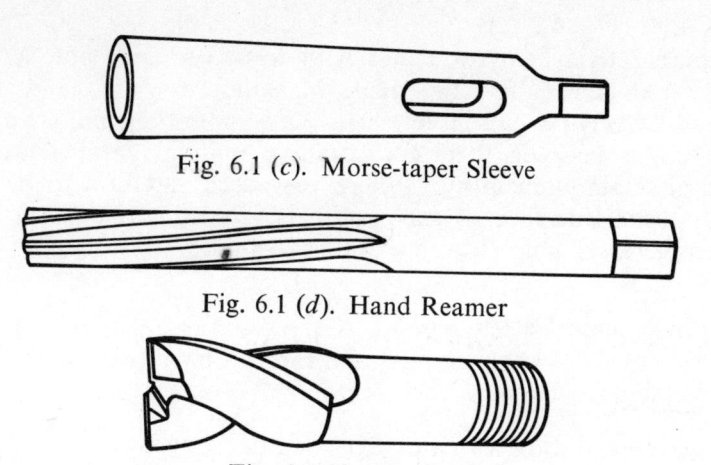

Fig. 6.1 (*d*). Hand Reamer

Fig. 6.1 (*e*). Slot Drill

Fig. 6.1 (*a*) to (*e*). Drills and Reamers

Slot Drill (Fig. 6.1 (*e*))

This cutter is of similar design to the end mill described below, but it has only two cutting teeth on the periphery, and these extend right across the end face of the cutter. The slot drill is specially suited for taking heavy cuts from solid metal and can be used as a form of drill to produce a hole in the workpiece to start the cut. They are often used for cutting deep slots or keyways for feather keys at high rates of feed.

MILLING CUTTERS

Cylindrical Cutter (Fig. 6.2 (*a*))

This cutter is often known as a slab cutter or roller mill and is used to produce a flat surface parallel to its axis. It is made in a wide range of diameters and widths to meet different requirements and has cutting teeth on its periphery only. Cutters less than 19 mm wide usually have straight teeth, but the wider cutters usually have helical teeth. These helical teeth impart a shearing action to the cut and so reduce the shock loading on the teeth when they start a cut. The surface finish obtained with helical teeth is superior to that produced with straight teeth, and less power is required to do the same amount of work.

End Mill (Fig. 6.2 (*b*))

This is a long and relatively slender, fragile cutter with teeth on the periphery and the end face. The teeth on the end face are relatively shallow and do not extend right across the end face, so this cutter is NOT intended to originate its own holes in workpieces, and the majority of the metal removed should be cut with the peripheral teeth. This cutter incorporates a shank, which is usually parallel but may be tapered, and can thus be held in a collet chuck or the spindle nose. Uses for end mills are numerous and include the milling of grooves which do not extend to the edge of the workpiece, milling around the outside of workpieces to bring them to a certain profile, and milling shallow depressions in the surfaces of workpieces.

Side and Face Cutter (Fig. 6.2 (c))

This is a comparatively narrow cutter with teeth on each side as well as on the periphery. Side and face cutters are made in standard widths and can be used to produce slots and keyways to close tolerances. Very often these cutters are used in pairs with a spacing collar between them for 'straddle milling' parallel faces on opposite sides of a workpiece simultaneously. Where very deep slots are to be milled in solid material, the opposite side face of each tooth is removed to make a staggered-tooth cutter which has increased chip clearance and rake angles.

Angle Cutters (Single-angle Cutter, Fig. 6.2 (d))

There are three types of angle cutters, and they all have two cutting faces which are located at specific angles relative to each other.

Standard angles
30°, 45°, 50°, 60°, 70°, 80°

Cutting faces

Standard angles
48°, 53°, 58°, 62°, 68°, 75°

12°

Cutting faces

Standard angles
45°, 60°, 90°

Cutting faces

Fig. 6.2 (d) (i). Single-angle Cutter

Used for cutting straight vee grooves or flutes only. May be right or left-handed

Fig. 6.2 (d) (ii). Combined (Equal-angle) Cutter

Used for cutting straight or helical vee grooves or flutes

Fig. 6.2 (d) (iii). Double-angle Cutter

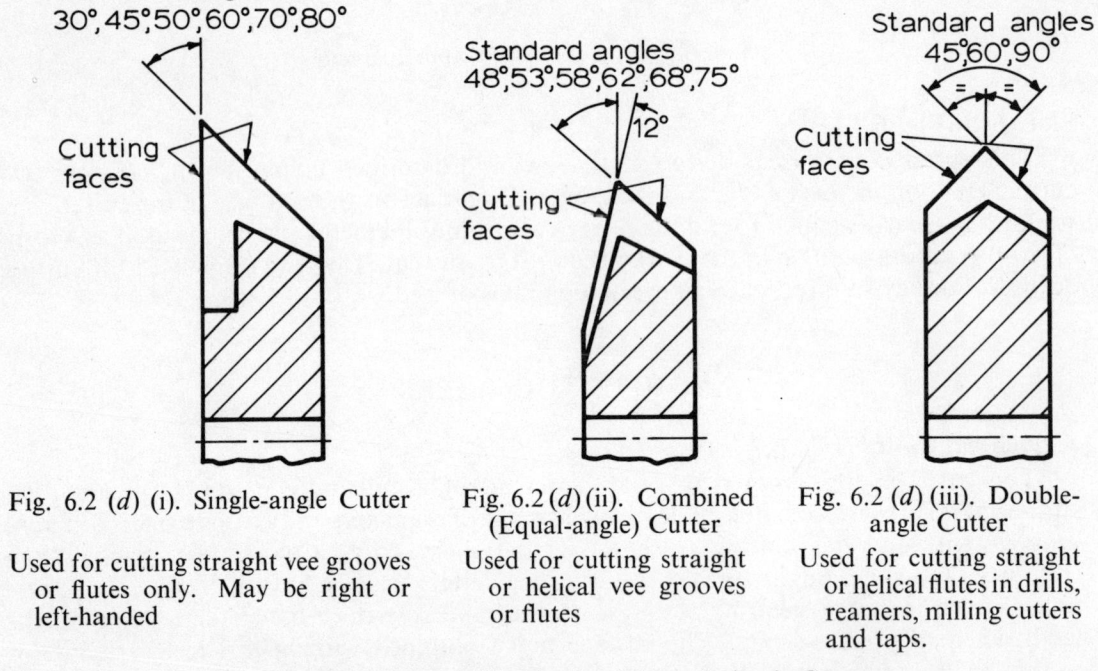

Used for cutting straight or helical flutes in drills, reamers, milling cutters and taps.

Fig. 6.2 (d) (i), (ii) and (iii). Section Through Angle Cutters

Shell End Mill (Fig. 6.2 (e))

As the name implies, these cutters are similar to end mills and perform the same work but on a larger scale. These cutters do not have an integral shank and are hollow so that they can be mounted on a stub arbor and are driven by a key in the arbor engaging in a slot cut across the rear face of the cutter.

Tee-slot Cutter (Fig. 6.2 (f))

This is a special cutter designed for finishing tee slots. It is rather like a small side and face cutter, attached to a shank by means of a small-diameter neck. The cutter has teeth on both sides as well as on the periphery.

Fig. 6.2 (a). Cylindrical Cutter

Fig. 6.2 (b). End Mill

Fig. 6.2 (c). Side and Face Cutter

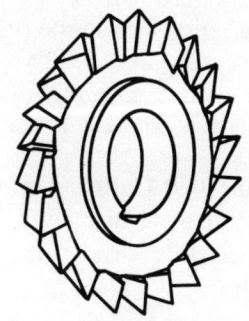

Fig. 6.2 (d). Single-angle Cutter

Fig. 6.2 (e). Shell End Mill

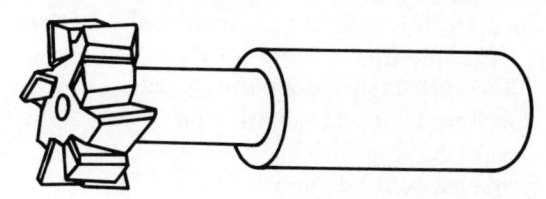

Fig. 6.2 (f). Tee-slot Cutter

Fig. 6.2 (g). Form Relieved Cutter

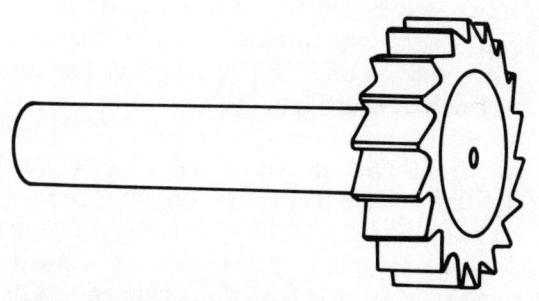

Fig. 6.2 (h). Woodruffe Key-seat Cutter

Fig. 6.2 (a) to (h). Milling Cutters

When a tee slot is produced, a side and face cutter first cuts a groove wide enough for the tee-bolt shank to fit in and of the correct depth. The tee-slot cutter then begins its cut from the end of the groove and undercuts each side of the groove to form a tee slot.

Form-relieved Cutters (Fig. 6.2 (*g*))

These cutters are given their tooth profile and relief angles on a relieving lathe and are the most expensive milling cutters. They are used to produce specially shaped workpieces with such features as concave or convex surfaces or even a combination of both, which could not be formed by the use of other cutters. A range of cutters with standard radii of both convex and concave form on the periphery are available, but other special shapes can be produced to order. Cutters used for gear cutting are of the form-relieved type. The shape produced on the work-piece is an exact negative copy of the profile of the cutter, and so great care must be taken in the manufacture and maintenance of the cutter, as any defects will be reproduced on the work-piece. The cutter illustrated at Fig. 6.2 (*g*) is a concave form-relieved cutter.

Woodruffe Key-seat Cutter (Fig. 6.2 (*h*))

This is a type of cutter which is specially manufactured for milling the keyways for standard Woodruffe keys. They are available in a standard range. It has teeth on the periphery only.

LATHE TOOLS

There are very many different kinds of lathe tools in use today. Illustrated at Fig. 6.3 (*a*)–(*h*), are some lathe tool holders and tools. Lathe tool holders are used to hold tool bits made from high-speed steel. As these tool bits are small they are relatively cheap to buy and can be discarded when worn or too small to grip in the holder.

Carbide-tipped lathe tools, of various shapes and sizes, are used today because they allow very high machining speeds. When the tip becomes damaged or worn it may be removed from the shank and a new one brazed in its place. Once tool holders and shanks have been obtained it is an easy and relatively cheap operation to replace the damaged tool bit or tip.

Knurling tools are used to emboss grooves on the surface of a work-piece so that handling is facilitated. The hardened knurling rollers are forced into the work so that the groove pattern on the rollers is reproduced on the work. The knurling tool illustrated (Fig. 6.3 (*e*)) has three pairs of rollers so that fine, medium, or coarse knurling can be obtained from one tool by selecting the appropriate rollers.

The Screwcutting tool shown has a circular cutter which may be adjusted vertically to suit the height of the work centre. The cutter has a hardened form ground thread and is easily removed, so that cutters of different thread forms may be mounted on the holder. This type of tool has a very long life, and will outlast many single-point screwcutting tools.

The Lathe Carriers shown at Fig. 6.3 (*g*) and (*h*) are clamped to the work-piece by means of the clamping screw and drive the work-piece when turning between centres. The tail of the straight lathe carrier butts against a stud on the catch plate of the lathe, and the tail of the bent-tail carrier engages in a slot in the catch plate. When the catch plate revolves it takes the carrier round with it, and so the work-piece is caused to rotate.

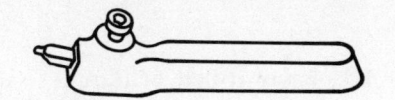

Fig. 6.3 (*a*). Right-hand Turning Tool

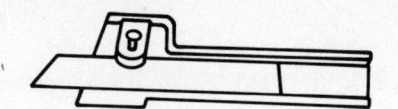

Fig. 6.3 (*b*). Parting-off Tool

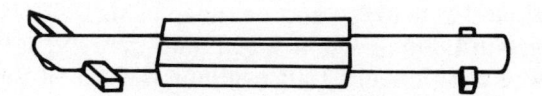

Fig. 6.3 (*c*). Boring Bar

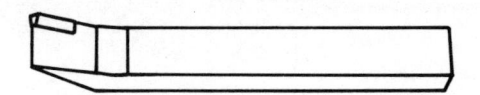

Fig. 6.3 (*d*). Carbide-tipped Lathe Tool

Fig. 6.3 (*g*). Straight Lathe Carrier

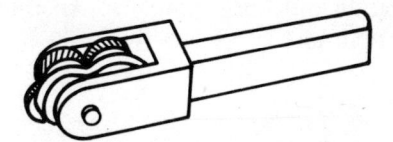

Fig. 6.3 (*e*). Knurling Tool

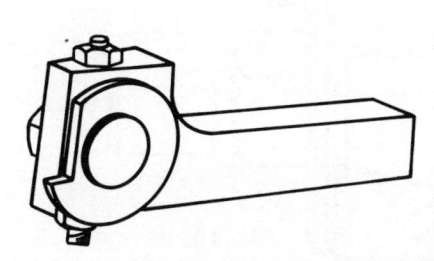

Fig. 6.3 (*f*). External Screwcutting Tool

Fig. 6.3 (*h*). Bent-tail Lathe Carrier

Fig. 6.3 (*a*) to (*h*). Lathe Tool Holders and Tools

MANDRELS

Mandrels are used for holding work which has already been drilled or bored, so that the outside diameter may be produced concentric with the drilled or bored hole in the centre. It is essential that the centre holes are in perfect alignment, as the accuracy of the running of the mandrel depends on this. The centre holes are recessed to avoid damage to the centres when the work is being fixed or taken off the mandrel.

Plain Mandrel (Fig. 6.4 (*a*))

This is the most common type of mandrel, and is made in a large range of sizes. They are usually made from a hardened and ground high-carbon steel, but may be left soft if required only for use on a single batch of components, thus enabling the size of the

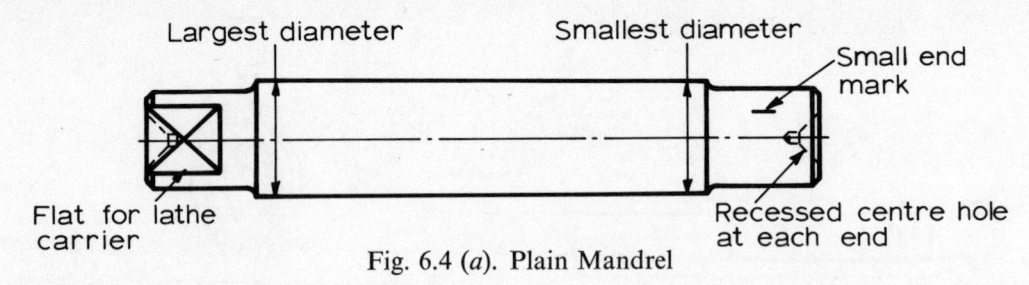

Fig. 6.4 (*a*). Plain Mandrel

mandrel to be altered to suit another batch of components. The smaller end is usually marked with a small dash (see drawing) for quick recognition. The component is loaded on to the mandrel, which is driven home by means of a mandrel press or a soft mallet. It is merely friction between the mandrel and the component which drives the component, so it is clear that heavy cuts may cause the component to slip on the mandrel. The disadvantage of this mandrel is that it will accommodate only one bore size, so that large stocks of mandrels are required where the bore sizes differ.

Gang or Screwed-collar Mandrel (Fig. 6.4 (*b*))

The loading, machining, and unloading of single components on a plain or stepped mandrel obviously takes time. It is far quicker to be able to load more than one component at a time on to the mandrel, and this type of mandrel achieves this aim. The components are loaded on to the parallel shank of the mandrel, and the loose collar and

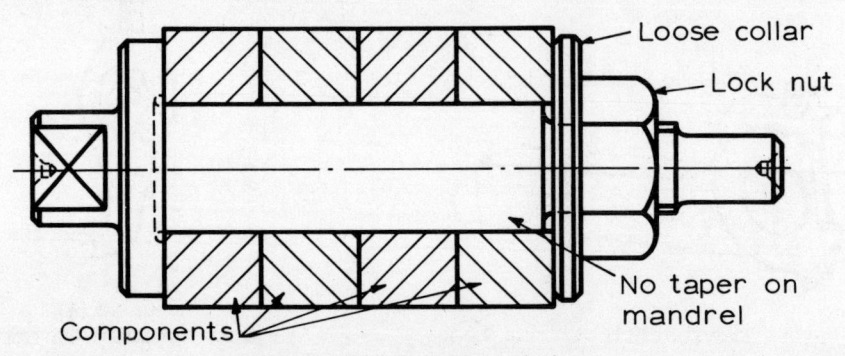

Fig. 6.4 (*b*). Gang Mandrel

nut are then put on. The components are then gripped between the shoulder on the mandrel and the loose collar, the shank of the mandrel serving only to provide a location for the components. The number of components which may be loaded on to the gang mandrel depends on the size and shape of the component only.

Expanding Mandrel (Fig. 6.4 (*c*))

The mandrels described previously have required that the bore of the component be held to reasonably close limits but, with the expanding mandrel, this is not necessary, although a reasonable standard of finish in the bore is required. With this mandrel the split bush with the tapered bore is inserted into the bore of the component. The tapered

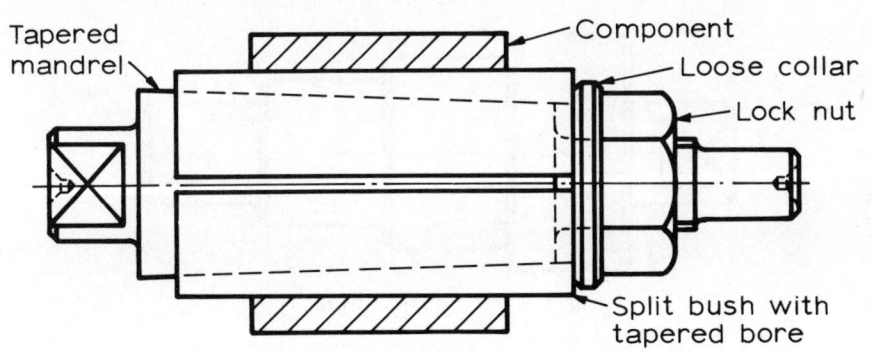

Fig. 6.4 (*c*). Expanding Mandrel

mandrel is fed into the split bush, the loose collar put on and the clamping nut tightened up. The action of tightening the nut forces the split bush farther on to the tapered mandrel, causing the bush to expand in diameter and grip the component. The bush will expand only a limited amount before gripping power is reduced owing to the bush becoming out of round, so it is usual to provide a series of split bushes with outside diameters to suit the range of work to be held.

Double-cone Mandrel (Fig. 6.4 (*d*))

Frequently components do not have a single-diameter bore, and this could mean the manufacture of special mandrels for each type of component. The use of the double-cone mandrel overcomes this problem, since each mandrel is capable of accommodating a wide range of machined bore diameters. The component automatically centralises itself on

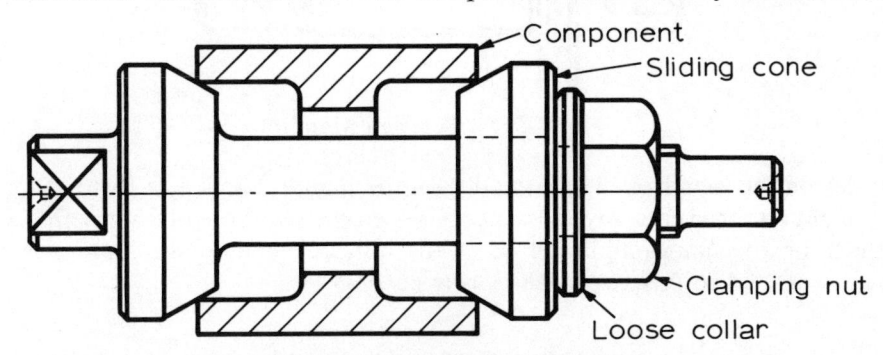

Fig. 6.4 (*d*). Double-cone Mandrel

Component centralises itself on cones when clamping nut is tightened up the two cones when the clamping nut is tightened up, and it does not matter if the locating machined diameters are of different sizes as long as they are concentric and the cones can accommodate their size. The disadvantage with this mandrel is that there is only line contact between the component and the cones, so that only light cuts can be accomplished, and often the edge of the locating diameters in contact with the cones becomes slightly burred.

Stepped Mandrel (Fig. 6.4 (*e*))

This is an attempt to reduce the number of mandrels required to accommodate a wide range of bore sizes, and is useful where lack of space or finance precludes the carrying of

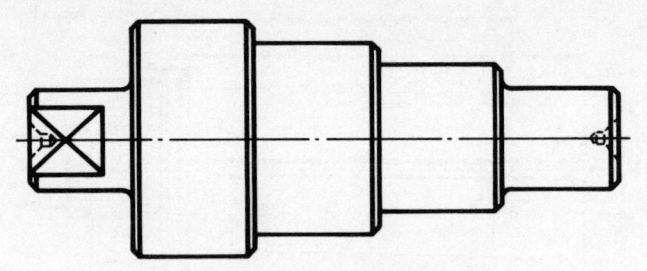

Fig. 6.4 (*e*). Stepped Mandrel

large stocks of tools. The steps are made to whatever diameters are required, and the number of steps on the mandrel may vary considerably; thus, stepped mandrels may replace plain mandrels.

Screwed Mandrels (Fig. 6.4 (*f*))

This type of mandrel is required when the bore of the component to be turned is threaded. The thread on the mandrel is the male counterpart to the female thread of the component. The component is screwed on to the mandrel until its end face butts against

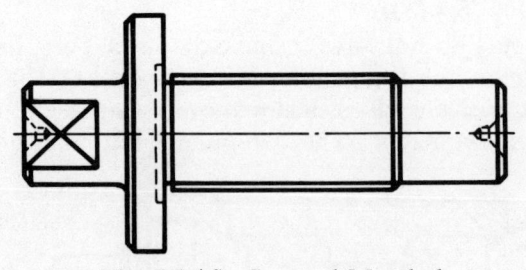

Fig. 6.4 (*f*). Screwed Mandrel

the shoulder on the mandrel. The shoulder on the mandrel acts as a form of lock-nut on the component and prevents any movement. When the component has a left-hand thread the shoulder on the mandrel should be at the tailstock end of the lathe, otherwise the component will tend to unscrew itself during cutting.

CHAPTER SEVEN
MARKING-OFF EQUIPMENT

Vernier Height Gauge (Fig. 7.1 (*a*))

The vernier allows the gauge to be set to any dimension with great accuracy. A chisel may be mounted on the gauge, as shown in the sketch, so that components may be marked out, or a dial gauge may be attached so that flatness or concentricity checks may be carried out on components. The sliding head may be readily moved up and down by releasing the locking screw and depressing the rapid-adjustment plungers. This method allows the head to be set approximately to the reading required, and then the fine-adjustment knob in the base is turned to obtain the exact reading.

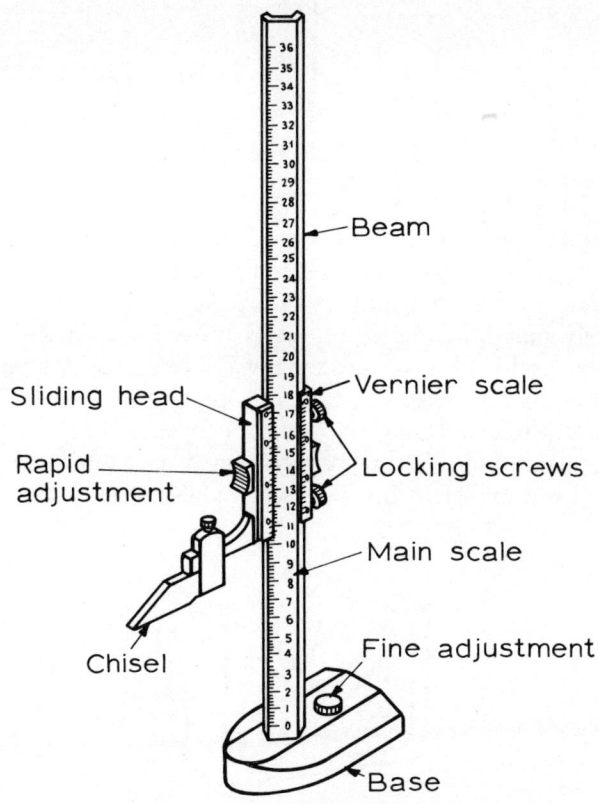

Fig. 7.1 (*a*). Vernier Height Gauge

Dial Gauge (Fig. 7.1 (*b*))

These are instruments fitted with dials for gauging in millimetres and parts of millimetres, but they may be used only to compare the variations in height of parts being checked. They are often used in setting up work accurately in the lathe, and can be used on concentricity checks to detect any out-of-roundness. Work set up on a sine bar may be checked for accuracy by running a dial gauge over the top face to check if it is level. The bezel may be rotated to 'zero' reading may be obtained as a datum point for future checks. Various sizes and shapes of buttons may be attached to the gauge to increase its range of usefulness.

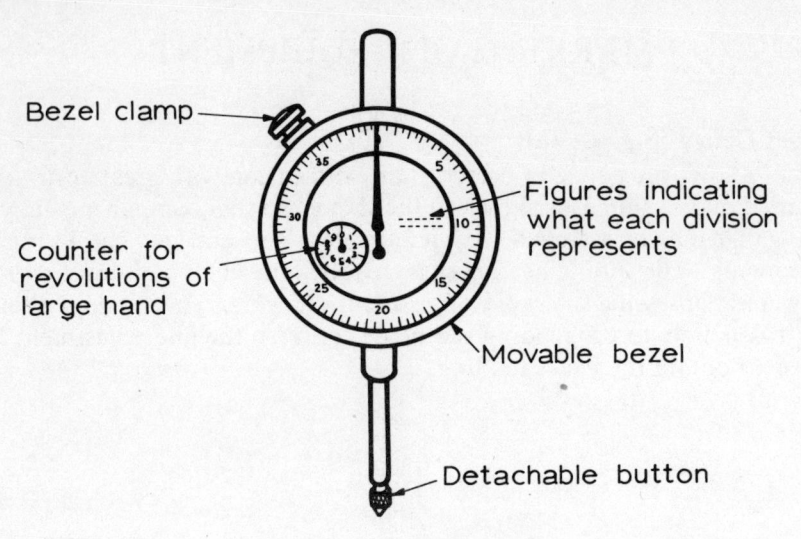

Fig. 7.1 (*b*). Dial Gauge

Vee Blocks (Fig. 7.1 (*c*))

These may be made from CAST IRON or STEEL, the latter being used mainly for the smaller sizes. Vee blocks and stirrups are used to grip round work when drilling at right angles to the work axis. When used for marking-out purposes they are usually used in pairs which have been accurately machined together. It is most important that 'vee' blocks which have been originally machined as a pair are always retained as a pair. Splitting of a pair may result in serious inaccuracies in marking out. Round work is often placed in vee blocks so that the end may be marked out for centre drilling or so that a keyway can be marked out. Concentricity checks can be performed on round components resting in vee blocks by rotating the component in the blocks while a dial gauge is in contact with the component.

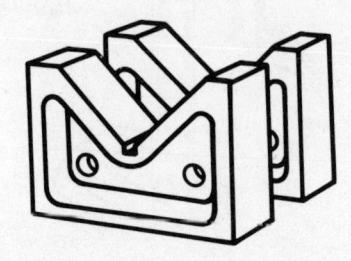

Fig. 7.1 (*c*). Pair of Cast-iron Vee Blocks

Surface Gauge (Fig. 7.1 (*d*))

This is often used for marking out, but is not as accurate as a vernier height gauge, although it is easier to handle. The curved end of the scriber is often used for checking

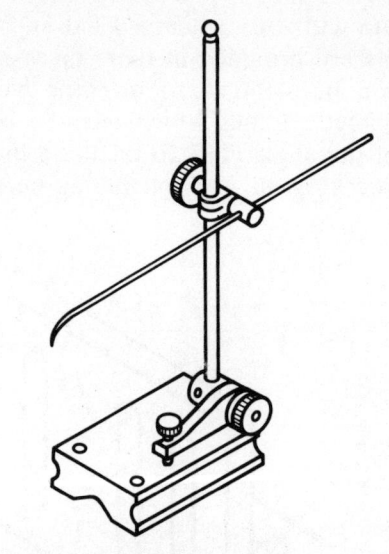

Fig. 7.1 (*d*). Surface Gauge

the true running of work in the lathe and for checking the flatness of surfaces when setting up.

Sine Bar (Fig. 7.1 (*e*))

This is a very simple device consisting of a hardened ground flat plate supported at each end by hardened rollers of identical diameter. These rollers are located a precise distance apart, which is chosen so as to simplify the trigonometry. When used with slip gauges and accurate trigonometrical tables, the sine bar can be set to measure shallow angles to an accuracy approaching 2 seconds of arc.

The sine bar should NOT be used to measure angles greater than 30° because it then tends to become unstable owing to the height of the slip blocks. Also the angular movement of the sine bar for a given change in the height of the slip blocks becomes too great for a high degree of accuracy to be maintained.

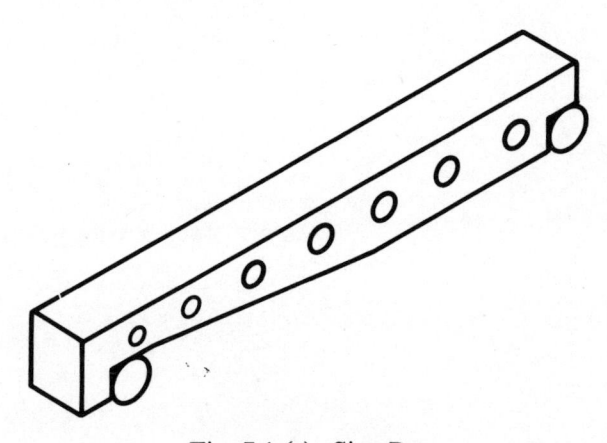

Fig. 7.1 (*e*). Sine Bar

Angle Plate (Fig. 7.1 (*f*))

This is a cast-iron plate with two machined flat surfaces located accurately at right angles to each other. Slots are provided in these faces so that work can be clamped to them so that the plate can be clamped to machine worktables after marking out or setting-up has been completed. Plates which have to be marked out can be held flat against the upright face of the angle plate to facilitate the marking out, and castings are often bolted to them for marking out and machining purposes.

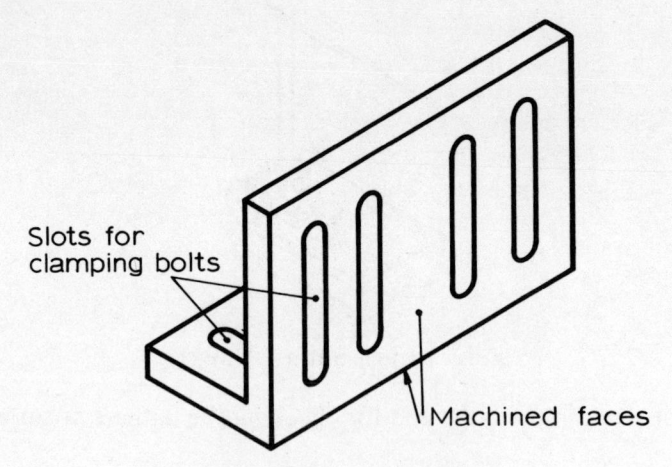

Fig. 7.1 (*f*). Angle Plate

CHAPTER EIGHT

LIMIT GAUGES

Limit gauges do not record the ACTUAL size of a component, but only whether the dimension being checked lies between specific limits of size. Limit gauges are thus extremely useful for checking mass-produced components, as no great skill in handling and no accurate readings are necessary; hence reduced gauging time and the possibility of employing unskilled personnel result. There are many types of limit gauges in use, but a selection of the main ones is shown below.

Snap or Gap Gauges (Fig. 8.1 (*a*), (*b*) and (*c*))

These are cheap and are easily made from gauge plate (ground flat stock), and after hardening are quite satisfactory for small dimensions. Large dimensions require a more sturdy gauge, and so cast or forged frames are used. These gauges are used for checking external dimensions and diameters and have the advantage that they can be used for checking work held between centres on a machine.

Separate 'GO' and 'NOT GO' gauges are sometimes used (Fig. 8.1 (*a*)), but it is usual to combine both 'GO' and 'NOT GO' dimensions on one gauge (Fig. 8.1 (*b*) and (*c*)). Care must be taken when using the gauge, as excessive force may distort the frame and so alter the gap between the jaws, which may result in the gauge accepting incorrect work.

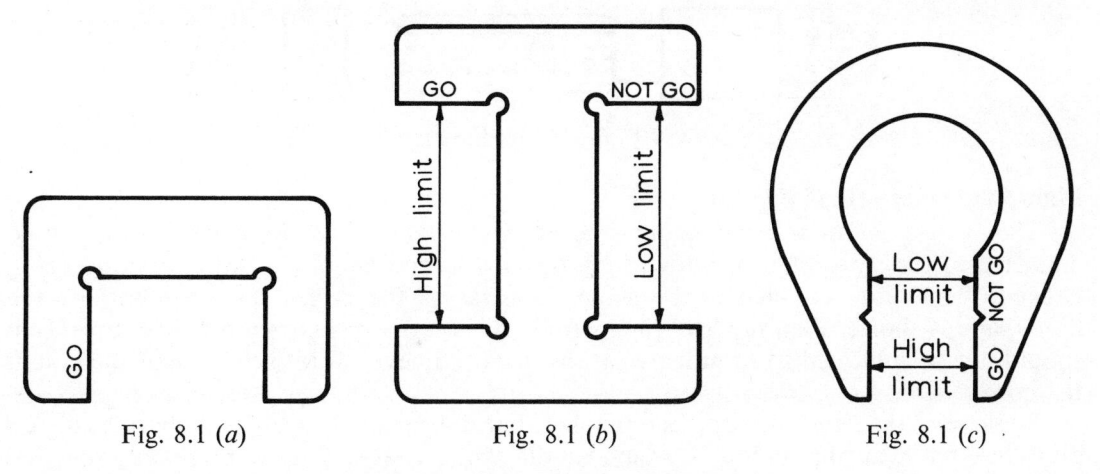

Fig. 8.1 (*a*) Fig. 8.1 (*b*) Fig. 8.1 (*c*)

Fig. 8.1 (*a*) to (*c*). Snap or Gap Gauges

Plate Depth Gauge (Fig. 8.1 (*d*))

This is a cheap and simple gauge made from gauge plate, and is used for checking the depths of slots, recesses, etc.

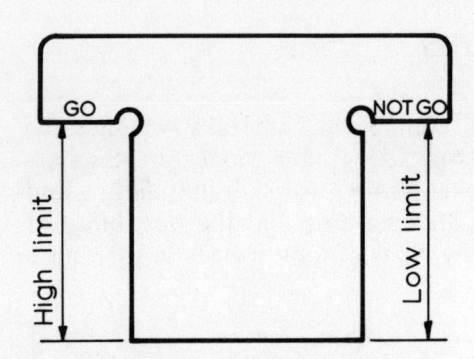

Fig. 8.1 (*d*). Plate Depth Gauge. 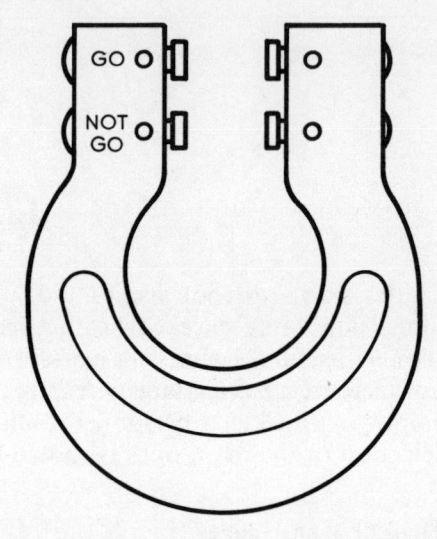 Fig. 8.1 (*e*). Adjustable Calliper Gauge

Adjustable Calliper Gauge (Fig. 8.1 (*e*))

This is used for the same purposes as the snap gauge, but is more robust and has adjustable anvils, so that the gauge may be used to check several different sizes after correct setting. The setting of the anvils may be altered by means of screw adjusters in the frame. After the anvils have been set to the correct dimensions in the standards room the adjusters are sealed to prevent unauthorised adjustment of the anvils.

Fig. 8.1 (*f*). Plain Plug Gauge

Plain Plug Gauge (Fig. 8.1 (*f*))

This gauge is used for gauging internal diameters. The 'GO' plug is the same diameter as the smallest hole allowed by the limits, and should fit into the hole being gauged. The 'NOT GO' plug is the same diameter as the largest hole allowed by the limits, and is shorter than the 'GO' plug, so that it is easily recognized and also because it should not be subjected to so much wear, as it should never fit into the hole if the hole is the correct size.

Sometimes the gauge is made in one piece, but the gauge illustrated has hardened steel plugs inserted in an aluminium or plastic handle, which enable plugs to be readily renewed when worn. This makes for a lighter and more easily handled gauge.

Plain Ring Gauge (Fig. 8.1 (*g*))

This is of simple design and is used as a 'GO' gauge for external diameters, as this gauge is NOT recommended for use as a 'NOT GO' type.

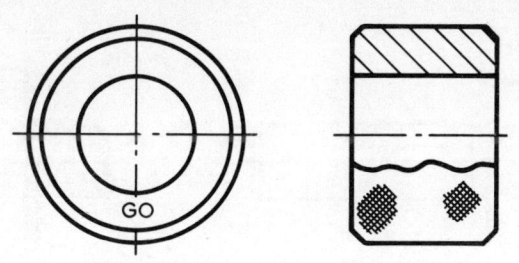

Fig. 8.1 (*g*). Plain Ring Gauge

Pin Gauge (Fig. 8.1 (*h*))

This again is of simple design and consists of a plain bar with conical ends. It is made of either tool steel or case-hardened mild steel, and is used for gauging large bores where a plug gauge would be clumsy and expensive.

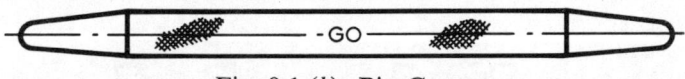

Fig. 8.1 (*h*). Pin Gauge

Bar Gauge (Fig. 8.1 (*j*))

This is used as a 'GO' and 'NOT GO' gauge for large internal diameters where a plug gauge would be very heavy and awkward to handle.

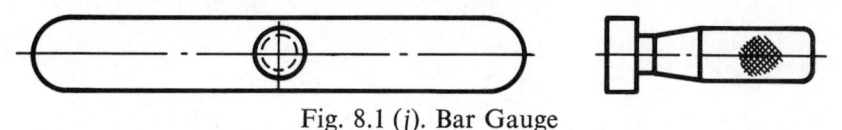

Fig. 8.1 (*j*). Bar Gauge

Plug Depth Gauge (Fig. 8.1 (*k*))

This gauge is similar to a plain plug gauge, except that it has two steps provided near the handle at specific distances from the leading face of the gauge. The diameter of this gauge is smaller than the smallest diameter of the acceptable hole, so that it should fit in all the holes it is to gauge. The hole is the correct depth when its surface lies between the two steps of the gauge.

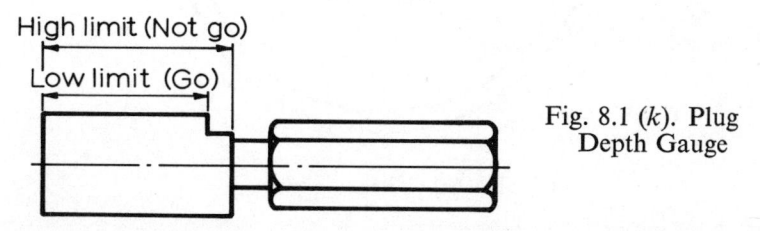

Fig. 8.1 (*k*). Plug Depth Gauge

Taper Plug Gauge (Fig. 8.1 (*l*))

This gauge checks a diameter at one end of a taper hole and also the angle of a taper. The diameter is checked by means of the two steps formed on the gauge. If the top face of the hole lies between the two steps, then the diameter is correct. If the gauge fits firmly into the tapered hole, then the angle of taper is correct but, if the gauge rocks in the hole, then the angle of the taper is incorrect, and the application of micrometer blue to the gauge will show where the fault lies.

Fig. 8.1 (*l*). Taper Plug Gauge

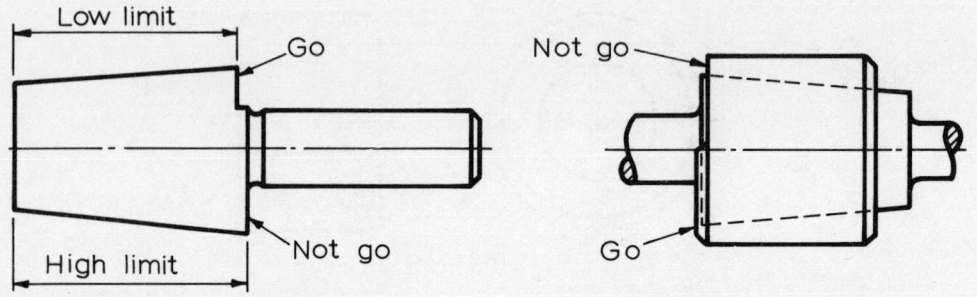

Fig. 8.1 (*m*). Taper Ring Gauge

Taper Ring Gauge (Fig. 8.1 (*m*))
This is used in a similar manner to the taper plug gauge, except that it is used to gauge male tapers. The end of the taper should lie between the two steps on the gauge if the size of the taper is correct.

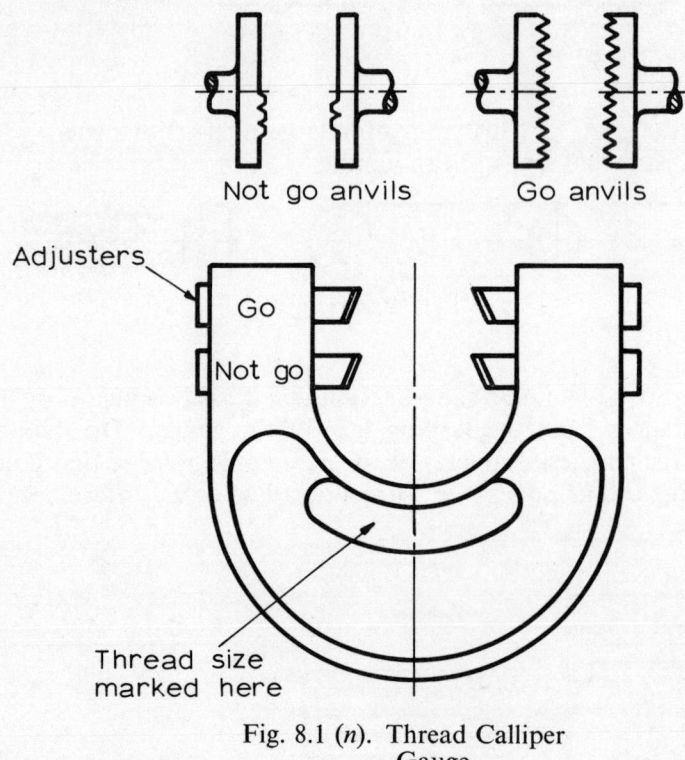

Fig. 8.1 (*n*). Thread Calliper Gauge

Thread Calliper Gauge (Fig. 8.1 (*n*))
This gauge resembles the adjustable calliper gauge, but the anvils are threaded and are used for checking external threads. The 'GO' anvils have the full form of thread on them, but the 'NOT GO' anvils have relieved threads, which check the effective diameter and which are only two or three pitches in length. To be acceptable, the component should pass through the 'GO' anvils but not through the 'NOT GO' anvils. Generally 'NOT GO' gauges should NOT be full-form.

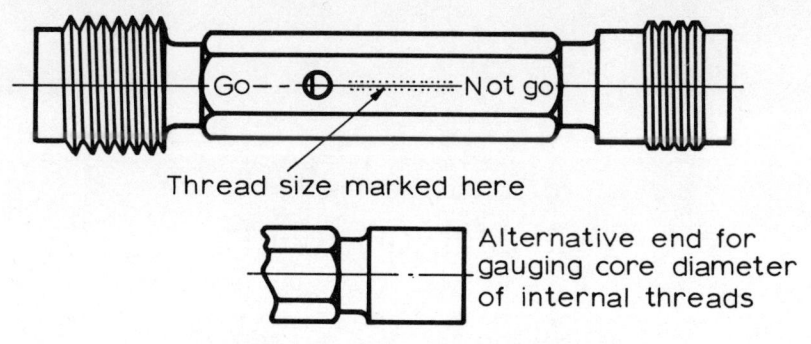

Fig. 8.1 (*o*). Thread Plug Gauge

Thread Plug Gauge (Fig. 8.1 (*o*))

This gauge is similar to the plain plug gauge, but may have 'GO' and 'NOT GO' ends, or both ends may be 'GO' or 'NOT GO'. Where the gauge has 'GO' and 'NOT GO' ends, these may be threaded or plain. The 'GO' threaded end is a full-form thread, and the 'NOT GO' thread is relieved to check the effective diameter and is only two or three pitches long. The plain 'GO' and 'NOT GO' plugs check the core diameter of the thread. Generally these gauges are similar to the plain plug gauges and usually have similar detachable ends and handles.

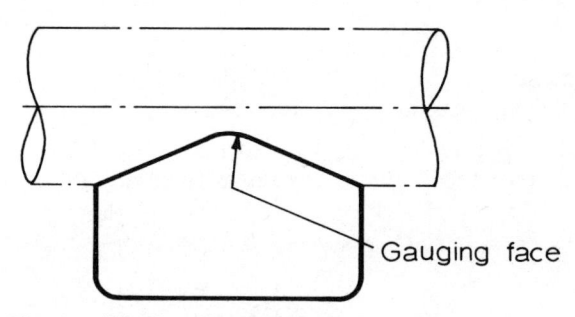

Fig. 8.1 (*p*). Profile or Template Gauge

Profile or Template Gauge (Fig. 8.1 (*p*))

This is generally made from gauge plate, one edge of which is made to the profile of the component. Feeler gauges may be used to check any variation in shape between the gauge and the component, or the gauge may be used in conjunction with a projector to check any errors in the component.

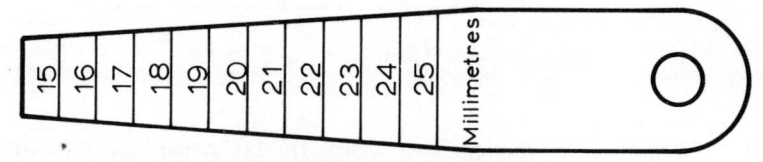

Fig. 8.1 (*q*). Taper Gauge

Taper Gauge (Fig. 8.1 (*q*))

This is used for measuring hole sizes, width of slots, and for setting callipers. The gauges are tapered strips of steel which have the width of the strip at certain points marked upon them. They are usually available in sets, like feeler gauges.

CHAPTER NINE

CLAMPING DEVICES

It is essential that, where clamps are used, they should clamp on to a solid section of the component which is also supported beneath the clamping point. Failure to do this may result in distortion of the component, and thus cause inaccurate machining. The clamp should be sufficiently strong so as not to bend under the clamping force, and it should be so arranged that the greater part of this force is used to hold the component in position.

The toe of the clamp should be RADIUSED, so that even if the clamp is not parallel to the machine table the gripping pressure is not affected. To prevent wear and marking of the clamping faces of the clamp it is preferable that the clamp be CASE-HARDENED to provide a hard, wear-resisting surface.

Common Plate Strap

Figs. 9.1 (*a*) and (*b*) show the COMMON PLATE STRAP which is widely used for clamping on all types of machine tools. Sometimes a spring is fitted beneath the clamp, as shown in Fig. 9.1 (*a*). This raises the clamp as the nut is released, and so prevents the bottom of the

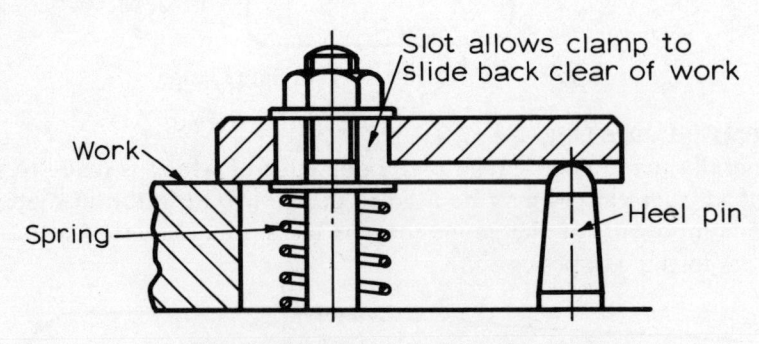

Fig. 9.1 (*a*). Common Plate Strap

clamp being fouled with any swarf which may be lying on the machine table. The clamping pressure may be obtained by the use of a nut and bolt, as shown in Fig. 9.1 (*a*), or by means of a cam, as shown in Fig. 9.1 (*b*). The cam is quicker-acting than the nut and bolt, but it is more expensive, and may tend to work loose under vibration unless properly designed. The heel pin may be of a fixed height or adjustable to suit the height of the clamping face on the work, but is often just a piece of rectangular steel bar.

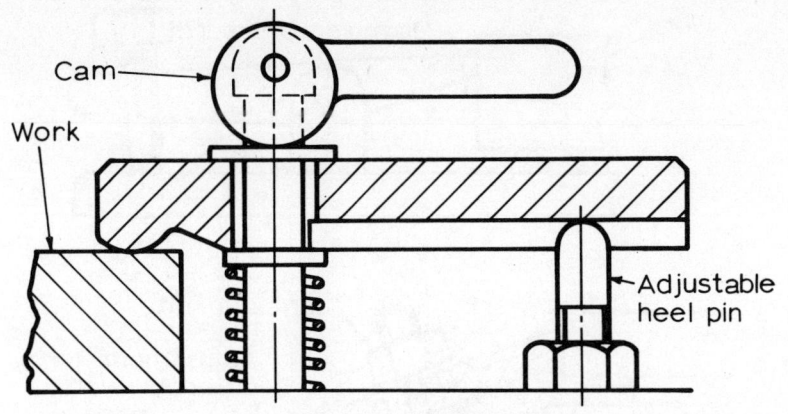

Fig. 9.1 (*b*). Common Plate Strap

Edge Clamps

Fig. 9.2 (*a*), (*b*), (*c*) and (*d*) show examples of EDGE CLAMPS which allow the whole top surface of the work to be machined. In each of these designs the clamping force acts sideways and downwards against a locating face. These clamps are often used on milling, shaping, and planing machines.

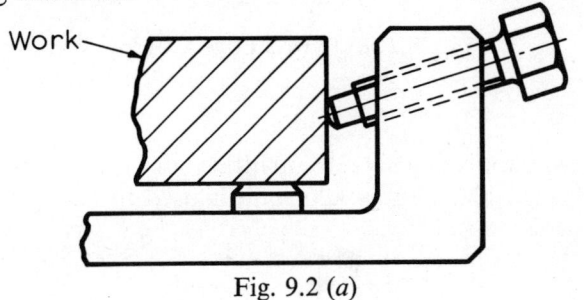

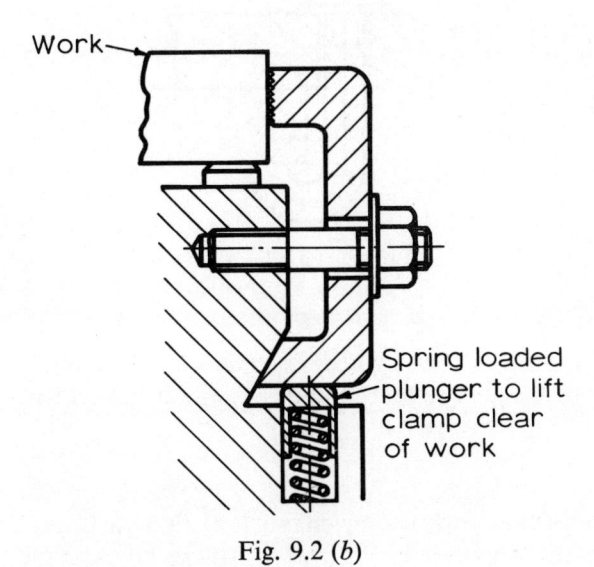

Fig. 9.2 (*a*)

Fig. 9.2 (*b*)

47

Fig. 9.2 (c)

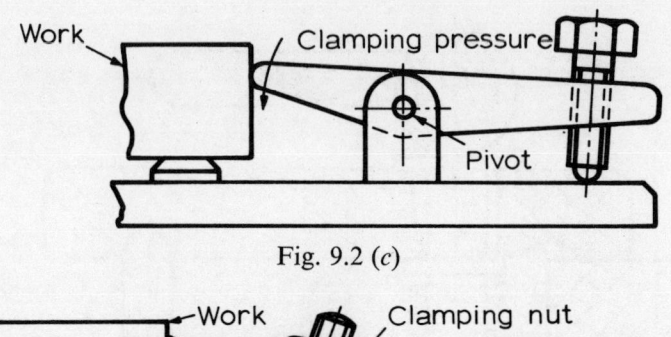

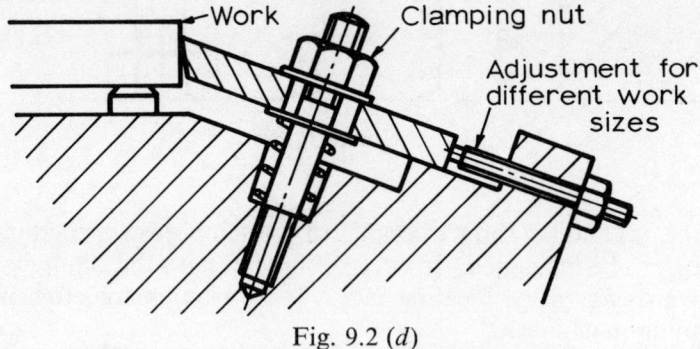

Fig. 9.2 (d)

Fig. 9.2 (a) to (d). Edge Clamps

Hook Bolt

Fig. 9.3 shows a HOOK BOLT, which takes up little room and is easy to manipulate, as the clamping nut is on the outside. This type of bolt is used to clamp loose plates to jigs or for securing door covers.

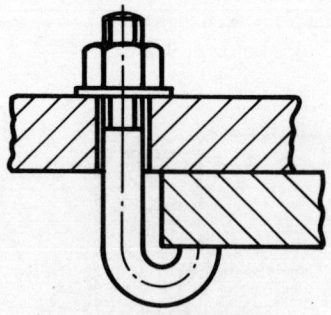

Fig. 9.3. Hook Bolt

Two-way Clamp

Fig. 9.4 shows a TWO-WAY CLAMP, which exerts both a horizontal and a vertical clamping force in one operation, thus saving loading time and the number of clamps required.

Equalising Clamps

Where the surface of the work is uneven, such as in a casting or a forging, the use of EQUALISING CLAMPS is recommended. Fig. 9.5 (a) shows an example of this type of clamp

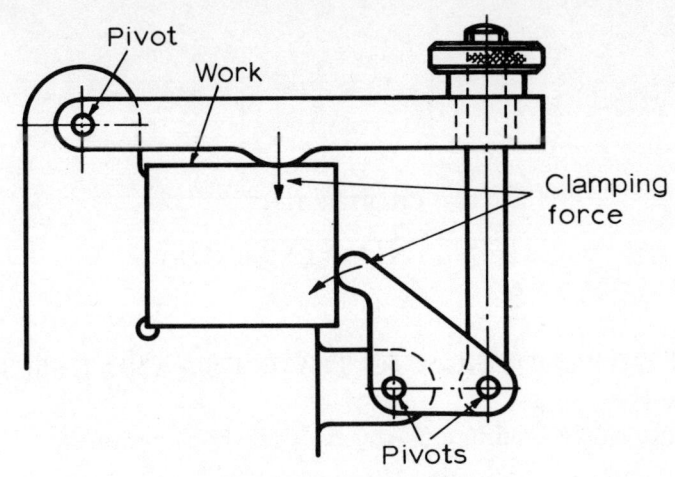

Fig. 9.4. Two-way Clamp

with a rounded pressure pad, which is in contact with the work and relieves bending stresses on the clamp bolts. The equalising clamp shown in Fig. 9.5 (b) may be used to grip two components as shown. Should the heights of the components vary slightly, the clamp will operate satisfactorily. This clamp may also be used on one component to distribute the clamping forces over a wider area or where the clamping surface is very rough.

Fig. 9.5 (a). Rounded Pressure Pad

Fig. 9.5 (b). Gripping Two Components

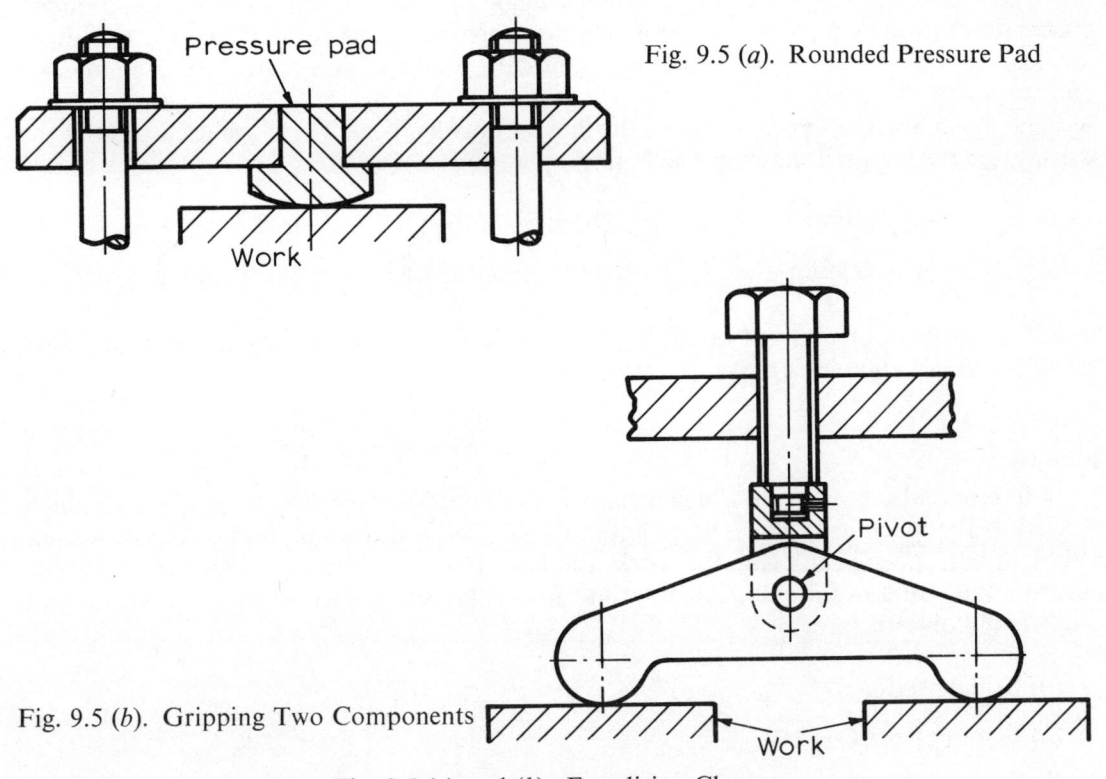

Fig. 9.5 (a) and (b). Equalising Clamps

CHAPTER TEN

JIGS AND FIXTURES

AN INTRODUCTION TO THEIR USE AND DESIGN

Jigs and fixtures are widely used in engineering workshops because:
  (a) They enable components to be produced more quickly and thus more cheaply.
  (b) They enable components to be produced with a constant accuracy which gives them greater interchangeability and saves time during subsequent assembly.
  (c) Production costs can be reduced because semi-skilled or even unskilled labour can be employed on machines when jigs or fixtures are used, without loss of accuracy in the finished product.

Jigs

A jig is a structure, plate, or box, usually made of metal, which holds the component, guides the cutting tools to the correct machining position on the component, and positively locates the component so that subsequent ones are produced in exactly the same manner and to exactly the same size.

The most common types of jig are drilling and boring jigs. These are used to hold the work-piece during the following machining operations:

| (a) Drilling | (c) Countersinking | (e) Spotfacing |
| (b) Reaming | (d) Counterboring | (f) Tapping. |

In all these operations, except tapping, the tool is accurately guided by the jig to produce results to an acceptable degree of accuracy.

Fixtures

A fixture is also a structure which usually is of heavier construction than a jig and which is fixed to the machine table. The essential difference between a jig and a fixture is that, although both positively locate the work, the fixture—unlike the jig—does NOT guide the cutting tools. Fixtures are used mainly on milling, grinding, and turning operations and are broadly divided into:

  (a) Milling fixtures

  (b) Planing fixtures

  (c) Splining fixtures.

JIGS

Template

Possibly the simplest form of jig is the well-known template which has many practical uses in the engineering workshop. It is essentially a flat plate made to a required shape, which is used to guide the cutting tools to the correct position for machining the component. The simple template shown at Fig. 10.1 (*a*) indicates how it locates the position of two holes which have to be drilled in the work-piece to which the template is attached.

Plate-type Jig

The plate-type jig, illustrated at Fig. 10.1 (*b*), is an improvement on the simpler template in that it carries drill bushes so that holes can be readily located and accurately drilled. In this illustration the work-piece has a central bore. Once this has been accurately machined the central pillar of the jig locates the work-piece in position so that subsequent machining operations can be accurately performed.

Box-type Jig

A typical box-type jig is shown at Fig. 10.1 (*c*), which illustrates how it can be used to enable holes to be drilled in the periphery of a cylindrical component. The cylindrical component is located in the central hole and secured in position by the clamping screw shown in the right face of the jig. The holes to be drilled in the work-piece are located in the various faces of the jig by the drill bushes shown. (Here only one drill bush is shown.) The jig is clamped to the worktable to secure it while drilling takes place. Burr grooves, opposite the drill bushes, must be provided in this type of jig to enable the work-piece to be withdrawn without damage after the holes have been drilled.

Swinging Arm Jig

Fig. 10.1 (*d*) shows a swinging arm jig which is so called because one side of what is virtually a box-type jig is hinged to enable it to be swung open and thus facilitate loading and unloading. The work-piece is located in the vee groove in the main body of the jig and the swinging arm is positioned over the work-piece and clamped in position by the eye-bolt and nut. When the hole in the work-piece has been drilled the retaining bolt is slacked off and the side folded back so that the work-piece can be easily removed. In this type of jig no burr grooves are needed.

Jig Bushes

The jig is required to guide the cutting tool so that it performs its machining operation in accordance with the specification. Drill jigs must, therefore, provide an acceptable means of guiding the drill and, at the same time, incorporate location and clamping devices. The usual way of guiding a drill is by means of a drill bush suitably incorporated in the jig. Drill bushes are broadly divided into the following categories:

(*a*) Headed drill bushes
(*b*) Headless drill bushes
(*c*) Special drill bushes
(*d*) Bushes used for light clamping
(*e*) Bushes providing depth control.

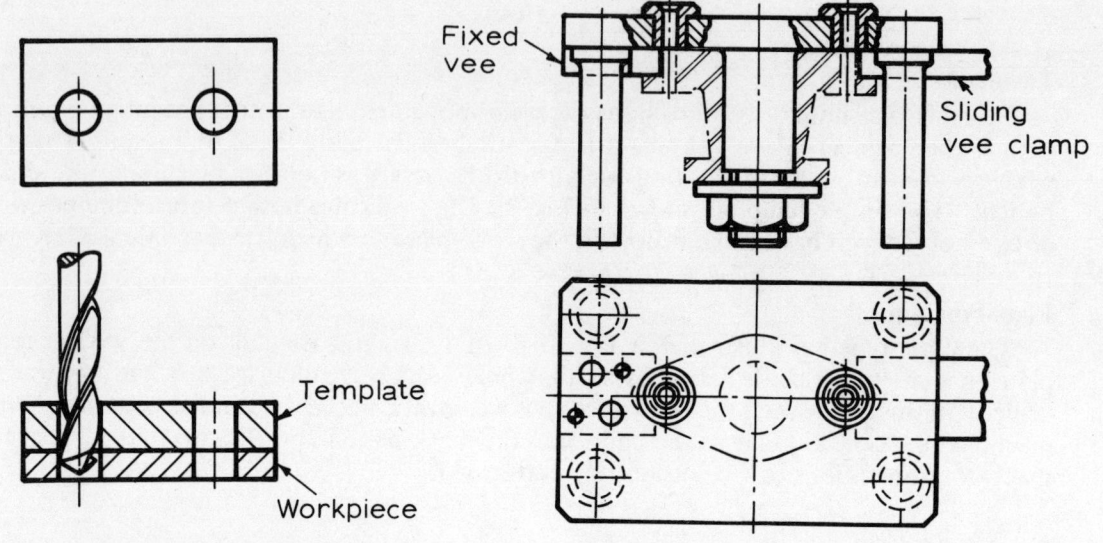

Fig. 10.1 (a). Template

Fig. 10.1 (b). Plate-type Jig

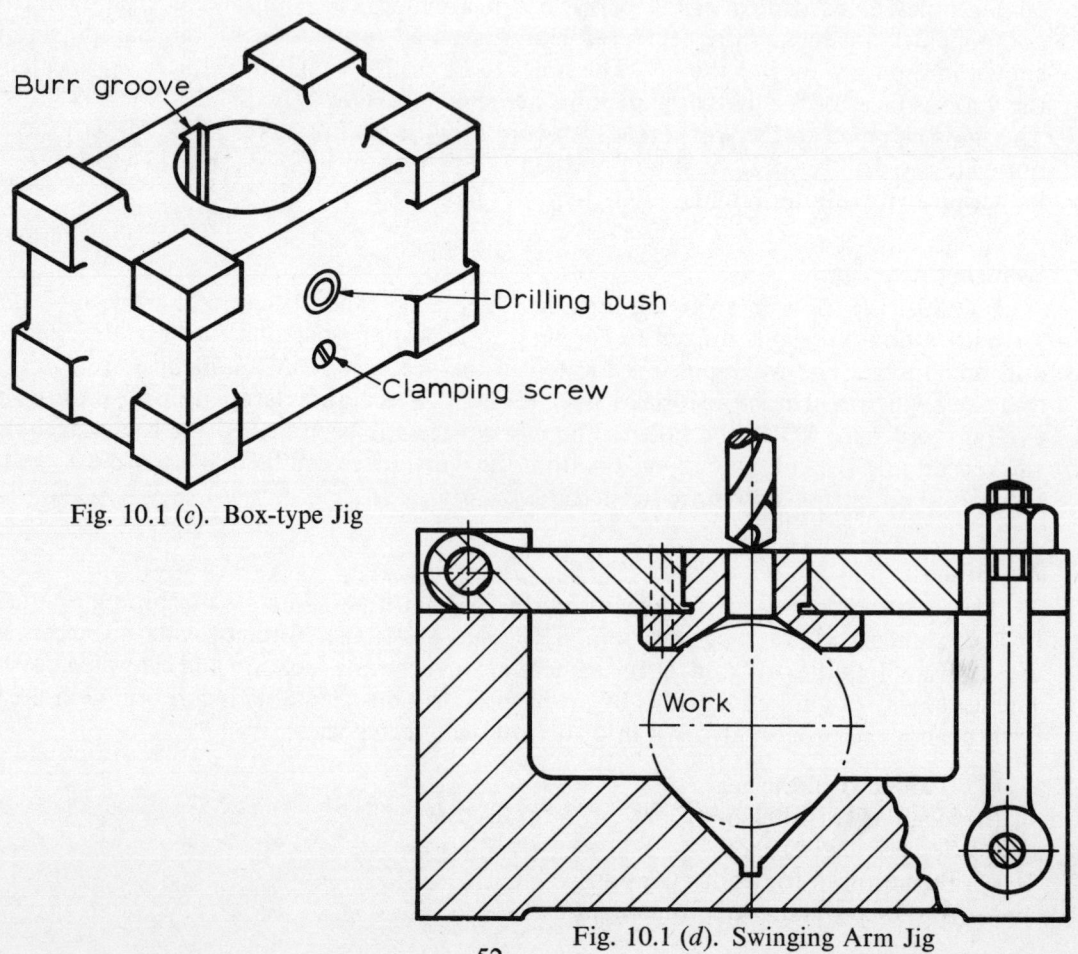

Fig. 10.1 (c). Box-type Jig

Fig. 10.1 (d). Swinging Arm Jig

52

Headed Drill Bushes

A headed drill bush must seat properly in the hole in the drill plate. This is usually accomplished by chamfering the hole in the drill plate and undercutting the head of the bush. A generous lead is provided and, in order to prevent swarf from becoming jammed between the drill plate and the work-piece, the bush is either placed close to the work-piece so that the swarf can escape only through the bush, as shown in Fig. 10.2 (*a*) or the bush is placed far enough away to allow the swarf to escape between it and the work-piece as shown in Fig. 10.2 (*b*).

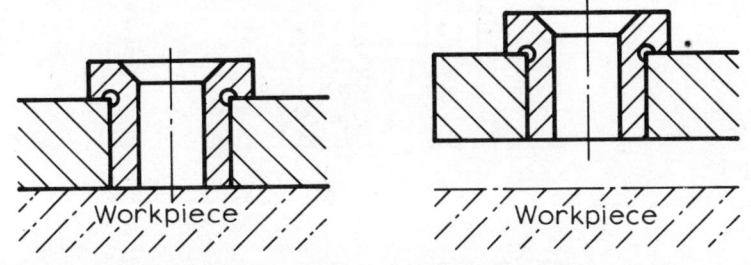

Fig. 10.2 (*a*) and (*b*). Headed Drill Bushes

Headless Drill Bushes

The headless drill bush, shown at Fig. 10.3, is often used as a liner bush for accommodating the headed-type bush. Should a hole be required which has two different diameters two headed bushes of different diameters would be inserted in turn in the headless liner bush.

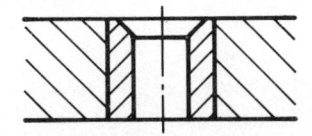

Fig. 10.3. Headless Drill Bush

Special Bushes

Special bushes are required for awkwardly shaped work-pieces, such as that shown at Fig. 10.4. Here an extended drill bush is required to guide the drill to the work-piece which is some distance below the drill plate. In these circumstances it would be usual to relieve the bore of the bush to reduce friction with the drill. This is shown in Fig. 10.4 where it is clear that only the end of the bush towards the work-piece controls the drill.

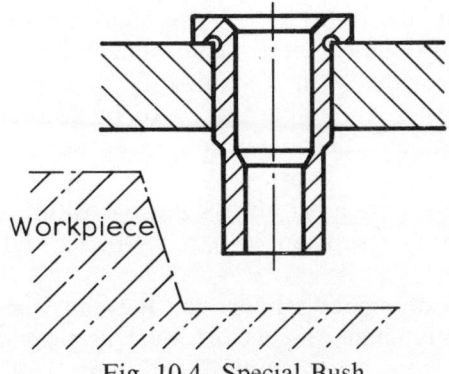

Fig. 10.4. Special Bush

Drill Bush Used for Light Clamping

In the example shown the axis of the drill bush is located positively, and it also lightly clamps the work-piece in the region of the cutting operation.

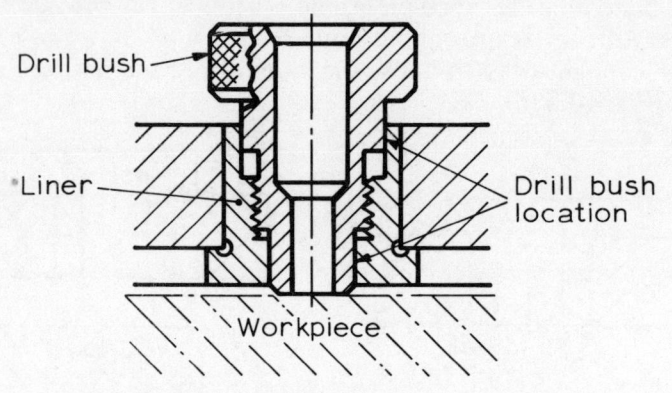

Fig. 10.5. Drill Bush Used for Light Clamping

The Design of Jigs

When a jig has to be designed various factors have to be considered of which the four listed below are possibly of major importance.

(a) The number and type of operations to be performed on the component.
(b) The best sequence for performing the required operations.
(c) The number of location points needed for the various operations.
(d) The clamping arrangements which will be needed to secure the work-piece firmly during each operation, preferably without moving the work-piece from its original position.

When these fundamental requirements have been decided there are still many practical considerations to be taken into account. These are listed below.

(a) The jig must be made as fool-proof as possible so that the operator cannot put the work-piece into the jig the wrong way round.
(b) The jig must be strong enough to withstand the pressure needed to secure the work-piece, yet it must be reasonably light in weight, rigid, and as compact as possible.
(c) Sharp corners should be avoided as they are areas where a concentration of stress could occur and, additionally, they might damage the surface of the work-piece.
(d) The jig should be provided with machined feet, on the surfaces opposite to those containing guide bushes, to enable the jig to be securely fixed to the drill table. Such feet not only cut down the area of contact of the jig with the worktable but they also facilitate the removal of swarf.
(e) Clamps used to secure a jig must always be so positioned that the pressure of the cutting tool is taken by a substantial part of the jig and is NOT against the clamp itself.
(f) The jig should provide sighting holes so that the operator can ensure that the work-piece is correctly sited, and means must be provided to enable swarf to be readily cleared both from the work-piece and from the jig itself.

(g) Quick-release clamps should be used whenever possible as this cuts down operating time with a consequent reduction in the cost of production.

(h) When jigs are large and cumbersome they should be provided with handles so that the operator may handle them more readily.

(j) Before a jig is put to use in the production shop it must always be checked most carefully to ensure that it will enable the various operations to be performed within the desired limits of accuracy.

FIXTURES

Fixtures may be broadly classified as follows:

(a) Those which hold a single component and locate it for single operations.

(b) Multiple fixtures for holding a row of components.

(c) Fixtures in which the component can be located in different positions for different operations.

When designing milling or other fixtures care must be taken to ensure that they can be easily loaded or unloaded, that the operator cannot get the work-piece in an incorrect position and that the fixture is as open as possible so that the operator can see and check each operation as it progresses and clear away swarf without difficulty.

CHAPTER ELEVEN

DEVELOPMENT OF SURFACES

During the first year the student was introduced to the need for developing the surfaces of well-known geometrical objects, to determine the shape which should be marked out on sheet metal so that, when bent into shape, it would produce the geometrical object desired. The objects dealt with in Volume I were relatively easy. Those that follow, although more complex, are still capable of being dealt with by a series of logical steps. All the developments shown should be familiar to mechanical-engineering technicians who have had two or more years' experience in an engineering workshop. The dimensions chosen for various developments which follow are appropriate to an A2 size drawing board. Students should construct each development as an exercise, following closely the series of steps given for each.

In many of the developments which follow it will be found that TRUE LENGTHS OF LINES are required to develop the true shape. The student must learn to recognise them on drawings and the methods of obtaining them. Let us now consider a few examples.

To Obtain the True Length of a Line Parallel to the Vertical Plane and Inclined to the Horizontal Plane (Fig. 11.1 (*a*))

1. The projection of the given line AB is clearly seen to be A_1B_1 on the horizontal plane. This is LESS than AB.
2. The projection of the given line AB on the vertical plane is A_2B_2.
3. It can be seen that the line A_2B_2 is the SAME length as the given line AB. Thus A_2B_2 is the TRUE length of the line AB.

Therefore when the line is parallel to the vertical plane THE PROJECTION OF IT ON THIS PLANE GIVES THE TRUE LENGTH.

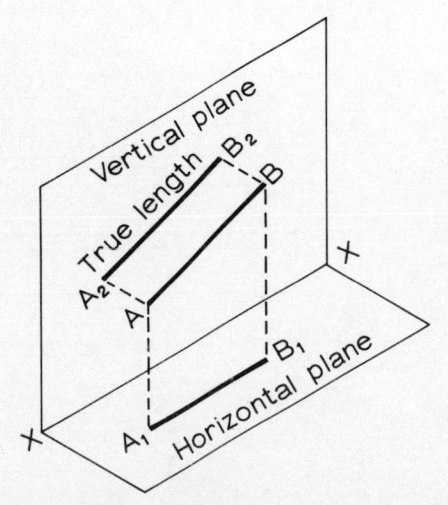

Fig. 11.1 (*a*). Obtaining a True Length (i)

To Obtain the True Length of a Line Inclined to the Vertical Plane and Parallel to the Horizontal Plane (Fig. 11.1 (b))

1. AB represents the given line inclined to the vertical plane and parallel to the horizontal plane.
2. A_2B_2 is the projection of the given line on the vertical plane. It can be seen that it is LESS than the length of AB.
3. A_1B_1 is the projection of the given line AB on the horizontal plane. It can be seen that it is EQUAL in length to the given line AB. Thus A_1B_1 is the TRUE length of the line AB.

Therefore when a line is parallel to the horizontal plane THE PROJECTION ON THAT PLANE GIVES THE TRUE LENGTH.

In general, the projection of a line on a plane parallel to it ALWAYS gives the TRUE LENGTH of the line.

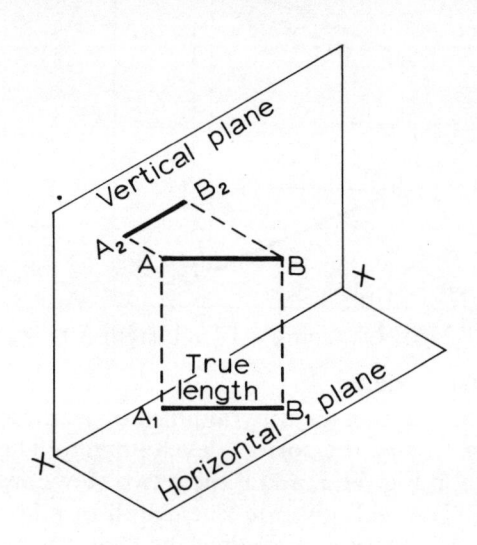

Fig. 11.1 (b). Obtaining a True Length (ii)

To Obtain the True Length of a Line Which Is Inclined to All Three Planes of Projection (Fig. 11.2 (a) and (b))

We were lucky in the two previous examples because the line whose true length we required happened to be parallel to ONE of the planes of projection. It often happens that we need to find the true length of a line which is inclined to ALL THREE planes of projection. A ready example would be the true length of the longest rod which could be put into a rectangular box. Here the length required is that of the transverse diagonal, which is inclined to all three 'sides' or 'planes' of the box. Let AB (Fig. 11.2 (a)) be the straight line inclined to all three planes of projection. For convenience we will deal only with its projections on the Vertical and Horizontal planes.

1. Project AB to A_2B_2 on the vertical plane.
2. Project AB to A_1B_1 on the horizontal plane.
   NOTE that neither A_1B_1 nor A_2B_2 is a TRUE length.

To find the TRUE length proceed as follows (Fig. 11.2 (b)).
3. Draw the projection on the vertical plane at A_2B_2 above XX.
4. Draw below it the projection A_1B_1 on the horizontal plane below XX.
   NOTE that A_1 is vertically below A_2 and B_1 is vertically below B_2.

5. With centre A_1 and radius A_1B_1 draw an arc.
6. Through A_1 draw a straight line parallel to XX to cut this arc at D.
7. Through B_2 draw a horizontal line parallel to XX.
8. Through D erect a perpendicular to cut the horizontal through B_2 at B.

A_2B is the TRUE LENGTH of the line whose projections on the vertical and horizontal planes are A_2B_2 and A_1B_1 respectively.

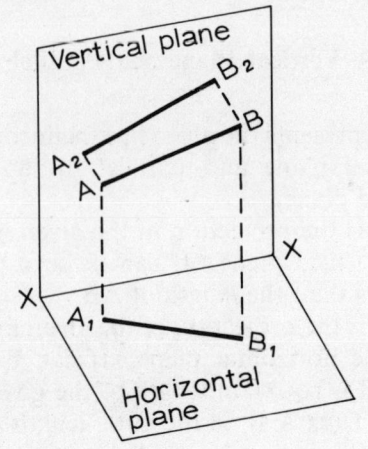

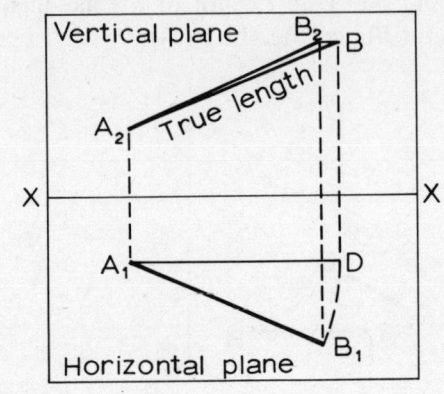

Fig. 11.2 (*a*). Obtaining a True Length (i)   Fig. 11.2 (*b*). Obtaining a True Length (ii)

To Obtain the True Lengths of the Sides of a Square Pyramid

Students are very often required to develop the surfaces of a pyramid and, in these problems, the TRUE LENGTH of lines must be found to give the correct development. The elevation and plan views are usually given as shown in Fig. 11.3, and if these two views are studied it can be clearly seen that neither of these views will give the true length of a line from the base corners to the apex of the pyramid. The method of finding the true lengths is as follows:

1. OA is the projection of the side in the vertical plane.
2. O_1A_1 is the projection of the side in the horizontal plane.
3. With centre O_1 and radius O_1A_1 draw an arc, to give point A_2 such that O_1A_2 is horizontal.
4. Project A_2 vertically to give point A_3 on the vertical plane such that AA_3 is horizontal.
5. Join O to A_3.

OA_3 is the TRUE length of the side.

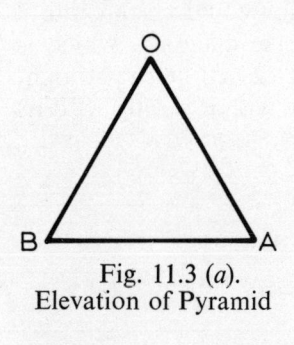

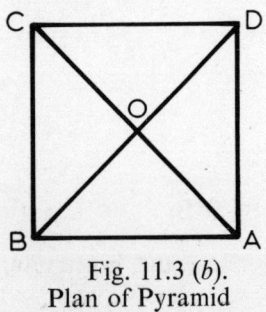

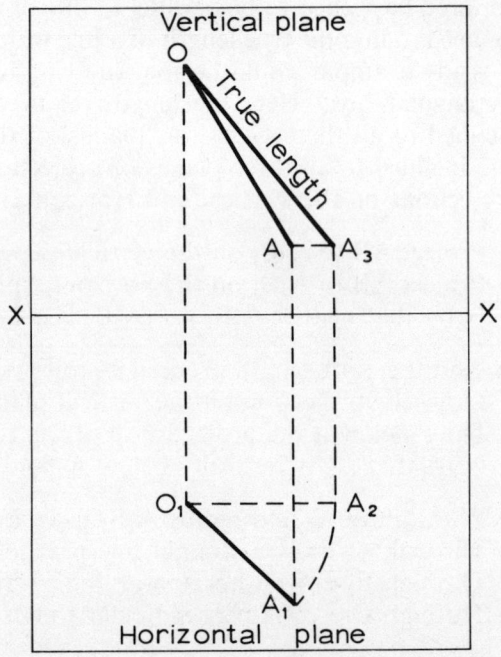

Fig. 11.3 (*a*). Elevation of Pyramid

Fig. 11.3 (*b*). Plan of Pyramid

Fig. 11.3 (*c*). True Length of Sloping Side of a Square Pyramid

DEVELOPMENT OF THE CURVED SURFACE OF AN OBLIQUE CONE

An oblique cone is a solid figure with a circular base tapering to an apex which does NOT lie directly above the centre point of the circular base. In other words, the cone leans over to one side as shown in Fig. 11.4 (a). Note that in Fig. 11.4 (a) the long axis of the cone through the apex is parallel to the vertical plane.

In order to develop the surface of an oblique cone we must obtain the true lengths of straight lines drawn on the curved surface of the cone from the apex to the base. Note that, since the axis of the cone is parallel to the VERTICAL plane the bounding lines Oa and Ob, which also are parallel to the vertical plane, are TRUE LENGTHS. No other lines drawn from the apex to the base appear as true lengths on either the elevation or the plan. Let Oc, in Fig. 11.4 (b), be any straight line drawn from the apex O to meet the base of the cone in the point c. Clearly Oc is inclined to both the vertical and the horizontal planes so that neither Oc nor O'c' can be true lengths.

To obtain the TRUE LENGTH of Oc we proceed as follows:
1. Draw the front elevation and half-plan as shown in Fig. 11.4 (b).
2. With centre O' and radius O'c' describe an arc to cut a'O' at d'.
3. Project d' vertically upwards to cut ab produced at d.
4. Join Od. Then Od is the TRUE LENGTH of the line Oc.

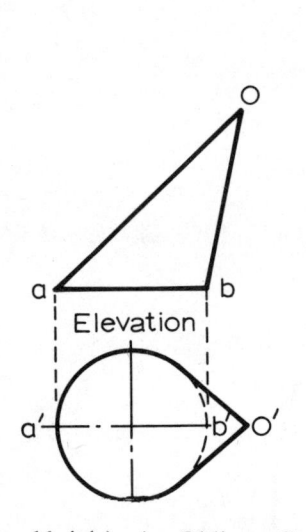

Fig. 11.4 (a). An Oblique Cone

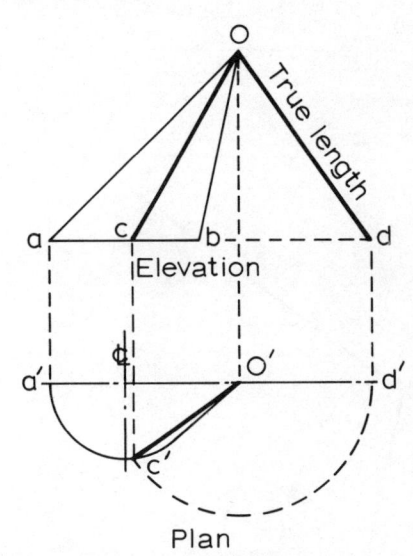

Fig. 11.4 (b). To Find True Length

In order to obtain the development of the curved surface of the oblique cone we must know the true lengths of a sufficient number of the 'generating' lines, as lines such as Oc are called, to enable the curved surface to be 'opened out'.

We proceed as follows (see Fig. 11.5 (a) and (b)):

1. Draw the front elevation and half-plan of the base of the cone (Fig. 11.5 (a)).
2. Divide the half-plan of the base of the cone into six equal parts, and number as shown.
3. Drop a perpendicular from the apex of the cone O to the horizontal base line produced, and mark the intersection point A. Join A2', A3', A4', A5', and A6' on the half-plan.

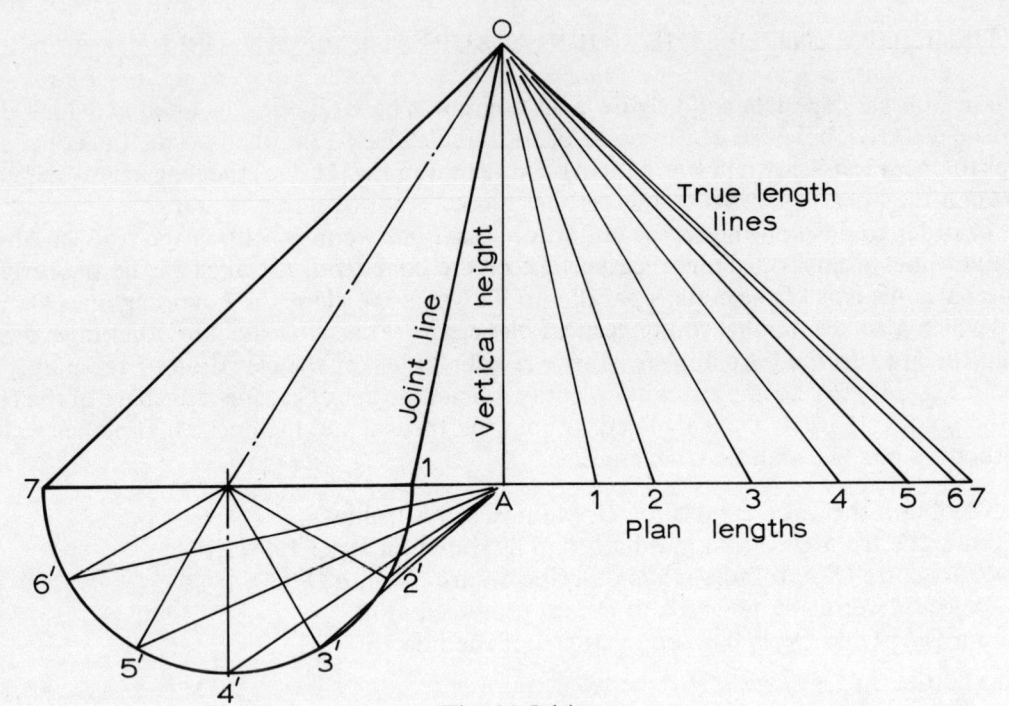

Fig. 11.5 (*a*)

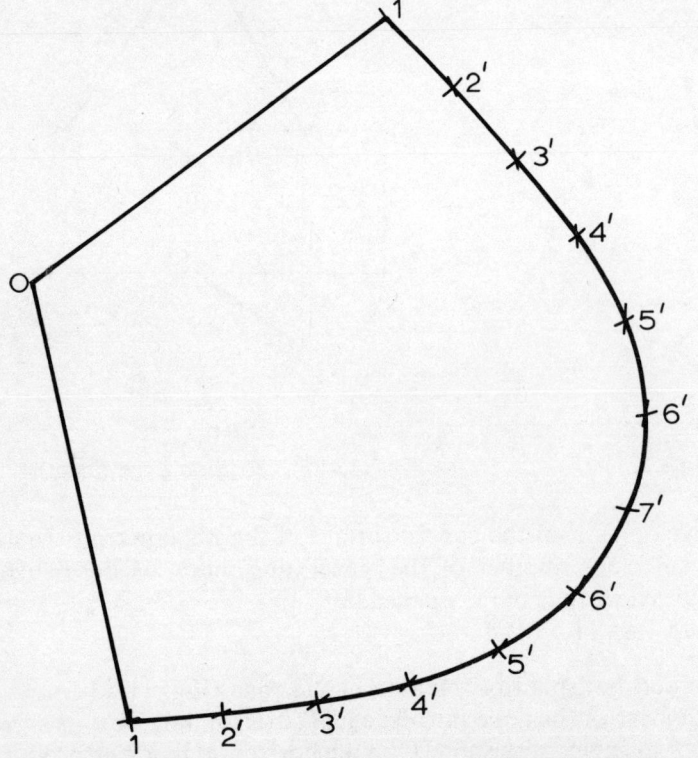

Fig. 11.5 (*b*). Development

4. Obtain the TRUE lengths of lines A1 to A7 by the method previously described.
5. To start the development draw a line equal to the TRUE length of O1 and mark the ends 0 and 1 (Fig. 11.5 (b)).
6. With centre 1 draw an arc of radius equal to the chordal distance 1–2′ on the half-plan.
7. With centre O draw an intersecting arc of radius equal to the TRUE length of line O2. The intersection of these arcs gives the point 2′ on the development.
8. In a similar way repeat steps 6 and 7 to obtain the other points.
9. Join these points by a smooth curve. This is the development of one half of the curved surface.
10. To complete the full development construct on O7′ a mirror image of the area O12′ ... 6′7′O. Then the area O17′1O is the REQUIRED DEVELOPMENT.

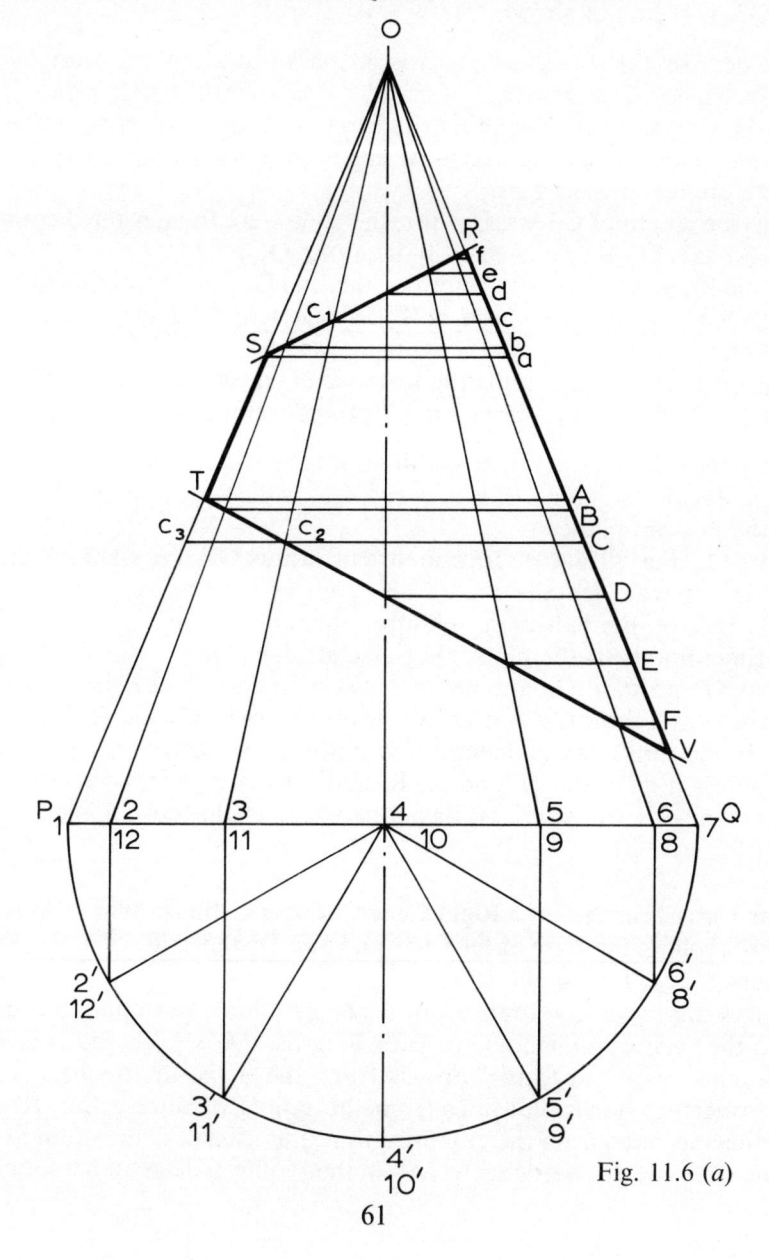

Fig. 11.6 (a)

To develop the Curved Surface of the Frustum of a Right Cone Which Is Cut by Two Planes, Both of Which Are at Right Angles to the Vertical Plane but Inclined at Different Angles to the Horizontal Plane (Fig. 11.6 (*a*) and (*b*))

Let VRST (Fig. 11.6 (*a*)) be the frustum of the right cone whose development is required. SR and VT are the traces of the cutting planes.

1. Complete the full outline of the original cone OPQ by fine lines (Fig. 11.6 (*a*)).
2. On the base PQ draw a half-plan of the cone.
3. Divide the half-plan into six equal parts and number them as shown.
4. Project the points 2′, 3′, 4′, 5′, etc., vertically to cut the base PQ at 2, 3, 4, 5, etc., respectively.
5. Join O2, O3, O4, etc., as shown.

In order to develop the surface of the frustum we must know the TRUE lengths of lines on the curved surface of the frustum. Consider one such line O3, which intersects the cutting planes at c_1 and c_2. We need the true length of c_1c_2. This presents no problem for a right cone, for we know that the bounding edges OP and OQ are parallel to the vertical plane and therefore are true lengths.

Clearly the true length of O3 is OQ, for if the cone were to be rotated counterclockwise about its vertical axis O3 would eventually lie along OQ.

In exactly the same way the true length of the line Oc_2 can be obtained by completing the right cone Oc_3C. Oc_3 and OC are both the true length of Oc_2. Similarly, O*c* is the true length of Oc_1.

Hence the TRUE LENGTH of c_1c_2 is the distance *c*C measured along OQ.

We are now in a position to carry on with the development.

6. Where the lines O2, O3, etc., intersect the traces of the cutting planes draw horizontal lines to meet OQ in the points *a, b, c, d, e, f*, R, for the upper plane, and A, B, C, D, E, F, V for the bottom plane.
7. With centre O, (Fig. 11.6 (*b*)), draw an arc of radius OP, the slant height of the cone.
8. Mark off the chordal lengths 1–2′, 2′–3′, etc., as shown, each equal to the lengths 1–2′, 2′–3′, etc., on the half-plan. Number them as shown.
9. Join ALL these points to the point O by fine straight lines.
10. With centre O and radii O*a* and OA draw arcs to cut O1 at *a* and A respectively.
11. With centre O and radii O*b* and OB draw arcs to cut O2′ and O12′ at *b* and B.
12. Continue in the same way and step off two points on each of the other lines.
13. Join the points *a, b, c, d, e, f*, and A, B, C, D, E, F by a smooth curve and join *a*A by straight lines as shown. The enclosed space is the development of the curved surface of the frustum.

To Develop the Curved Surface of a Right Cone Cut by a Cylinder Whose Axis is Horizontal and at a height 'h' above the Base of the Cone and at a Distance 'd' from the Vertical Centre Line of the Cone (Fig. 11.7 (*a*) and (*b*))

In the last example we saw that, when dealing with a right cone, the bounding lines are parallel to the vertical plane and are TRUE lengths. Moreover, the TRUE length of any 'generator' or part of a 'generator' drawn from the apex to the base can always be obtained by projecting horizontal lines from the points of intersection to the bounding lines of the cone and measuring the TRUE length required ALONG the bounding line.

We shall need to use TRUE lengths to obtain the required development, but these can be

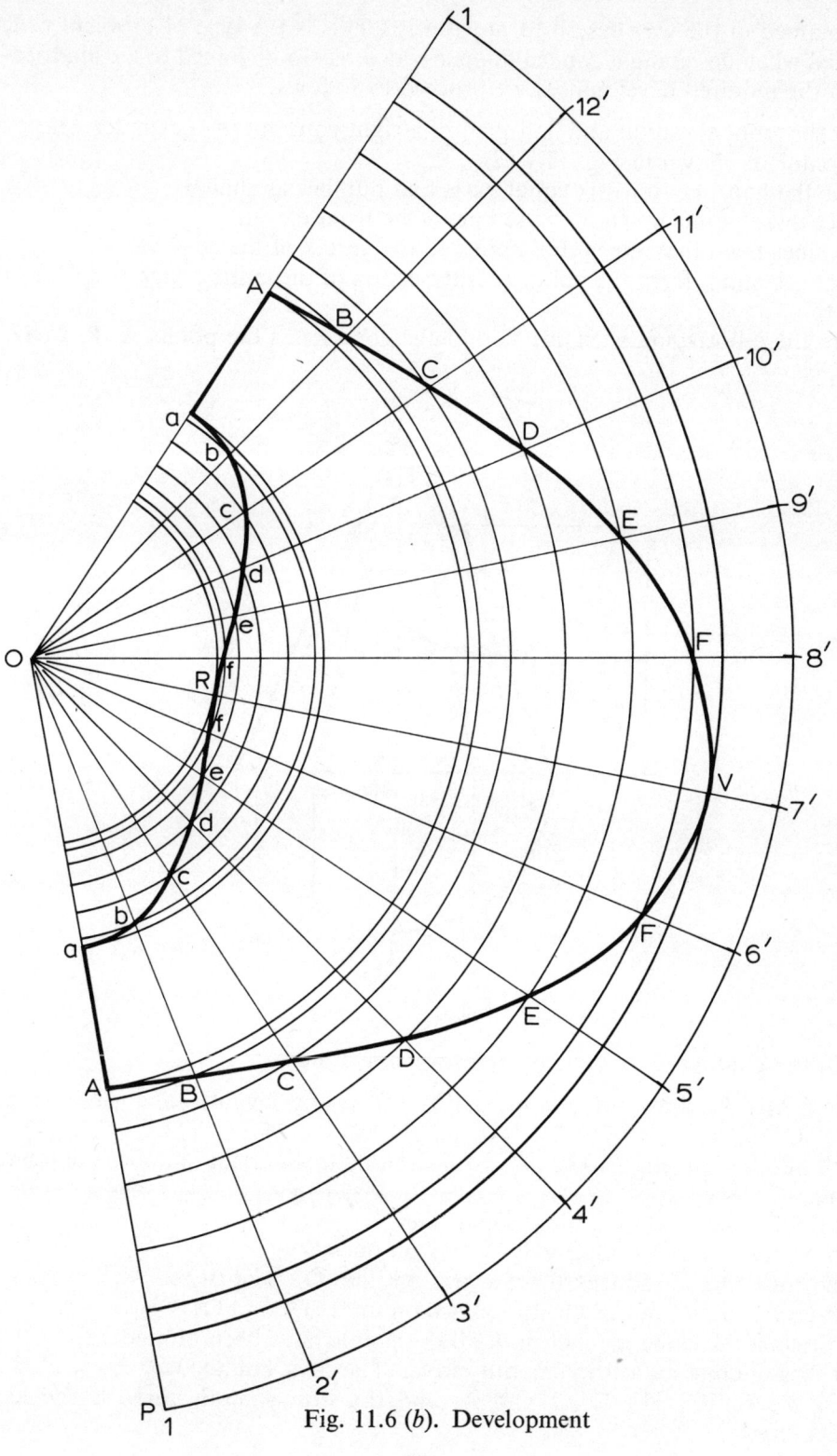

Fig. 11.6 (*b*). Development

readily obtained in the way described previously. This is the type of problem which has to be solved when designing a conical hopper which has to be joined to a cylindrical pipe. To obtain the required development we proceed as follows:

1. Draw the front elevation and half-plan of a right cone cut by a cylinder whose axis is horizontal, as shown in Fig. 11.7 (*a*).
2. Divide the half-plan into six equal parts and number as shown.
3. Project these points up to the base line in the front elevation.
4. Draw lines from these projected points to the vertex of the cone O.
5. Draw horizontals from the points of intersection of the cutting edge and lines O1, O2, O3, etc.
6. Where these horizontals cut the side of the cone letter the points A, B, C, D, E, F, and G.

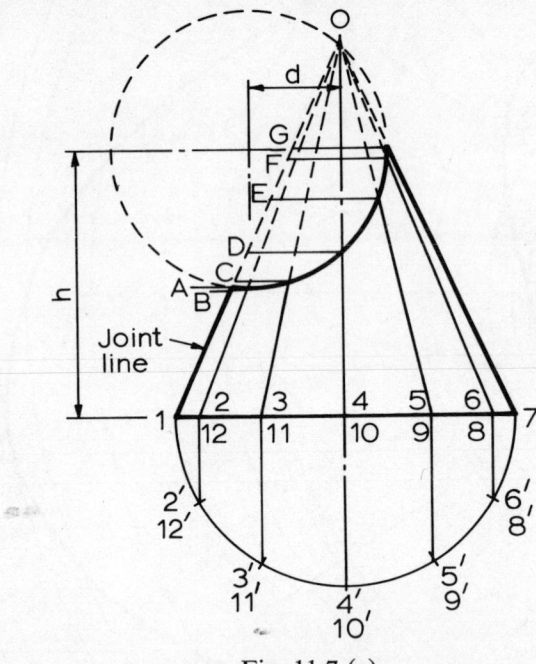

Fig. 11.7 (*a*)

To obtain the required development we proceed as follows:

7. With centre O draw an arc of radius O1 (slant height) in a suitable position (Fig. 11.7 (*b*)).
8. Mark off chordal lengths 1–2′, 2′–3′, etc., along this arc and number the points 1, 2′, 3′, etc.
9. Join these points to O by fine straight lines.
10. With centre O and radius OA draw arcs on lines O1.
11. With centre O and radius OB draw arcs on lines O2′ and 012′.
12. With centre O and radius OC draw arcs on lines O3′ and O11′.
13. Continue in the same manner until all the points have been plotted.
14. Join these points by a firm smooth curve. The area bounded by A, 1, 2′, 3′, 4′, 5′, 6′, 7′, 8′, 9′, 10′, 11′, 12′, 1 and A, and the firm smooth curve is the REQUIRED DEVELOPMENT.

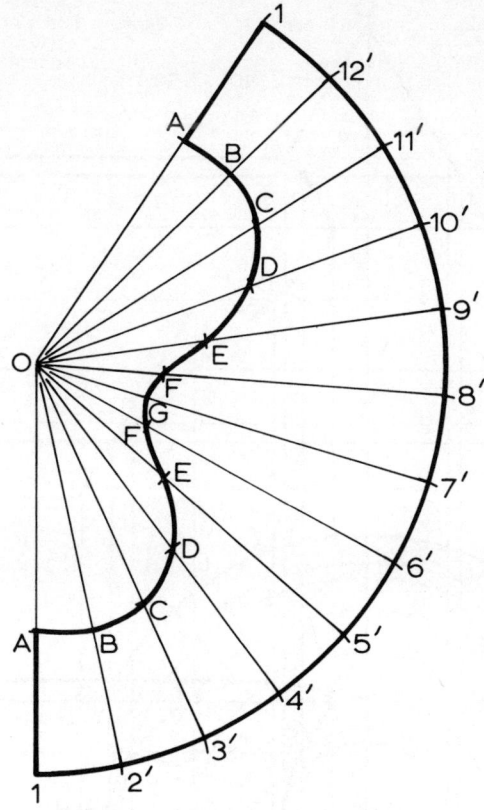

Fig. 11.7 (b). Development

To Draw the Development of the Intersection of a Right Cone and a Round Pipe
(Fig. 11.8 (a), (b), and (c))

In this example, which often occurs in the design of hoods or hoppers, the axis of the round pipe is horizontal and passes through the vertical axis of the cone. This tends to make the problem easier, for it is a symmetrical arrangement and we can readily work from centre lines. This problem is best tackled in three stages. The first stage is to obtain the shape of the JOINT LINE ABCDEFG in the front elevation (Fig. 11.8 (a)), for this will clearly be needed before we can attempt to develop either the curved surface of the cone or the surface of the intersecting pipe.

The second stage is to develop the surface of the cone; the third stage will be the development of the portion of the pipe. We proceed as follows:

1. Draw the front elevation and plan of the cone and pipe (Fig. 11.8 (a))
2. Construct semicircles on the ends of the round pipe, and divide them into six equal parts and number them 1–7 as shown in the elevation and correspondingly in the plan.
3. From these points project horizontals across the cone in both views.
4. Where the projected horizontals from the points 1, 2, 3, etc. (front elevation), cut the slant side of the cone, number the points 1′, 2′, 3′, etc., as shown.
5. Project the points 1′, 2′, 3′, etc., to the horizontal centre line of the plan.
6. With centre O (plan view) and radii O1′, O2′, O3′, etc., draw concentric circles.
7. Where the circle radius O7′ cuts the horizontal projected from point 7 on the pipe is point A on the curve of intersection.

Fig. 11.8 (a)

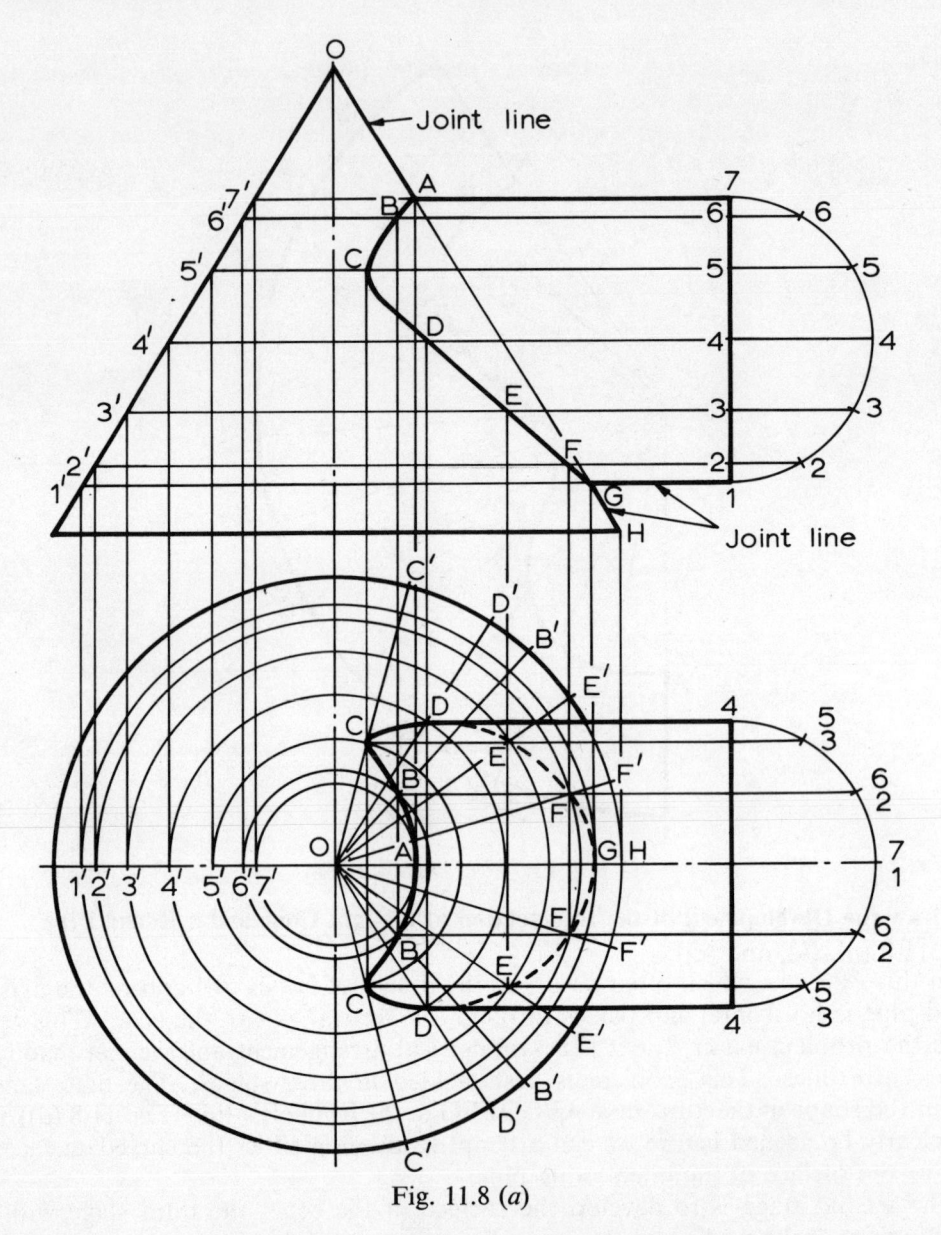

8. Where the circle radius O6′ cuts the horizontal projected from points 6 on the pipe are points B on the curve of intersection.
9. Continue in this manner until points C, D, E, F, and G are plotted.
10. Join these points by a smooth curve as shown, to obtain THE CURVE OF INTERSECTION.
11. Project points A, B, C, D, E, F, and G from the plan view to intersect their respective horizontals in the front elevation to obtain points A, B, C, D, E, F, and G in the front elevation.
12. Join these points by a smooth curve.

Now that the exact position of the joint line has been obtained we are in a position to develop the curved surface of the cone. We proceed as follows:

13. From point O (plan) draw radial lines through points B, C, D, E, and F on the curve of intersection to intersect the outer circumference of the cone at points B′, C′, D′, E′, and F′. Mark the intersection of the horizontal centre line and the outer circumference of the cone H.
14. Mark the point O (Fig. 11.8 (b)) in a suitable position.
15. With centre O and radius equal to the slant height of the cone, draw an arc of length equal to the circumference of the base of the cone.
16. Step off the plan chordal length HF′ from the ends of the arc to obtain points F′ on the arc.
17. From F′ step off chord lengths F′E′ to obtain points E′ on the arc.

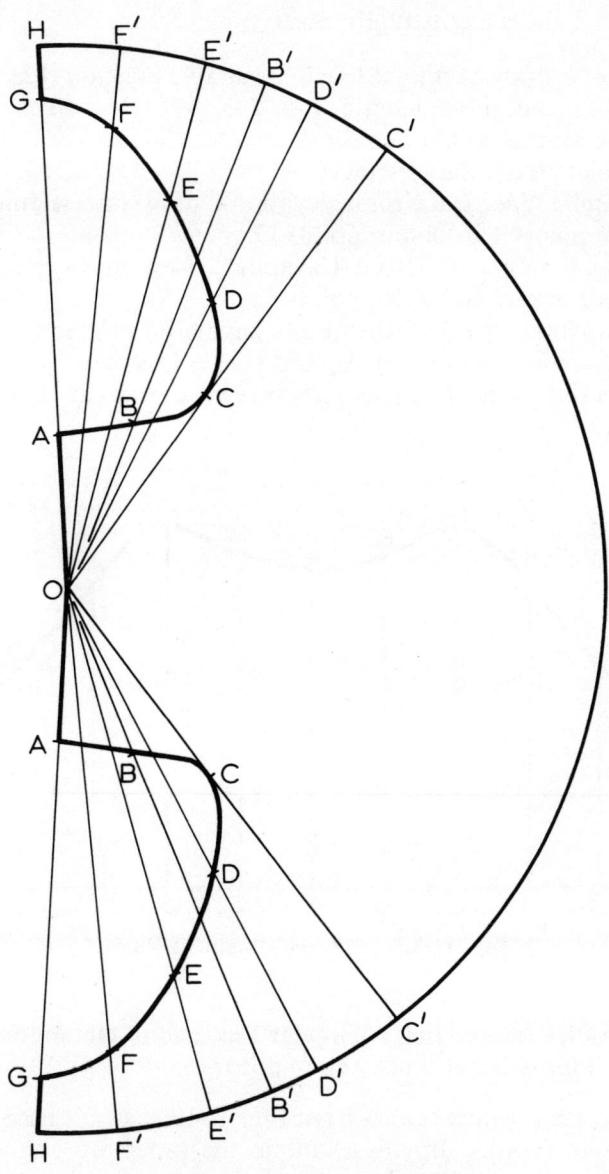

Fig. 11.8 (b). Development of Cone

18. Continue in this manner until points B′, D′, and C′ are also plotted.
19. Join these points to point O by fine straight lines.
20. With centre O and radius O7′ (front elevation) draw intersecting arcs on radial lines OH to obtain points A.
21. With centre O and radius O6′ (front elevation) draw intersecting arcs on radial lines OB′ to obtain points B.
22. Continue in this manner until points C, D, E, F, and G have been plotted.
23. Join these points with smooth curves and lines GH and AO by firm straight lines.

THIS IS THE REQUIRED DEVELOPMENT OF THE CONE.

This completes Stage 2 and we go straight on to Stage 3.

24. To develop the pipe, draw a straight line in a suitable position (Fig. 11.8 (c)).
25. Along this line step off chord lengths 1–2, 2–3, 3–4, etc., taken from the elevation (Fig. 11·8 (a)), to obtain points 1 to 7.
26. Erect perpendiculars from these points.
27. With centre 1 and radius G1 (front elevation), draw intersecting arcs on the perpendiculars from points 1 to obtain points G.
28. With centre 2 and radius F2 (front elevation), draw intersecting arcs on the perpendiculars from points 2 to obtain points F.
29. Continue in this manner until all the points have been plotted.
30. Join these points with a smooth curve, and points G and 1 by firm straight lines, as shown (Fig. 11.8 (c)). THIS IS THE REQUIRED DEVELOPMENT OF THE PIPE.

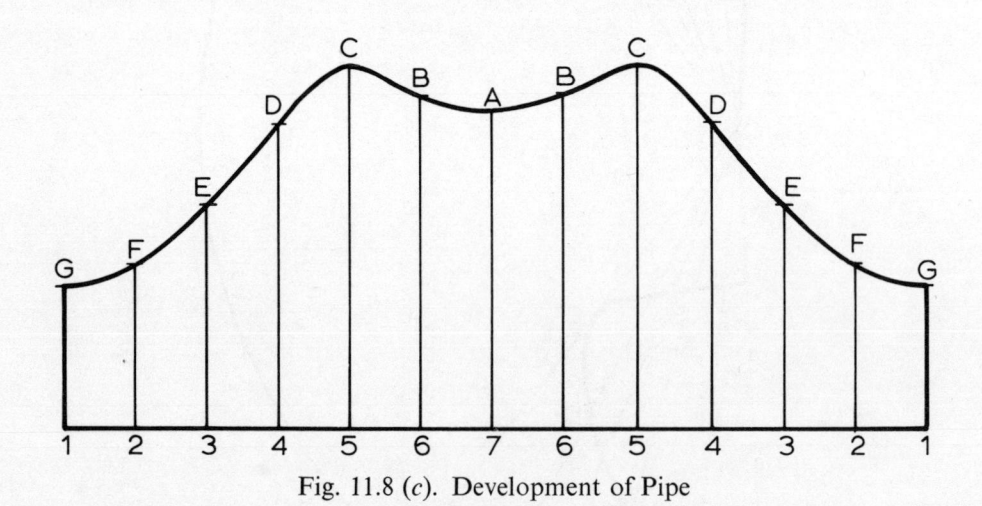

Fig. 11.8 (c). Development of Pipe

To Develop a Square Pipe Intersecting a Circular Pipe and to Obtain the Shape of the Hole of Penetration in the Pipe (Fig. 11.9 (a), (b), and (c))

This is the development which occurs from time to time and is used where a square tee branches from a circular pipe. In this example the pipes are NOT of the same cross-sectional area; a pictorial view of the branch pipe is shown in Fig. 11.9 (a).

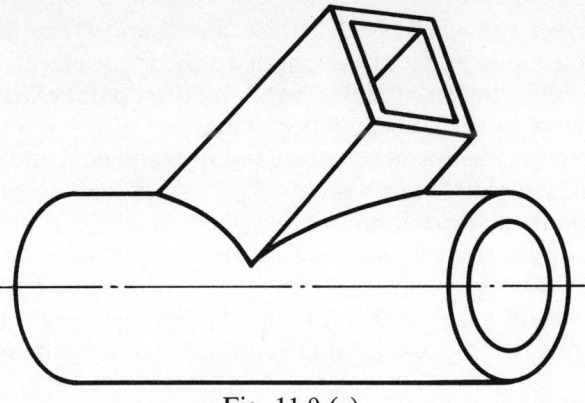

Fig. 11.9 (a)

To obtain the required development proceed as follows:

1. Draw the front elevation and end elevation as shown in Fig. 11.9 (b).
2. Divide the sides AB and BC on the front elevation of the square pipe into four equal parts and number the points as shown.
3. Project horizontals from these points to the end elevation to intersect the top edges of the square pipe, and number 1 to 6 as shown.
4. From these points draw vertical lines to intersect the circular pipe.

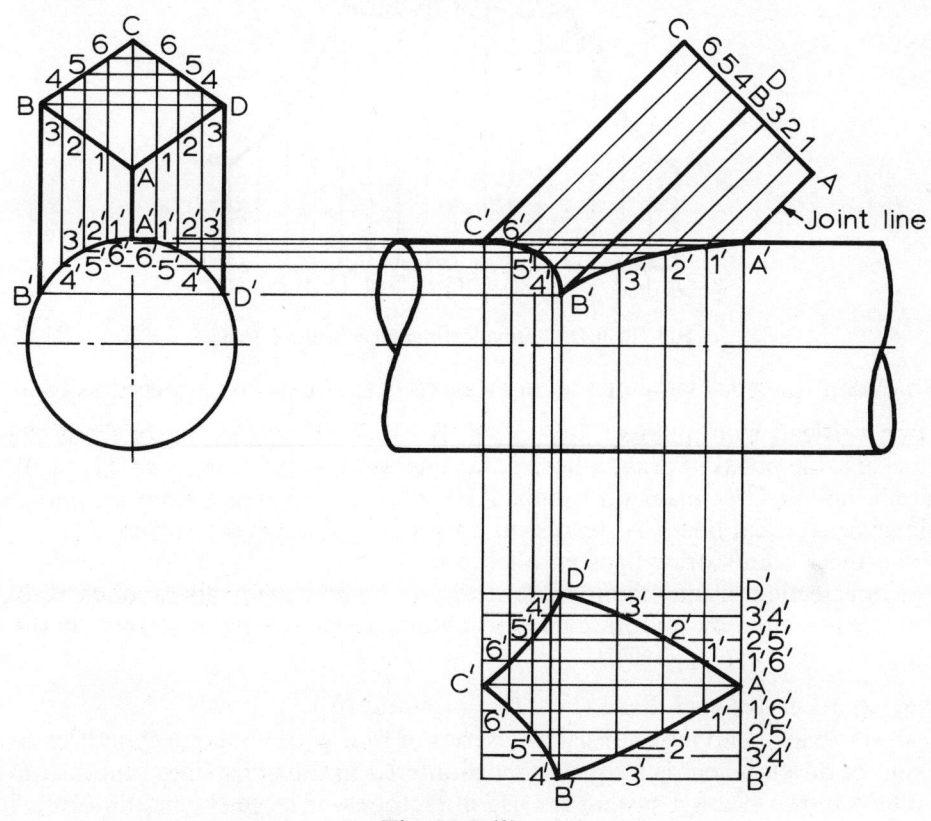

Fig. 11.9 (b)

69

5. Mark these intersections A′, 1′, 2′, 3′, B′, 4′, 5′, 6′, and D′ as shown.
6. From these intersections project horizontals to the front elevation.
7. From points 1 to 6 on the front elevation, draw lines parallel to the centre line of the square pipe to intersect the projected horizontals.
8. The intersection of the lines projected from points 6 and 6′, 5 and 5′, 4 and 4′, B and B′, 3 and 3′, 2 and 2′, 1 and 1′ gives points 6′, 5′, 4′, B′, 3′, 2′, and 1′ on the curve of intersection in the front elevation.
9. Join these points by a smooth curve to obtain the CURVE OF INTERSECTION.
10. To develop the square pipe draw a straight line in a suitable position, and step off the TRUE lengths of AB, BC, CD, and DA along the line AA (Fig. 11.9 (c)).
11. Divide these lengths AB, BC, CD, and DA, into four equal parts to obtain points 1, 2, 3, 4, 5, and 6.
12. Erect perpendiculars from these points.
13. With centre A step off length AA′ (front elevation) along the perpendicular to obtain points A′.
14. With centre 1 step off length 1–1′ (front elevation) along the perpendicular to obtain points 1′.
15. Continue in this manner until all the points have been plotted.
16. Join these points. THIS IS THE DEVELOPMENT OF THE SQUARE PIPE.

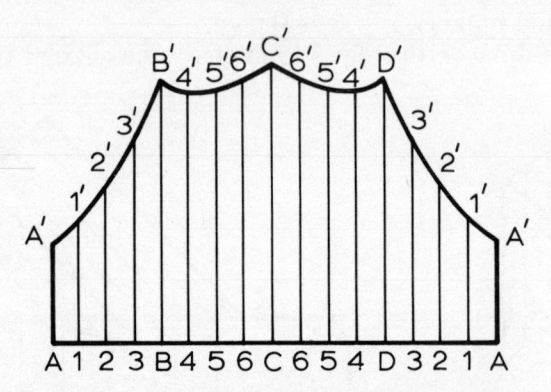

Fig. 11.9 (c). Development of Square Pipe

To obtain the PLAN VIEW OF THE HOLE IN THE CIRCULAR PIPE proceed as follows:

17. Drop verticals from points C′, 6′, 5′, 4′, B′, 3′, 2′, 1′, and A′ in the front elevation.
18. In a suitable position draw a horizontal intersecting line C′A′ (Fig. 11.9 (b))
19. From the line C′A′ mark off lengths A′1′, 1′2′, etc., obtained from the end elevation, along the vertical line A′A′ to obtain points 1′, 2′, 3′, D′, 4′, 5′, and 6′.
20. From these points draw lines parallel to C′A′.
21. The intersection of lines from points 1′–1′, 2′–2′, 3′–3′, etc., gives points 1′, 2′, 3′, etc.
22. Join these points by smooth curves to obtain the plan view of the hole in the circular pipe.

To Develop a Lobster-back Bend (Fig. 11.10 (a) and (b))

A lobster-back bend may consist of a series of four equal oblique cylindrical segments. This kind of development is frequently encountered in the main lines of a dust-extraction system or a blown heating system for use in factories or large shops or stores. It can be clearly seen that special bends can be made by this method, but right-angled bends are by far the most common. The lobster-back bend now dealt with consists of four equal segments, but the method is the same irrespective of the number of segments. The method of procedure is as follows:

1. Draw the front elevation of the complete bend (Fig. 11.10 (a)), so that one edge AB is vertical.
2. Label the corners of the end segment A and B as shown.
3. Construct a semicircle on the vertical line AB and divide it into six equal parts. Number the points 1, 2, 3, 4, and 5, as shown.
4. Project these points horizontally to the line AB and number the intersections 1', 2', 3', 4', and 5'.
5. From these intersections project lines across the segment parallel to the lines BB and AA.
6. Construct a perpendicular bisector to these lines and label the intersections C, D, E, F, G, H, and I, as shown.

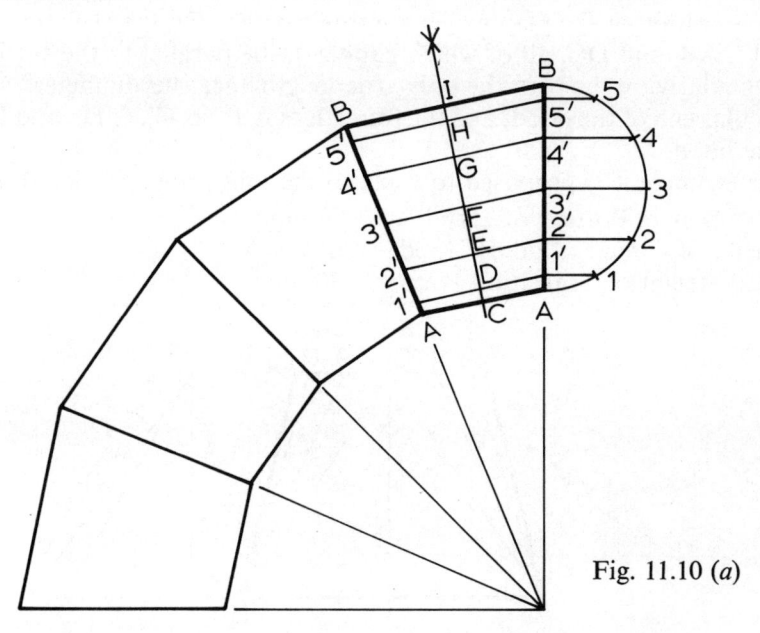

Fig. 11.10 (a)

7. To obtain the development draw a horizontal straight line in a suitable position and label one point on it C (Fig. 11.10 (b)).

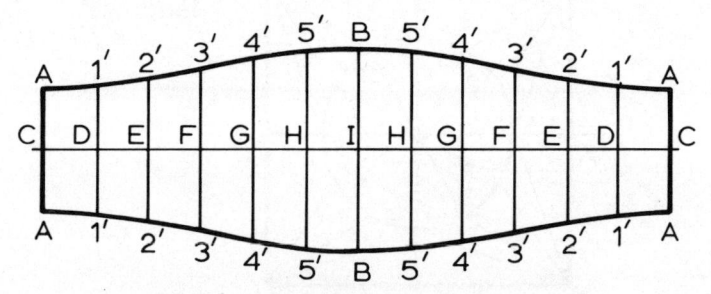

Fig. 11.10 (b). Development of One Segment
(Four required for the Complete Bend)

8. From C along this line step off lengths of chords A–1, 1–2, 2–3, 3–4, 4–5, 5–B, B–5, 5–4, 4–3, 3–2, 2–1, and 1–A taken from the elevation and label these points D, E, F, G, H, I, H, G, F, E, D, and C respectively.
9. Erect perpendiculars through these points.
10. With centre C (Fig. 11.10 (*b*)) and radius CA (Fig. 11.10 (*a*)), draw intersecting arcs on the perpendiculars through points C and label the intersections A.
11. With centre D (Fig. 11.10 (*b*)) and radius D1′ (Fig. 11.10 (*a*)), draw intersecting arcs on the perpendiculars through points D and label the intersections 1′.
12. Continue in this manner until all the points have been plotted.
13. Join these points by smooth curves. THIS IS THE REQUIRED DEVELOPMENT OF ONE OF THE SEGMENTS AB, BB, BA, AA. The full bend comprises four such segments.

Development of Square to Round Hood (Fig. 11.11 (*a*) and (*b*))

In this example, as in the earlier ones dealing with the development of cones, we must work from true lengths. Here it will at once be seen that there are only a few lines on either the elevation or the plan which are true lengths. On the elevation these are the lines X1, Y7, 17, AB, and DC, all of which happen to be parallel to the vertical plane of projection. Similarly, in the plan the only true lengths are the diameters and circumference of the circular end of the hood, and the four edges A′B′, B′C′, C′D′, and D′A′ of the square end of the hood.

In this example it is proposed to work to the following specified dimensions:

Sides of Square Portion of Hood: 90 mm.
Diameter of Circular End of Hood: 65 mm.
Vertical Height of Transition Piece: 70 mm.

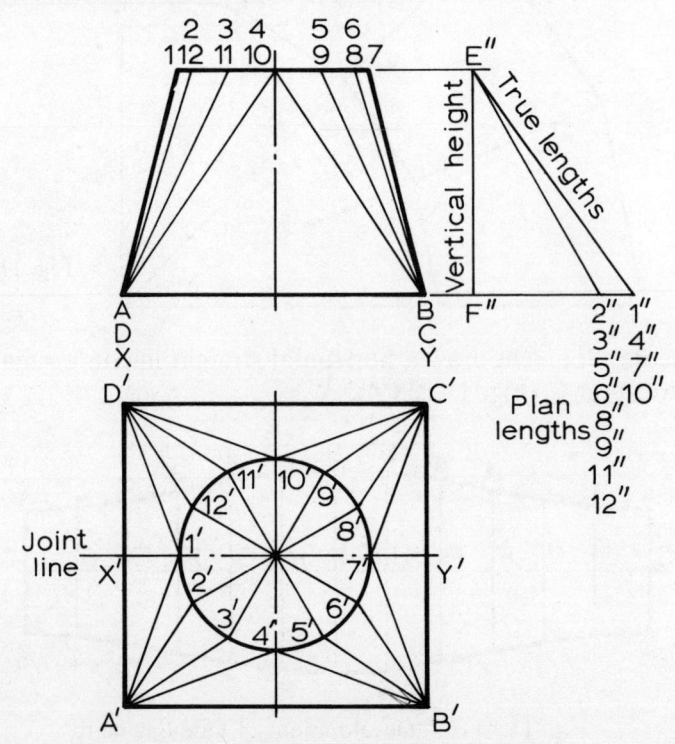

Fig. 11.11 (*a*). Elevation and Plan of Hood

To obtain the required development of the surface of the transition piece we proceed as follows:

1. Draw the front elevation and plan (Fig. 11.11 (a)).
2. Divide the plan of the circular top into twelve equal parts and number as shown.
3. From the corners of the square draw straight lines to the twelve points as shown.
4. Extend the top and base lines in the front elevation and erect a perpendicular, labelling the intersections E″ and F″ respectively.
5. From point F″ mark off a length F″1″ horizontally equal to the length of A′1′ (plan view).
6. Join E″ to point 1″ to obtain the TRUE LENGTH OF THE LINE A1. (Also the TRUE LENGTHS OF LINES A4, B4, B7, C7, C10, D10, and D1.)
7. From point F″ mark off a length F″2″ horizontally equal to the length of A′2′ (plan view).
8. Join E″ to point 2″ to obtain the TRUE LENGTH OF THE LINE A2. (Also the TRUE LENGTHS OF LINES A3, B5, B6, C8, C9, D11, and D12.)

The TRUE LENGTH of the JOINT LINE X1 is obtained from the front elevation.

To obtain the required development we proceed as follows (Fig. 11.11 (b)):

9. In a suitable position draw a straight line equal in length to the TRUE LENGTH of X1, and mark its ends X and 1′.

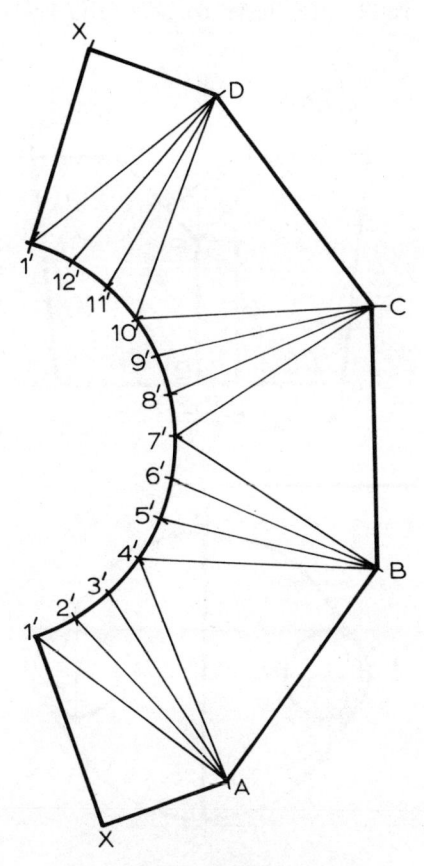

Fig. 11.11 (b). Development

10. From point X erect a perpendicular equal in length to A′X′ (plan view) and mark the end A.
11. With centre 1′ and radius equal to the length of chord 1′–2′ (plan view) draw an arc.
12. With centre A and radius equal to the TRUE LENGTH E″2″, draw an intersecting arc to obtain point 2′.
13. Join A to point 2′.
14. Repeat steps 11 to 13 to obtain points 3′ and 4′.
15. With centre A and radius A′B′ (plan view) draw an arc.
16. With centre 4′ and radius equal to the TRUE LENGTH E″1″, draw an intersecting arc to obtain point B.
17. Join points A, B, and 4′ to obtain triangle AB4′.
18. Repeat steps 11 to 17 until all the points have been plotted.
19. Join the points 1′–1′ by a smooth curve. THIS IS THE REQUIRED DEVELOPMENT.

To Draw the Development of One Branch of a Two-way Branch Pipe (Figs. 11.12 and 11.13 (*a*) and (*b*)).

This type of component occurs in ventilating systems which convey fumes from forge fires. It provides an interesting exercise in development, because we must obtain the true lengths of a convenient number of straight lines drawn on the surface of the component. As in the last exercise, only a small number of lines on either the plan or the end elevation appear as true lengths, the remainder have to be found by an appropriate construction.

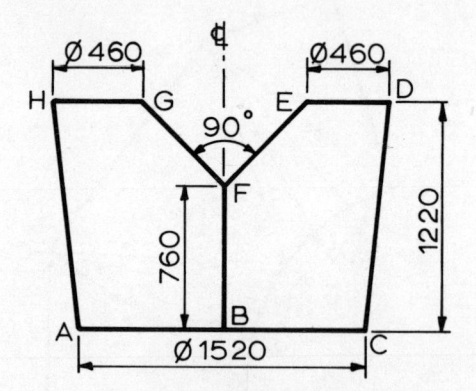

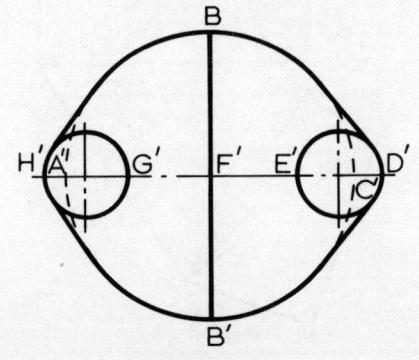

Fig. 11.12

The Branch Pipe shown in Fig. 11.12 is symmetrical about the ℄ through FB. We propose to develop the right-hand portion BCDEF, and to draw the development.

In the elevation (Fig. 11.12) the only true lengths are the sides AH and CD of the component and the diameters AC, ED, and HG of the circular ends of the branch pipe. All these are parallel to the vertical plane of projection. Similarly, in the plan, the only true lengths are the diameters and circumferences of the circular ends of the Branch Pipe, for these are parallel to the horizontal plane of projection.

To obtain the required development of the portion BCDEF we must treat it in a similar way to that which we adopted earlier when dealing with the development of the surface of an oblique cone (Fig. 11.4). We need a number of true lengths of convenient lines drawn on the surface of the component. At Fig. 11.13 (*a*) the portion CDEF has been continued upwards to the point O to complete the oblique cone of which the one-half of the pipe is a part. The component may, in fact, be regarded as being two oblique cones with a common joint line of intersection. If treated in this way the required development of one-half of the pipe becomes relatively straightforward. We proceed as follows (Fig. 11.13 (*a*) and (*b*)):

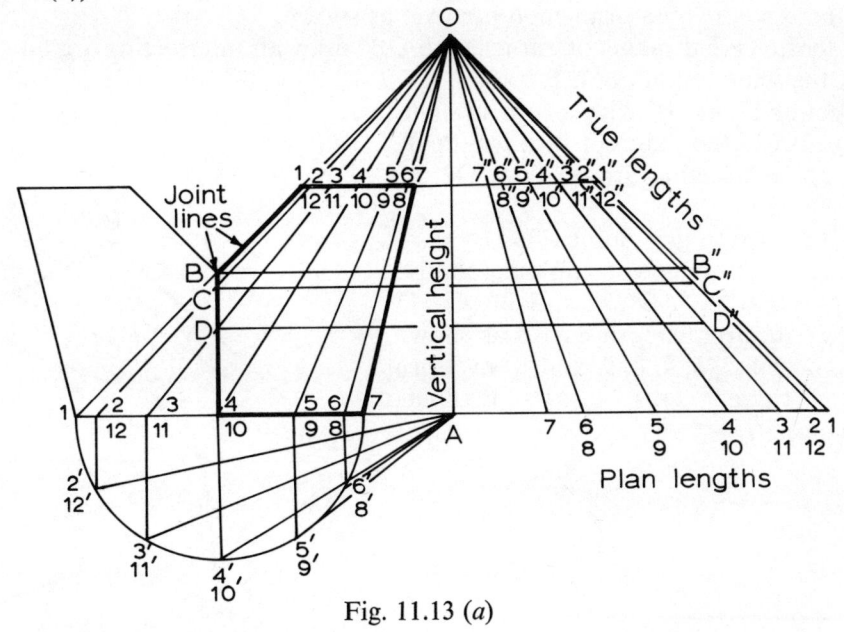

Fig. 11.13 (*a*)

1. Draw the front elevation and half-plan of the base of the pipe (Fig. 11.13 (*a*)).
2. Produce the sides to give a full cone.
3. From the vertex O of the cone, drop a perpendicular to the base line produced, and label the intersection point A.
4. Divide the half-plan into six equal parts and number 1 to 12' as shown.
5. Project these points vertically to the base line of the cone.
6. Join the points on the base to the vertex O.
7. From point A mark off plan lengths A1, A2', A3', etc., along the base line produced as shown.
8. Join these points to the vertex O to obtain the TRUE lengths of the lines O1, O2, O3, etc.
9. Produce the top edge of the branch across the true lengths, and number the intersections 7″, 6″, 5″, etc., where they cross the lines O7, O6, O5, etc.

75

10. Where the vertical joint line intersects lines O1, O2, O3, etc., in the front elevation, mark the intersections B, C, and D, as shown.
11. Project horizontals from points B, C, and D, to intersect the true lengths O1, O2, and O3, respectively.
12. Mark the intersections B″, C″, and D″.
13. Mark point O (Fig. 11.13 (*b*)) in a suitable position to start the development.
14. From O draw a line O1 of length equal to the TRUE length O1.
15. With centre 1 and radius equal to the length of the chord 1–2′ draw an arc.
16. With centre O and radius of TRUE length O2 draw an intersecting arc.
17. Mark the intersection point 2.
18. Continue in this manner until all the points on the base line have been plotted.
19. With centre O and radius of TRUE length O1″ drawn an intersecting arc on lines O1.
20. Mark the intersection point 1″.
21. With centre O and radius of TRUE length O2″ draw an intersecting arc on the line O2.
22. Mark the intersection point 2″.
23. Continue in this manner until all the points on the top edge have been plotted.
24. Join these points by a firm smooth curve, as shown,
25. With centre O and radius of TRUE length OB″ draw an intersecting arc on lines O1.
26. Mark the intersection point B″.
27. Join points 1″ and B″ with a firm straight line.
28. With centre O and radius of TRUE length OC″ draw an intersecting arc on lines O2 and O12.
29. Mark the intersection point C″.
30. Continue in this manner to obtain point D″.
31. Join points B″, C″, D″, 4, and B″, C″, D″ and 10 with firm smooth curves as shown.
32. Join points 4, 5, 6, 7, 8, 9, and 10 by a firm smooth curve. THIS IS THE REQUIRED DEVELOPMENT.

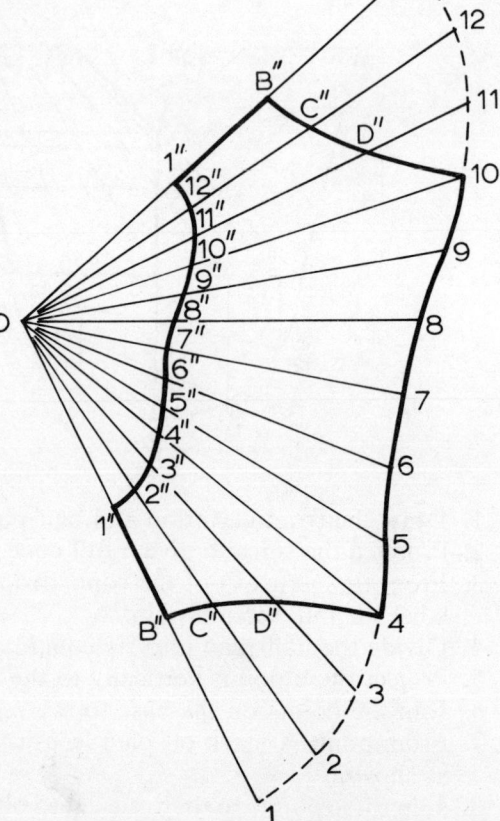

Fig. 11.13 (*b*). Development

PART TWO

MATERIALS

CHAPTER TWELVE
CAST IRONS

These are essentially alloys of iron and carbon with a carbon content of between 2·4% and 4·5%. They are produced by the resmelting of pig iron with steel scrap, and then the metal is cast into moulds. Cast iron is very fluid when molten enabling intricate castings to be produced, but neither hot nor cold working can be performed because of the brittleness of the metal.

In CAST IRON the carbon exists partly in the 'free' state and partly in chemical combination with the iron. In GREY cast iron the carbon is mostly in the 'free' state in the form of flakes of graphite, and it is this which gives the grey iron its dark appearance. In WHITE cast iron the carbon is combined with the iron to give iron carbide, and this gives a whitish colour to the metal. Between these two comes a cast iron, which is a mixture of both, called MOTTLED cast iron.

Grey cast iron (BS 1452: 1961) is mostly used because it has a low melting point (1150–1200 °C), it is easily machined and has excellent self-lubricating properties. Unfortunately it is brittle and is easily broken by shock loads. The compressive strength is high, often reaching 770 MN/m^2, but the tensile and shear strengths are low (108–216 MN/m^2). Grey cast iron SHOULD NOT therefore be used for parts which have to resist high tensile and shear stresses. It is often used for machine beds and frames, as it is able to damp down vibrations and provide a self-lubricating, hard-wearing, bearing surface.

The structure and properties of cast iron may be altered by several different methods as follows:

(*a*) By the use of special techniques in melting the metal and casting it.

(*b*) By means of heat treatment, especially white cast irons.

(*c*) By the addition of alloying elements.

Method (*a*)

Low-carbon cast iron which has a tensile strength of 260–355 MN/m^2 is produced by adding steel to the charge in the foundry cupola and is generally known as 'semi-steel'. High-duty cast irons can also be obtained by 'inoculation' which consists of the addition of certain compounds to white cast irons in the ladle. These compounds break up the graphite into a very fine form, producing a grey cast iron which is easily machined, and which has a tensile strength of 325–370 MN/m^2. MEEHANITE and SPHEROIDAL GRAPHITE cast irons are examples of 'inoculated' cast irons. The strength of cast irons may be improved still further by centrifugal casting, a method often employed for pipe sections.

Method (b)

Malleable cast irons are used where ordinary grey cast iron would be too brittle and possibly too weak. The two main methods are the WHITEHEART (BS 309: 1958) and BLACKHEART (BS 310: 1958) processes; both use white cast iron castings as the basis of the processes.

Malleable cast irons are cast to their required shape in the usual way and then, by suitable heat treatment, their ductility and malleability are increased considerably.

Method (c)

The addition of alloying elements to cast iron to change its structure and physical properties is probably the most important of the three methods listed above. Nickel, chromium, molybdenum, and copper are all used to provide desirable properties and they produce a range of metals which can be classed as ALLOY CAST IRONS. These are dealt with in more detail in the following paragraphs.

ALLOY CAST IRONS

To overcome the deficiencies of ordinary cast iron, while retaining the advantages, a wide range of alloy cast irons have been developed. The addition of alloying elements in sufficient amounts provides a range of cast irons with good wearing qualities, heat resistance and tensile strength. Components, such as gear wheels, camshafts, and crankshafts, made from alloy cast irons, are equal in all respects to those made from alloy-steel forgings, with the benefit of a considerable reduction in the amount of machining required to finish the component, and therefore a saving in cost.

Nickel Cast Irons

The addition of up to 2% of nickel refines the grains of low-silicon cast iron, making it stronger. It also eliminates 'chilling' of the iron, thus preventing the formation of hard spots in thin sections or corners, with a consequent improvement in machinability. The refining of the grains gives the iron a better wear resistance and a more uniform density, making it suitable for applications where high pressures are encountered; thus it finds many uses in hydraulic equipment and pumping machinery.

High-duty nickel cast irons can have a tensile strength of 465 MN/m^2 which may be improved to 540 MN/m^2 by heat treatment. These cast irons are suitable for uses where weight reduction with strength is important or where parts are severely loaded.

Nickel and nickel–chromium irons have extremely good resistance to abrasion, coupled with good machinability, and are used for components such as cylinder blocks, valve-guides, and brake drums. The influence of nickel in making the density more uniform means that internal casting stresses are reduced, and so castings do not have to undergo long periods of 'weathering' after manufacture. There is therefore much less risk of distortion occurring during service.

The resistance of grey cast iron to corrosion by caustic compounds can be improved by the addition of 2–5% nickel, but better results are obtainable with the austenitic cast irons dealt with later.

Irons containing up to 2% nickel and up to 0·5% molybdenum provide machinable castings with a strength up to 385 MN/m^2, and they are outstanding where high strength coupled with wear resistance is important. Typical uses are press dies, gears, cams, hydraulic equipment, and highly stressed components. Increasing the nickel content from 2 to 6% and molybdenum from 0·7 to 1·2% results in improved mechanical properties, and strengths up to 540 MN/m² are easily obtained. The unusual microstructure leads to their being called 'Acicular' cast irons. They have very much greater resistance to shock loading than any other grey cast iron and give excellent service in forging and forming dies and tools.

The hardness of grey iron castings increases progressively as the nickel content is increased up to 6%, and it is possible to obtain up to 300 Brinell Hardness Number (BHN), together with machinability, with a 3% nickel content. These irons are useful where severe abrasion has to be withstood, such as in gears, cams, and engine cylinders. Hardnesses up to 400 BHN can be obtained with 5% nickel cast iron, although then the only method of machining is by grinding.

Where it is not convenient to machine hard castings it is advisable to use heat-treatable alloy cast irons. The addition of 2% nickel allows full hardening (400 BHN) to be obtained with an oil quench, and this hardness can also be obtained by adding 4% nickel and quenching in an air blast. Tempering is recommended after hardening to obtain improved tensile strength. The depth of hardness is considerable, and these irons are used for gear wheels, cams, dies, cylinder liners, and pumps.

When good resistance to corrosion and heat is required an iron containing about 15% nickel, 7–8% copper, and 2–5% chromium produces an austenitic cast iron with an excellent corrosion resistance equal, or even superior, to phosphor-bronze and is used for pipes, valves, and pumps in contact with caustic alkalis or weak mineral acids. The standard austenitic cast irons are non-magnetic and, unlike brass and bronze, they have a high electrical resistance and are used where non-magnetic protective castings are required, such as terminal boxes and alternator end rings.

Chromium Cast Irons

Chromium may be added singly or with nickel, and it is similar to nickel in that it makes the iron stronger, but it does tend to prevent the formation of graphite by forming very hard carbides. It therefore increases any chilling effect, and may be added where hardness and increased resistance to wear are required. Small amounts of chromium refine the grain structure, making the iron suitable for 'rolls' and for moulds used in the production of steel ingots.

Since the formation of these hard carbide spots makes machining difficult, this can be counteracted by an increase in the silicon content. The best combination of strength and machinability is obtained by adding both nickel and chromium.

Copper in Cast Irons

Copper refines the graphite and strengthens and toughens the matrix of cast iron, making it a useful alloying element when used for internal-combustion engine cylinders and other castings subjected to pressures, as it prevents 'chill' in thin sections and helps to maintain a dense structure in thick ones.

Copper can be used to replace some of the silicon, and results in a noticeable improvement in the mechanical properties as well as giving a more uniform structure throughout the casting. The effects of small variations in the composition of the cast iron such as may be experienced during a daily production, are less significant and this is of benefit where mass production machining of light sections is carried out.

Copper is used to counteract the chilling effect of alloying elements, such as manganese, molybdenum, and chromium, which are added to high-duty cast irons to increase hardness, otherwise these cast irons would be very hard and brittle, and consequently extremely difficult to machine.

Phosphorus

This element tends to give a greater fluidity to the metal when hot and reduces shrinkage and density. Too much phosphorus, however, results in increased brittleness and so only very small percentages are used.

Manganese

This metal seems to oppose the formation of graphite and to lessen the unfavourable effects of any sulphur that may be present in the cast iron. It makes the iron harder but more brittle and it refines the grain structure.

Details of other cast irons are found in the following British Standards:

BS 3333: 1961. *Pearlitic Malleable Iron Castings.*
BS 2789: 1961. *Iron Castings with Spheroidal or Nodular Graphite.*
BS 3468: 1962. *Austenitic Cast Iron.*

The student is strongly advised to study the above British Standards and also to read further books on this subject.

Suggested Books

Teach Yourself Engineering Materials by M. H. A. Kempster.
Engineering Drawing and Materials, Vols 3 and 4 by H. Ord.
The above books are published by The English Universities Press Ltd, London.

CHAPTER THIRTEEN

STEELS

Steel is essentially an alloy of iron (Fe) and iron carbide (Fe_3C), in which the iron is in the combined form. Steel also contains other elements in controlled amounts.

Steel is produced from pig iron by oxidation which is a chemical process in which oxygen is introduced and combines with the carbon and other impurities so that they are removed in a converter or open-hearth furnace.

Carbon plays an important part in steels, it can be present in small amounts as part of ferrite (pure iron grains or crystals which are very soft and ductile) or combined with iron to form cementite (iron carbide Fe_3C) which is hard and brittle.

Other constituents such as sulphur, manganese, and phosphorus are usually present in amounts too small to have any real effect on the properties of steel.

The following British Standards are applicable to various steels:

BS 971: 1950. *Wrought Steels. En Series.*
BS 3100: 1967. *Steel Castings for General Engineering Purposes.*

The amount of carbon determines the type of steel and the following table gives four of the principal steels and their uses.

Fig. 13.1 illustrates the relationship between the carbon content in steel and its strength, hardness, and ductility. Here the base of the graph shows the percentage of carbon in the steel, the left-hand vertical shows the Ultimate Tensile Strength in MN/m^2 and the right-hand vertical gives the measure of the hardness of the steel in terms of its 'Brinell' Hardness Number. It will be seen from the graph that ductility decreases as the carbon content increases, but that ultimate strength and hardness increase as the carbon content increases.

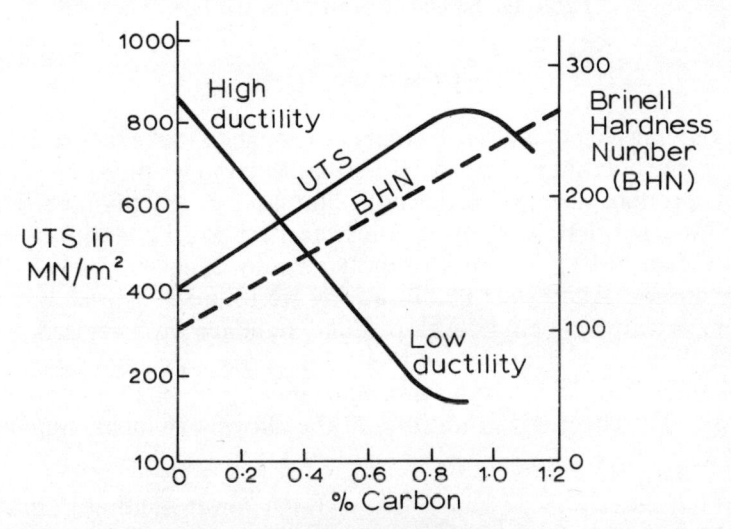

Fig. 13.1 Graph Showing the Relationship Between the Carbon Content in Steel and its Strength, Hardness, and Ductility.

Type of steel	Form of supply	Carbon, %	Uses and properties
Dead Mild or Low Carbon	Black and bright bars, tubes, wire	0·07–0·15	Pipes, chains, rivets, screws, nails, wire, boiler plates Easily worked when HOT, but difficult to machine owing to tendency to tear
Mild	Black bar sections and sheet Bright bar strip and tubing Forgings	0·15–0·25	Ship plates and forgings, gears, shafts, nuts, bolts, washers, rivets, chains Easily machined and welded, and is cheapest steel
Medium Carbon	Black bar, sheet, sections and plate Bright bar, rod, flats and strip Forgings	0·25–0·5	Machine parts and forgings, castings, springs, drop hammer dies Responds to heat treatment and can be machined satisfactorily
High Carbon	Black bar and strip	0·5–0·7	Hammers, sledges, stamping and pressing dies, drop-forging dies, screwdrivers, hammers, set-screws
	Silver steel rod	0·7–0·8	Punches, cold chisels, hammers, shear blades, drop-forging dies, lathe centres, spanners, band saws, rivet sets, vice jaws
		0·8–1·0	Punches, rivets, sets, screwing dies, screwing taps, shear blades, drop-forging dies, saws, hammers, cold chisels, springs, axes, rock drills, milling cutters, lathe centres, reamers
		1·0–1·5	Drills, milling cutters, lathe tools, files, wire drawing dies, hacksaw blades, ball bearings, screwing dies and taps

Table II. Steels—Carbon Content and Uses

ALLOY STEELS

The addition of alloying elements to steel is generally done to make the steel more responsive to heat treatment, thus obtaining improved mechanical and/or physical properties. Some alloying elements produce new properties not obtainable in any plain carbon steel.

The British Standard definition of an alloy steel is: 'Steel containing 0·40% or more of chromium or nickel; 0·10% or more of molybdenum, tungsten, or vanadium; or 10% or more of manganese'. Alloy steel specifications are found in British Standard 970, but new specifications are always being developed and standard ones revised.

The principal alloying elements added to steel in widely varying amounts, either singly or in complex mixtures are: nickel, chromium, manganese, molybdenum, vanadium, tungsten, silicon, and cobalt. The effect of the addition of the alloying elements may be one or more of the following:

(a) Increased hardness.
(b) Increased tensile strength, toughness, or elasticity.
(c) A lower melting point.
(d) A modified colour or structure.
(e) An increased resistance to corrosion.

Nickel Steels

The addition of nickel to steel makes the heat treatment required to obtain a hard surface less drastic, with consequent reduction in the possibility of distortion or cracking occurring in the component. It also imparts great strength with considerable ductility and toughness.

Up to 6% nickel may be added to steel for highly stressed machine parts, the alloy being suitable for heat treatment or case-hardening.

Steels with 20–30% nickel are highly resistant to corrosion by steam, hot gases, and sea-water. They have a low coefficient of thermal expansion and are used for steam-turbine blades, internal-combustion-engine valves, and for machine parts which are subject to wide ranges of temperature.

Among the 30–40% nickel steels the notable one is INVAR, which contains 36% nickel and 0·2% carbon. It is non-magnetic, stainless, has a low coefficient of thermal expansion, and so finds many uses in measuring instruments; but care should be taken in deciding its applications, as it has the property of increasing in length over a period of time.

Steels containing 50% or more of nickel have high magnetic permeability.

Chromium Steels

Chromium is often used in conjunction with nickel, as it neutralises the tendency of nickel to graphitise steel, but it makes heat treatment more difficult, although nickel counteracts this tendency.

There are several types of chromium steels. For example, one type has 1% carbon and 1·4% chromium and is used in ball and roller race parts. Another type, a corrosion-resisting steel containing 0·04% carbon and 13% chromium, cannot be heat treated but will work harden and is very often known as 'stainless iron'. Yet another, containing 0·3% carbon and 13% chromium, is known as Martenistic Stainless Steel and cannot be hardened. High carbon chrome steels are used for magnets.

Nickel–Chrome Steels

These are some of the most important alloy steels used for general engineering since, by varied heat treatments, an enormous range of mechanical properties may be obtained. These steels have a good resistance to impact and good ductility. The undesirable effects of nickel and chromium are cancelled by each other when both are used together, but the steel suffers from 'TEMPER BRITTLENESS', which is a low impact resistance at certain tempering temperatures.

Steels can be supplied in the oil-quenched and tempered condition ready for machining. and they give tensile strengths up to 1000 MN/m^2.

In addition, if 3·5% nickel and 0·75% chromium is added to 0·3% carbon steel the tensile strength is about 930 MN/m^2 after heat treatment, and this steel is used for components such as heavily loaded shafts and high-tensile bolts. Steels containing 4·25% nickel and 1·25% chromium can be hardened by heating and cooling in air (air-hardening steel). Their strength can reach 155 MN/m^2 or more, and they are used for tools, gear wheels, and the like.

A cold-working range of steels is formed by 8% nickel and 18% chromium. When heated and quenched they are fairly soft and easily cold worked. They are used for containers and tools which require high corrosion resistance.

Nickel–Chrome–Vanadium Steels

The addition of vanadium improves the mechanical properties generally, and increases the effects of the other elements. About 0·1–0·2% vanadium is generally present, and it helps produce sound ingots, and is excellent in removing oxides from the steel.

Nickel–Chrome–Molybdenum Steels

The addition of 0·3–0·6% of molybdenum reduces the 'temper brittleness' of nickel–chrome steels and, when used for dies in drop forging, they do not scale so readily and have a longer life than those which do not contain molybdenum. This steel is also used in steam plants, where it resists the tendency of the continuously elevated temperatures to make the steel brittle.

Silicon Steels

Silicon is often used in alloy steels in amounts up to 0·8%, which increases the tensile strength but decreases the ductility. Steels containing up to 2·5% silicon are used for making springs, as the fatigue strength is high. About 3·5% silicon is used in steel for valves for internal-combustion engines.

Tungsten Steels (High-Speed)

About 18% of tungsten is added to high-carbon steels, with 4% chromium and 1% vanadium to counteract the softening of these steels at high temperatures. These alloys are known as 'high-speed steels'; they retain their hardness up to 600 °C, and intermittent heating to this temperature tends to harden the steel even more. These properties are obtained only after correct heat treatment. High-speed steels are used for many types of cutting tools.

Manganese Steels

Steels with 1–2% manganese make an alloy frequently used in structural work and in motor cars, as it has higher tensile and impact strengths than plain carbon steels. High-carbon steel with 12–14% manganese makes it work-hardened to a higher degree. It can be hot worked, but it is extremely difficult to machine, as this leads to a hard surface being formed on the steel. The corrosion resistance is good and it is non-magnetic, but it is mostly used where a high degree of resistance to abrasion is required, as the abrasion tends to make the surface of the steel harder (up to 600 BHN). It is used for railway points and rock-crushing machinery.

Tool Steels

Plain carbon steels tend to crack during hardening, but some alloy tool steels have been developed which are called 'non-shrinking steels'. These are high-carbon steels to which manganese, tungsten, and chromium have been added. They are useful for dies and thin tools which have to be hardened. A typical non-shrinking die steel contains 1% carbon, 0·9% molybdenum, 0·5% tungsten, and 0·75% chromium. As the amount of the alloying elements is small, the steel is not very expensive.

Effects of Alloying Elements in Steels

Table III shows the effects (approximately stated) of individual alloying elements on steels. They depend, of course, upon the other constituents in the steel and it is to be noted that, in general, the purposes of the alloying elements are NOT achieved unless the steel has been suitably heat treated.

Alloying element	Percentage	Effect
Chromium	Up to $1\frac{1}{2}$	Used with nickel and/or molybdenum increases hardness and allows high UTS with considerable ductility
Cobalt	12–18 5–10 Up to 40	Increased corrosion resistance in stainless steel Retention of hardness at elevated temperatures Improves coercive force in magnet steels
Nickel	$1\frac{1}{2}$–5 20+	Increases tensile strength and toughness Used in corrosion- and heat-resisting steels
Tungsten		Strengthens steels at normal and high temperatures
Molybdenum		Used in stainless steels to provide resistance to sulphuric and other acids
Vanadium		Increases hardenability
Niobium Tantalum Titanium		Prevents 'weld decay' in chromium steels and in nickel stainless steels
Boron	0·003	Great increase in hardenability
Copper	0·2–1·0	Increases corrosion resistance

Table III. The Effects of Individual Alloying Elements on Steels

CHAPTER FOURTEEN

NON-FERROUS METALS AND ALLOYS

The non-ferrous metals and alloys are those in which iron is not the chief constituent. It may be present in minute quantities as an unavoidable impurity but in some instances it is a deliberate addition to obtain improved properties.

The pure metals are NOT used much in engineering, as improved properties are obtained by the addition of various amounts of other elements.

The most important non-ferrous alloys used in engineering are those containing large amounts of COPPER or ALUMINIUM.

COPPER AND ITS ALLOYS

Pure copper is too soft and weak for most engineering purposes although large amounts are used in electrical engineering. It is used extensively in engineering in the alloyed state as it is ductile, malleable, and has high thermal and electrical conductivity. It has extremely good resistance to corrosion by the atmosphere and other corrosive agents. It is unsuitable for castings owing to the difficulty of obtaining sound castings free from blow holes. There are ten grades of copper which are divided into three main groups:

(a) High conductivity copper. This is the best quality and has the highest electrical and thermal conductivity.
(b) Best select copper. This contains more impurities and has a lower conductivity. It is cheaper and is suitable for most uses.
(c) Arsenical copper. This contains 0·25%–0·50% arsenic which increases the tensile strength up to 260 MN/m^2. It is used in fire boxes, boiler tubes, rivets, and in domestic plumbing.

Copper, when cold drawn, can have a tensile strength up to 495 MN/m^2 but its ductility is greatly reduced so annealing is necessary. This is carried out by heating to 500 °C and then quenching in water.

A free cutting copper is produced by including approximately 0·5% tellurium which is insoluble in copper but is dispersed throughout the copper when the alloy is molten and remains in fine particles after the alloy has cooled. During machining operations it breaks up the chips.

If 20% beryllium is added to copper it increases the strength to about 1235 MN/m^2 and the resulting alloy is very hard. It is then used in bourdon tubes, bellows, and diaphragms.

BRASS

This is an alloy of copper and zinc with a wide range of properties and uses. Brass, except for manganese bronze, is usually available in bar form for automatic and capstan lathes or as sheet and strip to be cut into blanks for press work. Castings are, of course, available to special order. A great many small parts are made from extruded sections cut to length and machined where necessary. Any cold working of brass will tend to harden it, so before any subsequent operations can be carried out it is nearly always necessary to anneal the brass by heating to about 500 °C and quenching in water.

Brass may be subdivided into THREE main groups depending upon the zinc content,

(*a*) *The Alpha* (α) *Brasses* contain up to 39% zinc and are used for cold working. They are extremely malleable and may be cold rolled into sheets, drawn into tubes, wire and rod and used for cold stamping. The best combination of tensile strength and ductility is found in 'cartridge brass' (70% Cu, 30% Zn), which is used for deep-drawn articles, deep pressings, and applications where high ductility allied to high tensile strength is required, such as in condenser tubes, cartridge cases, gas tubes, gas and electric light fittings, architectural fittings, and sanitary ware.

Although these brasses may be severely cold worked, they are 'hot short', i.e. they tend to crack and disintegrate at high temperatures.

(*b*) *The Alpha–Beta* ($\alpha\beta$) *Brasses* contain 39–46% zinc and are specially suited for hot-working operations, although a very slight degree of cold working is possible if required. The most common brass in this group is 'Muntz Metal' (60% Cu, 40% Zn), which has a high corrosion resistance. It is readily hot worked and is used for extrusions of various sections such as small gears, hot-stampings for pipe junction pieces, water-tap bodies, gear housings, and for rolling into sheets and rods. Bolts, pins, spindles, and nuts are manufactured from bar stock by automatic lathes, and pump components are frequently made from these brasses.

This group of brasses is suitable for the production of castings, but care must be taken because stresses may be set up during cooling, resulting in considerable distortion when machining is carried out. An annealing process at 600–650 °C carried out prior to machining will prevent this trouble occurring. This group of brasses is rather difficult to machine, but this defect can be put right by the addition of 1–3% of lead to the brass to make it 'free cutting'.

(*c*) *Beta–Brass* (β) containing 46–49% zinc is used frequently in marine engineering because of its excellent corrosion resistance. It has a tensile strength of 385–465 MN/m^2 and a low ductility, but it cannot be cold worked without possibility of fracture. It is primarily a hot-working metal.

Above 49% zinc the alloys are very hard, but are so brittle that they are useless for most engineering purposes. An exception to this is 'brazing brass', with 50% zinc, which is used because of its comparatively low melting-point.

Season Cracking

Cold worked alpha and alpha–beta brasses are liable to season cracking. This is the development of cracks in components in service, probably after years of service. This defect is due to internal stresses set up by cold working, and by the component being used in a contaminated atmosphere (such as may be found in many industrial areas), and is especially prevalent where small traces of ammonia are present. Season cracking may be overcome by tempering cold-worked components at 250–270 °C for a period of ½–1 hour. The possibility of season cracking occurring can be reduced by increasing the copper content of the brass.

Effects of Alloying Elements

The addition of lead reduces the cold-working properties and lowers the tensile strength and ductility, so it is desirable that not more than 0·1% be present. On the other hand, it is sometimes added to improve machinability and surface finish, and up to 2% is then present.

Manganese Bronze

This is not a bronze at all, but a 60% copper, 33% zinc, high-tensile brass with about 7% manganese added. The tensile strength is high, being about 430–510 MN/m². It has an excellent resistance to corrosion by sea-water and so finds many marine applications as ships' fittings, propellers, etc. It can be cast and may also be forged and stamped at temperatures between 600 and 750 °C.

Delta Metal

This is an alpha–beta brass with about 2% iron and 1% manganese. It can be extruded, forged, rolled, stamped, or pressed into almost any required shape when heated to above 550 °C. Its corrosion resistance is excellent and it is a useful substitute for mild steel.

BRONZE

This is a copper–tin alloy which has high electrical conductivity, and so is used a great deal in electrical work, but it is also used for bushes and parts of hydraulic machinery.

With up to 6% tin, the bronzes can be compared with alpha brasses, though the bronzes are stronger. The maximum tensile strength is obtained with 9–10% tin, and ductility falls rapidly with a higher tin content. Cast bronze with 10% tin has a tensile strength of 216–247 MN/m² and finds many engineering applications where strength is required, e.g. bearings, nuts, and gears. Annealing will improve the ductility, but may give rise to porosity in the bronze so for components such as pumps or steam fittings it is advisable to avoid annealing. Bronze which is to be used for bearings should NOT be annealed, as the rate of wear is greatly increased. When bronze is annealed at a very high temperature it becomes hard and difficult to machine. Best results are obtained when it is quenched at about 550 °C.

Gunmetal

This is a bronze with 2% zinc and was once used to produce artillery, hence the name. The zinc helps to produce sounder castings, as it increases the fluidity of the bronze when molten and also hardens the bronze, counteracting the effect of the lead, which is sometimes added to improve machinability. Gunmetal is used chiefly for castings, particularly when they are of a complicated form. It also finds many uses in marine engineering and for steam-plant work. Improved properties can be obtained by an annealing process at about 700 °C.

Lead Bronze

Although bronze is a soft metal, it is not easy to machine, so lead is frequently introduced to improve machinability. Bronzes containing 8–10% lead are often used for locomotive slide valves and other heavily loaded bearings.

'PLASTIC BRONZES', containing up to 35% lead, are frequently used in shell bearings. The lead softens the bronze and assists in rapid bedding down of the bearing surfaces, while resistance to wear is increased without the coefficient of friction being raised.

Phosphor-bronze

True phosphor-bronzes contain not less than 0·1% phosphorus. A bronze containing 0·1–0·3% phosphorus and 5% tin is readily cold worked into rods, wires, and sheets and sometimes used for turbine blades and valves. The tensile strength is about 215 MN/m^2, and the bronze has an excellent resistance to sea-water corrosion. Bronzes containing 0·5–1·0% phosphorus and 10–13% tin are used for heavy-duty bearings and gears; they have a low coefficient of friction, great hardness, and good wearing resistance.

COPPER–NICKEL ALLOYS

There is an extremely wide range of these alloys, and they find many engineering applications. They will withstand considerable cold working after annealing and are also readily hot worked, being obtainable in almost any size and shape.

Alloys containing about 2% nickel combine excellent corrosion resistance, good ductility, and the retention of strength at high temperatures.

Alloys with 15–20% nickel are extremely malleable, with a tensile strength of 280–340 MN/m^2. They also have good corrosion resistance and ductility, and they retain their strength at elevated temperatures better than most other bronzes and brasses. These alloys do not appear to be liable to season cracking.

Alloys containing 40–45% nickel are readily cold worked and find use in electrical equipment due to their high resistivity and low resistance temperature coefficient.

Alloys containing 70% nickel are the most widely used of this range and have excellent mechanical properties. These alloys are known as MONEL METAL and contain iron, manganese, and other elements in addition to copper and nickel. These combine the strength of steel with excellent corrosion resistance to sea-water, steam, salt solutions, fatty and organic acids, and oils, but possess poor resistance to mineral oils, cyanide solutions, and molten lead or zinc. Monel metal is stronger than most non-ferrous alloys, having a tensile strength of up to 775 MN/m^2 in the normal state, but heat treatment can raise this to about 1160 MN/m^2. The alloy may be cast, soldered, or brazed, and is readily hot or cold worked, although annealing may be required in cold working. Its ability to retain its strength at high temperatures, coupled with its excellent corrosion resistance, makes Monel metal suitable for parts in contact with high-pressure steam, hospital and ships' fittings, and measuring and recording instruments. Monel metal makes good forgings, but it is affected by scale, prolonged heat, or extreme heat, so great care is required in the forge shop. Suitable forging temperatures are between 1050 and 1150 °C. For further information on these alloys the student is recommended to consult BS 3071: 1959 and BS 3072–6: 1968.

Nickel Brass (Nickel Silver or German Silver)

This is a copper, nickel, and zinc alloy with a copper/zinc ratio of 70/30, while the nickel content ranges from 5 to 30%. The alloys have a silver appearance, will take a high polish, and have excellent resistance to corrosion, leading to their widespread use in motor cars, railway, marine, and sanitary fittings, as well as for springs and electrical components. The alloys are readily cold worked, but annealing will be required between each operation as ductility is lowered although strength is increased by cold working. The machinability of the alloys is improved by the addition of about 2% of lead, but too much lead will lead to reduced strength, ductility, and malleability. These alloys are sometimes used for the brazing of iron and steel. BS 790: 1963 contains further information on Nickel Brass.

COPPER–ALUMINIUM ALLOYS (ALUMINIUM BRONZES)

There is a wide range of these alloys, from those predominantly copper to those predominantly aluminium. Only those alloys rich in copper will be dealt with in this section, and they are very suitable for gravity die-casting. Those rich in aluminium will be dealt with under aluminium alloys.

Copper alloys with 5–7% aluminium have a golden appearance, fairly high tensile strength and good resistance to corrosion. They also possess good ductility and find uses in jewellery, seamless tubing, and in wire drawing. Cold working will increase the strength of the alloy, but ductility is lowered and can be restored only by an annealing process.

Alloys with 10–12% aluminium may be heat-treated to increase their hardness, and are sometimes used where strength is required but where steel would be unsuitable. These alloys are suitable for sand or gravity die-castings, and they retain their strength at high temperatures. Typical uses are valve seats in petrol and diesel engines, worm gears, chemical plant, and marine equipment.

ALUMINIUM

Pure aluminium is a soft, weak (60–140 MN/m^2 UTS) ductile white metal noted for its light weight and high resistance to corrosion. It is the low density of aluminium and its alloys which is generally the deciding factor when they are chosen for some engineering project, and they are eminently suitable for many purposes. Aluminium is available in a range of standard grades from 99·0 to 99·99% purity, and it has a melting-point of 658 °C. It has good thermal and electrical conductivity, being second only to copper among the commercial metals. The electrical conductivity is approximately two-thirds that of copper, but on a weight-for-weight basis the aluminium is twice as efficient. The addition of alloying elements reduces the conductivity to some extent, but the alloys continue to compare favourably with iron and steel. Cables of aluminium are to be found in the British National Grid and in other grid systems all over the world, but the cables have a steel-wire core because a cable made of pure aluminium would be too weak to support its own weight over a long span.

The high corrosion resistance of aluminium and its alloys to atmospheric conditions and many chemical substances such as ammonia and nitric acid is provided by a thin inert film of oxide on the surface of the aluminium. Certain chemicals, such as caustic soda, some acids and alkalis, dissolve this oxide film so that the aluminium beneath is no longer protected and corrosion can take place. The corrosion resistance can be improved if the surface of the aluminium is anodised, a process in which the oxide film is thickened by means of an electrolytic process. The thick oxide film thus produced has an outstanding resistance to chemical attack. The anodised surface can be dyed in a wide range of heat- and light-resistant colours for decorative or identification purposes. By means of a special treatment it is possible to reproduce photographs or designs on the surface of the aluminium.

The immunity of aluminium and many of its alloys to chemical attack, and the fact that it is non-toxic, are the main reasons for its wide use for utensils used in the preparation of foods. The high thermal conductivity, the ductility, which allows deep vessels to be easily spun or pressed to shape, and the low density, which makes for easy handling, all make aluminium an extremely useful material in the kitchen and catering trades.

A very high polish can be obtained on aluminium by a burnishing or an electro-brightening process, and this makes it a useful material for reflectors. The polished surface does not readily tarnish and is used for mirrors, motor-car headlamp reflectors and also for paraffin- and electric-fire reflectors and vacuum flasks, for it reflects heat as well as light. Owing to its heat-reflecting qualities, aluminium is also used in the form of foil, sometimes laminated to paper or board as a heat insulator to enable even temperatures to be maintained in containers, buildings, vehicles, and ships.

Aluminium and its alloys are widely used in the field of transport, especially in the aircraft industry, where light weight is very important. Other transport applications are bodies for railway coaches and trucks, commercial-vehicle and motor-car bodies and engine parts for road transport, and superstructures and lifeboats for marine use. As a structural material aluminium has been used for bridges, wall panels, window frames, and prefabricated houses.

Electrical applications are due to the high conductivity of aluminium; it is used for steel-cored overhead conductors, busbars and risers, condenser plates, cable sheathing, and in the form of foil for capacitors.

In the food and chemical industries aluminium is used for brewing vats, beer barrels, refrigerators, and cold storage rooms. Aluminium foil is used for bottle-tops and wrapping such foodstuffs as chocolate and tea, and also for tobacco and cigarettes.

Aluminium and its alloys are available in a wide variety of forms which can be broadly divided into the wrought and the cast groups. The common forms of supply of the wrought materials are rolled sheet, plate, strip, and foil, extruded bars, rods, and sections, drawn tubes and wire, forgings, and stampings.

Castings are available in both sand and diecast forms, and the choice of method used will depend upon the quality of castings required and the size and intricacy of the casting.

Aluminium can be sprayed on surfaces to form a protective metallic skin, and in powder form it is also used to make aluminium paint, which gives a durable protective coating. Metal coatings of nickel, silver, and chromium can also be applied to aluminium by an electro-plating process if required.

High-purity aluminium has very poor machinability, as it tends to tear badly and is so weak that fine threads will very easily strip. Aluminium and many of its alloys are readily welded by both gas and arc processes, although a different technique is required to that used for steel. Brazing and soldering can also be carried out, but soldering should be restricted to joints where no moisture will be present. Probably the most common method of joining aluminium and its alloys is by means of rivets, and this method is extensively used on aircraft for safety reasons.

Pure aluminium is not a suitable material for many engineering purposes but, if small amounts of alloying elements are introduced, there is a great improvement in the mechanical properties, without the low density being materially increased.

ALUMINIUM ALLOYS

Aluminium–Copper Alloys

The addition of copper hardens and strengthens the aluminium. Two alloys are in common use in this group.

(a) 4L11, containing 6–8% copper, which is used as a good all-round sand-casting metal, but should not be used where it may be exposed to a marine atmosphere, as severe corrosion will take place.

(b) 3L8, containing 12% copper, which is used for castings having to withstand shocks and severe stresses. It has good strength at elevated temperatures, so being suitable for engine pistons. The additional copper also improves the machinability.

These alloys are amenable to heat treatment, resulting in an increase in strength and hardness.

Duralumin

This is a most important aluminium alloy with a specification of 3·5–4·5% copper, 0·4–0·7% manganese, 0·4–0·7% magnesium, with about 0·4% silicon and up to 0·5% iron present as impurities. It is easily hot worked, but is only readily cold worked after forging or annealing owing to the phenomenon of 'age-hardening'. This is an increase in the hardness value after a period of time although no heat treatment or cold working has been carried out. Age hardening can be suppressed by keeping parts at a low temperature in a refrigerator.

Duralumin is widely used in the wrought condition for forgings, stampings, tubes, and rivets, but it is NOT a suitable material for castings. The strength may be as much as 400 MN/m^2 after ageing, and this is fairly well retained up to about 200 °C, when a value of 310 MN/m^2 is obtained but, above this temperature, it rapidly falls off, thus making this alloy unsuitable for pistons.

'Y' Alloy

This is an aluminium alloy with the specification of 4% copper, 2% nickel, and 1·5% magnesium, and was developed by the National Physical Laboratory. It is mostly used for castings, but may be mechanically worked, and is sometimes used for forgings. The best properties are obtained by heat treatment followed by an 'ageing' process carried out over five days, resulting in 50% increase in strength up to 310 MN/m^2. 'Y' alloy retains its strength well at high temperatures and is widely used for the pistons and cylinder-heads of internal-combustion engines. It possesses good machining properties and has a better resistance to corrosion than duralumin.

RR Alloys

These are a series of alloys developed by Rolls-Royce Ltd. There are four main alloys containing copper, nickel, iron, magnesium, titanium, and silicon.

RR50 is used for general castings and has a UTS of 170 MN/m^2.
RR53 is used for die-castings (pistons, etc.) and has a UTS of 370 MN/m^2.
RR56 is used for general forgings and has a UTS of 465 MN/m^2.
RR59 is used for forgings and has a UTS of 370 NM/m^2.

These alloys require to be heat-treated to obtain their best properties, and RR53 and RR59 both retain their properties well at high temperatures.

Aluminium–Copper–Zinc Alloys

These alloys have a low melting-point and are easily cast, finding uses as crankcases, brake-shoes, gear-boxes, and other similar components. The alloys are inexpensive and have good machining properties, but the resistance to corrosion is not very high.

Aluminium–Silicon Alloys

These alloys are even lighter than aluminium itself, and so find many uses where lightness is important. Those containing 10–14% silicon have the best corrosion resistance and are used a great deal in marine work. The alloys retain their strength well at elevated temperatures and are often used in internal-combustion engines. Sound non-porous pressure die-castings are produced even when of complicated shape. The alloys may undergo a 'modification' process which improves the structure and strength of the alloy, up to 215 MN/m^2 being obtained. BS 1490 lists twenty-four alloys for general engineering purposes; the student is advised to read this publication.

MAGNESIUM AND ITS ALLOYS

Magnesium is one of the lightest metals, having a density only two-thirds that of aluminium, and it is this lightness of magnesium and its alloys which is extremely useful where high power/weight ratios are desired. Pure magnesium is very weak and has a strength of about 110 MN/m^2, which may be increased to about 185 MN/m^2 by rolling.

The most common alloying elements are aluminium, zinc, and manganese. The aluminium and zinc harden the alloy and improve the mechanical properties, while the manganese is added to improve the resistance to corrosion. Cast alloys have a strength of 125 MN/m^2, while wrought alloys attain 170–215 MN/m^2. These alloys are considerably improved by heat treatment. The latest alloying element is zirconium, which has the effect of reducing the grain size of magnesium, resulting in a stronger, more ductile metal which retains its strength at elevated temperatures.

Magnesium alloys may be rolled, die-cast, forged, pressed, extruded, and welded. They can be machined at extremely high speeds (50 metres per second), but there is a danger that the friction of the tool on the work may generate enough heat to ignite the swarf, so tools should be VERY SHARP. The student is advised to consult BS 2970: 1959.

The corrosion resistance of magnesium alloys may be considerably improved by chromating or painting the surfaces of components.

NICKEL AND ITS ALLOYS

Malleable nickel contains up to 0·5% impurities and is readily hot or cold worked. Nickel has excellent resistance to corrosion to various acids, caustic alkalis, ammonia, and salt solutions, and so it finds uses in chemical plant and foodstuff-handling equipment. It has a fine white colour and takes a brilliant polish, making it useful for decorative work and as a plating on steel parts to improve appearance and corrosion resistance.

Nickel–Chromium Alloys

Alloys with 80% nickel and 20% chromium have a high electrical resistance, a high corrosion resistance, and a good resistance to scaling at red heat, making them useful for resistance wires in electrical appliances. The student is advised to read BS 3072–6 entitled *Nickel and Nickel Alloys*.

Nimonic Alloys

This is a range of alloys which are basically composed of nickel and chromium, with the addition of titanium and carbon. They are capable of withstanding temperatures of the order of 900 °C, and will withstand high stresses. Having these properties, they are ideally suited for gas-turbine engine applications, where materials are required to withstand a combination of high stresses and temperatures, and also resist the corrosive action of the products of combustion.

CHAPTER FIFTEEN
BEARING METALS

Pure metals and some alloys are unsuitable for use as bearing metals. The compositions of bearing alloys vary a great deal and depend largely upon the working conditions of the bearing. Usually the object is to produce an alloy having hard particles embedded in a soft matrix. The function of the soft matrix is to deform sufficiently to allow the bearing to conform to the journal and to absorb any particles of foreign matter that may get into the bearing, thus preventing scoring of the journal. The hard particles resist wear and provide a surface with a low coefficient of friction. During use the soft matrix wears away slightly, leaving the hard particles protruding from the matrix surface sufficiently to support the journal. The lower level of the matrix helps to maintain a film of lubricant in the bearing.

Lead–Copper Alloys (Leaded Bronze) (*see also* **Non-ferrous Metals**)

These alloys have been fairly recently developed and have largely displaced white metals in high-duty bearings. Typical compositions contain 25–45% lead and 75–55% copper, together with small amounts of other elements, such as tin, nickel, and iron.

Lead and copper do not dissolve in each other at all, and leaded bronzes are merely mixtures of the two metals, so great care is required in their manufacture, or they will separate out from each other. The function of lead in a bearing bronze is to act as a sort of metallic lubricant should the oil film break down.

The copper provides high thermal conductivity, which assists in avoiding overheating, while the presence of the minor alloying elements improves the lead distribution and the mechanical strength of the bearing.

White-metal Alloys (Babbitt's Metal)

These are tin-based alloys which also contain copper and antimony. Antimony is a constituent of most anti-friction alloys and up to about 15% may be present, but greater amounts will make the alloys very brittle. The antimony gives rise to the hard particles which support the journal. A typical composition is 85% tin, 5% copper, and 10% antimony. These are expensive alloys and are used for heavy-duty and high-speed applications.

Lead-base Alloys

These are not quite so satisfactory as tin-based alloys or leaded bronze for severe conditions of high-speed service, but for medium speeds and loads they are quite adequate, and their low cost is an advantage. They usually contain lead, antimony, and tin, but more recently types having 98% or more of lead with calcium and lithium have been introduced. The calcium produces an age-hardening effect which trebles the strength of the lead.

Phosphor-bronze (*see* **Non-ferrous Metals**)

Phosphor-bronzes with a tin content of 10–13% and 0·5–1·0% phosphorus are used for heavy-duty bearings. They have a low coefficient of friction, great hardness, and an excellent resistance to wear, together with a very good resistance to corrosion by sea-water. These alloys may be obtained in the form of cast hollow sticks, which save material and machining time.

Aluminium-base Alloys

These alloys contain: (*a*) tin, nickel, magnesium, and copper, or (*b*) tin, nickel, magnesium, antimony, manganese, and silicon, the balance in each case being aluminium. Composition (*a*) is used for big-end bearings and (*b*) is used for main bearings. They retain their hardness at normal bearing temperatures better than other bearing alloys and their hardness is TWICE that of copper–lead alloys.

Indium

This is a rare and precious metal which is used as a surface coating for bearings to give increased resistance to corrosion and wear.

CHAPTER SIXTEEN

PLASTICS

The term 'plastics' is used to cover the very wide range of man-made complex organic, organo-metallic, or completely inorganic compounds which are made plastic by heating and are then moulded into the required shape by the application of pressure.

The raw materials used for the production of plastics are easily obtained, and include water, wood, coal, petroleum, cloth, cereal husks, nut shells, and animal secretions.

Although the plastic known as 'celluloid' was produced as long ago as 1870, it is only in the last thirty years or so that plastics have become widely used in engineering. In this short time they have had a great influence on the design of many commonplace articles, and have also made it possible to produce articles which could not have been made in any other material.

There are two main groups into which all plastics may be divided, namely, thermoplastic and thermosetting materials.

Thermoplastic Materials

These become soft and pliable when heated and can be moulded under pressure into the required shape. The article will hold this shape only after cooling to room temperature. If the article is reheated it will become soft and can be remoulded into another shape. Repeated heating and cooling will have no chemical effect upon the plastic, and so can be carried out repeatedly.

The range of thermoplastics includes:

(*a*) *The Acrylic Resins.* An example of these is perspex, which has good optical properties and which can be moulded to shape to make lenses, whereas glass has to be ground and polished. Acrylic resins are also used for the production of dentures, edge-lighted signs, and in fibre form are made into 'Orlon' and 'Acrilan' fabrics for the manufacture of clothing and yacht sails.

(*b*) *The Polyvinyl Plastics.* An example of these is polyvinyl chloride (PVC), which is often used as sheathing for electrical cables, gramophone records, non-slip floor tiles and flexible sheets. PVC is flame and water resistant, but can be attacked by organic solvents of a similar nature.

(*c*) *The Polystyrene Plastics.* These are easily moulded into complicated shapes with intricate detail, as can be seen in the plastic model construction kits for motor cars, aeroplanes, ships, and railway stock which are on sale today. Other major uses are for refrigerator panels and parts and wall tiles, where the dimensional stability, unlimited colour range and water resistance of the plastics are of great importance. Polystyrene is resistant to water solutions, but it is readily attacked by most organic solvents and oils. It is an excellent electrical insulator, but it is not weather resistant, and so is not suitable for outdoor applications.

(*d*) *The Cellulose Plastics.* An example of these is 'Celluloid', which is often used for drawing office equipment because of its good moisture resistance and the ease with which printing may be done on it. Other examples are 'Cellophane', which, in film form, is used for packaging; 'Rayon', which, in fibre form, is used in clothing and for other applications, such as household cements, photographic safety film, and petrol and gas pipes.

Thermosetting Materials

These also require heat and pressure to make them plastic and to enable them to be moulded into the shape required. This shape is maintained after cooling to room temperature. The heat and pressure used to make the materials plastic also causes a chemical change to occur in them and, after hardening by cooling, these materials cannot be softened by further application of heat. The two main groups of thermosetting plastics are:

(*a*) *The Phenolic Plastics*, such as 'Bakelite'. They are among the cheapest plastics and so are used extensively for bottle tops, tool and utensil handles, foam packing, bonding, material for grinding wheels and for parts of the ignition system of internal-combustion engines where complex insulating pieces have metal conductors moulded into them, such as in distributor caps. Unfortunately the phenolic plastics cannot be recommended for outdoor applications because they deteriorate when exposed to ozone or ultra-violet light.

(*b*) *The Amino Plastics*, which include the urea, melamine, and aniline formaldehydes. Typical uses for the urea–formaldehyde plastics are for colour-coded electrical switch parts and circuit-breakers which do not carbonise in the event of flashover. Other uses are for lamp shades, glues, adhesives, the treatment of paper to improve wet strength, and the treatment of textiles to improve crease and crush resistance.

The melamine plastics have similar properties to the urea plastics, but have superior performance and are also more expensive. Typical uses are for plastic tableware, laminates for table tops, resins for adhesives, and the treatment of paper and textiles.

Aniline formaldehyde is used for electrical terminal strips and blocks because of its high insulation resistance and low loss factor.

Originally plastics were used mainly in the form of 'moulding powders' to be used in compression or injection moulding machines, but nowadays they are widely used in the form of sheets, rods, and tubes in the same way as the metallic engineering materials.

Laminated plastics are thermosetting plastics containing layers of paper, cloth, asbestos, or wood which have been heated when under pressure to form sheets or special shapes. These laminated plastics can be used to replace wood, metal, or fibre. They have the advantage of having a uniform structure, and so are less liable to fracture than wood or metal. Their specific gravity is low, being only half that of aluminium, while tensile strengths can be up to 90% that of the metal. This means that they could be very suitable materials for applications where light weights with moderate strength are required. These laminates are resistant to many oils, alkalis, and dilute acids and, when fully hardened, are chemically inert. This means that the electrical insulation properties are maintained in conditions which might lead to a breakdown in other materials. Sheets of laminated plastics are available in a wide range of colours and in thicknesses ranging from 2 mm–100 mm. Typical uses for laminated plastics are for high-voltage fuses, printed circuits for electrical work, high-speed cams which can stop and start rapidly because of their light weight, quiet-running timing gears for internal-combustion engines, because the natural resilience of the plastic absorbs the shocks applied by varying loads, and also for heavy-duty bearings in steel rolling mills where the low coefficient of friction of the laminates gives a long bearing life and reduced power consumption. Some types of pump also use these plastics for thrust bearings, gears, and seals.

Examples of the laminated plastics are 'Bakelite' and 'Tufnol', but the range is very wide and often combines the outstanding properties of both plastic and traditional materials. An example of this is the coating of steel sheet with PVC so that the laminated plastic has the strength of the steel and the decorative appearance and corrosion resistance of the plastic, making it useful material for structural purposes.

Most of the normal requirements of engineering can be met by the use of plastics if they are specially selected to suit their application and are used in combination with traditional materials if necessary. However, the drawback of most plastics is their poor resistance to heat or open flame, when they will eventually collapse or decompose. Special plastics are available which will not soften until temperatures exceeding 200 °C are reached, and others have a good flame resistance.

Plastics have a low thermal conductivity, and so give a pleasant sensation to the touch, and this has led to their use for tool and machine handles, table tops, and thermal insulation in refrigerators.

The tensile strength of plastics is generally satisfactory, especially when their light weight is taken into account, but thermoplastic materials suffer a decrease in strength with increase in temperatures, so that care should be taken to see that the operating temperature for these plastics does not become too high.

In general, plastics have an excellent corrosion resistance and are being widely used as a corrosion-resistant coating for metals.

Typical applications of plastics in the electrical engineering industry today are for radio and television cabinets, personal hearing aids, switches, junction boxes, lampshades, and copper-clad laminates for computer printed circuits.

In the field of transport there are 'fibreglass' car bodies, motor-cycle fairings, nose cones for rockets and aircraft, sailing-dinghy hulls, and of course many of the smaller fittings which are to be found in these means of transport.

The chemical industry uses plastic linings on storage tanks, plastic pipes, ducts, guttering, valve seats, and glands. Where increased corrosion resistance is required use is being made of plastic-coated metals in place of the lacquered metals previously used.

In engineering workshops plastics are to be found as handles for tools and machines, safety guards, especially where electrical equipment is concerned, and moulds. Plastics are also used for press tools, as they give a lower power consumption, greater accuracy, and increased life as compared with the more traditional materials. The shapes of moulds made of plastic are easily altered if required, and the time required to cast the mould is very short; all these combine to make them an attractive proposition for this kind of work. Plastic adhesives are now being increasingly used in structural work, because the life of the joints made by this method often exceeds that which would be obtained by using nuts and bolts.

Plastics are becoming an increasingly common sight in modern life, and their influence will extend even more as their properties are improved and developed.

Nomenclature of Plastics

Many of the plastics which are now widely used by engineers are known by trade names which are easier to remember and pronounce than are their chemical equivalents. Nevertheless, the student who may wish to study these materials more deeply should be aware of the correct chemical term for these plastics. To meet this need the following table relates some of the better known plastics to their chemical equivalents.

Trade Name	Chemical Equivalent
Alkathene	Polyethylene
Celluloid	Nitrocellulose
Perspex	Polymethyl methacrylate
PVC	Polyvinyl chloride
Fluon and Teflon	Polytetrafluoroethylene

Nylon, Fluon, and Teflon are plastics with a low coefficient of friction and are now being used in motor-car accessories and domestic equipment.

The student is advised to consult the following British Standards:

BS 1493: 1967. *Polystyrene Moulding Materials.*
BS 1524: 1955. *Cellulose Acetate Moulding Materials.*
BS 1322: 1956. *Aminoplastic Moulding Materials.*
BS 771: 1959. *Phenolic Moulding Materials.*
BS 1755: 1961. *Glossary of Terms Used in the Plastics Industry.*
BS 3396: 1961–6. *Woven Glass Fibre Fabrics for Plastics Reinforcement.*
BS 3502: 1967. *Schedule of Common Names and Abbreviations for Plastics and Rubbers.*

The following books are recommended to the student who wishes to pursue his study of plastics and other materials further than is possible in this volume:

Kempster, M. H. A. *Introduction to Engineering Materials.* The English Universities Press Ltd.
Kempster, M. H. A. *Materials for Engineers.* The English Universities Press Ltd.

CHAPTER SEVENTEEN
TESTING OF MATERIALS

The following are some of the types of machines used for the testing of materials:

Avery Universal Testing Machine (Fig. 17.1 (*a*))

At Fig. 17.1 (*a*) is a simplified diagram of the Avery Universal Testing Machine. This is a typical testing machine in which the load is applied hydraulically. The specimen to be tested is either secured in the self-aligning grips on the right of the diagram for tensile tests or placed between the two compression platens for compression tests.

The load is applied hydraulically by means of an electric motor driving a pump which

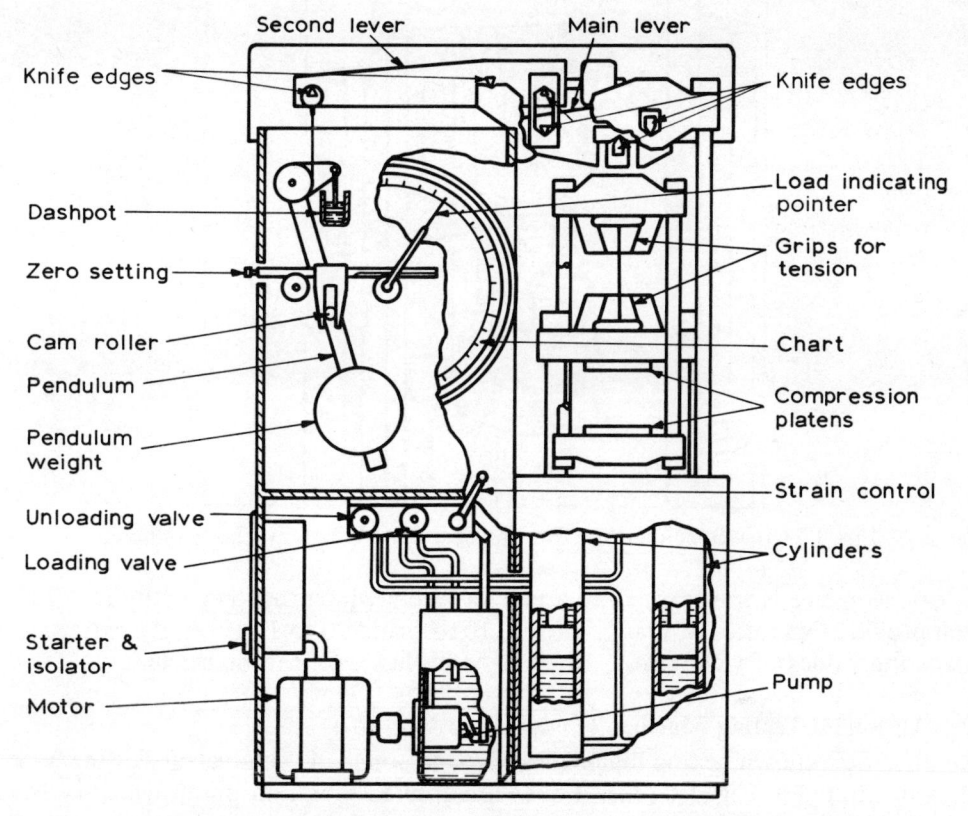

Fig. 17.1 (*a*). Diagram of an Avery Universal Testing Machine

forces oil into the cylinders, shown at the bottom of the diagram, through suitable valves, shown to the left. Clearly a loading and an unloading valve are needed.

When the load is applied the downward pull exerted by the specimen is transmitted to the load-indicating pointer via the main lever and the second lever. The second lever is connected to a circular drum on the axis of the pendulum. The movement of the second lever displaces the pendulum which, in turn, causes a rack-and-pinion mechanism, operating through the cam roller on the pendulum itself, to rotate the load-indicating pointer and register the load on the test piece. The dash-pot shown at the upper end of the pendulum is to damp the movement of the pendulum when the test piece fractures under the load.

This is an extremely sensitive machine. The levers are most carefully supported on the knife edges shown in the diagram, and it is most important that they are kept clean and are not subjected to undue jolts or shocks.

For tensile tests the specimen should conform to British Standards and the extension produced should be measured by means of an extensometer.

Fig. 17.1 (*b*) shows a gauge-length extensometer which is suitable for round or flat specimens. This extensometer is provided with spring-loaded follow-up plungers which enable it to remain on a metal specimen right up to the point of fracture. The movement

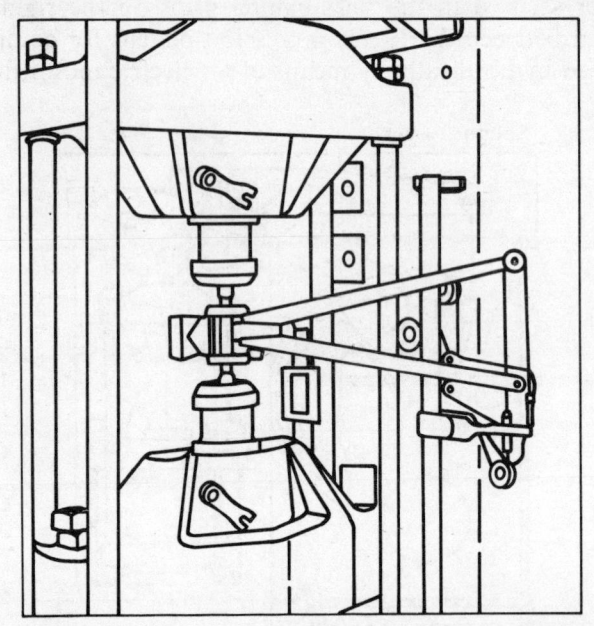

Fig. 17.1 (*b*). Specimen for Tensile Test Fitted with an Extensometer

of the extensometer is transmitted by a pair of levers which together with the cord transmission provide two ratios of magnification, 10 to 1 and 20 to 1. From the extensions and the loads the values of yield stress, Young's Modulus, etc., can be calculated.

Denison Universal Testing Machine (Fig. 17.2 (*a*) and (*b*))

Another well-known testing machine is the Denison (T.42) Universal Testing Machine, which is illustrated at Fig. 17.2 (*a*). Loads are applied by an oil pump which is driven at constant speed by an electric motor. This pump, which is controlled by the pump-displacement control wheel on the lower right-hand side of the machine, supplies oil under pressure to the two cylinders on either side of the test piece. A bleed valve permits excess oil to escape from the cylinders to the main oil tank and, by this means, an exceedingly fine control of the load on the specimen is achieved. Moreover, a given load can be maintained on the test piece almost indefinitely.

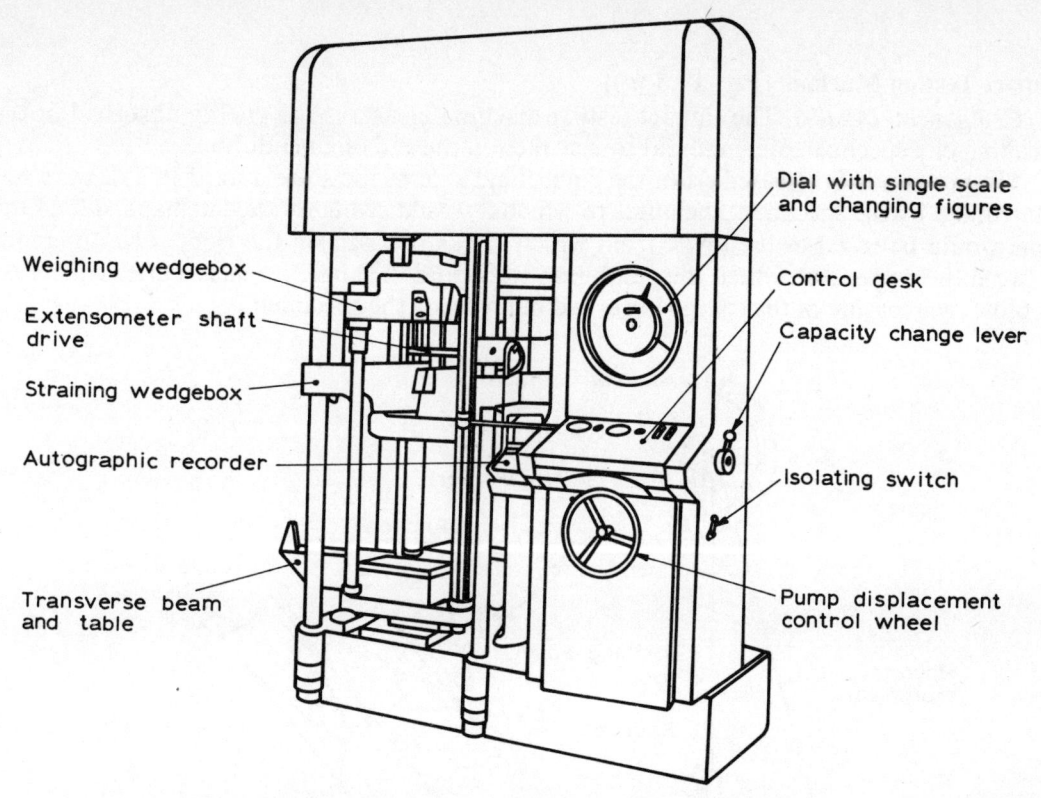

Fig. 17.2 (*a*). Denison (T.42) Universal Testing Machine

The load on the specimen is transmitted to a dial pointer through the weighing wedge box and the series of beams and linkages shown diagrammatically at Fig. 17.2 (*b*). The beams are most carefully balanced on knife edges and enable very accurate readings to be made.

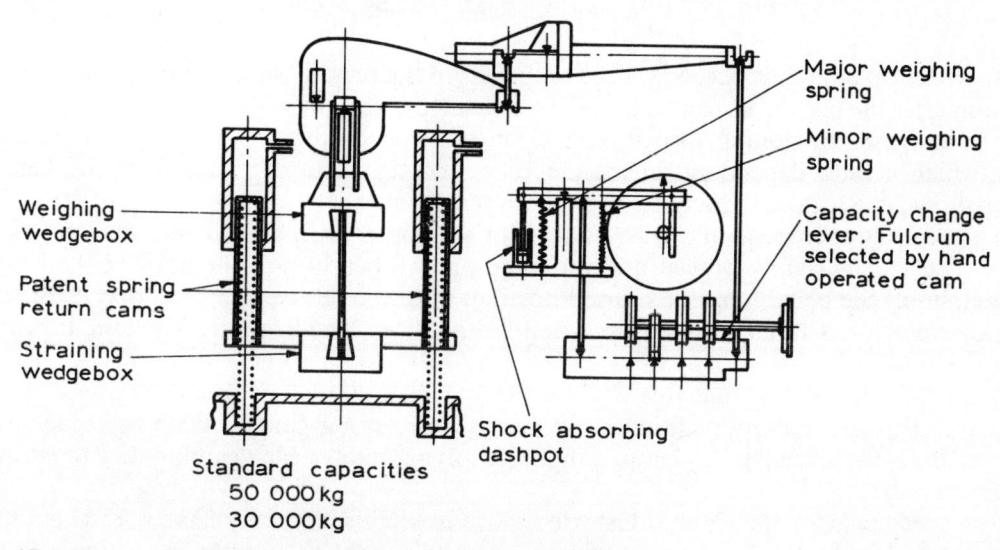

Fig. 17.2 (*b*). Arrangement of Weighing and Load Indicating Mechanism on a Denison (T.42) Universal Testing Machine

Impact Testing Machine (Fig. 17.3 (*a*))

Component Details. The impact testing machine measures the energy absorbed in the breaking of a specimen of a material by a striker on the end of a pendulum.

The pendulum is released from the right-hand side of the scale and, if its fall were not interrupted by the specimen, the angle to which it would swing on the left-hand side of the scale would be equal to the angle from which it was released on the right. The difference between the angle from which the pendulum starts and the angle it reaches after delivering its blow is a measure of the energy absorbed in breaking the specimen.

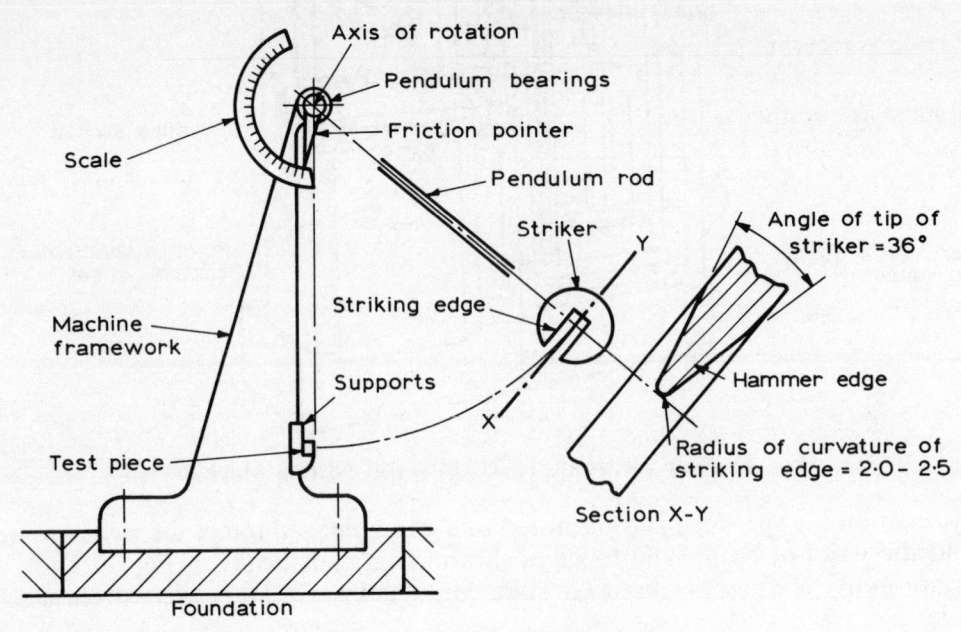

Fig. 17.3 (*a*). Charpy Impact Testing Machine

The friction pointer is zeroed on the scale before the pendulum is released and from its position after the test the impact value of the specimen is read off. The range of the machine may be increased by bolting special weights onto the pendulum or by changing the height from which it falls, depending on the machine, and the scale has, therefore, two sets of graduations, one for each range.

The pendulum consists of a tube fitted with a hammer with a hardened steel precision edge. The unit is rigidly braced and mounted on ball-bearings in the apex of the frame. A catch holds the pendulum in its raised position until the release trigger is operated. The striking velocity, hammer dimensions and foundation specifications are laid down in BS 131.

With the Charpy test machine shown, the specimen is placed on two support blocks (Fig. 17.3 (*b*)) and rapidly positioned by means of a setting gauge. With the older Izod test machine, the specimen is clamped in a vice having removable gripping dies to suit the specimen to be tested.

The specimens for the Charpy test are square in section and may have a V, U or 'keyhole' notch (Fig. 17.4). The Izod specimens may be square or circular in section and are V-notched. Dimensions of specimens are laid down in BS 131.

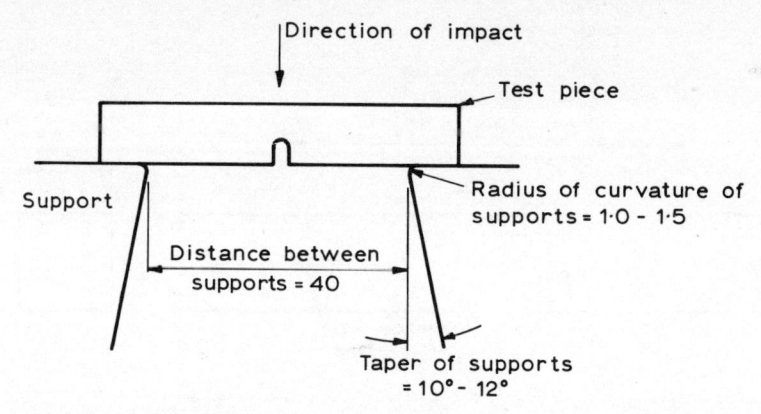

Fig. 17.3 (b). Specimen Support on a Charpy Impact Testing Machine

Cast iron is tested under Izod conditions using an unnotched specimen and special gripping dies.

Method of Making Tests. The specimen is placed on the supports as in Fig. 17.3 (b), being positioned by setting gauge. The pendulum is raised to its maximum position and released by a trigger; it then swings down and breaks the specimen, the residual energy in the pendulum carrying it forward. The distance it travels is shown on the graduated scale by the loose pointer, and this reading gives the impact value.

While the specimen is being removed, the pendulum is supported by a rest on the frames. This rest falls away when the pendulum is raised. Examination of the fractured surface is helpful in judging certain qualities of the material under test. The broken specimen should therefore be retained.

Brinell Hardness Testing Machine (Fig. 17.5 (a))

Description. The load is applied by a lever mounted on knife-edges and carrying a hanger for loose weights. The hanger, without weights, is equivalent to a load of 250 kg and the load can be increased, in 250 kg stages, up to 3000 kg. The specimen to be tested is carried on a hardened steel table, which is removable so that alternative supports for specimens can be used. The table is raised or lowered by a robust steel screw operated by a large hand-wheel. Contact is made between the specimen and the ball penetrator by turning the wheel fitted on the penetrator column. When testing, the load is applied and removed by hydraulic power controlled by a hand-lever. An indicator shows the position of the load-bearing lever, the rate at which the load is applied, and whether the test has been correctly carried out.

General Information. The Brinell test for hardness consists in applying a hardened steel ball of known diameter to the surface of the specimen to be tested under a known loading for a specified minimum period of time. The diameter of the resulting impression on the specimen's surface is measured with a microscope. Hardness is indicated by the Brinell Number, derived by dividing the applied load in kilogrammes by the spherical area of the impression in square millimetres. The harder the material, the smaller the impression and, consequently, the higher is the Brinell Number.

Choice of Ball. So that the relation between the diameter of the ball and the impression produced on different metals can be held within limits, standard ratios of P/D^2 are used, where P is the load in kilogrammes and D^2 is the square of the diameter of the ball in millimetres.

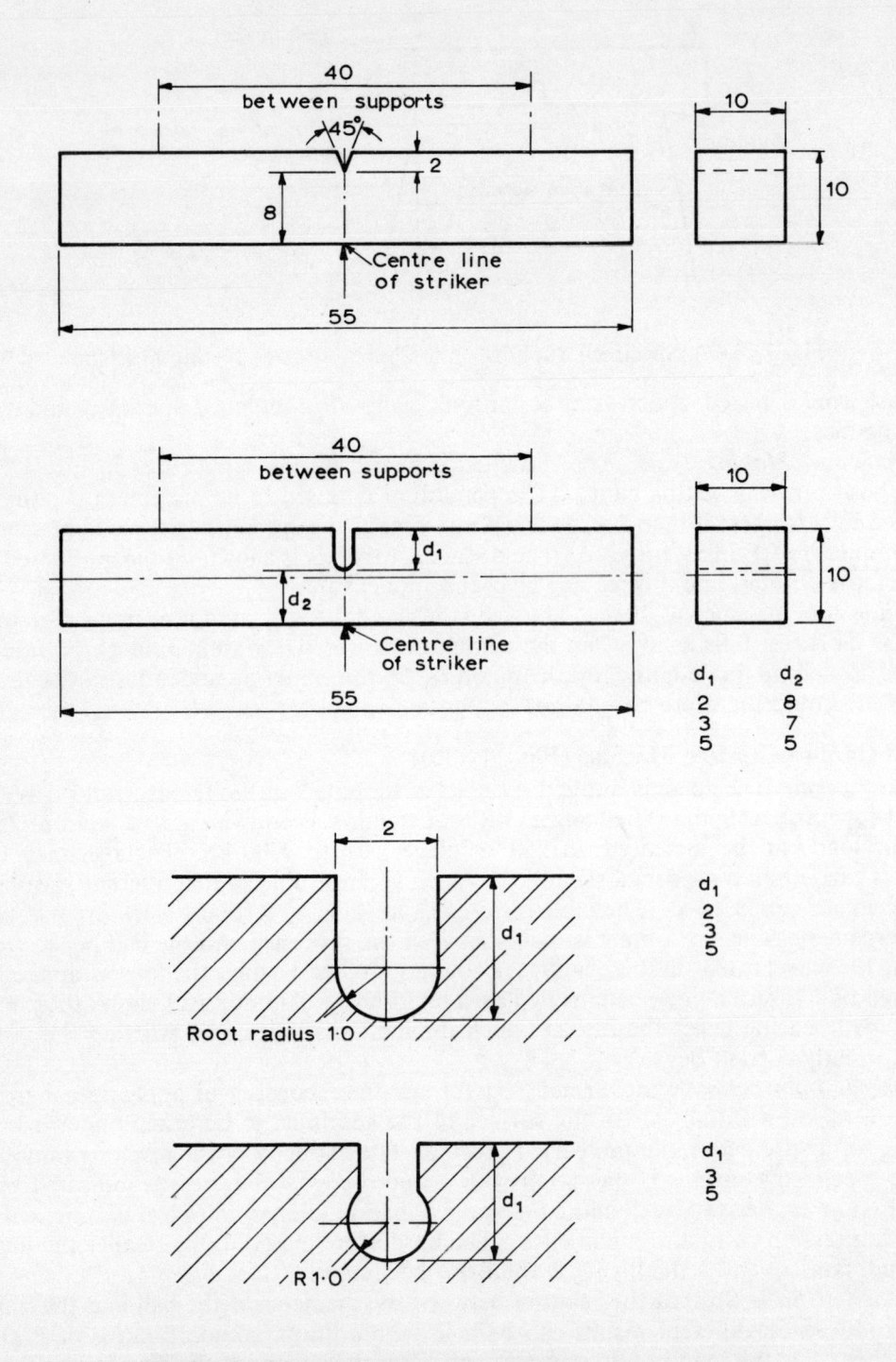

Fig. 17.4. Dimensions of Standard Charpy Test Specimens

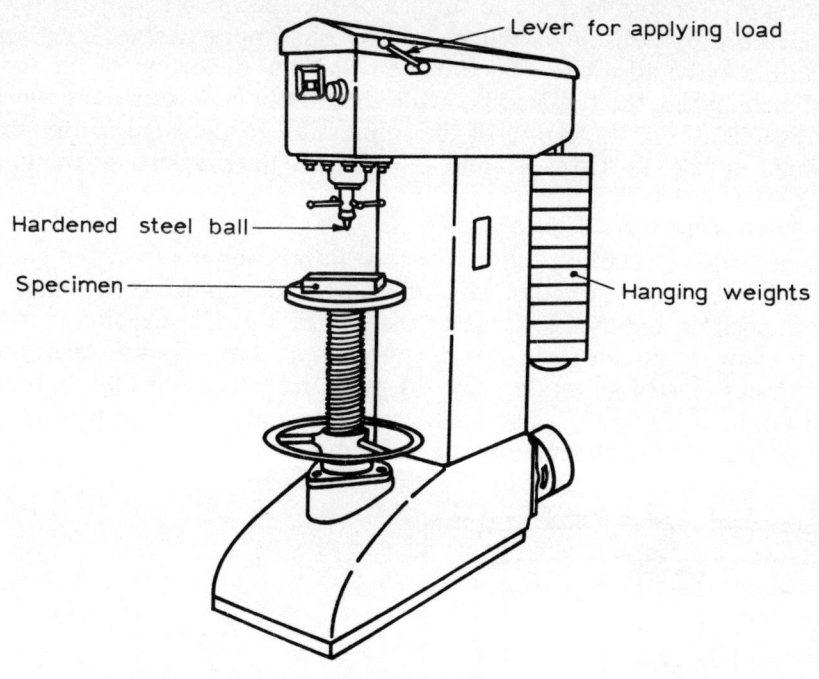

Fig. 17.5 (a)

Load. The loads most used are 3000 kg and 500 kg with ball 10 mm diameter and 750 kg with ball 5 mm diameter. Choice of the most suitable P/D^2 ratio for the testing of a material depends on the average hardness of such material. Desirable values are broadly indicated in Tables IV and V.

TABLE IV

Dia of ball (D), in mm	Load (P), in kg		
	$\dfrac{P}{D^2} = 5$	$\dfrac{P}{D^2} = 10$	$\dfrac{P}{D^2} = 30$
5	—	250	750
10	500	1000	3000

TABLE V

Approx. Brinell Hardness No.	$\dfrac{P}{D^2}$ ratio	Representative material
Above 160	30	Steels, cast iron
160 to 60	10	Copper alloys and aluminium alloys
60 to 20	5	Copper, aluminium

Preparation of Test Specimen. The surface of the specimen should be made flat and smooth, preferably by polishing. Where polishing is impracticable, filing, grinding, or fine machining may be adequate. To avoid errors from distortion of the test body, the thickness of metal where the test is to be made should not be less than ten times the depth of the impression. From the centre of the impression to the edge of the test body the distance should not be less than two and a half times the diameter of the impression.

The Brinell Microscope (Fig. 17.5 (*b*))

This instrument is placed in position over the impression made by the ball so that the diameter can be measured. An adjustable tube carries the optical components, which can be clamped in position and used to focus on the impression. The eyepiece is independently adjustable to allow a graticule scale (on which the impression appears superimposed) to be brought into focus. Divisions on the scale 0·1 mm, and impressions up to 7 mm diameter can be measured (Fig. 17.5 (*c*)). The diameter of the indentation shown in Fig. 17.5 (*c*) as recorded on the scale of the microscope is 4·1 mm.

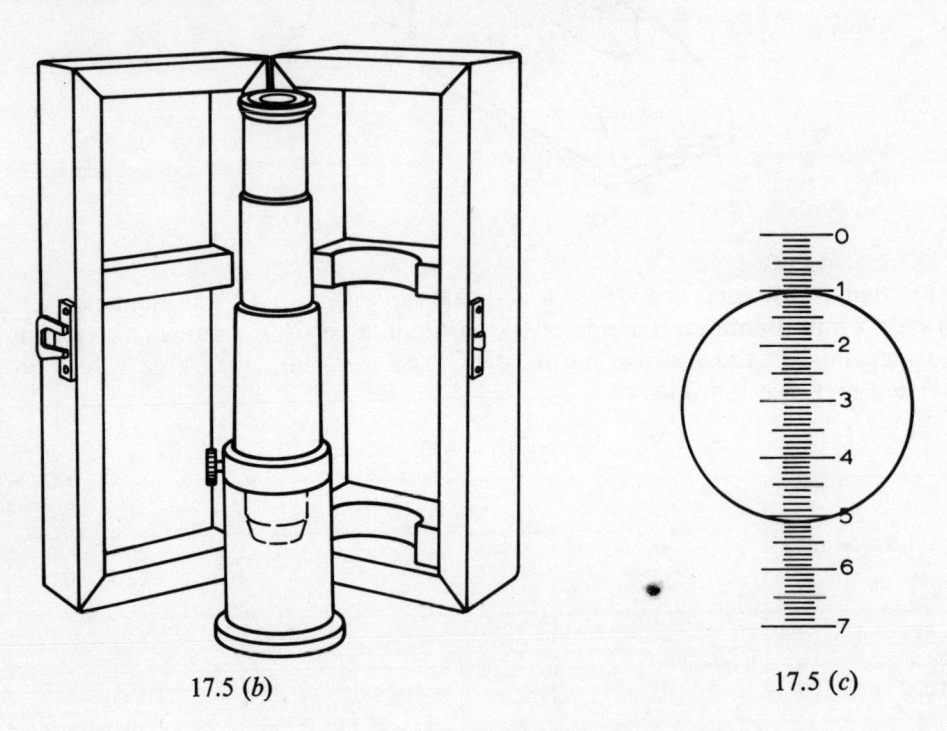

17.5 (*b*)   17.5 (*c*)

PART THREE
EXERCISES

TEST QUESTIONS

The following questions have been prepared to enable the student to apply himself to typical problems which might well be set in an examination paper.

1. Sketch a Woodruffe key. Where would such a key be used? What are its advantages and disadvantages over other types of key?
2. Sketch an isometric view of a lathe tailstock. Give sectional views where necessary to show the internal construction.
3. Draw neat sketches to show how the hand feed and driving mechanism for a power-driven pillar drill works.
4. Explain, using sketches where necessary, how an independent four-jaw chuck operates. State any advantages or disadvantages it has over other types of chuck.
5. Make a freehand sketch of a hand-operated press for pressing-in small bushes.
6. Explain, using sketches where necessary, how the length of the stroke of a shaping machine ram may be altered.
7. Sketch freehand: (*a*) a milling machine vice; (*b*) a three-jaw concentric lathe chuck.
8. Make sketches of the nose of a milling-machine spindle, showing how the drive is transmitted to the cutter arbor. It is essential that one of the sketches is a section.
9. Sketch and describe the ratchet feed device suitable for a grinding machine.
10. Sketch freehand: (*a*) a plain mandrel, (*b*) a double cone mandrel. State for what purpose each is used.
11. Sketch and describe the type of cutter used for milling: (*a*) 'vee' grooves; (*b*) flat surfaces; (*c*) vertical surfaces. Sketch also and describe the type of cutter which could be used for cutting flutes in milling cutters.
12. Sketch the essential features of a taper-turning attachment for use with a centre lathe.
13. Explain, using sketches where necessary, how the quick-return mechanism of a shaping machine operates.
14. Write a short account of each of the following methods of lubrication: (*a*) drip feed; (*b*) a lubricator using grease; (*c*) a force-feed system as used in the modern motor car.
15. Sketch and describe: (*a*) a parallel-shank twist drill; (*b*) a hand reamer. What is the purpose of each? What materials could each be made from? State why you have chosen these materials.
16. A shaft requires a short taper at one end (30 mm × 7°). Describe in detail, using sketches where necessary, how this taper may be obtained using the compound slide.
17. Write a short account of the advantages of using roller and ball bearings, illustrating your answer with sketches where necessary.
18. Choosing your own dimensions, draw, in accordance with BS 308, the conventional representation of:
    (*a*) an internal thread; (*b*) an external thread; (*c*) a compression spring.

19. (*a*) Using sketches, explain how a suitable dial gauge and accessories could be used:
    (i) to check that the tailstock spindle of a lathe is co-axial with the headstock spindle;
    (ii) to act as a comparator for checking a quantity of ϕ 25 mm rollers.
    (*b*) For case (ii) above, explain how you would decide the accuracy of measurement.
    (CGLI) *Modified*

20. Sketch and explain how a vernier height gauge works. Give TWO examples of how it may be used in the workshop.

21. Describe with the aid of sketches the BS method of dimensioning each of the following.

    (*a*) A spot faced hole.
    (*b*) A counter bored hole.
    (*c*) A countersunk hole.
    (*d*) A keyway in a shaft.
    (*e*) A keyway in the bore of a gear wheel.

22. Describe with the aid of sketches how the following features should be shown on engineering drawings using BS 308 recommendations.

    (*a*) Holes equally spaced on a circular pitch.
    (*b*) A machined surface.
    (*c*) A stud assembled in a blind hole.

23. What is the difference between a spot face and a counterbore? Give an example of where each is used.

24. (*a*) List briefly the main points to be considered in deciding whether to employ casting or forging to produce a component. A particular component may be chosen to illustrate the points.
    (*b*) Discuss the different reasons why it is a great advantage for both a casting and a forging to be as uniform as possible in section. (CGLI)

25. What is the difference between measuring and gauging?

26. A dial gauge can be used to determine the roundness and concentricity of a component. A scribing block can also be used for this purpose but has certain disadvantages. What are these disadvantages?

27. Discuss the properties of wrought iron and show how these properties affect its uses in modern engineering.

28. State the percentage of carbon in (*a*) a medium carbon steel, and (*b*) a high carbon steel. Give two applications for each of these steels.

29. State the composition of a bronze that could be used for a bearing bush, giving reasons for such a choice. Name two other bearing metals.

30. Brass, bronze, and white metal are all used for plain bearings. Explain briefly a type of bearing application for which each of these metals should be used. Give an example, with reasons, of an UNSUITABLE application in each case. (CGLI)

31. State the main characteristics of anti-friction metal. State why it is used for a bearing. What are the principal properties of aluminium-bronze?

32. In plain carbon steel there are other elements in addition to carbon. Name these elements and state their effects on the characteristics of the steel.

33. Name one aluminium alloy which has the property of 'age hardening'. What difficulties are caused by this condition?
34. State, giving the size and/or form, what material would be suitable for the following parts, giving reasons for your choice: (*a*) a non-adjustable horseshoe-type gauge; (*b*) the nut for a lathe cross-slide screw.
35. Write down the average composition of: (*a*) brass; (*b*) high-tensile steel.
What results would you expect from an impact test on these metals? State why these results should be expected.
36. You are required to carry out a tensile test on mild steel in the laboratory. Give a brief description of how you would carry out such a test, using sketches where necessary.
37. Describe the physical properties of: (*a*) gunmetal; (*b*) phosphor-bronze; (*c*) duralumin. Give TWO examples of where each could be used in an engineering component.
38. What are the particular properties of bearing white metal which make it suitable for its particular purpose? In what forms can it be obtained commercially? (CGLI)
39. What characteristics do you consider to be essential in a good bearing metal?
Name three bearing metals, give their main composition, and state one use of each type.
40. Anti-friction alloys are sometimes used as bearing metals. Name two and state their constituents.
Compare the relative merits of the two you have chosen.
41. Brass has special properties which make it suitable and valuable as an engineering material. What are these special properties?
Give examples of TWO types of brass which have special properties and give reasons for your choice.
42. What is the difference between a jig and a fixture? List TWELVE basic essentials in the design of a good jig.
43. Sketch TWO types of: (*a*) edge clamps; (*b*) equalising clamps. State where each type is used, and list the fundamental differences between them.
44. Give neat freehand sketches of TWO types of clamps that may be used on milling fixtures or drilling jigs. Indicate an application for each type of clamp.
45. Draw a neat freehand sketch of a 'Go' and 'Not go' plug gauge. Show on your drawing:

   (*a*) the 'Go' end
   (*b*) the 'Not go' end
   (*c*) surfaces which must be ground
   (*d*) any other information which should be engraved on the gauge.

46. Various types and parts of gauges are made from certain materials. List these, giving reasons for your choice.
47. (*a*) Distinguish in a general way between thermoplastics and thermosetting plastics.
    (*b*) Name one type of material in each of the above groups and give an example of its application in engineering.
    (*c*) What are the main advantages and disadvantages of thermoplastic materials as compared with metals? (CGLI)
48. Name TWO kinds of hardness tests which can be applied to materials. Describe in detail, using sketches where necessary, one of the tests which you have carried out.

EXERCISES ON DEVELOPMENTS

The following exercises are based on the developments which have already been dealt with earlier in the book. It is recommended that the student should study the appropriate development and then attempt the exercise without further reference to the textbook unless he finds himself unable to continue.

In most examinations where questions on developments are set the student is required to show his construction lines so that the examiner can see at a glance whether the candidate has used the correct method for obtaining the required development. It is strongly recommended that the student should show all his construction lines on the solutions to these exercises, for they will help him to remember how his solution was obtained. All such lines should be fine and faint, but clear.

In the following questions ALL DIMENSIONS ARE GIVEN IN MILLIMETRES.

1. Fig. E1 shows an oblique cone. Draw the development of the COMPLETE SURFACE of the cone. (The complete development is the curved surface and the base.)

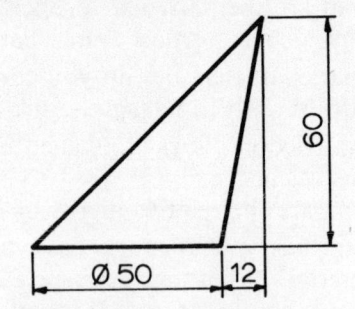

Fig. E1. An Oblique Cone

2. Fig. E2 shows a branch pipe. Draw the development of the COMPLETE branch, and draw the curve of intersection between the two branches of the pipe.

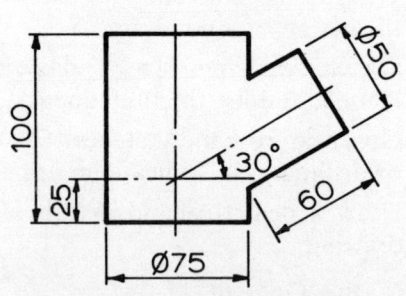

Fig. E2. A Branch Pipe

3. Fig. E3 shows a cone cut by a circular pipe. Develop the CURVED SURFACE of the RIGHT CONE and draw the curve of intersection between the pipe and the cone.

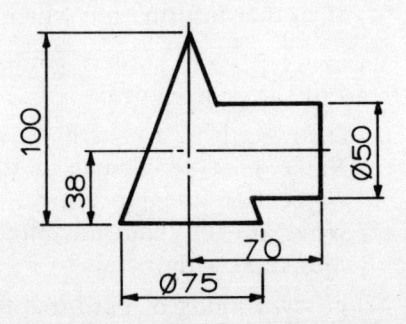

Fig. E3. A Cone Cut by a Circular Pipe

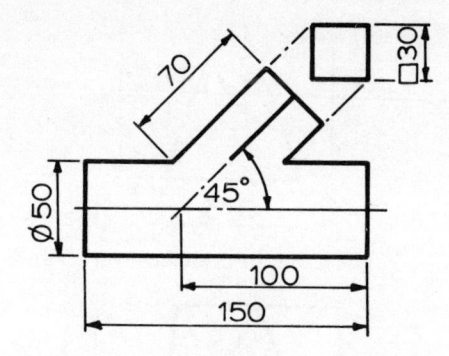

Fig. E4. A Square Pipe Intersecting a Circular Pipe

4. Fig. E4 shows a square pipe intersecting a circular pipe. Draw:
   (i) the development of the SQUARE PIPE;
   (ii) the plan view of the hole in the circular pipe.

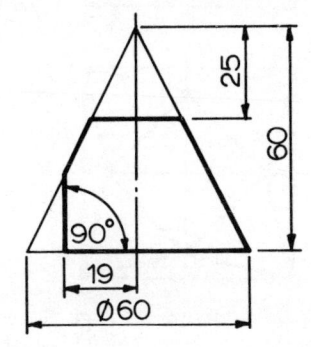

Fig. E5. Frustum of a Right Cone Cut by Two Planes at Right Angles to Each Other

5. Fig. E5 shows the frustum of a right cone which is cut by two planes at right angles to each other.
Develop the CURVED surface of the frustum.

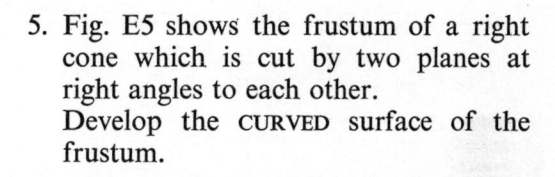

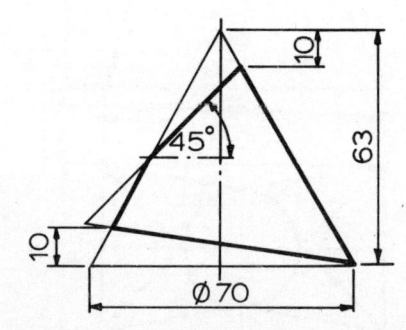

Fig. E6. Frustum of a Right Cone Cut by Two Planes NOT at Right Angles to Each Other

6. Fig. E6 shows the frustum of a right cone which is cut by two planes NOT at right angles to each other.
Draw the development of the CURVED SURFACE of the frustum.

7. Fig. E7 shows a right cone which is intersected by a cylinder.
   Draw the development of the CURVED SURFACE of the right cone.

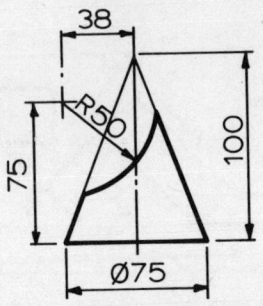

Fig. E7. A Right Cone Intersected by a Cylinder

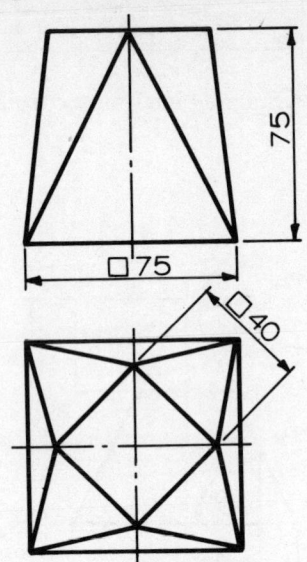

8. Fig. E8 shows a transition from a large square to a small square rotated through 45° to the larger.
   Draw the development.

Fig. E8. Transition from a Large Square to a Smaller Square Rotated through 45° to the Larger

9. Fig. E9 shows an oblong to round transition piece.
   Draw the development.

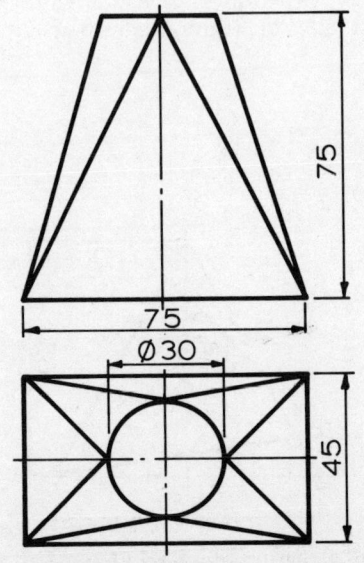

Fig. E9. Oblong to Round Transition Piece

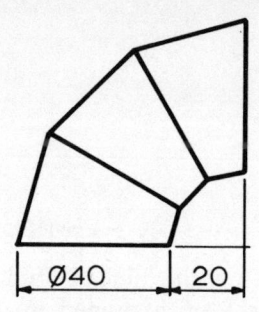

Fig. E10. A 90° Lobster-back Bend with Three Segments

10. Fig. E10 shows a 90° lobster-back bend which comprises three full segments.
    Draw the development.

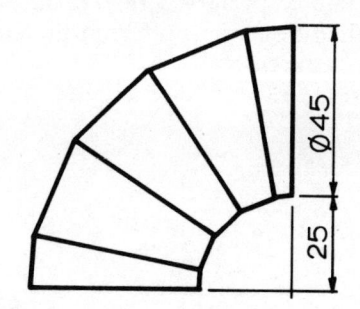

Fig. E11. A 90° Lobster-back Bend with Three Full and Two Half Segments

11. Fig. E11 shows a 90° lobster-back bend which comprises three full and two half segments.
    Draw the development.

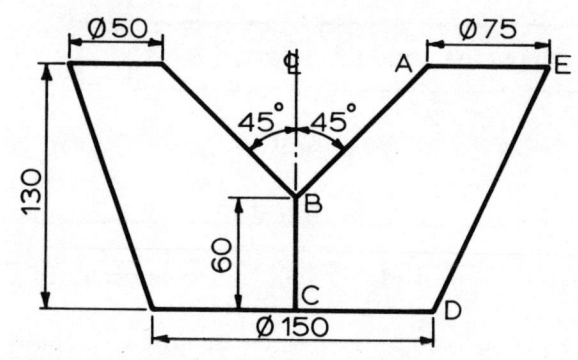

Fig. E12. A Circular Branch Pipe

12. Fig. E12 shows a circular branch pipe. Draw the development of the branch ABCDE.

DRAWING EXERCISES

The exercises which follow deal with engineering components with which all students taking the T2 course should be reasonably familiar. They have been arranged in progressive order of difficulty, and a time scale has been given for each exercise. This should help the student to assess his ability to work to the time scale of an examination and to gauge his relative progress in using his drawing instruments accurately and quickly.

Wherever possible, BS 4318 first, second, or third choice preferred metric basic sizes for engineering have been used, but, due to design difficulties, non-preferred dimensions have been used in places. ALL DIMENSIONS ARE GIVEN IN MILLIMETRES.

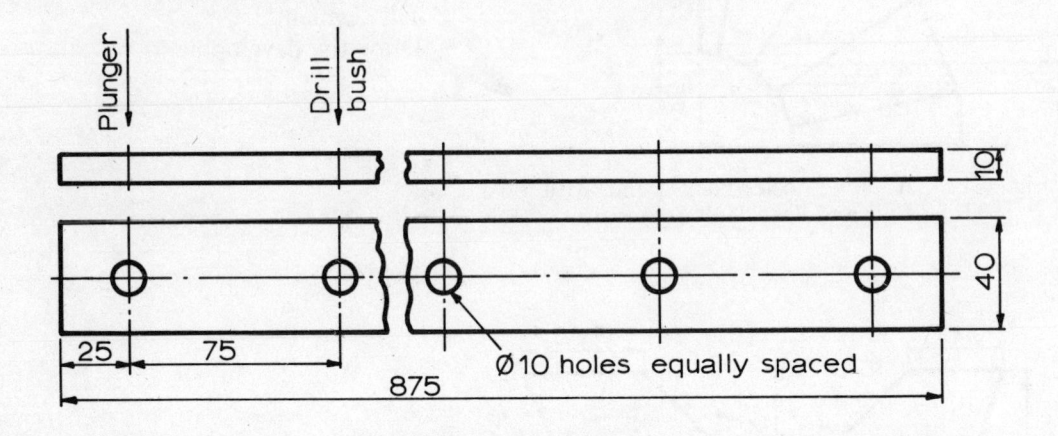

METAL STRIP

DRAWING EXERCISE 1. The METAL STRIP shown above is to be drilled with holes at equal intervals along its length as shown.

The drilling can be done using a simple channel-type drill-jig having one drill bush and a locating plunger.

Make a sketch or drawing of a suitable jig in good proportion. Indicate how you would position the first hole. (CGLI) *Modified*

Estimated time for completion:

　　　　Sketch ¼ HOUR
　　　　Drawing ½ HOUR

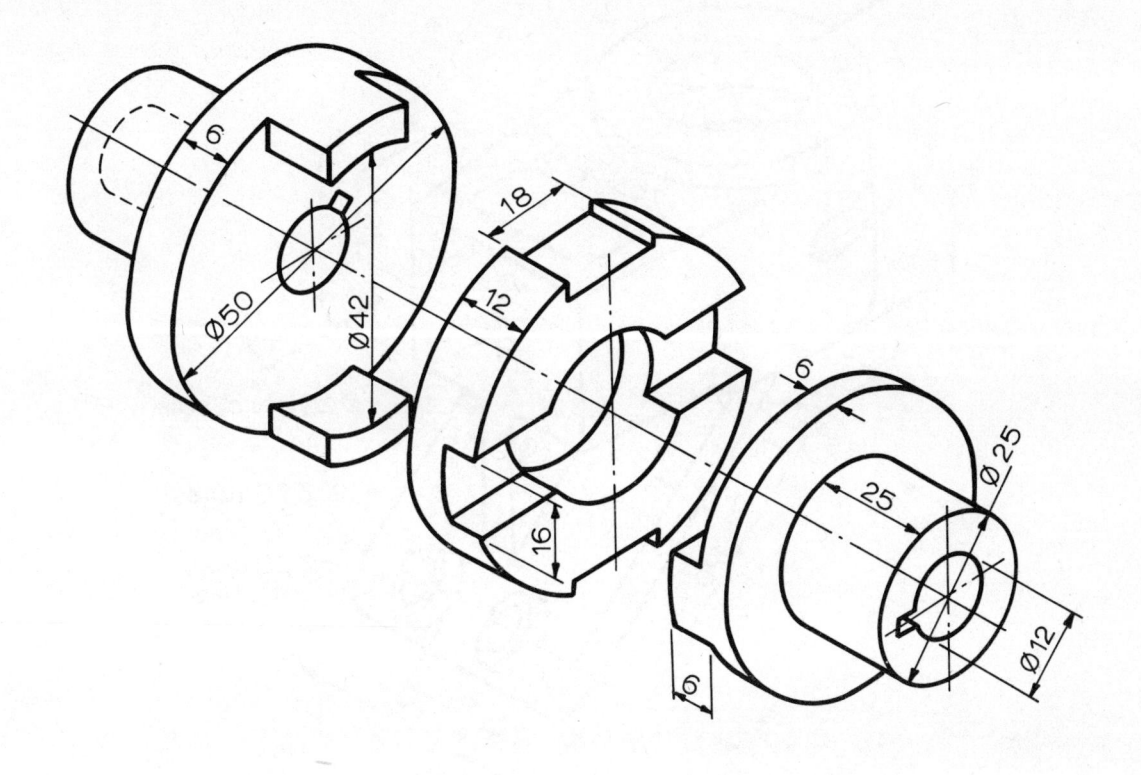

Claw Coupling

DRAWING EXERCISE 2. Draw, to a suitable scale, using first-angle projection, the following views of the completely assembled CLAW COUPLING shown above:

(a) A sectional front elevation, the cutting plane to be taken on the vertical centre line of the assembled coupling.

(b) A plan.

Show a length of shaft in both ends of the coupling. Any dimensions omitted must be supplied by the student. Dimension the drawing, and give suitable limits where necessary to ensure interchangeability and satisfactory working conditions.

Estimated time for completion: 1½ HOURS.

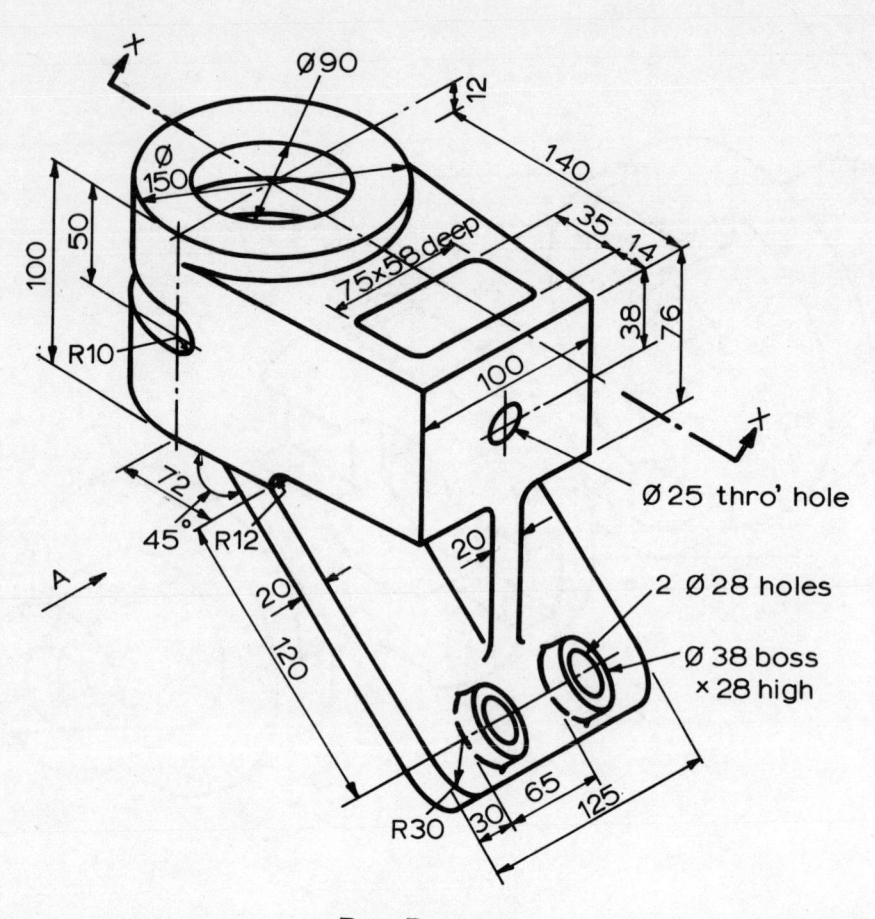

PIPE BRACKET

DRAWING EXERCISE 3. Draw to a suitable scale and using first-angle projection the following views of the PIPE BRACKET shown above:

(a) A sectional front elevation in the direction of the arrow A taken on the cutting plane X–X which passes centrally through the 20 mm web in the vertical plane.
(b) An end elevation.
(c) A plan.

Fully dimension the drawing.
Estimated time for completion: $2\frac{1}{4}$ HOURS.

As a further exercise, sketch the set-up and give a list of tools required for the operation of boring the 90 mm diameter boss using a centre lathe, assuming only one component is required. You may assume that all other machining has been carried out, and that the bracket is to be made of malleable cast iron.

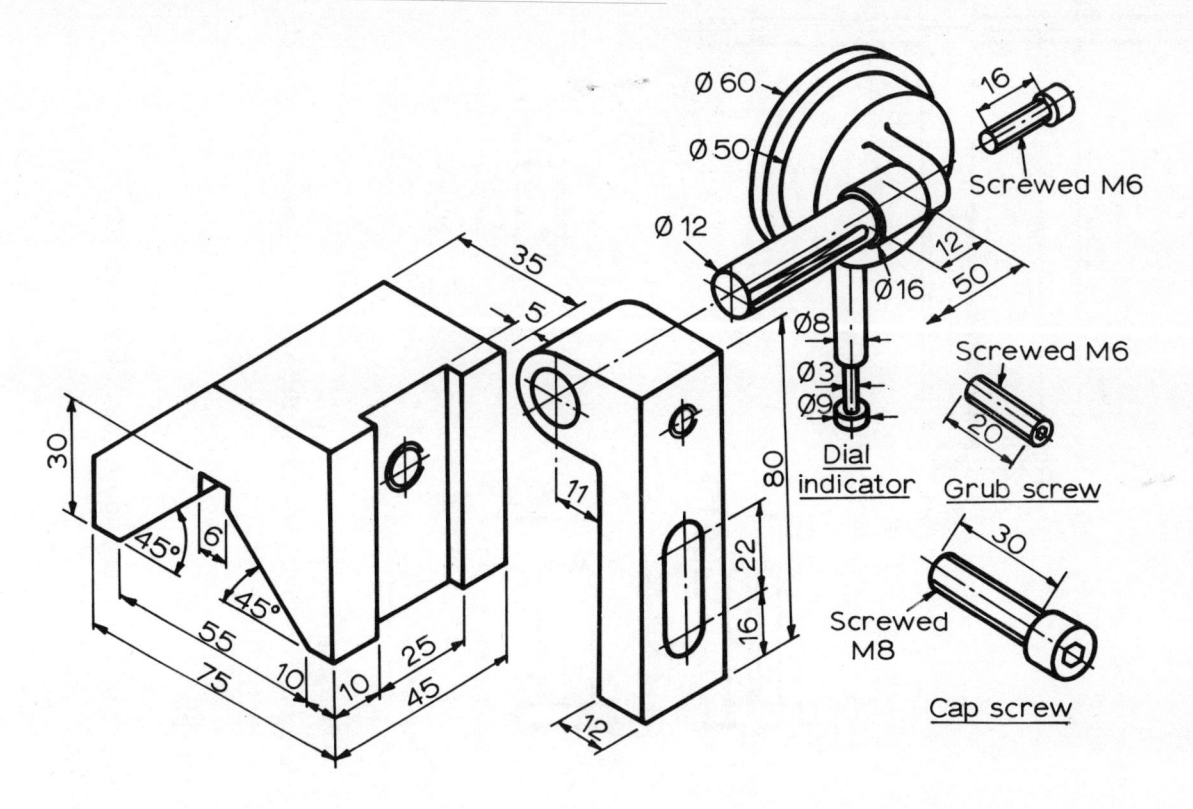

Tool Setting Gauge for Boring Bar

DRAWING EXERCISE 4. Draw, to a suitable scale, using first-angle projection, the following views of the completely assembled TOOL SETTING GAUGE for a boring bar:

(*a*) A front elevation.
(*b*) An end elevation.

Do NOT dimension the drawing, but number the parts and draw-up a parts list. The dial gauge can be assumed as a stock part. Any dimensions omitted must be supplied by the student.

As a further exercise, draw to a suitable scale, the separate parts giving ALL necessary dimensions, tolerances, and machining marks required for production. State the materials each part could be made from, giving your reasons for such a choice.

Estimated time for completion: 3 HOURS.

DRAWING EXERCISE 5. Draw to a suitable scale, and using first-angle projection, the following views of the completely assembled BAR BENDER, showing a 25 mm diameter bar in position for bending:

(a) A front elevation in direction of arrow X.
(b) A sectional end elevation taken on the cutting plane A–A.
(c) A plan.

Show all necessary machining marks, and any other information required for production.
Estimated time for completion: 2½ HOURS.

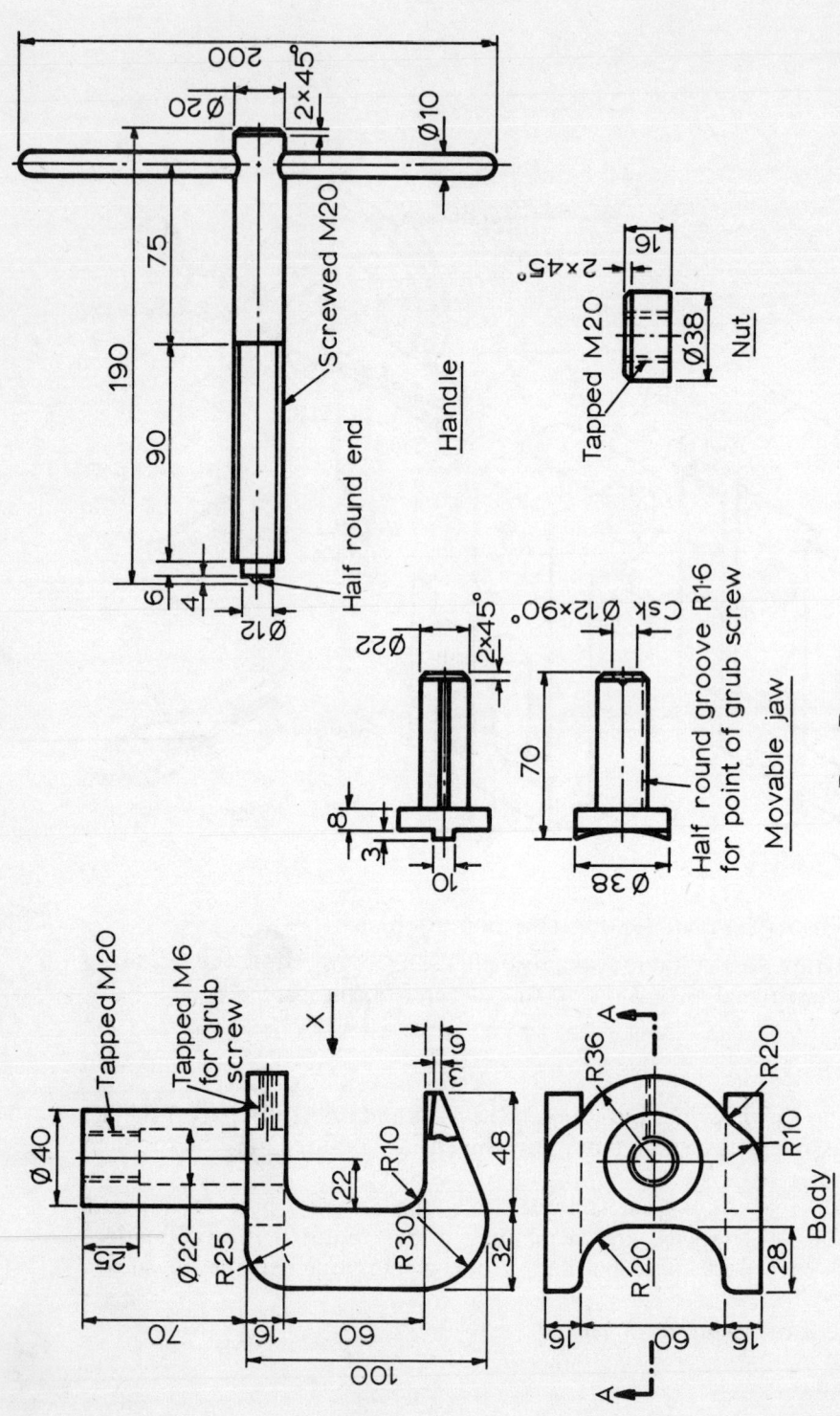

Travelling Steady for a Centre Lathe

Drawing Exercise 6. The main dimensions of a TRAVELLING STEADY for a centre lathe are given above. Two supports S contact the rotating workpiece when the steady is in use. The base B is bolted to the cross slide of the lathe. The supports have provision for fine adjustment and for being locked in position. Using not more than two views in orthographic projection, draw FULL SIZE the assembled steady with the supports set as for a 25 mm work-piece. No dimensions need be given. The dimensions shown are given as a guide and you must decide the other sizes. State:

(*a*) The material from which each part would be made.
(*b*) The parts requiring heat treatment.
   Estimated time for completion: 2½ HOURS.   (CGLI)

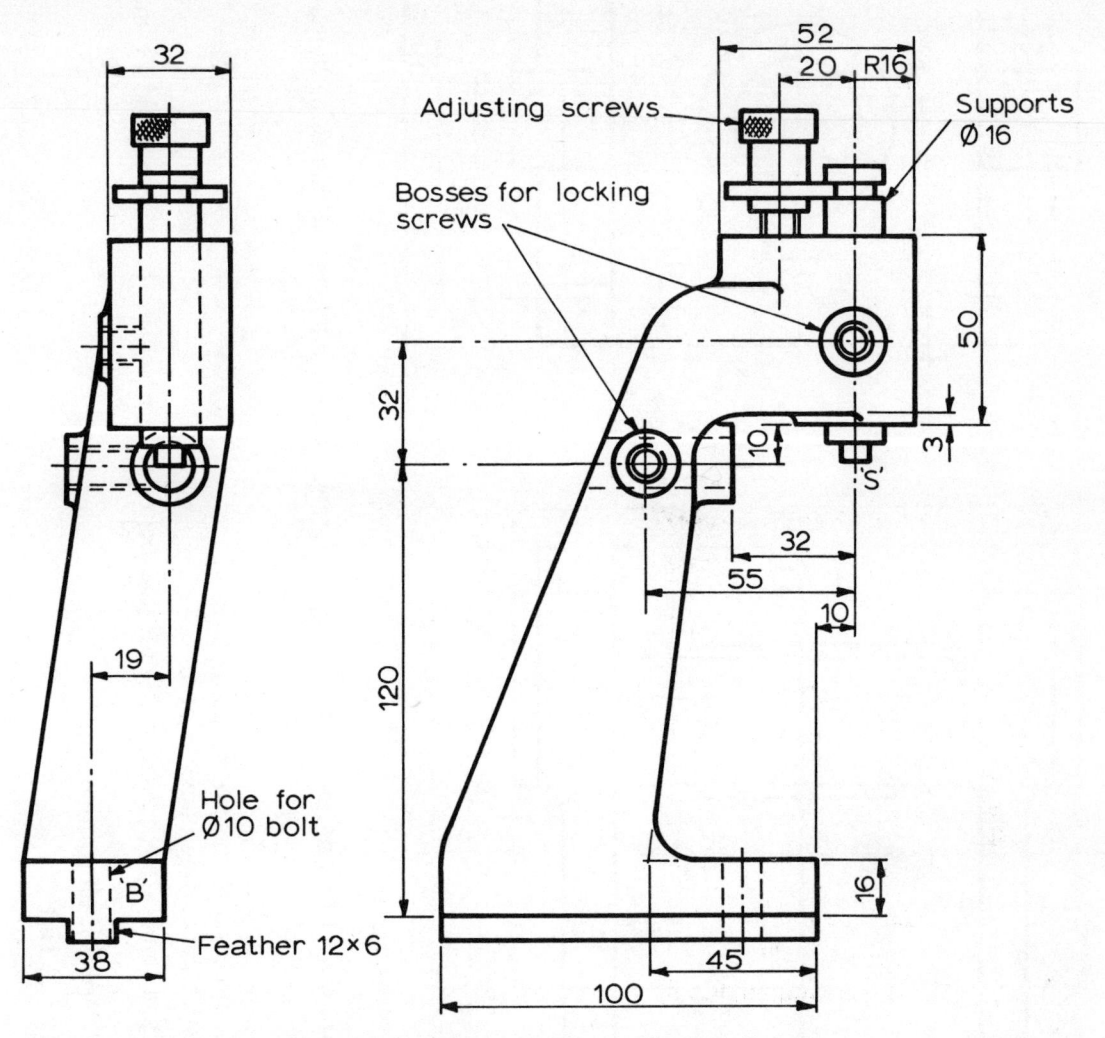

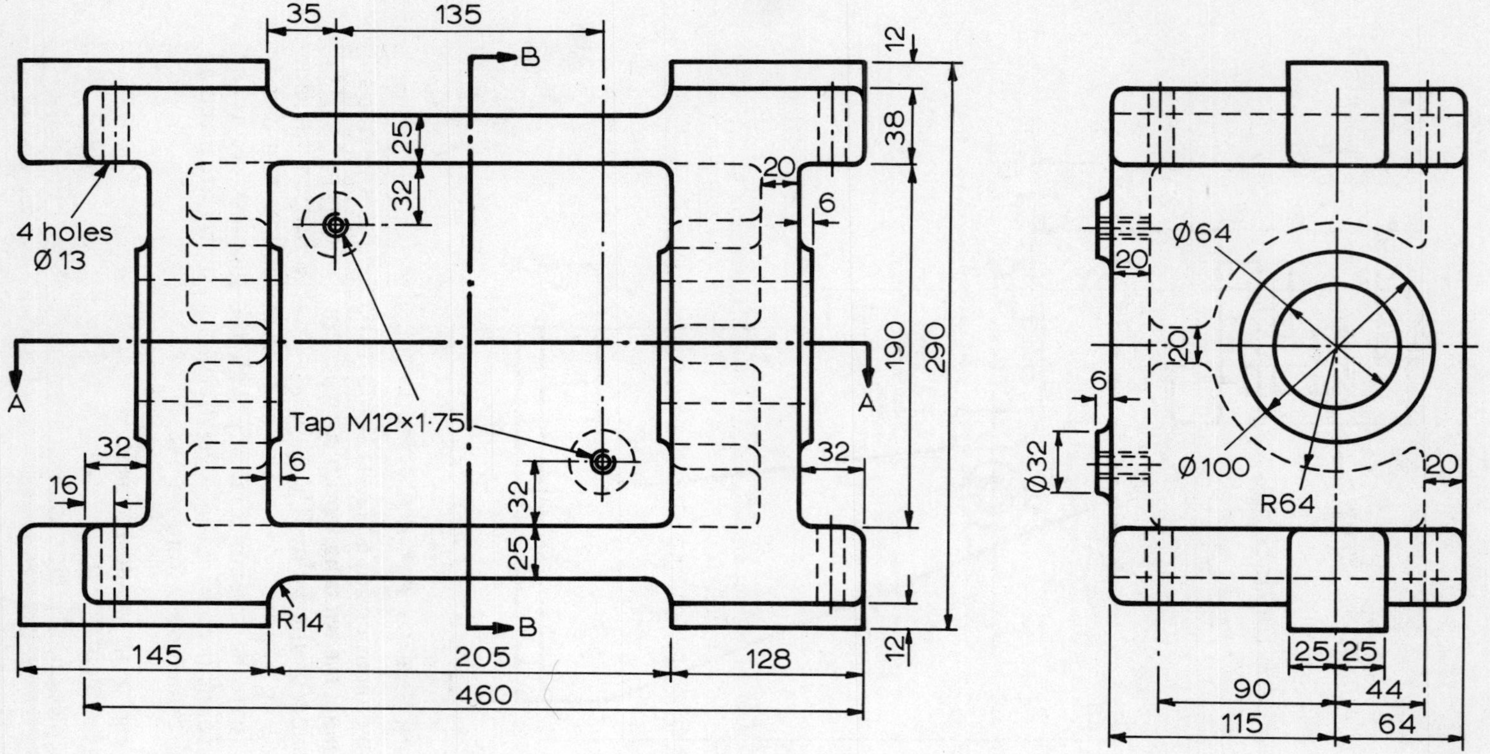

Oil Separator Casing

DRAWING EXERCISE 7. Two views are given of an OIL SEPARATOR CASING. Draw, using a suitable scale and using first angle projection, the following views:

(a) The given front elevation.
(b) A sectional end elevation in the direction of the cutting-plane B–B.
(c) A sectional plan in the direction of the cutting plane A–A.

Show any machining marks you think are required, and state the material from which the casing could be made, giving reasons for your choice.

Print title and scale, and add twelve leading dimensions.

Estimated time for completion: 2½ HOURS.

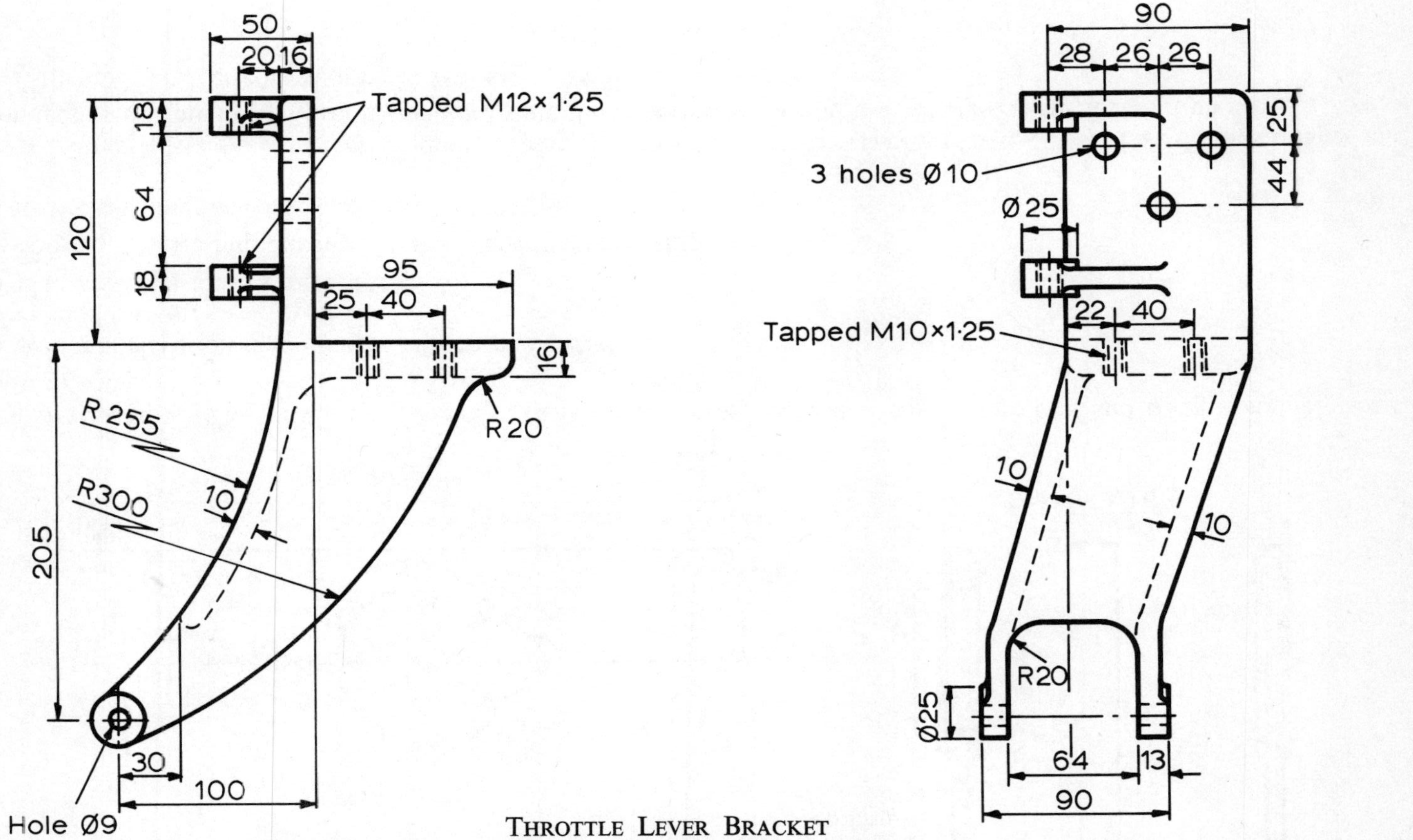

THROTTLE LEVER BRACKET

DRAWING EXERCISE 8. Two views are given of a THROTTLE LEVER BRACKET. Draw, using first- or third-angle projection, and using a suitable scale, the following views:

(a) The given front elevation.
(b) The given end elevation.
(c) A plan.

Show twelve leading dimensions, all necessary machining marks and the material from which you think the component could be made, giving reasons for your choice.

Estimated time for completion: 2½ HOURS.

127

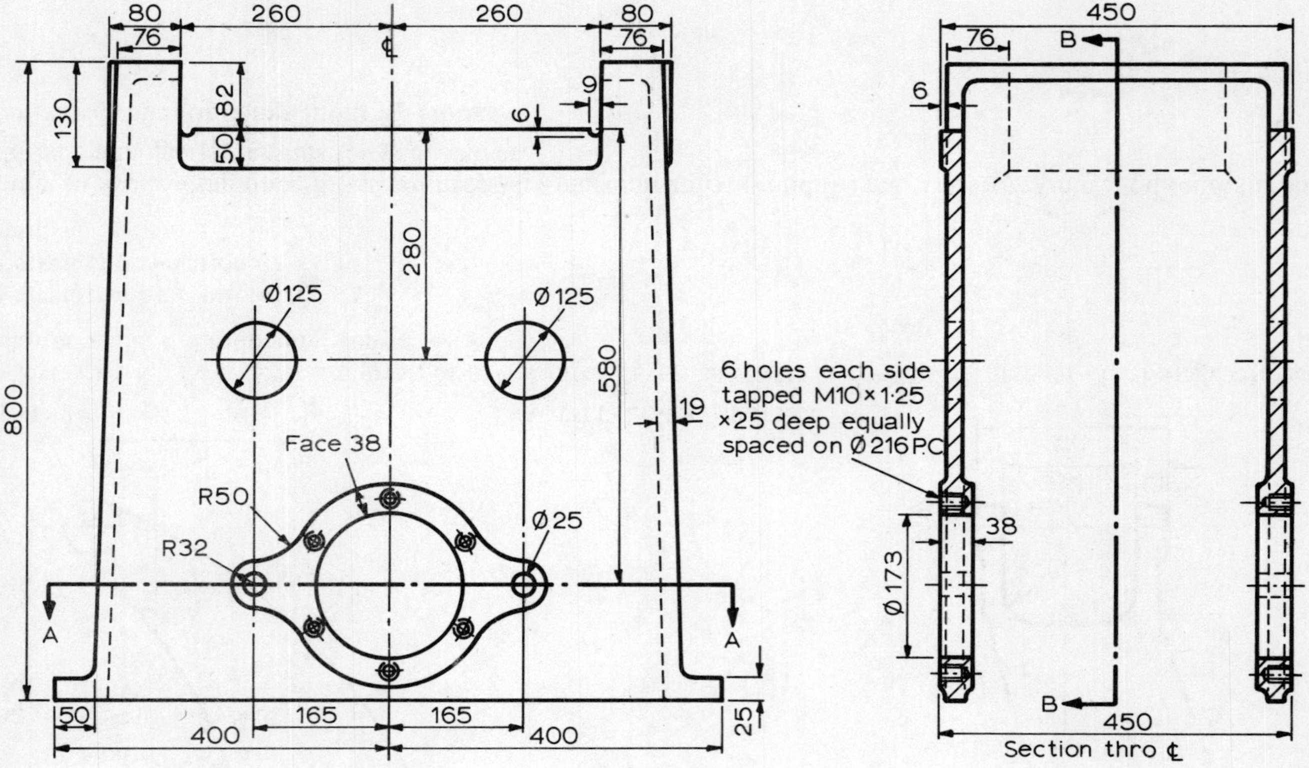

GEAR CASE

DRAWING EXERCISE 9. Two views are given of a GEAR CASE. Draw, using first-angle projection and using a suitable scale, the following views:

(a) A sectional elevation taken on the cutting plane B–B.
(b) An end elevation.
(c) A plan taken on the cutting plane A–A.

Show twelve leading dimensions and all necessary machining marks.
Estimated time for completion: 2½ HOURS.

DRAWING EXERCISE 10. As a further exercise redesign the GEAR CASE as a WELDED FABRICATION. List the advantages and disadvantages of this method of production, and state the material you would use, giving reasons for your choice.
Estimated time for completion: 2½ HOURS.

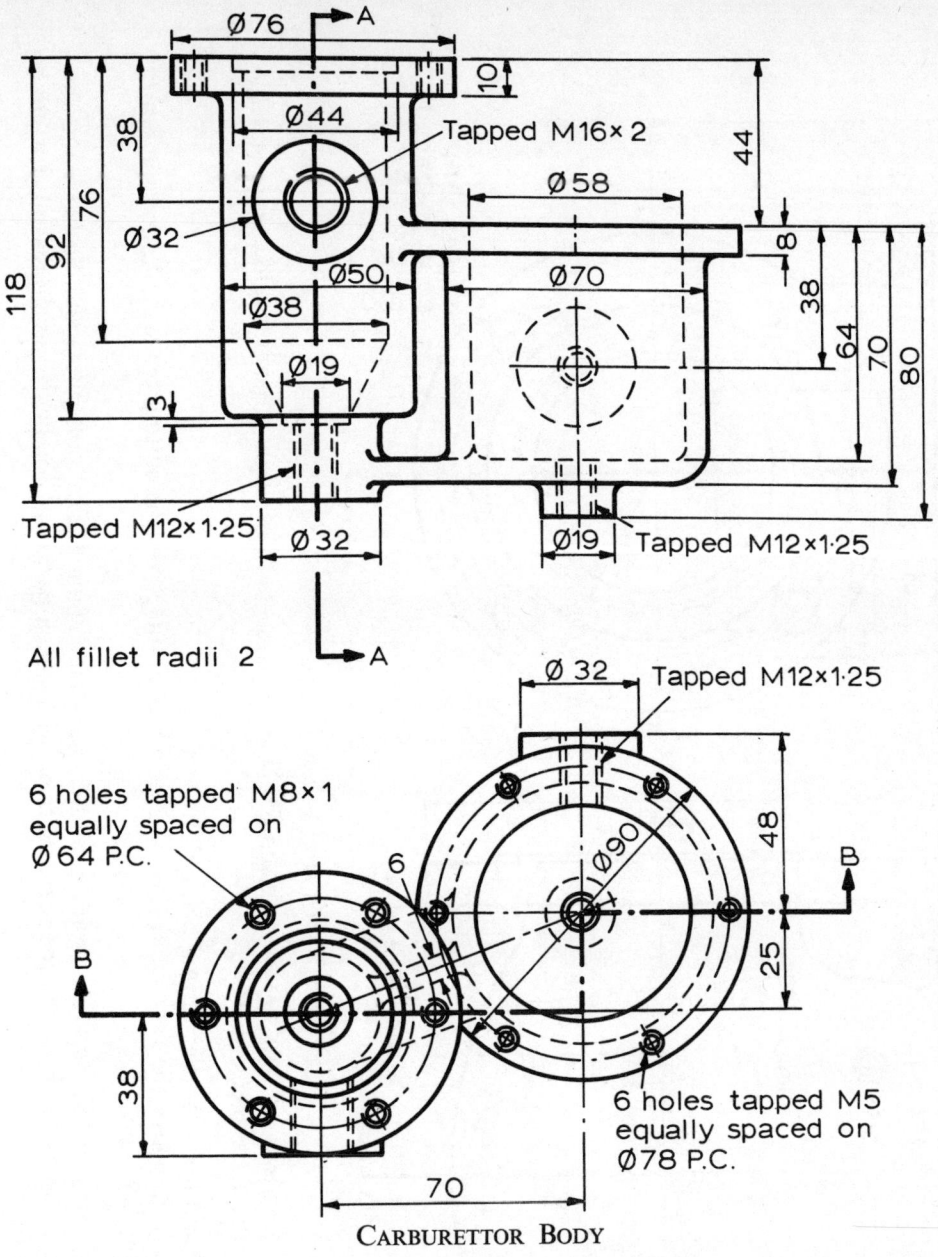

CARBURETTOR BODY

DRAWING EXERCISE 11. Two views are given of a CARBURETTOR BODY. Draw, using first- or third-angle projection and a suitable scale, the following views:

(a) A sectional front elevation taken on the cutting plane B–B.
(b) A sectional end elevation taken on the cutting plane A–A.
(c) The given plan.

Fully dimension the drawing, and show all necessary machining marks. Suggest a material the component could be made from if it were to be mass produced at the lowest possible cost. Give reasons for your choice.

Estimated time for completion: 3 HOURS.

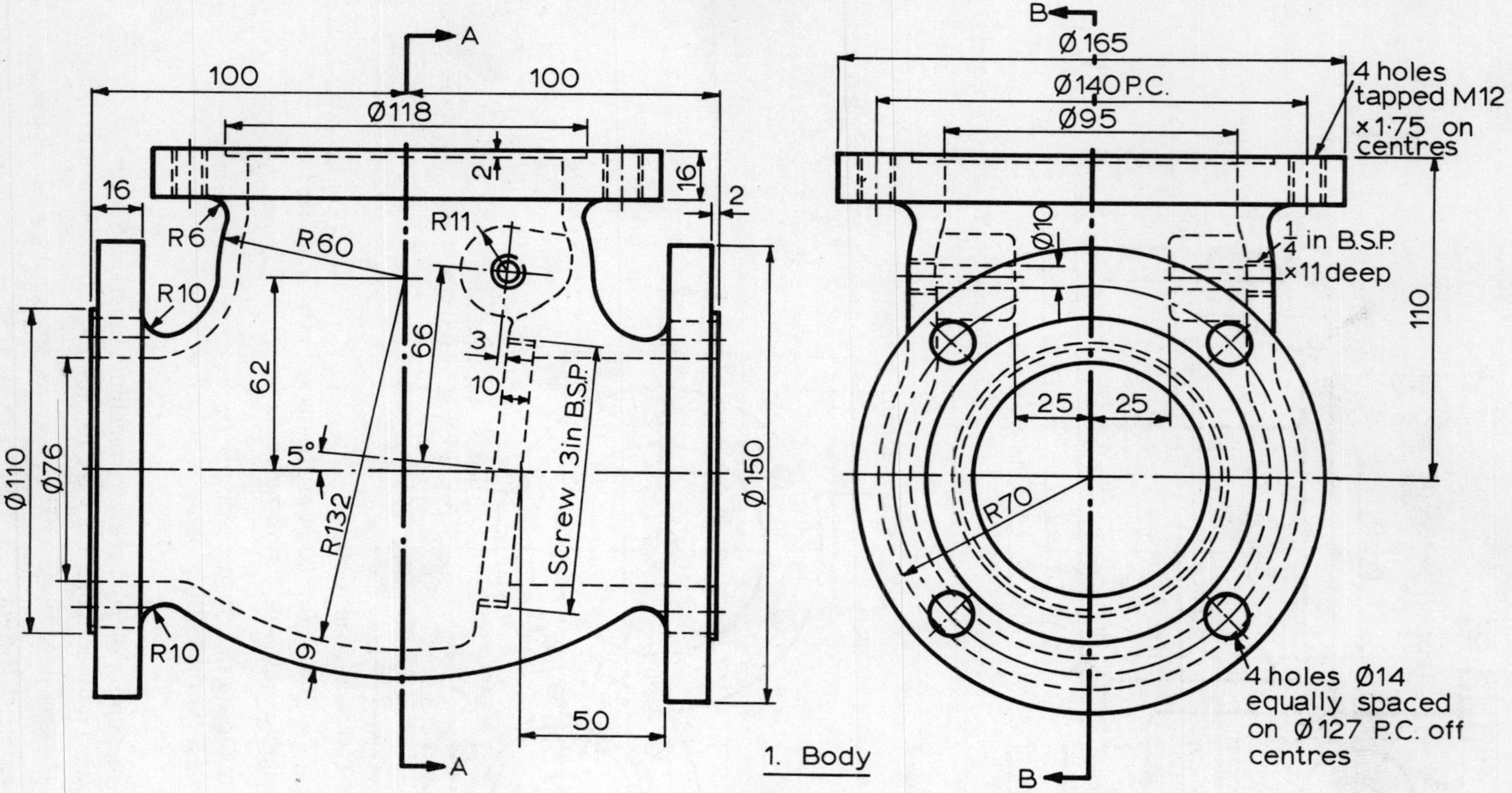

CLACK VALVE

DRAWING EXERCISE 12. Part details of a CLACK VALVE are given. Draw, using first- or third-angle projection and using a suitable scale, the following views of the assembled valve:

(a) A sectional front elevation taken on the cutting plane B–B.
(b) A sectional end elevation in which the LEFT hand side is to be a section taken on the cutting plane A–A, and the RIGHT hand side is to be an outside view.

You are required to show, in their correct position, all necessary machining marks, bolts, nuts and washers, and the gasket. Show twelve leading dimensions and the material from which each part could be made, giving reasons for your choice. Draw up a parts list.

Estimated time for completion: 3 HOURS.

130

4. Cover
Ø165, Ø115, 16, 12
4 holes Ø17 on Ø140 P.C.

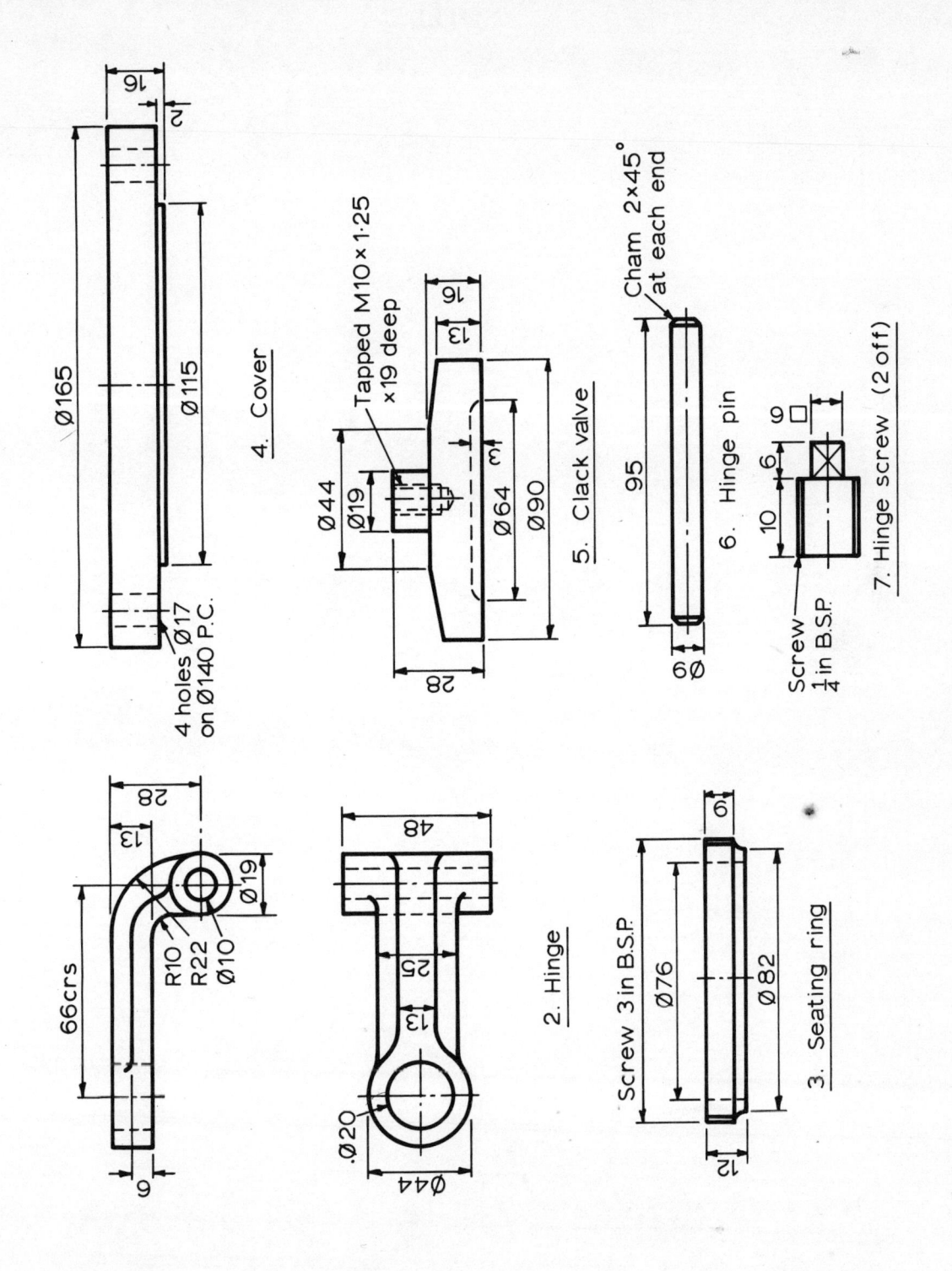

5. Clack valve
Tapped M10 × 1.25 × 19 deep
Ø44, Ø19, Ø64, Ø90, 16, 13, 4, 28

6. Hinge pin
Cham 2×45° at each end
95, Ø6

7. Hinge screw (2 off)
Screw ¼ in B.S.P.
9, 6, 10

2. Hinge
28, 13, Ø19, R10, R22, Ø10, 66 crs, 6
48, 25, 13, Ø20, Ø44

3. Seating ring
Screw 3 in B.S.P.
Ø76, Ø82, 6, 12

131

NOTES

NOTES

NOTES

NOTES

NOTES